The Economics of Business Enterprise

International Student Edition

In grateful memory of two people who might have been relied upon to admire this book.

Gertrude Dorothy Ricketts (Née Elgar) 1913–97
Leonard Alfred Ricketts 1912–2000

The Economics of Business Enterprise

An Introduction to Economic Organisation and the Theory of the Firm

INTERNATIONAL STUDENT EDITION

Martin Ricketts

University of Buckingham, UK

Edward Elgar

Cheltenham, UK • Northampton, MA, USA

Published by
Edward Elgar Publishing Limited
Glensanda House
Montpellier Parade
Cheltenham
Glos GL50 1UA
UK

Edward Elgar Publishing, Inc.
136 West Street
Suite 202
Northampton
Massachusetts 01060
USA

Coventry University

Third Edition published 2002
International Student Edition published 2003

A catalogue record for this book
is available from the British Library

ISBN 1 84064 524 5 (Third Edition, cased)
     1 84064 905 4 (Third Edition, paperback)
     1 84376 420 2 (International Student Editon)

Printed and bound in Great Britain by MPG Books Ltd, Bodmin, Cornwall

Contents

Figures

Tables

Preface

Two features distinguish the third from the earlier editions of this book. Firstly I have been encouraged by a number of users of the book to incorporate a discussion of the implications of the theory of economic organisation for public policy. In earlier editions my objectives were limited to setting out various approaches to the positive analysis of business structure. However, such has been the welter of experiment across the globe over the last twenty years and such has been the controversy surrounding it that a discussion of policy issues seems to be a desirable feature of a book on economic organisation. Interest in the theory of economic organisation will often be motivated by a desire to understand why privatisation has been pursued in so many countries, whether 'brown outs' in California or train crashes in the UK have anything to do with the reformed structures of the electricity and rail industries, whether the government should give 'stakeholders' more power to influence corporate decisions and so forth. Part 3 of the book is devoted to an investigation of this type of question. It could not provide a detailed review of every policy area for obvious reasons of space constraints not to mention my own limited expertise. Its aim, however, is to show how the theory introduced in Part 1 can be used to provide a framework for criticising public policy. Transactions cost theory, the theory of property rights, the theory of principal and agent, public choice theory and evolutionary or Austrian considerations all play a part in understanding public policy. The book does not provide definitive 'answers' to specific questions of policy but investigates alternative theoretical approaches and their inter-connections.

The second major change is the incorporation of more material on the theory of property rights. Although property rights featured prominently in earlier editions the focus was mainly on claims to the residual. More recent analysis associated with Oliver Hart, Sanford Grossman and John Moore has highlighted the allocation of residual control rights as the crucial issue. Clearer distinctions are therefore drawn in this edition between the transactions cost tradition associated with Coase and Williamson, the property rights theory of Grossman, Hart and Moore and the principal–agent or optimal contracting tradition of writers such as Holstrom, Stiglitz and others. The implications of property rights analysis for financial structure are introduced in Chapters 4 and 9. Chapter 10 has also been extended to include more material on Henry Hansmann's approach to 'the ownership of enterprise'. Consumer cooperation, for example, was discussed in earlier editions but marketing and supply co-operatives as well as mutual enterprises now receive more detailed treatment.

Recent years have seen the publication of some excellent books on the New Institutional Economics. Notable examples are Kasper and Streit (1998) and Furubotn and Richter (1997). These works cover a wide spectrum of institutional analysis including markets, the firm, the state and even the international order. This book follows earlier editions in being more focused on the organisation of the firm. It draws heavily on modern institutional economics at certain points (for example when discussing the evolution of rules of behaviour or of property) but does not aim to provide a comprehensive treatment. The sub-title thus continues to emphasise 'economic organisation' (the structure of firms and contractual relations) rather than 'economic institutions' (the system of end-independent rules which governs social inter-action).

Buckingham, 22nd January, 2001

Preface to the first edition

For many years, the study of business enterprise has been a relatively neglected facet of economic theory. Most theoretical developments from the mid-1950s onwards involved areas remote from the preoccupations of everyday business life. The internal structure of enterprises was left to organisation theorists, the strategic development of individual firms to business historians, and the analysis of entrepreneurial endeavour to biographers. Indeed economists in the universities and people working in the world of business, at least in the United Kingdom, appeared to have little to say to one another. This was not merely the result of a prejudice against abstract theory on the part of business people. Most of them, perhaps, had neither the leisure nor the inclination for reading much economic theory, but, in addition, their patience would have been tried by an approach which, even allowing for the demands of simplifications and abstraction, appeared unrecognisable as a representation of the world in which they lived.

In this book I have attempted to present a review of certain theoretical developments that have become increasingly important during the last decade but which inevitably have their roots further back. These developments all derive from an interest in the problem of information and the transactional difficulties which are encountered in a world where people can never be fully informed. The result is a body of theory which, even when involving a high degree of abstraction, relates to problems of immediate interest to business people. It also provides greater coherence to the business economics that was the product of an era in which economists still communicated with the business world. It is uncanny how close are textbooks such as Edwards and Townsend's *Business Enterprise* (the result of a series of seminars at the London School of Economics in the early 1950s) to the spirit and content of modern transactions costs theory. Their emphasis on entrepreneurial judgement in a world of continuing change would now be called 'Austrian', while their description of the transactional problems encountered with suppliers of customers and the resulting tendency towards integration (p. 206) has not been improved upon in the modern literature. Before the late 1970s, however, the transactions costs view of the world had not been developed systematically, and it was always possible to characterise business economics as comprising practical wisdom rather than respectable theory. Once the information problem began to command attention as the central problem in economics, however, this attitude changed. The objective of this book is to show how transactions cost theory affects our view of business enterprise.

It is important to be clear at the outset that the theory of the firm expounded here is not a theory of production as conventionally defined. The entire book is about exchange. The reader will look in vain for detailed discussions of the properties of production functions or cost functions; estimates of economies of scale or minimum efficient scale of plant; elaboration of the 'structure, conduct and performance' paradigm, and many other areas which make up the core of most established textbooks in industrial economics. It is no accident that the central tool of analysis used in this book is not the usual production function diagram, but the Edgeworth box. This emphasis permeates every chapter. It explains the content of the opening chapter on costless exchange and the chapter which succeeds it on transactions costs. It explains the subject matter of Chapter 3 on the entrepreneur as an intermediator of exchange transactions, and of chapter 4 on the policing and enforcement of property rights. Throughout Part 2 it is asymmetric information and the resulting view of the firm as a governance structure for complex and implicit exchange transactions, associated with the names of Ronald Coase and Oliver Williamson, which is at the centre of the stage.

The development of the book as a whole should not be considered as a set of more or less disconnected topics, but as a gradual elaboration of a particular 'view of the world'. In the first few chapters the barest outline of the landscape is informally sketched in, while in Part 2 extra colour, missing structural features and additional detail are superimposed. The reader may like the final picture or he may hate it, but he should at least be aware that what he is looking at is intended to be a single item and not a sequence of independent exhibits. A determination to stick to a central theme is also reflected in the choice of empirical work which is cited. Reference is made to some of those studies which impinge most closely on the transactions costs view of the firm. The literature on quasi-vertical, vertical and international integration, for example, is outlined in Chapter 7; while that on managerial incentives and the effects of differing property rights structures is reviewed in Chapter 8. No attempt has been made to cover comprehensively the existing empirical literature in industrial economics however, as this would have involved an enormous increase in the scope of the book.

If the analytical foundations of the book are neoclassical, they are supplemented by a rhetoric which is distinctly 'Austrian'. This combination of neoclassical analysis and Austrian rhetoric has always seemed to the writer to be of great persuasive power, and it may therefore be appropriate that a health warning should appear in the preface. Historically it seems to have been a combination favoured by many of the writers who developed the transactions costs approach to the firm. Knight used perfectly competitive theory as a benchmark against which to compare the world of profit and uncertainty; Schumpeter is said to have admired Walras above all other economists; Coase, who has a claim to be considered the father of the modern theory of the firm, was also instrumental in developing the neoclassical theory of externalities; and Hayek, for whom the information problem has always been central, produced work in the inter-war years which was formally close to the tradition of neoclassical equilibrium theory.

With exchange transactions as the central issue, the analysis is for the most part individualistic and concentrates on the behaviour of individual economic agents. These agents are also narrowly self-interested. They will shirk as soon as it is in their own perceived interest to do so, and they will rob you if they think they can get away with it. People are not, of course, like this; at least not universally and not all the time. To find the book bearable the reader merely has to believe that it is more likely to be rewarding to analyse the world on the assumption of selfishness than selflessness. Other social scientists including psychologists and sociologists may have alternative methods of approaching the analysis of institutions and I have no interest in asserting the exclusive claims of economics in this area, least of all an economics based entirely on self-interest. I hope the book demonstrates however, that the economic approach and the self-interest assumption are capable of providing a framework for the analysis of business institutions which is both coherent and enlightening.

Thanks are due to many colleagues and friends who have discussed the issues presented in these pages over several years. Norman Barry has been particularly helpful in discussions on the subjectivist tradition in economics. In addition it is necessary to mention my teachers: Stanley Dennison whilst at Newcastle and John Jewkes for whom I worked for two years at the Industrial Policy Group in London were both closely interested in the subject of economic organisation and will find novelty in the book, less in the ideas it describes than in the way they are presented. Jack Wiseman at York is responsible for much of the 'Austrian' influence although he will find in these pages that three years as his research assistant left me a somewhat wayward convert. Tony Culyer, my DPhil supervisor, first introduced me to the work of Armen Alchian and the literature on property rights, and Alan Peacock, first at York and then at the University of Buckingham, has been unstinting in his support. In a jointly written book at present under preparation[1] we hope to discuss problems of public policy and of

---

[1] This book was produced as part of the Heriot-Watt distance learning MBA course under the title *Government and Industry* (1991).

government–industry inter-reaction. Space constraints have prevented any extended discussion of policy issues in this book.

To Mrs Linda Waterman at the University of Buckingham I owe a great debt of gratitude for deciphering my handwriting, typing the manuscript, checking the spelling, and keeping a watchful eye for split infinitives. To complete this task accurately in conjunction with the other demands of the School of Accounting, Business and Economics was a notable achievement.

October 1985

Preface to the second edition

In the eight years that have elapsed between preparing the first and second editions of this book, institutional change has been a subject of continuing practical as well as theoretical interest. Debates about privatisation, the contracting out of government services, the regulation of public utilities, the role of takeovers in systems of corporate governance and many other issues have concerned matters of property rights and transactions costs that were at the heart of the first edition. The literature on economic organisation has expanded rapidly and this is reflected in the increased scope of the book.

The most obvious difference is that eight chapters have now become twelve. In the first edition, the final Chapter 8 covered a vast range of topics all associated with 'control' or 'governance' problems in organisations. The second edition extends this material over four chapters. Chapter 8 considers management incentives, Chapter 9 investigates the takeover mechanism, chapter 10 introduces the theory of profit sharing enterprises, and chapter 11 is devoted to nonprofit and government enterprise. A final chapter relates some of the earlier material to the evolutionary tradition in economic thought. This extension of Part 2 of the book has been accompanied by some reorganisation of the rest of the material. Chapter 5, which introduces the theory of principal and agent, now moves to part 1 where it properly belongs as part of the theoretical foundation of the theory of economic organisation.

There are more subtle, if equally important, changes in the intellectual framework of the book. The preface to the first edition draws attention to the methodological individualism of the exposition and the self-interest assumption which permeates the text. This remains broadly true of the second edition. However, much theoretical work has recently emphasised the role of 'cultural' factors in establishing a suitable environment in which exchange can take place. Business pursuits require a social environment which supports exchange, and creating such a background is not simply a matter of individual choice but may be more appropriately regarded as a matter of cultural evolution. At various points, the text reflects a greater awareness of this thinking and provides some elementary background on the literature concerning the evolution of social norms and property rights.

The book remains true to its original conception in introducing various theoretical approaches to economic organisation not 'one after the other' but in a comparative setting. The contribution of neoclassical, Austrian, and evolutionary thinking is contrasted in the setting of the particular issue being discussed. Reference to empirical work is not intended to be comprehensive. I have attempted to cite papers where they are particularly relevant to a theoretical point under discussion. Usually papers are cited on different sides of a particular issue and, if possible, a survey paper is mentioned which interested students can consult as a first stage in developing their own expertise.

Public policy is never central to the exposition. The extension of the book to a more systematic analysis of takeovers, corporate governance, nonprofit enterprise and so forth means that policy implications are inevitably nearer the surface than was the case in the first edition. However, they are not scrutinised in detail although the economic analysis covered in the book should form a precondition for any worthwhile excursion into questions of public policy.

As with the first edition, thanks are due to the many colleagues and students who have discussed the evolving content of this book, to my parents who provided me with a 'safe house' where drafting was possible without interruption, and to my wife and children for tolerating these absences along with even more protracted absences of mind. Mrs Linda Waterman provided invaluable assistance by processing the files of the first edition produced by optical scanning thus enabling me to edit them using my personal computer.

Buckingham, November 1993

Acknowledgement

The publishers wish to thank the Polish Cultural Foundation Limited for their kind permission to reprint the excerpt from pp. 88 and 92 of *Pan Tadeusz* by Adam Mickiewicz, translated from the Polish by Kenneth Mackenzie and published by the Polish Cultural Foundation, London in 1999.

PART ONE

Basic Concepts

'In conditions of perfect knowledge, the theory of the firm is very simple: there are no firms.'
(Brian J. Loasby)[1]

1. The gains from trade

'A vast range, therefore, of our relations with others enters into a system of mutual adjustment by which we further each other's purposes simply as an indirect way of furthering our own. All such relations may be fitly called "economic". The range of activity they cover is "business".'
(Philip H. Wicksteed)[2]

1. PRODUCTION AND THE FIRM

The firm is not an easy economic concept to define. Everyone accepts that IBM or ICI or Ford constitute 'firms', but from an economic as distinct from a purely legal point of view it is necessary to discover what underlying principles enable us to refer to such international giants using the same word as might be used for the local grocer's retail outlet. Further, if the local grocer's shop is a 'firm' would the same be true of a small hospital run by a charitable foundation, or a church, or even a family? Established textbooks on the principles of economics typically reveal little curiosity about this issue. The firm is simply the fundamental microeconomic unit in the theory of supply. Firms exist and can be recognised by their function, which is to transform inputs of factors of production into outputs of goods and services. With some notable exceptions, the implied asymmetry between the theory of demand, with its emphasis on the individual consumer as the ultimate microeconomic building block, and the theory of supply, with its emphasis on the firm, is rarely explored.

Conventional theory does, however, provide a clue to the nature of 'the firm'. The process of production usually involves coordinating the activities of different individuals. Suppliers of labour, capital, intermediate inputs, raw materials and land cooperate with one another to produce outputs of goods and services. The institutional setting in which this coordination of activity is attempted may vary enormously, but where economic agents cooperate with one another not through a system of explicit contracts that bind each to every other member of the group but through a system of bilateral contracts in which each comes to an agreement with a 'single contractual agent', the essential ingredient of 'the firm' is present. It is therefore the nature of the contractual arrangements that bind individuals together which, at least from the point of view of economic theory, constitutes the central preoccupation of the theory of the firm. Much of this book will be concerned to elaborate upon this basic idea and to investigate the insights that flow from it.

2. SCARCITY

Most expositions of elementary economic analysis start with a statement to the effect that economics is concerned with choice. If individuals are confronted by limited resources they must choose between alternatives. Following the definition of Robbins (1935, p. 16), 'Economics is the science which studies human behaviour as a relationship between ends and scarce means which have alternative uses.' As Robbins recognised, this definition is not of very great interest when applied to isolated individuals. A lone individual would have an allocation problem to solve, but a student of such a person's activities would find it difficult to go further than asserting the proposition that out of all the perceived available courses of action, the isolated decision-maker chooses the alternative that he or she most prefers.

As part of a community of individuals, however, individuals are confronted with a more complex problem. They will usually find that their best strategy is not to cut themselves off from all communication with their fellows, but rather to coordinate their activity with that of other people. Making the best use of scarce resources will therefore involve forming agreements with others, and economics then becomes the study of the social mechanisms which facilitate such agreements. Hidden in this statement, however, are two rather different preoccupations.

First, it is possible to ask in any given situation what particular allocation (or allocations) of resources, what set of agreements, would be best in the sense that no individual or set of individuals within the entire community could gain by opting out and substituting alternative feasible arrangements. Economists express this idea in the technical language of game theory as identifying allocations of resources which are in 'the core' of a market exchange game.[3] Suppose there were a community of four individuals. Each, we may assume, could live the life of a recluse, but none wishes to do so if cooperation with the others is capable of adding to his or her perceived satisfaction. The four meet and discuss various proposals which will make them all better off. No one will accept a deal which reduces their well-being below that of an isolated recluse, and similarly no final agreement would hold if any two or possibly three out of four could benefit by coming to some alternative arrangement between themselves. A set of agreements which it is in no single individual's or group's interests to renounce in favour of an available alternative, is said to be in the 'core'. Allocations of resources that are 'core' allocations represent in one sense a 'solution' to the resource allocation problem. Sections 3 to 6, below, present a brief description of this tradition in economics using a very simple example. Proceeding in this way, the unsuitability of the theoretical apparatus of general economic equilibrium for the investigation of economic organisation is thrown into sharp relief.

Economic organisation is more closely concerned with the process by which agreements are formulated. If the tastes and preferences of our four individuals are known to the economist; if their skills and endowments of resources including tools and equipment as well as natural resources, raw materials and land are likewise clearly defined; and if all the feasible options technically available from using these resources in various combinations can be listed, it should be possible in principle to work out all the mutually advantageous agreements which potentially exist. Working out allocations of resources which are in the 'core' becomes a matter of mere 'calculation'. All the necessary information which is formally required to uncover a 'solution' is present, and the rest can be accomplished by a sufficiently devoted mathematician or adequately powerful computer. This, though, tells us nothing about the methods adopted by our four individuals to solve their resource allocation problem.

Imagine, for example, that by some fluke of history the four people meet on an otherwise uninhabited island (the sole survivors from four separate shipwrecks). Each person will have little idea of the skills possessed by his or her associates. Indeed each may be in some doubt about his or her own capabilities in the new and unfamiliar environment. The potential of the island to sustain life, the characteristics and uses of the available resources, the best methods of using these resources for various purposes (making clothes, building shelter, finding food, and so on) are all a matter of guesswork and hunch. Setting up the problem in this way makes it clear that what our four individuals lack most is not a calculator, but information.

Facing the appalling problems of survival, the four islanders are likely to agree to cooperate with one another. These agreements will not represent a 'solution' to the problem of resource allocation in any ideal sense, since no one can possibly know what the ideal way of proceeding entails. Instead, agreements between the four represent stages in a process of discovery.[4] As time advances, experience will reveal something of the relative talents of the individuals and the properties and potential of the available resources. Arrangements between the individuals are continually modified in the light of past experience and of expectations about the future. In this framework it is still possible to argue that the subject matter of economics is the allocation of scarce means between competing uses, but it is clear that the nature of the economic problem when opportunities are not fully known is quite different from the problem conceived of as making the best of available resources in the context of perfect information.

3.   THE ALLOCATION PROBLEM

At this stage it will prove useful to develop the theme further by reference to a simple example of the sort frequently encountered in basic textbooks on the principles of economics. We continue to assume that the world consists of four individuals who possess differing endowments of resources. Conventional analysis then proceeds on the assumption that the limited resources available to each individual permit them to produce various known combinations of goods and services. Suppose for simplicity that people desire only two goods (x and y). With the resources at his or her disposal, person A can produce any combination of x and y in the area $aa'0$ illustrated in Figure 1.1. Given that both x and y confer benefits on person A, it is inconceivable that he or she would choose to produce at any point inside the line aa'. This line aa' is called person A's production possibility curve. Its downward slope reflects the fact that the production of more of any one good requires resources to be diverted from the production of the

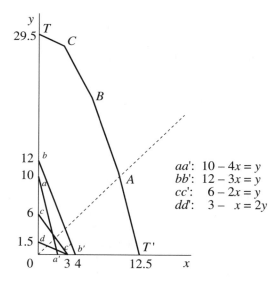

$$aa': \quad 10 - 4x = y$$
$$bb': \quad 12 - 3x = y$$
$$cc': \quad \ 6 - 2x = y$$
$$dd': \quad \ 3 - \ x = 2y$$

Figure 1.1   Production possibilities in a four-person community

other. The steepness of the curve indicates the amount of y which has to be sacrificed to produce an extra unit of x. In the case of person A, one more unit of x entails the sacrifice of four units of y. Thus the slope of the production possibility curve indicates the marginal opportunity cost of an extra unit of x. If person A produces more x its marginal cost will be $4y$. Note that the cost of x can be interpreted as a physical and objective measure (the amount of y forgone) only because we have assumed that all the options available to A are known to him or her with complete certainty.

Each of the other people (labelled B, C and D) will also face constraints on their ability to produce. The constraints are represented by the lines bb', cc' and dc' in Figure 1.1. Notice that some individuals are luckier than others. All points on person B's production possibility curve are unattainable by any other person. Notice also that the marginal costs of production differ for each person. Person D, for example, is relatively poor but in terms of y sacrificed he or she is the cheapest producer of x.

As solitary individuals, each person will have to pick a point on his or her production possibility curve. Suppose, for example, that x and y were not substitutable in consumption and that everyone consumed these goods in fixed proportions (say equal quantities of each). In the absence of trade, consumption points would be given where production possibility curves intersect a 45° line through the origin. The total output of the community will be $8x$ and $8y$. The individual consumption and production levels of each person are recorded in Table 1.1.

Table 1.1   Consumption levels with no trade

	x	y
A	2	2
B	3	3
C	2	2
D	1	1
Total output	8	8

One of the most enduring discoveries in economic theory, first fully established by David Ricardo, suggests, however, that these four individuals could do much better through specialisation and exchange. Consider the curve TT' in Figure 1.1. This is referred to as the 'community outer-bound production possibility curve' or the 'community transformation curve'. Given the production constraints facing each individual, it is easy to see that if all four people produced product x they could between them achieve 12.5 units of output. If now some y is to be produced, it will entail the sacrifice of some x and it seems reasonable to allocate the person to y production who can produce it at least cost. This person is A, for whom each unit of y will entail the sacrifice of only 0.25 units of x. Person A has the greatest 'comparative advantage' in y production of the four individuals. If A specialises in y production and persons B, C and D specialise in x production, the community in total will achieve an output of ten units of x and ten units of y (point A). Further y production can only be achieved by using another person in addition to A. The person who can produce further y at least marginal cost is now person B for whom the marginal cost of y is 0.33x. Complete specialisation of both A and B in y production and of C and D in x production would enable the community to achieve six units of x and 22 units of y (point B). Yet further y production must now involve person C, for whom the marginal cost is 0.5x, and so forth.

Given the rather extreme assumptions we have made about consumption patterns, it is clear that point A will represent the best production point. Specialisation has resulted in an increase of community output of two units of x and two of y. No alternative arrangements exist which would permit the achievement of any points further out along the 45° line. We would expect, therefore, that any agreement between the four individuals would involve A specialising in y production and B, C and D specialising in x production.

This still leaves open the question of how the benefits of specialisation are to be distributed. We might, for example, envisage one of the transactors making the following suggestion. 'Since our joint efforts will result in a total increase in output of 2x and 2y above that achievable by our original uncoordinated activity, let us each share equally in this benefit. Final consumption levels would then be as recorded in Table 1.2. All individuals achieve a consumption level 0.5 units higher than those recorded in Table 1.1.

Table 1.2   A possible allocation that is outside the 'core'

	A	B	C	D	Total
Units of x and y	2.5	3.5	2.5	1.5	10.0

Note: Specialisation and exchange increases combined output from eight to ten units of x and y, but increasing each person's consumption by 0.5 does not produce a 'core' allocation.

This attempted solution will not work, however. To see why, it is necessary to consider all the trading options available to the various transactors. There is nothing to stop A and B, for example, from getting together and agreeing to collaborate without the others. Similarly, persons C and D might come to a separate agreement. The total output or 'payoff' achievable by all the conceivable 'coalitions' of people is recorded in Table 1.3.

The reader should take an entry at random and check that its meaning is clear.[5] If persons C and D collaborated they could achieve a combined output of four units of x and four units of y, as is illustrated in Figure 1.2. D would specialise in x production thus yielding three units of x, while C would produce one unit of x and four units of y. In total, they therefore produce four units of each commodity.

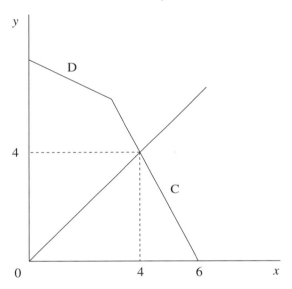

Figure 1.2   Person C and Person D together can produce four units of x *and four units of* y

Now consider the position of persons A and D. If they accept the deal offered in Table 1.2 they will join in an agreement which involves all four transactors with a total payoff to the 'coalition' of ten units of x and ten of y. Out of this, A will receive 2.5 units of each commodity and D will receive 1.5 units of each, but from Table 1.3 we see that simply by ignoring the others and striking a deal between themselves, A and D could receive a combined payoff of 4.4 units of each commodity instead of the 4.0 of Table 1.2. It follows that the 'allocation' of Table 1.2 is not in the 'core'. Persons A and D could both be better off by renouncing the allocation of Table 1.2 and agreeing an alternative between themselves.

To illustrate the case of an allocation which *is* in the 'core', consider the entries of Table 1.4. Comparing the entries in Table 1.4 with those in Table 1.3, it will be confirmed that no coalition of individuals could do better by striking a separate bargain between themselves. An alliance of B, C and D,

Table 1.3   Joint payoff to every possible coalition

'Coalition'	'Payoff' (units of x and y achievable)	'Coalition'	'Payoff' (units of x and y achievable)
A	2.00	BC	5.25
B	3.00	BD	5.25
C	2.00	CD	4.00
D	1.00	ABC	7.60
		ABD	7.60
AB	5.20	BCD	7.50
AC	4.40	ACD	6.80
AD	4.40	ABCD	10.00

Table 1.4   An allocation of consumption that is in the 'core'

	A	B	C	D	Total
Units of x and y	2.40	3.10	2.30	2.20	10.00

for example, could produce a payoff of 7.5, but their combined allocation in Table 1.4 is 7.6. A similar calculation can be performed for every other possible coalition. Thus the allocation of Table 1.4 is in the 'core' of the exchange game.

An agreement to specialise in accordance with comparative advantage and then to allocate the output as described in Table 1.4 is therefore one 'solution' to the economic problem of making the best out of scarce resources. It is not, however, a unique solution, as the reader can verify by checking the entries of Table 1.5 against those in Table 1.3. The three allocations recorded in Table 1.5 are also in the 'core'.

Table 1.5   A second allocation of consumption that is in the 'core'

	A	B	C	D	Total
Units of x and y	2.50	3.00	2.25	2.25	10.00
Units of x and y	2.00	3.20	2.40	2.40	10.00
Units of x and y	2.22	3.11	2.33	2.33	10.00

Note: The 'core' of an exchange game is not unique. The allocations recorded in this table are also in the 'core'.

4. RECONTRACTING AND THE ALLOCATION PROBLEM

In the section above, attention was focused primarily on calculating a 'solution' to the allocation problem under certain specific conditions. Little was said explicitly about the mechanism by which a solution might be achieved. Specialisation implies the existence of a coordinating mechanism by which one person's activities are made compatible with the actions of others. One mechanism consistent with the example of section 3 is a bargaining process. The four individuals could be seen as initially forming provisional agreements. If it then transpired that alternative more beneficial arrangements were possible for some individual or set of individuals (the provisional agreements did not represent a 'core' allocation) then the parties could 'recontract'. The process of recontracting would continue until it was in no one's interest to renounce the existing provisional agreement. At this point the agreement would be finalised.[6] The provisional agreement summarised in Table 1.2, for example, was renounced by persons A and D. If at the end of further negotiations the agreement summarised in the first line of Table 1.5 were hit upon, this would hold and the process of recontracting would cease.

The recontracting process just described does present some awkward dilemmas for the theorist, however, for if this process means anything, it must imply that the individuals involved possess incomplete information about the production possibilities and preferences of others. If information were perfect, there would be no purpose in conducting 'negotiations'. All the potential 'core allocations' or 'solutions' could be computed mathematically, as indeed we computed some in Tables 1.4 and 1.5. The big problem would then be that of choosing between a number of possible known solutions rather than discovering some particular solution or other. Choice between multiple solutions raises extremely difficult issues, since a move from one possibility to another involves some people becoming better off and others worse off (compare lines 1 and 2 of Table 1.5). Which of the many possible options available might eventually be agreed upon is therefore not easy to determine, and it is at least conceivable that no agreement would be forthcoming. Faced with this problem, economic theorists have developed an ingenious escape route. It is possible to show that as the number of contractors in a market increases, then under certain conditions the set of 'core' allocations diminishes in size. Indeed, in the limit, with an infinite number of contractors the 'core' shrinks to a single allocation.[7] No longer is there a problem of choosing between multiple solutions since only a single determinate solution exists.

For a theorist working with the full-information assumption and anxious to show the existence of a unique solution to the allocation problem, a shrinking core is no doubt a matter of some satisfaction. It is difficult to suppress the feeling, however, that where search is a costly activity, the smaller the core the more tiresome and protracted is the process of finding it. In a world in which information is discovered through the process of negotiation there would not appear to be the same compelling reasons to expect any particular outcome to occur. Indeed, it is not even clear that the final agreement will represent a core allocation. After some provisional contracts have been made the parties search around for a better deal. Nothing is finalised until each contractor finds that he or she cannot improve on his or her allocation. This, however, raises the question of how long people are prepared to search for coalitions which improve on their present position. As the number of contractors increases, so the number of potential coalitions increases exponentially and the number of core allocations declines. Any commitment to try all conceivable possibilities could be likely to imply never coming to a final agreed solution.

If the process of forming contracts with one another involves the use of scarce resources, then the 'best' use of these scarce resources cannot be said to reside entirely in the discovery of a 'core' allocation. A more crucial question concerns how scarce resources are used in the process of contracting itself. Conventional expositions of the recontracting process and the discovery of an allocation of resources which is in the core of the exchange game are therefore suspect. Either the process described is itself a user of scarce resources, in which case it cannot be inferred that search will continue indefinitely until a solution is found, or the process does not use scarce resources, in which case it is merely an unnecessary story to cloak the 'full-information' assumption.

5.   TATÔNNEMENT

The bargaining framework outlined in sections 3 and 4 deriving from the work of Edgeworth is not the usual approach adopted in elementary treatments of economics. It is more conventional to concentrate on the role of markets and the price system as a device for coordinating activity. Suppose, for example, that all contractors were able to exchange x for y at a ratio of one for one. For every person, the market price of x is one y and vice versa. Returning to Figure 1.1, it is seen that person A must sacrifice only 0.25 units of x in production to obtain a unit of y whereas in the market the price of y is $1x$. With the marginal cost to person A of y production so much less than the prevailing price, it will be in his or her interest to specialise in y production and exchange in the market. By this means, the

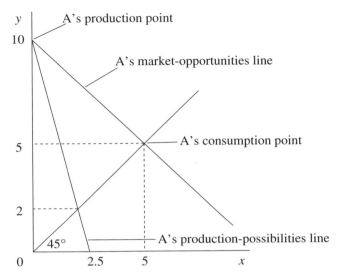

Note: Facing a market exchange ratio of 1x for 1y, person A can, by specialisation and exchange, achieve five units of each commodity instead of only two by isolated effort.

Figure 1.3   How person A gains from specialisation and exchange

person can achieve a production level of ten units of y and a consumption level of five units of each commodity (see Figure 1.3).

The marginal cost of y production, however, is less than the assumed prevailing market price for both persons B and C as well. Only person D will find it advantageous to specialise in x production, since for him or her the marginal cost of y exceeds the market price (the marginal cost of x on the other hand is less than its market price). Faced, therefore, with this ratio of exchange, the four individuals will be induced to specialise according to their area of comparative advantage and between them they will produce at point C in Figure 1.1.

Given the special nature of consumers' preferences, however, it is clear that with production of 28 units of y and only three units of x there will be enormous excess demand for x. Equilibrium in the market requires quantities demanded and supplied at the prevailing price to be the same. Clearly a higher price of x relative to y is required to induce persons B and C to change their area of specialisation. Point A will be achieved if the price ratio is set between $3y$ for $1x$ and $4y$ for $1x$. A single ratio of exchange applying to all transactors will result in a market equilibrium at point A.

This market 'solution' to the resource allocation problem turns out to be closely related to the concept of the 'core' mentioned in the last section. Suppose, for example, that the ratio of exchange were $3y$ for $1x$. These market opportunities clearly do not affect person B, since they are exactly the same as the opportunities which confront him or her in production. He/she will continue to consume three units of each commodity. Person A, on the other hand, will specialise in y production (ten units) and exchange 7.5 units of y for 2.5 units of x, thus achieving 2.5 units of each. Both persons C and D will specialise in x (three units each) and exchange 0.75 units for 2.25 units of y, thus achieving 2.25 units of each. Comparing these results with Table 1.5, the reader can verify that they correspond with the entries on the first line. A market ratio of exchange of $3y$ per $1x$ will produce an allocation of resources in the conditions specified, equivalent to the first 'core' allocation of Table 1.5. As an exercise, the reader should verify that a market rate of exchange of $4y$ per $1x$ will produce a result equivalent to the 'core' allocation recorded on the second line of Table 1.5. Indeed, it can be rigorously proved that any competitive equilibrium will imply an allocation which is in the 'core'.[8] A given ratio of exchange applying to all contractors of $3.5y$ per $1x$ will produce the third allocation of Table 1.5.

This theory of competitive equilibrium, however, suffers from similar difficulties to the exchange theory of Edgeworth discussed above. In its most general form, the theory indicates that there will exist, under specified conditions, a set of relative prices such that individual responses to these given prices will be compatible with equilibrium in every market. The question which the theory does not attempt to answer is precisely how this equilibrium set of prices is to be discovered. As Shackle (1972) puts it 'what (general equilibrium) theory neglects is the epistemic problem, the problem of how the necessary knowledge on which reason can base itself is to be gained' (p. 447). Like the recontracting process of Edgeworth, the theory of competitive market equilibrium has an equivalent story to tell. In this case it is supposed that an 'auctioneer' sets prices and that people form provisional agreements at these given prices. If it transpires that excess demands or supplies exist, the provisional agreements lapse and the auctioneer modifies prices in an attempt to eliminate any disequilibria. This process is termed the 'tatônnement' process and is associated primarily with the name of Leon Walras.[9]

The major problem with the Walrasian auction is not simply that it does not represent an accurate representation of reality. Resource allocation is not conducted by means of Walrasian auctions and, more to the point, the reason why is not difficult to understand. Such a process would be enormously costly. Indeed, such is the complexity characteristic of exchange relationships that an attempt to proceed along Walrasian lines would absorb all the energies and resources of contractors without perhaps ever achieving a 'solution'. Once more, the paradox of equilibrium theory is exposed. If all information is costlessly available, the auctioneer will get it right first time. If the process of acquiring information is costly, endless pursuit of a general equilibrium is the ultimate example of the ideal becoming the enemy of the good.

6.   THE EQUILIBRIUM METHOD

The purpose of our brief discussion of the salient features of general equilibrium theorising conducted above is not to develop a detailed critique or to question the intellectual achievement which it represents. It is important, however, to appreciate the nature of that achievement and the implications which it holds for the theory of the firm and of economic organisation more generally. General equilibrium theory represents an existence proof. Under tightly specified conditions in a world consisting of many individuals all with different tastes, skills and other endowments of resources, there will exist a set of relative prices of goods and factors compatible with universal market clearing. Equivalently there will exist a set of agreements between the individuals which no one will wish to change. The activities of all contractors will be perfectly reconciled. For any given set of preferences, resources and technological possibilities a 'solution' to the resource allocation problem exists in terms of specific outcomes.

Such a perfect coordination of all activity requires that agreements are concluded simultaneously and that transactions costs are zero. Knowledge of all technical possibilities both now and in the future must be assumed to be complete. The very passage of time itself can be admitted only in a very artificial sense. By extending the concept of consumers' preferences to embrace consumption in future time periods, and of production possibilities to include the 'transformation' via investment of goods today into goods tomorrow, it is possible to envisage a set of equilibrium intertemporal prices. At some price ratio, the right to consume apples in period 2 may be exchanged for the right to consume nuts in period 5. The final set of agreements will then embrace transactions extending over all future time periods. Time exists as a dimension on a graph, but outcomes over time are completely predetermined at the moment of general agreement. Time is incorporated into the analysis but only at the price of robbing the concept of all meaning. Formally, 'apples today' and 'apples tomorrow' are simply two different commodities. Decisions concerning consumption and production levels are made 'now'.

Time implies uncertainty, and the uncertain future poses intractable

problems for any theory of rational choice. For general equilibrium theorists, a further extension of the Walrasian system to embrace transactions
in 'state-contingent claims' is a possibility. Each transactor is assumed to
possess a list of all possible future 'states of the world' along with some
probability estimates attached to each state. Given initial resource endowments, the transactors exchange claims to resources contingent upon
specified events. For example, a claim to one kilogram of cocoa in period 3
contingent upon heavy rainfall in Ghana, might exchange in equilibrium
for two claims to one kilogram of coffee in period 4 contingent upon no
frost in Brazil.

Quite apart from the transactions costs problem mentioned earlier, this
effort to achieve a determinate equilibrium in the face of uncertainty
encounters even more fundamental difficulties. For the transactors are
'unboundedly rational'. All possible future states of the world are imagin-
able and nothing can occur which has not been imagined. Yet, when the
future is concerned, there would appear to be no limits on the agenda of
possible events, no boundaries on the contingencies which might be considered. Decision-making in the face of such uncertainty cannot then be
rational in the sense of making one best choice in the face of known opportunities. To quote Shackle (1972): 'it is plain that in order to achieve a
theory of value applicable to the real human situation, reason must compromise with time' (p. 269).

7.   INSTITUTIONS AND INFORMATION

For the purposes of the theory of the firm, the important point about the
general equilibrium method is that by effectively excluding time and uncertainty from the analysis, all transactions are costlessly and instantaneously
reconciled. In this environment there are no institutional structures called
firms. The efforts of all individuals are coordinated by a gigantic and
complex web of contractual commitments simultaneously entered into.
The economy is made up of a myriad of individual contractors, each one
in an intricate and complex pattern of interrelationships with every other.
As a description of economic life, however, this is clearly not very accurate.
Institutions such as firms, clubs, political parties, trade unions and bureaucracies exist, and their existence, if it is not to be left unexplained or put
down to chance, can be viewed as the outcome of the attempts by rational
individuals to solve the resource allocation problems which confront them.

If firms help in the process of resource allocation they must represent a
response to factors from which general equilibrium theory abstracts. The
economy, to use the analogy of Simon (1969) and Loasby (1976), is not like

a watch made up of thousands of parts placed separately in an appropriate position relative to all the others, but is more equivalent to a mechanism made up of several subassemblies, the operating principles of which may be analysed separately even if their ultimate purposes may be fully understood only in the context of the complete item. A system of subassemblies places limits on the number of linkages which must simultaneously be considered and thereby reduces the costs of establishing them.

Firms are formed and survive as an institutional response to transactions costs. In a world of costless knowledge they have no rationale, but in a world in which opportunities are continually being discovered and in which the formation of agreements between individuals is a costly activity, firms may be seen as devices for reducing the costs of achieving coordinated effort. The ways in which transactions costs are reduced and the problems which arise as a result will be discussed in greater detail in future chapters. For present purposes it is sufficient to remember that 'firms' are characterised by a system of bilateral contracts. Each person comes to an agreement with 'the firm'. In the case of a small business a single proprietor might be the central contractual agent. In more complex cases the agreement will be between employees, managers, bondholders or landowners and a 'legal fiction' such as BP or US Steel. The firm is a 'nexus of contracts'.[10]

The nature of this set of contracts is of very great importance. They are not highly specific contracts. They will not normally lay down extremely detailed provisions concerning when, where and how particular tasks are to be performed. When we join a firm as an employee we agree, within certain limits, to do whatever we are asked to do. We agree to be 'organised'. When we join as a manager we agree to organise resources, and have considerable discretion as to the way this may be done. Contracts, in other words, are imperfectly specified. This lack of specificity derives from the simple fact that the precise details of the actions required of the employees of a firm may be unknown at the time the contract is made. The decision-making process continues through time, and only time will reveal the decisions which may be made in the future concerning the best plan of action for the firm. If contracts had to be renegotiated with every small change of policy, the firm as a useful device for allocating resources would disappear.

Within the firm, information is collected concerning opportunities for productive collaboration, on the skills and attributes of employees, on new technical innovations, on the demands of consumers and so forth. This information must be transmitted to the relevant decision-makers who must then choose and implement a plan of action. Resource allocation within the firm is not therefore the outcome of entirely decentralised decisions by individual people in response to their particular circumstances as in a market process. Nor is it the result of simultaneous agreement between all contractors as in a state of general equilibrium. Resources within firms are allocated by the conscious decisions of planners. The market process is replaced in the firm by a planning process. Firms are 'islands of conscious power in an ocean of unconscious co-operation' to use D.H. Robertson's vivid metaphor.[11]

It is important for readers to recognise that this initial characterisation of the firm will be amended in important respects in future chapters. As presented here, our definition depends upon a clear distinction being possible between a 'market process' and a 'planning process'. Later, we shall question whether a clear dividing line can be drawn, and we will investigate in greater detail the spectrum of contractual relations which ranges from relatively arm's length market types towards contracts involving more 'firm-like' characteristics.[12] Certainly it should not be inferred from the above paragraph that firms must be monolithic organisations with highly centralised planning arrangements. As will be seen in Chapters 6 and 7, contractual relations can vary substantially both within and between firms.

The existence of firms suggests, however, that up to a point, at least, a structure of loosely specified and durable contracts with a central agent may have advantages over the market. Groups of people may find it expedient to accept these arrangements if they permit the more effective generation and use of information. It can be advantageous to be told what to do if the decision-making processes used within the firm make it possible to coordinate activities more productively than would otherwise be possible.

8.   INSTITUTIONS AND CONTRACT ENFORCEMENT

8.1   The Exchange Game

The firm as a method of enabling contractors to adjust to change and of encouraging the discovery of new possibilities for mutually advantageous cooperation will be a major theme running through this book. Alongside it there will be developed a different, though complementary, perspective. In section 2 we supposed that a number of people found themselves stranded in unfamiliar circumstances and we argued that generating information about the possibilities technically achievable would be their most important problem. Of equal significance, however, is their lack of information about how far they can trust each other. The possible advantages flowing from cooperative effort through division of labour and exchange were clear enough (sections 3 to 5) but these gains to the group as a whole could only be achieved if people could be relied upon to abide by the terms of an agreement and not to cheat.

Exchange requires that each contractor accepts the right of the other to the resources at present in their possession. Rights to the resources available to people stranded on a desert island would not be well established. No doubt the stranded travellers would apply some of the conventions about property which were familiar in their place of origin. But with no agency to enforce property rights, the danger of a Hobbesian war of all against all would be a real one. Looked at from this perspective, therefore, the assertion in section 2 that the four stranded individuals lacked information about technical possibilities is only one part of the story. They also lack conventions upon which they can rely in their dealings with one another. More generally, they require a trade-sustaining culture.

The difficulty in establishing such a culture can be seen by looking at each potential trade in the form of a game. Two people may see a potential advantage in exchanging x for y. Person C (as in the coalition illustrated in Figure 1.2) might therefore suggest that person D should provide 1.5 units of x and that, after receiving the x, C will return in exchange 1.5 units of y. Person D replies that this is an excellent idea but that it would be even better if C would first provide the 1.5 units of y and that, on receipt of the y, person D would immediately return 1.5 units of x. If neither party is able to trust the other, no trade takes place and the payoff is zero. If both are trustworthy and the trade is honestly made, they will each receive some net benefit from the exchange (let us say this has a value of unity to each person). Finally, if one party mistakenly trusts the other, sending the x or y but receiving nothing in return, the payoff to the cheater we may suppose is two while that to the trusting party is -1. This structure of payoffs is recorded in Table 1.6.

Table 1.6   The structure of payoffs in a game of exchange

		Person D	
		Cooperate	Cheat
Person C	Cooperate	1, 1	−1, 2
	Cheat	2, −1	0, 0

Person C's payoffs are given on the left of each pair and person D's on the right. The game is symmetrical in terms of outcomes. The precise numbers attached to the outcomes are not crucial to the discussion, however. It is the structure of the game as a whole which matters. As presented in Table 1.6, the game of exchange is an example of a prisoner's dilemma. Consider the situation from the point of view of person C. If D cooperates and provides C with the agreed units of x, person C will receive a higher payoff if he cheats. On the other hand, if D cheats and does not send the agreed units of x, it is still true that person C will do better by also being uncooperative. The worst outcome is to be a 'sucker'. Cheating is therefore a dominant strategy in a prisoner's dilemma. This is so even though, from a social point of view, the combined payoff to persons C and D from their both being cooperative exceeds that available from the other alternatives.

Many situations in economic life which require cooperative effort can be modelled in the form of a prisoner's dilemma. In Chapter 2 the problem of providing public goods is briefly discussed, while in Chapter 4 the difficulty of providing incentives to cooperate in a team activity provides the basis for much of the analysis of Part 2. Here it is necessary merely to note the possible responses to the prisoner's dilemma which have been suggested and which can be seen reflected in the institutional arrangements which have developed. If cooperation is so difficult, how is it that we observe as much cooperative activity as we do? Four possible answers are proposed below, which will receive varying amounts of attention in future chapters. These may be summarised as the development of reputation, the evolution of norms, the use of outside monitoring and penalties, and finally the creation of a cooperative ethos through leadership.

8.2   Conventions and Norms

The most obvious objection to the simple exposition of the prisoner's dilemma in Table 1.6 is that it presents trade as a single, never to be repeated encounter between two people who have no knowledge of each other. If, instead, we consider the possibility that persons C and D might repeat their exchange transaction many times in the future, the game changes its nature. Repeated games or 'supergames' can be complex to deal with because the number of possible individual strategies rises exponentially with the number of iterations of the game. It is no longer simply a question of whether to cooperate or cheat in the first round, but whether to cooperate or cheat in the second, conditional upon what had happened in the first and so forth. Nevertheless, both intuition and formal analysis confirm that a sufficiently high probability of repeated dealing will provide a framework in which cooperation can take root.[13] The strategy which has attracted the most theoretical attention and which has performed well in simulations of repeated prisoner's dilemma games is 'tit for tat'.[14]

A person playing 'tit for tat' cooperates in the first encounter and thereafter cooperates or cheats according to the behaviour of his or her opponent. The obvious advantage of this strategy is that two people playing 'tit for tat' will cooperate with one another in the first and all subsequent rounds while limiting their vulnerability to cheaters. Suppose, for example, that after each play of the game there is a probability of 3/4 that another round will be played (that is, there is a one in four chance that it will be the last). The players do not know how many times they will actually play the game but the expected number of iterations will be four. Even this may be enough to make 'tit for tat' worth considering as a strategy. The expected payoffs to the players are recorded in Table 1.7.

Table 1.7   Expected payoffs in the exchange game when the probability of repetition is 3/4

		Person D	
		'Tit for tat'	Always cheat
Person C	'Tit for tat'	4, 4	−1, 2
	Always cheat	2, −1	0, 0

Clearly, if persons C and D both play 'tit for tat' they receive an expected payoff of four each. They both cooperate in round one and then, because each has cooperated, they continue to do so in future rounds. If both cheat in every round their payoff is zero as before. Where one person cheats and the other plays 'tit for tat', the latter is exploited in the first round only – the cheater receiving two and the cooperator −1. In subsequent rounds, both cheat and receive zero payoffs.

A sufficiently high probability of repetition thus changes the structure of the exchange game. When confronted with a certain cheater it remains the best strategy to cheat. But cheating is no longer the dominant strategy. If someone is playing 'tit for tat' it is better to respond in kind than to cheat. Assuming that it is impossible to know in advance which strategy particular individuals are going to play, strategy choice will depend upon what probability people attach to meeting a person playing 'tit for tat'. Let the probability of meeting an opponent playing 'tit for tat' be p^* and the probability of meeting a cheater be $(1-p^*)$. Our expected return to 'tit for tat' will then be

$$4p^* + (-1)(1-p^*).$$

Similarly our expected return to cheating will be

$$2p^* + (0)(1 - p^*).$$

Thus, 'tit for tat' will give us a higher expected payoff providing that

$$5p^* - 1 > 2p^*$$

that is

$$p^* > 1/3.$$

If the probability of meeting a person playing 'tit for tat' exceeds 1/3, it will pay us to adopt that strategy also. Thus, once this critical proportion of 'tit for tat' strategists in a population is exceeded, there will be a tendency for it to grow. People will learn that cooperation is in their own interests. It is also evident that the higher the probability of repeat dealing, and hence the higher the expected number of iterations of the game, the lower this critical probability p^* will be. With the payoffs of Table 1.6, if the chance of any given play of the game being the final one is only 1/100 (and hence the expected number of plays is 100) 'tit for tat' would give a greater expected return than continual cheating, even if the chance of finding another 'tit for tat' player was as low as 1/99. Such are the enormous potential rewards from finding someone cooperative, that quite large losses in first-round plays with cheaters are worth incurring in the search.

It is therefore possible to tell a plausible story about the evolution of cooperative behaviour.[15] Mathematical biologists use the concept of the 'evolutionary stable strategy' to describe a strategy which is immune to invasion by a group of mutants playing any other strategy (see John Maynard Smith, 1982, *Evolution and the Theory of Games*). In certain conditions, self-interested behaviour may result in the widespread adoption of the 'tit for tat' strategy in trading games. 'Tit for tat' becomes what Sugden (1986) calls a convention. Once established, there are powerful forces of self-interest tending to maintain it, even though alternative conventions might equally well have developed. People comply with established norms of behaviour not necessarily because they think these are worthy of respect from an ethical perspective but because they accord with their own selfish interests.

It can be argued, however, that once conventions have become established they gradually accumulate about them an aura of moral acceptability. People may begin to follow norms of behaviour not merely because it is in their interests to do so but because they believe these norms have moral force.[16] They feel they ought to cooperate in the exchange game and would feel a sense of guilt if they did not do so, even in situations where a single round of the game is all that is expected. Tourists, for example, may be in no greater danger of cheating in a small local hotel than in an international chain that hopes to attract their custom again in a different location. In general, however, the existence of the 'traveller's tax' is not widely doubted, although whether it derives from poor knowledge of local conventions on the part of travellers, or poor adherence to more universal conventions on the part of local inhabitants, is perhaps a moot point.

8.3 Reputation

According to the argument of subsection 8.2, cooperative behaviour developed because successive rounds of the exchange game are played with the same person. The non-repeated prisoner's dilemma is a game in which the players know nothing of one another except that, in the absence of a moral imperative, the players are virtually impelled to cheat. Repetition enabled knowledge of an opponent to build up, and cheating could be punished by lack of cooperation in the future. Each person was assumed to develop knowledge about other contractors in the market entirely by personal experience. Those playing a 'tit for tat' strategy would remember those who had cheated and those who had cooperated on their last acquaintance. This memory would determine the strategy played in any future encounter with these people. Strategy choice becomes, to this extent, personalised.

Clearly the forces leading to cooperation would be greatly reinforced if information about strategy choice in an encounter with one person were available to other potential transactors thereafter. A person observed cheating in the first round would then know that all future encounters would yield nothing, even if these encounters were with 'new' opponents. The new opponents would know that the person played the cheating strategy in round one, and would respond with the like strategy in future rounds. People who might otherwise have played 'tit for tat' on their first encounter with the cheater will be warned off and will defect. Only a period of cooperation in the face of defection by others might re-establish a person's 'standing' after the initial decision to cheat.

8.4 Monitoring and Penalties

To achieve a cooperative outcome given the payoffs in the trading game recorded in Table 1.6, something has to happen to change the structure of the game. In subsection 8.2 the possibility of repetition was enough to produce this effect. An obvious alternative is for some third party to monitor compliance with the agreed deal and to punish a transactor who cheats. If this monitor can, for example impose a 'fine' in excess of one on anyone who cheats, the payoffs in Table 1.6 will be such that cooperation is the dominant strategy even in a single encounter.

The monitoring solution is particularly likely where information about behaviour is otherwise poor. In the case of our exchange game it is at least clear to each transactor what strategy their opponent has played and the 'discipline of continuous dealings' may then be sufficient to ensure cooperative behaviour. In many of the contexts with which we shall be concerned later in this book, however, it may not be possible to tell whether someone has cooperated simply by looking at the outcome of an agreement. Especially when many people are trying to cooperate on some joint enterprise, apportioning responsibility for the final outcome may not be feasible. Transactors again face a prisoner's dilemma, but the 'tit for tat' repeated game solution will not work. Not only may it be impossible to determine who has cooperated and who has not, but the rational response to this information is not obvious. Do I withdraw my cooperation in the next round when a single other person in the group cheats? Or do I cooperate providing a sufficient number of others do likewise? If the latter, how big does the cheating group have to be before I join them?

Where individual behaviour can be fairly accurately gauged by other transactors in a group, and where punishment can be focused on the non-cooperative person, the forces of spontaneous order may operate to a degree. In Chapter 10, for example, the use of peer pressure and 'shame' to induce cooperative behaviour in a profit-sharing enterprise is discussed. The need for a specialist monitor and enforcer plays a major role in much modern analysis of economic organisation, however. The firm as a device for policing and enforcing contracts will therefore be a continually recurring theme throughout the book.

8.5 Moral Leadership

Imposing a sufficiently large fine for cheating may, in principle, turn the exchange game from a prisoner's dilemma into a game of harmonious coordination. It is usual to see the punishment or fine as administered by some monitor as discussed in subsection 8.4. Casson (1991) argues, however, that, especially where the costs of monitoring are high, it is the task of leadership through 'moral manipulation' to associate cheating or slacking with a guilt penalty. Thus, the penalty is psychological rather than material. It may be powerful because it operates even in circumstances where a person's cheating is not discovered by other people. Obviously, if people feel bad about cheating, more possibilities for beneficial exchange will be realised. A trusting culture sustains trade.

We have already seen in section 8.2 that rules having moral force might evolve over time. People might abide by such rules even when flouting them is in their purely material interests. Casson admits that trust can emerge naturally but 'in many cases it needs to be engineered' (p. 28). Leaders are in the business of moral propaganda and preference manipulation. Expenditures on guilt-enhancing propaganda are a substitute for monitoring expenditure. Some further discussion of the role of guilt and shame in economic organisation will take place in Chapters 10 and 11, but the role of leadership in setting the general moral climate will not be pursued further.

9. CONCLUSION

The firm can be seen as a response to two major economic problems. First, people face the problem of adjusting their economic activities to continually changing conditions. They also need the flexibility to make use of new information generated by their own operations. This leads to the idea of the firm as a device for coping with change. Second, agreements between contractors require enforcement. This enforcement problem may give rise to the development of close, durable relationships based on trust and the generation of reputational capital, or it may lead to systems of monitoring behaviour backed up by sanctions.

Before investigating these problems in detail and analysing their effect on the internal structure of firms, it is time to look more closely at the general nature of 'transactions costs' which play such a central part in the theory of economic organisation.

NOTES

1. Loasby (1976, p. 70).
2. Philip H. Wicksteed (1946), *The Common Sense of Political Economy*, Vol. 1, p. 166, Routledge, London (first published in 1910).
3. For an elementary introduction to game theory see M. Bacharach (1976) *Economics and the Theory of Games*, Macmillan, London. The classic reference is J. von Neumann and O. Morgenstern (1944).
4. Perceiving economic life as a discovery procedure and, by implication, the primary economic problem as an information problem, is especially associated with 'Austrian' thinkers; see Hayek (1978). The approach lends itself to the use of biological and, particularly, evolutionary analogies as new ideas are tried out and submitted to the test of survival in the market. A major contribution in this tradition is Alchian (1950). A more detailed discussion of the evolutionary tradition is presented in Chapter 12.
5. Game theorists will recognise this table as representing the complete 'characteristic function' of our exchange game. For each possible coalition the joint payoff is recorded; see Bacharach (1976, pp. 121–4).

6. This description of a bargaining process was used in the theoretical work of F.Y. Edgeworth, especially in his Mathematical Physics. See also 'On the determinateness of economic equilibrium' in Edgeworth (1925) Vol. II. Thus: 'A "final settlement" is not reached until the market has hit upon a set of agreements which cannot be varied with advantage to all the re-contracting parties' (p. 314).

7. Gravelle and Rees (1981) present an intuitive discussion of the conditions under which this theorem will hold (pp. 266–70).

8. E.g. Gravelle and Rees (1981, pp. 263–5).

9. Walras (1954), *Elements of Pure Economics*, translated by William Jaffe.

10. The 'nexus of contracts' idea goes back to Coase (1937). A more detailed discussion is undertaken in Chapter 2, and it forms the foundation for most of the rest of the analysis in this book.

11. D.H. Robertson and S.R. Dennison (1960, p. 73).

12. See especially Chapter 7, section 3.

13. In any game repeated a finite number of times, it can be shown that the dominant strategy is still to shirk. Since defection of one's opponent is certain in the last round of the game, it is rational to defect in the penultimate round. Since both defect in the penultimate round, they both find it rational to defect in the round before the penultimate one and so forth back to the very first round of the game. This totally 'non-cooperative' result is felt by many to be counterintuitive as well as being contradicted by experiments. Much effort has been devoted to achieving more 'plausible' results; for example, Luce and Raiffa (1957, pp. 97–102). See also Radner (1981). In the text, we consider situations in which there is always a given positive probability that the game will be repeated.

14. For a fascinating exposition of the theory of 'spontaneous order' and the social evolution of cooperative behaviour see Sugden (1986).

15. The classic reference is Axelrod (1984), *The Evolution of Cooperation*.

16. Sugden (1986) discusses the relationship between evolved conventions and moral judgements (Chapters 8 and 9). 'There is more to spontaneous order than a set of conventions that it is in everyone's interest to follow; these conventions are likely to be supported by a system of morality' (p. 140). This derivation of moral judgements is particularly associated with David Hume (1740), *A Treatise of Human Nature*.

2. Transactions costs

*'The main reason why it is profitable to establish a firm would seem to be
that there is a cost of using the price mechanism'*
(Ronald Coase)[1]

1. THE PROCESS OF EXCHANGE

All exchange transactions encounter problems of information and enforcement. Consider, for example, the process of building houses. Suppose that
a person, A, who, for the sake of convenience, we shall call a 'he', wishes to
build an extension to his home. One possibility is that he will draw up some
plans, submit them to the relevant public authorities, dig the foundations,
order the bricks, mix the cement, build the walls, plaster the interior, put in
the doors and windows and undertake to install any electrical fitments and
plumbing. Elementary economic principles, however, suggest this is
unlikely. Recognising the advantages to be gained from specialisation and
exchange, person A might instead decide to spend his time in a suitably
remunerative occupation and then to purchase the services of specialist
help. He could, for example, pay an architect to draw plans, another agent
to obtain the necessary planning consent, a bricklayer to build walls and
an electrician, carpenter, plumber and so forth to fulfil their respective
tasks.

By forming agreements with specialists, person A will gain the
classic advantages from exchange. But he has also given himself some
problems.

1. Like a cook consulting Hannah Glasse's *Art of Cookery* who is there
   advised 'first catch your hare', A has to find the people who are going
   to help him. As may be subtly suggested in this celebrated misquote,
   obtaining the constituent ingredients is not necessarily the easiest part
   in any process of coordination.
2. Having located his bricklayer, architect and electrician, A has to form
   some assessment of their professional competence. If the bricklayer
   is more productive at laying bricks than is person A there should be

some advantage in using his or her services, but how does A acquire such information? The existence of some other examples of the brick-layer's handiwork which A can inspect, or the recommendation of other satisfied clients, are obvious possibilities. Inspecting other ser-vices and goods, however, may present greater difficulties. Person A may never be quite sure that he is not risking life and limb each time he switches on his electric kettle!

3.   With each of his contacts, A will draw up a separate agreement, but this will not necessarily be as straightforward as it sounds. Person A knows what he wants to do in a very general sense: he wants to extend his house. The technical details of how this can be accomplished and the options available may, however, be quite beyond him. When he approaches his architect with a request to produce some plans, he therefore confronts a significant problem. He cannot ask the architect to undertake a highly specific and carefully delineated task, since at this level of detail A quite literally does not know what he wants. Instead he must ask the architect to act on his behalf. The architect is A's agent and is asked to make specific recommendations which are likely to satisfy the general requirements laid down by person A. Proceeding in this way enables A to gain the advantages of specialised advice, but as an intelligent and shrewd individual he is sure to be beset by a few nagging doubts.

If, for example, A does not like the architect's suggested plans and does not wish to proceed with the project, will he have to pay a fee to the architect? Clearly the architect is unlikely to agree to waive his or her fee simply because the client is dissatisfied. Such an arrangement would provide an enormous incentive to person A to dissemble. He would claim to see no merit in the plans whatever whilst secretly taking careful note of their contents. The alternative arrangement, however, by which the architect is paid a fee irrespective of the quality of his or her work, is likewise fraught with difficulties, this time from the perspective of person A. Person A may wonder whether the archi-tect has given his problem more than a moment's thought, or has perhaps delegated the case to some assistant of little talent and even less experience.

Similar considerations will play a part in person A's dealings with each of the other tradespeople involved in his project. The plumber, for example, cannot be told in detail how to proceed, since only the broad objectives are defined by A. Technicalities such as the gauge and type of piping to be used, the potential heat output required of the boiler, the positioning of thermostats, the siting of the pumps, are all matters upon which A will have to accept the advice of the expert.

The plumber will be asked to solve these detailed problems in ways which serve the interests of A. He or she should not install a boiler with the wrong characteristics simply because he/she stands to gain from an agreement with the suppliers, but the client will be in a weak position from which to detect such behaviour.

4. Overcoming the difficulties of formulating enforceable agreements with each individual is an important prerequisite to the success of A's plans. Of equal significance, however, is A's ability to coordinate the activities of each of his helpers. To build an extension to a house using specialist help involves many people cooperating together. Only in the simplest cases will the provisions of one person's contract be entirely independent of the provisions in another's. A decision, for example, to lay a concrete floor rather than a wooden suspended floor will influence the way in which the heating system is installed. Likewise, the electrician and plumber may have to work closely together at various stages. Thus, A will find it difficult to finalise his agreement with any one person in the absence of agreements with all the others. Stolidly, he contacts first one and then another, asking advice, modifying his original proposals and renegotiating terms until eventually he calculates that construction can begin. Inevitably there will be some residual uncertainty about his plans, some unforeseen difficulties which will arise and which will result in a continuing process of bargaining. Within rather vaguely defined limits, his craftsmen accept the obligation to be flexible. Outside these limits, they will claim that the job they are doing was not part of their original agreement and will therefore wish to renegotiate terms.

As building starts, A becomes painfully aware that delays and problems in one area have implications for his plans in others. Bricklayers turn up but cannot build because the inspector has yet to see the foundations. Person A nevertheless pays them for their time. The nagging doubts which afflicted A at the beginning now turn to serious concern. Indeed, he begins to have nightmares. In his sleep he sees the extension to his house. Were those gaps in the roof really the latest thing in ventilation? Is it usual for walls to sway so far in the breeze? In the nearby hotel, his architect and lawyer share a joke over a glass of whisky. It seems they are using his wallet to pay for their drinks. His gaze returns to his extension, only to see the whole structure collapse in a cloud of dust. Across the rubble a shadowy figure advances towards him coughing and dusting his pin-stripe suit. The planner from the local authority serves him with a demolition order as a result of failure to comply with all necessary regulations. Person A wakes up sweating. He, at least, has discovered the primary message

of this chapter. Whatever may be the potential advantages of specialisation and exchange, they certainly do not come free.

2.   CONTRACTS AND INFORMATION

Our fictional story of person A's building project was designed to highlight
some of the difficulties everyone encounters at some time or other in the
process of contracting. It is now necessary to look at the issues involved
from a more analytical viewpoint. Perhaps the most important point about
the hapless A is that his problems all derive from various forms of *information deficiency*. Were information costlessly available and all transactions costlessly enforceable most of his worries would be over. Consider
now the various points at which A confronts the problem of his own ignorance.

2.1   Adverse Selection or 'Hidden Information'

2.1.1   Examples of adverse selection
The first problem was that A did not know the location, skills or reliability of the tradespeople he required. Finding out this type of information
requires time spent in search. More consideration will be given to the question of search in Chapter 3, but it should be evident from the discussion
in Chapter 1 that to search exhaustively – that is to search until information is complete – would be to do nothing else. At some stage the costs of
further search in terms of the perceived opportunities forgone will outweigh the benefits in terms of the expected new opportunities potentially
discoverable. Further, certain types of ignorance are in their nature costly
to dispel through search. Ignorance of the price of a very well-defined
product can be mitigated by asking for quotes from an increasing number
of sellers, but overcoming ignorance of product quality is more difficult.
It may be worth paying more for the services of a more skilled person, but
how is person A to tell a good and reliable craftsperson from a poor one
ex ante? Clearly, this problem ultimately derives from the difficulty of precisely specifying what services are required in a contract. If a contract
between person A and a craftsperson were clearly and unambiguously
specified the 'reliability' or 'skill' of that person would not be an issue.
Either the provisions of the contract are fulfilled and the craftsperson
demonstrates sufficient skill or they are not fulfilled in which case the
absence of sufficient skill results in a specified penalty. A skilled and reliable craftsperson is valuable to person A because he may not have the technical knowledge required to specify precisely what is to be done. The

absence of this knowledge, however, will make it difficult for A to discover the credentials of his potential workforce. All craftspeople, skilled or otherwise, will have an incentive to overstate their expertise in the process of negotiation, and the truly skilled will have difficulty in communicating their status to the doubting person A.

The problem which we have uncovered here is in fact of very widespread interest in economics. Essentially it relates to any transaction in which one of the parties is better informed than the other. Such transactions are said to be characterised by a structure of information which is *asymmetric*. Akerlof (1970) gives as an example of a market with asymmetric information; transactions in second-hand cars. It will often be very costly for a buyer of a second-hand car to determine accurately its true quality. He or she may or may not buy a 'lemon' (an American expression for a bad car) but *ex ante* there is not much that can be done to avoid it. Ignorance on the part of buyers will imply therefore that both good and bad second-hand cars sell for the same price. Sellers of these cars, however, will have much better knowledge of their history and characteristics and therefore correspondingly better judgement about the probability of obtaining good or bad service in the future. The upshot will be that owners of good cars will tend to feel that the second-hand market value seriously understates their (better informed) valuation. The owners of 'lemons', on the other hand, are more likely to sell. As the average quality of second-hand cars offered for sale falls, the price that they fetch falls with it, and this accentuates the tendency for only the worst to be offered. It is at least possible to develop a model in which this *adverse selection* problem is so serious that no transactions will take place at all, even though better-informed buyers would stand to gain.[2] Note the implied assumption, however, that contracts cannot be drawn up in such a way that failure of a car to meet the standards claimed for it would elicit penalties from the seller.

Perhaps the classic instance of adverse selection brought about by asymmetric information is in the realm of insurance. A provider of insurance against some undesired contingency (say ill health) may be less well informed about the probability of the occurrence of this event than the person seeking insurance. The terms quoted by an insurance company will be based upon certain basic pieces of information such as the age and medical history of the person buying the insurance; information which may be obtained at relatively low cost. This information may not be detailed enough, however, to distinguish with sufficient subtlety between relatively good and bad risks. Once more, people with good health prospects will regard the insurance terms offered as rather unfavourable while people with bad prospects will find the terms attractive. The people who are therefore most inclined to take out health insurance are those most likely to require health care. There is an 'adverse selection' problem based upon asymmetric information. *Ex ante* it may be very costly for an insurance company to distinguish between good and bad risks, just as, by assumption, buyers of cars in the last paragraph could not distinguish good and bad cars, and person A in our story found it difficult to distinguish between good and bad craftspeople.

2.1.2 Adverse selection and 'reputation'
In this context it is useful to note the importance of 'reputation' or 'goodwill' in markets with asymmetric information. As was seen in the exchange game of Chapter 1, if knowledge of cheating becomes widely known *ex post*, traders will have an incentive to remain in good standing. A seller of second-hand cars who has established a reputation for providing good cars will be able to charge higher prices or establish markets where none existed before. Similarly, person A found it expedient to use craftspeople with a good local reputation. The existence of 'goodwill' economises on transactions costs by reducing search, thus enabling trade to take place in higher-quality products and services than might otherwise be possible.

2.1.3 Adverse selection and 'signalling'
Another response to the adverse selection problem is to think of 'signalling' or 'screening' mechanisms. A signal is an activity which convinces buyers of the quality of a seller's wares. It is convincing because it is so structured that a seller of poor-quality products would be irrational to undertake the activity. As Hirshleifer and Riley (1979, p. 1406) express it: 'Signalling takes place when sellers of truly higher-quality products engage in some activity that would not be rational for those selling lower quality products.' Examples of possible signalling devices include the following:

- *Advertising* Advertising may be more rational for producers of high-quality goods than for providers of low-quality goods. By engaging in an expensive advertising campaign, producers are expressing confidence in the ability of their product to attract and keep customers. A shoddy product that may fool customers on a single occasion but for no longer is unlikely to be worth extensive advertising.
- *Education qualifications* Educational credentials can act as a signal if the marginal cost of education is lower for higher-quality workers. Offering higher wages for people with certain qualifications will be most attractive for those who find these qualifications the least costly to achieve. A more detailed exposition of this mechanism will be presented in Chapter 6.

- *Insurance deductibles* In insurance markets, higher quality risks can signal their status to insurance companies by a willingness to accept a big deductible (that is, less than full coverage).

Signalling may develop in the presence of information asymmetry and adverse selection. It should not be assumed that the results are always socially advantageous. As will be seen later, signalling can lead to a waste of resources. If the signal is costly to transmit and the private gains to signalling are all derived from someone else's private losses, the end result will be a simple redistribution of income with resources dissipated in the process. Where, therefore, the information conveyed by a signal permits a more effective allocation of resources, signalling may be both privately and socially beneficial. Some signals, though, may have the opposite effect. In Chapter 9, for example, we will discuss how 'signalling' to the stock market by managers of joint-stock companies might result in a form of 'short termism'.

2.1.4 Ignorance of contractual results

Where information remains hidden *ex post* and the buyer can never really tell the quality of the services he or she has received, the adverse selection problem is yet more difficult to overcome. Suppose, for example, that A attempts to draw up a set of state-contingent contracts with his workpeople. He agrees, for example, that *if* certain geological conditions are found to prevail, the foundations will need to be strengthened or extra drainage installed. He agrees that *if* weather conditions are unfavourable, construction may be delayed and specified extra expenses incurred and so forth. This type of contract clearly requires that A and his workpeople can agree on what 'state of the world' actually pertains. If, for example, it proved very costly for A to verify the correct position, the workers would have an incentive to 'observe' any state of the world which they felt was most favourable to their own interests. Where it is expedient to discover problems, the worker will duly discover them, and where it is inexpedient they will be ignored. When workers inform person A that they have 'hit problems', they are saying 'I have observed a state of the world which permits me to take the following actions under the terms of our contract and which commits you to extra expenditure.' In many cases, the problem will be sufficiently obvious to both parties, but in others person A may have to trust the worker. Asymmetric information therefore turns out to be at the root of A's difficulties once more.

In the circumstances of person A's building project it is perhaps unlikely that this extreme form of information asymmetry will pose intractable difficulties. Nevertheless, there are situations in which the quality of a service is difficult to assess by the purchaser even after it has been delivered. As will be seen in Chapter 11, this possibility lies behind some recent thinking concerning the rationale of the non-profit enterprise.

2.2 Moral Hazard or 'Hidden Action'

A second important problem facing A was that even after striking a bargain he did not know whether the other parties were fulfilling their obligations. The electrician seemed to have wired his house, but was it safe? Was the architect actually exerting him or herself on A's behalf? Was the plumber using unnecessarily expensive equipment? Whereas under section 2.1 the problem was that *ex ante* a buyer might be ill-informed about the qualities of a potential purchase or the difficulties encountered by people working on their behalf, the problem being considered now concerns the difficulty of observing or deducing the *actions* of the supplier.

Moral hazard exists when the probability of a given 'state of the world' occurring is influenced by one of the parties to a contract but when the behaviour of this contractor cannot be observed. Insurance contracts again supply the classic case. Suppose that person A, in return for a specified payment now (an insurance premium), promises to pay to person B (who we will assume to be female) another specified sum in the event of person B being robbed. Our discussion so far has been limited to A's problem of deciding whether B is telling the truth when she claims to have been robbed or whether in reality the only person being 'robbed' is person A. Even when the prevailing 'state of the world' is easily verified, however, there remains the possibility that the outcome was materially influenced by the activities of B. In other words, the probability of being robbed is not entirely independent of B's behaviour. She is obviously more likely to be robbed if she spends long periods of time away from her house and habitually leaves the door open than if she installs a system of locks and alarms and never leaves her property unattended. This suggests the possibility that the insurance contract could specify conditions which commit person B to take certain precautions. Once more, the problem of asymmetric information is confronted, however. If the contract states that B must always lock her door when leaving her house, how is A to know whether this provision was or was not complied with when B was robbed? Further, although it is easy enough to think of a few basic precautions against robbery, it would be extremely costly to investigate the detailed circumstances of person B in order to establish the actions required of her in every particular. Only B can have the kind of knowledge concerning specific circumstances necessary to determine all the options available to discourage thieves. Once the insurance contract is agreed, however, B will clearly have a much smaller incentive to engage in thief-discouraging activities than before.

This general problem of verifying *ex post* whether a person's actions have been compatible with the provisions of a contract is called the problem of moral hazard. In the context of insurance markets, Arrow (1962) summarises the issue as follows: 'The general principle is the difficulty of distinguishing between a state of nature and a decision by the insured. As a result, any insurance policy and in general any device for shifting risks can have the effect of dulling incentives' (p. 145). As we have already seen, however, these problems are not confined to insurance markets. Any contracts drawn up in conditions of asymmetric information may give rise to moral hazard. As Demsetz (1969) puts it: 'Moral hazard is a relevant cost of producing insurance; it is not different from the cost that arises from the tendency of men to shirk when their employer is not watching them' (p. 167).

2.3 Bounded Rationality

The third broad class of transactional problem facing person A which we may identify was the simple magnitude of the potential task of coordinating the activities of his workpeople. This problem would exist even were information symmetrical; that is, available equally to A and the people he employs; and it is therefore logically distinct from the issues discussed earlier in this section. Not only were the provisions of each person's contract interdependent but they would vary with all sorts of possible contingencies which might arise as work proceeded. The capacity of person A to imagine all possible future contingencies and then process the information required to allow for these different contingencies in the contracts of each person he hires is obviously limited. Person A faces, in other words, a problem which is now usually referred to as 'bounded rationality'.

The idea of 'bounded rationality' is especially associated with the work of H.A. Simon (1957, 1969, 1979) and O.E. Williamson (1975, 1985). Both writers use the example of the game of chess to illustrate the issues involved. Given the rules which govern the movement of the pieces on a chessboard, we might in principle consider constructing a list of all possible games. We might start by recording all possible opening moves and then, for each one, record all possible legal responses, and so on, until we have built up an entire 'decision tree'. The problem, of course, and the factor which prevents chess becoming a totally trivial pastime, is that the decision tree would be of such size and complexity that it beggars the imagination. Even the best chess players must make their decisions in the absence of a complete list of future contingencies which might possibly flow from them, and resort must be made to a limited set of considerations which experience has suggested are important.

If rationality is conceived as selecting the best possible course of action for achieving a specified objective, chess moves evidently do not qualify. Yet most people would baulk at describing chess decisions as irrational. Indeed, chess is widely regarded as the board game requiring powers of reason in the highest degree. Chess problems are susceptible to the application of reason, but the complexity of the game is such that decisions are effectively taken under conditions of uncertainty. This is why Williamson (1975, p. 23) argues that 'the distinction between deterministic complexity and uncertainty is inessential . . . As long as either uncertainty or complexity is present in requisite degree, the bounded rationality problem arises.'

2.4   Asset Specificity and 'Hold-up'

There is a final contractual problem which plays an important role in the transactions costs theory of economic organisation. Where situations are complex and contracts are not absolutely 'cast iron' and perfectly enforceable, there will be room for adjustments to contractual terms over time in response to changes in the bargaining power of the contractors. This problem is particularly serious when assets become 'transaction specific'.

Consider once more the relationship between person A and his architect. It is likely that, over time, the architect has accumulated all sorts of special information about the circumstances and preferences of A, the nature of his property, and the engineering and other difficulties associated with construction work in the area. Were A to change his architect, the new person would not have access to the same stock of information and might, therefore, be much less effective whilst undergoing the initial process of 'learning' about the background. The existing architect has an advantage over an outsider in serving person A – a so called 'first-mover advantage'. Notice that, by assumption, person A has financed the accumulation of this useful information by paying the architect a fee at least as great as could have been achieved elsewhere during the initial period of their association, but the information is in the form of 'human capital', and the human form is that of the architect, not person A. The architect, realising that he or she is a much more productive resource than any outsider, may therefore be tempted to raise his or her fee. Person A will not like this, but may be prepared to pay some increase because the alternative of employing a new architect carries an even higher cost.

The architect is more productive than any outsider, and this return in excess of what would be achievable using alternative human resources is a form of 'rent'.[3] There is a surplus associated with the use of the existing architect, a surplus accruing to a type of specific capital (specialised knowledge), and there is a danger that much effort can be taken up in a fight over who should receive it. Although person A has financed it, the architect may attempt to take some of it by implicitly threatening termination. If person A succumbs to this threat, he is the victim of 'hold-up'.

It is not necessarily always the buyer in a transaction who is vulnerable to 'hold-up', however. Suppose, for example, that A has such eccentric ideas that the plumber has to invest in material and equipment which he or she is most unlikely ever to find a use for again and which has a very low value on the second-hand market. Once the plumber has invested in these assets, s/he in turn will be vulnerable to contract renegotiation. They are transaction-specific physical assets, and any return above their value in alternative uses is again a 'rent'. Person A may try to push down the agreed price of the work thus appropriating some of the rent which accrues to these assets. The plumber will feel aggrieved but may be in a poor bargaining position for resisting some adjustment to contract terms. Any return on the assets in excess of their value elsewhere is, in principle, better than terminating the contract.

In practice, of course, these problems are unlikely to be of great significance in a local community where reputational effects are significant. Further, a simple solution to the specific physical assets problem is for the plumber to insist that person A should finance them in the first place. Person A will buy the specialised equipment and the plumber will use it when undertaking the work. The plumber cannot 'hold up' person A, since a threat to raise the agreed fee will be met with the use of another plumber. Person A cannot 'hold up' the plumber because a threat to lower the fee will result in the plumber working elsewhere. In other words, there is no longer a 'rent' element associated with the plumber's services. The rent accrues to person A's services as a provider of capital to himself, and it does not matter whether the return is seen as accruing to the provider or the user. That particular transaction has been 'internalised'.

Although there are circumstances, therefore, in which asset specificity poses no great problem, vulnerability to 'hold-up' in general plays a large part in the theory of economic organisation. The existence of transaction-specific assets (either human or physical) will play a significant role in our discussion of the firm's relationship with its employees (Chapter 6), its suppliers (Chapter 7) and its financiers (Chapter 9). It is also associated with the question of the viability of cooperative and other forms of enterprise (Chapter 10). As will be seen, the modern approach to the firm emphasises that its capabilities are highly specific and related to the information and experience accumulated in its membership. This implies that a significant part of any firm's return is rent on its specific human assets. A high degree of trust is required if these rents are not to be dissipated in distributional squabbles. Casson (1991) argues that it is a crucial role of the business leader to engineer this trusting environment. We will concentrate more on the power of repeat dealing and reputation. There can be no doubt, however, that business structure both reflects the degree of trust that exists between transactors and influences its future development.

In the following section, consideration is given to a number of different institutional responses to the problems we have been considering. Search costs, asymmetric information leading to adverse selection and moral hazard, bounded rationality, and vulnerability to 'hold-up' are factors which inevitably influence the ways in which people contract with one another. If gains from trade are potentially available, it might be expected that institutions will be developed to facilitate their realisation, and this will involve mitigating the effects of some of the forces which stand in the way.

3.   INSTITUTIONAL RESPONSES TO TRANSACTIONS COSTS

Information is costly to obtain. Finding out about the opportunities which are potentially available, about the quality of the goods and services on offer, and about the appropriate responses to various possible future contingencies, involves time and effort. The absence of information, as we have seen, can inhibit the process of exchange, but if the costs of acquiring the relevant information are too great the failure of exchange to occur is both predictable and efficient. This was the essential bone of contention in the celebrated exchange between Arrow (1962) and Demsetz (1969) already referred to in the section above. To observe the failure of exchange to take place is not to prove inefficiency if information costs exist. To assert otherwise is, according to Demsetz, to commit the fallacy of the 'free lunch' (that is, to assume that information is potentially available without cost). Alternatively, the fallacy involved might be described as the 'people could be different' fallacy (that is, that somehow or other people could be induced not to exploit asymmetries in information and that the problem of moral hazard might go away).

As we have taken some pains to elaborate, however, the process of exchange inevitably entails overcoming these transactional difficulties. To assume away the problem of information is not very helpful if the object of study is the theory of the firm, but it would be equally unhelpful to assume that no attempts are made to mitigate the problem. If exchange is potentially advantageous we would expect the would-be transactors to devise mechanisms which enable it to proceed. Institutions will develop which economise on information costs and permit trades which would otherwise be impossible to take place.

3.1 Money

The idea that institutions develop in response to transactions costs is familiar enough in certain areas. All students learn at an early stage the advantages associated with the use of money as a medium of exchange relative to a system of barter. Elementary textbooks will usually contain examples of the difficulties faced by a fisherman vainly searching for a cobbler who wants a piece of haddock, to use D.H. Robertson's example. The problem of establishing a 'double coincidence of wants' is a slightly misleading way of looking at the issue of barter, however. A barter system – that is, a system involving the direct exchange of goods and services without the use of money – does not strictly require a 'double coincidence of wants' unless it is stipulated that all exchange transactions must be bilateral ones. A fisherman can obtain shoes from a cobbler under a system of barter even if the cobbler has no taste for fish, but to do so it will be necessary to involve other parties in a joint multilateral agreement. For example, a baker may agree to provide a certain quantity of bread to the cobbler. In exchange the fisherman provides the baker with fish and receives shoes from the cobbler. Finding the parties willing to take part in this 'triangular trade' and negotiating the terms of the contract, however, is clearly going to be more costly and require greater information than a simple bilateral deal. In principle, it is possible to envisage more and more individuals taking part in these multilateral negotiations, but, as discussed in Chapter 1, obtaining a simultaneous agreement between many contractors is likely to be extremely difficult.

Money enables contractors to escape from the requirement of forming agreements simultaneously. A complex pattern of exchange relationships can instead be entered into through a sequence of bilateral arrangements. To return to our simple example, the shoemaker might accept fish in exchange for his shoes even when he dislikes fish if he knows of a baker who will be happy to exchange bread for fish. In this case, the fish is being used in the form of a medium of exchange since its value to the shoemaker depends entirely on its ability to procure him something else. Clearly, if the agreements described here are not entered into simultaneously the cobbler will want to be confident of the willingness of the baker to accept fish, and it is apparent that this is not necessarily or usually going to be the case. A medium of exchange will be more acceptable to the shoemaker the more widely acceptable it is known to be to other people. Where confidence in the

wide acceptability of a medium of exchange is strong, it will not be necessary for the shoemaker to have knowledge of the demands of any particular baker. Any baker he knows will be happy to supply him with bread in
exchange for money. This view of the origins of money is particularly associated with Carl Menger.[4]

> As each economising individual becomes increasingly more aware of his eco-
> nomic interest, he is led by this interest, without any agreement, without legisla-
> tive compulsion and even without regard to the public interest, to give his
> commodities in exchange for other, more saleable, commodities, even if he does
> not need them for any immediate consumption purpose.

This passage from Menger effectively describes the evolution of what
Sugden (1986) calls a *convention*. As we saw in Chapter 1, conventions can
develop gradually over time in response to the self-interested choices of
contractors. People accept money because everyone else does, and a particular form of money may survive for long periods even if a different type,
and hence a different convention, might have had better properties. Menger
does hint, however, that 'more saleable' commodities are the ones that convention will tend to favour as money, and this raises the question of what
is meant by that phrase. Alchian (1977a) provides a persuasive answer.

Imagine a world in which four commodities exist; Alchian supposes that
these are called oil, wheat, diamonds and '*C*'. He notes that people cannot
be expected to have expert knowledge of the characteristics of all the commodities in which they trade. Transactions costs, he assumes, will be highest
when two 'novices' trade together, and will be lowest when the two traders
are 'experts' in both commodities traded. We have already noted in our
earlier discussion of asymmetric information that traders in certain products will have to establish a 'reputation' for trustworthiness if exchange is
to take place. Let us suppose that by specialising in the trade of wheat in
the sense that every exchange involves either its purchase or sale, a person
becomes both an expert in assessing its quality and comes to command a
high reputation. Such a reputation in a single commodity will be of little
use, however, if the 'expert' wheat dealer is faced with the problem of
assessing the qualities of oil or diamonds in the process of exchange. What
is required if transactions costs are to be substantially reduced is a commodity in which everyone is an 'expert'. Such a commodity will be one the
qualities of which are very easy to assay. This is the primary characteristic
of 'money' and is implicit in Menger's use of the term 'more saleable commodities' as a description of money. Commodities are 'more saleable' if
large numbers of people find their qualities can be assessed at very low cost.
The use of money as an exchange medium reduces transactions costs
because, in conjunction with the existence of specialist traders in other

commodities, it increases the knowledge possessed by each contractor involved in an exchange. The specialist wheat trader will be an 'expert' in both wheat and money, while a customer (either a buyer or seller of wheat) will at least be an 'expert' in money. Of course, this in no way alters the fact that most of the specialist traders' customers will be novices in wheat, and the implications of this have already been considered in the context of second-hand cars. In the absence of money, however, both parties to an exchange would usually be novices, while it is the use of money which permits the growth of specialised traders whose accumulated expertise and pursuit of goodwill are a response to the twin problems of asymmetric information and adverse selection.

Although a person accepting money in exchange for some good or service will feel confident that it can be used to procure other things, the precise terms of any future trades will not be known with certainty. Money is accepted in the expectation that it will permit the achievement of desired ends. It may even be the case that money is accepted with no specific and determinate ideas as to what is to be done with it. Instead, the person may prefer to wait upon events, and spend time searching for suitable opportunities. By reducing transactions costs, in other words, money permits wider search, and a more extensive and complex system of exchange transactions can occur than would otherwise be possible. Pigou (1949, p. 25) likened money to 'a railway through the air, the loss of which would inflict on us the same sort of damage as we should suffer if the actual railways and roads, by which the different parts of the country are physically linked together were destroyed'. Money, that is, like the transport system, enables a wider range of transactions to take place.

But the existence of money implies more than a simple widening of possibilities. It implies that these possibilities are discovered by a process which continues over time. People hold money speculatively in the hope that to commit themselves later will be advantageous compared with deciding on a course of action immediately. The cobbler, for example, might have bartered his shoes immediately for fish. In fact, he preferred money because he expected to be able to use it later in ways yielding him greater satisfaction. The fact that in many everyday cases the time period involved might be quite short, and the cobbler may have intentions concerning the use of his money which are usually and routinely realised (he is very sure of the terms on which he can buy bread at the bakers) in no way changes the general principle.

Ignorance inevitably restricts exchange. Institutions which help to overcome the problems posed by ignorance are therefore expected to take root. To quote Loasby (1976): 'Money, like the firm, is a means of handling the consequences of the excessive cost or the sheer impossibility of abolishing ignorance . . . both imply a negation of the concept of general equilibrium in favour of the continuing management of emerging events' (p. 165).

3.2   Political Institutions

The idea that a fundamental political institution such as 'the state' might be interpreted as a means of overcoming impediments to the process of exchange has a long history. Consider for example a celebrated passage from Hume:

> Two neighbours may agree to drain a meadow, which they possess in common: because it is easy for them to know each other's mind; and each must perceive, that the immediate consequence of his failing in his part, is the abandoning of the whole project. But it is very difficult, and indeed impossible, that a thousand persons should agree in any such action; it being difficult for them to concert so complicated a design, and still more difficult for them to execute it; while each seeks a pretext to free himself of the trouble and expense, and would lay the whole burden on others. Political society easily remedies both these inconveniences . . .[5]

The focus of attention here is on the problem of 'public goods' (Samuelson, 1954; Musgrave, 1959). Some goods confer benefits not merely on a single consumer of the good but on a whole population of consumers simultaneously. Standard examples include defence, public health provisions, the services of lighthouses and so forth. Pure public goods are said to be 'non-rival' in consumption and 'non-excludable' (that is, it is technically not possible, or at least enormously costly, to prevent any individual person from enjoying the benefits of a public good provided by others). The result of these two characteristics is that ordinary market processes 'fail' in the sense that a multilateral agreement which might potentially benefit all the parties to it will not emerge spontaneously. In Chapter 1, the costs of simultaneous multilateral contracting have already been discussed in the context of private goods. There it was argued that although simultaneous agreement would be impossibly costly to achieve, alternatives existed which would be preferable to completely independent activity for the parties concerned. Resources would be allocated not in a single all-embracing moment of universal agreement but in a process involving bilateral exchanges and the use of money or the forming of institutions such as 'firms' to manage events as time advanced. Public goods, however, present us with a severe problem in that apparently the only alternative to a widespread multilateral agreement is no agreement. Resolution of this dilemma requires the existence of the 'productive state' and the institution of collective processes in place of market processes. Buchanan (1975, p. 97) re-emphasises Hume's point if in somewhat different style:

Only through governmental-collective processes can individuals secure the net benefits of goods and services that are characterised by extreme jointness efficiencies and by extreme non-excludability, goods and services which would tend to be provided suboptimally or not at all in the absence of collective-governmental action.

Public goods present obstacles to the formation of agreements of a particularly intractable nature, but they are not in principle different from those difficulties discussed in detail in section 2.2. There it was seen that the failure of transactors honestly to declare information could conceivably totally inhibit the development of certain insurance or other markets. Second-hand-car salesmen would always maintain that their wares were more reliable than they really were, and purchasers of insurance that the risks they faced were less than they really were. People, in other words, cannot be expected to declare honestly and voluntarily information which adversely influences the terms upon which they will trade when there are no cost-effective means of verifying the information. Trade in public goods is no exception. Further, where the simultaneous agreement of large numbers of individuals is involved, the problem of 'bounded rationality' cannot be overlooked. Thus, Hume's two 'inconveniences' which, he argues, political society remedies, amount to the problems analysed earlier: 'bounded rationality' ('it being difficult for them to concert so complicated a design') and an extreme form of information asymmetry leading to opportunistic behaviour ('each seeks a pretext to free himself of the trouble and expense').

3.3 The Firm as a Nexus of Contracts

A provisional rationalisation of the emergence of 'firms' was suggested at the end of Chapter 1. From the standpoint of economic theory, the firm represented a 'nexus of contracts' so framed as to provide flexibility in the face of unpredictable events. Uncertainty, and the resulting difficulty of precisely specifying the terms of each person's contract, thus constituted the starting point for the theory of the firm. This approach has its origins in a celebrated paper by Coase (1937), and the discussion of transactional difficulties above (section 2), now permits a further appraisal.

For Coase: 'The main reason why it is profitable to establish a firm would seem to be that there is a cost of using the price mechanism' (p. 336). Coase is here referring to such matters as 'negotiating and concluding a separate contract for each exchange transaction' (p. 336). In the absence of a firm, each factor of production must contract with every other factor whose cooperation is required. Within the firm, each factor negotiates a single contract. In an extreme case where 'n' individuals must all cooperate closely, a set of $n(n-1)/2$ bilateral contracts would be required to bind the parties together. For five individuals, Figure 2.1 illustrates that ten agreements would be necessary. In a slightly different context, Williamson (1975, p.46) refers to this as the 'all-channel network'. In the firm, on the other hand, one person would become the central contractual agent and a total of four contracts would be sufficient to link all the parties together.

The firm   The market

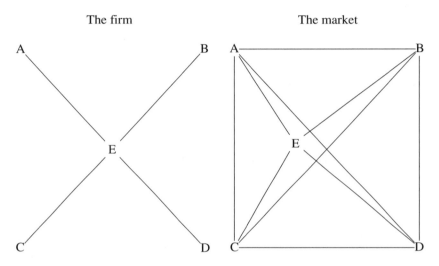

Figure 2.1   A central contractual agent economises on contractual links

It is important always to remember, however, that the advantages of the firm in terms of savings in contracting costs presuppose conditions of uncertainty. With costless knowledge there would be no advantages accruing to a reduced number of transactional bonds, since these bonds would be costless to establish. In Coase's view of things the firm economises on transactions costs because bargaining over what has to be done, and on what precise terms, does not take place. The firm is characterised by the conscious organisation or direction of resources over time: 'When the direction of resources (within the limits of the contract) becomes dependent on the buyer in this way, that relationship which I term a "firm" may be obtained' (p.337). Within the firm, people do what they are told to do.

More recent contributions to this literature have modified Coase's conception in important respects. Below we look at several 'contractual modes' and discuss what distinguishes 'market-like' from 'firm-like' arrangements.

3.3.1 The deterministic contract

Under this scheme the contractors agree to perform specific services at certain future points in time. The obvious problem is that, in the extreme, it completely lacks flexibility and presupposes that the contracting parties are able to determine exactly what they will require at all relevant times in the future. It will be recalled that person A found it difficult to formulate a deterministic contract with his craftspeople because of the problem of predicting exactly what would be required of them at each stage.

This type of contracting is only likely to be observed, therefore, where the duration of an association is expected to be short, where conditions are stable and predictable so that routine procedures can be adopted, and where problems of information asymmetry are not serious.

3.3.2 The state-contingent contract

In a state-contingent contract, obligations are no longer deterministic and fixed. The requirements vary with the 'state of the world' which occurs. An example of such a contract was discussed in section 2. There it was argued that the specification of such a contract would be enormously time-consuming and complex. Ultimately, it would encounter the problem of 'bounded rationality'; the sheer impossibility of imagining all the future contingencies which might arise along with the appropriate responses to them. We also noted that information about the 'state of the world' might be distributed asymmetrically between the contractors, thus leading to problems of 'adverse selection' and 'moral hazard'.

3.3.3 Sequential spot contracting

Instead of a single contract, deterministic or probabilistic, involving commitments in future time periods, the parties involved in a project might contract period by period. As time gradually reveals what has to be done, the contracts are drawn up and the specified tasks are accomplished in a sequence. This solution faces the objection emphasised by Coase that the number of contracts required to accomplish a given objective will be very large if they are continually renegotiated over time. The number of contracts, however, will not be the only problem. An equally important issue is the cost of establishing each one. In principle we might imagine the process of recontracting as a relatively simple operation. The buyer of labour services, for example, would ask a worker to do something at the established wage rate and acceptance of this 'request' would imply that the 'contract' had been duly renegotiated. According to this view, associated with Alchian and Demsetz (1972), the type of contract observed within a 'firm' is not a single long-term contract of employment involving 'direction' of resources by the buyer, as claimed by Coase. Instead, there is an implicit process of continual renegotiation as in a system of sequential spot contracting.

3.3.4   The contract of employment

Where the process of recontracting operates as smoothly as suggested above there would be no advantage attached to a contract of employment. Indeed, it would arguably be extremely difficult in practice to distinguish between the two methods of contracting. Whether an 'employee' is considered to 'renegotiate' his or her contract continually, or is seen as accepting contractually permissible 'instructions', may not in some circumstances be a matter of very great practical importance. Analytically, however, the distinction is significant. The Coasian view of the employment contract requires that it is possible to specify a list of 'acceptable' tasks from which the employer can choose. Any attempt at such exhaustive listing must, however, confront the information problem. The employer simply will not have sufficient knowledge to draw up a contract of this nature. If, on the other hand, information is revealed gradually over time, and if, further, this information accrues not to everyone equally but to particular individuals (it is 'impacted', to use Williamson's jargon), the crucial problem will be to set an environment in which people have an incentive to act cooperatively rather than opportunistically. Thus the employer is not a giver of instructions, as in Coase's model, but a provider of incentives. The employee becomes not a passive receiver and executor of orders but an active agent of the employer.

3.3.5   The agency contract

Under an agency contract, one party (the agent) agrees to act in the interests of another party (the principal). The example of the architect and person A has already been discussed earlier in this chapter. Note that two important features are required to hold if the agency relation is to be interesting. Firstly, there must be a conflict of interest. The architect, by assumption, was interested in giving A's plans the minimum amount of attention he or she could get away with. Person A, of course, was interested in eliciting from his architect the greatest attention that was possible. Secondly, there must be an asymmetry in the information available to principal and agent. Person A may simply not know what actions are possible and how they may affect him. He may not be in a position even to tell what action if any, his agent has taken.

Clearly if there were no conflict of interest, the existence of asymmetric information would not matter. The agent would always choose an action which accorded with the preferences of the principal. Similarly, if the information available to both principal and agent were the same, the conflict of interest would not matter since the principal would immediately detect any 'opportunistic' behaviour on the part of the agent. Where both asymmetric information and conflict of interest are present, the problem facing the principal will be to present the agent with a 'system of remuneration' sometimes called a 'fee structure' or 'incentive structure', which will provide the principal with the greatest payoff.

In the case of the relationship between employer and employee, there are obvious parallels with the principal–agent problem. This was recognised by Coase, who, in a footnote in his 1937 paper (p. 337), wrote:

> Of course, it is not possible to draw a hard and fast line which determines whether there is a firm or not. There may be more or less direction. It is similar to the legal question of whether there is the relationship of master and servant or principal and agent.

The clear implication here is that only a contract of 'master and servant', which implies the direction of resources, will be found in the Coasian firm. The relationship of principal and agent would not be compatible with the existence of a 'firm'. More recent theorists would not accept this judgement. Once the problem of asymmetrically distributed knowledge within the firm is recognised, together with the accompanying possibility of moral hazard, it becomes useful to view the employee as an 'agent', and the firm as a response to the agency problem. The Coasian insight that the firm replaces a whole system of multilateral contracts with bilateral contracts between employer and employee is maintained, but the nature of the contract between employee and firm is no longer seen exclusively in terms of the *direction* of resources. Whatever the strictly legal position, the economist can argue that perceiving the relationship between 'firm' and employee in terms of principal and agent may provide valuable insights into the way resources are allocated within the firm.

3.3.6 Relational contracting

All of the contractual forms discussed above have one thing in common. The agreements are all well specified and complete. In the spot contract, the deterministic contract, the state-contingent contract, the agency contract or even the Coasian employment contract, the obligations of each of the parties under the contract are clear. An instruction under a contract of employment is either permissible or not. The quality of a product or service traded in a spot contract is clear and unambiguous. The agent's fee will be related to results which will be easily observed by both parties while *actions* may not figure in the contract at all (in a sense, *all* lawful actions of the agent would then be contractually permissible).

In practice, of course, things are never that simple. As we emphasised in

Chapter 1, the firm is a device for handling change and coping with the problem of lack of trust. The essence of the firm from this point of view is not simply that it involves fewer contractual linkages than would the market, or even that dealings are repeated period by period. The main point is that bounded rationality inevitably implies that contracts will be incomplete, and incomplete contracts are vulnerable to opportunism. Williamson (1985) is particularly associated with this view.[6] The contracts discussed above were all from the world of 'classical contracting' in which clear agreements could be formulated and, if necessary, enforced by an outside agency (the state). There are many circumstances, however, in which such enforcement mechanisms will be ineffective and the contractors themselves will have to develop a system of 'governance'. The firm is then a system of governance for incompletely specified contracts. It establishes a framework in which the benefits from a continuing association can be achieved. Because potential conflicts will inevitably arise over time, procedures are devised to minimise their destructive consequences and induce as much cooperative behaviour as possible.

Contracting within the firm is not 'classical' but 'relational'. Implicit exchanges are going on continuously, but they are not formalised in specific 'contracts'. People are cooperative because they perceive it to be in their own long-term interests and because they come to trust the governance structures of the firm. Williamson emphasises that governance arrangements within the firm will not always be necessary. Where, for example, very specific services are required of someone at a particular point in time, and the quality of these services is easy to define and assay, there is no advantage to establishing a specialised 'governance structure'. The spot market is the arrangement which minimises the cost of the transaction. Even where a continuing association is desirable, a firm may not evolve. Repeat dealing is a perfectly reasonable way of establishing trust and reputation in some market settings, as was seen in Chapter 1. The crucial element, for Williamson, is vulnerability to opportunism deriving from the existence of transaction-specific assets.

As explained in section 2.4, a provider of a service may gain knowledge and experience over time which is specific to a particular buyer. A workforce in a firm can also accumulate similarly specific skills. This is not, of course, undesirable in itself. The problem is simply the transactional one that continual renegotiation of contracts in these circumstances puts the employer in the sort of position faced by person A in our example of the building project. Each person with whom he or she is negotiating is in the possession of skills and information which he/she does not fully share. Further, once individuals or groups of individuals are more productive within the firm than they would be outside, the income generated by their efforts is a form of 'rent'. Striking a bargain is then inhibited by asymmetric information and there is an incentive to act 'opportunistically' in pursuit of these 'rents'.[7]

For Williamson (1985), therefore, special governance arrangements within the firm develop when specific assets require protection which classical forms of contracting cannot provide. Frequency of repeat dealing is still important, both because it is repetition which generates transaction-specific knowledge and because infrequent dealing would not warrant the development of an expensive governance structure. Further, an ever-changing and uncertain environment favours the evolution of a firm because in very stable and unchanging circumstances, trust engendered by repeat dealing might be a cost-minimising response. Thus, frequent contracting with highly transaction-specific resources in an uncertain environment leads to the evolution of 'unified governance'.

4. CONCLUSION

In Part 2 of this book we shall be using the ideas surveyed in this chapter to consider many different aspects of a firm's structure. Already it can be seen that several overlapping intellectual traditions are developing.

1. There is first the application of standard neoclassical economic reasoning to the design of contracts. If information is asymmetrically distributed it is still possible to consider what will be the 'best' contract achievable in the circumstances. The theory of principal and agent concerns precisely this problem. If information can be collected through some 'monitoring technology', it is possible to investigate how this technology will be used and how its intensity of use will be related to the punishments available. The consequences for optimal contract design of the presence or absence of 'good reputation' and hence trust on the side of the buyer or the seller can also be investigated. In short, this tradition simply uses the tools of neoclassical economics to see what contracts utility-maximising people would use assuming that enforcement is not costless. The problem of enforcement becomes part of contract design. Bowles and Gintis (1993) refer to this area of study as *contested exchange*. It differs from the exchange theory discussed in sections 3 to 5 of Chapter 1 in recognising the problem of contract enforcement.
2. The Coase/Williamson transactions cost tradition is somewhat different in that it emphasises bounded rationality and contractual incompleteness as the major issue. Firms are a response to the *process*

of contracting over time in an environment of continual change and contractual hazards. Contract enforcement is still a central concern, but bounded rationality means that the techniques of neoclassical-constrained maximisation cannot be used to *calculate* ideal solutions to contractual problems. The approach is inevitably less rigorous than principal–agent theory but draws on wider traditions than simple neo-classical economics. By emphasising uncertainty and the accumulation of knowledge over time, the transactions cost tradition has affinities with the 'Austrian' school of thought which will be introduced in Chapter 3.

In Chapter 5 the theory of principal and agent will be developed more formally. This will prepare the ground for an investigation in Chapter 6 of how both neoclassical contract theory and transactions cost theory have been used to explain some of the internal characteristics of firms. The existence of a hierarchical structure, with the possibility of promotion through the various grades from points of entry to compulsory retire-ment, can be explained in terms of the provision of a system of incentives which encourage cooperative behaviour, and which permit transactions to take place which would otherwise be inhibited by 'opportunistic' responses to informational asymmetries. The principal–agent and incom-plete-contracts paradigms will also permit us to discuss other important issues such as 'the division of ownership from control' in Chapter 8 (man-agers as agents of shareholders), the control of non-profit and public enterprises in Chapter 11 (managers as agents of politicians, donors or consumers), and a number of topics in the economics of bureaucracy. Before pursuing this analysis further, however, it is necessary to introduce another component which will play an important role in our general framework, the entrepreneur.

NOTES

1. Coase (1937, p. 390).
2. Akerlof's model is outlined in the Appendix at the end of this chapter.
3. An economic rent is a return in excess of that which is achievable in the next best employ-ment. Any payment to factor owners greater than the minimum required to compensate them (that is, greater than that strictly required to induce them to supply the services instead of going elsewhere) is a rent. Conversely, if a buyer would have been prepared to pay more for a resource than was actually necessary to secure its services, the buyer receives a rent. In any bilateral exchange relationship, these rents will exist. They are the 'gains from trade'. Economic organisation is therefore about encouraging the generation of these rents, but it is also about protecting them from being dissipated by opportunism or 'rent seeking'.
4. Carl Menger (1950), *Principles of Economics*, Chapter VIII, p. 260.

5. David Hume (1978), *A Treatise of Human Nature* (edited by P.H. Nidditch), Oxford: Clarendon Press, p. 538. Originally published 1740.
6. See especially Williamson (1985), Chapters 1–3.
7. A more detailed discussion of the problem of 'rent-seeking' behaviour can be found in Chapter 6.

APPENDIX

Akerlof (1970, pp. 490–1) presents the following purely illustrative model. Suppose there are two types of transactor. Type-1 transactors have a stock of N cars with quality q uniformly distributed $0 < q < 2$. A type-1 person knows the quality of each car with certainty. The utility (U) of type-1 transactors is given by

$$U_1 = G + \sum_{i=1}^{n} q_i$$

where G = consumption of goods other than cars. Type-2 transactors have no cars to begin with and their utility is given by

$$U_2 = G + \sum_{i=1}^{n} kq_i$$

The linear utility functions postulated might seem strange but the objective is merely to illustrate a possibility using as simple a framework as possible. Suppose that each transactor wishes to maximise expected utility. Further, let the price of other goods (G) be unity. Consider first the supply of cars. Suppose the market price of second-hand cars were p – how would type-1 transactors respond? Clearly, those holding cars with quality $q_i > p$ will not sell them, since to do so would reduce their utility. They would lose utility q_i from selling the car and gain utility p from buying other goods with the proceeds. Since $q_i > p$ there is a net loss. Those holding cars with quality $q_i < p$ will hasten to sell, however, since their utility index will rise. Given that the distribution of quality is uniform, the proportion of cars offered for sale will be given by the shaded area in Figure 2.2. This shaded area will equal $p/2$ and the number of cars offered for sale will be $Np/2$. Given that the cars offered for sale are of uniformly distributed quality between 0 and p, the average quality of car offered (q_a) will be $p/2$.

Now consider the demand side. Transactors of either type will only demand cars if the expected utility obtained per unit of expenditure on cars is greater than on other goods (that is, greater than unity). The *expected* number of units of quality obtained per unit of expenditure on a car will be q_a/p. For transactors of type 1, therefore, cars will be demanded only if $q_a/p > 1$. Since $q_a = p/2$, this condition can clearly never be fulfilled. For

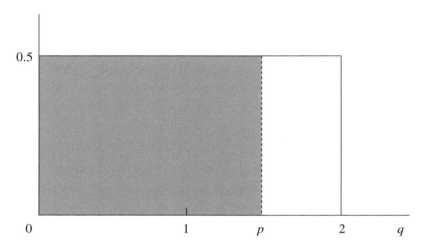

Figure 2.2   Probability distribution of quality (q): $f(q) = 0.5,\ 0 \leqslant q \leqslant 2$.

transactors of type 2, cars will be demanded if $kq_d/p > 1$. Again since $q_a = p/2$ we deduce that type-2 contractors will demand cars only if $k/2 > 1$; that is, if $k > 2$.

Thus, if type-2 transactors have utility functions as specified with $0 < k < 2$, no cars will be demanded. This will be so even though examples can be constructed in which some type-1 transactors are prepared to supply cars of a quality and at a price that type-2 transactors would have been prepared to pay *if only they knew* the precise qualities of the cars on offer. Suppose for example k were 2. At a price of 1, a type-2 transactor would be prepared to buy any car with quality greater than $q_i = 1/2$. And at a price of 1, there will be $N/4$ such cars offered for sale. The problem, of course, is that there will also be $N/4$ cars offered for sale with quality less than $1/2$ and our type-2 transactor by hypothesis cannot *ex ante* tell the difference between these two classes of car.

Kim (1985) presents a model in which traders are not designated as buyers or sellers but may choose whether to buy or sell. Traders are of differing types. They may also trade in the new-car market. It is possible, using this type of framework, to derive results which contradict Akerlof's lemons principle. Traded used cars may be, on average, of higher quality than non-traded used cars.

3. The entrepreneur

'The pivot on which everything turns'.
(J.A. Schumpeter)[1]

1. INTRODUCTION

In everyday parlance the word 'entrepreneur' has wide-ranging connotations. Certain individuals, both contemporary and historical, might by common consent be described as entrepreneurs. J. Pierpont Morgan, J.D. Rockefeller, A. Carnegie and other personalities associated with the development of banking and finance, railroads, and oil and steel in nineteenth-century America (sometimes collectively referred to as the 'robber barons') would each seem to warrant the label 'entrepreneur'. Yet the pure scale of a person's activity, the opening up of whole continents, the development of entirely new industries, does not seem to be crucial. We might as easily apply the term to a local person often engaged in conventional, long-established trades, who nevertheless appears to possess those characteristics of energy, drive, inquisitiveness, acquisitiveness, shrewdness and perhaps even deviousness in the proportions required.

Energy and drive are, in themselves, insufficient to produce an entrepreneur. An entrepreneur must certainly have energy to act and the drive not to be discouraged by obstacles, but the blinkered determination of the fanatic is not an entrepreneurial quality. Entrepreneurs require not simply the momentum of the bulldozer to demolish all before them, but rather the agility and flexibility of the Land Rover to circumvent the difficulties. Clearly, such a strategy requires that the entrepreneur should look about, and the acquisitive and inquisitive aspects of the entrepreneurial character relate to this process. Both words derive from the Latin 'quaero', to seek, and the modern theory of the entrepreneur is concerned primarily with elaborating on this primary characteristic – the search for, or discovery of, new knowledge.

Entrepreneurs use the knowledge they have acquired to their own advantage by reallocating resources. This process of resource reallocation involves forming agreements with others, and it is here that the qualities of shrewdness and deviousness enter: shrewdness to judge the character and reliability of the people with whom agreements are formed, and deviousness to get the best of the bargains struck. As was noted in Chapter 2, in the process of bilateral bargaining it will be advantageous for each party to give the other a misleading impression of their true preferences. It is perhaps this component of the entrepreneurial character which gives the word entrepreneur its somewhat disparaging flavour, and helps to explain research findings which point to the success of poor immigrant people in entrepreneurial endeavours (see Hannah, 1983b). Immigrants will look on established procedures with a new perspective, well aware that things may be done differently; the very act of migration suggests energy and ambition; while the costs of incurring the disapprobation of those inconvenienced by change will be lower for the outsider.[2]

The purpose of this chapter is not, however, to discuss the social origins of the entrepreneur or popular perceptions of the nature of entrepreneurship, but rather to outline the role of the entrepreneur in economic theory. A number of significant questions will arise. Are 'the firm' and 'the entrepreneur' necessarily always observed together or can we conceive of a firm without an entrepreneur? Are some people entrepreneurs and others not, or does the quality of entrepreneurship, as has been hinted above, inhere to a greater or lesser extent in all participants in the market? Is entrepreneurship a factor of production, a resource akin to land, capital or labour, receiving as its reward a factor payment; or is the return to the entrepreneur qualitatively different from the return to other factors? What exactly does the entrepreneur do?

2.　CONTRASTING VIEWS OF THE ENTREPRENEUR

2.1　The Classical Tradition

To summarise in a few lines the views of a range of writers spanning more than a century from the time of Adam Smith onwards is clearly a hazardous undertaking and one which is liable to result in severe distortions to the work of some economists. As a generalisation, however, the classical tradition, at least in England, did not offer a very sophisticated account of the entrepreneur. Indeed this state of affairs has continued in the neoclassical analysis of the late nineteenth and twentieth centuries and for substantially similar reasons. Both traditions are concerned primarily with the analysis of the establishment of 'natural' or as we would now say 'equilibrium' prices. The emphasis on the final state rather than the process of getting there inevitably diverts attention from the distinctive contribution of the entrepreneur. Classical analysis recognised the role of superintendence and organisation in economic life; and, in the conditions prevailing in the late eighteenth century, the provider of capital and the organiser of production would usually be the same person. The result was a tendency to muddle together some sources of income and to reduce the significance of others. Thus the English classical writers, including Smith, Ricardo and Mill[3], used the word 'profit' to describe the total return to the provider of capital even though this included elements which might more properly be termed 'wages of management', 'interest on capital', 'monopoly rents', 'windfalls' and so forth.

It is to the French classical tradition we must look for the origins of the idea that profit is a type of income quite distinct from that received by capital and that it goes to the entrepreneur. The early French contribution in this field is perhaps appropriately reflected in the fact that English economists have come to use the French word 'entrepreneur' rather than any English equivalent such as the term 'venturer'. J.B. Say[4], building on the ideas of Cantillon[5], insisted that profit was a quite separate category of income from interest, thus establishing the major distinction between English and French classical schools in this area. He did not, however, emphasise as did Cantillon the importance of risk, but initially viewed profit as a wage accruing to the organiser of production. Within the French school, Knight (1921) in his review of theories of profit (p. 25) singles out Courcelle-Seneuil[6] as the contributor who most clearly argued that profit was a reward for the assumption of risk and was not in any sense a wage.

Mention should also be made of the German, and especially Von Thünen's, contribution. Von Thünen[7] is most well known for his work on transport costs, land rents and the consequent spatial pattern of agricultural land-use around a city. In the development of this analysis, Von Thünen, who is said to have made extensive use of the financial records of his own estates, defines profit as a residual after the expenses of interest, insurance, and the wages of management have been met. By seeing profit as essentially a return for bearing uninsurable risks, Von Thünen was a close forerunner of Knight.

2.2 Knight

Knight (1921) developed and elaborated the view that entrepreneurs receive a return for bearing uncertainty. His major criticism of theory up to that date was that even those who appreciated the importance of uncertainty were unclear about its nature and implications. One view, for example, was that profit arose from the fact of continuous change and development over time. Knight did not dispute that radical and less radical changes occurred continuously and that these could give rise to uncertainty and hence to profits, but he insisted that change *per se* was not the issue. If, for example, changes occurred, the consequences of which were entirely foreseeable, no profits would be generated. Perfectly foreseen changes were compatible with a state of 'equilibrium' in which no profits would appear. This type of equilibrium is now often referred to as a 'Hayekian' equilibrium.[8] Change occurs, but, because it is perfectly foreseen, no expectations are ever disappointed. A famous example is that of an approaching meteorite, the impact of which will occasion many changes but all of which may be calculated perfectly accurately (fire damage, loss of crops and buildings, and so on). The actual collision of the meteorite with the earth will then produce no profits, since the prices of resources have long since adjusted to the certainty of the impact and nothing unforeseen has occurred. Correct expectations, however, are critical to this result. No change is compatible with profits and losses if change is confidently expected. If contrary to all known laws of physics the meteorite suddenly veers away from the earth and disappears into outer space, people will have to adjust to this unexpected continuation of the status quo, expectations will have been disappointed and profits and losses will appear.

According to Knight, therefore, it is not change but uncertainty and the possibility of incorrect expectations which give rise to profit. Further, the term uncertainty is used by Knight only to describe circumstances in which reliable probability values cannot be attached to possible future outcomes. Where future events can be assigned probabilities, Knight uses the term 'risk' to describe the situation, and argues that the existence of insurance markets will often enable people to avoid such risk.[9] True uncertainty cannot be avoided by paying an insurance premium. Important consequences follow from the recognition that much of economic life represents a response to the existence of uncertainty. As Knight puts it: 'With Uncertainty present doing things, the actual execution of activity becomes in a real sense a secondary part of life; the primary problem or function is deciding what to do and how to do it' (p. 268).

This 'primary function' is the entrepreneurial function. The job of deciding how various objectives are to be achieved and of predicting what objectives are worth achieving devolves on the entrepreneur, a specialist who is prepared to bear the costs of uncertainty. 'The confident and venturesome assume the risk or insure the doubtful and timid by guaranteeing to the latter a specified income in return for an assignment of the actual result' (pp. 269–70).

It is not clear from this that the confident and venturesome should employ the doubtful and timid, or that the entrepreneur should own and organise 'a firm', although Knight appears to have thought that this necessarily follows. This point will be taken up later on. For present purposes, however, the main result of Knight's analysis is that the entrepreneur's function is to make judgements about the uncertain future, and the reward associated with this function 'profit' is a return to uncertainty bearing. 'It is our imperfect knowledge of the future . . . which is crucial for the understanding of our problem' (p. 198).

This 'Knightian' view of the entrepreneur has a powerful intuitive appeal. Clearly the exercise of entrepreneurship is usually associated with uncertainty bearing and has something to do with imperfect knowledge, but there are equally powerful objections to it. As Schumpeter emphasised (1954, p. 556) if a person is to make a profit from uncertain turns of events, that person will do so as the owner of some marketable resource. Thus, uncertainty is borne by resource owners who have to accept the consequences for the value on the market of their resources of unexpected change. If we are prepared to define resource owners as 'capitalists' (that is, we suppress the distinctions between land, natural resources, buildings, physical and human capital) then uninsurable risks must be borne by capitalists. It may be objected that the entrepreneur may borrow from the capitalist at a fixed interest and that, if so, the entrepreneur not the capitalist bears the risk, but in this case, if the entrepreneur has no independent resources, failure of the enterprise must mean default on the loan and the capitalist is an uncertainty bearer. Where the entrepreneur has other resources which permit repayment of the debt in the event of failure, clearly the entrepreneur bears the uncertainty but only in so far as he or she is also a capitalist.

If uninsurable risk is borne by resource owners, what becomes of the distinctive contribution of 'the entrepreneur'? Modern analysis of the entrepreneur reverts to and develops Say's insight that the organisation of production, the combining together of resource inputs, requires skills of a different order than those of routine labour. Knights' 'primary function' of 'deciding what to do and how to do it' is indeed an entrepreneurial activity, but it is conceptually a quite separate activity from bearing uninsurable risks, even though the latter may be associated with it. Recent theory therefore emphasises that the entrepreneur does not merely put up with the consequences of imperfect knowledge, but rather reaps the rewards of discovering and using new knowledge. The English tradition, in which industry appears to 'run itself' using inputs of capital and labour in an apparently routine and 'mindless' fashion, failed to recognise the importance of the coordinator; the person who decides how and what things shall be done as distinct from the person who merely ensures that they are done. In the next section a more careful elaboration of this view of the entrepreneur is attempted using the work of the most influential modern theorist in the subject, Israel Kirzner.

2.3 Kirzner

In Chapter 1 we spent some time on the elementary task of showing how a community of four individuals (A, B, C and D) could gain through specialisation and exchange. Each person, we assumed, faced different 'production possibilities'. If each remained independent and isolated, their consumption patterns would be those of Table 1.1. Total output would be eight units of x and eight units of y. Specialisation, it was found, enabled total output to rise to ten units of x and ten units of y. Agreements to specialise in the appropriate way and distribute the output as in Tables 1.4 and 1.5 represented various 'solutions' to the exchange game (the 'core'). We further saw that the establishment of appropriate prices for x and y would induce people to specialise and exchange their output on the market, and that the final position would be equivalent to a 'core' solution. At each stage it was emphasised that the theory as presented did not provide a persuasive account of the exchange process. 'Core' solutions could be calculated and equilibrium prices deduced once all the information necessary had been acquired, but there was only a limited discussion of how and to whom this information is made available.

In Edgeworth's bargaining approach, the 'core' solution emerges after a process of haggling involving all the contractors in the market. In Walras's 'tatônnement', the solution emerges from a trial and error sequence of price-setting by the auctioneer. In both cases it is assumed that no final decisions concerning the allocation of resources are made until the bargaining or tatônnement processes are completed. As we have seen, this is paradoxical, for it effectively implies that the information problem has to be completely solved before the stage of actual resource allocation can begin, and yet this solution of the information problem apparently requires no resources itself and hence involves no opportunity costs. These two ideas that contractors in the market must all be fully informed before anything of consequence can happen, and that the achievement of this state of full information does not in itself imply that anything of consequence has already happened, should not be rejected simply on the grounds that they are 'unrealistic'. Within the framework of general equilibrium theory, and given the objectives and purposes of that theory, they may be perfectly defensible. Further, it is by considering the conditions imposed by the requirements of general equilibrium that the role of the entrepreneur is perhaps most easily appreciated.[10]

The entrepreneur is central to the process by which contractors come to perceive the opportunities presented by specialisation and exchange. Clearly, if everyone already knows the production-possibility curves and preferences of each contractor, and if everyone is a rational, calculating, individual, one of the suggested solutions of Tables 1.4 and 1.5 will be adopted, but if each person is only partially informed, the acquisition of knowledge about potential gains from exchange becomes the pivotal economic problem. It is at this point that the 'Austrian' tradition in economic theory, here represented mainly by the work of Kirzner, emphasises the role of the entrepreneur. Essentially, an entrepreneur is any person who is 'alert' to hitherto unexploited possibilities for exchange. Spotting such possibilities enables the entrepreneur to benefit by acting as the 'middleman' who effects the change.

2.3.1   The entrepreneur as a 'middleman'

Consider once more the four individuals in Chapter 1. The production possibilities facing each were assumed to be:

A: $10 - 4x = y$
B: $12 - 3x = y$
C: $6 - 2x = y$
D: $3 - x = 2y$.

Suppose now that another individual (an entrepreneur E) turns up on the scene (there is yet another shipwreck). This individual is washed up with no resources to his or her name but, being alert to new opportunities, s/he rapidly observes that the four inhabitants s/he meets would be much better off if they specialised along the lines we have already discussed and thus coordinated their activities. It will be recalled that the 'no trade' consumption pattern was as shown in the left-hand side of Table 3.1. Imagine that E first contacts A and persuades A to provide him/her with eight units of y in exchange for two units of x. Person A will just be prepared to do this since by specialising in y production (ten units) and accepting E's offer, his or her final consumption level of two units of each commodity will be unchanged. E then approaches person B and suggests that the latter should provide one unit of x in exchange for three units of y. Once more, if person B specialises in x production (four units) and accepts E's offer, his or her final consumption level of three units of each commodity would be unchanged. These are, of course, very 'hard bargains' and we might expect in general A and B to benefit from their acquaintance with E. For the moment, however, we will assume simply that E offers to purchase y at a price of $\frac{1}{4}x$ (that is, sell x at price of $4y$), and sell y at a price of $\frac{1}{3}x$ (that is, purchase x at a price of $3y$) and we have seen that this would leave A and

B no better or worse off than before. Person C on the other hand, will benefit noticeably from trade with E assuming he or she faces the same price ratio as B. By specialising in x (three units), C can trade 0.75 units of x for 2.25 units of y. Similarly, person D can specialise in x (three units) and through trade achieve the same position as C. The argument is precisely the same as was presented in Chapter 1 and the entries on the right-hand side of Table 3.1 are a combination of the first two lines of Table 1.5.

Table 3.1   The gains to entrepreneurial activity

	No Trade		With Entrepreneur		
	x	y	x	y	Gain
A	2.00	2.00	2.00	2.00	(0.00)
B	3.00	3.00	3.00	3.00	(0.00)
C	2.00	2.00	2.25	2.25	(+0.25)
D	1.00	1.00	2.25	2.25	(+1.25)
E	–	–	0.50	0.50	(+0.50)
Total	8.00	8.00	10.00	10.00	(+2.00)

The important difference is that, whereas we assumed in each line of Table 1.5 that every contractor faced the same price ratio set by an auctioneer, in Table 3.1 we have assumed that contractors B, C and D faced a different price ratio from contractor A, and that these price ratios were negotiated with an entrepreneur. The entrepreneur in this simple situation acts merely as an *intermediary*. By spotting that currently unexploited gains from trade existed, the entrepreneur was able to use that knowledge both to realise the gains and to appropriate a proportion of them for him or herself. Each person's individual benefit (in terms of units of x and y) from the realloca-tion of resources initiated by the entrepreneur is recorded in parenthesis in the last column of Table 3.1. Person D appears to have gained most of all, but this, of course, is the result of our simple assumption that E offered the same terms of trade to all sellers of x. If the entrepreneur could have kept B, C and D apart and negotiated individually with them, then a sufficiently 'hardnosed' approach might have diverted a larger proportion of the gains from trade in E's direction. However, in the particular arithmetical example presented, the entrepreneur gains 0.5 units of x and 0.5 of y. Of the units of y supplied by person A, 7.5 units are in total given to B, C and D; while of the 2.5 units of x supplied altogether by B, C and D, only two units are given to A.

Person E achieves a consumption level of $0.5x$ and $0.5y$. This represents 'pure entrepreneurial profit'. It has nothing to do with interest payments on capital employed. Indeed, it has nothing to do with a return to any 'factor' as conventionally defined. It arises out of entrepreneurial activity and the possession of a particular kind of knowledge: the knowledge that opportunities exist which no one has spotted before. The entrepreneur acts as a coordinator of resources, and his or her profit is taken from the gains in efficiency which accompany his/her activity. Note that the gains to persons C and D recorded in Table 3.1 are not entrepreneurial profits even though they also are part of the efficiency gain resulting from the reallocation of resources. Persons C and D did not spot the potential benefits available from change; they merely responded to the entrepreneur's offer. Their gain is therefore a type of 'windfall'; a portion of the increased output which eluded the grasp of the entrepreneur.

An important problem was studiously ignored in the paragraphs above, however. Clearly the entrepreneur does not negotiate simultaneously with all the people playing a part in his or her plans. Had s/he done so, s/he would be unable to offer person A different terms of trade from the others, and the mechanism which enables some profit to be realised would be ineffective. In effect, the entrepreneur's knowledge would be instantly available to the others and no entrepreneurial profit could therefore be derived from it. As Richardson (1960, p. 57) puts it: 'a general profit opportunity, which is both known to everyone and equally capable of being exploited by everyone, is, in an important sense, a profit opportunity for no one in particular'. On the other hand, if the entrepreneur, who it will be recalled has no resources of his or her own, is to trade with A first, where is s/he to find the units of x required to make an offer? One solution to this problem might involve E persuading person A to supply the eight units of y in advance of E's delivery of the x. In this case, person A would be acting as a capitalist supplying the entrepreneur with the resources required to test his or her hunch in the market. We would then expect that person A would require compensation both for the delay and for the perceived uncertainty associated with the ultimate delivery of x. Person A would have to take the risk that E's confidence in her ability to deliver a given quantity of x by a certain date is misplaced and that the entrepreneurial plan might fail. For Knight, as we have seen, this bearing of uncertainty would make person A an entrepreneur, but for Kirzner this is not necessarily the case. E is the person who thinks s/he has spotted new opportunities, and it is E who stands to gain pure entrepreneurial profits if this judgement proves correct. Kirzner (1979) is quite specific on this point: 'Entrepreneurial profits . . . are not captured by owners, in their capacity as owners, at all. They are captured, instead, by men who exercise pure entrepreneurship, for which ownership is never a condition' (p. 94). Where time must elapse between purchase and sale: 'It is still correct to insist that the entrepreneur requires no investment of any kind. If the surplus . . . is sufficient to enable the entrepreneur to offer an interest payment attractive enough to persuade someone to advance the necessary funds . . . the entrepreneur has discovered a way of obtaining pure profit, without the need to invest anything at all' (Kirzner, 1973, p. 49).[11]

Of course, nothing guarantees that the penniless entrepreneur will succeed in persuading capitalists to advance their funds, but, as was emphasised in Chapter 2: 'These costs of securing recognition of one's competence and trustworthiness are truly social costs. They would exist under any system of economic organisation' (Kirzner, 1979, p. 101). All that can be said is that an entrepreneur who is also a resource owner will find it easier to back his or her hunches and benefit from his or her knowledge since these transactions costs can be avoided.[12] The entrepreneur lends to him or herself.[13]

2.3.2 Entrepreneurship and knowledge

For Kirzner, the entrepreneur is the person who perceives the opportunities and hence benefits from the possession of knowledge not apparently possessed by others. Thus entrepreneurship is central to the process by which information is disseminated throughout the economy. This emphasis on process is distinctive of the modern 'Austrian' school of thought, and it was noted in Chapter 1 that the major Austrian criticism of neoclassical equilibrium theory is the implicit assumption of perfect knowledge which underlies it.

It would, however, be totally misleading simply to leave the impression that neoclassical theory has nothing of substance to say about the problem of information. Our discussion of the information requirements underlying general equilibrium theory still stands, but neoclassical economists have developed tools which enable them to handle some problems in the economics of information very effectively. Since the early 1960s, the assumption of 'costless knowledge' has been dropped and replaced by the idea that knowledge is a valuable good which it is costly to acquire. This opens the way to the study of the behaviour of rational, maximising, calculating agents in the field of acquiring knowledge. A good example of such an approach is the analysis of 'search behaviour', a literature which emanates from Stigler's (1961) paper on the economics of information. Essentially the idea is simply that resources will be invested in search (that is, acquiring information) up to the point at which the marginal expected benefits of the information thus obtained equal the marginal costs of obtaining it.

It is worth taking a brief look at the elements of this literature in order to draw out the contrast between the approach of the Austrians and that of 'standard' theory to the problem of information. Take the very simplest case discussed by Stigler (1961). Suppose that a person wishes to purchase a certain commodity. In the textbook world of perfect competition, the price of this commodity is known with certainty by every transactor. But in reality, of course, the price quoted by some sellers will be higher than others, and consumers will usually benefit by 'shopping around'. Imagine now that the consumer knows something about the probability of being quoted a price within certain ranges upon any given enquiry. Indeed, suppose that s/he knows that the distribution of quoted prices is rectangular and that the price quoted may vary between £0 and £1. Such a person might argue that if s/he simply plans to buy from the first person s/he contacts s/he will expect to pay a price of £0.5, but, of course, there is a 0.5 probability that s/he will pay a price greater than £0.5. If s/he obtains two price quotes and then accepts the minimum of these two prices, the person will reduce the expected price that s/he pays. The probability of paying more than £0.5 for the item (that is, that both quotes turn out to be greater than £0.5) will be reduced to 0.25, while the probability that at least one of the two quotes is less than £0.5 would be 0.75. Clearly, 'shopping around' favourably affects the probability distribution of the minimum price encountered. It can be shown in this case[14] that if n is the number of price quotes obtained, the mathematical expectation of the price paid will be $1/(n+1)$.

If we now assume that the person intends to buy a quantity q of the commodity (which for simplicity we take as independent of the minimum price quoted) and that the extra cost of getting one more price quote is a constant c, it is a routine minimisation problem to calculate the number of searches which will minimise the expected total cost (expenditure plus search costs) of buying q units of the commodity. The expected total cost $E(T)$ of buying q units of the commodity will be

$$E(T) = [q/(n+1)] + nc.$$

The value of n that minimises this expression is given by

$$n^* = (q/c) - 1.$$

If, for example, the person is to purchase a single unit of the commodity (Stigler uses once more the example of a second-hand car!) and if $c = 1/9$ then the first-order condition tells us that two price quotes will be optimal. Clearly the lower the cost of search c, the greater the optimal number of searches (if $c = 1/100$, $n = 9$). Not surprisingly, the more units of the commodity to be purchased, the greater the optimal search effort (with $q = 100$ and $c = 1/100$, $n = 99$).

Stigler's analysis therefore involves the searcher in calculating the best sample size of price offers to choose. Once the problem is solved, the searcher goes out into the market and contacts the requisite number of sellers. This *predetermined-sample-size* strategy, however, clearly has its disadvantages. If $q = 1$ and $c = 1/9$ and the buyer approaches the first of the two sellers s/he is going to sample and finds that s/he is offered a price of £0.1, it is not at all clear that the person should bother to contact anyone else. Rather than a predetermined sample-size strategy, therefore, it has been suggested that a sequential-search strategy would be more sensible. At each stage, the searcher asks whether, given the known frequency distribution of price offers and the lowest price so far encountered, a further unit of search would be worthwhile.

Assuming that $q = 1$ and the frequency distribution is rectangular, as above, it is a simple matter to show[15] that further search at any stage will not be worthwhile (in terms of reducing expected costs) if

$$p^* < \sqrt{(2c)}.$$

If the most recent price offer is less than $\sqrt{(2c)}$ it is best to accept it and search no more. $\sqrt{(2c)}$ is called a 'reservation price'. The sequential-search strategy therefore comes down to the calculation of the optimal reservation price. Search then continues until a price below this level is quoted.[16]

This brief excursion into neoclassical search theory is sufficient at least to uncover the essential rationale of the approach. Neoclassical theory is evidently quite capable of analysing some types of search, but, if this is so, what is it that distinguishes Kirzner's 'alert' entrepreneur who discovers new information from Stigler's searcher after new information, and is the distinction of any importance?

The idea of a rational investment programme in the acquisition of new knowledge, as suggested by neoclassical search theory, is in some respects rather odd, for it implies that it is possible to estimate the value of new knowledge in advance of its discovery. Presumably, though, this will only be possible if, in some sense, we already know what we are looking for along with the probability of finding it. It is rather as if we are searching for something of which we once had full knowledge but have inadvertently mislaid. Stigler's searcher decides how much time it is worth spending rummaging through dusty attics and untidy drawers looking for a sketch which (the family recalls) Aunt Enid thought might be by Lautrec. Kirzner's entrepreneur enters a house and glances lazily at the pictures which have been hanging in the same place for years. 'Isn't that a Lautrec on the wall?'[17]

For Kirzner, entrepreneurial knowledge is not the sort of knowledge which is the yield to a rational investment policy in search. Entrepreneurial knowledge does not involve resource inputs but is 'costless'. It arises when someone notices an opportunity which may have been available all along – something which was staring everyone in the face but had somehow escaped their attention (Kirzner, 1979, pp. 129–31).[18] 'Why didn't I think of that?' is the exasperated cry of most of us when confronted with some simple and effective piece of enterprise. Part of our exasperation derives from the appreciation that we may have possessed all the individual pieces of information required to perceive the same opportunity. The significance of the information somehow unfortunately escaped us, and we failed to 'put it together' to form a coherent and profitable picture. Such self-admonishment is quite out of place in the world of neoclassical search. For in that world there are no mistakes and regrets whether deriving from omission or commission. True, a decision having been made, a person may later acquire knowledge which reveals how much better some alternative decision might have been, but, providing that within the context of the knowledge available at the time the decision was correct and providing that investment in information had been carried to the optimal point, no real 'error' can be said to have occurred. The neoclassical world must always ultimately be a world of calculation in which 'observation' is taken for granted.

2.4 Schumpeter

2.4.1 Entrepreneurship and equilibrium

As we have seen, Kirzner's approach to the entrepreneur is that s/he is alert to hitherto unexploited gains from trade. At any one time, economic life consists of a complex pattern of exchange relationships. The entrepreneur acts as the catalyst which loosens some transactional bonds and forges new ones. In our simple example above, the entrepreneur was the motive force impelling society towards some ultimate 'solution' represented by the figures in Tables 1.4 and 1.5. Once this position is achieved, no further possible entrepreneurial profits are available. By definition, if the allocation of resources is a 'core' allocation, no reallocation can benefit any group of people, and hence all the 'alertness' in the world will be of no avail in the spotting of further efficiency gains. Thus, for Kirzner, entrepreneurship is associated with disequilibrium, and concerns the process by which the economy moves towards equilibrium.

The very notion of the entrepreneur as a trader and middleman suggests the gradual and incremental approach to equilibrium, as differences in relative prices are spotted and arbitrage takes place. As Loasby (1982) emphasises, there is a similarity here with Marshall's[19] approach to economic change, with its emphasis on numberless small modifications of established procedures tested out in the marketplace by 'the alert businessman'. It is the tradition of Mises and of Hayek, who both emphasise the small-scale and 'local' character of much entrepreneurship and the dependence of this entrepreneurship on 'knowledge of time and place' or 'tacit knowledge'[20] which 'by its nature cannot enter into statistics' (Hayek, 1945, p. 21).

There is, however, a more heroic conception of the entrepreneur than this. It is easy to see how Kirzner's approach might lead to the conclusion that virtually everyone acts entrepreneurially, at least to some degree. For Schumpeter (1943), on the other hand, the entrepreneur is an extraordinary person who brings about extraordinary events. In Schumpeter's view, the entrepreneur is a revolutionary, an innovator overturning tried and tested convention and producing novelty. Such boldness and confidence 'requires aptitudes that are present only in a small fraction of the population' (p. 132) and represents a 'distinct economic function'. This function of the entrepreneur 'is to reform or revolutionise the pattern of production by exploiting an invention or, more generally, an untried technological possibility for producing a new commodity or producing an old one in a new way, by opening up a new source of supply of materials or a new outlet for products, by reorganising an industry and so on' (p. 132).

In order not to give a misleading impression, it should be added that Schumpeter is careful to say that railroad construction or the generation of electrical power were 'spectacular instances' and that his conception of entrepreneurship would include introducing a new kind of 'sausage or toothbrush'. The crucial characteristic is not scale as such but novelty in a technological sense. New products, new processes or new types of organisation are thrust upon the world, often in the face of violent opposition. The military analogy with generalship or the 'medieval warlords, great or small' (p. 133) is considered by Schumpeter most appropriate because of the importance of 'individual leadership acting by virtue of personal force and personal responsibility for success'.

Because of this emphasis on the energy of individual entrepreneurs and the introduction of new products and processes, Schumpeter sees entrepreneurship as a disruptive, destabilising force, responsible for cycles of prosperity and depression. He refers explicitly to the *disequilibrating* impact of the new products or methods' (p. 132, emphasis added). This is clearly a rather different conception from that of Kirzner. Kirzner's entrepreneur is engaged in spotting ways of making the best of a given set of technical circumstances. Technology, the state of the arts, of skills and scientific knowledge, are a backdrop to, rather than the outcome of, entrepreneurial activities. The possibilities for the full use of available resources in given technical circumstances still have to be uncovered, but this is all the entrepreneur is seen as doing. The production-possibility curves applying to each of the four contractors in our arithmetical example were drawn on the assumption that they represented the outer bound of all the possible points attainable in the prevailing state of technological knowledge available to each individual. These curves would alter with changes in scientific and technical information. Thus, it is usual to contrast Kirzner's approach with Schumpeter's by arguing that Kirzner's entrepreneur will get us to point A in Figure 1.1, a point on the community-production-possibility frontier representing a given state of technical knowledge; while Schumpeter's entrepreneur is engaged in *shifting* the production-possibility frontier by instituting innovations. It is in this sense that Kirzner's entrepreneur gets us to an equilibrium point A, while Schumpeter's entrepreneur disturbs this position of equilibrium by redefining the technical constraints.

This distinction between two types of entrepreneur, one an equilibrating and the other a disequilibrating force, is not, however, as clear-cut as at first sight it might appear. It would seem inconsistent with Kirzner's basic philosophy to assume that people are aware of all the purely technical possibilities available to them, and that their lack of knowledge concerns only the possibilities of benefiting through the process of exchange. Rather, consistency requires us to argue that each person will have limited technical knowledge; that over time, whether by accident or design, they will acquire additional technical knowledge; and that entrepreneurial perception will be as significant in appreciating the consequences of newly acquired technical knowledge as knowledge of price differentials or any other objective pieces of information. It is difficult to see why the person who, upon becoming acquainted with the properties of some artificial fibre, realises that, using this fibre, toothbrushes might be made more cheaply than with natural fibre, is acting as a Schumpeterian rather than Kirznerian entrepreneur. If, ultimately, it is the perception of opportunities which defines the entrepreneur, then Kirzner's framework must surely embrace the marketing of new sausages and toothbrushes.

To maintain the distinction between equilibrating and disequilibrating entrepreneurs therefore seems to require that we distinguish between the use of 'new' technical knowledge, and the new use of technical knowledge which has been known for some time – at least, known to some people. Thus, the person who first manufactures and uses an artificial fibre is Schumpeterian, whereas the people who gradually come to perceive the multifarious possible applications are Kirznerian. This distinction would certainly seem consistent with the 'flavour' of the two writers, but whether it is tenable is a question which, for the present, we will simply ignore.

2.4.2 The fate of the entrepreneur
Given the differences in emphasis between Schumpeter and Kirzner it is somewhat surprising to find one strand of thought common to both.

Entrepreneurial activity serves to render obsolete the entrepreneur. This is perhaps easier to understand in the case of Kirzner since we have already drawn attention to the fact that, as advantage is taken of the available opportunities, the approach of equilibrium reduces the scope for further entrepreneurial insights. Kirzner, it should be emphasised, does not explicitly predict the demise of the entrepreneur, as does Schumpeter. Exogenous changes in tastes and technology can be relied upon to create continuous opportunities for entrepreneurship, but it does appear to be a characteristic of Kirzner's system that it would run down in the absence of these outside forces.

In the case of Schumpeter, the idea of the entrepreneur as a destabiliser might suggest the conclusion that the commercial exploitation of new inventions could go on indefinitely and with it the distinctive role of the entrepreneur. Schumpeter, however, took a quite different view. The progress of capitalism, he asserted, would eventually reduce the importance of the entrepreneur. The entrepreneur was required initially to overcome resistance to change but now 'innovation itself is being reduced to routine. Technological progress is increasingly becoming the business of teams of trained specialists who turn out what is required and make it work in predictable ways' (p. 132). 'Economic progress tends to become depersonalised and automatised' (p. 133). The giant industrial unit 'ousts the entrepreneur' and the specialist instigators of progress eventually receive 'wages such as are paid for current administrative work' (p. 134).

This conception is, of course, quite alien to Kirzner since 'alertness' to new opportunities could hardly be 'depersonalised' as envisaged by Schumpeter. Clearly 'perception' as such is not considered by Schumpeter to give rise to any special problems. Progress derives from technological change, and this can apparently develop a momentum of its own. The entrepreneur is required to galvanise the economic system into motion after which, like some material object in Newtonian physics, all resisting forces having been removed, it continues indefinitely along its predicted path.[21]

Schumpeter's prediction of the obsolescence of the entrepreneur is one of the most celebrated aspects of his work. It has naturally attracted considerable critical attention which cannot be considered here in detail. However, the different interpretations that can be placed on similar observations are startling in the study of economics. Whereas large corporate entities in Schumpeter's view 'oust the entrepreneur', Kirzner sees them as magnets attracting entrepreneurial talent. The corporation is 'an ingenious, unplanned device that eases the access of entrepreneurial talent to sources of large-scale financing' (1979, p. 105). It reduces the transactions costs, considered earlier, involved in gaining access to capitalists' funds.[22] Schumpeter observes the large corporation and finds in it an environment unconducive to the survival of the entrepreneur. Kirzner observes the same phenomenon and pronounces it a structure which has evolved to permit a more effective use of entrepreneurial alertness. Further, Schumpeter's view that, within the corporation, technical progress becomes automatic was greeted even at the time with scepticism if not disbelief in some quarters. One such critic (Jewkes, 1948), with barely concealed contempt for a view which so contradicted his experience of aircraft production and research during the Second World War in the UK, wrote that: 'Left to themselves, and having no particular reasons for taking risks, teams of technicians will almost invariably bog themselves down without direction or purpose . . . Take away the motive force of innovation – the business man – and the cautious and conservative habits of the consumer and technician would roll back over us with deadening effect' (p. 21).

2.5 Shackle

Shackle is celebrated not so much for his specific views on the entrepreneur as for his writing on the nature of choice in general. A brief consideration of his work is relevant here, however, because it impinges directly on the issues under discussion. We have seen how, in Kirzner's conception of things, the entrepreneur perceives opportunities. Shackle would insist that the entrepreneur must imagine these opportunities. This is not to use the word 'imagine' in the popular sense, to imply that the opportunities are illusions, but rather simply to assert that any choice involves the exercise of imagining a possible future state of affairs. We do not choose between 'facts' or 'certainties'. When we act, it is on the basis of the imagined consequences. Even in the simplest possible case of choosing between a loaf of bread and a pint of beer we must choose on the basis of how we imagine our feelings will be when we actually get round to eating the bread or drinking the beer. This is so even if this occurrence follows the act of choice by a mere fraction of a second. Once we have drunk the beer we know what it was like, but this information is not relevant to any act of choice. When we approach the bar for our second pint we will of course, remember the experience of drinking the first, but it is strictly not this recollection of past drinks which determines our choice, but the consequent expectation of the future drink. Thus, Shackle is the complete subjectivist. All neoclassical economists are subjectivists in the sense that they accept that my valuation of beer in terms of the amount of something else I am prepared to sacrifice to get another pint is simply an expression of my own subjective preferences. Shackle, however, goes further to argue that the so-called 'objects of choice' (the bread and the beer) are not objects at all, but subjective impressions about the future: 'If my theme be accepted, there is nothing among which the individual can make a choice, except the creations of his own thought' (1979b, p. 26).

Such radical subjectivism has immediate implications for his view of the entrepreneur. Shackle, like Kirzner, is often placed within the group of writers called 'Austrian', yet the implications of his philosophy are so subversive that by comparison the main Austrian camp appears a haven of conservatism. Kirzner's entrepreneur gradually uncovers the opportunities presented by objectively given constraints. In the process, s/he takes us to an equilibrium in which all opportunities are finally exploited. If, though, opportunities do not have an objective existence independent of their discoverer, but spring rather from each person's imagination, they cannot be recorded, even conceptually, in a finite list unless the human imagination itself is capable of exhaustion. Thus, for Shackle there can be no state of 'full coordination'; no equilibrium representing the final resting place of the economy. Underlying Kirzner, there is a form of historical determinism, a final destination. Underlying Shackle, there is simply 'the anarchy of history' (1979b, p. 31). His view is clearly anti-determinist, and rejects the whole concept of equilibrium.[23]

To refer once more to our arithmetical illustration of the four individuals, Kirzner's entrepreneur spots the possibilities presented by four different, but objectively existing, production-possibility curves, but these constraints and the opportunities delimited by them are, for Shackle, simply what people at any given time think they are, and can never have the status of ultimate objective unchanging facts. Tomorrow, person A may imagine new ways of using his or her resources for different or for similar purposes. Either way, the established pattern is upset and new opportunities for entrepreneurship are created. As Loasby (1982b) puts it: 'Kirzner's entrepreneurs are alert, Shackle's are creative' (p. 119). Shackle rejects conceptions of the economic process which 'rule a line under the sum of human knowledge, the total human inventive accomplishment' (Shackle, 1982, p. 225).

If comparisons are to be made, Shackle's entrepreneur has perhaps a greater affinity with that of Schumpeter than with that of Kirzner. The emphasis on innovation on the one hand (Schumpeter) and the creative imagination on the other (Shackle) are closely related.[24] Further, the ideas that entrepreneurial activity disrupts equilibrium on the one hand (Schumpeter) and denies the possibility of equilibrium on the other (Shackle), while clearly not formally compatible, nevertheless suggest a similar conception of its impact. In other ways, however, Schumpeter and Shackle are far apart. Neither Schumpeter's view that only a small proportion of people have the qualities to be entrepreneurs, nor his view that the entrepreneurial function is doomed to extinction, seem compatible with

Shackle's philosophy, for Shackle's view is ultimately grounded on his response to the most fundamental question of what it really means 'to choose'. Everyone faces the necessity of choice, and in choosing they exercise the entrepreneurial faculty of imagination. Thus, so long as there are human beings and choices to be made, so too will there be entrepreneurs. Shackle's approach to the entrepreneur, therefore, is not part of a theory of business enterprise as commonly understood, nor is it like Kirzner's framework an attempt to consider the process by which equilibrium is attained; rather it is an integral part of his whole approach to the theory of individual choice.

2.6 Casson

To be told that entrepreneurship is an inevitable concomitant of the human condition, while important conceptually and philosophically, is light years away from the popular conception of the entrepreneur with which we started. In principle we may accept the case that all decisions are speculative, but we may also accept that some decisions are more speculative than others, and that some people are better at making these more speculative decisions than others. If the entrepreneur is ultimately to play a part within a theory of the firm, there seems no escaping the idea that the entrepreneur possesses skills which are special, if not in kind then in degree. Thus, Knight's entrepreneur is unusually willing to tolerate uncertainty, Kirzner's is especially alert, Schumpeter's is ruthlessly capable of smashing the opposition, and Shackle's is endowed with a particularly creative imagination.

Casson (1982) attempts to synthesise and extend these conceptions of the entrepreneur. His definition is as follows: 'An entrepreneur is someone who specialises in taking judgemental decisions about the coordination of scarce resources' (p. 23). Central to this definition is the notion of a judgemental decision. This, Casson defines as a decision 'where different individuals, sharing the same objectives and acting under similar circumstances, would make different decisions' (p. 24). They would make different decisions because they have 'different access to information, or different interpretation of it'. It follows from this definition that an entrepreneur will be a person whose judgement inevitably differs from the judgement of others. The reward, then, for an entrepreneur derives from backing his or her judgement and being proved right by subsequent events.

A single chapter does not allow the space carefully to develop every point of comparison between Casson's view of the entrepreneur and those which we have already encountered. Nevertheless a few observations may help to make clear the distinctive contribution of Casson and at the same time clarify some of the issues discussed in earlier sections.

Casson has one fundamental point of agreement with the 'Austrian' theorists. The entrepreneur's reward is a residual income not a contractual income, and it is derived from the process of exchange or 'market-making activities'. For Casson, the middleman is an entrepreneur, just as for Kirzner. Entrepreneurs reallocate resources. To achieve such a resource reallocation they must trade in property rights (see Chapter 4) and if their attempts at coordination (that is, resource reallocation) are successful they will derive a pure entrepreneurial profit. The person who judges that a firm could be reorganised profitably, purchases the firm, changes its operations (by recontracting with the inputs) and sells it for a gain is clearly an entrepreneur. The person who thinks that a group of people, at present working independently, would be more effective as a team, and who forms the team by employing each at a wage equivalent to their existing income, thereby appropriates the productivity gains achievable through team effort. Such a person is also clearly an entrepreneur.[25]

Even at this level there are, of course, differences of emphasis. Thus, as we have seen, Casson insists that these 'market makers' or 'coordinators' are specialists, whereas Kirzner sees any alert person as a potential entrepreneur. Further, Casson emphasises that entrepreneurs require command over resources if they are to back their judgements and that this is likely to imply personal wealth. He refers to people with entrepreneurial ability but no access to capital as 'unqualified' (p. 333). Kirzner would accept that lack of personal capital presents extra transactional difficulties (see above section 2.3.1) but would almost certainly argue that anyone with entrepreneurial talent could never be in an objective sense totally 'unqualified'. Entrepreneurial talent will find ways of securing control of resources, and 'alertness' to possible new ways of doing so is as much a part of entrepreneurial talent as alertness to possible new uses for the resources themselves.

In other respects, Casson and the Austrian theorists are far apart. For Schumpeter, Kirzner and Shackle, the 'pace of change' is determined by the activities of the entrepreneurs. Each had different ideas of the personal qualities which were important in instigating change, and they differed on the question of whether change thus instigated was disequilibrating or equilibrating, but each was clear that change and entrepreneurship go together like a horse and cart and that the entrepreneur is the horse. In Casson's scheme, however, there is a tendency to view 'the pace of change' as an accompaniment to entrepreneurial activity rather than as its result. This makes Casson's entrepreneur more akin to that of Knight – the person who, in an uncertain (changing) world, specialises in making difficult judgements and receives a profit for bearing uninsurable risk (Casson would say for exhibiting superior judgement). Indeed, Casson himself writes that his work on the entrepreneur is in many parts 'simply a reformulation of ideas first presented by Knight' (p. 373).

Casson's entrepreneur perhaps requires Kirznerian perception to spot the information most pertinent to the judgemental decision at hand, and requires Shackle's imaginative faculty to ponder future possibilities, but these features are not greatly emphasised. The reason is straightforward and fundamental. Casson wants to discuss more than the rationale of the entrepreneur. He realises the importance of the entrepreneur to the process of resource coordination and wishes to consider further questions upon which an economic theory might cast some light. Ultimately, Casson wishes to construct a predictive theory of entrepreneurship. Shackle's sublime epistemology is all very well but there are some important down-to-earth issues which it does not really help us to address. Why are some economic systems apparently more successful at resource reallocation than others? How are entrepreneurs 'allocated' to the task of making judgemental decisions? What institutional arrangements facilitate the exercise of entrepreneurship? What factors determine the 'supply' of entrepreneurial talent? The language in these questions, which clearly implies the notion of entrepreneurship as a 'resource' similar to other factors of production to be 'allocated', is clearly alien to the Austrian conception. Yet, as Casson recognises early on (p. 9), 'the Austrian school . . . is committed to extreme subjectivism – a philosophical standpoint which makes a predictive theory of the entrepreneur impossible'. He accepts that no predictive theory of the behaviour of an individual entrepreneur is possible, but this does not rule out, he argues, a theory of the aggregate behaviour of a population of entrepreneurs. Fortified with this thought, Casson braces the hostility of the entire Austrian camp and proceeds to consider entrepreneurship within a supply and demand framework.

Figure 3.1 reproduces Casson's diagrammatic apparatus. The curves, though labelled DD' and SS' should not be regarded as supply and demand curves as conventionally interpreted. Consider the DD' curve first. Along this curve is plotted the expected reward per entrepreneur as the number of active entrepreneurs increases. It is drawn *assuming a given pace of change* in the economy. Thus, new opportunities are cropping up at a certain pace and it is the task of the entrepreneurs to spot them and take advantage of them. Notice how similar to Kirzner's is this conception. Whereas Kirzner sees the entrepreneur as gradually coming to perceive the opportunities latent *in given circumstances*, Casson sees the entrepreneur as spotting a certain proportion of the opportunities thrown up *as circumstances change*. It is as if Schumpeter's entrepreneurial horse has done its work and the cart is proceeding under its own momentum directed not by teams of experts, as Schumpeter expected, but by specialist Kirznerian entrepreneurs placed in this slightly different environment by Casson.

As the number of active entrepreneurs increases, the expected return to each declines. This is to imply the usual competitive postulate in a slightly unfamiliar guise. The more active entrepreneurs there are, the more likely it is that any given opportunity will have already been spotted by someone else, and the length of time elapsing before a newly spotted opportunity is emulated by others is reduced. Thus the curve DD' slopes downwards to the right and its position is dependent upon the pace of change. Curve SS', on the other hand, is the supply curve of 'qualified' entrepreneurs (those with access to resources). It has a lower bound at the prevailing real wage on the reasonable grounds that no one will be an entrepreneur if the expected reward is below the wage rate. (This would, of course, not necessarily follow if entrepreneurs could be found who were risk lovers.) As the expected return to entrepreneurship rises above the wage rate, 'qualified' people desert employment to become specialist entrepreneurs. Further rises in the expected return induce yet others to become entrepreneurs who had before preferred leisure.

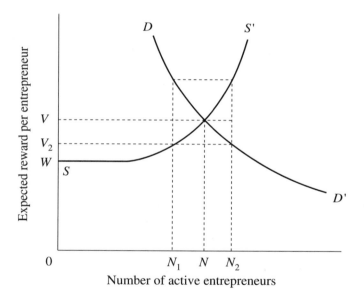

Figure 3.1   Casson's theory of entrepreneurship

The position of the curve SS' depends on the stock of entrepreneurial talent existing in the population (that is, the number of people who have the necessary judgemental qualities) and the proportion of these who are 'qualified' in Casson's sense of having command over resources. People can become 'qualified' in three possible ways. They can have wealth of their own with which to pursue entrepreneurial ideas, they can have social contacts with wealthy individuals who know their character and appreciate their entrepreneurial potential, and they can gain command of resources from venture capitalists who do not know them but are specialists in screening for entrepreneurial flair, or from holding a senior position in a corporation.[26] Thus, *SS'* will shift with changes in the distribution of wealth, changes in social mobility, and changes in institutional mechanisms for screening for entrepreneurial ability.

Intersection of the two curves *DD'* and *SS'* gives an 'equilibrium' solution and determines the number of active entrepreneurs (N) and their expected rewards (V). These long-run 'equilibrium' expected rewards to entrepreneurship Casson interprets as a form of wage. In the short run, the return to each entrepreneur is a return to superior (monopoly) knowledge. In the long run, the expected return is 'simply compensation for time and effort, namely for the time and effort spent in identifying and making judgemental decisions' (p. 337). This long-run conception is not unlike that of J.B. Say which we encountered early on in this chapter. The number of active entrepreneurs (N), given the pace of change, will determine the proportion of new job opportunities that are exploited.

If this equilibrium or steady state is to be achieved, it is necessary that potential entrepreneurs should know the total number of entrepreneurs operating at any given time, along with the underlying pace of change of the economy. This information will be required if the expected return to entrepreneurship is to be assessed at each point and a decision made about the desirability of entry. It is worth noting that this mechanism will not necessarily lead smoothly to the equilibrium point. Suppose, for example, there were N_1 active entrepreneurs, all those entrepreneurs in the interval $N_1 N_2$ would be attracted to enter. Casson supposes that the numbers gradually rise and the expected reward gradually falls until equilibrium is achieved, but since we have not assumed that each entrepreneur knows the opportunity costs faced by other entrepreneurs, all we can really tell is that all entrepreneurs in the interval $N_1 N_2$ will enter. Such a *mass* entry, however, will greatly depress the expected reward per entrepreneur (V_2). In this way, a cycle could be generated not unlike the 'cobweb cycle' of principles of economics textbooks. It is also similar in conception to Schumpeter's view of cycles of entrepreneurial activity. Clearly the decision whether or not to become an entrepreneur is as 'judgemental' as the individual decisions the entrepreneur makes after he or she has entered. It would be ironical indeed to have to conclude that markets in general are coordinated by entrepreneurial activity, but that the market for entrepreneurs requires an auctioneer.

Casson's presentation of the market for entrepreneurs has many of the strengths which are associated with neoclassical ways of thinking. Drawing supply and demand curves can be a powerful aid to thought, which is presumably why they were invented and have proved so popular. Such diagrams immediately require us to specify what determines the shapes and positions of the curves, and in so doing we isolate what we think are the important influences on the market. Whether the concept of a steady-state equilibrium in the market for entrepreneurs is a theoretical advance, however, will have to be judged by future research effort. In principle the framework should permit comparative static properties to be deduced which are testable statistically. In practice it is not clear that some of the crucial variables in the model are amenable to statistical measurement; for example, the social and institutional factors behind the supply curve. Further, economists of the Austrian school would argue that the attempt to introduce the equilibrium method into studies of entrepreneurship is fundamentally misconceived. For the DD' curve to mean anything it has to be assumed that all entrepreneurs know 'the pace of economic change' and can calculate the expected rewards from their entrepreneurial efforts. There seems to be no very clear explanation as to why such a construction is likely to exhibit much stability. In the context of a firm's market demand curve, Shackle (1982, p. 230) defends the geometrical figure as an aid to thought, but dismisses the possibility of knowing much about it in practice: 'It is a mere thread floating wildly in the gale.' There seems little possibility that he would take a different view of the demand for entrepreneurs.

3.   THE ENTREPRENEUR AND THE FIRM

We have now considered in some detail the contribution of those economic theorists who have given the entrepreneur a place of importance in their thinking. There are clearly many different conceptions of the entrepreneur, but complex and subtle as are some of the arguments and distinctions that we have encountered, a few fundamental points seem particularly relevant for the theory of the firm. Entrepreneurs are concerned with the process of coordination. It is time and change which give rise to the possibility of entrepreneurial profit. This is so whether we emphasise alertness, imagination, skill in making judgemental decisions, willingness to bear uncertainty or energy to overcome resistance as the ultimate source of entrepreneurship. In Chapter 1, much space was devoted to the proposition that a world of perfect information required no firms and that the firm was an institutional response to uncertainty. Clearly, therefore, at this very fundamental level the entrepreneur and the firm are closely associated. Both are concerned with managing change.

It is important to remember that the entrepreneur is not a prisoner in the firm, and it is interesting that most of the theoretical work in the Austrian school concentrates, as we have seen, on intermediation in the market. This, though, is simply because these theorists are particularly interested in uncovering the ultimate source of entrepreneurial profit, and wish to emphasise their view that all economic life can be seen as a changing network of exchange relationships. Thus, as we saw in Chapter 2, the firm itself can be viewed as a set of contracts with a central authority; contracts so framed as to reduce the transactions costs associated with exchange in the market. Those who spot that possibilities for profitable collaboration exist, who put together the necessary set of contracts between themselves and the collaborating agents, and thus establish a new enterprise or firm, are acting as entrepreneurs in the same way as the middleman in our earlier example. The difference between simple arbitrage and setting up a firm is one of the degree of complexity and the type of contract involved rather than any difference of economic principle. In both cases, resources are reallocated, and if the reallocation makes it possible for everyone to benefit thereby the entrepreneur stands to gain a pure entrepreneurial profit. Entrepreneurship is central, therefore, to the establishment of new enterprises. As Knight recognised, 'A considerable and increasing number of individual promoters and corporations give their exclusive attention to the launching of new enterprises, withdrawing entirely as soon as the prospects of the business become fairly determinate' (p. 257).

3.1 The Small Entrepreneurial Firm

Casson's supply curve of entrepreneurs is not easy to estimate empirically, but in recent years a significant amount of academic research has attempted to investigate the factors determining the establishment of new entrepreneurial firms. As we saw above, the position of the supply curve is expected to depend upon the prevailing return to normal employment, the judgemental qualities of the population and the information flows which they encounter, and access to finance (especially private wealth or some other means of surmounting the hazards associated with the capitalist–entrepreneur relationship).

In the United Kingdom, for example, Storey and Johnson (1987) have studied regional variations in entrepreneurship. The authors construct an 'entrepreneurship index' for each region. Factors such as the percentage of small firms in a region or the proportion of the population in managerial groups can be associated with the accumulation of relevant knowledge and experience on the part of potential entrepreneurs. Educational information, such as the proportion of the population with degrees, may correlate with the ability of people to draw up and act upon simple business plans. Savings per head, house price indices, and measures of the house-owning population are related to access to capital. Indices of 'entry barriers' attempt to measure the height of the capital 'qualification' which would have to be surmounted by new entrepreneurs in the industries of the region. Storey and Johnson find that variation between the regions in new firm formation rates in manufacturing cannot be explained simply by differing industrial structures. 'Fertility', that is the propensity for new firms to be set up, was a more important factor than regional industrial structure. Further, government policies to encourage small firm formation were not equally effective in all the regions.[27] Indeed, 'the entrepreneurship index performs remarkably well in predicting the regional take-up of small firms policy' (p. 170).

In another paper, Storey and Johnson (1987b) concentrate on the opportunity cost side of the decision to become an entrepreneur. They use an index of labour shedding as a measure of local labour market conditions. Unemployment may reduce the opportunity costs of becoming an entrepreneur although it may also have adverse effects on asset values – both human and physical. Using data on new manufacturing firms in Northern England between 1965 and 1978 they found that it was not the lure of high profitability that influenced new firm formation so much as local labour market conditions.[28]

Other work focuses on the entrepreneur's problem of obtaining finance. In the United States, Evans and Leighton (1989) and Evans and Jovanovic (1989) find that switches out of employment into self-employment are more likely to occur as family assets rise. They argue that this evidence is consistent with the existence of binding financial constraints deriving from the contractual hazards discussed earlier. Blanchflower and Oswald (1991) also use a neoclassical supply and demand framework to investigate this issue. Data from the National Child Development Study in the United Kingdom were used to estimate the probability of a person being self-employed. The role of gifts or inheritance proved to be significant. 'A gift or inheritance of £5,000 approximately doubles a typical young individual's probability, ceteris paribus, of setting up his or her own business' (p. 22).

At the macroeconomic level, King and Levine (1993) propose a model of the connection between finance, entrepreneurship and growth. In their work, financial intermediaries specialise in evaluating prospective entrepreneurs and thus overcoming the adverse selection problem. Some people have the capacity to be successful entrepreneurs and others do not. Expenditure of resources in the activity of assessment is capable of distinguishing competent from incompetent entrepreneurs. When competent entrepreneurs and potentially successful projects have been identified, the intermediaries raise finance and diversify risk. They do this by providing equity capital in the manner of venture capitalists. The hypothesis is that a more developed financial system will facilitate entrepreneurship and hence will be associated with higher levels of national income and with a higher growth rate. King and Levine use data from over eighty countries for the years 1960–89 to evaluate this hypothesis. Their proxies for the degree of development of the financial system include the ratio of liquid liabilities (currency plus interest and non-interest-bearing liabilities) to GDP, the relative size of central bank assets to total bank assets and the proportion of credit advanced to private enterprises rather than the government sector. Econometric analysis indicated strong links between these characteristics of the financial system and overall productivity growth and growth in per capita output.

Small businesses rely heavily on the banks for the provision of finance. It has been argued that the problems of information asymmetry which confront entrepreneur and financier will depend to some extent on the nature of the banking system. More discussion of this issue can be found at the end of Chapter 9 in the context of corporate governance. Here we merely note that the commercial banks in the United Kingdom have not traditionally been seen as appropriate sources of venture capital or long-term industrial investment.[29] They developed as deposit-taking institutions that would provide relatively short-term finance on good security. No very deep knowledge of particular industries or entrepreneurial prospects was required in this system on the part of banks. Quite different traditions evolved in other countries with respect to the channelling of savings to investment opportunities. Stanworth and Gray (1991, p. 70) write that 'by retaining a more separate and isolationist role from industry in the UK, the banks may be less able to provide this transformation process than are their counterparts in other countries'. Entrepreneurs require appropriate supporting institutions. Reid and Jacobsen (1988, p. 6) in their study of the small entrepreneurial firm in Scotland, however, do not see the policies of commercial banks as representing a significant barrier to the raising of outside finance by new small firms. Further discussion of the finance of the entrepreneur can be found in section 8 of Chapter 4, where the role of instruments of debt compared with instruments of ownership is specifically investigated.

Once the enterprise is established, the scope for entrepreneurship does not cease. In principle, the continuation of the same arrangements, the monitoring of the inputs and routine management are not entrepreneurial activities, but continuing change elsewhere is likely to involve a continuous process of adaptation by the firm, and no firm is likely to survive for long without the exercise of some entrepreneurial talent. It is in this context that Casson's approach has most to commend it. All firms require entrepreneurs, and a significant problem is how to make the most of available talent in the making of judgemental decisions. One of the most obvious problems faced by closely owned businesses is what happens when the sons or daughters of the founder lack their parent's business acumen. Indeed, the growth of transferable shares and limited liability can be seen as a response to this very problem.[30]

The entrepreneur and the proprietor of a business enterprise are not synonymous. Clearly, the single owner of the classical capitalist firm who supplies the capital and performs routine managerial tasks may also exercise entrepreneurial skills, but the owner is not necessarily an entrepreneur. Neither should we think in terms of a single entrepreneur associated with each firm. Especially in larger firms, entrepreneurship, alertness to new opportunities, may exist throughout the organisation. Indeed it is possible to regard 'the firm' itself as a 'coalition' of entrepreneurs.

3.2 The Firm as a Coalition of Entrepreneurs

Wu (1989) has developed the idea that markets can evolve over time to permit trade in commodities, labour and capital, but that 'all the services provided by entrepreneurs are nontradeable' (p. 103). Moral hazard is such a severe problem with entrepreneurial services that a market can never exist and 'entrepreneurs must take the initiative to organise production through non market means, that is, by organising a firm' (p. 232). In the era of the medieval guilds, a craftsman would supply capital labour and entrepreneurial talent together. Gradually, however, separate markets in labour and capital developed. For several centuries, entrepreneurship was still associated with the provision of capital, but the development of the joint-stock company has permitted further specialisation. Pure entrepreneurs are taking control of production while capitalists become providers of funds. 'The long historical evolution toward functional specialisation among the factors of production had reached its destination' (p. 224).

For Wu, a firm is a coalition of entrepreneurs which agrees a production policy, an organisational structure, and a rule for sharing the residual profits. The entrepreneur's reward is the result of bargaining within the firm over a share of the surplus. This does not mean that pure entrepreneurs can easily set up a new firm. Start-up firms in risky industries cannot be founded by pure entrepreneurs because of the difficulty of raising funds. Such firms will require innovator-entrepreneurs with private sources of finance, but established firms can generate a sufficient reputation in the market to attract finance, and hence can be managed by pure entrepreneurs.

Further reference to this conception of the firm and the role of the entrepreneur is made in Chapter 8 in the context of corporate governance. It is clearly a controversial view because it implies that market evolution and the power of reputation is enough to overcome the hazards associated with the relationship between entrepreneur and financier. It is also heavily influenced by 'Austrian' ideas. The main resources harnessed by each firm are the entrepreneurial talents of the coalition. These will be highly 'coalition specific' and the surplus generated by the mutual efforts of the entrepreneurs will not necessarily be competed away in the long run. Thus, Wu's approach has affinities with those who emphasise the importance of the generation of 'competitive advantages' within the firm – advantages which cannot be replicated at low cost and derive from the special experience and make-up of a given coalition.

If the firm is a vehicle for the exercise of entrepreneurship we have to get used to the idea that a significant proportion of the income received by those who work in the firm is entrepreneurial profit. This applies not merely to those who have Board appointments, and possess the more obvious claims to profits such as stock options and deferred pension rights, but also to those who work throughout the organisation. The means by which people lay claim to these profits is important. In Chapter 6, for example, we will look at the structure of hierarchies. Promotion can be seen as a way of inducing effort. It might also be part of the mechanism whereby the pure surplus of the organisation is distributed between the entrepreneurs who created it. The important thing is that entrepreneurs have the means of transferring their insights into personal gain. To consider the mechanisms by which this can be accomplished requires us to investigate in much more detail the nature of property rights and the way that different types of organisation reflect different structures of rights.

NOTES

1. Schumpeter (1954, p. 555).
2. Binks and Coyne (1983) briefly discuss the origins of entrepreneurs (pp. 15–16). In recent years, the success of British-Asian entrepreneurs has been noted (Forester, 1978) while Bannock (1981) identifies (among others) 'the desperate, the non-conformist and the odd man out' as the instigator of new business enterprise. A useful survey of the literature on the psychology and socioeconomic background of the small business owner-manager can be found in Stanworth and Gray (1991), chapter 7, pp. 151–77.
3. A. Smith (1776) *The Wealth of Nations*; D. Ricardo (1817), *Principles of Political Economy and Taxation*; J.S. Mill (1848), *Principles of Political Economy with some of their Applications to Social Philosophy*.
4. Schumpeter (1954) writes of Say's work: 'His contribution is summed up in the pithy statement that the entrepreneur's function is to combine the factors of production into a producing organism. Such a statement may indeed mean much or little. He certainly

    failed to make full use of it and presumably did not see all its analytic possibilities.' (p. 555). Say's major work was the *Traite d'economie politique* (1803).

5.   It is not clear that Say was consciously influenced by Cantillon. Richard Cantillon's 'Essai sur la nature de commerce en general' was in circulation around 1730. He saw the farmer as an entrepreneur paying contractual sums to landlords and labourers and receiving an 'uncertain' revenue from the sale of crops. This is a clear statement of the view of the entrepreneur as a recipient of 'residual' rather than 'contractual' income.

6.   Schumpeter takes a less exalted view of Courcelle-Seneuil's analytical contributions: 'His work illustrates our old truth that it is one thing to be a good economist and quite another to be a theorist.' (p. 498). Given his acknowledged 'practical turn of mind' however, it is appropriate, and perhaps even to be expected, that his view of profit and the entrepreneur was an advance on those of many more accomplished theorists. For, as Knight emphasises at many points, 'the absence of profit is the essential distinction between theoretical and actual economic society' (p. 51). In 'actual' economic society profits exist, and observers of such a society are therefore more likely to be interested in an explanation than are observers of 'theoretical' societies.

7.   Von Thünen's major work, *Der Isolierte Staat*, was published in three volumes over a substantial period of time. The first volume was published in 1826: the third not until 1863.

8.   For a discussion see Littlechild (1982).

9.   Knight accepts that the 'moral factor' may make ordinary insurance inapplicable, but 'some other method of securing the same result will be developed and employed' (p. 47). The principal mechanism which Knight appears to have in mind is 'self-insurance' by taking on a variety of independent risks and increasing the scope of the operations of a single person or organisation (pp. 252–5). The growth of the corporate form of enterprise permits enormous size and scope and hence the pooling of risks, but is of course exposed to other moral hazards. These issues will be examined in detail in a later chapter.

10.   Knight (1921) felt justified in devoting the whole of Part 2 of his book (over 140 pages) to a discussion of perfect competition, a state which involved 'the possession of accurate and certain knowledge of the whole economic situation by all the competitors' (p. 48). Similarly, Schumpeter (1954) argued that all sound reasoning about the entrepreneur started from an appreciation of equilibrium theory, and the economist whose work he most admired was Walras: 'With perfect competition prevailing, firms would break-even in an equilibrium state – the proposition from which starts all clear thinking on profits' (p. 893).

11.   Discussion and criticism of this point can also be found in Chapter 4, section 8.

12.   Kirzner suggests at one point that capitalists must inevitably exercise the quality of entrepreneurship, and quotes Mises to the effect that every human decision is speculative. This appears to the present writer to muddy the distinction between profit as a reward for 'perception' and as a reward for uncertainty bearing. The capitalist may be an entrepreneur but it is difficult to see why he or she must be so in Kirzner's sense. True, if a capitalist lends to an entrepreneur s/he may trivially have perceived what it is that the entrepreneur is trying to accomplish, but there is a difference between perceiving a possible opportunity which is being, so to speak, presented on a plate by someone else and independently perceiving the opportunity to begin with. Again, if the entrepreneur feels unwilling to divulge his/her plans to the capitalist for obvious reasons, the capitalist will lend only if s/he is convinced that the entrepreneur is a person of sound judgement. Being a good judge of character may therefore be a crucial part of becoming a successful capitalist, but it is not, in itself, the defining characteristic of an entrepreneur.

13.   Borrowing from capitalists constitutes only one method by which an entrepreneur can obtain profit in the absence of resource ownership. We might have envisaged person E drawing up a contract with (say) person A by which E agreed to inform A about her entrepreneurial idea in exchange for a share in any resulting profit. This possible solution requires considerable trust between A and E, of course, but we have seen that the problem of establishing a reputation for integrity is common to virtually any contractual arrangement. Venture capitalists can be seen as specialists in assessing entrepre-

neurial talent and arranging suitable financial contracts. Another possibility is that E negotiates with all the parties independently but arranges for all deliveries of goods to take place at the same time, thus eliminating the need to carry stock (the case of 'instantaneous arbitrage'). Again a substantial portion of Chapter 1 was devoted to the proposition that arranging for events to occur simultaneously is a costly activity.

14. See Appendix, Technical Note 1.
15. See Appendix, Technical Note 2.
16. For a more detailed discussion of search models and an excellent introduction to the whole neoclassical framework for dealing with uncertainty, see Hey (1979).
17. As a successful entrepreneur s/he will presumably express this possibility in tones sufficiently muted to be inaudible to any other occupant of the room!
18. Klein (1997a) characterises Kirznerian alertness as discovery by 'epiphany' – a sudden 'awakening' or 'awareness' – which he distinguishes from discovery through 'serendipity' or pure chance.
19. Marshall did not expect all firms to adopt the same solutions to the problems they faced. People do not have the same information which will always lead to the same decisions: 'The tendency to variation is a chief cause of progress; and the abler are the undertakers in any trade the greater will this tendency be' (Marshall, 1925, p. 355). Different variations are then submitted to the test of the market. As Loasby (1982a) puts it, 'Marshallian competition is a Hayekian discovery process' (p. 236) and his theory of economic progress is 'an incremental, experimental, evolutionary theory' (p. 239). For further discussion of these matters, see Chapter 12.
20. The concept of 'tacit knowledge' is of great importance to the understanding of the modern 'Austrian' writers. The term was coined by Polanyi (1958, 1967): 'We know more than we can tell' (1967, p. 4). In the neoclassical world, as was seen in section 2.3.2, all knowledge is objective and hence discoverable by routine search and, potentially at least, communicable to everyone. The prices quoted by sellers in the example of search considered earlier, constitute objective pieces of information. Austrian theorists have argued that there is a category of knowledge which is of a different kind; information which cannot be communicated in simple statistical form to other people; information which can be acquired only through close association with particular circumstances, 'knowledge of people, of local conditions and of special circumstances' (Hayek, 1945, p. 20). Later in the same paper, Hayek refers to 'knowledge of circumstances of the fleeting moment not known to others' (p. 20). In principle, the fundamental distinction is between knowledge of objective facts and knowledge of the opportunities which are present in any given situation (entrepreneurial knowledge in Kirzner's sense). The fact that circumstances are fleeting does not imply that the bits of information that make up these circumstances are not objective. Neither would the complexity of the information, as, for example, knowledge of character, necessarily imply lack of objectivity, but the ability to perceive the possibilities inherent in such fleeting or complex information is clearly to perceive information of a different order from the objective facts themselves. It is clear, however, that tacit knowledge will be particularly associated with the response to fleeting, complex, local conditions.
21. Schumpeter expresses the opinion that apart from special interests threatened by an innovation 'every other kind of resistance – the resistance, in particular, of consumers and producers to a new kind of thing because it is new – has well-nigh vanished already' (p. 133). Compare with Jewkes (1948, p. 21) quoted in the text.
22. The corporate form of enterprise will be considered in detail in Chapters 8 and 9.
23. Littlechild (1979b) considers this point in greater detail.
24. It should be said, however, that Schumpeter did not really see the entrepreneur as 'creating' new possibilities so much as forcing through those that existed.
25. See Chapter 4 for a fuller discussion of team production and the firm.
26. We have already met the idea of the corporation as a device to make use of otherwise 'unqualified' entrepreneurial talent in the section on Kirzner above.
27. Policies such as the Loan Guarantee Scheme, the Business Expansion Scheme, the Enterprise Allowance Scheme and so on.

28. Storey (1991) and Audretsch and Jin (1994) investigate the forces leading to new firm for-
     mation. The focus of their discussion is the role of unemployment in encouraging or dis-
     couraging entrepreneurship. See also Rees and Shah (1986) on self-employment in the
     UK.
29. As discussed above, King and Levine (1993) measure the depth of the financial system
     by liquid liabilities, yet their model of entrepreneurial finance is in the tradition of
     venture capitalism with the financiers taking a major equity stake in the enterprise. In
     the UK, banks have not traditionally behaved in this way and have tended to lend for
     short periods on good security.
30. See Ekelund and Tollison (1980). Further discussion of this point can be found in
     Chapter 4, section 5.3 and in Chapter 13, section 5.1.

APPENDIX

Technical Notes

1. If the distribution of quoted prices is rectangular we have

$$f(p)=1, 0<p<1.$$

The probability that the price quoted is less than or equal to p^* on any one
occasion will be

$$F(p^*)=p^*$$

where F is the cumulative distribution function. The probability that in n
searches, all price quotes are above p^* will therefore be $(1-p^*)^n$ and hence
the probability that at least one quote will be less than or equal to p^* will
be $1-(1-p^*)^n$. This therefore gives us an expression for the cumulative distribution function of p^* over n searches ($F_n(p^*)$). Thus, the probability
density function *pdf* of p^* for n searches will be

$$f_n(p^*)=n(1-p^*)^{n-1}$$

Thus:

$$E_n(p^*)=n\int_0^1 p^* (1-p^*)^{n-1}dp^*$$

Integrating by parts we obtain

$$E_n(p^*)=\left[-p^*(1-p^*)^n - \frac{1}{(n+1)}(1-p^*)^{n+1} \right]_0^1$$

Thus

$$E_n(p^*) = 1/(n+1)$$

2. If the most recent price quote is accepted (p^*), this will be the 'cost' of the transaction. (Past search is a 'bygone'.) If an extra unit of search is undertaken, what will be the expected cost of the transaction T?

$$T = c + p^* (1 - F(p^*)) + \int_0^{p^*} pf(p)dp$$

where c = search cost as before and $p^*(1 - F(p^*))$ is the current lowest price times the probability that it continues to be the lowest price even after extra search. Thus:

$$p^*(1 - F(p^*)) + \int_0^{p^*} pf(p)dp$$

is the mathematical expectation of the lowest price available after one more search. In the present case, we simply substitute $f(p) = 1$ and $F(p^*) = p^*$ into the above expression and obtain:

$$T = c + p^* - 1/2p^{*2}.$$

Clearly it is not worth searching any more if $T > p^*$; that is, if $c > 1/2p^{*2}$. Thus we stop searching when $p^* < \surd(2c)$.

4.   Property rights

'If we concentrate attention on constraints and classes of permissible action we find ourselves studying the property *aspect of behaviour.'*
(Armen Alchian)[1]

1.   INTRODUCTION

In earlier chapters we have discussed at length the phenomenon of 'exchange', but until now it has simply been assumed that exchange takes place in goods or services (or in the x and y of our arithmetical example) and that these goods and services are valued because of some physical or technical characteristics. Further progress in piecing together a coherent picture of the firm requires that we refine our concept of what it is that people trade with one another. Occasionally in microeconomics textbooks, the idea is encountered that utility or satisfaction derives not from 'goods' in themselves but from their 'characteristics'. Thus, in Lancaster's (1966) framework we gain satisfaction not from toothpaste as such but from 'decay prevention' and 'mouth freshening' qualities which the toothpaste provides. Similarly, in Becker's (1965) approach, households are ultimately concerned with 'commodities' which may be produced by using inputs of various market goods. Thus, a visit to friends may be the desired end (the 'commodity') which requires us to use the 'goods' car service, petrol, shoe leather and so forth, along with a certain amount of time, if we are to achieve it.

These ideas suggest an even more general proposition. It is not goods in themselves which give satisfaction. It is what people are entitled to do with these goods which really counts. Of course, in the simple case involving an exchange of apples and nuts, so often explored in the economics textbook, the question of the ways in which we could use these physical entities to yield utility barely arises. Even here, however, we might observe that whereas the purchase of an apple entitles us to eat it, or cook it, we are not (say) entitled to propel it through our neighbour's window, or to drop the core carelessly on the public highway, or to ferment more than certain limited amounts of cider, and so forth. Thus, when people exchange apples and nuts, the physical goods change hands, but that physical transaction is the visible manifestation of something more fundamental. The trade is more correctly seen as an *exchange of property rights* in the apples and the nuts.

In the case of more complex commodities, the idea is more obvious. The market in the stock of housing, for example, involves the exchange of rights in the stock, and these property rights can be subdivided in such a way that several different people may have different rights in the same physical asset. Consider the legal 'owner' of a house. Such a person has the right to occupy the premises ('*usus*'); may alternatively let the house to someone else and charge that person (the tenant) a rent ('*usus fructus*'); may, within limits, allow the house to deteriorate; or may improve it and change it in a beneficial way ('*abusus*'). In all these things, the owner is not entirely unconstrained. Ownership does not imply being able to do anything we like.

1. If the owner occupies the premises, there may be limitations on its use. He or she may be forbidden from keeping a caravan in the front garden or chickens in the back, or from painting the windows red. These activities may be forbidden because the original builder or developer of the house, wishing to create a favourable environment and thus to sell the houses for the highest possible price, judged that people will be prepared to pay more for houses free from the possible disamenities of neighbouring painters in tasteless red or lovers of noisy animals. By maintaining a right to prevent such activities, the developer is effectively instituting private 'zoning' arrangements which may be a less costly solution to these environmental problems than relying on negotiations between the occupants of neighbouring houses after they have all moved in. Whatever may be the economic rationale of the privately established 'chicken-free zone', for the moment the important point is that the bundle of rights purchased by the 'buyer' of a house is not all encompassing.

2. If the owner lets the property, he or she thereby transfers the rights of use to the tenant. The tenant now has a bundle of rights in the use of the house. The landlord can no longer enter the house when he or she likes, may possibly be forbidden from charging more than a specified rent (if there is rent control), and may have to give a certain length of notice to the tenant. The tenant on the other hand has the right to live in the house and use the assets for a specified period of time. Under rent control the tenant may have 'security of tenure' so that he or she has the right to use the stock for as long as desired providing he or she pays the rent. This right of use might even be inherited by descendants of the tenant.

3. The right of an owner (or a tenant) to change the asset may be severely
    limited. As was mentioned in Chapter 2, building an extension to a
    house will normally require gaining the consent of the local authority
    planning department who thereby have considerable influence on the
    amount and type of development.

All these factors influence what a person can do with housing resources and
hence the benefit that is derivable from them. The value to an individual of
any resource thus depends on the property rights associated with it. As
Demsetz (1967) puts it: 'Property rights are an instrument of society and
derive their significance from the fact that they help a man form those
expectations which he can reasonably hold in his dealings with others . . .
An owner of property rights possesses the consent of fellow men to allow
him to act in particular ways' (p. 31).

2. TYPES OF PROPERTY RIGHTS

2.1 Private Rights

When it is said that a person has private rights in any resource, it means that
the particular person concerned and no one else has the authority to decide
how the resource should be used. As we have seen, this does not imply that
the person is unconstrained in his or her choice. The choice must be from
a 'non-prohibited class of uses' (Alchian, 1977b, p. 130), but the individual
person with private property rights can prevent other people from using the
resource in ways of which he or she does not approve. It is important to
understand that this definition does not imply that all the property rights
associated with a given resource are in the hands of a single person. Rights
to use a resource may be partitioned between two or more individuals, as
in the case of landlord and tenant, but the rights held by the landlord and
the rights held by the tenant in the housing stock are private rights. The
landlord can prevent the tenant, or anyone else, physically changing the
housing stock or subletting it to another person (unless, of course, the
tenant has purchased the latter right from the landlord). The tenant can
prevent the landlord from using the stock for his or her own private purposes. Thus, the fact that different people have rights in the same physical
asset does not necessarily imply that these rights are not private. So long as
each person holds different rights, and the exercise of one person's rights in
no way impinges upon the exercise of the other person's rights, both people
have private rights in the resource.

2.2   Communal Rights

There are instances in which a person's right to use a resource in a certain way is held in common with another person or group of people. My right to walk across common land is the same right as that held by everyone else with access to that land. I may use the resource for the purposes of walking, or gathering firewood, or grazing animals, or whatever, but so also can other people. Other important examples of communal rights might include the right to use a watercourse for the disposal of waste products, or the right to fish on a particular stretch of water or at sea, or the right to allow smoke or other waste gases to escape into the air. In each case, a resource (a river, a lake, the sea or the air) may be used for the same purpose by many individuals. The analytical consequences of communal property will be discussed in a later section, but it will be obvious enough that the problems of 'congestion', 'over-fishing', and water and air 'pollution' are bound up with this question of property rights. Communal property rights, however, do not necessarily imply 'overuse' of resources if the group of people who hold these rights in common is restricted to an 'appropriate' size.[2] Thus, a landowner with private rights to the fishing on a particular stretch of river may decide to restrict the use of the river to a selected group of other people. These people can buy a communal right to fish from the landlord, and any landlord wishing to maximise his or her income from selling these communal rights (licences) will wish to restrict their number.

2.3   Collective Rights

With communal rights, each individual makes his or her decision as to when or how to exercise it. If I am going fishing, I do not have to consult the other people who may also have this right. In the case of a *collective* right or *shared* right, the decision about the use of a resource is taken as a group. For example, a group of individuals may form a consortium which 'owns' a racehorse. This does not imply that individual members of the consortium can enter the horse in whatever race they please, or that they can decide independently on how the horse should be treated. Rather, it implies that some *collective decision* has to be taken about the training and sporting commitments of the horse. This will usually (though not necessarily) imply using some voting process to choose a particular person who will make the detailed decisions which most of the members of the consortium may be ill equipped to make. Once a person has been appointed to this position, the necessary private property rights which will enable him or her to execute decisions and prevent other non-qualified people from making decisions will inhere in that person. A *collective* right to determine the use of a resource and to share in the results is quite different therefore from a *private* or indeed *communal* right. The manager of the resource will exercise the private rights which go with executive decision-making.[3] These rights will remain for so long as the consortium believes they are being exercised sufficiently effectively on their behalf and it is therefore not worth the time and trouble involved in changing the manager.

2.4 Exchangeable Rights

All trade concerns the exchange of property rights, but not all property rights are tradable. Consider, for example, the tenant in a rent-controlled apartment. Such a tenant has the rights of use which we discussed earlier. These rights have no market value, however. The tenant cannot sell the rights to live in a particular house at a controlled rent to anyone else. This lack of tradability can have important consequences, as the eclipse of the private rented sector in the UK helps to testify. Suppose, for example, the value of a house available for owner-occupation on the market was £50,000. Now imagine that the same house has a tenant paying a below-market rent set by a controlling agency. Clearly, the value of the house with a sitting tenant will be less than £50,000 (perhaps £30,000) depending upon the level of the controlled rent, expectations concerning the future of rent control, or the likelihood that the tenant will move. The result is that the market value of the tenant's rights (zero) plus those of the landlord (£30,000) falls short of the value of the property unencumbered by the tenant (£50,000). It follows that both landlord and tenant will have a mutual interest in changing the allocation of property rights in the house. By creating a freehold, there is a potential £20,000 of capital gain to be shared between them. Thus the tenant might offer the landlord (say) £40,000 for his or her rights in the house. This is £10,000 more than their value on the market, but by combining the landlord's and tenant's rights in this way, the tenant creates the freehold which, as we saw, was worth £50,000. Both landlord and tenant thus each make a gain of £10,000.

This example is an illustration of an important principle which will be encountered again in differing disguises. The nature of property rights in resources is expected to change when someone perceives that existing rights holders could all be better off by agreeing to such a change. Sometimes this will involve combining hitherto separately held rights in a single holder (as in the landlord–tenant example under rent control). Sometimes, though, it might involve disentangling different rights, at present held by a single person, and then allocating them to different people. Financial markets provide examples of this process. A government bond which promises to pay £5 per year until repayment of the principal in the year 2010 can be held by a single person, but the right to £5 per year until 2010, and the right to the principal (say £100) in 2010, are quite distinct and could be sold separately on the market. If the market values of the two separate rights sum to more than the market value of the combined rights (the bond) it will pay some financial intermediary to buy bonds and split them down into their component parts.[4]

Just as private rights may be exchangeable or non-exchangeable, the same applies to collective and communal rights. Consider first the case of communal rights. The purchase of a licence to fish in a particular area results, as we saw, in a communal right (unless of course there is only a single licence). This right may or may not be tradable. If I break my arm after buying the licence, I may be able to sell it to someone else, in which case possession of some document is presumably sufficient to procure admission. If, on the other hand, the licence applies to a single named individual, it is worthless to anyone else, and will have no exchangeable value. Membership of a club which allows people access to some communal property constitutes another example. Usually such communal rights are not marketable for the simple reason that when communal access to some resource is involved, the other members of the club will want a say in deciding the eligibility of new members.[5] Willingness to pay the highest entry fee may not be the deciding criterion. Assessment of character and the probability that the new member will take due care of the communal property may be equally important. On the other hand, the incentive to take care of communal property would appear to be stronger when rights of access are exchangeable than when they are not, since failure to do so will be reflected in a falling market value of club membership as facilities deteriorate.

Company shares represent the classic case of exchangeable collective rights. Members of the consortium that owned the racehorse in our earlier example would normally be able to sell their 'share' in the racehorse to another person. We will be investigating the property rights structure of different types of company in more detail shortly. Collective rights in assets taken into 'public ownership', such as nationalised undertakings and departments of state, are clearly not exchangeable. This lack of transferability is the crucial distinction between collective rights in the assets of the state and collective rights in the private sector. As Alchian (1965) expresses it: 'The differences between public and private ownership arise from the inability of a public owner to sell his share of public ownership' (p. 138).

The right of exchange may be exercised privately or collectively. In the case of the shares of a joint-stock company, the shareholder can trade his or her holdings without gaining the approval of other people. An individual decision to buy and sell shares can be made at any time. It is for this reason that shares in a joint-stock company are usually regarded as *private* assets. In fact they are *privately exchangeable* titles to *collective rights*. The share is a bundle of rights, one of which (the right to exchange) is a private right. It is slightly paradoxical to note that in 'private' companies the right to exchange shares is more circumscribed and cannot be exercised purely privately. In the case of public ownership mentioned by Alchian, we might insist that a public owner *can* sell his or her share of ownership but only through the exercise of a collective right of exchange. Presumably this is what happened in the privatisation programmes pursued in many countries during the 1980s. Taxpayers collectively 'decided' through their representative institutions of government to sell their collective rights in the assets of the nationalised industries.

2.5   Alienable and Inalienable Rights

Rights which cannot be reassigned to someone else are sometimes called 'inalienable rights'. Because they cannot be reassigned, the entrepreneurial function of intermediation which we discussed in Chapter 3 has no scope to operate in a world of inalienable rights. Some rights must be alienable if there is to be any coordination problem to solve. Exchangeable rights are clearly alienable, but the converse does not hold. A manager's rights to make decisions about the allocation of shared resources are not exchangeable but they are certainly alienable. A collective decision by shareholders can dismiss the manager.

2.6   Exclusion

If rights are to be exchangeable on the market they must, of course, be denied to people who have not acquired them through gift or exchange. If people cannot effectively be excluded from fishing a stretch of river because the costs of policing the river bank are very high, the market price of a licence will be zero. No one will voluntarily pay for a right they can without penalty acquire for nothing.[6] Thus the ability to exclude others from using a resource is a necessary condition of exchangeability and hence of markets in property rights. If exclusion cannot be effected, the resource is perforce 'communal'; we all have a right to grab what we can get. The converse does not hold: communal property may or may not permit exclusion, as was seen in the section on communal rights.

3.   THE DEVELOPMENT OF PROPERTY RIGHTS

Thus far, our attention has primarily been confined to describing property rights and presenting a simple taxonomy. Several questions now arise. Can we explain the development of different types of property rights? How will the nature of a person's rights influence behaviour? Do property rights matter? One possible response to these questions is that of Demsetz (1967, 1979). Demsetz concentrates on the issue of economic efficiency. We have already seen how the process of exchange gives rise to efficiency gains. If, as a result of resource reallocation, everyone is made better off (as in the example of Chapter 1) the new allocation of resources is said to be 'Pareto superior' to the old allocation. It was from these 'efficiency gains' that the entrepreneur was seen to draw 'pure entrepreneurial profit' in Chapter 3. In Chapter 2, on the other hand, the obstacles to the realisation of gains from exchange, 'transactions costs', were considered. Demsetz makes the point that transactions costs are not independent of the types of property rights in which trade is taking place. As a result, some change in the structure of property rights in a resource may be required before potential efficiency gains can be appropriated.

Consider once more the case of the four islanders A, B, C and D. Let us suppose that somewhere on the island is a freshwater lake containing fish. Each person is equally skilled at catching fish and equally conveniently located with respect to access to the lake. The fish are a delicate species living in a finely balanced harmony with predators and prey. One person fishing the lake can take ten fish per day, but two people fishing will find that only 16 fish per day are sustainable. A maximum yield per day of 18 fish can be achieved with three people, and any further fishing effort will actually reduce the sustainable yield of fish obtainable from the lake by depleting the stock of fish by more than can be compensated by the greater fishing effort. Table 4.1 records these illustrative figures for total social product of fish along with average and marginal social product schedules.

Table 4.1   The fishery – an illustrative table

Number of Fishers	Total social product	Average social product	Marginal social product	Surplus
1	10	10	10	6
2	16	8	6	8
3	18	6	2	6
4	16	4	-2	0

From the figures in Table 4.1, we see that each person fishing in the lake imposes on the others an 'external diseconomy'. Suppose that A is fishing alone and taking home ten fish per day. Person B now comes along and starts fishing. Both A and B each take home eight fish per day. B's fishing has reduced A's catch by two fish per day. It would, however, be equally correct to say that A's presence at the lake reduced B's catch by two fish per day. The relationship is perfectly reciprocal. Each person imposes external diseconomies on the other. Real external diseconomies in production occur when one person's actions affect the production possibilities faced by others, and the four individuals around the island lake are clearly interdependent in this way. The fishing resource is subject to congestion as reflected in the declining schedule of average social product (ASP) as the number of people fishing increases.

Assume now that all four islanders have a communal right to fish in the lake. No one is excluded from fishing, and hence the right to fish there has no market value. Each person will therefore fish as long as the product he or she takes home exceeds the value of the alternative uses of the time expended (the value of the fish exceeds its opportunity cost). Let this opportunity cost be the equivalent of four fish per day.[7] Since the private return to each person is the average social product (ASP), extra people will fish if ASP is greater than four and this implies that all four people on the island will fish in the lake.

Of course, from the point of view of the group of islanders as a whole, this outcome is not ideal. They could all be better off by restricting access to the lake. This is more easily seen by considering the 'surplus' which the community as a whole has derived from the resource. The 'surplus' is simply the total social product of fish minus the opportunity costs of catching it. For the case of three fishermen, total product is 18 and total social cost is 12, thus resulting in a 'surplus' of six. With four people fishing, this surplus has declined to zero. The presence of the lake has conferred no net benefit on the four individuals. Between them, they have managed to sacrifice elsewhere things equivalent in value to the fish they have caught. If access to the lake were restricted to two people, the social product would be unchanged at 16, while the other two people would be free to take leisure or to produce additional goods elsewhere, goods or leisure which we have assumed are valued as equivalent to eight fish.

Restricting access to the lake implies changing the nature of the property rights which people hold. The lake can no longer be unrestricted common property. We can imagine many different ways in which this might come about.

1. All four islanders might come to some mutual agreement whereby they renounce their communal rights in exchange for a collective right to a share in the produce of the lake. This 'fisheries consortium' will then have an incentive to ensure that only two people actually fish in the lake.
2. One of the islanders, perhaps the entrepreneur E of Chapter 3, might simply try to buy up the common rights of the others. Providing that

the price of these rights is less than the surplus expected from the commercial exploitation of the lake, a profit will be achieved on the transactions. The bargaining and transactions costs involved in this strategy are likely to be considerable, however, because those who 'hold out' against the offers made by person E will in the end find themselves in a very strong bargaining position.[8] It is this problem which is often used to justify an element of coercion by the state when bargaining costs threaten the achievement of potential efficiency gains. The power of compulsory purchase, for example, has been defended as a method of reducing transactions costs in situations which would otherwise be subject to the problem of 'hold-out'.

3. A third possibility is that one of the islanders announces to the others that from henceforth they cannot fish in the lake without his or her consent. Common rights are confiscated by force and replaced by private rights.

The establishment of property rights may be modelled as a Hawk–Dove game. Suppose, for example, that the social gains available from the more effective use of the lake are valued at two. Two 'Doves' would meet and split the benefit between them (as in the first of our three scenarios). A 'Hawk' meeting a 'Dove' would take all the gains by the threat of force. Two 'Hawks' meeting, however, might do each other great damage. Let us suppose the payoff to each in this situation is -2. The payoffs are recorded in Table 4.2.

Table 4.2   The Hawk–Dove game

		Islander A	
		Dove	Hawk
Islander B	Dove	1, 1	0, 2
	Hawk	2, 0	$-2, -2$

If all of the islanders are equally equipped to fight and equally likely to win in the event of a fight, the *expected* payoff to the two possible strategies will depend upon the probability of meeting a 'Hawk' or a 'Dove'. A high probability of meeting a 'Hawk' makes a 'Dove' strategy more attractive, and vice versa. With the payoffs as recorded, a probability of meeting a 'Dove' of 2/3 will result in the same *expected* payoff to each strategy. Biologists use this type of argument to model the evolution of a stable proportion of aggressive to non-aggressive animals in a certain species.

The outcome would be different, however, if the islanders could be distinguished in some way and if this distinction began to be associated with the probability of their playing a 'Hawk' or 'Dove' strategy.[9] Islander B might, for example, live closer to the lake, or have fished in the lake for longer. If proximity to or use of a resource is recognised by the players as conditioning the likelihood of playing a given strategy in the Hawk–Dove game, *conventions of property* can evolve. A convention might become established such as 'play the Hawk strategy if you live closer to the resource than your opponent' or 'play the Dove strategy if your opponent has used the resource for longer than you have' and so forth. Just as in the repeated exchange game of Chapter 1, these property conventions could become self-enforcing. As an islander it would be in my self-interest to recognise the sorts of characteristics likely to determine whether an opponent would fight or not. In other words it pays me to recognise emergent rules of property.

Whatever the mechanism by which changes in property rights are effected, one result is the same. By restricting access to the resource, efficiency gains are achievable. The distribution of these gains will depend on the property assignment between the islanders. They may all accrue to the strongest person, to the person who lives closest to the lake, to the only person with a gun, to the entrepreneur E, or they may be shared between members of the fisheries consortium. Whatever the rights assignment turns out to be, a licence to fish in the lake set at a price equivalent to four fish would reduce the number of people fishing to two, and procure an income of eight fish for the resource owner or owners.

Figure 4.1 illustrates the entire argument geometrically. The average social product of fishing effort is depicted by curve ASP. Since, by assumption, all people are equally skilled at fishing, the private return to extra fishing effort will equal the average social return. This implies that people will continue to supply more fishing effort as long as average social product exceeds marginal private cost. Marginal private costs (equal to social costs) are assumed constant at c. Thus, with unrestricted entry into fishing we find a quantity of fishing effort F_1 provided. This is inefficient, since the marginal social product of fishing effort (MSP) is well below marginal social cost (MSC) at this level of effort. Efficiency requires a level of fishing effort F_2, where MSP = MSC. The vertical distance between ASP and MSP represents the external cost imposed on others by extra fishing effort. Similarly the vertical distance between ASP and MPC represents the private benefit accruing to extra fishing effort. Clearly, if external costs exceed private benefit it will be possible for people to get together to bribe some of their number not to fish, since the bribers will gain from reduced congestion more than they have to pay in compensation to the people being bribed (see especially Coase, 1960).

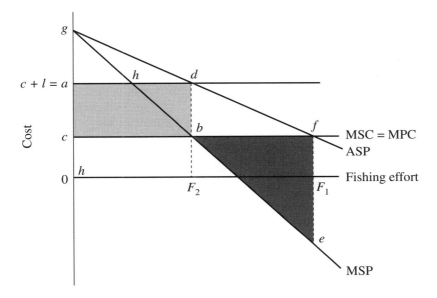

Figure 4.1   External effects result in overfishing

The gain to restricting fishing effort in this way is given by area *bfe*. Once private rights to fishing have been established, a licence fee per unit of fishing effort (*l*) can be introduced, the private marginal costs of fishing will increase to $l + c = a$ and fishing effort will fall to F_2. Total revenue from the sale of licences will be area *acbd* and in these circumstances will precisely equal the efficiency gains achieved (area *bfe*).[10]

For Demsetz, therefore, property rights will change when people find that there are substantial efficiency gains (mutual benefits) to be derived from such a change. These benefits must be sufficient to compensate for the transactions costs involved in establishing and in policing the new structure of rights. If people cannot, except at prohibitively high cost, be prevented from fishing in the lake, no changes in the structure of rights will emerge. On the other hand 'prohibitive' here means 'relative to potential benefits', and the more congested the lake becomes the larger become the efficiency gains from mitigating the problem, and the more likely therefore that the policing costs are worth incurring.

Demsetz cites as an example of this process changes in the rights to use land among the Indians of Labrador. It appears that in the seventeenth century there was no restriction on hunting rights. The development of the fur trade, however, gave rise, according to this theory, to the division of territory among hunting bands. Clearly, without such rights each hunting party could impose severe external disbenefits on the others. When animals were hunted merely for food and clothing for the Indian population, the problem of external costs was insignificant, but with commercial development this was no longer the case and more restrictive property rights emerged. Demsetz then poses the question: why did a similar process not occur among the plains Indians of the south west? One answer is that the cost of defining and policing property rights on the plains would have been much higher than in the forests. Animals grazing on the plains wander over vast areas; those in the forests are more restricted in their movements. Thus, simple delineation of a given policeable area is not sufficient to appropriate a right to tend and harvest a particular herd on the plains, and property rights remained common and open. The consequence of this structure of property rights for the buffalo herds is, of course, well known.

Although property rights may develop in ways conducive to the more efficient use of economic resources, it should not be assumed that this tendency is inevitable. The point about conventions is that there are many possible ones that might evolve and that, once evolved, they are self-enforcing. Whether the conventions most likely to evolve turn out to be the ones that, once established, are the most efficient, is not certain. As we have seen, some writers have tended to assume that a benign process of social development can be expected over time. Others are less sure. Further discussion of this issue must await Chapter 12.

4. TEAM PRODUCTION AND THE CLASSICAL CAPITALIST FIRM

Just as the development of property rights in resources subject to congestion can be seen as an attempt to achieve efficiency gains, so the development of institutional structures such as firms can be viewed in the same light. In Chapter 2, the firm as a device to economise on transactions costs was considered in some detail. We did not emphasise at that stage, however, that the contractual relationships found within 'the firm' establish a structure of property rights in the use of resources. In a classic paper, Alchian and Demsetz (1972) elaborated on this theme and argued that the structure of property rights observed in the classical capitalist firm was a response to transactional problems, and in particular to the problem of 'team production'.

The essence of the firm for Alchian and Demsetz is that it permits people to work as a team. Team production occurs when an output is produced by the simultaneous cooperation of several team members. Production is not a sequence of identifiable stages by which a series of intermediate products are gradually transformed into the final output. Rather, the final output is the joint result of the combined efforts of all the inputs working at the same time. It follows that the individual contribution of each member of the team to the final output cannot be isolated and observed. All that can be observed in terms of output is the combined result of the entire team's efforts.

A further complication is that any one person's activity may affect the productivity of the other members of the team. In these circumstances there will exist an incentive for people to get together and agree to take account of external effects in their behaviour. In the last section, we showed how people could gain by forming a 'fisheries consortium' if their fishing activities imposed external disbenefits on each other. Here, the same argument can be used to show that a collective agreement to modify behaviour may be useful in the presence of external benefits. Person A agrees to work a little harder on the understanding that person B will do likewise. The benefits in terms of higher output of their joint decision to work harder will be sufficient to compensate them both, although any individual commitment to greater effort in the absence of the other party would not have conferred net private benefits on the person undertaking the extra work.

The situation is analogous to the public goods problem discussed in Chapter 2. No individual person may have an incentive to provide a public good, although a joint decision to produce one may confer benefits on everyone. It will be recalled that a joint decision was difficult to arrange because each person had an incentive to understate his or her true valuation of the public good in the hope that other people would pay to provide it. People, in other words, would tend 'to shirk' and fail voluntarily to pay their contributions. In the same way, a joint agreement to work harder in order to increase team output will be difficult to implement unless each person's behaviour can be monitored. Without monitoring, each person will 'shirk' and hope to 'free ride' on the effort of other people. Note that this problem would not arise if an identifiable output could be assigned costlessly to each person, for then a contract linking reward to performance would be possible. In the case of 'team production', however, there is a single output produced by the simultaneous cooperation of all members of the team, and the individual contribution of each member cannot be separately identified.

Problems of 'moral hazard' will therefore have to be overcome if the potential advantages of team production are to be achieved. The 'solution' suggested by Alchian and Demsetz is that the team requires a 'monitor' to observe the individual members and to check that their effort is satisfactory.

Clearly, this solution requires that effort is observable and this will obviously not always be the case. Where the team is concerned with the coordination of fairly simple 'manual' operations, the observation of the inputs to ensure that they perform the tasks they contract to perform may not be very costly. In other cases, observation of behaviour may be a very imperfect guide to the effective input of the team member involved. Further, as we saw in Chapter 2, a monitor may not have the information to judge whether the actions taken by a particular person are or are not in the interests of the team as a whole. The problem is equivalent to person A's difficulty of contracting with his or her architect.

Assuming for the time being that a monitor is capable of observing the effort of team members, the problem remains of providing the monitor with some incentive to bother. If the monitor is simply another member of the team whose job is to check that all other team members are fulfilling their contractual commitments, the monitor would have as much incentive to shirk as anyone else. It is for this reason, argue Alchian and Demsetz, that the monitor becomes a residual claimant. Each team member receives a contractual reward in the form of a wage, and the monitor receives whatever remains after these payments have been made. The more effectively the team operates, the bigger the residual will be, and hence the monitor will have a definite interest in promoting the efficiency of the team. All the benefits from improved coordination will accrue to the monitor instead of being shared amongst the team members.

If the status of residual claimant is to provide the monitor with an incentive rather than merely an interest, he or she must be able to discipline team members. It would be pointless monitoring the behaviour of team members if they could then ignore the monitor's criticisms. Thus, the monitor becomes the common party to all contracts with the power to alter these contractual arrangements and to add and subtract from the team (to hire and fire). Note the difference here from Coase's view of the firm. Coase emphasised the costs of arranging detailed multilateral contracts as an explanation of the firm. Alchian and Demsetz emphasise the necessity of the monitor having control of contractual arrangements in the context of team production if shirking is to be reduced.

From the perspective of property rights theory, therefore, the traditional single proprietorship can be seen as a form of enterprise which concentrates property rights in the hands of a single person. The 'private' nature of these property rights gives the possessor the maximum incentive to consider the consequences of his or her actions for the market value of the rights. The more effectively the single contractual agent or proprietor monitors and organises the team, the greater is the residual claim and the more valuable will be his or her property rights on the market. Exchangeable private rights to determine the use of team resources, monitor operations and claim the residual, represent a response to the moral hazard problem posed by shirking in the context of team production.

Although Alchian and Demsetz in their original (1972) paper saw team production as the primary source of the moral hazard problem, it is evident from the arguments reviewed in Chapter 2 that, even in the absence of team production as we have conceived it, asymmetric information can lead to problems of moral hazard. Whenever it is difficult to assess the quality of an intermediate product, for example, the supplier may have an incentive to shirk and there will be an advantage in appointing a specialist monitor. In this way, a purely market transaction becomes a transaction conducted within a firm. We will consider this process in more detail in a later chapter on the subject of vertical integration. For the present, it is merely necessary to note that the single proprietorship can be considered as a response to the 'shirking' problem and that this does not require us to assume conditions of team production rather, as Williamson (1975, pp. 49–50) emphasises, this may be an appropriate view wherever information difficulties lead to opportunistic behaviour.[11]

5. ALTERNATIVE STRUCTURES OF PROPERTY RIGHTS

In the last section we focused attention on the structure of property rights characteristic of the single proprietorship. Common observation tells us, however, that, numerous and economically important though such arrangements are (for example, Storey, 1982; Bolton, 1971), the modern economy has developed institutions of far greater complexity. An explanation of these more complex institutions must ultimately reflect the idea that concentrating property rights in a single holder is not necessarily the most efficient structure. Sometimes the sharing of rights between people or the apportioning of different private rights between people may be efficient. Thus the full package of property rights held by a proprietor may instead be shared between two or more people in a 'partnership', or alternatively the right to claim the residual may be shared between one group of people and the right to monitor the inputs may be held by another as in a 'joint stock' company.

At first sight such a statement appears to contradict flatly all that was argued in the previous section concerning the necessity of overcoming the moral hazard problem posed by shirking and the resulting concentration of property rights. It is evident, however, that the complete avoidance of all moral hazard problems is neither feasible nor efficient. If this were not so it would be a simple matter to circumvent moral hazard by refraining from all contractual relations with other people and forgoing the benefits of division of labour and exchange. The maximum concern for fire prevention and theft prevention can be achieved no doubt by abolishing insurance markets, but few people would advocate such a move or claim that economic efficiency would be enhanced. It may be worth while tolerating reduced incentives if the benefits of a more efficient distribution of risk taking are sufficiently great. Conversely (and this is something we shall discuss in more detail in Chapter 5 on principal and agent) if a perfectly efficient distribution of risk taking involves severe problems of moral hazard it may be worth while sacrificing risk-sharing benefits in the interests of providing incentives. In other words we might expect observed contractual relations to reflect the available trade-off between risk-sharing benefits and effort incentives, a trade-off which will be affected in any given case by the costs of monitoring.

5.1   The Single Proprietor

Consider once more the single proprietor. A team endeavour requires a monitor if it is to operate effectively. The problem of providing incentives to the monitor is then encountered. This can be viewed as a classic 'agency' problem. If members of the team cannot tell whether the monitor is performing the promised services, they have to devise some incentive structure based not on unobservable behaviour but on observable outcomes. The one thing that, by assumption, is observable by everyone is the final output of the entire team. Instead of a system in which this output is shared between all members of the team therefore, a form of organisation evolves in which team members receive a fixed wage (irrespective of overall team performance) and the monitor receives the residual. In Chapter 5 we shall investigate more carefully the circumstances in which we expect an agent to promise a principal a fixed sum in this way and thus to relieve the latter of all risk. However, it is not offensive to the intuition to learn that if the agent is risk neutral and the principal is risk averse the efficient contract between them will involve the agent bearing the entire risk.

It is very important to understand the nature of the 'thought experiment' conducted in the above paragraph. The single proprietor is clearly not an agent in a legal sense. As we saw in an earlier section, the proprietor must be the employer, not merely the agent of the team, if he or she is to have the authority to influence team behaviour. However, in piecing together a rationale of the proprietorship, it is defensible and indeed enlightening as a first approximation to regard the structure of incentives embodied in this form of organisation as a solution to an agency problem. In a similar spirit, we will later on consider how far and in what circumstances an employee might be considered an agent of the manager or the manager an agent of the shareholder.

Let us suppose now that the moral hazard problem is so severe that in the absence of a monitor-employer the team could not survive in any shape or form. On the other hand, assume that the returns to monitoring activities are substantial so that a proprietorship is viable. If the proprietor is risk neutral and the employees are risk averse, the traditional structure with the proprietor receiving the residual and the employees a given wage will be efficient. Notice how akin to Knight's is this conception with the 'confident and venturesome' providing insurance for the 'doubtful and timid'. Alchian and Demsetz, however, explicitly reject the Knightian risk-sharing approach to the firm and prefer to concentrate instead on the advantages of team production. Yet any final organisational form, with its structure of property rights held by the members of the organisation, will presumably reflect all the forces which we have so far discussed:

1. The potential advantages of further specialisation (division of labour) or team production.
2. The extent to which the exchange relationships involved in point 1 above give rise to problems of moral hazard.
3. The returns to monitoring.
4. The trade-off between risk-sharing benefits and incentives.

The single proprietorship is a 'solution' to the problem of organisational form under rather special circumstances:

1. The potential advantages of specialisation or of team operations are limited to groups sufficiently small to be efficiently monitored by a single person.
2. Moral hazard problems are severe, but . . .
3. The returns to monitoring are such that at least over a certain range the extra output of the monitored team is more than sufficient to compensate the monitor for his or her effort.
4. Either (a) the returns to monitoring effort are certain, or (b) monitoring effort favourably affects the probability distribution of the residual by increasing expected output net of monitoring and contractual costs, and the monitor is risk neutral.

By setting out the conditions most favourable to the establishment of a single proprietorship in this way we begin to perceive the circumstances in which alternative organisational forms might be observed.

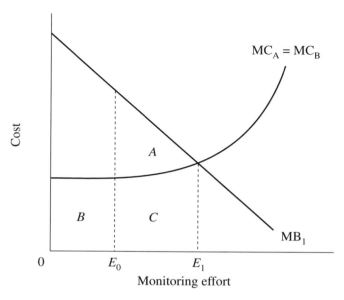

Figure 4.2   The team with a single monitor

5.2   The Partnership

5.2.1   Monitoring costs

We start by assuming that returns to monitoring effort are certain. In Figure 4.2, the curve labelled $MC_A = MC_B$ represents the marginal costs to monitors A and B of different levels of monitoring effort. It measures the extra monetary payment required to induce them to exert one more unit of effort. Curve MB_1 indicates the marginal returns to extra effort. We suppose that after a certain point (E_1) the marginal cost of monitoring effort rises and eventually becomes vertical as the limits of human endurance are reached. The returns to extra monitoring of the team decline throughout. A single proprietor (say person A) facing curve MB_1 would put in effort level E_1 where the extra returns from marginal effort are just equal to the compensation required. The final reward of the monitor will depend upon the level of effort required for the team to break even. Suppose for example, monitoring effort E_0 is required if contractual payments to other team members are to be met from the value of output. All further monitoring effort will produce a residual which can be claimed by the monitor. Since we have assumed that returns to monitoring effort are certain, we would expect this residual will just be sufficient to compensate the monitor for the costs he or she incurs (including wages forgone as a team member).[12] Thus, the additional benefit to monitoring effort above E_0 (the value of the residual, areas $A + C$) will be just equal to the costs incurred in being a monitor (areas $B + C$). Hence, under conditions of a certain return to monitoring effort, area $A =$ area B.

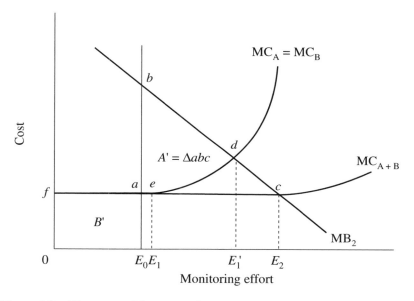

Figure 4.3   The team with two monitors

Now suppose that the returns to monitoring effort are given by MB_2 in Figure 4.3. Under these conditions a partnership of two people monitoring together will exert effort level $2E_1 = E_2$. The marginal cost of effort at this point is the same for each partner, but we might ask why a single proprietor should not monitor the team and exert effort level E_1'? The answer is that competition from the partnership form of organisation will undermine the single proprietorship. Once more, assume that effort level E_0 is required for the team to break even. It follows, as before, that where the returns to monitoring effort are certain, both partners will just be compensated for the costs of monitoring the team. Thus area $A'(abc) =$ area $B'($of $aE_0)$. But if area A' equals area B', a single proprietor exerting effort E_1' would not be able to earn enough to compensate for the work involved. Clearly, the residual of the single proprietor will be $bdE_1'E_0$ which will fall short of total monitoring costs (the total area under MC_A up to E_1') since area $aedb < B'$. The essential point is extremely obvious.

If a partnership can monitor at the same marginal cost as a proprietorship or lower up to E_1' and can further afford to monitor to a higher level of intensity (E_2), the partnership form of enterprise will take over from the proprietorship and the efficiency gains represented by area *edc* will be the prize.

The assumption that the monitoring costs faced by each individual are uninfluenced by the forms of organisation is, of course, crucial to this piece of analysis. A partnership involves an agreement between two or more people to perform certain monitoring services in exchange for a specified share in the residual. Even when the returns to monitoring effort are assumed to be certain, therefore, contractual difficulties are likely to be encountered. If the monitoring effort of each partner is perfectly and costlessly observable by all the others, partnership arrangements will be a predictable response to the increasing productivity of team effort and hence will permit larger team sizes than would otherwise be possible. Where, however, the behaviour of each monitor is costly to observe, Alchian and Demsetz's moral hazard problem reasserts itself. The effort of one monitor (partner) confers benefits on the others and the result will be an incentive to shirk. We therefore deduce that partnerships are more likely to evolve where the process of monitoring is itself routine and susceptible to a degree of accountability than where the effort of each partner is almost impossible to observe or deduce. Where the returns to monitoring are certain, two partners should each be able to police the activity of the other since each will know their own effort and can deduce the effort of the other from the final team output.[13] As the number of partners increases, however, the incentive to shirk will rise, since assigning individual responsibility for poor team performance may become impossible, and the effort of any individual partner will have a smaller and smaller effect on the value of his or her share.

Our discussion of the partnership, thus far, leads to the conclusion that sharing the right to the residual may hold out the possibility of potential efficiency gains by reducing the marginal cost of monitoring large teams. Against these potential gains we must set the extra problems of moral hazard which may arise when rights are shared in this way. If monitors begin to shirk, the efficiency gain (area *edc*) in Figure 4.3 may be dissipated and the single proprietorship will continue as the most effective organisational form. At any rate, partnerships are likely to be fairly small and, given the trust which must exist between partners if they are to avoid the losses involved in opportunistic behaviour, it is expected that the use of close family connections and those amenable to peer-group pressure will be frequent. A more extended discussion of profit sharing as an institutional form appears in Chapter 10.

5.2.2 Risk sharing

The assumption that returns to monitoring are certain is a convenient simplification when discussing the trade-off between monitoring costs and the hazards encountered when the residual is shared. As was noted earlier, however, the residual received by the monitor is unlikely to be deterministically related to monitoring effort. By accepting a residual reward, the monitor is exposed to risk. The fact that the residual may vary for reasons unrelated to monitoring effort has important implications.

1. In the first place the suppliers of 'contractual' resources to the team effort will want assurances that, if the residual turns out to be negative, they will still receive the promised payment for services rendered. This implies that a monitor will require some personal wealth to act as 'collateral security'. We discussed at some length in Chapter 3 the possibility that an entrepreneur with no wealth might persuade others to provide finance, but, accepting that this may occur, there are clear limits to the resource inputs which can be acquired in this way. Risk implies that the size of a single proprietorship will be limited by personal wealth and that partnerships will be necessary if firms are to grow beyond these limits.

    It is worth emphasising that the above argument relies on the premise that the risk faced by the monitor is 'uninsurable'. Even if the residual could be represented by a probability distribution conditional upon effort, and was thus 'risky' in Knight's strict sense, insurance markets would succumb to the moral hazard problem if the monitor's effort were not observable. If the monitor were certain of achieving a given residual through an insurance contract, the incentive to exert effort would be entirely lost, and with it the whole point of giving the monitor the residual claim.

2. Where the monitor is risk neutral, the concentration of risk is efficient as we have seen. Where, however, the monitor is risk averse along with other members of the team it makes no more sense to concentrate all the risk on such a person than to insist that someone confronting rapidly rising marginal costs of effort should do all the work. By taking a partner, the risks of the enterprise are shared, and where both partners are risk averse, total risk-bearing costs will decline. Thus, just as we showed in subsection 5.2.1 that partnerships might permit lower monitoring costs, they might also permit lower risk-bearing costs. It is then the sum total of these two possible efficiency gains which must be set against the moral hazard problems arising from sharing a property right in the residual.

The history of the partnership form of enterprise illustrates the operation of these conflicting forces. Each partner, in addition to sharing in the residual, has rights to use and manage the resources of the team. The decisions of each can therefore bind the others, and the partners are responsible for all debts, whether or not as individuals they were personally involved in incurring them. Indeed, the English law of partnership developed the rule that each partner was liable 'to his last shilling and acre'. In the face of this stringent legal background of unlimited liability, it is not surprising, as was noted earlier, that the property rights of each partner are not freely tradable. If a partner withdraws or dies, the partnership is broken and has to be reconstituted. Thus, it is very complicated and difficult for a partner to extricate his or her share of the resources from the business.

Because in the case of a partnership there is no single contractual agent but several agents capable of contracting on behalf of each other, the transactional difficulties involved in this type of enterprise are substantial. During the 1830s in the UK, when dissatisfaction with the law of partnership was growing, one of the major issues concerned the difficulty faced by a third party in suing a partnership or vice versa, and the difficulty involved in one partner suing another. Grievances between partners were particularly troublesome given the difficulties of acquiring information, and cases were reported 'which were upwards of thirty years in the Court of Chancery'.[14] The fact that the 1837 report on partnerships was particularly concerned 'with regard to the difficulties which exist in suing and being sued where partners are numerous' is indicative of the transactional problems encountered by large partnerships. These problems rapidly cancelled any risk-sharing or monitoring benefits available, and effectively placed a limit on the size to which a partnership could grow.[15]

5.3   The Joint-stock Company

Large-scale enterprises involving the cooperation of thousands and even hundreds of thousands of individuals would clearly not have evolved had the property rights structures characteristic of the single proprietorship and the partnership been the only possibilities available. The potential gains available from the monitoring of large teams – the 'visible hand' as Chandler (1977) has termed it – required a new structure of rights to emerge, a structure which did not expose the managers of large-scale enterprise to a degree of risk which they were not prepared to shoulder, and which permitted capital to be supplied by many people who would play no part in day-to-day business decisions. This particular combination of characteristics was impossible to achieve under the strict law of partnership. Capital could be borrowed, no doubt, at fixed interest from many people, but only at the cost of tolerating a very high 'gearing' or 'leverage' in the financial structure. Such high ratios of debt to proprietor's or partners' wealth would increase the risk of insolvency; a spectre made even more appalling by the provisions of unlimited liability which effectively meant personal ruin in the event of business failure on such a large scale. As we have seen, the alternative of growing through the addition of new partners was rendered unattractive because of the transactional difficulties involved and the enormous trust required in the integrity of other members of the partnership.

The joint-stock company developed as a response to these difficulties. For our purposes, there are three characteristics of great economic importance.

1. A joint-stock company has a legal existence quite distinct from the people who comprise the company at any given point in time. People may come and go but, unlike the partnership, the company continues in existence. Further, as a separate legal entity, a joint-stock company can sue and be sued. This greatly simplifies contractual relations with third parties and helps to overcome some of the difficulties alluded to in the previous section.

2. The shares of public companies are freely exchangeable. A market can therefore develop in these shared rights (the stock exchange) and it is a relatively costless exercise to buy or sell an interest in any particular company. Ekelund and Tollison (1980) argue that this ease of transferability was important in the early history of the development of the joint-stock form of enterprise. Lack of transferability would inhibit the most talented and qualified people gaining control of productive resources, which would instead remain in the same hands or in the same family for many years. Over the long run, the flexibility offered by joint-stock enterprises in reassigning property rights to more energetic people would give them an advantage over alternative institutional forms.[16]

3. The third important characteristic of joint-stock enterprises is that the liability of shareholders is limited.[17] With unlimited liability, people will naturally be chary of business associations involving people they do not know personally. With limited liability the prospect of subscribing relatively small amounts to an enterprise will be more tolerable, in the secure knowledge that the rest of a person's fortune is not inevitably at hazard in the same enterprise. Perhaps a more important implication of limited liability than the effect on the willingness of people to supply finance (as we have seen they could always lend at fixed interest to other types of enterprise) is the willingness of man-

agers to raise finance. For the directors of a joint-stock company are themselves liable only to the extent of the shares they hold in the company and indeed there is no legal requirement that they should hold any. With risk spread widely in this way, rising costs of risk-bearing do not constrain the size of operations as severely as they do in a partnership or proprietorship.

It is sometimes said that the coming of limited liability and the joint-stock enterprise lowered the 'cost' of finance. This is a somewhat misleading way of thinking, however. When people supply finance, whether by loan or by buying shares, they are aware of the institutional arrangements prevailing and are unlikely to ask for or expect a lower return when dealing with a limited liability company than with other forms of enterprise. They will 'pierce the veil of limited liability' and may adjust upwards their required return to allow for any perceived adverse effect on managerial incentives.[18] The advantage of limited liability is that even after these upward adjustments have been made, the possibilities opened up by large-scale operations may be more than adequate to compensate. Much depends here, however, on terminology. A single proprietor with unlimited liability would be expected to undertake fewer projects than would be the case after turning the enterprise into a limited company. Even if the available projects were identical in the two cases, the additional risks faced by a proprietor will induce him or her to apply a higher discount rate, and fewer of the projects will yield expected returns which exceed the 'cost of capital'. Thus, 'the cost of capital' to the enterprise, interpreted in this way, is very likely to be lower in the limited company, but this is just another way of saying that risk-bearing costs are lower to the decision-makers.

Although Ekelund and Tollison emphasise the transferability of shares as a crucial force in the origins of the corporation in the sixteenth and seventeenth centuries, by the mid-nineteenth century the risk-sharing characteristics of the corporate form with limited liability appear to be a more decisive consideration. Hannah (1983a, p. 23) reports that, in the UK, eighty per cent of joint-stock companies were private not public as late as 1914. Private companies are those which specifically restrict the right to transfer their shares while retaining the other characteristics of the joint-stock form, including limited liability. It is instructive to consider the possible reason for this popularity of the private company in the UK into the twentieth century.

In terms of property rights, the fundamental characteristic of the corporate form is that the 'right to claim the residual' is separated from the 'right to monitor the inputs'. This 'separation of ownership from control' has certain transactional advantages, as we have seen, and it permits the development of a class of specialist managers, but it also confronts the problem of managerial incentives which was so central to our earlier discussion of team production. The suspicion that joint-stock enterprises would result in inefficient if not corrupt management has a long history. Adam Smith, for example, wrote that 'negligence and profusion, therefore, must always prevail, more or less, in the management of the affairs of a joint stock company'.[19] Such 'negligence and profusion' will not prevent the emergence of the joint-stock form if potential efficiency gains exist which are sufficient to compensate, but it is clear that the problem of managerial incentives is central to this form of enterprise. The use of managers from a restricted family circle, each with a considerable shareholding and with limited ability to dispose of their holding, as in a private company, can obviously be viewed as a response to the incentives problem. Even successful public companies at the turn of the twentieth century in the UK used management from the families which founded and built the firms during the nineteenth century; firms such as J. and P. Coats, Imperial Tobacco, and Watney Combe Reid. As Hannah (1983, p. 24) remarks, 'while this solved a fundamental problem of the corporate economy – that of maintaining managerial efficiency while divorcing ownership from control – it did so more by avoiding the issue than by devising new techniques of incentive and control'. In the United States, on the other hand, the development of the corporate form occurred more rapidly than in the UK, and innovation in corporate structure was more advanced. Indeed Chandler (1977, 1990) attributes backwardness in the UK up to the 1940s to the influence of family management and the failure to develop sufficiently quickly a class of professional managers.[20] How far the former was the cause of, rather than a rational response to, the latter is, however, a moot point.

6. PROPERTY RIGHTS AND MANAGERIAL THEORIES OF THE FIRM

By the early 1960s, the large professionally managed corporation was such a familiar part of the institutional landscape that it began to influence the thinking of economists about the firm. A series of 'managerial' models of the firm appeared during these years. They all had the same essential structure. Surpluses could be generated within the large firm. These were interpreted as resulting from the exploitation of a degree of monopoly power rather than of entrepreneurial talents. The firms were under the 'control' of the managers but these managers faced constraints on their behaviour. Thus the managerial tradition in the theory of the firm was capable of generating an enormous variety of models depending upon the objectives assumed of the managers and the way the constraints on their behaviour were handled.

The most celebrated managerial models are those of Baumol (1959), Marris (1964) and Williamson (1964). They are distinguished primarily by the assumed objectives of the managers. Baumol suggested that managers maximise revenue from sales, Marris that they maximise growth, and Williamson that they maximise a utility function including 'staff' or 'emoluments'. In each case, the existence of monitoring from outside and limits to managerial discretion were recognised. Baumol included a minimum profit constraint in his model, and Marris similarly incorporated a valuation ratio constraint to reflect pressure from shareholders. The valuation ratio is the market value of outstanding equity shares divided by the book value of the assets of a firm. Too low a valuation ratio will involve a risk of takeover 'unacceptable' to the management (Marris, 1963, p. 205).

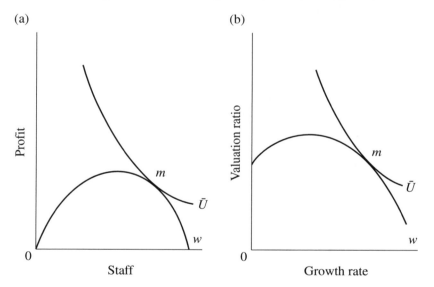

Figure 4.4   Two 'managerial' models of the firm: (a) Williamson's 'staff' model; (b) Marris's 'growth' model

In general, the conclusion of these models was that managerial firms would produce higher output, employ more staff, or grow faster than stockholder-controlled ones. In other words, the costs to the stockholders of asserting their influence gave a margin of discretion to managers which they were assumed to use in pursuit of whatever objectives the analyst felt could plausibly be imputed to them. Figure 4.4 provides a diagrammatic representation of Williamson's staff model and Marris's growth model. In the case of part (a), the recruitment of more staff is assumed first to add to profit but after a point to cause profits to decline. The manager's utility is maximised at point m to the right of the profit-maximising level of staff. For Marris, the figure (part (b)) is again basically the same, with the horizontal axis now measuring the rate of growth and the vertical axis the valuation ratio. The constraint will not emanate from the origin but is expected to have the same concave shape. If growth is pushed past a certain point the value of shares on the market will fall as diseconomies associated with staff training are encountered (Penrose effects[21]) and as a greater proportion of earnings are retained in the firm to finance expansion instead of being paid in dividends to shareholders.

Later in the 1960s and 1970s, the development of property rights theory and recognition of the importance of 'studying the property aspect of behaviour' led to the extension of managerial models into different institutional contexts. Niskanen (1968) introduced the property rights approach to the study of bureaucracy, Furubotn and Pejovich (1970, 1971 and 1974) analysed the labour-managed firm and the Soviet firm within a property rights framework. In Chapters 10 and 11, some of this literature is reviewed in more detail. At the most general level, however, the managerial tradition, while recognising that moral hazard problems were important in particular circumstances, did not directly address the question of the mechanisms which might be used to overcome them. Implicitly, the whole approach was concerned with the problem of the principal–agent relationship. Contractual and monitoring responses were not investigated in detail in the managerial tradition. Chapters 8 and 9 of this book are concerned with the modern analysis of the corporation from a principal–agent perspective.

7. PROPERTY RIGHTS AND TRANSACTIONS COST APPROACHES TO THE FIRM

7.1 'Ownership' of the Firm

The firm in transactions cost analysis is a 'nexus of contracts' as explored in Chapter 2. These 'contracts' represent promises between participants in the firm. The ability and incentive of the participants to fulfil their contractual obligations will depend upon their assignments of property rights. Within the firm, property rights in resources are assigned to the various participants. Different assignments of property rights can then be seen as characterising different types of organisation (for example, the proprietorship, the partnership and the joint-stock enterprise) as discussed in sections 5 and 6. If transactors successfully pursue efficiency gains, property rights will be assigned in such a way that the gains from trade net of all costs of transacting are maximised. This type of analysis of property rights is thus complementary with transactions cost theory.

An interesting aspect of the transactions cost theory as summarised above, however, is that the concept of 'ownership' is not well defined. Assets seem not to have 'owners'. Rights to use assets and to claim income flows are simply divided up between cooperating groups of people in ways which facilitate mutual gain. The quote from Demsetz (1967) at the end of section 1 simply mentions 'the owner of property rights', suggesting that the 'owner' is simply a 'possessor' or a 'holder' of rights. In so far as a more specific idea of 'ownership' has so far appeared in the analysis, it has implicitly been associated with residual claims. References, for example, to the 'division of ownership from control' suggest that the residual claimants (shareholders) are the 'owners' of the firm but no longer are really in a position to exercise control over the use of the assets.

Given the complexity of property rights assignments – the fact that many people may be contractually permitted to use an asset for specified purposes and may claim portions of the resulting profit – is it possible to identify an 'owner' from amongst all those who can be seen as holding property entitlements? The answer to this question has led to a view of the firm which differs from the pure 'nexus of contracts' approach. In modern property rights theory, the 'owner' of an asset possesses 'residual rights of control'. The word 'residual' here, does not refer to the right to receive profit (*the* residual). It is used as an adjective, not as a noun. It refers to those rights of control which have not explicitly been ceded to others by means of contract. They are residual rights in the sense that they are 'left over' and remain with the owner. The most important thing about these 'residual control rights' is that they cannot be exhaustively listed and written down. If they could be so listed, they would not be 'residual' rights. They would simply be one subset of specified property rights – no different in principle from anyone else's non-overlapping subset of specified rights which, when summed together, exhaust all possibilities. If every contingency can be contracted for, the 'owner' disappears. 'Ownership' is important because all contingencies cannot be contracted for. When contingencies occur for which there is no contractual provision, it is the 'owner' who has the right to determine how an asset should be used.

Ownership is thus intimately associated with contractual incompleteness. In subsection 2.1 we saw that 'private rights' in housing could be divided between landlord and tenant. What distinguishes these subsets of rights? In principle, the tenant's rights are delineated in a contract. The landlord retains all those rights which are not explicitly contracted away for a specified length of time. Thus, the landlord is the 'owner' of the housing even if he or she cannot live in it for the time being. It might be objected that even the tenant's rights cannot be exhaustively written down and that interpretation and 'gap filling' by the courts will be important. To this, the response is simply that, in their attempts to fill gaps in contracts, the courts are trying to discover what comes within the domain of the contract and what is outside it. Providing there is an acceptance that some matters are not, and were never intended to be, contractually determined (the tenant's subset of rights is in some sense 'bounded'), the 'owner' with his or her 'unbounded' set of residual rights has a distinct and important role.

Recognition of the distinct function of 'ownership' has resulted in the development of two rather different (though complementary) types of theoretical analysis. In the first, associated with the work of Hansmann (1996), the 'nexus of contracts' view of the firm is maintained and extended. In the second, associated with the work of Grossman and Hart (1986), attention is directed at the problem of determining the circumstances under which there will be advantages to different assets coming under the control of a single 'owner' (integration within the firm) and the circumstances when it will be better to leave the assets under the control of different owners. The 'firm' for Grossman and Hart is defined by the common ownership of a set of physical assets, not by the nature of the contracts which bind it to its suppliers. In subsections 7.2 and 7.3 we outline these two approaches to 'ownership'.

7.2 Hansmann and the Costs of Ownership

For Hansmann, the firm is the hub of a set of contracts with its 'patrons'. Patrons are simply any people who find it useful to deal with the firm. They might be workers, providers of capital, consumers of the firm's output, or suppliers of other inputs such as raw materials, professional services or intermediate goods. Hansmann is not concerned with the nature of these contracts. Whether they are durable and relational or arm's length and conducted on spot markets is not the focus of attention. The main feature of concern to Hansmann is that some patrons will be 'owners' and others will not. 'Owners' are those patrons who possess 'residual rights of control'. They are also likely to possess rights to the residual; that is, to the profit. It is usually efficient that control rights and profit rights are held together, although they might, in principle, be held by separate people.

What determines the allocation of ownership rights among the patrons? Efficiency requires that they are assigned to maximise the gains to trade after allowing for all costs of transacting and the costs of ownership. Transactions costs have been discussed in detail in Chapter 2 – the costs of search, bargaining and contractual opportunism. Ownership costs are new. In so far as ownership is associated with claims to profit, one cost is the bearing of Knight's 'uncertainty' – uninsurable risk. The owners have to accept fluctuations in the value of the firm's 'equity', which in the joint-stock enterprise is represented by the market value of shares but in other types of enterprise will not take such a clear-cut form. Another cost given a central role by Hansmann is the cost of exercising residual control rights. Again, it is possible to see this cost as bound up with entrepreneurship. At certain points, where contract is silent, owners determine the use of assets. If we envisage such owners as single individuals, they are entrepreneurs of the variety discussed by Casson – making judgemental decisions. If, as is common, ownership rights are shared between many patrons, they are the group which must determine overall priorities and appoint and monitor the managers and agents who will act on their behalf.

The cost of controlling managers and agents is of central importance in the theory of the firm and is discussed in detail in Chapters 8 and 9. We have already seen in section 5.3.2 that the incentive to monitor in a partnership is undermined as claims to the profit are shared more widely. Hansmann's distinctive contribution, however, is to emphasise the costs of collective decision-making as a category of 'ownership cost'. If ownership is shared between patrons, they must exercise their control rights by means of some 'collective choice mechanism'. The individual preferences of the owners have to be aggregated and somehow transformed into a decision which can be said to 'represent' them as a group. The ownership of enterprise is thus closely connected to the problems of 'public choice' – not at the level of the state, but at the microeconomic level of the firm. Each firm has a 'constitution' which will specify how the 'owners' are to exercise their collective rights. Collective choice processes are not costless, however. Each person faces the costs of becoming informed and deciding where their own interests lie. In this function, as in the monitoring function, each owner might try to free-ride on the work of others. They might calculate that their individual influence on the outcome was likely to be so slight that extensive information gathering and analysis would not be individually worthwhile (the problem of 'rational ignorance'). They might not even bother to register their preferences and take part in whatever voting processes are used (the problem of 'rational abstention'). Even where informed owners register their preferences, the choices of the group as a whole might be paradoxical and unrelated to these individual preferences (the problem of 'preference aggregation' or 'the paradox of voting').

The simplest and most famous demonstration of the 'paradox of voting' is as follows. Suppose there are three voters who must decide collectively which of three available mutually exclusive choices they should make. Voter 1 ranks the options in order of preference ABC. Voter 2 ranks them in the order BCA and voter 3 in the order CAB. If the three people take each pair of options in turn and vote according to a majority rule, they will find that, collectively, they prefer A to B, B to C, and C to A. This is the classic 'voting cycle'. Assuming the final choice to be made by elimination, the outcome would be arbitrary and depend entirely upon the order in which the options were put to the vote.[22] It is not true, of course, that a voting cycle will always be generated. If the rankings of the voters were 'sufficiently similar' the problem would not necessarily arise. Collective choice will obviously be a great deal easier in circumstances where there is a fair amount of agreement between the voters. This leads to the conclusion that, where ownership is shared between many patrons, collective decision-making costs will be lower if these patrons comprise a reasonably homogeneous group.

Hansmann argues, therefore, that minimising the costs of the firm's transactions will imply the allocation of ownership rights to two groups:

1. to those who would otherwise face relatively high costs of market transacting; and/or
2. to those for whom the costs of ownership are relatively low.

The first point above derives from the fact that ownership can be a substitute for contract. If post-contractual opportunism is a serious problem, for example, the patrons fearing 'hold-up' might become owners. They will now have control and will therefore avoid the dangers involved in 'contract renegotiation'. Similarly, if another group of patrons faces severe adverse selection or moral hazard problems, ownership might mitigate the difficulty, providing that monitoring costs and other costs of ownership are not too great. In Chapters 10 and 11, we will apply this type of reasoning to the worker-owned firm as well as to consumer cooperatives, mutual enterprises and non-profit firms.

The second point simply emphasises that it is no good avoiding the costs of contract if the costs of ownership are even greater. As will be seen later in Part 2, it is high costs of ownership that lie behind many of the problems of worker-owned firms and non-profits. Workers tend to have heterogeneous interests unless ownership is confined to a small group such as in a professional partnership. In contrast, a major advantage of the investor-owned joint-stock enterprise, notwithstanding the problem of managerial monitoring which will be discussed in Chapters 8 and 9, is the relatively homogeneous interests of the group of patrons who own it.

7.3   Grossman and Hart and the Property Rights Theory of the Firm

Hansmann's approach to the 'ownership' of the firm is rooted in transactions cost analysis. In contrast, the property rights approach to the firm as developed by Grossman, Hart and others does not focus on transactions costs. It starts by asking the question: why does it matter who holds residual rights of control in an asset? What is the nature of the social benefit derived from an 'efficient' rather than an 'inefficient' allocation of control rights? Hansmann and other transactions cost theorists would answer that the social benefit takes the form of lower costs of transacting. Property rights theorists argue that this answer is not precise enough. They show this by imagining a world in which bargaining costs are actually zero but in which long-term contracts are incomplete. Some promises are simply 'non-verifiable'. This does not necessarily mean that behaviour or results are unobservable. It means that it is impossible to construct a contract which a court or some third party can interpret accurately in order to tell whether a promise has or has not been met. One party might promise to publish a book of a particular word length. This would easily be verifiable. Once the nature and quality of the book become important, the terms of the contract become 'non-verifiable'. The manuscript exists, its contents are observable, but is it what the publisher was expecting and had contracted for?

The property rights theory of the firm is based upon the idea that the assignment of residual control rights matters in a world where some issues concerning 'quality' are non-contractible. Property rights matter not because they determine the costs of transacting. 'Quality' is non-contractible, irrespective of how property rights are assigned, thus effectively rendering a long-term enforceable contract 'infinitely costly'. Property rights matter because they influence the 'power' that transactors have in their (zero-cost) post-contractual bargaining when the provisions of a contract are non-verifiable. Why, though, should the distribution of such 'power' matter to society as a whole? Will not one person's loss be another person's gain when this post-contractual bargaining happens? The answer is that people are forward looking. They know that their contractual arrangements are incomplete and that they cannot rely on third parties to enforce all provisions. They know, therefore, that post-contractual bargaining will take place and that 'hold-up' will occur. This certain knowledge that they are vulnerable to hold-up will influence behaviour. In particular, it will influence each party's willingness to make '*ex ante*' transaction-specific investments.[23]

As we saw in Chapter 2, transaction-specific investments are those which raise the return to a particular contractual relationship but which have a lower payoff outside. A supplier, for example, may spend time and resources learning how best to satisfy the requirements of a buyer. These are investments in 'performance'. A buyer may expend resources preparing for the delivery of the supplier's goods or services. A restaurateur, for example, may invest in publicity and in planning menus prior to the delivery of interior designs. These are investments in 'reliance'. The essence of the property rights theory of the firm is that the combined incentive to invest in performance and reliance will depend upon how property rights in physical assets are assigned.

The contractors know that their *ex ante* investments are non-verifiable. They know that *after* they have made these investments they will bargain about the distribution of the *ex post* gains from trade. Each will want to be in as strong a position as possible when this bargaining takes place. A 'strong' position in this context is the ability to walk away from the agreement with as little penalty as possible. In other words, the person with the most valuable outside opportunities will be in a stronger position than a person who is very 'dependent' on the relationship and has few opportunities elsewhere. Each person, therefore, will have a 'threat point', a payoff below which he or she cannot be squeezed because they will be better off simply terminating their existing agreement and trading with someone else.

Holding residual control rights in physical assets is important because, in the event of a breakdown in an agreement, such rights might enable alternative possibilities to be pursued. Consider our example of the restaurant. Imagine that there is a single physical asset – the building itself. Who should be assigned the control rights in the building – the restaurateur (chef) or the interior designer? Each might be expected to make greater *ex ante* investments if they own the building than if they do not. If the designer owns the building and his or her contract with the restaurateur breaks down, he/she can at least open the restaurant using the services of some other chef hired in the market and so install his or her interior designs. Similarly, if the restaurateur owns the building s/he can, on the collapse of the original agreement, go ahead and open the restaurant even if the interior is not as attractive as s/he had hoped. The crucially important question is therefore the sensitivity of investments in performance and reliance to the possession of residual control rights. The greater the sensitivity of a contractor's *ex ante* investments to control of a physical asset, the more powerful the case for the assignment of ownership to that contractor.

Without the availability of the building, the restaurateur will find advertising and planning to no avail. Perhaps a different location could be found and a lease arranged, but geographical position and exterior appearance are important especially as these might have featured prominently in marketing efforts. Failure of the contract with the building-owning interior designer would therefore be expected to be serious for the restaurateur. He or she might consider the whole investment effectively wasted. Control of the building would be likely to provide a powerful incentive to greater investment on the part of the restaurateur because there is the reassurance that, even without the interior designs, the investment will be productive. Is the position of the interior designer similar?

For the sake of argument, suppose that the designer has other outlets for his or her services. Although the designs for the restaurant are, to some degree, specific to the original restaurateur's requirements, the ideas can be used, with some not too costly modifications, in restaurants, clubs or pubs elsewhere. This implies that, although his or her effort will be somewhat less if s/he does not own the building, the assignment of ownership to the restaurateur will not greatly diminish the designer's 'up front' commitment. Changing the ownership of the building from the designer to the restaurateur will radically increase the latter's *ex ante* investment and only marginally reduce that of the former. Thus, the restaurateur is the most efficient owner.

Another way of expressing this result is to note that, as this story has been set up, the restaurateur's human capital is complementary to the physical asset to a much greater extent than is the designer's human capital. Ownership of the physical asset does not help the designer much. S/he needs the chef's human capital before the project becomes really successful. In the absence of the chef's human capital (that is, if the contract breaks down and the agreement is terminated) the designer gains little from ownership of the building. The chef's human capital is thus 'essential' in the technical sense that, without it, the designer gains nothing from ownership of the physical asset. If the human capital of one of the parties to a contract is 'essential', it is this party that should own the asset.

Although the threat to trade elsewhere and renounce a non-verifiable agreement plays a central role in property rights theory, it would be wrong to conclude that agreements are likely to break down. On the contrary, because bargaining costs are assumed to be zero, *ex post* bargaining is always successful and the *ex ante* specific investments in human capital undertaken by the contracting parties are never (theoretically) wasted. It is this feature that points up the highly distinctive nature of modern property rights theory. A transactions-cost approach would tend to emphasise the use of governance mechanisms to make the breakdown of contract less likely. The property rights theorising sketched here does not investigate such issues because (perhaps somewhat paradoxically) contracts always survive *ex post* bargaining. In fact, it is usual to invoke the Nash solution to a cooperative two-person bargaining game which (assuming contractors have similar preferences) predicts that the gains from trade will be shared equally between the bargainers.[24] Thus, our contractors not only predict that they will have to engage in *ex post* bargaining; they also predict what will be the outcome of this *ex post* bargaining. They each receive their 'threat value' plus one half of the gains available from a successful agreement. Their *ex ante* investments are then based upon these accurate forecasts, and the optimum assignment of ownership rights maximises the resulting total investment in performance and reliance. An algebraic presentation of the theory based upon the work of Hart (1995a) is presented in the notes at the end of this chapter.

  Thus far the analysis has focused on the problem of deciding which of two contractors should hold the residual control rights to a single physical asset. If we now imagine that there are two assets involved, further conclusions can be drawn about how the rights in these will be distributed. The physical assets, to follow our example further, might be the building and kitchen equipment. It seems natural to expect the restaurateur will control both the building and the kitchen equipment. We would not anticipate the designer owning the kitchen equipment and the restaurateur the building. Why do we not think such an arrangement would be reasonable? The formal answer is once more based upon the willingness of the contractors to make *ex ante* transaction specific investments. The restaurateur will undoubtedly conclude that the control of the restaurant, in the event of termination of the agreement with the designer, will be of no avail unless he or she also has access to the kitchen equipment. Willingness to invest in reliance is not increased by control of just one of these assets; s/he requires control of both. Given that the designer will not increase his or her investment in performance if s/he controls the kitchen equipment, it is obvious that the chef should control both assets. They can be regarded as a single 'composite' asset, to be allocated on the principles discussed above. The two assets in this example are 'strictly complementary' and strictly complementary assets should be held together.

  In contrast, we might imagine that the second asset consists of some specialised computer equipment used in design work. No one would expect the restaurateur rather than the designer to own this equipment, but can we explain this commonsense response more formally? In the event of the termination of their agreement, the restaurateur gains nothing from his or her control of design equipment. On the other hand, the designer might find it impossible to undertake the modifications necessary to take advantage of alternative opportunities without it. His or her *ex ante* investment in performance will be adversely affected if s/he does not control the design equipment. The chef's *ex ante* investment in reliance is not affected either way. Thus, the designer should hold the residual control rights in the design equipment. The two assets are now 'independent' and independent assets should be held separately.

Coase's theory of the firm saw internalisation as a means of reducing the transactions costs of using markets. Given, however, that incentives are still a problem within the firm and that moral hazard and other difficulties do not go away just because a transaction is conducted within the firm rather than outside, the precise source of any advantage to integration is left unspecified in the Coasian analysis. Durable, long-term agreements supported by reputation or indeed supported by a degree of monitoring are possible across 'markets' as well as in 'firms'. As was seen in Chapter 2, Williamson (1985) emphasises the firm as a system of 'governance'. In a world of specific assets and opportunism, the firm establishes structures for the governance of long-term incomplete contracts. For Williamson, these governance arrangements lower the cost of long-term contracting. Property rights theory also starts from the acceptance of contractual incompleteness, asset specificity and opportunistic post-contractual bargaining. The essence of the firm, however, is not that it is an effective governor of contracts but that it owns a set of physical assets which induce optimal *ex ante* investment in performance and reliance between contractual agents.

8.   ENTREPRENEURSHIP AND PROPERTY RIGHTS

8.1   'Ownership' and the Entrepreneur

Property rights theory as developed by Grossman, Hart and others in recent years is in the neoclassical tradition of analysis. It assumes rational utility-maximising behaviour in the presence of a known set of constraints. It is not Walrasian in the sense described in Chapter 1, with its assumption of a full set of markets for all goods and services. In property rights theory, some things are not contractible. Property rights theory is thus in the tradition of 'contested exchange'.[25] There are elements to the theory, however, which have implications for the issues which we began to develop in Chapter 3. There we argued that although conceptions of the role of the entrepreneur varied – whether the entrepreneur was an uncertainty bearer (after Knight), an alert intermediator (after Kirzner), a maker of judgemental decisions (after Casson), or a technological innovator (after Schumpeter) – the one feature in common was that entrepreneurial services were themselves not contractible. You cannot promise to supply entrepreneurial services because (in the language of property rights theory) such a contract would be unverifiable.

Entrepreneurs achieve pure profits through trading in property rights. These property rights do not have to be residual control rights. Any exchangeable right is capable of generating pure profit to the entrepreneur. From Kirzner's point of view, for example, a person who buys a lease on some domestic property and then sells to a person who values it more highly gains an entrepreneurial rent. The fact that 'ownership' of the property has not changed hands does not matter; the entrepreneur might or might not be the 'owner' of the property. However, although ownership is not a necessary condition for the exercise of the entrepreneurial function, we might still wonder whether ownership is sometimes helpful to the entrepreneur.

The property rights theory reviewed in section 7.3 hinges on the idea that 'ownership' matters when contract fails. Consider now the position of an entrepreneur wishing to undertake a particular plan of action. If the entrepreneur owns the physical assets which are necessary to the successful completion of the plan, there is no need to ask anyone else's permission to go ahead. The danger with having to negotiate with an owner is that the owner will then be able to demand a share in the entrepreneurial profit. Does this matter? Somewhat paradoxically, an Austrian theorist such as Kirzner would find it difficult to prove that it did matter. This is because Kirzner asserts that entrepreneurial insight is 'costless'. Combine Kirzner's costless alertness with Hart's costless bargaining and the sharing of some of the profit with an asset owner will not reduce the amount of entrepreneurial alertness or the social gains achieved.[26] Relaxing these assumptions of costless alertness and bargaining, however, makes the assignment of ownership rights important for entrepreneurial activity.

If bargaining is not a costless and efficient process, ownership of residual control rights by the entrepreneur will economise on bargaining costs and greatly facilitate entrepreneurial activity. This is an important 'Austrian' theme which is taken up in Part 3 where the social importance of the assignment of control rights to 'competence' is discussed in more detail. Similarly, if entrepreneurial ideas require the commitment of time, energy and resources in *ex ante* non-contractible investments, the Grossman–Hart property rights approach can be applied directly to conclude that the necessary physical assets should be owned by the entrepreneur whose human capital is likely to be 'essential' to achieving the best results. This would be so, even if the cost of bargaining with the asset owner were zero *ex post*. The entrepreneur would predict that a portion of the value of his or her discoveries would be appropriated by the asset owner and would thus cut back on the level of *ex ante* investment.

A major reason for the lack of dynamism associated with socialist regimes during the twentieth century was the difficulty faced by most people in putting any entrepreneurial plan into action, because rights of control were not assigned privately. These control rights were also separated from profit rights. In fact, profit rights and control rights are highly complementary. If I possess profit rights but no control rights, I will expect to have to share some of my profit with the controller before I am permitted to go ahead with an entrepreneurial initiative. Conversely, if I have control rights but no profit rights, I will expect much of the value of my entrepreneurial activities to be harvested by the holder of profit rights. Holding one of these rights is not enough. I need to hold both together before the return to my non-contractible investments is protected. The close association between profit rights and control rights – the fact that these are usually seen as a 'package' constituting 'ownership' – thus follows naturally from property rights analysis.

8.2   The Property Rights Approach to the Finance of the Entrepreneur

In Chapter 3 we introduced Kirzner's (1979, p. 94) idea that entrepreneurial profits are captured by those 'who exercise pure entrepreneurship, for which ownership is never a condition'. By this statement, Kirzner is emphasising the point that entrepreneurial gains are a distinct category and nothing to do with the conventional return to capital. Precise textual analysis of Kirzner's treatise does not concern us here, but it will be useful to interpret his use of the word 'ownership' at this point as meaning simply 'wealth'. Kirzner is not making distinctions between ownership and other property rights but is simply making the challenging point that you do not have to be wealthy to be an entrepreneur. He notes that a capitalist might be induced to lend funds at interest and that this might permit pure profit to be earned without any net investment on the part of the entrepreneur.

Property rights theory provides a tool for investigating this claim in more detail. Obviously there is a level at which the possibility of successful entrepreneurship with zero wealth is a matter of pure tautology rather than positive economics. Maybe there really are capitalists somewhere who might be induced to lend to entrepreneurs with zero wealth. Possibly the entrepreneur has discovered an opportunity that can be pursued by means that are not inherently non-contractible. Nevertheless, the commonsense observation that it is less difficult to act entrepreneurially if you have some wealth than if you do not can be analysed more systematically and is capable of yielding insights concerning the use of debt in financial contracting.[27]

Consider, for example, an entrepreneur who has no wealth (for the sake of convenience we shall take this entrepreneur to be a woman). She discovers an opportunity that will result in a flow of revenue in the future. The revenue flow will be R_1 at the end of period 1 and R_2 at the end of period 2. There is no uncertainty in this model which gives it a rather Kirznerian flavour. In order to achieve this revenue flow, the entrepreneur must invest in an asset costing K_0 at the beginning of period 1. The asset depreciates over the two periods. At the end of period 2 it is worthless. Assume that the rate of interest is zero so that this project is worth undertaking if

$$K_0 < R_1 + R_2 \qquad (4.1)$$

If there are no contractual difficulties confronting capitalist and entrepreneur, we can imagine the entrepreneur borrowing K_0 from the capitalist. The entrepreneur could make repayments from the revenue stream spread over the life of the project. The pure profit might be split between capitalist and entrepreneur.

In fact, of course, the entrepreneur and the capitalist face a very hazardous contractual environment. These hazards can be introduced by assuming that R_1 and R_2 are unverifiable. It is always possible for the entrepreneur to claim that she had not, after all, received any revenues and that the project had failed. She could regretfully announce this news even as she is making secret deposits in a foreign bank account. This is an extreme situation. It is not denied that social mechanisms exist to help enforce debt repayments and overcome hazards. If the project is a local one, and if the lenders of funds are neighbours, the power of peer pressure and other monitoring devices might be used. These matters will be considered in Chapters 10 and 11. The assumption of the non-verifiability of revenue flows, however, helps to focus attention on the root of the contractual problem and is a useful basis for modelling potential responses.

The first thing to note is that, with non-contractible flows of revenue, the project is unlikely to get financed if the entrepreneur has no wealth. There is, however, one possible escape route. If the asset does not depreciate at all during period 1, the entrepreneur could make the following offer to the capitalist. 'If you will lend me a sum K_0, I will undertake to repay this sum at the end of period 1. If I fail to make this repayment, you may take over the ownership rights in the assets which will have a liquidation value at that time of K_0.' This has the features of a classic debt contract. Ownership of the asset resides with the entrepreneur for so long as an agreed schedule of repayments is adhered to. Failure to meet this schedule of payments will lead to ownership rights passing to the capitalist. Clearly, if K_0 is used to acquire assets these will normally depreciate so that the entrepreneur's offer mentioned above will not generally be possible. Perhaps the nearest approach in practice would be the finance of a farmer by a mortgage on the land. Nevertheless, the main point is that the entrepreneur can gain access to debt finance providing she has wealth enough to cover the depreciation on the asset during period 1. If the asset has a liquidation value of K_1 at the end of period 1, the entrepreneur will be able to borrow K_1 during that period of time. She will therefore require wealth of $K_0 - K_1$ to start her project. We will assume initially that the entrepreneur uses all her available wealth (W) to get her project off the ground ($W = K_0 - K_1$).

Starting the project is all very well, but will she be able to finish it? It is not obvious that it will be worth borrowing K_1 and investing her personal wealth $K_0 - K_1$, in the certain knowledge that liquidation will occur at the end of period 1. How will she make the payment K_1 at that point? One answer might be that the revenue R_1 is more than enough to pay off the debt; that is, $R_1 > K_1$. The project would certainly have to be extremely profitable for this to be the case but it is a logical possibility. Notice that, if the entrepreneur is not to liquidate the project herself, the revenue at the end of period 2 must also exceed K_1. Thus we assume $R_2 > K_1$ to ensure that liquidation of the project at the end of period 1 is not the efficient thing to do in any case. We conclude that there might exist some projects with such attractive cash flows that the entrepreneur will be able to use them to finance her borrowing. The capitalist will have security for his loan and the entrepreneur the means and the incentive to repay at the end of period 1. Note also that, for a given level of investment K_0, the smaller is the depreciation of the assets during period 1 the more the entrepreneur can borrow, but the greater the cash flows have to be at the end of periods 1 and 2 to enable and to warrant the repayment of debt. Entrepreneurs with very modest wealth will therefore only be able to finance projects using assets which depreciate slowly at first, which are not highly project-specific and which have cash flows which imply a very high level of profitability.

There is, however, another possibility. In the above paragraph, the implicit assumption was made that the full project either achieved completion at the end of period 2 or was liquidated at the end of period 1. Perhaps, however, the entrepreneur could herself partially liquidate the project at the end of period 1 using the proceeds of asset sales to repay her loan to the capitalist – thus retaining control rights in the assets that remain. Even with $R_1 < K_1$, therefore, the entrepreneur need not give up her plans for period 2, pocket R_1, go into liquidation and hand over all control rights to the capitalist. She could borrow K_1 and repay partly from period 1 revenues but partly from asset sales. This would only be possible, of course, if the project were flexible enough to be scaled back. In order to meet her obligations to the capitalist she would have to sell a proportion $(K_1 - R_1)/K_1$ of the assets at the end of period 1. This would leave her in possession of R_1/K_1 of the assets from which we assume she could derive a revenue of $(R_1/K_1)R_2$ at the end of period 2. The entrepreneur therefore invests $K_0 - K_1$ (still assumed to be equal to her personal wealth) at the beginning of period 1 and receives the return $(R_1/K_1)R_2$ at the end of period 2. This will be profitable providing that

$$K_0 - K_1 < (R_1/K_1)R_2.$$

Since $K_1 = R_1 + (1 - R_1/K_1)K_1$, this condition for the entrepreneur to invest can also be written

$$K_0 < R_1 + (1 - R_1/K_1)K_1 + (R_1/K_1)R_2. \qquad (4.1')$$

The last two terms on the right hand side of 4.1' constitute a weighted average of K_1 and R_2. Since $K_1 < R_2$ we deduce that

$$K_0 < R_1 + (1 - R_1/K_1)K_1 + (R_1/K_1)R_2 < R_1 + R_2.$$

In other words, the entrepreneur will not undertake all projects for which the revenues exceed K_0. She will undertake only those projects for which the cash flows (allowing for partial liquidation at the end of period 1) exceed K_0. Clearly if $R_1 = K_1$, the entrepreneur will be able to undertake the project with no inefficient early liquidation, just as discussed in an earlier paragraph.

Up to this point, the entrepreneur's personal wealth has served entirely to finance the depreciation of the asset during period 1. If she does not have access to this level of wealth, she cannot get the project through the first period. This is because, by assumption, she cannot commit to pay the capitalist more than the liquidation value of the asset at the end of period 1.[28] If, however, her wealth is more than sufficient to cover asset depreciation during the first period she might use the remaining portion, in conjunction with revenue accruing at the end of period 1, to repay the capitalist and avoid some of the inefficient liquidation which might otherwise be necessary. This partial liquidation of assets occurs because she cannot commit to pay the capitalist any of the non-verifiable revenue accruing at the end of period 2.

An entrepreneur will be able to finance a project without partial liquidation of assets along the way providing her wealth (W) exceeds asset depreciation in the first period ($K_0 - K_1$) plus any shortfall in period 1's revenue below the liquidation value of the assets ($K_1 - R_1$). Thus:

$$W \geq (K_0 - K_1) + (K_1 - R_1) \text{ or } W \geq K_0 - R_1$$

ensures that the entrepreneur's plan can be financed without liquidating assets. If wealth exceeds $K_0 - K_1$ but is less than $K_0 - R_1$ the proportion of the project liquidated at the end of period 1 will be $(K_0 - R_1 - W)/K_1$.

Private wealth is thus important to entrepreneurial initiative in a property rights analysis. The contract of debt whereby control rights pass to the capitalist in the event of default is indeed a method whereby entrepreneurs can pursue their ideas without having to finance it all themselves. But some private wealth assists entrepreneurship. The greater the depreciation of assets in period 1 (perhaps the more project specific the capital) the more private wealth is required to finance the project. Similarly, the more end-weighted the project returns (the smaller the revenues accruing at the end of period 1) the more private wealth will be required to avoid partial liqui-dation of assets.

The role of private wealth in economic development is of considerable theoretical and practical interest. In a recent book, for example, de Soto (2000) asks why it is that capitalism seems to be successful in some coun-tries but apparently fails in others. His answer is that even people living in conditions of great poverty have accumulated in aggregate vast resources which eclipse flows of aid and even far exceed the capitalisation of compa-nies quoted on the local stock exchanges. His main point is that these assets held by the poor constitute 'dead capital' because legal title to the assets is absent or hugely expensive to assert. He estimates untitled real estate hold-ings in Haiti to be worth $5.2 billion, in Peru $74 billion, in the Philippines $133 billion, in Egypt $240 billion and, in the third world as a whole, $9.3 trillion.[29] Without legal title, the potential energy contained within these assets cannot be realised. 'What creates capital in the West, in other words, is an implicit process buried in the intricacies of its formal property systems' (p. 39).

In the context of this chapter, we might interpret de Soto's argument along the following lines. The existence of legal title and the ability to trade ownership rights cheaply and freely is a determinant of the level of per-sonal wealth that people can bring to bear on their entrepreneurial projects. People in many countries live in poverty unable to exercise entrepreneurial talent because the assets which they have developed, which are part of their everyday existence and whose value is collectively enormous, cannot be used in the type of bargains that we have been discussing in section 8. Untitled assets might be valued by 'think-tanks' at $9.3 trillion throughout the world, but, for the mass of people, W is effectively zero.

9.   CONCLUSION

The assignment of control rights and rights to profit streams is of funda-mental importance to the theory of economic organisation. We expect the behaviour of economic agents to be profoundly influenced by the property rights which they hold. For some theorists, the allocation of property rights has a direct bearing on the level of transactions costs. For others, the assignment of residual control rights determines investments in contractual performance and reliance, even when enforceable long-term contracts are ruled out and outcomes depend upon *ex post* bargaining. The application of these ideas to organisational structure will be pursued further in Part 2. Before proceeding to a more extended discussion of enterprise structure and governance, however, it will be useful in Chapter 5 to outline some of the main results of principal–agent theory.

NOTES

1. Alchian (1977b, p.128) – a reprint of Alchian (1965).
2. The meaning of the words 'overuse' and 'appropriate' will be considered in a later section.
3. 'Public' property is often extremely 'private', as has frequently been noted. Custodians of assets which are collectively owned have little incentive to grant access to outsiders or even members of the owning consortium.
4. In a world of perfect certainty and no taxation, of course, the bond should sell for precisely the same sum as the right to interest plus the right to repayment of the principal. Where interest income and capital gains are taxed at different rates and the relative advantage of taking income in one form rather than another varies between people, this conclusion no longer holds.
5. Further discussion of 'the club' occurs in Chapter 11.
6. This statement may appear rather strong to some people. It should be interpreted more as a basic assumption upon which much of the future analysis will depend rather than a complete denial of a 'social conscience' in individual people. Clearly people do leave money by an unattended pile of newspapers if the vendor is momentarily not there, but it would be difficult to maintain that social institutions have developed on the assumption that they will always do so. The evolution of moral 'norms' mentioned in Chapter 1 might be sufficient to support many uncoerced acts of cooperation, but they are not powerful enough to overcome every prisoner's dilemma.
7. 'Leisure' might be valued by each person at four fish per day. Alternatively, we have to imagine that a market in fish exists, perhaps involving other groups on the island and possibly on nearby islands. The product of a day's labour at x or y production might then exchange for four fish on this market.
8. The problem is identical to that of site assembly in the context of urban land development. A developer finds him or herself playing a game of 'chicken' (see note 13) with the last remaining holder of a parcel of land that is required if the project is to go ahead. The existing owner of this parcel of land effectively has a 'veto' on the development, and can hold out for a price which will appropriate as much of the developer's profit as possible (see Davis and Whinston, 1961). In principle, of course, it would be foolish of an owner to so overplay his or her hand that the project did not go ahead and any potential efficiency gain should therefore be achieved. In practice, however, the possibility of being thwarted by a single person may act as a distinct disincentive to development.
9. Sugden (1986) refers to games in which players have distinguishing features as 'asymmetrical' games even if the payoffs are symmetrical. Asymmetry is required if conventions are to evolve. Sugden discusses conventions of property in his Chapter 4.
10. $\Delta gcb \equiv \Delta bfe$. Also $\Delta gah \equiv \Delta hdb$, thus area $ahbc$ + area hdb = area bfe.
11. The definition of the term 'team production' given by Alchian and Demsetz does not accord perfectly with the interpretation of this chapter. In their original presentation, Alchian and Demsetz (1972, p.779) cite the case of two people jointly lifting heavy cargo into trucks. They point out that 'it is impossible to determine each person's marginal productivity'. More formally, 'Team production of z involves at least two inputs, X_i and X_j, with $\partial^2 z/(\partial X_i \partial X_j) \neq 0$.'
    There seems to be a clear implication here that 'technological nonseparabilities' are

central to the concept of team production and lead to the difficulty of identifying the output attributable to each cooperating agent. If $\partial^2 z/(\partial X_i \partial X_j) = 0$ so that the marginal productivity of each input is independent of the activity of other inputs (the production function is separable) then 'this is not team production'. At the level of pure principle, however, it is difficult to see why a separable production function is sufficient to rule out team production in the sense of the impossibility of observing individual marginal products. Observability and separability are surely not synonymous, although Alchian and Demsetz appear to treat them as if they were.

Williamson (1975, p. 61) argues that 'most tasks appear to be separable in a buffer inventory sense'; that is, production can usually be seen as a succession of stages with the possibility of an inventory of the intermediate product at each stage. This does not, however, imply that the productivity of the resources used at each stage is easy to assess, and a monitor may still be necessary. The extreme case of a *single team output* produced simultaneously by all cooperating inputs presents particularly severe problems for monitoring. But 'regarded in transactional terms, technological nonseparability represents a case where information impactedness is particularly severe; but I emphasise that this is merely a matter of degree'.

12. We are here assuming 'free entry' into monitoring.

13. In the two-partner case, the situation can be envisaged as a game of 'chicken'. This has the same structure as the Hawk–Dove game analysed earlier in this chapter. Each partner has two strategies: 'monitor' and 'shirk'. If B monitors, it is better for A to shirk; whatever A does, he or she is better off if B monitors; but if B shirks it is better for A to monitor. This game will lead to 'bluffing'. Each partner will have an incentive to convince the other of his or her idleness in the hope that the other will be frightened into working. The 'chicken' game is representative of many situations which arise in the field of litigation (see Goetz, 1984). In the situation analysed in the text, however, it is necessary to remember that the game is repeated for as long as the partnership lasts. This 'discipline of continuous dealings' is likely to limit the advantage that will accrue to a partner from adopting a stance of exaggerated non-cooperation. As the number of partners increases, however, the nature of the 'game' changes. Eventually, if the others shirk it is better for A to shirk also. This turns the game into a 'prisoner's dilemma'. Shirking is a 'dominant strategy', since A is better off shirking whatever his or her partners do. Clearly, a partnership will find it difficult to operate under these conditions. We may surmise that 'unlimited liability' would delay their establishment. Again, we must bear in mind that the 'game' is repeated and we might expect partners to cooperate until the others cheat, if they have reasonable information about each other's behaviour.

14. See H.A. Shannon (1931, pp. 270–74). The quote, as reported by Shannon, is from Lord Ashburton's evidence to the Report on Partnership (1837).

15. There is in the UK a statutory limit to the number of partners. In general, there should be no more than twenty.

16. 'The Cartel owner-managers had wealth-maximising incentives to seek the development of a legal form of organisation under which they could more easily trade their property rights in these firms' (Ekelund and Tollison, 1980, p. 717). In Chapter 13, the 'Austrian' argument that effectiveness in the assignment of resources to 'competence' is one of the most important factors determining economic development is discussed in more detail.

17. General Limited Liability in the UK came with the Joint Stock Companies Act, 1856.

18. See R. Meiners *et al.* (1979) and C.M. Jensen and W.H. Meckling (1976).

19. *Wealth of Nations*, Vol. 2, p. 233.

20. Chandler (1990) provides a monumental survey of the two hundred largest manufacturing companies before the Second World War. He contrasts the early growth of managerial capitalism in the United States during the latter part of the nineteenth century with the continuation of 'personal capitalism' in the United Kingdom and the development of 'cooperative managerial capitalism' in Germany. Some discussion of different models of capitalism is offered in Chapter 9. In the last half-century, the UK model seems to have moved gradually but decisively in the US direction. Managerial capitalism

has become established in each country. Discussions of finance and governance tend now to contrast the 'market-orientated' system of the US and the UK with the more 'cooperative' German and Japanese systems.

21. See E.T. Penrose (1959), *The Theory of the Growth of the Firm.*

22. Public Choice Theory is now treated in most Public Finance textbooks, and concerns the application of traditional microeconomic methodology (rational self-interested utility-maximising people facing known constraints) to the study of behaviour in the political arena. See, for example, Brown and Jackson (1986), Chapter 4. Further discussion is delayed until Chapter 13. The theory concerned with voting systems and the problem of deriving a social welfare ordering from a set of individual orderings is called 'Social Choice Theory'. A fundamental contribution to social choice theory was Arrow (1951) in which he established his 'Impossibility Theorem'. No social decision rule exists capable of producing non-paradoxical outcomes which simultaneously satisfies certain 'desirable' properties. These properties (the 'conditions' of the theorem) include the unanimity or Pareto principle (if everyone prefers A to B then 'society' should prefer A to B); the universality principle (individuals are free to declare any ordering they like); the non-dictatorship principle (there should not be a single individual whose preference ordering always determines the social choice irrespective of the preferences of others); and the independence-of-irrelevant-alternatives principle (if 'society' ranks A above B when these two options are considered, it should not end up selecting B just because some other 'irrelevant' options such as C or D have been added for consideration). A statement of Arrow's theorem can be found in Varian (1999) and a proof in Quirk and Saposnik (1968), pp. 108–16.

23. See again, Chapter 2, section 2.4 for a discussion of specific investments and 'hold-up'.

24. See, for example, Rasmusen (1989), Chapter 10. This bargaining theory has a somewhat normative flavour. The 'solution' derives from a set of axioms. Whether actual bargaining satisfies the axioms is perhaps doubtful.

25. See again, Chapter 2, section 4.

26. To avoid confusion it should be pointed out that Kirzner does not actually assume costless bargaining. He recognises the costs of the entrepreneur bargaining with an asset owner but tends to play down the social significance of these costs on the grounds that they are unavoidable under any social system. The fact that they are unavoidable, however, does not imply that they are the same under any system. See again, Chapter 3, section 2.3.1.

27. A more formal development of the following model can be found in Hart (1995a) Chapter 5.

28. This is an extreme assumption which nevertheless simplifies matters and makes for clearer exposition. By threatening to liquidate the project, a capitalist might be able to force the entrepreneur to honour a promise to pay more than the liquidation value of the asset. In other words, we might expect him to achieve more than his 'threat value' at the end of period 1 especially if, by liquidating the project, he can deny the entrepreneur access to significant profits at the end of period 2.

29. De Soto (2000), pp. 27–8.

APPENDIX*   THE ASSIGNMENT OF RESIDUAL CONTROL RIGHTS

Let *B* be the maximum a buyer (say a male chef) is prepared to pay for an input (say the interior design for a restaurant). Let *S* be the minimum that a seller (a female designer) is prepared to accept for her services (assumed constant). The benefit to the buyer depends positively on his *ex ante* non-contractible investments in 'reliance' (*r*) – preparing for the restaurant's launch. The value of the designs to the buyer also depends upon *ex ante* non-contractible investments of the designer in performance (*p*). These investments in performance by the supplier are assumed to benefit the buyer only if the supplier is present to make use of them. They take the form of 'human capital' and cannot be transferred to an alternative supplier.

Ideally the contractors would maximise the gains to trade

$$G(r,p) = B(r,p) - S - r - p$$

with partial derivatives

$$\partial B/\partial r > 0; \ \partial^2 B/\partial r^2 < 0; \ \partial B/\partial p > 0 \text{ and } \partial^2 B/\partial p^2 < 0.$$

First order conditions require $\partial B/\partial r = 1$ and $\partial B/\partial p = 1$.

These investments in performance and reliance are unverifiable. Let the value to the buyer of recontracting with some other person after the investments *r* and *p* have been undertaken be $b(r) < B(r,p)$. Similarly, let the value of the designs (after modification) on the open market be $s(p)$.

The gains to trade after the 'up front' investments have been made will therefore be $(B - S) - (b + s)$. The term $(b + s)$ is the sum of the contractors' threat values. The excess of the mutual gain to a successful agreement $(B - S)$ above the combined threat values of the contractors is the rent which is subject to this *ex post* bargaining. Each contractor will receive one half of these gains. Thus the buyer will achieve (*ex post*):

$$\pi_B = b + 0.5(B - b - S - s) = 0.5(B + b) - 0.5(S + s) \qquad (4A.1)$$

The seller will achieve (*ex post*):

$$\pi_s = s + 0.5(B - b - S - s) = 0.5(s - S) + 0.5(B - b) \qquad (4A.2)$$

The buyer will invest (*ex ante*) in reliance such that:

$$\partial \pi_B/\partial r = 1$$

which from (4A.1) implies that

$$0.5\partial B/\partial r + 0.5\partial b/\partial r = 1 \qquad (4A.3)$$

The seller will invest *ex ante* in performance such that:

$$\partial \pi_s/\partial p = 1$$

which from (4A.2) implies that

$$0.5\partial s/\partial p + 0.5\partial B/\partial p = 1 \qquad (4A.4)$$

Underinvestment in both performance and reliance compared with a situation in which both are contractible follows from (4A.3) and (4A.4). It is assumed that $\partial b/\partial r < \partial B/\partial r$ (investments in reliance on the part of the chef will be less productive in the absence of the designer's human capital). Similarly $\partial s/\partial p < \partial B/\partial p$ (the designer's investment in performance is less productive when diverted to serve other contractors rather than the restaurateur).

A Single Asset

Now assume there is a single asset A_1 (the building). If possession of the asset does not reduce and can increase the productivity of *ex ante* investments in the event of contractual breakdown we have

$$(\partial b/\partial r) \leq (\partial b/\partial r)_{A1} \qquad (4A.5)$$

and

$$(\partial s/\partial p) \leq (\partial s/\partial p)_{A1} \qquad (4A.6)$$

where the subscript A1 refers to ownership of the asset.

Ownership of the asset is best assigned so as to achieve the highest *ex ante* investments on the part of the contractors. Clearly, if (as in the text) Equation 4A.6. were a strict equality, possession of the asset would not increase the designer's incentive to invest in performance. If Equation 4A.5, on the other hand, were a strict inequality, the chef will invest more if he owns the asset than if he does not. Thus the conditions

$$(\partial b/\partial r) < (\partial b/\partial r)_{A1} \qquad (4A.5')$$

and

$$(\partial s/\partial p) = (\partial s/\partial p)_{A1} \qquad (4A.6')$$

imply that the asset should be assigned to the chef. Equation (4A.6') means that the chef's human capital is 'essential' and that, without it, the designer gains nothing from possession of A_1.

Two Assets

Complementary assets

We now suppose that there exists another asset A_2 (the kitchen equipment). Let

$$(\partial b/\partial r) = (\partial b/\partial r)_{A1} = (\partial b/\partial r)_{A2} < (\partial b/\partial r)_{A1A2} \qquad (4A.5'')$$

and

$$(\partial s/\partial p) = (\partial s/\partial p)_{A2} = (\partial s/\partial p)_{A1} = (\partial s/\partial p)_{A1A2} \qquad (4A.6'')$$

Once more the objective is to so distribute ownership of the assets that the first best level of *ex ante* investment is approached as closely as possible. The assets are strictly complementary because the possession of a single asset does not raise the productivity of the chef's investment in reliance $(\partial b/\partial r) = (\partial b/\partial r)_{A1} = (\partial b/\partial r)_{A2}$. Possession of both assets is required before the chef is prepared to invest more as reflected in the strict inequality in expression 4A.5''. Expression 4A.6'' indicates that the chef's human capital is still 'essential' since $(\partial B/\partial p) > (\partial s/\partial p) = (\partial s/\partial p)_{A1A2}$ so that asset ownership is of no use to the designer in the absence of the chef. Even with a set of strict inequalities in expression 4A.6'', however (thus dispensing with the 'essential' nature of the chef's human capital), the strict complementarity of the assets for the chef is enough to establish that they should be held together. If the chef holds just one asset, his investments will not be reduced if control of this asset is transferred to the designer. On the other hand, transferring both assets back to the chef might be better than their both being owned by the designer (as assumed in the text). Either way, both assets should be held together – either both held by the designer or both held by the chef.

Independent assets

Suppose now that asset A_1 is the building and A_2 is the design equipment. Let

$$(\partial b/\partial r) = (\partial b/\partial r)_{A2} < (\partial b/\partial r)_{A1} = (\partial b/\partial r)_{A1A2} \qquad (4A.5''')$$

and

$$(\partial s/\partial p) = (\partial s/\partial p)_{A1} < (\partial s/\partial p)_{A2} = (\partial s/\partial p)_{A1A2} \qquad (4A.6''')$$

The assets are independent because $(\partial b/\partial r)_{A1} = (\partial b/\partial r)_{A1A2}$ for the buyer (chef). Similarly $(\partial s/\partial p)_{A2} = (\partial s/\partial p)_{A1A2}$ for the seller (designer). Given that he controls the building, the chef gets no additional benefit from control of the design equipment, and given that she controls the design equipment, the designer gets no additional benefit from control of the building. If the chef holds both assets, the transfer of the design equipment will raise the designer's *ex ante* investment without harming that of the chef. If the designer holds both assets, the transfer of the building will raise the chef's *ex ante* investments without harming those of the designer. Independent assets should be held separately.

NOTE

* This appendix follows the approach of Hart (1995a), Chapter 2.

5. Principal and agent

'Cremated . . . 10% of his ashes to be thrown in his agent's face.'
(Ted Ray)

1. INTRODUCTION

In chapters 1 to 4, attention has been focused on the difficulties inherent in formulating agreements which permit specialisation and exchange to occur, when information is not 'public'; that is, costlessly and equally available to everyone. Specialisation permits people to concentrate on those tasks in which they have a comparative advantage (Chapter 1), and it also has more dynamic effects. As Adam Smith[1] noted, specialisation results in the acquisition of enhanced levels of skill in particular operations as experience accumulates, it may permit the introduction of specialised machinery as various activities are broken down into basic components, and it may reduce the time which would otherwise be spent transferring attention from one job to the next.[2] If 'many hands make light work' however, they may also give rise to new problems. A person who 'saunters a little' between tasks will at least face the costs of that sauntering if he or she is responsible for all stages in the production process. Much of Chapter 4 was devoted to the analysis of situations in which specialisation results in Adam Smith's 'sauntering' turning into Alchian and Demsetz's 'shirking' as people attempt to transfer the costs of their wavering attention on to others. Clearly, Smith, in his example of pin making, was considering a case of division of labour which, we may infer, he did not expect would encounter substantial coordination and policing costs. In general, however, costs of coordination and policing are not negligible (Chapter 2) and the firm itself can be seen as a response to them. These costs underlie the saying that 'too many cooks spoil the broth', as well as the often heard remark 'if you want a job done properly you must do it yourself'.

The tension between the advantages of 'specialisation' and the costs of policing and monitoring (the advantages of 'integration') is a leitmotif which returns constantly in the theory of the firm. Already in Chapter 4 we have seen how different types of firm represent compromise solutions to the conflicting requirements of specialisation and incentives. In the classical proprietorship, the tasks of capitalist, monitor and risk bearer are 'integrated' and the problem of managerial incentives thereby mitigated. The partnership and, even more, the joint-stock company permit the 'disintegration' of these functions and hence the potential advantages which may accrue from exchange – a specialised management and widely spread risks – but the problem of policing and incentives is more pronounced.

In this chapter our objective is to consider the contractual problem faced by principal and agent in greater analytical detail. This will help to clarify the nature of the trade-off between risk-sharing benefits and effort incentives, and will provide a useful framework for rationalising various contractual arrangements which are observed in practice. At the outset, it is necessary to remember that the economist uses the word 'agent' in a much looser sense than does the lawyer. For the lawyer, an agent is 'a person invested with a legal power to alter the principal's legal relations with third parties'.[3] Thus two partners are one another's agents in a strict legal sense, since each can bind the other in contractual arrangements with third parties. The economist, however, is, for once, more in line with common usage in seeing the agent as a person who is employed to undertake some activity on behalf of someone else (the principal). This will cover cases of agency in the strict sense, but will also include other cases in which the same or similar incentive problems arise, although the legal term 'agent' would not be accurate.[4]

2. OBSERVABILITY AND THE SHARECROPPER

As we have seen in chapter 2, a principal–agent relation exists when one party (the agent) agrees to act on behalf of another party (the principal). (For the sake of convenience we will take the principal agent, and workers in this chapter to be male.) The problem then exists of devising a 'contract' which provides incentives for the agent to work in ways which benefit the principal. Let π be the final *outcome* of the agent's activities, and let e represent his level of *effort*. Sharecropping represents the most commonly used illustrative case for discussing incentive contracts, with the landlord as the 'principal' and the sharecropper as his 'agent' (in the loose rather than the legal sense of these terms). In this case, π might represent the volume of the crop finally harvested (say bushels of wheat), while e would represent the input of the sharecropper's time and skill. Now suppose that the final outcome is deterministically related to the sharecropper's effort

$$\pi = \pi(e) \tag{5.1}$$

Assuming that both sharecropper and landlord can observe the final outcome and that this outcome is conceptually simple enough to appear in a contract, it is clear that there is no reason for the landlord to monitor effort. The contract merely has to stipulate the outcome desired (say π), and the payment to be made when it is achieved. Under these circumstances, perfect knowledge of the outcome gives us perfect information about the effort expended, and the result is a contract which is not a 'sharecropping' arrangement at all but simply a paid worker contract. The worker receives a specified reward upon completing the job he was hired to do. There is no incentive problem.

A case more germane to the problem of incentives occurs when the outcome depends not only on the labourer's effort but also upon other chance factors. In the agricultural example, the harvest may depend upon climatic conditions as well as work effort. Thus we might write

$$\pi = \pi^*(e, \theta) \tag{5.2}$$

where θ represents the 'state of the world'. For example, θ might measure 'inches of rainfall' or 'hours of sunshine' or 'average temperature in July' and so forth. Any contract will now involve the sharing of risk in addition to the provision of incentives. Consider, once more, the paid worker contract which depends only on the achievement of a target outcome π. The labourer is unlikely to accept such an arrangement since it exposes him to considerable risk. The most careful husbandry could be powerless against adverse weather conditions and the labourer, if he is risk averse, will prefer that some account is taken either of his effort level, or of the state of the world prevailing. Clearly, however, the prospect of including e or θ in a contract depends upon whether or not they are 'observable'. Suppose, first of all, that θ can easily be verified by both parties. It follows, once more, that observation of the labourer's effort is unnecessary to provide incentives, and that a preferred distribution of risk can be achieved without confronting the shirking problem.

From (5.2) both landlord and labourer will be able to work out the result (π) of a given amount of effort (e) in different states of the world (θ). The labourer's reward (A) can therefore be made to depend upon both outcome and state of the world: $A = A(\pi, \theta)$. If the landlord receives an amount (P) which depends only on the state of the world $P(\theta)$, the labourer's return would be given by

$$A = \pi - P(\theta). \tag{5.3}$$

In other words, the labourer would pay to the landlord an amount $P(\theta)$ which depended on the weather, and would keep the rest of the harvest for himself. The results of additional effort always accrue to the labourer, so that no incentive problem arises, while the characteristics of $P(\theta)$ enable risks to be shared between landlord and labourer in any way desired. Such arrangements typify the 'sharecropping' contract. If, for example, $P(\theta)$ were a constant P', so that the labourer paid the same amount to the landlord in every state of the world, the labourer would effectively be bearing the entire risk and insuring the landlord against the vagaries of the weather. On the other hand, the landlord's share $P(\theta)$ could be so arranged that the remainder left for the labourer is always the same, providing the labourer puts in the standard effort e'. In this case, it would be the landlord who would bear the risk and the labourer who would receive a definite predetermined return providing the standard effort e' was forthcoming. If both landlord and labourer were risk averse, we would not expect either to bear the entire risk. Instead $P(\theta)$ would be defined so as to share risk efficiently between them. In the next section we will discuss in more detail what it means to share risk 'efficiently'.

Specifying a mutually agreeable contract becomes more complicated when we assume that the state of the world θ is not observable by the landlord (or principal). If effort e is unobservable also, then clearly any contract must of necessity depend upon the outcome π alone. It is this case which we will discuss in detail in section 4. Even at this stage, however, the essential character of the problem can be appreciated. The unobservability of the state variable θ and effort e means that it will, in general, be impossible to achieve an ideal distribution of risk between the parties without sacrificing effort incentives. Conversely, the 'best' contract achievable will usually involve the sacrifice of risk-sharing benefits in the interests of providing incentives.

Consider the case in which the landlord or principal is risk neutral and the labourer or agent is risk averse. Intuitively, we have already accepted that the risk-neutral partner should ideally bear the entire risk (a proposition which we will justify in more detail in the next section). Where the state of the world θ is observable, it has already been shown how this distribution of risk could be arranged whilst still eliciting the standard effort e' from the labourer. The labourer would receive the same reward whatever the state of the world, but only if he exerted the standard effort. Where the contract must depend on the outcome alone, however, assuring the labourer of a given reward is to leave him with no incentive to do anything. If the principal can never form the faintest conception of how hard the agent worked, and can never become acquainted with the difficulties he encountered, these factors cannot enter the contract. In such a case, however, a promise to pay a fixed determinate sum to the agent would be to make his remuneration completely independent of effort. The labourer would receive the same number of bushels of wheat from the landlord even if his only acquaintance with the fields to be cultivated occurred as he passed through them during his daily journeys to and from the village pub. Clearly, the provision of effort incentives requires that the labourer receives a bigger payment if the harvest is big than if the harvest is small, but because the harvest depends on the chance factors θ, this implies that the labourer must shoulder some risk, even though his landlord is risk neutral and would, in conditions of 'observability', provide him with complete insurance.

The above paragraph suggests that information about the labourer's effort would be valuable in enabling both parties to a contract to achieve preferred positions. If we continue to assume that θ is unobservable by the principal, some observation of the agent's effort e might clearly benefit both parties. By checking that the labourer sowed the correct type of seed, applied the appropriate fertiliser and so forth, it would be possible to move towards the ideal distribution of risk without diminishing effort incentives. In the extreme case of perfectly observable effort, the (risk-averse) labourer would receive a payment dependent entirely on effort and would thus face no risk, while the (risk-neutral) landlord would receive the residual harvest. Monitoring will not usually be so reliable, however, and a further interesting question is whether information about effort containing errors, which are subject to a known statistical distribution, could be incorporated in a contract to the advantage of both parties. The landlord might check at random whether the labourer is actually working in the field. An unlucky labourer could find that the spot check occurred during the only five minutes he was away, and a lucky one that it occurred during the only five minutes he was there. A series of such checks will provide information which, although not perfectly accurate, nevertheless contains potentially usable information about effort. Indeed it can be shown,[5] that, irrespective of the 'noise' associated with the information, there will always be an advantage to incorporating an informative signal into a contract if the agent is risk averse (assuming that the signal is costlessly received and that costs of writing the contract can be ignored). A more detailed illustration of what it means for a noisy signal to be 'informative' will be given in section 4.

In the case of a risk-neutral labourer or agent, information about effort or state of the world will be valueless. Even in conditions of complete non-observability of effort and state, all available risk-sharing benefits can be achieved without sacrificing incentives. As we noted above, a risk-neutral labourer will shoulder the entire risk and pay a fixed fee to the landlord. Because the fee is the same whatever the state of the world that occurs, it is clearly not necessary to observe the state. Neither will observation of the agent's effort confer any benefits, since the agent will personally face the consequences of any 'sauntering' and cannot unload the costs on to the landlord. In effect, the agent simply pays a fixed fee for the use of the resources owned by the landlord for a specified period of time. This will obviously avoid any dangers associated with shirking, while the risk-neutrality assumption ensures that this arrangement is compatible with the efficient distribution of risk. The next two sections illustrate some of the above results using a set of simple diagrams.

3.   RISK SHARING

Consider a case in which two people (person A and person P) wish to share the risk implied by a fluctuating harvest. Suppose that the harvest or outcome can take only two values π_1 and π_2 with $\pi_1 > \pi_2$. For the present, we ignore the influence of effort on the harvest and simply assume that π_1 and π_2 occur with probabilities p_1 and $P_2 = (1 - P_1)$ respectively. Each person, we assume, will be entitled to a given portion of the harvest depending on whether the harvest is good or bad. Thus,

$$\pi_{1A} + \pi_{1P} = \pi_1$$

and

$$\pi_{2A} + \pi_{2P} = \pi_2$$

where π_{1A} is person A's entitlement when the harvest is good, π_{2P} is person P's entitlement when the harvest is bad, and so forth. Presented with various different combinations of π_{1A} and π_{2A}, it is assumed, as in elementary consumer theory, that person A is capable of ranking them in a weak ordering. The outcome of this ranking process can then be illustrated on a two-dimensional diagram using indifference curves. If person A's preferences accord with certain axioms – the von Neumann–Morgenstern axioms[6] – it can be shown that a utility function for person A can be constructed $U_A(\pi_A)$ such that his preferences over risky prospects are consistent with the *expected utility* attached to the prospects. Indifference curves can then be thought of as lines of constant expected utility.[7]

The shape of A's indifference curves will depend upon his attitude to risk. In Figure 5.1, each point (π_{1A}, π_{2A}) represents a prospect. At point '*a*' for example, person A has a claim or entitlement to π'_{1A} if the harvest is good and π'_{2A} if the harvest is bad. Since, as drawn, $\pi'_{1A} = \pi'_{2A}$, this implies that, at such a point, person A would be *certain* of the outcome and would be bearing no risk. Given the probability of a good harvest P_1, it is clear that any portfolio of claims represented by a point in the shaded set to the north-east of '*a*' will be more preferred, and any portfolio represented by a point in the shaded set to the south-west of '*a*' will be less preferred, than the portfolio at '*a*'. Thus, just as in conventional consumer theory, indifference curves are expected to slope downwards from left to right. The curvature properties of the indifference curves are more complex, however.

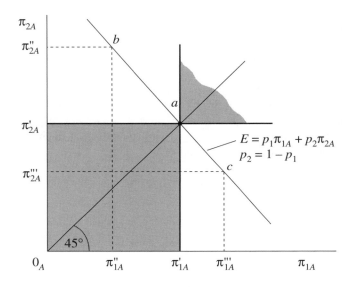

Figure 5.1   State-contingent claims: a line of constant expected outcome

Consider the straight line $p_1\pi_{1A} + p_2\pi_{2A} = E$ drawn through point '*a*'. By definition, all prospects along this line produce the same mathematical expectation (E) of the outcome as at point '*a*'. The slope of the line will be $-(p_1/p_2)$. Now consider a point such as *b* on this line. Will person A prefer '*b*' to '*a*' or vice versa? To answer this question, we note that a move from *a* to *b* implies a move from a riskless environment to a risky one. Person A would risk losing $(\pi'_{1A} - \pi''_{1A})$ in the event of the harvest being good, but would stand the chance of gaining $(\pi''_{2A} - \pi'_{2A})$ in the event of the harvest being bad. However, since the *expected* outcome for person A is constant all along the straight line, we know that the gamble involved in moving from '*a*' to '*b*' is a 'fair' gamble. A 'fair' gamble is one with an expected value of zero. Person A would expect, in a mathematical sense, neither to gain nor to lose because

$$p_2\,(\pi''_{2A}-\pi'_{2A})-p_1\,(\pi'_{1A}-\pi''_{1A})=0.$$

Whether person A would prefer point *a* or point *b* therefore reduces to the question of whether or not person A is prepared to take a 'fair' gamble. Any person who always rejects a 'fair' bet will prefer *a* to *b*. Such a person is 'risk averse'. A risk-averse person will move to lower and lower levels of satisfaction (expected utility) as he or she moves away from point *a* in either direction along the line of constant expected outcome. Thus, the indifference curves of a risk-averse person will have the conventional convex shape familiar from elementary consumer theory. Figure 5.2 illustrates the preference map of a typical risk-averse person. An important characteristic of this preference map is that the slope of the indifference curves along the 45° line from the origin (for example, at point *a*) will be equal to the slope of the constant expected outcome line $-(p_1/p_2)$. In other words, along the certainty line where $\pi_{1A}=\pi_{2A}$, each person will be prepared to exchange claims contingent upon a bad harvest for claims contingent on a good harvest in the ratio (p_1/p_2). This applies only to 'points such as *a*' and is therefore a proposition about limits. Although the person is risk averse, he will *approach* indifference between point *a* and a fair gamble, as the 'stakes' become vanishingly small. Some use will be made of this property of indifference curves in future sections.

Returning to Figure 5.1, a person who is indifferent between point *a* and

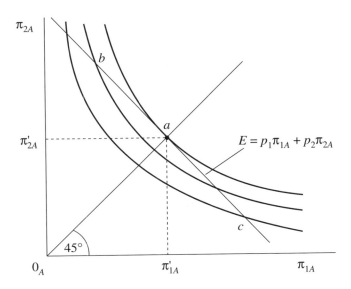

Figure 5.2   Risk-averse people have convex indifference curves

any 'fair' gamble represented by another point on the constant expected outcome line (such as point b or point c) is termed 'risk neutral'. Variability of the outcome is of no consequence for such a person. The only matter of interest is the expected value of the outcome, and all combinations of claims which yield the same mathematical expectation of the outcome are equally preferred. Thus, the indifference curves of a risk-neutral person will be straight lines with slope $-(p_1/p_2)$ corresponding to lines of constant expected outcome. Maximising expected utility for this person will be the same as maximising the expected outcome. For completeness, we should add that a person who *enjoys* taking fair bets will prefer point b to point a, and hence a 'risk-preferring' person will have concave indifference curves. The case is not illustrated and no future use will be made of it.

We are now in a position to discuss the risk-sharing problem. Figure 5.3 is a 'box diagram' with A's origin at the bottom left-hand corner and P's origin at the top right-hand corner. The horizontal dimension of the box represents the total harvest if yields are good (π_1) and the vertical dimension represents the total harvest if the yields are bad (π_2). Any point within the box represents a division of the total harvest between the two people in both good times and bad. Thus, point r, for example, illustrates a case in which person A has entitlements given by distance $O_A\pi'_{1A}$ if the harvest is good and $O_A\pi'_{2A}$ if the harvest is bad; while person P has entitlements given by distance $O_P\pi'_{1P}$ if the harvest is good and $O_P\pi'_{2P}$ if the harvest is bad. Person A's claims plus person P's claims sum to the total harvest.

The question now arises: does point r represent an 'efficient' allocation of claims between persons A and P? The answer will depend upon the preferences of the people concerned and therefore Figure 5.3 illustrates one particular case. As drawn, person A is risk averse and his convex indifference curves are drawn with respect to an origin at O_A; while person P is assumed to be risk neutral and his straight line indifference curves are drawn with respect to an origin at O_P. At point r, person A has utility index $\bar{U}_A$ and person P has utility index $\bar{U}_P$. It is clear, however, that by exchanging claims with one another, both could be made better off; there are gains from trade to be had. Any allocation of claims represented by a point in the shaded set in Figure 5.3 will benefit at least one of the parties without harming the other; that is, they represent 'Pareto improvements' on point r. 'Efficiency' is characterised by the absence of gains from trade, as was seen in Chapter 1 of this book. Points of tangency between A's indifference curves and P's indifference curves will be efficient points. An allocation represented by a point such as s, for example, is 'efficient'. Any move away from s must harm one or both of the parties, and therefore agreement to a move will be impossible to achieve.

As drawn in Figure 5.3, the locus of points of tangency between the

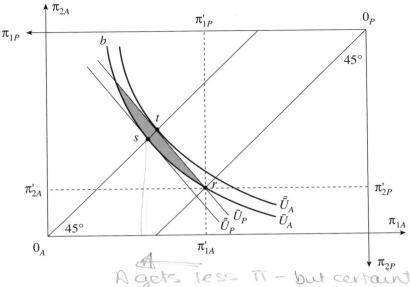

Figure 5.3   *Optimal risk sharing with a risk-neutral party. The risk-averse person takes no risk*

indifference curves of the two parties lies along the 45° line out of A's origin. It will be recalled that P's indifference curves have a slope of (p_1/p_2) along their entire length, whilst A's curves have a slope of (p_1/p_2) along A's certainty line. Thus, tangency must occur along A's 45° line. The line between s and t represents the set of efficient allocations which are Pareto improvements on point r. By moving from point r to point t, for example, person P will be supplying person A with fair insurance. Fair insurance will benefit risk-averse A, whose utility index increases to $\bar{\bar{U}}_A$. The risk taken by person P will be increased, but, for him, point t represents a fair gamble relative to point r and, being risk neutral, person P's utility index will be the same at t as at r. A move from r to s, on the other hand, will confer all the gains from trade on person P. Person P shoulders the entire risk still, but now on somewhat 'unfair' terms (in an actuarial sense) relative to point r. P's expected return and hence expected utility has increased, while A's expected return has decreased. The fall in the expected return to A does not result in a fall in expected utility because the greater certainty of the return at s compared with r is sufficient to compensate.

Figure 5.3 illustrates our earlier contention that efficient sharing of risk will involve a risk-neutral party providing complete insurance to the risk-averse party. Thus, in section 2, we saw that, where the state of the world θ was observable and the effort-incentive problem could therefore be overcome, a risk-neutral landlord (employer) would take the entire risk and a risk-averse labourer (worker) would receive the same amount irrespective of whether the harvest turned out to be good or bad. Conversely, a risk-neutral labourer would pay a fixed fee to a risk-averse landlord and keep the residual harvest. Where both persons are risk averse, efficient allocations of claims will be between the two 45° lines in Figure 5.3 and both parties will bear some of the risk.

4. EFFORT INCENTIVES

The principal–agent problem proper can now be considered by assuming that the probability of a good harvest is not given and unalterable, but can be influenced by the activity of the agent, person A. To keep matters as simple as it is possible to make them, let us assume that by exerting effort e, the agent is capable of changing the probability of a good harvest from p_1 to p_1^e where $p_1^e > p_1$. The agent has a simple choice between two levels of effort, zero or e. His effort, however, is assumed to be totally unobservable by the principal, P. The final outcome or harvest can be observed by both parties, but this is all. Let the agent be risk averse and the principal be risk neutral.

Consider now the effect of effort on the agent's indifference map. Because effort increases the probability of a good harvest to p_1^e, the slope of all the agent's indifference curves along A's certainty line will steepen to $-p_1^e/(1 - p_1^e)$. At any particular point on this certainty line, however, the utility index will be lower, because effort we assume is unpleasant and reduces A's level of utility. In Figure 5.4 the indifference curve of the agent through θ is drawn assuming no effort is exerted. The slope at θ is $-p_1/(1-p_1)$ and the utility index is $\bar{U}_A$. The curve through α is drawn on the assumption that effort e is exerted. Its slope at α is $(-p_1^e/(1 - p_1^e))$ and the utility index is also $\bar{U}_A$. To show that it applies to situations where effort is being exerted, the curve is labelled $\bar{U}_A^e$. Distance $\theta\alpha$ is a measure of the 'cost' to A of effort e.

These two curves $\bar{U}_A^e$ and $\bar{U}_A$ intersect at point r. A portfolio of claims represented by point r would just leave the agent indifferent between exerting effort e and not exerting any effort. At any point to the right of r and between $\bar{U}_A$ and $\bar{U}_A^e$, the agent would strictly prefer effort to no effort. At point s, for example, the agent will achieve a higher utility index by operating on his 'with effort' set of indifference curves than his 'without effort' set. By providing the agent with a portfolio of claims at s, we can induce the effort e. No monitoring is possible and none is required. The agent's own self-interest will be sufficient to produce the effort. We have loaded his claims sufficiently heavily in favour of the good harvest that he has an interest in increasing the probability of this favoured event occurring; an interest powerful enough at s to overcome the disutility associated with effort.

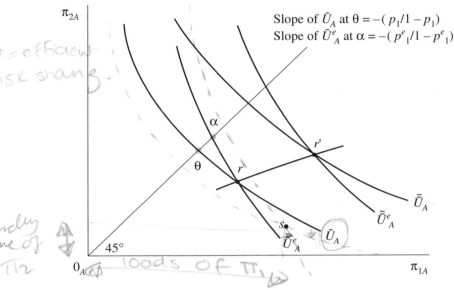

Figure 5.4   Contracts on rr′ *will just induce effort level* e

By an identical process of reasoning, we can deduce that at point r' in Figure 5.4, the agent is also indifferent between effort and no effort. At this point, the agent's utility index is $\bar{U}_A > \bar{U}_A$, whether or not effort is forthcoming. Joining up the points of intersection between 'with effort' and 'without effort' indifference curves applying to the same utility index, a locus such as rr' is traced out. Points to the right of rr' will induce effort e. Points to the left will not.

If it is possible to induce effort e from the agent, we still do not know whether both parties would *agree* to such a contract, or whether the principal would be as well off leaving the agent to relax in security at a point along his certainty line. It is this question which Figure 5.5 attempts to answer. At a point such as θ, risk would be efficiently shared between persons A and P as was shown in section 3. For effort to be forthcoming from the agent, however, a contract to the right of rr' must be agreed. Such a contract, by increasing the probability of a good harvest to p_1^e, will affect P's indifference curves and not merely person A's. P's indifference curves will now have a slope of $-p_1^e/(1-p_1^e)$ along their entire length. The new P indifference curve yielding the same utility index as at θ, but applying to a situation in which the agent is exerting effort, is labelled $\bar{U}_p^A$. Note that it cuts P's original indifference curve $\bar{U}_P$ at φ along P's certainty line. Clearly a given point on P's certainty line will yield the same utility index irrespective of the probability of a good harvest since, along that line, P is completely insulated from the effects of variations in the harvest.

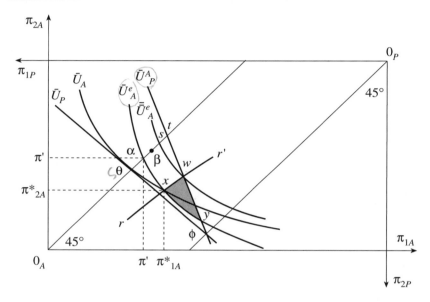

Figure 5.5   All contracts in set xwy *will induce effort level* e *and are Pareto preferred to a contract at* θ

Inspection of Figure 5.5 reveals that there exists a set of contracts (the shaded set *wxy*) which consists of Pareto improvements on the contract at θ. Points in the set *wxy* are between the curves $\bar{U}_A^e$ and $\bar{U}_p^A$, thus ensuring that the utility index of both principal and agent will be at least as great as at θ, and to the right of *rr'*, thus ensuring that it is the 'with effort' indifference curves that will be relevant and that effort *e* will be forthcoming from the agent. Of this set of Pareto improvements on θ, Pareto-efficient contracts will lie along the boundary between *x* and *w*. A move from point *w*, for example, to any other point in the shaded set will harm person A. A move from point *x* would harm person P. Conversely, from any point within the shaded set, it will be possible to find a point on the boundary which is preferred by both A and P.

It is important to notice that along the boundary *xw*, risk is not shared efficiently between principal and agent. The indifference curves of principal and agent intersect (for example, at point *w*) indicating that ideally there are risk-sharing benefits to be achieved by a move to A's certainty line between *s* and *t*. These benefits are unachievable, however, because of the observability problem. Figure 5.5 therefore illustrates clearly the distinction drawn in principal–agent theory between 'first-best' solutions (achievable only in an ideal world of perfect observability) which lie along A's certainty line and involve the efficient sharing of risk, and 'Pareto-efficient contracts' which lie along *xw* and are the best that can be achieved in the context of unobservable effort and state. Along *xw*, risk-sharing benefits are sacrificed in the interests of providing incentives. The sacrifice will be worthwhile, providing that the agent's effort is not too costly to him for any given effect on the probability of a good harvest, or, conversely, that for any given level of the disutility of effort the effect on the probability of a good harvest is sufficiently pronounced. It is possible to envisage a case in which the distance $\theta\alpha$ in Figure 5.5 is so large and $(p_1^e - p_1)$ is so small that the set of Pareto improvements on θ is empty.

Although a risk-averse agent may be made to bear some risk in the efficient contract, it is worth noting that we will never observe him bearing the entire risk. For a risk-averse agent to bear the entire risk we would have to imagine an efficient contract existing somewhere along P's certainty line. In terms of Figure 5.5, the locus *xw* would have to cross P's certainty line at some point. Risk aversion and the resulting convexity of A's indifference curves ensure, however, that the point *x* must always lie to the right of $\bar{U}_P$. But points to the right of $\bar{U}_P$ along P's certainty line will leave person P with a lower utility index than at θ. Thus, there can never be an efficient contract on P's certainty line which is Pareto preferred to θ when A is risk averse.

Where the agent is risk neutral, however, and the principal is risk averse it is no longer necessary to sacrifice risk-sharing benefits to achieve incentives. Incentives and risk sharing are compatible, as can be seen from Figure 5.6, and the agent will optimally bear the entire risk. The structure of the figure is the same as that of Figure 5.5. Once more contracts to the right of *rr'* provide an incentive to A to exert effort level *e*. The set of contracts Pareto preferred to θ is given by the shaded area. In this case, however, the boundary *xw* no longer represents the set of Pareto-efficient contracts. At *w*, for example, the agent could be made better off without harming the principal by a move to point ϕ, thereby achieving a more efficient distribution of risk. Points along P's certainty line share risk efficiently and induce effort *e* from the agent. 'Pareto efficient contracts' are 'first best' even under conditions of unobservability. Information on

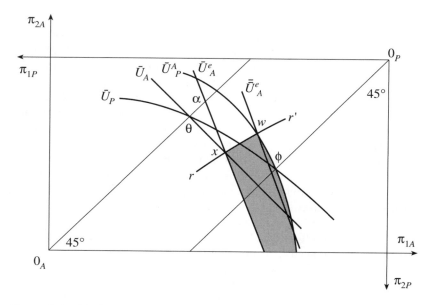

Figure 5.6   With a risk-neutral agent, a 'first-best' outcome is achievable at
           ϕ

the agent's effort or on the state of the world has no value to the principal.
At ϕ, the agent pays a fixed fee to the principal and is entitled to keep whatever remains of the harvest.

5.   INFORMATION

A risk-averse agent and a risk-neutral principal (Figure 5.5) will have to
sacrifice risk-sharing benefits if effort is to be induced under conditions of
'unobservability'. The ability to observe the agent's effort is therefore valuable because it enables risk-sharing benefits to be captured. Information
about the agent's effort may be subject to error, however, and it is not immediately obvious whether principal and agent would both agree to use this
kind of information in their contractual arrangements. As reported in
section 2, abstracting from the costs of writing and enforcing an increasingly complex contract, an informative signal, no matter how noisy, can be
used to increase the utility of both parties. In this section we illustrate this
proposition using the simple example of principal and agent discussed in
section 4.

    Suppose to begin with that no information about the agent's effort is used in the contract. Efficient contracts will then lie along the locus rr' in Figure 5.5. Consider the efficient contract at x. As argued at length earlier, the agent at x will just be indifferent between effort and no effort. By exerting effort the agent faces one gamble and by not exerting effort he faces another (different) gamble. He is just indifferent between these two gambles. Specifically, if the agent remains idle he faces the following gamble:

$$G = (p_1, \pi^*_{1A}; 1 - p_1, \pi^*_{2A})$$

Effort, on the other hand, produces a different gamble:

$$G^e = (p^e_1, \pi^{*e}_{1A}; 1 - p^e_1, \pi^{*e}_{2A})$$

where in this case π^{*e}_{1A} represents the outcome π^*_{1A} bushels having exerted effort level e. From our diagram we know that for person A, GIG^e, where I represents indifference.

Now let the principal (landlord) monitor the agent (labourer) through a series of spot checks mentioned in section 2. He may visit the field at random a given number of times. If the labourer is never there, the landlord will conclude (perhaps wrongly) that his effort level has been zero. Providing the labourer is there at least once, the landlord will conclude (again perhaps wrongly) that effort level e has been forthcoming. Satisfying this crude spot-check test will yield a reward of $+ \delta_e$ and not satisfying it will incur a penalty of $- \delta_o$. Might such an arrangement be agreeable to both principal and agent?

Ignore for the present the problem of how the labourer is to know whether the landlord is telling the truth when the latter claims to have seen neither hide nor hair of the former. This is an important issue which will be taken up later in Chapter 6 on hierarchies. Assuming that the landlord monitors in the way described, the labourer will be able to calculate the probability that he is observed hard at work when in fact he has been idle, as well as the probability that he is observed to be idle when in fact he has been hard at work and so forth. Let the first subscript represent the landlord's observation of effort and the second subscript the tenant's actual effort. Thus let

q_{oe} = probability that landlord observes zero effort when actual effort is e;
q_{ee} = probability that landlord observes effort e when actual effort is e;
q_{eo} = probability that landlord observes effort e when actual effort is zero;
q_{oo} = probability that landlord observes zero effort when actual effort is zero.

With these probabilities, we can construct a number of new gambles which we might call 'monitoring gambles'. Consider, for example, the following prospects:

$$m_{1A} = (q_{eo}, \pi^*_{1A} + \delta_e; q_{oo}, \pi^*_{1A} - \delta_o)$$

and

$$m_{2A} = (q_{eo}, \pi^*_{2A} + \delta_e; q_{oo}, \pi^*_{2A} - \delta_o)$$

These are the gambles the labourer would face if his effort level were zero. They depend upon the harvest. If the harvest turned out to be good and the labourer had agreed to be monitored, he would then face gamble m_{1A}. Similarly, if the harvest were bad, the labourer would then face gamble m_{2A}. By agreeing to be monitored, therefore, the *idle* labourer would change the original gamble G into the complex gamble G_m where

$$G_m = (p_1, m_{1A}; 1 - p_1; m_{2A}).$$

Suppose now that $q_{oo} > q_{eo}$; that is, the landlord is more likely to observe 'correctly' than 'incorrectly'. If the labourer is idle, it is more likely that he will be observed as such than that he will be observed exerting effort e. This is our minimal requirement for the landlord's monitoring to be 'informative'. If $q_{oo} = q_{eo}$, the spot checks would produce a signal that was all 'noise' and no information. If $q_{oo} < q_{eo}$, the signal would be positively misleading. Further, assume that $\delta_e < \delta_o$.

Clearly, if $q_{oo} > q_{eo}$, and $\delta_o > \delta_e$, gambles m_{1A} and m_{2A} are statistically 'unfair'. The labourer would prefer π^*_{1A} to the gamble m_{1A}, and π^*_{2A} to the gamble m_{2A}, assuming that he is risk averse. Thus, we deduce that the idle labourer will not want to be monitored and that he will prefer G to G_m.

For the industrious labourer, the situation is rather different, however. He will face the 'monitoring gambles':

$$m^e_{1A} = (q_{ee}, \pi^{*e}_{1A} + \delta_e; q_{oe}, \pi^{*e}_{1A} - \delta_o)$$

and

$$m^e_{2A} = (q_{ee}, \pi^{*e}_{2A} + \delta_e; q_{oe}, \pi^{*e}_{2A} - \delta_o).$$

If he consents to be monitored, the original gamble G^e will change to the more complex gamble

$$G_m^e = (p^e_1, m^e_{1A}; 1 - p^e_1, m^e_{2A}).$$

Again, suppose that the monitoring of the landlord is 'informative' so that $q_{ee} > q_{oe}$ and that the industrious labourer is more likely to be seen as industrious than idle. Further, assume that the reward δ_e and the penalty δ_o are set such that $\delta_e < \delta_o$ as above, but also $q_{ee}\delta_e = q_{oe}\delta_o$. Gambles m^e_{1A} and m^e_{2A} will then both be 'fair' gambles.

As was seen in section 3, a risk-averse labourer will reject a fair bet. However, we also saw in section 3 that as the 'stakes' were reduced a risk-averse person would approach indifference between taking and not taking a fair bet. People are risk neutral 'in the limit'. Thus, we might imagine δ_e and δ_o being reduced in size whilst always maintaining the ratio $\delta_e/\delta_o = q_{oe}/q_{ee}$. In the limit, the industrious labourer will be indifferent between G_m^e and G_e. Because the 'monitoring gambles' m_{1A} and m_{2A} are statistically unfavourable, the idle labourer, on the other hand, will always strictly prefer G to G_m and can never be brought to indifference no matter how tiny the stakes.

At point x, therefore, we have the following results as δ_e, δ_o tend to zero with $\delta_e/\delta_o = q_{oe}/q_{ee}$

(i) $G_m^e I G^e$,

(ii) $G P G_m$

(iii) $G I G^e$ (by original assumption).

Thus, $G_m^e P G_m$. *Without* the monitor, the labourer at x is just indifferent between effort and no effort. *With* the monitor and an 'informative signal', we can construct a situation in which the labourer strictly prefers effort to no effort at x and is no worse off in his own estimation than he was in the absence of the monitor ($G_m^e I G^e I G$).

Consider now how the principal is affected by these arrangements. We continue to assume that the signal is costlessly observed. Providing that the monitoring gambles m^e_{1A} and m^e_{2A} are 'fair', the risk-neutral principal will be prepared to offer them to the agent whatever the absolute sizes of δ_e and δ_o. Even if the principal were risk averse, we could apply the same argument used above for the agent to show that he would approach indifference as the stakes declined. Thus, in the limit, neither principal nor agent will be any worse off from a risk-bearing point of view as a result of the 'monitoring gambles'. Work incentives, however, have changed, as we have seen, and the benefits from this enhanced work incentive can be used to increase the utility index of either the principal or agent.

The argument is illustrated diagrammatically in Figure 5.7. The locus rr' represents, as before, points at which the agent is indifferent between effort and no effort, when no information about effort is used in the contract. Monitoring, as described in the earlier paragraphs of this section, using noisy but informative signals, results in effort being strictly preferred by the agent at x. It will therefore be possible to find another point such as y at which the agent is once more indifferent between effort and no effort even in the context of monitoring.[8] The locus of all such points might be represented by the curve mm'. At y, the utility of the industrious labourer will be the same as at x, but the utility of the landlord will be greater than at x. Monitoring, by providing a source of additional effort incentives, enables risk-sharing benefits to be achieved without reducing the amount of effort forthcoming. In effect, monitoring is being used as a substitute for a more inefficient distribution of risk as a means of inducing effort.

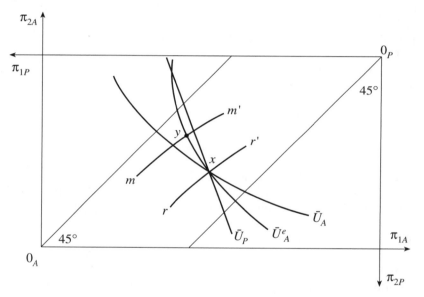

Figure 5.7   With an informative signal, costless monitoring can save on risk-bearing costs

6.   EXAMPLES OF INCENTIVE CONTRACTS

The principles which have been outlined in the first five sections of this chapter have applications which are more wide ranging than the share-cropping case which we have thus far been using for illustrative purposes. Harris and Raviv (1978) provide a number of interesting examples.

6.1 Health and Motor Insurance

Moral hazard in insurance markets is a classic problem, as was seen in Chapter 2. In terms of the content of Chapter 5, however, what kind of insurance contracts are likely to be observed and in what situations? Let θ, the state of the world, stand for 'degree of illness' instead of weather conditions. Let e stand for 'health effort' (for example, not smoking, taking safety precautions in dangerous tasks and so forth). Finally, let π represent 'amount of healthcare used'; that is, the outcome.

A contract which depends on the outcome alone (that is, simply on the amount of healthcare someone consumes) will, according to the earlier discussion, be inefficient relative to a contract which depends on both the outcome and the state if the latter is observable. Thus, if 'degree of illness' can be observed, we would expect contracts to specify payments conditional upon the degree of illness, just as payments to the labourer in the earlier example depended if possible on the weather and not merely the harvest. Assuming 'degree of illness' is unobservable, information about 'health effort' should be valuable. If health effort is observable, again we would expect this to be reflected in contracts; for example, lower premiums for non-smokers, higher premiums for those who refuse to wear seat belts in cars, and so on.

In the case of motor insurance, θ could represent 'difficulty of driving conditions', e 'safety effort', and π 'damage to the insured and to third parties'. Clearly, a contract which depends only on damage will be inferior to one based on both π and θ if the latter is observable. Thus, we might expect insurance contracts to vary by geographical area if 'driving conditions' differ. If θ is not observable, information on safety effort will be valuable. This too may be very difficult to observe, but if driving care is perfectly correlated with age, for example, we would expect to see insurance contracts varying with the age of the insured.

6.2 Law Enforcement

Here the principal is seen as the political representative of the general public, while the agent is the policeman whose task it is to detect and punish crime. Suppose the outcome π in this case is revenue generated by fines. Effort e will be 'policing effort' such as patrols, observations and whatever other activities compatible with the law raise the total of fines collected. θ represents the 'state of crime'. It reflects the type and seriousness of crimes committed and, to fit into the principal–agent framework of this chapter, it is assumed that this 'state of crime' is independent of policing effort e.

Applying the sharecropping results to this new situation, an efficient contract would be expected to involve both the outcome, 'fines generated', and the 'state of crime'. The government would receive a payment from the police which depended only on the state of crime and the police would keep the residual fines. Risk could then be distributed in accordance with the principles of section 3. If the government were risk neutral and the police were risk averse, the residual fines in each 'state of crime', given that the standard policing effort had been applied, would ideally be constant. On the other hand, if the police were risk neutral, no information about effort or state would be necessary for the efficient contract. The police would pay a flat fee to the government independent of the state of crime and would keep whatever revenue in excess of this fee they succeeded in generating. Effectively, the police would be paying a certain sum for the 'policing franchise' of an area and would be rewarded by their success in levying fines. Unsettling though such arrangements undoubtedly appear, there seems little doubt that they are well designed to produce a dedicated police force (dedicated, that is, to collecting fines). A more detailed discussion of 'franchising' as an incentive device and form of business organisation occurs in Chapter 7, while Chapter 15 contains a discussion of the role of franchising in government regulation.

Assuming that the state of crime is unobservable, information on effort is valuable if the police are risk averse. Even if the information is ' noisy', it may be used to improve incentives, as we have seen in section 5. A policeman's contract might, for example, be designed so that effectively he 'posted a bond' which would be returned to him providing that malfeasance remained undetected over a specified period. Corruption or negligence would result, if observed, in the loss of the value of the bond. In other words, loss of the bond would be equivalent to the term $-\delta_o$ which appears in the monitoring gambles of section 5.

6.3   Employment Contracts

Consider first a case in which the employee's output is observable, whilst effort and state are unobservable. This case is identical with the sharecropping example discussed in section 4. The employee must take some risk if effort is to be induced, and this will involve inefficient risk sharing unless the employee is risk neutral. In the latter case, we once more observe the 'franchising' solution, with the 'employee' paying a fee to the 'employer' for permission to use specified resources for a given period of time.

Where employees are risk averse, a contract involving both outcome and state will be preferred to a contract involving just the outcome. The state variable θ might represent 'market conditions', in which case, if these were 'observable', contracts might be expected to link remuneration to some economic indicators of these conditions. Employees could be envisaged to pay a fee to the employer conditional only upon the state. This fee would presumably be lower in times of depression and higher in times of prosperity if workers were risk averse. The employer effectively offers insurance to the workers and takes the brunt of economic fluctuations. In the extreme case of a perfectly observable state variable θ, and a known function $\pi = \pi$ (θ, e), the worker's remuneration would be constant in both prosperity and depression. Although practical examples of contracts *explicitly* written in this way are not easy to find, it has been argued that many contracts of employment are implicit.[9] The employer accepts an *implicit* unwritten obligation to insure the workforce against fluctuations in the way described. It is suggested that this *implicit* obligation helps to explain the 'stickiness' or 'inflexibility' of wage rates over the business cycle. Along with supplementary assumptions about the type of social security system operating, or the nature of information about θ (it may be asymmetrically distributed and available to employers but not employees), the implicit contracts literature has attempted to explain the existence of levels of employment greater than or less than would be observed under symmetric information. We shall discuss some of the ideas of the implicit contracts literature in a little more detail in Chapter 6.

Another application of the principal-agent results to employment contracts concerns the use of educational qualifications. Suppose that output depended not only on effort e but also on 'native ability' (Harris and Raviv, 1978). The state variable θ would now refer to the 'native ability' of the worker. Clearly this is not easy to observe, but if employers believed that 'native ability' was reflected in educational attainment we would expect remuneration to depend on qualifications and not just on the outcome. According to this view of things, education does not necessarily equip people with specific skills, but provides them through a series of tests, no matter how pointless in other respects, with evidence about their 'native ability'. Education is a 'screening procedure'[10] which tests for a particular type of attribute. This evidence can then be used by employers when contracting with employees.

Where the state variable is unobservable and workers are risk averse, information about effort is valuable. Perfect observability of the employees' effort by the employer would simply result, of course, in a contract dependent on effort alone. The risk-averse employee would again be assured of the outcome, and the risk-neutral employer would take the risk. This, it will be recalled, is the principal and agent result considered in Chapter 4, where the 'single proprietorship' was discussed. There, however, it was assumed that monitoring was costly and there was no presumption that effort was perfectly observable. It is worthwhile remembering, therefore, why it was that, even with costly monitoring, the contract did not involve the outcome and depended on effort alone. Conditions of team production implied that output could not be ascribed to particular members of the team, and the incentive effects of linking individual rewards to the collective outcome are minimal for large teams. In terms of our discussion of this chapter, therefore, contracts dependent upon the outcome will not induce effort under conditions of team production, because the probability of a preferred outcome is perceived to be only very weakly related to individual effort. A large individual effort (distance $\theta\alpha$ in Figure 5.4) will not greatly affect the slope of the indifference curves so that the set of contracts xyw in Figure 5.5 disappears and there are no Pareto improvements on θ. From an individual point of view, the 'efficiency of effort' is small, even though jointly it may be very high.

7. MONITORING THE EFFORT OF TEAM MEMBERS

In the light of the above, the individual employer under conditions of team production must therefore rely on monitoring to induce effort. We have already surmised in Chapter 4 that the proprietorship will be viable only if the returns to monitoring are 'sufficiently great'. Again, to reinterpret this observation in the light of the analysis of Chapter 5 may be useful. Assume, as above, that there are only two effort levels, zero and e, which employees can choose. Assume further that if *everyone* chooses effort e the probability of outcome π_1 will increase to p_1^e from p_1; otherwise the probability of π_1 will remain at p_1.[11] Figure 5.5 can be reinterpreted to apply to the employer P and the 'typical employee' A, with indifference curves $\bar{U}_A^e$ now reflecting the utility index of the employee when the whole team is exerting effort e. If the employer could be *absolutely certain* of every employee's effort simply by monitoring at a given level of intensity, the team would obviously be viable, providing the potential benefits, distance αt, multiplied by the number of employees, exceeded the costs to the employer of the critical level of monitoring required. Each employee would have a contract at α and would be monitored sufficiently intensely to determine with certainty that effort e was forthcoming. Providing the average monitoring cost per employee fell short of αt, both employer and employee are capable of becoming better off than remaining at θ.

A natural extension of this analysis is to consider what would happen if the employer could observe the employee's effort only with some accompanying error. In section 5 it was shown how even a very 'noisy' signal could, in principle, improve the positions of both principal and agent.

However, in that section we were considering a case in which there existed a contract x involving the outcome alone which was Pareto preferred to the original position at θ in Figure 5.5. The addition of any informative, though noisy, signal could be used to improve further on such a contract. In the case here, however, we have assumed that no contract based on the outcome alone is viable, and our point of departure is from θ. Clearly, from this inauspicious starting point the principal's information about the agent's effort will have to be reasonably good if it is going to make much difference. Some signals may simply not be 'informative enough' to be capable of providing opportunities for mutual benefit. On the other hand, intuition suggests that *perfect* information may not be necessary, and that a 'sufficiently informative' signal, which was nevertheless subject to error, might be useful.

That such a possibility exists can be seen by considering once more the monitoring gambles of section 5. There we saw that the labourer could, providing the monitor was more likely to observe 'correctly' than 'incorrectly', be presented with a reward structure which implied that an idle labourer would be taking an 'unfavourable' gamble while an industrious labourer would be taking a 'fair' one. Now, unlike the labourer at point x in section 5, this will not be sufficient, in itself, to ensure that the labourer at a point such as α will prefer effort to no effort. The idle labourer at α will not like having to take an unfavourable gamble if he is monitored, but he does not like exerting effort e either, and the 'effort price' of avoiding the unfavourable gamble may be too high for him. (By contrast it will be recalled that at point x in the example of section 5, the labourer was indifferent between effort and no effort, so that there was no 'effort price' of avoiding the unfavourable gamble.)

Although the prospect of *any* unfavourable gamble will not automatically induce effort at point α, it is clearly possible that the prospect of an *extremely unfavourable* gamble might do the trick. At point α, the employee or agent would face the 'monitoring gamble':

$$m^{\alpha}{}_A = (q_{eo}, \pi^1 + \delta_e; \; q_{oo}, \pi^1 - \delta_o)$$

assuming that effort zero were chosen. If the principal's information is very good, so that both q_{eo} (that is, the probability of being observed working when the agent is in fact idle) and q_{oe} (the probability of being observed shirking when the agent is really working) are very small, the gamble $m_A{}^{\alpha}$ will be extremely unfavourable. Thus, the more *reliable* the information of the principal, the more *adverse* is the monitoring gamble taken by the shirker. It is at least possible to envisage a point at which work becomes more attractive than the monitoring gamble associated with idleness.

We cannot appeal to the limit theorem used in section 5 to prove this proposition, since it is clear that the 'stakes' cannot be infinitesimally small if the jump in effort from zero to e is to be forthcoming. The employee, or agent, will have to face values of δ_e and δ_o sufficiently large to induce effort e whilst the value of π must be chosen so as to leave him as well off as he was at α. It is not, therefore, sufficient for the industrious labourer to be offered a 'fair' monitoring gamble at α, since risk-averse people will be made worse off by non-infinitesimal fair bets. The monitoring gamble will have to be favourable at α, or, if it is fair, the contract point must be to the right of α along A's certainty line. In the latter case, providing a point exists to the left of t (say point β) where the agent is as well off exerting effort and taking a fair monitoring gamble as he was at θ, and providing the monitoring gambles are so constructed that effort is preferred to idleness at β, the use of the principal's less than completely reliable information may permit Pareto improvements on θ. Distance $\alpha\beta$ in Figure 5.5 represents the cost to the risk-averse agent of taking the fair monitoring bet. Clearly, other things constant, the bigger are δ_o and δ_e the bigger will be the distance $\alpha\beta$, but the more reliable the principal's information the more adverse is the monitoring gamble of the shirker and the smaller can be the value of δ_o and δ_e compatible with making effort the preferred option on the part of the agent. Thus, more reliable information will be associated with a smaller distance $\alpha\beta$.

Figure 5.8 may help to illustrate the relationship between effort costs $\theta\alpha$, risk-bearing costs $\alpha\beta$, and the monitoring gambles. At point β, the agent receives π_1 with certainty. This gives no incentive to exert effort. Now offer the agent a monitoring gamble, $\pi_1 + \delta_e$, conditional upon being observed working, and $\pi_1 - \delta_0$, conditional upon being observed idle. Further, ensure that this monitoring gamble is 'fair' for the industrious worker so that $q_{ee}\delta_e = q_{0e}\delta_0$ with $q_{ee} > q_{0e}$. Call this monitoring gamble point m_β. Clearly, the agent will be worse off at m_β than at β. The cost of bearing the uncertainty of the fair monitoring gamble is $\alpha\beta$. For the idle labourer, however, fair gambles occur along the line through β slope $-q_{00}/q_{0e}$ and hence the gamble at m_β is clearly unfavourable. Draw the idle labourer's indifference curve through m_β and let it cut the certainty line at θ. If distance $\theta\alpha$ is the cost to the agent of exerting effort level e, the agent will be indifferent at m_β between effort and no effort; m_β will represent the least costly monitoring gamble which is 'fair' to the industrious labourer and is just able to induce effort e.

The effect of more reliable information can now be deduced from the figure. An increase in q_{00}/q_{eo} (that is, better information about the shirker) will steepen A's indifference curve through θ. It follows that, at m_β, A's utility index will be lower than before if he shirks, and he will strictly prefer effort to no effort. Thus, a less costly monitoring gamble between m_β and

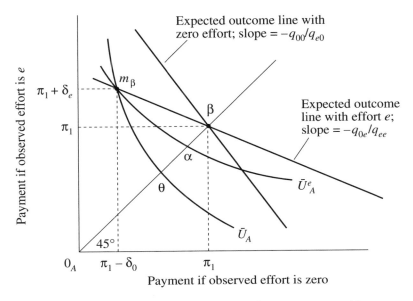

Figure 5.8   Effort costs, risk-bearing costs and monitoring gambles

β can be found. Even perfect information about the shirker will not remove risk-bearing costs entirely, however, if there is a chance of perceiving an industrious labourer as idle. Zero risk-bearing costs would require perfect information about the industrious worker; that is, $q_{oe}/q_{ee}=0$.

If we now introduce the complication that reliability of information may depend upon the monitoring costs incurred by the principal, we see that the distance βt in Figure 5.5 will exaggerate the gains to be had from monitoring by the amount of these costs. This suggests that there may be some efficient amount of monitoring effort on the part of the principal. At very *low* levels of monitoring effort, the information may be so unreliable that β lies to the right of point t and no Pareto improvement on θ is possible. At very *high* levels of monitoring effort, point β may lie close to point α. The risk-bearing costs associated with the monitoring gamble are low because information is very reliable, but in this case the monitoring costs may be so big that they more than absorb the potential benefits βt, and there is still no Pareto improvement on θ. If monitoring is to be viable, there must be a point at which the distance βt minus total monitoring costs is positive, and the efficient amount of monitoring effort will be that at which distance βt minus costs of monitoring is maximised. This gives us a new perspective on Figure 4.2 in Chapter 4. There we argued that monitoring effort would be applied to the point at which marginal benefits and costs were equal. Here we are looking behind the MB_1 schedule. The benefit of additional monitoring in this framework is more reliable information. A given amount of effort e can thus be induced from each employee using monitoring gambles involving lower risk-bearing costs.

8.   INCENTIVE CONTRACTS AND THE FIRM

In this chapter our primary task has been to consider in some detail the contractual problems which face two parties when outcomes are uncertain, and when information cannot be observed or is costly to observe and subject to error. It is appropriate at this point to discuss explicitly the significance for the theory of the firm of the issues covered in the first six sections. Sharecropping, franchising, insurance contracts, police incentives, and even some of the employment contracts discussed earlier, may at first appear rather specialised and peripheral concerns rather than of central importance. Yet, as has been emphasised from the very outset, the firm is a particular type of contractual environment, and its characteristics would be expected therefore to be moulded by the sorts of considerations which formed the basis of our discussion above. In Chapter 1, the firm was rationalised as a device for coping with uncertainty and the passage of time; in Chapter 2 it was seen as a response to 'opportunistic behaviour' resulting from 'information asymmetry', in Chapter 4 the firm evolved to permit policing and monitoring of cooperating inputs in conditions of 'team production'. All these ideas are closely interrelated. They all reduce ultimately to the firm as an institutional consequence of imperfect information, and they all have in common the idea of the firm as a *nexus of contracts* with a central agent.

   Within the nexus of contracts called the firm, however, there is scope for considerable variety. The nature of the contracts is not absolutely standard and will vary as conditions vary. As we saw in Chapter 2, Coase (1937) stressed the *direction* of resources and the employment or 'authority' relation as characterising the typical contract. No doubt there are particular cases in which this is descriptively not unrealistic, but labour is not the only type of input used by the firm and, as pointed out at the end of Chapter 2, positive monitoring costs associated with less than perfect 'observability' (Williamson would say 'information asymmetry') will usually mean that employer–employee relationships have attributes similar to those of principal and agent. The sections above have indicated, however, that there are many possible 'solutions' to the principal–agent problem, depending on assumptions about what is and what is not observable, the risk preferences of the parties, the costs of monitoring and so forth.

In some firms, people will be closely monitored, whereas in others they may have wider discretion. Some will be paid according to their own particular *output* (for example, by piece rates), others in 'team' environments (in the sense of Alchian and Demsetz) may be paid according to their *effort*. Payment according to effort will involve 'monitoring gambles' as described above, and the nature of these may also vary between firms. If monitoring of effort is very efficient and reliable, the risk involved in being monitored may be small, perhaps involving small bonuses or other prizes. Where monitoring is less reliable, the gamble may be substantial, as when promotion to a higher grade involves a considerable pay rise. Thus, the structure of a hierarchy can be seen as being closely related to the provision of incentives through what we have called 'monitoring gambles' and this is a topic which will be taken further in Chapter 6.

It is important to remember also that *within a single firm* different people will have different types of contract. A senior manager whose performance is difficult to monitor by shareholders may have a contract which links remuneration to the outcome through stock options or bonuses linked to profits. Similarly, a travelling salesman for the company may depend heavily on his particular sales record, the difficulty of monitoring implying that the salesman has to tolerate considerable risks. The professional designers of the product, on the other hand, are also difficult to monitor, but because individual 'output' may be impossible to measure, 'effort' may be monitored and incentives given by means of promotion through a hierarchy. At least a design team is likely to be concentrated in a particular geographical location, and members may thus be assessed by more senior leaders of the team. The people who actually fabricate the product could have quite different contracts again, depending on the technological context and its implications for monitoring. To take just one example, a simple production-line process involving little chance for 'shirking', with the line speed predetermined by the manager, could result in a standard payment per 'shift'. Providing the number of 'shifts' worked per week does not vary, the employee would be relieved of all risk. For a risk-averse employee, this would be preferred to a contract dependent upon output, since output would vary with technical problems such as 'breakdowns' or poor components. Where, however, as is almost invariably the case in practice, the chance of a breakdown or the quality of the final product depends to some degree on the alertness, concentration, or dexterity of the employee, incentives via the possibility of promotion may still be used even on production lines.

Where monitoring is very costly, and effort and state of the world are effectively 'unobservable', contracts will depend upon the outcome alone. A particular example of this arrangement is the franchise contract, and we have discussed some of its properties in an earlier section. In the present context, however, the franchise contract warrants closer inspection because it represents a relationship which leaves the franchisee with a large area of discretion as to how affairs should be conducted. It is thus far distant from the 'authority relation' discussed by Coase, or the exercise of 'conscious power' mentioned by Robertson. From the point of view of economic principle, however, a franchise chain would seem to have the major characteristic required to make it a single 'firm'. A franchise chain is a 'nexus of contracts' in which each franchisee has a contract with a single contractual agent or franchisor. Legally, these contractual arrangements exist between separate 'firms', yet economically the transactions might be regarded as taking place within a single firm. This is the essence of a contribution by Rubin (1978, p. 225) which emphasises the somewhat arbitrary distinction between interfirm and intrafirm transactions and argues that 'the economic concept of a "firm" does not have clear boundaries'.[12]

The theoretical developments reported in this chapter are in the neoclassical 'contracts' tradition. There are several features of firms which need to be borne in mind when interpreting the results.

a. Firms will usually be contracting with several agents (whether workers or suppliers) and if all agents face similar environmental conditions (even if these are not observable by the principal) *relative* performance may be used to assess an agent's effort. Providing the agents do not conspire against the principal, information on *relative* performance can be used in contracting. The firm, in other words, runs a tournament. Further analysis of the tournament as an incentive device is provided in Chapter 6.

b. In a market setting, repeat dealing may be important. Similarly, within a firm contracts continue over time and are not isolated events. This means that information on an agent's *past* performance can be used in future contracts. Shirking can result in a process of settling up *ex post*, and agents will have to consider the implications of a poor outcome for the terms of future agreements.

c. If agents differ from one another in their level of skill, the problem of choosing the agent and adapting the contract to his or her particular attributes becomes important. In the case of risk-neutral agents, the choice might be made by auctioning a contract to the highest bidder. Some of the contractual difficulties with this approach are considered in Chapters 11 and 15 in the context of the contracting-out of government services. If competitive bidding is not suitable, screening devices may, in some circumstances, be used to separate agents of differing quality. Chapter 6 explains the principles of screening mechanisms in more detail.

d. The agency contracts investigated in the earlier sections of this chapter were complete. Because there were only two possible outcomes, two possible effort levels, and a single period of time, the contract could be specified relatively simply. Contracts within the firm, as emphasised in earlier chapters, are incompletely specified as a result of bounded rationality. In this respect, principal–agent theory does not take into account one of the major elements of the nexus of contracts conception of the firm.

9. CONCLUSION

Our discussion of the many different contractual forms which may be found within the firm and the inevitable fuzziness accompanying the economic as distinct from the strictly legal view of the firm, leads to some important implications concerning the place of the entrepreneur and hence the relevance of Chapter 3 in the theoretical framework of principal and agent. The results stated in sections 1 and 2, especially as illustrated in the figures of sections 3, 4, and 5, may give a rather misleading impression of 'determinateness' about the whole problem. It must be remembered that the theoretical apparatus developed above is not intended to convey the conclusion that there is an 'answer' to the principal–agent problem for any given set of circumstances, and that, therefore, this 'answer' will be recognised by everyone and implemented. Such a conclusion would no more follow from the analysis of Chapter 5 than it would follow from the analysis of the gains from trade in Chapter 1. All that has been shown in this chapter is that *once the conditions are correctly recognised and interpreted* there may in principle be efficiency gains to be derived from an appropriately specified contract. Noticing the availability of these gains (Kirzner), developing entirely new institutional forms incorporating different incentive structures (Schumpeter), making 'judgemental decisions' about what form of contract would be best for a particular activity of the firm (Casson): these are entrepreneurial functions.

Impressions about risk preferences; judgements about what can be observed, how, and at what cost; guesses about the probability distribution of various states of the world: these are the forces which mould contractual relations, and in so doing throw up the institutional structures which are observed at any one time. There is nothing immutable about these structures. New or modified institutional forms embodying differing contractual relations compete in a continuing process of trial and error. A chain of restaurants run by professional managers suddenly faces competition from a chain of restaurants run by franchisees. The franchise chain switches to professional managers in large cities where the proximity of many outlets makes monitoring less costly. This, however, is anticipating some of the discussion of Chapter 7, where the nature of the competitive process is considered in more detail.

Chapter 5 completes the process of outlining the nature and historical development of the basic concepts used in much modern work on economic organisation. It is the task of Part 2 of this book to take the theoretical ideas discussed in Part 1 and to apply them to more specific areas of organisational structure.

NOTES

1. *Wealth of Nations*, Book 1, pp. 9–12. Edwin Cannan Edition.
2. Smith's views concerning the degree of application exhibited by people undertaking a variety of jobs seem strange to modern ways of thinking. 'A man commonly saunters a little in turning his hand from one sort of employment to another. When he first begins the new work he is seldom very keen and hearty . . . and for some time he rather trifles than applies to good purpose. The habit of sauntering and of indolent careless application . . . renders (the country workman) almost always slothful and lazy' (p.10). From this quote it appears that Smith associates division of labour with greater diligence presumably because, in his example of pin making, monitoring costs would be relatively low. Smith does not, however, seem to distinguish between the effects of division of labour *per se* and the consequences for the costs of monitoring. It is plausible that in eighteenth-century conditions a country workman asked to perform a whole range of tasks in different places would be difficult to monitor, but an independent craftsman (such as a blacksmith) would presumably have had a smaller incentive to be careless since he would personally bear the costs.
3. *Towle and Co.* v. *White* (1873).
4. For a recent and accessible review, see Sappington (1991).
5. See Holmstrom (1979).
6. A list of these axioms is provided in the notes at the end of this chapter.
7. For an exposition of the theory of choice under uncertainty, see Hey (1979).
8. The locus of such points must lie to the left of rr'. Only if GPG^e; that is, if idleness is preferred to effort in the absence of monitoring; can we construct an example in which $G_m IG_m^e$; that is, the agent is indifferent between effort and idleness in the presence of monitoring.
9. Early papers on implicit contracts were those of Baily (1974) and Azariadis (1975). Okun (1981) has termed the implicit contract 'the invisible handshake'.
10. See K. Arrow (1973), Higher education as a filter', *Journal of Public Economics*, July Vol. 2, No. 3, pp.193–216.
11. The predicament of the team here resembles that analysed by Hirshleifer (1983). The payoff to each member depends upon the 'weakest link'. Hirshleifer gives the example of an island inhabited by a group of people, where each person is responsible for a portion of the sea defences. The land is flat so that the probability of inundation is dependent upon the strength of the weakest portion of the sea defences and hence the effort of the person responsible for the poorest section. This contrasts with a 'best shot' collective outcome in which everything depends upon the best effort forthcoming. The example given here is of an incoming missile which will damage all members of the group but which can be destroyed by any single member with a well-aimed shot.
12. For further discussion of the franchise chain see Chapter 7, section 3.

APPENDIX THE VON NEUMANN–MORGENSTERN AXIOMS OF CHOICE UNDER UNCERTAINTY

The Von Neumann–Morgenstern axioms extend the standard axioms of consumer theory to take account of uncertainty. It is assumed that:

1. Each person can order the basic outcomes (π_i) which go to make up the gambles (G_i). A gamble is simply a probability distribution of outcomes. Thus

$$G_1 = (p_1\pi_1; 1 - p_1, \pi_2)$$

   is a simple gamble involving two possible outcomes π_1 and π_2 with probabilities p_1 and $1 - p_1$ respectively. This is the form which the 'monitoring gambles' are assumed to take in section 5.

2. Each person can order the gambles G_i transitively. Thus, when confronted with any two gambles, the chooser will state either that G_1RG_2, G_2RG_1, or both, where R means 'is at least as preferred as'. Further if G_1RG_2 and G_2RG_3 then by transitivity G_1RG_3.

3. The axiom of continuity states that for all outcomes π_i there exists a probability v_i such that $\pi_iI[v_i,\pi_b; 1 - v_i,\pi_w]$ where π_b and π_w are the 'best' and 'worst' outcomes respectively. If the best outcome were one hundred and the worst were zero, the axiom means that for any outcome between these figures (say eighty) the chooser can be made indifferent between the certainty of eighty and a gamble involving one hundred with probability v_i and zero with probability $1 - v_i$. Clearly, as v_i approaches unity, we will eventually prefer the gamble. As it approaches zero, we prefer the sure prospect. At some point in between, we can be made indifferent.

4. In any gamble G_i it is possible to substitute for a basic outcome, π_i, another gamble g_i where π_iIg_i. Thus, the components of a gamble can be other gambles, and this will make no difference to the consumer providing he or she is indifferent between the sure prospect and the gamble g_i which replaces it.

5. The complexity of a gamble is of no consequence. All gambles are eventually reducible to a probability distribution over outcomes, and this is always the choice perceived by the consumer. The consumer attaches the same utility number to all gambles representing the same probability distribution. Notice that this axiom puts considerable strain on the information-processing capacity of individuals. In the case of extremely complex gambles, it could fall foul of the 'bounded rationality' problem mentioned in Chapters 1 and 2.

6.   If G_1 and G_2 are two gambles involving the same two outcomes π_1 and
     π_2 with $\pi_1 P \pi_2$, the consumer will prefer the gamble involving the
     greater probability of π_1. A proof that a utility function may be derived
     from these axioms may be found in Hey (1979), pp. 30–33. The classic
     reference in this field is J. von Neumann and O. Morgenstern, *The
     Theory of Games and Economic Behaviour* (1944).

PART 2

The Structure of Economic Organisations

'Capital consists in a great part of knowledge and organisation.'
(Alfred Marshall)[1]

6. Hierarchies

*'I polished that handle so carefully,
That now I am the ruler of the Queen's Navy.'*
(W.S. Gilbert)[2]

1. INTRODUCTION

The firm in conventional neoclassical economics is a curiously underdeveloped concept; an 'empty box', to use Clapham's (1922) phrase. As will be seen in more detail in Chapter 7, the firm of the standard textbook is no more than a 'production function', a mathematical abstraction indicating the relationship between 'inputs' and 'outputs'. The firm's operations are therefore defined technologically, the outcome of physical laws defined by a given state of the arts and known to everyone. For some purposes, this approach to the firm may serve well enough, and it is not intended to discuss explicitly the purely methodological issues which permeate disputes in this area. An approach, however, that abstracts from the information problem abstracts from institutions (Chapter 1), and an institution-free analysis is simply not very useful if our purpose is to consider the structure of institutions such as firms. In this chapter, therefore, an attempt is made to outline some more recent developments (still mainly within the neoclassical tradition) which specifically concern information problems, incentives and internal structure.

If economists have become interested in the application of their techniques to institutional issues relatively recently, other social scientists have been concerned with them for many years. It is to the literature of 'organisation theory' and 'management science' that we must turn for early attempts to add substance to the firm and to analyse its internal structure.[3] Much of this work, however, was normative, and represented a desire to discover 'ideal' arrangements for manufacturing operations, rather than a desire simply to explain observed structures or analyse the causes of differences between structures. Taylor (1911), for example, was imbued with an almost messianic desire to rid the world of shirking ('underworking') through the establishment of 'work study' techniques and scientific management. His name has therefore become associated with systems of remorseless drudgery which pay scant attention to the individual characteristics of employees. Urwick (1943) was likewise concerned 'to establish a general set of principles or laws for designing organisational structures' (Jackson, 1982, p. 21). Principles were sought for establishing the correct division of labour, instituting the appropriate 'span of control' (number of subordinates per supervisor), defining a clear command structure and so forth. The result was a somewhat impersonal, mechanistic approach to organisations, which was criticised for overlooking more human and social factors. These factors such as management style, establishing friendly personal relationships and mutual respect, peer group constraints and effective communication were emphasised in the celebrated 'Hawthorne Studies'[4] and led to the development of the 'human relations school'. The approach was still normative, however, either because good human relations were seen as ends in themselves, or because a satisfying work environment was regarded as automatically conducive to physical productivity.

This chapter draws on a rather different tradition. The aim is not to be prescriptive but simply to make sense of the varying institutional arrangements which are observed in practice. Our starting point is an appreciation of transactions costs (Chapter 2) and the problems of contract enforcement to which they give rise (Chapter 5). In the tradition pioneered by Coase, the firm is seen as a response to these problems, and we show how various theorists have attempted to explain basic hierarchical characteristics by reference to the theory of principal and agent. From the early work of Weber (1947) onwards, bureaucracies or hierarchies have been recognised as having certain standard features.

1. The organisation is made up of people assigned to the various layers in the hierarchy. These layers may be defined in terms of 'authority', so that those assigned to a higher rank supervise those in the subordinate layer. In this case, the number of layers in the organisation will depend upon the size of the base and the 'span of control' exercised by supervisors. Clearly, the bigger the 'span of control' the flatter is the pyramid and the fewer the layers in the organisation for any given size of base. Williamson (1967), for example, used the idea of a fixed 'span of control' combined with the concept of 'control loss' (only a certain fraction of a supervisor's intentions are effectively implemented at each stage) to discuss the profit-maximising number of layers in a hierarchical organisation.[5] Hierarchical layers do not necessarily, however, have to be defined by authority and supervision. The organisation may be purely a 'wage hierarchy', with positions in some layers paid more than positions in others. Of course the two types of hierarchy may go

together, as when supervisors are paid more than the people they supervise. It is not obvious, however, why this is usually so. Further, more senior posts do not always imply supervision. In British universities, senior lecturers do not monitor lecturers. They often do essentially the same job, even though the former are paid more than the latter.

2. The number of people in higher positions in a hierarchy is fewer than the number in the immediately subordinate position. This is a rather mechanical implication of a hierarchy based on authority with an assumed 'span of control' greater than one. But in a wage hierarchy, it is not immediately clear why there should be fewer people in higher-paid positions than in lower-paid ones. Why, for example, do we not tend to observe departments in universities in which every member of staff is a full professor?

3. Positions higher up a hierarchy are filled predominantly by promoting people from lower positions in the hierarchy. To use Williamson's (1975) terminology, the 'ports of entry' into the hierarchy are mainly at lower levels. Promotion is often associated with a fixed retirement date so that people cannot linger too long in the most senior posts.

4. Hierarchies are characterised by Weber's quality of 'impersonality'. People are treated alike once they have been assigned to a position in the hierarchy. Williamson sees this 'impersonality' in the lack of scope for individual bargaining and the necessity of accepting 'standard' terms and conditions of employment applicable to a particular hierarchical level (see section 9). When a hierarchy offers 'advancement' to a person, it is not tailored to that person's special circumstances but takes the form of a change from one standard contract to another.

These broad characteristics of hierarchies have attracted considerable attention from economists in recent years, and much of the later part of this chapter is concerned with them. As a preliminary exercise, however, we reformulate the analysis of incentive contracts to show how it relates to the choice of methods of payment adopted by the firm.[6]

2. PIECE-RATES AND TIME-RATES

2.1 Payment Schedules, Moral Hazard and Effort

Although employment contracts were discussed at various points in Chapter 5, it will be useful to reinterpret some of the principal–agent results in terms of more conventional concepts. Our analysis thus far has been conducted with the aid of a simple box diagram, with each point in the box representing a 'contract'. Implicitly, therefore, each point represents a primitive 'payment schedule' or 'incentive structure'. It determines what contractually accrues to the agent or employee in given circumstances. Suppose, as we did initially in section 4 of Chapter 5, that only the final outcome of the employees' effort is observable, then each point in the box diagram can be interpreted as implying a payment schedule made up of a time-rate and a piece-rate. Consider Figure 6.1 in which we reproduce a box diagram with the risk-neutral employer's indifference curve $\bar{U}_p^e$. Along $\bar{U}_p^e$ we identify four possible contractual positions labelled a, b, c and d respectively. The locus rr' which will just induce effort e from the risk-averse employee is drawn through point b. Point c lies on a diagonal drawn through the principal's origin and the agent's origin. Point a and point d are on the agent's certainty line and the principal's certainty line respectively.

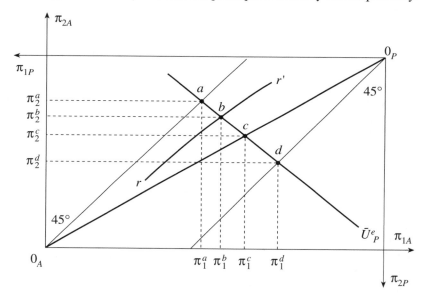

Figure 6.1   Alternative contractual arrangements

Each of the identified contracts can be illustrated in a different way in Figure 6.2. Along the horizontal axis in Figure 6.2 is measured the actual outcome and along the vertical axis the payment to the employee. Since there are only two possible outcomes in our simple formulation, each contract point in Figure 6.1 is represented by two points in Figure 6.2. Thus, contract a in Figure 6.1 is equivalent to the two points a' and a'' in Figure

6.2. A straight line drawn through these two points is horizontal, indicating that the payment to the employee is independent of the outcome. This can therefore be regarded as a pure time-rate system. The employee receives a *certain* payment $\pi^a_1 = \pi^a_2$. Interpreting the 'outcomes' measured by the dimensions of the box as referring to particular intervals of time (in Chapter 5 it might have been a year, since there we were discussing the size of the harvest, but here we could regard the outcomes as applying to weekly intervals), $\pi^a_1 = \pi^a_2$ would represent a weekly wage.

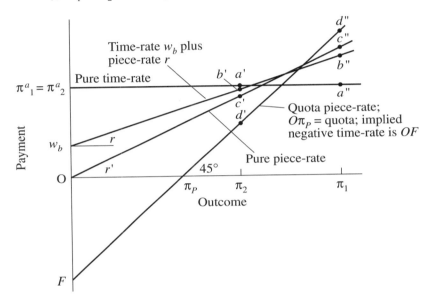

Figure 6.2   Time-rates and piece-rates

As was seen in Chapter 5, a weekly wage in the context of total lack of observability of effort would not produce the required work incentives. To induce effort, the employee had to take some risk, and in the present context this implies an element of piece-rate payment. Point b in Figure 6.1 transfers to the two points b', b'' in Figure 6.2. A straight line through these points cuts the vertical axis at w_b. It is therefore possible to interpret the contract at b in Figure 6.1 as a combination of a time-rate or weekly wage w_b and a payment per unit of outcome or piece-rate given by the slope of the line through b' and b''. Designate the slope of this line as r, then the payment to the employee $\pi_A = w_b + r\pi$ where π is the actual outcome. This payment schedule will just induce the risk-averse employee to exert effort e, as was seen in Chapter 5. A contract at point c in Figure 6.1, it will be recalled, would involve risk-sharing losses relative to point b and (given the assumption of only two effort levels, zero and e) would result in no compensating increase in effort. The contract at c lies on the diagonal through the origins of the box and thus implies that the agent is paid the same proportion of the outcome, whichever outcome occurs. There is thus no time-rate at all but just a pure piece-rate, as shown in Figure 6.2 by the straight line through the origin. Of course there is no reason in principle why a contract at c, and hence a pure piece-rate, might not be an efficient solution to the contractual problem, given the right circumstances (the degree of risk aversion of the employee, the cost of effort to the employee, the effect of effort on the probability of π_1, and so forth).

Indeed, although a risk-averse employee will never, according to the results of Chapter 5, be observed accepting a contract at d (since another contract will exist preferred by both employer and employee), a risk-neutral employee may do so. The resulting payment schedule is shown as the straight line through d' and d'' in Figure 6.2. Note that the implied time-rate is now negative and represents the 'franchise fee' discussed in the last chapter. It should not be concluded, however, that this fee has actually to be paid to the employer in the form of cash for the incentive structure to be operating. The fee can be paid 'implicitly' by effectively forgoing any reward over a certain range of outcomes, and hence paying the fee 'in kind' to the employer. Thus a piece-rate system can involve a 'quota' below which the employee receives nothing. In the case of the contract at d, the employee receives whatever is produced,[7] but only above the quota π_p.

The fact that only two outcomes were assumed to be possible meant that the various incentive structures could be represented by points lying along the straight lines in Figure 6.2. In the general case, where any number of outcomes might occur and effort levels can vary continuously, there is absolutely no reason to suppose that the efficient contract will imply a linear incentive structure. Indeed, the informational and computational requirements involved in 'calculating' the best contract will be formidable and the result could be a highly complex structure. Once more, therefore, we are led back to the basic arguments of Chapters 1 and 2 and the proposition that bounded rationality and other information problems will imply continual experiment rather than perfectly stable 'solutions'. Stiglitz (1975) recognises this point and argues in terms reminiscent of Alchian (1950) or even Hayek (1937, 1945) that: 'If there are large and significant advantages of one contractual arrangement over another, firms that 'discover' (this) will find they can increase profits and the particular contractual arrangement will be imitated. Thus, it might be argued that there is an evolutionary tendency of the economy to gravitate to the contractual arrangements analysed here' (p. 556). Stiglitz proceeds to investigate the properties of linear payment schedules where employees are risk averse and employers are risk neutral, and derives results which may be intuitively understood in the context of the model presented in Chapter 5: 'The piece rate is higher the smaller the risk, the lower the risk aversion, and the higher the supply elasticity of effort (the greater the incentive effects)' (p. 560).

In other words, if output is very closely related to effort and only weakly influenced by chance elements (the risk is small) the payment schedule will emphasise the piece-rate, and the time-rate will be low. By opting for piece-rates, the employee does not expose him- or herself to great risk but there is a clear advantage in providing incentives to effort. The impact of risk aversion also accords with *a priori* expectations. Where, as in Stiglitz's model, the outcome alone is observable, contracts which induce effort will involve the employee in *some* risk (unless of course there is no environmental risk and $\pi = \pi(e)$). As we saw in Chapter 5, the risk-sharing losses were worth incurring provided that the incentive effects were big enough. There we were considering a case in which effort could take only two values, but where effort can vary continuously the efficient contract will be so adjusted that the *additional* risk-sharing losses associated with inducing an extra unit of effort from the employee are just equal to the marginal benefits derivable from the extra effort. Clearly, the more risk averse the employee the greater will be the risk-sharing losses involved in any given modifications of the incentive structure away from time-rates towards piece-rates. Marginal risk-sharing losses will exceed marginal benefits from greater effort sooner as the importance of piece-rates is increased, and higher risk aversion is therefore expected to favour the time-rate. By a similar process of reasoning it is clear that for any given degree of risk aversion the marginal benefits of a move towards piece-rates will be higher the greater the resulting incentive effects, and thus large incentive effects favour the piece-rate. A final conclusion from Stiglitz's analysis also accords with the results of our simple framework: 'If individuals are perfectly well informed about their own abilities' (that is, they know the cost of effort and the effect on the probability distribution of outcomes) 'and there are no other sources of risk' (or people are risk neutral) 'then equilibrium will entail . . . auctioning off the jobs to the highest bidder; that is, a non-positive time rate' (p. 563). This corresponds, of course, to our conclusion that with risk-neutral employees the incentive structure $d'd''$ in Figure 6.2 will be efficient.

2.2 Payment Schedules, Adverse Selection and Worker Sorting

Choice of incentive structure will also have an impact on the quality of worker recruited when this quality or 'ability' is unobservable and adverse selection is a problem. A simple demonstration that firms with higher piece-rates tend to prevail when the ability level of workers is unobservable can be derived by assuming that workers' (observable) output is closely corre-lated to their 'ability'. If, subject to meeting a competitive profit constraint, firms can offer different contracts (such as those in Figure 6.2) high piece-rate firms will dominate low piece-rate firms. Suppose we have just two qualities of worker. Effort is either zero, in which case nothing is produced, or one. For effort level one, quality-1 workers will produce output π_1 and quality 2 workers will produce π_2. Higher output is thus linked to higher quality not to higher effort. The worker knows his or her productivity with certainty. Clearly quality-1 workers will receive a higher payment under a quota piece-rate than under the other schedules (compare d' with c'' and b'' in Figure 6.2) while for quality-2 workers it will be the other way around (compare b', c' and d').[8] Low-quality workers will therefore offer their ser-vices to firms with low-powered incentives and high-quality workers will seek employment in firms with high-powered incentives.

Assume now that the distance OF (the payment to the principal) in Figure 6.2 represents a competitive payment for capital per worker which all firms must achieve. Firms offering schedules $c'c''$ or $b'b''$ would make a loss. They would attract quality-2 workers and their output would be π_2. The output available for paying the worker after the demands of capital had been satisfied would be $\pi_2 - \pi_P$ which equals vertical distance $d'\pi_2$, but the amount promised to the worker would be greater than this, implying a loss per worker of vertical distance $c'd'$ or $b'd'$. To make profits, firms offering payment schedules $c'c''$ or $b'b''$ require quality-1 workers, but quality-1 workers prefer to work in firms offering payment schedule $d'd''$.

Clearly, the argument sketched in the previous paragraphs abstracts from many important considerations. However, it produces some clear predic-tions. A firm moving from time-rates to piece-rates under conditions in which individual output is measurable at fairly low cost would expect to encounter two effects. Work effort is expected to rise as shown in section 2.1 and the average quality of the workforce is also expected to rise as high-quality workers choose to work in firms offering piece-rates. Lazear (2000b) reports strong support for both of these predictions from a study of Safelite; a US autoglass installer which switched from hourly wages to piece-rates in the mid-1990s. An overall rise in productivity of 44 per cent could be divided into two components – a rise in the productivity of exist-ing workers as their effort responded to the new incentives and a rise due to the recruitment of workers attracted by the new regime.

3. THE ROLE OF THE MONITOR

The linear incentive structures of section 2 do not imply hierarchical relationships; they are simply a reformulation of the contractual issues discussed in Chapter 5, sections 3 and 4. We saw in section 5 of Chapter 5, however, how monitoring could result in both parties to a contract becoming better off. It is this use of a monitor or supervisor which is the distinguishing mark of what Williamson (1975) terms a 'simple hierarchy'. One person or group of people does the work, and another person monitors and assesses performance, as discussed in Chapter 4 in the context of Alchian and Demsetz's view of the firm. In fact, monitoring can be considered as having two conceptually distinct roles.

3.1 Monitoring and Moral Hazard

Monitoring is a response to the problem of 'moral hazard'. Because people, by assumption, cannot be relied upon to keep a promise to exert effort e, 'direct incentives' via piece-rates are required to ensure compliance. The risk-sharing losses involved are the result of moral hazard, but they may be reduced by monitoring. As Stiglitz (1975) puts it 'workers voluntarily undertake to be supervised . . . They submit to being compelled to work harder than direct incentives provide for because the consequence is a higher expected utility' (p. 571). Against these potential benefits it is necessary to set the costs of monitoring, as we saw in Chapter 5. It may also be that individuals will resent the presence of a monitor, and extra costs (utility losses) will result from working in a less pleasant 'atmosphere'.

In Chapter 5 we analysed 'monitoring gambles' which involved the imperfect observations of an agent's effort. In practice, of course, many jobs are very complex and the relatively simple 'principal and agent' approach which assumes observable and 'verifiable' outcomes does not fully encapsulate the contractual difficulties. Many aspects of complex management jobs are difficult to contract over. As was emphasised in Chapter 4, subsection 7.3, some outcomes are non-contractible because, while 'observable', they are nonverifiable. If, as a principal, we were to draw up contracts simply using a verifiable subset of the outcomes that we wish our agent to achieve, we would run the risk of encouraging severely dysfunctional behaviour. Teachers paid by the examination results of their pupils, for example, might ignore less able children or divert attention from non-contractible outcomes such as inculcating enthusiasm for a wide range of cultural activities. Surgeons penalised for deaths might become highly risk averse and not take actions which are actually in the interests of certain categories of patient. 'Lower-powered' incentives might be more appropriate if these dangers are serious.

One response to this problem of complex non-verifiable objectives is to monitor using 'subjective' measures of performance. An obvious immediate objection is that the agent might not trust the monitor to be honest in his or her 'subjective' evaluation. The system would seem to constitute an open invitation to the principal–monitor to 'move the goalposts' by claiming to have observed deficiency in some non-verifiable realm of activity. Clearly, repeat dealing and the game-theoretic mechanisms for the evolution of 'trust' and 'reputation' discussed in Chapter 1, section 8, are significant elements in a solution to this problem. Further comments on this subject appear below in the context of 'bond posting' and the 'tournament'. A further problem with subjective criteria occurs when the monitor is not the same person as the principal. If monitors are themselves agents of the principal and their decisions are not verifiable, they will be subject to pressure from the people they are monitoring. This pressure might take the form, for example, of personal unwillingness to 'judge' unfavourably the performance of a close colleague.[9] Attempts to influence the decisions of a monitor through 'influence activities' could range, however, all the way from flattery to blackmail or outright bribery.[10]

3.2   Monitoring and Adverse Selection

Monitoring may also be required to cope with a quite separate problem; that of 'adverse selection'. A simple model of adverse selection has already been considered in section 2.2. Here the analysis is extended to incorporate risk aversion, while the contractors are assumed to vary in the cost of exerting effort. Suppose that there are two groups of employees with two different skill levels and that the principal cannot by simple observation determine which person belongs to which group. The problem may be illustrated in Figure 6.3. The indifference curve $\bar{U}_{AS} = \bar{U}_{AU}$ indicates the locus of prospects yielding the same utility index to the skilled person S and the unskilled person U when neither is exerting effort. Thus, we are assuming that both skilled and unskilled persons have the same risk preferences. When the skilled person exerts effort e, his or her indifference curve becomes $\bar{U}^e_{AS}$ through point α. As usual, $\alpha\theta$ represents the cost of effort to the skilled person. For the unskilled person, however, greater effort may be required to change the probability of outcome 1 from p_1 to p^e_1 and his/her indifference curve is therefore labelled $\bar{U}^{e'}_{AU}$. Distance $\alpha'\theta$ is the cost of effort to the unskilled person. The upshot is that efficient contracts involving skilled people will lie along $r_s r_s'$ while contracts involving unskilled people will lie along $r_u r_u'$. Indifference curve $E(\pi)$ represents the constant expected profits line for the risk-neutral principal assuming that the required effort is being exerted. The firm or principal can therefore offer a contract at *a* to the unskilled, or, compatible with maintaining the same expected profit, a contract at *b* to the skilled. If we assume for the moment that $E(\pi)$ represents some competitive level of profits, we would expect firms to sort themselves into groups: one group specialising in employing the skilled, the other group specialising in the unskilled.

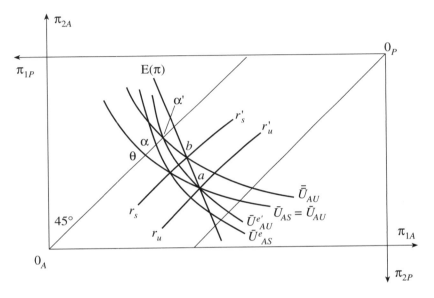

Figure 6.3   Adverse selection in recruitment

This process of sorting employees into groups, however, requires that ability is observable, and we have assumed that ability cannot be observed. Of course unobservability would not matter if people could be trusted to declare accurately their level of skill assuming that they, at least, know what it is. But Figure 6.3 illustrates that the unskilled will have an incentive to lie about their ability. An unskilled person will have a higher utility index if he or she can obtain a contract at *b* ($\bar{U}_{AU}$) than he would have at *a* ($\bar{U}_{AU}$). Thus, like the craftspeople in their dealings with person A in Chapter 2, unskilled people may misrepresent their skill level and attempt to 'contaminate' high-skill-level firms. By undermining the firms with contracts at *b*, the forces of adverse selection thus lead to generally higher levels of incentive pay in the surviving firms with contracts at *a*.

Will it be worth monitoring workers in order to discover their true quality? If output is observable at negligible cost, as assumed above, and there are no sources of risk (or contractors are all risk neutral) monitoring is not necessary. High- and low-quality workers face the same payment schedule. Quality-1 workers receive d' and quality-2 workers receive d' in Figure 6.2. If, however, we return to the case where the less skilled could undermine risk sharing benefits otherwise available to the skilled, or if we assume that individual output is not costlessly observable but is linked to ability, the monitor can potentially achieve benefits. Using a monitor to ascertain a worker's true quality could be used to reassign workers to tasks appropriate to their skills and thus to raise total output. The more heterogeneous are workers the larger are the potential benefits from correct assignment.[11] Monitoring might also be used to prevent the adverse-selection effects analysed in Figure 6.3. Workers are all appointed to a contract at a and then, after a period of monitoring, a suitable sub-group are moved to a contract at b. On the other hand, monitoring is itself costly. If monitoring costs exceed the gains to sorting derived from a more efficient assignment of workers to jobs or a more efficient sharing of risk between contractors, it will be better to avoid monitoring. On the other hand, again, this does not imply that all workers should be offered the same contract. As was the case with moral hazard, monitoring and purely contractual responses to adverse selection are substitutes. In section 4, the role of contractual devices to cope with adverse selection is discussed.

4.   CONTRACTS AND ADVERSE SELECTION: THE SCREENING MECHANISM

Contractual responses to the adverse-selection problem are possible, although they will not always be effective. The firm may employ screening devices or skill indicators, as was briefly mentioned in Chapter 2, subsection 2.1.3. In Figure 6.4 we illustrate the case of an educational-screening mechanism. Let there be two types of potential employee with productivity (skill) levels s_1 and s_2 respectively. The average productivity of potential employees is w^* and a firm can break even by paying skilled and unskilled alike a wage of w^*. Now suppose that educational qualifications are more costly to achieve for the unskilled than the skilled. In both cases it will be necessary to pay a higher wage to persuade potential employees to acquire qualifications.[12] However, the lower costs faced by the skilled will mean that they will require a smaller upward adjustment to the wage for any given level of educational attainment than will the unskilled. Thus, in Figure 6.4 the indifference curves with the subscript s_1 apply to the relatively skilled individuals, while the indifference curves with the subscript s_2 apply to the less skilled. The curves of the skilled are less steep, at any given level of education, than are those of the unskilled.

Instead of offering a contract at w^* for all its employees, the firm could instead try to separate the skilled from the unskilled. In Figure 6.4 this can be accomplished by offering a choice of two contracts, one at A and one at B. The contract at A offers a wage of w_1 contingent upon the applicant achieving educational level e_1. The contract at B offers a wage of w_2 with no stipulation about educational attainment. Points A and B are both on an indifference curve applying to skill-level 2. Thus, a relatively unskilled person will be indifferent between the two contracts. A skilled person, in contrast, is better off at A than at B. In this case, therefore, a 'separating equilibrium' exists. A contract at A (or fractionally to the right of A) will be accepted by the skilled and rejected by the unskilled in favour of B.

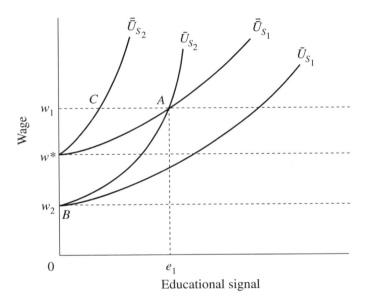

Figure 6.4   Education as a screening device

It is worth noticing that, as the figure is drawn, the screening mechanism has harmed the less skilled while leaving the more skilled at the same utility level as they would have enjoyed if a single contract at w^* had been offered. From a social point of view, therefore, screening or signalling may not always result in benefits. Further, the social opportunity cost of the resources used in providing the signal does not appear in the figure. However, the model has been presented in a particularly extreme form. If the process of acquiring the education itself increases productivity, or if the internal training procedures of the firm are more effective because of the information provided by the signal, signalling or screening can have productive and not merely redistributional consequences.

It should also be noted that a simple separating equilibrium is not always assured. If, for example, the contract at point A were less preferred than one at w^* by the skilled individuals, it would be open to a firm to avoid screening, offer a contract at w^* to skilled and unskilled alike and still break even. The situation would be unstable, however, because another firm could counter by offering a contract just below or to the right of point C, thereby attracting all the skilled individuals but forcing adjustments on the 'pooling' firms.[13] Contractual responses to adverse selection can be expected to be only partially effective, therefore, and should be regarded as complementary with rather than complete substitutes for internal monitoring.

5. MORAL HAZARD, PENALTIES AND WAGE PAYMENTS

The transactions-based view of the firm provides a rationalisation of simple hierarchy (interpreted loosely as the use of monitors) based upon an attempt to cope with moral hazard and adverse selection. As yet, however, we have no explanation of why the monitors in the hierarchy should be paid more than the people they are monitoring, why the people being monitored should have 'standard' contracts with the terms specified collectively rather than subject to individual bargaining, why recruitment into the hierarchy will occur at the lower levels, and so forth. These matters will be considered in later sections. For the moment, it is possible to lead into these areas by investigating another fundamental problem. Monitoring employees will be useless unless the monitor can apply some sanctions in the event of shirking being detected. The 'monitoring gambles' of Chapter 5 had to involve the employee in the risk of loss if observed effort were below standard. The precise mechanism involved in these monitoring gambles was not discussed in detail, however.

Suppose that a 'team' enterprise requires a monitor to ensure effort e is forthcoming from all its members. If effort is satisfactory, a certain payment (or wage) will be paid. Where shirking is observed, a penalty is exacted. The nature of this penalty is important. A reduction in the wage paid for bad service would create moral hazard problems of its own. The employee would have to trust that the firm would not deliberately 'observe' a low effort and penalise him or her dishonestly. Later, we will discuss mechanisms which may help to mitigate this problem. For the present, let us assume that the objection to relying on the 'observations' of only *one* of the contracting parties is overwhelming and consider the consequences. How is a firm to penalise an employee observed shirking? The obvious answer, and one which we encountered in Chapter 4, is that the firm can simply fire the shirker and not use his or her services henceforth. This was the rationale behind the necessity of making Alchian and Demsetz's monitor a central contractual agent with the power to hire and fire. But, as Shapiro and Stiglitz (1984) recognise, the theoretical objection to this mechanism as it stands is that the 'penalty' depends upon general labour market conditions outside the firm. To take an extreme case, suppose that full employment prevailed and that any fired worker could immediately be re-employed elsewhere at the going competitive wage. The so-called penalty for being observed shirking is in fact completely absent and with it the incentive effects of monitoring.

It is tempting to object that people fired for shirking will not find re-employment easy, but this is to confuse the two separate problems of moral hazard and adverse selection. Employers may use indicators such as employment history to counter adverse selection, but Shapiro and Stiglitz explicitly assume that all workers are identical in order to abstract from this problem. Thus, firms in this situation *know* that there is no reason to prefer one person over another on grounds of differential skill or propensity to shirk. If a fired person comes to them for a job they will conclude either that the person was wrongly fired, as is always a possibility with monitoring gambles (as we saw in Chapter 5), or that the previous employer was not clever enough in setting the appropriate incentive structure and that *anyone* would have shirked in the same circumstances. How, then, is the firm to devise a credible threat?

5.1 The Efficiency Wage

In the conditions specified, being fired *will* be a penalty to an employee if the firm pays a wage higher than that paid by other firms. Being a 'good employer' and paying higher wages can therefore be seen as part of the process of constructing monitoring gambles which will induce effort. Employees wish to avoid being fired because this will involve taking a lower wage elsewhere. Unfortunately, all firms can play the same game, and if each acts independently their common policy of raising wages above the 'norm' will sabotage any incentive effects from differential wages. All will end up paying higher wages and each will find the incentive effects much smaller than expected. If the differential wage mechanism fails to produce incentives, however, the overall result of a *general* increase in the wage level is to produce monitoring incentives from a different source. As the wage level rises with each firm's efforts to attach a penalty to being fired, the higher price of labour reduces the quantity demanded and increases the quantity supplied. An unemployment pool is the result. It is this unemployment pool, in Shapiro and Stiglitz's framework, which provides the 'penalty' required if monitoring is to be viable within the firm. With a pool of unemployment a fired worker will not be able to find new employment immediately. The expected length of time unemployed will be directly related to the size of the pool. Thus, if x workers are fired per period of time and x workers are hired and if the pool of unemployed is $10x$, there will be ten potential applicants for each available job per period, and hence a one in ten chance of gaining employment. The expected duration of unemployment will be ten periods.[14]

Shapiro and Stiglitz thus provide us with a model which predicts unemployment not as a short-term aberration, nor as a result of 'voluntary' job search along the lines of Stigler's approach to information acquisition discussed in Chapter 3, but as the outcome of attempts by firms to provide effort incentives through monitoring.[15] The resulting unemployment is clearly 'involuntary' in the sense that all the unemployed are prepared to accept jobs at the proffered wage level, but wage reductions will not occur because of each firm's desire to maintain an appropriate 'penalty' associated with terminating the contract of employment. As we saw in Chapter 5, not all monitoring gambles will be the same, and firms facing differing monitoring costs or differing consequences of shirking may construct different gambles. If monitoring costs are high, and the adverse consequences of shirking on the team are severe, a firm may wish to have a particularly substantial penalty associated with being fired. This will result in some firms paying higher wages for the same labour than other firms, and continuing to do so as a deliberate policy over time. Clearly this approach to unemployment is of considerable interest to macroeconomists, and the formal model can be manipulated to show how the size of the unemployment pool is expected to depend on factors such as unemployment pay.[16] Our purpose in discussing it here, however, is to show how it relates to the moral hazard problem and the internal monitoring environment of the firm.

The class of models discussed in this section relies on what is termed the 'efficiency wage' hypothesis. This idea originated in the development-economics literature, where it was observed that higher wages by improving nutrition and health might increase the productivity of the worker. Thus, physical productivity and wages are not independent and the 'efficiency wage' might fall after an increase in the real wage rate. In the context of developed economies, the argument is still that effort (and hence productivity) is not independent of the wage.[17]

For monitoring to be effective, the worker must be dependent on the firm. Dependency implies that he or she has something to lose by being dismissed from the firm. Employment in the firm must be more highly valued than outside available opportunities. Some of the worker's remuneration, in other words, must be a form of rent.[18] In this particular setting, the rent has been artificially contrived in order to raise the productivity of monitoring. Bowles and Gintis (1993) refer to rents of this nature as *enforcement rents*. In the absence of trust, unemployment can result, as we have seen, and this leads Bowles and Gintis to characterise contested exchange as a system which 'allocates power to agents on the short sides of non-clearing markets' (p. 90).

The payment of wages above the market norm can also be seen as a response to the adverse selection problem in certain circumstances. If firms cannot tell skilled from unskilled workers and simply pick at random from a group of applicants, they will wish to increase the proportion of skilled applicants to total applicants. Where the 'reservation wage' of people (that is, the wage below which they simply will not apply for the job) is positively related to their level of skill, the firms can persuade more skilled people to offer themselves for employment by setting a higher wage (Malcolmson, 1981). The use of this kind of mechanism implies, however, that internal monitoring of effort or skill is ineffective either for technical reasons or for the moral hazard reasons mentioned earlier. It also assumes that 'screening' devices are not available.

5.2 Deferred Compensation and 'Bond-posting'

Our discussion of incentives thus far has proceeded on the assumption that moral hazard prevents agreements which use the observations of the monitor to determine rewards. The result has been a system which uses the threat of terminating the agreement to induce effort; a threat which requires unemployment if it is to be effective. Implicitly, therefore, the 'hierarchy' under consideration is a very simple one in which monitors observe employees and fire those observed shirking. This incentive mechanism would not involve the necessity of a pool of unemployment if the employee could be brought to trust the integrity of the firm. As in the example of police incentives in Chapter 5, each employee could then 'post a bond' which he or she would forfeit if discovered shirking.

'Posting a bond' does not have to be interpreted literally in this context. An equivalent incentive is provided if the employee agrees to receive his or her remuneration not in a constant stream over time but in a stream which starts lower and rises through time. The employer gains at first by paying a relatively low wage but will have to repay the employee later when the wage is relatively high. Clearly the employee will have an incentive to avoid being fired, and monitoring will therefore involve a credible threat (Lazear, 1979, 1981). Working for a relatively low wage early on implies that the employee provides a 'hostage to fortune', and demonstrates in so doing a serious commitment to the firm. The firm offers a 'career path' by which the worker's employment income will include 'seniority payments'. Remuneration rises with years of service even when productivity has not changed. The wage is below the worker's productivity at first and rises above this level later.[19]

This brings us at last to the important question of what induces the firm to demonstrate a serious commitment to the employee? What induces the firm to monitor honestly and to refrain from firing the employee as soon as his or her wage reaches a level which implies repayment of his/her bond? As with the second-hand car salesman of Chapter 2 the answer to this question revolves around the value to the firm of a 'reputation' for honesty.

Although there are obvious short-term gains to cheating the employee, firing people dishonestly is not costless for the firm. If people begin to doubt the firm's integrity, they will no longer be willing to enter a long-term relationship involving bond-posting, and hence the incentive effects of this system will no longer be available to the firm. The firm will have to pay higher wages to new entrants, the value of the bond will be lower or zero, and monitoring will be more costly and less effective. Thus, an agreement between firm and employee is not something which can be considered as a single isolated event. If each bargain represented the outcome of a game between the two parties and was never to be repeated, the firm would have a clear incentive to cheat the employee if the latter agreed to the bond-posting scheme, but, of course, in such circumstances no employee would do so. It is the fact that the game is repeated continuously, and that cheating by the firm will have serious consequences for future agreements, which induces the firm to comply, and gives the employee the confidence to enter this kind of implicit contract (Radner, 1981). We cannot, however, conclude that the firm will never cheat. Clearly, there would be circumstances in which the gains from reneging on the implicit contract are so great that they outweigh the future costs. Thus, as Lazear (1979) puts it 'minimising cheating costs . . . will therefore trade off reduced worker cheating against increased firm cheating as (the time profile of wages) becomes more end weighted' (p. 1271).

'Reputation' and 'goodwill' are clearly central to the problem of establishing the viability of implicit contracts. These concepts can appear somewhat abstract at first, and they are certainly difficult to observe and measure objectively. This does not mean, however, that we have to accept them as exogenous and mysterious forces out of the reach of economic analysis.

Building a reputation amounts to thinking of ways of making implicit agreements enforceable. An important factor will therefore involve demonstrating to potential employees that the firm is fulfilling its implicit obligations. In the case of the rising time profile of wages discussed by Lazear, how are the employees to know whether any workers fired were honestly considered by the firm to be shirking? What is required, it might be argued, is some *observable* signal which induces this type of confidence in employees.

Malcolmson (1984) suggests that the mechanism of promotion through a hierarchy is capable of generating just this kind of confidence. Instead of promising to pay everyone a higher wage later, conditional upon their avoiding being fired by exerting 'sufficient' effort, the firm offers to pay a specified proportion of the workforce a higher wage later. The firm gives assurances that it will promote to higher-paid positions a certain fraction of its employees and that those people promoted will be the ones observed to be exerting the greatest effort. Such a scheme offers a number of advantages. First, it does not require any attempt to define what is a 'sufficient' level of effort to achieve promotion, although such an effort level may be implicit in the scheme. Second, implementation of the policy gives rise to an observable signal (the number of people actually promoted), which acts as an assurance that the firm is indeed sticking to its side of the bargain. Of course, it could be questioned whether those promoted really were those who were observed to have the highest productivity. The firm might economise on monitoring costs by promoting the required proportion at random. Once again, if it did so, all the incentive properties of the scheme would disappear and it will therefore be important to the firm to convince the workforce of its monitoring integrity.[20] Effort devoted to monitoring by the firm is observable by the employees, however, and this observability of monitoring effort combined with the promotions commitment provides an assurance of the firm's honesty, unless there is some perverse reason for the firm to promote those who appear the least productive.[21]

6. THE RANK-ORDER TOURNAMENT

6.1 Incentives and the Structure of a Tournament

This suggestion that a proportion of the workforce be offered a 'prize' (promotion) is an application of the incentive structure underlying the rank-order tournament. In a tournament, compensation is based not on the absolute level of individual output, but simply on the rank order of contestants. Prizes are fixed in advance, and then allocated to contestants according to their position in the ranking. As in a sporting contest, the 'closeness' of the match in no way determines the rewards. Some contestants may be so evenly matched that separating them in the final may be a matter of the merest chance, and yet the ultimate winner may receive many times the reward of the runner-up. This type of incentive structure has been analysed by Lazear and Rosen (1981). They show that 'under certain conditions, a scheme which rewards rank yields an allocation of resources identical to that generated by the efficient piece rate' (p. 863). Here, we present a very simple special case of Lazear and Rosen's result, in order to illustrate in more detail how the tournament works.

Suppose that employees are risk neutral. Using the results of Chapter 5, it was indicated in section 2 of this chapter that if individual output is perfectly observable, a piece-rate by which each employee receives his or her full marginal product will be efficient. The analysis up to that point had assumed only two effort levels, zero and e, but the efficiency property of the piece-rate under risk neutrality is maintained even when effort can take on a continuum of values. Since the person exerting additional effort receives the entire extra output produced under this piece-rate scheme, effort will be applied until the marginal costs incurred just equal the resulting output.

To make the example more concrete, let person j's output be directly related to his or her effort, as follows:

$$\pi_j = e_j + \theta_j,$$

where π_j is person j's output, e_j is person j's level of effort, and θ_j is a random element with mean zero. Further, let person j's marginal cost of effort be represented by the expression

$$\text{MC}_j = ae_j. \tag{6.1}$$

Clearly, the expected marginal return to an extra unit of effort is unity. The marginal cost of extra effort is simply ae_j. Thus, equating marginal cost to marginal benefit, the simple condition for maximising output net of effort costs will result in a level of effort

$$e_j = 1/a. \tag{6.2}$$

Now consider the case of a tournament.[22] We will assume that two people are involved, persons j and k, and that their individual outputs are impossible to observe. Thus, although they are both risk neutral, a piece-rate scheme cannot be devised and they will be rewarded on the basis of observed effort. Even the observation of effort is subject to error, however, and we suppose for the sake of the argument that the distribution of this error is known to both people. Two prizes are set in advance (π_1 and π_2, with $\pi_1 > \pi_2$). The person with the highest observed effort will receive π_1; the other will receive π_2. How will the behaviour of persons j and k be affected by this scheme?

As usual in neoclassical microeconomics, we expect both persons j and k to equate marginal benefits and costs of extra effort. Assume the individuals are identical. Both will face a rising marginal cost of effort equal to ae_j or ae_k. Marginal benefits of effort are more complex to calculate, however. The gain to greater effort will derive from its effect on the probability of winning the tournament and, through this, to the expected size of the prize. Indeed, we can write the expected gain to greater effort as the product of $(\pi_1 - \pi_2)$ and the change in the probability of winning the largest prize Δp_1. Thus

$$\text{MB}_j = (\pi_1 - \pi_2) \Delta p_1 \qquad (6.3)$$

The problem for each contestant is therefore to decide how their effort affects the probability of winning the tournament. Two factors will figure most prominently in j's decision – the accuracy of the monitor in assessing each person's effort, and the actual level of effort chosen by person k. If person k is not working at all, the benefit to person j of exerting some positive level of effort might be substantial. At a zero effort level, both k and j have a 0.5 probability of winning the tournament. Either might be perceived as the hardest worker and we assume that the monitor's errors are symmetrical. Marginal benefits will exceed marginal costs of effort in this situation and person j will increase his or her work effort until they are equated. Depending on the accuracy of the monitor, person j will increase the probability of winning by working harder than k.

If k now matches the work effort of j, the probability of winning returns to 0.5 and j has to decide whether yet further effort would be worthwhile. Once more, harder work will raise the probability of winning above 0.5, but the marginal costs of effort are now higher than they were, while the marginal benefits from establishing any given differential in effort levels have not changed. Person j may calculate that *some* attempt to distinguish him or herself from k is still worthwhile and j's effort will rise further until marginal benefits and costs are once more brought to equality. However, the differential in effort levels between j and k that maximises j's expected payoff will be lower than it was before. Indeed, eventually, if k always responds by matching j's effort, a point will come when both feel that there is no gain to be had from a further increase in effort. This will be the equilibrium level of effort induced by the tournament.

From Equation 6.3, it is clear that the marginal benefit of extra effort to a player in the tournament will rise with $\pi_1 - \pi_2 = \pi^*$ (the differential between the prizes). A larger spread can therefore be expected to increase the resulting level of effort. Similarly, a smaller value of a in Equation 6.1 will lower the marginal costs of effort and stimulate a higher equilibrium effort level.[23] Indeed, it is possible to show that with a uniform distribution of observational errors on the part of the monitor (observations of effort varying between $+\frac{1}{2}$ and $-\frac{1}{2}$ of their true value) the amount of effort stimulated by the tournament will be precisely π^*/a.

The above argument can be summarised in the form of Figure 6.5. By plotting utility maximising values of e_j for different values of e_k, person j's 'reaction curve' is traced out. Conversely, the optimal values of e_k corresponding to given levels of e_j trace out k's 'reaction curve'. In Figure 6.5, j's reaction curve is labelled jcj' while k's reaction curve is kck'. The reaction curves of persons j and k intersect at point c. This point is called a Cournot or Nash equilibrium. Given k's effort, person j is maximising his or her utility; and, given j's effort, person k is doing the same. Neither person j nor person k will wish to move away from point c, therefore. We might envisage the approach to point c in dynamic terms, with each person responding to the moves of the other along a path such as j, l, m, n, in the diagram. Given

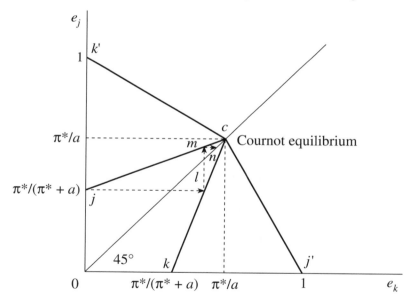

Notes:
$jcj' = j$'s reaction curve
$kck' = k$'s reaction curve

Figure 6.5   The tournament

the symmetry of the two reaction curves, it is seen that point c lies on a 45° line and hence that persons j and k end up working equally hard.

Notice that this result is a distinctive feature of the 'rat race'. If both individuals could arrange to limit their efforts, both would be better off. With $e_k = e_j = 0$, each person will still have a 0.5 probability of winning the tournament and will have saved all the effort costs. The two persons could agree never to turn up to work early in the morning or to leave late at night, never to take less than an hour and a half for lunch, never to work at home, never to flatter the boss, and so forth, but if this type of agreement cannot be enforced and policed, or if we envisage each individual as competing against large numbers of other people whose behaviour is taken as largely beyond any personal influence, the efforts of each person to 'get ahead' will be mutually frustrating. All people finish the week tired out from their efforts to win the tournament, and none of them are any more likely to do so than they would have been had they all stayed in bed.

As seen from Equation 6.3, the amount of effort stimulated by the tournament depends upon π^*, the difference between the two prizes. If π^* were set equal to one, the Cournot equilibrium would involve each person exerting effort equal to $1/a$, but this level of effort is precisely that forthcoming under the efficient piece-rate scheme outlined at the beginning of this section (Equation 6.2). Thus, the two prizes $\pi_1 = (1/a) + \frac{1}{2}$, and $\pi_2 = (1/a) - \frac{1}{2}$ will induce the same effort from the two contestants as the efficient piece-rate. Because the contestants are risk neutral, they will be equally happy under a piece-rate scheme or competing in a tournament with the prizes set so as to induce the same level of effort. Unlike the piece-rate scheme, however, the tournament does not require us to be able to measure on a cardinal scale each person's output: it merely requires that we can rank individual performance in terms of more or less, better or worse. On the other hand, the tournament does require that the 'correct' prizes are set, and here we may once again imagine a competitive process of trial and error at work. A firm which sets $\pi^* > 1$ will obtain greater effort from the contestants. The extra output generated by this additional effort, however, will fall short of the costs incurred by the employees, and their expected utility will fall. Thus, a firm which hits upon the 'correct' structure of prizes will be able to attract contestants from firms who encourage 'too much' or 'too little' effort.

Notice the similarity between the 'monitoring gambles' discussed in Chapter 5, the 'bond-posting' incentive structure discussed in subsection 5.2 of this chapter, and the tournament. In the tournament, the employee receives $(1/a) + \frac{1}{2}$ if he or she is lucky, and $(1/a) - \frac{1}{2}$ if he or she is unlucky. Thus, it looks similar to any other monitoring gamble. The only difference is that receiving the bigger prize does not depend upon achieving any particular satisfactory level of performance; it depends entirely on how a person performs relative to others. With the monitoring gambles of Chapter 5, all employees might have been observed working, and hence all would have their bond returned. Indeed, if a worker could never be mistaken for an idler ($q_{oe}=0$) all people putting in the required effort would certainly receive the larger reward. In the case of the tournament discussed above, however, one person wins and the other loses, even though they are both predicted to exert the same level of effort.

It is important to remember that our exposition of the tournament assumed that employees were risk neutral. The fact that piece-rates and tournaments can be made equivalent under these conditions does not mean that they can always be made equivalent. Risk aversion will obviously complicate matters considerably, and everything will depend upon the risks associated with piece-rates compared with the risks associated with the best-constructed tournament. The tournament replaces a whole distribution of possible outcomes with just two prizes. In so doing, it removes many possible outcomes in the 'middle' of the distribution (in our example around $1/a$). This will clearly not be attractive to a risk-averse person. On the other hand, the two prizes set a limit on the range of possible outcomes and may rule out extremely disastrous or very favourable occurrences, and this is obviously attractive in the context of risk aversion.[24] A direct comparison between piece-rates and tournaments is not of central concern here, however. The important point is that tournaments may be a viable form of incentive structure in circumstances where piece-rates are not feasible because individual marginal products cannot be observed.

Lazear and Rosen's analysis of the tournament helps to make sense of many features of hierarchical firms which would otherwise be very perplexing. The high salaries of top corporate executives often draw adverse comment from people who correctly observe that these salaries can hardly be explained on the basis of very high productivity. 'Productivity', however, is not objectively measurable in many circumstances, and it seems reasonable to suppose that the observed salary structure represents a set of tournament prizes: 'This interpretation suggests that presidents of large corporations do not necessarily earn high wages because they are more productive as presidents but because this particular type of payment structure makes them more productive over their entire working lives' (p. 847). Reward at any one time will not reflect actual or even expected product. In our example, both people worked equally hard and produced the same output $1/a$, yet their rewards differed, with one person getting more and the other less than his or her product. Monitoring costs will play a crucial role in determining whether or not tournaments are used. Tournaments require that each person's performance is compared qualitatively with that of everyone else, whereas with piece-rates each person can be rewarded without reference to other people. Thus 'salesmen, whose output level is easily observed, typically are paid by piece rates, whereas corporate executives, whose output is more difficult to observe, engage in contests' (p. 848). A similar observation was made at the end of Chapter 5, but promotion through a hierarchy was seen there as dependent upon achieving satisfactory effort, whereas here we are perceiving it as a prize in a tournament.

6.2 Further Problems with High-powered Incentives

6.2.1 Sabotage

One important aspect of the tournament or other 'high-powered' systems of incentives concerns the effect that it has on cooperative behaviour in team environments. Clearly, no participant in a tournament will have an incentive to make a colleague look good to the monitor unless such 'selfless' behaviour is itself fairly visible. Indeed, there is a danger that super-competitive 'win at all costs' characters might be tempted into a spot of sabotage. As has been noted at various points throughout the text, these 'dysfunctional' effects are a danger in any environment where contracts are incomplete but high-powered incentives are in place. If sabotage is costly to observe, at least part of j's effort might go into undermining the success of k rather than improving his or her own performance, and vice versa.

Sometimes, therefore, it will be necessary to weaken these temptations by adjusting downwards the spread between the prizes ('pay compression'). Sabotage is then reduced at the price of somewhat lower effort incentives all round. If the tendency towards sabotage is partly a matter of innate 'personality', so that very aggressive individuals (Hawks) are more prone to 'cheat' in this way than others (Doves), the establishment of a suitable 'ethos' in the firm can be a matter of great importance. A firm that screens for 'Doves' will be able to increase the difference between the tournament prizes at a lower cost in terms of sabotage. A firm that employs 'Hawks' will have to compress the differential between the prizes. Paradoxically, therefore, Dove-employing firms can use higher-powered incentives than can Hawk-employing firms. On the other hand, 'Hawks' will try to infiltrate 'Dove' firms so that, if they cannot be successfully identified, there will be a tendency for high-incentive firms to be undermined.

This conclusion that adverse selection might work to reduce the spread of prizes in tournaments is heavily dependent on the assumption that 'Hawks' and 'Doves' are personality types and not influenced by their peers. Further, it is one thing for 'Doves' not to engage in sabotage but quite another for them to be fully cooperative. In a team environment, as defined by Alchian and Demsetz, encouraging active cooperation will be important. If the firm can be broken down into non-overlapping groups of people, then prizes might be awarded for relative team performance, but then sabotage between teams might still be a problem. Producing a contractual environment that supports cooperative effort might therefore require lower-powered incentives than would emerge from situations where individual performance is the paramount consideration. In Chapters 10 and 11, some of these issues are discussed in the context of profit-sharing and non-profit enterprise.

6.2.2   The crowding out of intrinsic motivation

A further possibility investigated by Frey (1994) is that a person's 'intrinsic motivation' might be affected by the contractual setting of the firm. This is a subversive idea from the point of view of neoclassical economics because it calls into question the independence of a person's 'preferences' from the 'constraints' that they face. The idea is simply that close monitoring or the payment of rewards might reduce a person's willingness to act cooperatively and to perform to a high standard out of a sense of professional pride, social obligation, duty or whatever words we use to describe an intrinsic desire to cooperate with others or to achieve some goal for its own sake. Extrinsic motivation concerns responses to rewards and penalties imposed from outside. It is 'calculative' in the conventional economic sense of comparing marginal benefits (perhaps a wage received) and marginal costs (perhaps effort expended). Intrinsic motivation concerns a desire to achieve particular ends with which the person is personally identified. Such motivation, argues Frey, 'leads to playfulness and idiosyncrasy, convictedness and amateurish actions, as well as more innovativeness' (p. 336). The problem is that extrinsic intervention in the form of incentive payments or monitoring might 'crowd out' intrinsically motivated behaviour. Frey (1994, p. 335) gives as examples a boy who stops mowing the lawn voluntarily after his father begins to pay him a fee, or a professor in a state university who cuts down on teaching to a minimum once the government carefully monitors her hours.

The pure psychology of this 'crowding-out' effect does not directly concern us here. Assuming that people do respond to intrinsic motivation and that external intervention causes this motivation to diminish, then we would expect this effect to be taken into account in any principal–agent relationship. The disciplining effect of additional monitoring or the incentive effect of high-powered monetary rewards would have to be traded off against the possible loss in intrinsic motivation. Frey argues, for example, that a number of propositions associated with the hypothesis of the crowding out of intrinsic motivation are testable. Personal relationships between principal and agent, for example, are expected to increase the importance of intrinsic motivation as also are interesting and complex tasks. The more uniformly and highly regulated the agent, the less will be the agent's intrinsic motivation. Incentives via money payments will be less destructive of intrinsic motivation than close monitoring and regulation because 'rewards shift the locus of control less than commands do' (p. 345). In other words, monetary rewards (like economic instruments of control generally) leave the agent to adjust in ways that they think are best.[25]

Observations compatible with the crowding out of intrinsic motivation include the fact that incentive schemes are used more commonly for managers than for lower-level employees. The latter look at incentive schemes as a sign of lack of trust and therefore as a means of control. Morale and intrinsic motivation decline as a result. Managers are prepared to view incentive schemes more positively as a means of measuring performance. On the other hand, workers doing repetitive tasks are often rewarded by high-powered piece-rates because 'they typically have little if any work morale which would be crowded out' (Frey, 1995, p. 17). Similarly, payment schedules appropriate for private profit-oriented firms might be inappropriate for a non-profit enterprise. If workers in the latter already accept lower payments in exchange for non-pecuniary intrinsic benefits, attempts to regulate and monitor too closely might be expected to be destructive of morale and of intrinsic motivation.[26]

7.   IDIOSYNCRATIC EXCHANGE

The analysis of sections 3 to 6 helps us to rationalise some of the characteristics of hierarchical structures. Even in the context of *identical* employees performing *identical* tasks it is possible to understand the development of recognisable hierarchies. We have seen that the provision of effort incentives where individual output cannot be identified or where employees are risk averse may involve the use of monitoring gambles and hence (i) the use of monitors to measure effort; (ii) wages rising faster than productivity over time (Lazear) with mandatory retirement after a certain point; or, (iii) the use of 'tournament-like' incentive schemes whereby the firm undertakes to pronounce a certain fraction of its employees as 'winners' by promoting them to higher-paid positions (Lazear and Rosen, 1981; Malcolmson, 1984).

These ideas depend simply on the existence of moral hazard and the assumed propensity of people to shirk if they are not being monitored. They thus relate most closely to the discussion of 'team production' in Chapter 4. The fact that certain hierarchical features are explicable on this basis alone is significant, since theorists usually prefer their work to depend upon the weakest assumptions possible. Yet, it has to be admitted that the models discussed so far produce only the barest outlines of a hierarchy, stripped of the complexity associated with the organisation of large firms. For a less austere approach, richer in its implications for internal structure, we now return to the work of Williamson (1975).

It will be recalled from Chapter 2 that person A, in his attempts to extend his house, faced many transactional problems other than the simple inability to observe the effort of the workpeople involved. It was of the essence of person A's problem that potential craftspeople were not of identical ability, that the different people in the team had different jobs to do, and that person A was not, and could not become, apprised of the best way of performing the different tasks involved. Certain information and certain types of skill were inevitably associated with the actual business of performing the job in question and would not be available on equal terms to person A. This type of knowledge was considered also in Chapter 3, where the scope for entrepreneurial reward from Hayek's 'knowledge of time and place' was discussed. Further, A confronted the 'bounded rationality' problem; the plain incapacity to calculate all possible best responses to every conceivable set of contingencies. Williamson's approach to hierarchies is rooted in an appreciation of these more varied but very fundamental transactional difficulties.

All people have their own special skills and attributes, and all tasks are idiosyncratic to some degree. As Doeringer and Piore (1971) put it: 'almost every job involves some specific skills . . . The apparently routine operation of standard machines can be importantly aided by familiarity with the particular piece of operating equipment . . . Moreover . . . a critical skill is the ability to operate effectively with the given members of the team' (p. 15). At the risk of repetition, note again the difference between this observation as the starting point for analysis, and the models of sections 5 and 6 which assume away task idiosyncrasy and differential skills. If, as a matter of observation, people and jobs are all special to some degree, transactions cannot be regarded as 'standard'. Each transaction has its own features which are unique, and the central agent or firm will find itself bargaining continually in a situation of bilateral monopoly and with asymmetrically distributed information. The possibilities available to the employee in these circumstances for 'opportunistic behaviour' were discussed in detail in Chapter 2. As Williamson defines it (Williamson *et al.*, 1975, pp. 258–9): 'opportunism is an effort to realise individual gains through a lack of candour or honesty in transactions. It is a somewhat deeper variety of self-interest seeking assumption than is ordinarily employed in economics; opportunism is self-interest seeking with guile.' Employees enter the firm and gradually become skilled and adept at specific tasks. This specialised knowledge gives the incumbent employee 'first-mover advantages' over potential replacements from outside and thus places the employee in a bargaining position which he or she may try to exploit in negotiations with the firm. Essentially, Williamson sees most of the characteristics of employment hierarchies as a response to the transactional difficulties posed by 'small-numbers bargaining' and 'opportunistic behaviour'. Before proceeding to outline the mechanisms which are supposed to cope with 'opportunism', it will be useful to reflect in more detail on its nature and in particular on its relationship to the subject matter of Chapter 3 – 'entrepreneurship'.

8. RENT SEEKING, ENTREPRENEURSHIP AND OPPORTUNISM

The entrepreneur is nothing if not an opportunist. Without the ability to perceive opportunities and to make use of them while they last, resource reallocation and the efficiency gains which accompany them could not occur. From the hero of Chapter 3, however, the opportunist has unaccountably become the villain of Chapter 6, whose fiendish unreliability the whole paraphernalia of hierarchical organisations are designed to counteract. How are we to explain this unexpected change of view? The answer is basically simple in outline although often extraordinarily complex in detail. It revolves around the distinction between rent seeking and entrepreneurship. Entrepreneurship, as we saw at length in Chapter 3, produces efficiency gains. It extends our knowledge of the available possibilities for division of labour and exchange. The entrepreneur trades in property rights and, if successful, receives an entrepreneurial profit from the efficiency gains he or she has created. Rent seeking is behaviour aimed at acquiring or asserting property rights other than by voluntary exchange. Resources are expended in efforts merely to redistribute income.

Tullock (1980a) defines rent seeking as follows: 'an individual who invests in something that will not actually improve productivity or will actually lower it, but that does raise his income because it gives him some special position or monopoly power, is 'rent seeking' and the 'rent' is the 'income derived' (p. 17). The idea grew initially out of dissatisfaction with the conventional approach to measuring social losses due to monopoly. Monopoly profits in received theory are not part of the social costs of monopoly. They merely represent transfers from consumers who are worse off to monopoly producers who are better off. Tullock argued, however, that if it were possible to receive profits by creating monopolies, people would invest resources in 'monopoly-creating activities'. Further, the resources 'invested' in total could equal or even on occasions far exceed

(Tullock, 1980b) the monopoly profits obtained by the eventual holder of the monopoly. Thus, the profits of monopolists attract attempts to gain monopoly privileges, and the resources expended in these attempts are part of the 'efficiency loss' associated with monopoly. A similar argument applies in cases where tariff protection is sought. Consumers lose and protected producers gain from measures to restrict foreign trade, but if these producer 'gains' are available, producers will expend effort and resources in lobbying and pressuring politicians to grant them protection. These political efforts are 'rent seeking' and represent social losses.

The archetypal form of rent seeking is theft. Theft involves a simple redistribution of resources and diverts activity from production and exchange to either thieving itself or protection from thieving. Burglar alarms, locks and other security devices use up scarce resources and are a response to a purely redistributional activity. To quote Tullock again: 'as a successful theft will stimulate other thieves to greater industry and require greater investment in protective measures, so each successful establishment of a monopoly or creation of a tariff will stimulate greater diversion of resources to attempts to organise further transfers of income' (1980c, pp. 48–9). The contrast between gaining from theft and gaining from the encouragement of fully voluntary exchange is the essential contrast between rent seeking and entrepreneurship. Readers should be aware that this use of the terms 'rent seeking' and 'entrepreneurship' is not fully agreed upon. Rent seeking is sometimes broken down into different types and an entrepreneur is often simply viewed as any rent seeker. Entrepreneurs do seek, and if successful receive, a form of rent (the efficiency gains created) and thus it is understandable that they should be seen as rent seekers. But the term 'rent seeking' is now so closely associated with the pursuit of income transfers, and the theory of entrepreneurship so intimately associated with the pursuit of efficiency gains, that the suggested distinction between rent seeking and entrepreneurship seems both useful and tenable.

When presented as the difference between theft and voluntary exchange, nothing might seem more clear-cut than the difference between rent seeking and entrepreneurship.[27] Yet detailed cases can give rise to conceptual problems. These problems will ultimately derive from ambiguities about property rights. If rent seeking involves a form of theft, it must, as Sisk (1985) emphasises, imply the infringement of someone's property rights: 'Rent-seeking emerges when rights are challengeable' (p. 96). In the case of monopoly, considered above, the right of people to use resources in the monopolised trade was restricted by government decree. Thus, people's rights to use their resources (their property rights, see Chapter 4) have been restricted by the activities of the rent seeker, and the result is an uncompensated transfer. Similarly, if person A pays another to do some shopping and the shopper (an opportunist) lies about the price of the items purchased, a theft has taken place. The fact that person A may not know with certainty that he has been robbed does not affect the issue. His property rights have been infringed by the rent seeker and the knowledge that he is vulnerable to this type of rent seeking will presumably reduce his use of the shopper, or restrict it to items for which receipts (somehow made tamper proof) can be obtained.

Consider now the case of the artistically inclined entrepreneur of Chapter 3 who notices a valuable picture hanging in the house of an unsuspecting old lady. He offers her a sum sufficient to acquire the picture and makes a fortune. Has the old lady been robbed? Most of us would be inclined initially to say that she had, and that this action was rent seeking. Yet, in principle, this is clearly not the case. No uncompensated transfer took place and no property rights were infringed. Our trader with knowledge of the art market was an entrepreneur. There is no economic principle which says that entrepreneurs, even as we have defined them, will be generous to old ladies (which is not to say, of course, that they *ought* not to be). Suppose, however, that we change the story so that the old lady shrewdly suspects that her picture is valuable and approaches an expert with an offer to pay for his or her professional advice. The professional adviser lies to her, purchases the item, and again makes a fortune by reselling at a huge profit. This is rent seeking because it involves the adviser implicitly challenging the old lady's right to the information for which she had paid. Trade in information gives rise to many problems, but the most fundamental is that of establishing clear and policeable property rights. It would, no doubt, be difficult to prove that the adviser had abridged the lady's property rights: 'I really had no idea at the time that the picture would prove to be so valuable.' This, though, is simply to reiterate the basic point that the lower the cost of challenging a person's property rights, the more likely such rights are to be challenged, and hence the greater will be the amount of rent seeking. Property rights in information are eminently challengeable.

The use of the word 'theft' in the context of rent seeking requires care. It is clearly a useful analogy, but the more neutral 'uncompensated transfer' is a less value-laden term. If a group of businessmen lobby politicians and receive a subsidy for their industry, they are rent seeking. The tax mechanism is used to transfer resources from one group of people to another. An uncompensated transfer occurs and, with it, the attenuation of taxpayers' property rights, but although some of us are apt to declaim on occasions that 'all taxation is theft', from a legal point of view this is obviously not so, and to avoid confusion it is better that theft be considered the archetypal case rather than the defining characteristic of rent seeking.

A case closer to the problem of employer and employee is that of the plumber and person A in Chapter 2. A plumber who installs a system of unnecessary technical sophistication to heat a customer's house is a rent seeker. The resources expended are pure waste and the customer's rights to the information possessed by the plumber have been implicitly challenged. Contrast this with a plumber who, after finalising an agreement with person A, perceives new opportunities which will enable the same objectives to be achieved at much lower cost. The plumber returns to person A and renegotiates the agreement. In the process he or she deliberately understates the cost-reducing characteristics of his/her discovery and succeeds in making a large profit. Is he/she a rent seeker or an entrepreneur? Everything depends upon our understanding of the contractual relationship between the plumber and person A. If the plumber had signed a contract saying 'I undertake to serve person A in the capacity of plumber over the following period and faithfully promise to use all the information at my disposal during this period in the interests of person A', the activities of the plumber in attempting to mislead person A could be construed as rent seeking. The plumber is renouncing the provisions of a contract. This is, of course, precisely what happens when a person paid by time-rate shirks. If, though, the plumber's contract merely states 'I undertake to install a heating system which meets the following specifications', the use of new information to achieve this end at lower cost is pure entrepreneurship. If the contract actually specifies the exact equipment to be installed so that renegotiation is necessary before the new information can be used, the plumber may be less than candid about the cost advantages of the new system and vastly underestimate them, but no one has ever claimed that entrepreneurs must be frank. They merely fulfil their contractual obligations. A person paid by piece-rate who discovers methods of improving his or her output is an entrepreneur, and may not be required contractually to inform his/her employer of these developments.[28]

Our discussion of principal and agent in Chapter 5 can thus be recast in terms of rent seeking and entrepreneurship. The contractual problem was to find mechanisms which would reduce rent seeking and channel attention away from attempts to challenge property rights towards attempts to achieve more effective coordination of resources. For Williamson, this is also the function of hierarchical organisations. Both rent seekers and entrepreneurs are opportunists, but institutional structures determine the returns available from opportunist contract-breaking and opportunist contract-making and contract fulfilment. The baby of entrepreneurship sits, if we can adapt a popular metaphor, in the bathwater of rent seeking, and the function of hierarchies is to jettison the latter whilst somehow retaining the former. This manoeuvre is beset with difficulty and not infrequently ends with the baby ousted and the performer drenched with the bathwater. In the next section, however, we consider Williamson's observations on the procedures which make this result less likely.

9. THE FIRM AS A GOVERNANCE STRUCTURE

9.1 The Internal Labour Market

A description of the major 'contracting modes' (the spot contract, the state-contingent contract and the authority relation) has already been presented at the end of Chapter 2, along with a brief outline of Williamson's criticism of these modes. Bounded rationality and opportunistic behaviour deriving from task idiosyncrasy, he argues, imply that alternative contractual arrangements have advantages over each of these forms of contract. As has been recognised at many points in this book, contracting in circumstances of asymmetrically distributed information is facilitated by 'reputation' and 'trust', but it is fundamental to our approach to the firm that instead of *assuming* the existence of this 'reputation' and 'trust', institutional mechanisms are seen as the means by which confidence in the integrity of others can be encouraged.

In Williamson's view, the internal labour market represents an institutional response to the problem of opportunism, and elicits more cooperative behaviour from employees than would be possible under spot or state-contingent contracting. As seen in Chapter 2, Williamson (1985) sees 'unified governance' as becoming established under conditions of uncertainty, transaction-specificity and high frequency of repeat dealing. More recently, Williamson (2000) succinctly distinguishes the transactions cost and principal–agent approaches to contract. 'Moving beyond the agency theory tradition of ex ante incentive alignment, transaction cost economics turns its attention – additionally and predominantly – to the ex post stage of contract' (p. 599). In other words, the theory which was reviewed in sections 2 to 6 above concerned the problem of selecting the right transactional terms *ex ante* (the best payment schedule or the best distribution of prizes in a tournament) – before the outcomes are known. Even when the passage of time was explicitly recognised – as in the sections on seniority payments and bond-posting – implicit contracts were simply seen as being put into effect supported by the forces of reputation. Transactions cost theory asks what happens at the post-contractual stage. As information is revealed how will the transactors behave? Will they try to renegotiate the contract? How disruptive and costly will this process be? What mechanisms will be used to reduce the costs of *ex post* adjustment? Notice here that the Grossman–Hart–Moore property rights theory of the firm introduced in Chapter 4, while emphasising *ex post* opportunism as a problem, is not a transactions cost approach in the spirit of Coase or Williamson. This is because *ex post* hold-up is accurately predicted by the transactors *ex ante* while *ex post* bargaining costs are assumed to be zero. Transactions cost economics, in contrast, is largely about the costs of *ex post* bargaining.

9.2   Specific Human Capital

Consider yet again the problem faced by the firm. It requires a person to perform some task. This task involves skills which are not general and cannot be used to aid performance in other lines of activity. They are *specific* skills (to use Becker's (1964) terminology). They are useful in the highly particular context of the firm, and some may be acquired only by on-the-job training, as in the case of 'knowledge of time and place' mentioned in section 7. Human capital theory concludes that the costs of *general* training, which increases the productivity of people in lines of activity both inside and outside the firm, will be borne by the individual concerned, whereas the costs of *specific* training will be borne by the firm. This argument depends on the idea that the firm will not pay for the general training of employees because they may then be enticed away to higher-paid jobs elsewhere and the firm will lose its investment. The firm cannot trust the employee. On the other hand, the employee will not pay the cost of specific training because this implies accepting a lower reward than could be obtained elsewhere during the training period. Higher rewards would be forthcoming *after* the training period, but this implies that the employee must trust the firm, and the traditional argument of human capital theory assumes this will not happen. Instead the firm pays for the specific training.

As we saw in section 7, however, a firm which pays for specific training might still itself be the victim of opportunism. An employee, by threatening to leave, is capable of inflicting large costs on the firm which would face the prospect of having to invest more resources in the training of another outsider. In the context of full employment the threat would be costless and hence credible (see section 5). Thus, the conventional distinction between types of training, general and specific, and the conclusion that these are financed by the individual and the firm respectively, depends upon the assumption that employees do not trust firms but that in the realm of specific training firms have to trust employees.[29] Note that the opportunism of the employee is here a form of rent seeking and that the implicit challenge is to the employer's property rights in the 'specific human capital' he or she has financed. Just as with property rights in information, property rights in human capital[30] are difficult to establish and police for obvious reasons, and are therefore challengeable.

Unlike the conclusions of human capital theory, the upshot of Williamson's approach is a greater emphasis on the employee trusting the firm. The primary characteristic of the 'internal labour market' is that employees do not bargain individually over terms and conditions with the employer. Instead, a person joining a firm will be assigned to a certain grade in the hierarchy and will receive whatever remuneration attaches to that grade: 'The internal labour market achieves a fundamental transformation by shifting to a system where wage rates attach mainly to jobs rather than to workers' (Williamson *et al.*, 1975, p. 270). By 'job', here, the authors are not referring to a single idiosyncratic task but to a broad category of tasks attached to which are standard terms of employment. Because individual bargaining is ruled out, 'the incentives to behave opportunistically . . . are correspondingly attenuated' (p. 271). The employee voluntarily accepts these constraints on his or her freedom of action in the knowledge that others will be similarly constrained. Of course, while this procedure mitigates the problem of rent seeking through attempts to mislead the employer in an unending bargaining process, it does not in itself prevent shirking. Williamson argues, however, that the promotion ladder is designed to counter this form of rent seeking and to encourage 'consummate' instead of 'perfunctory' cooperation. 'Consummate cooperation is an affirmative job attitude – to include the use of judgement, filling gaps, and taking initiative in an instrumental way. Perfunctory cooperation, by contrast, involves job performance of a minimally acceptable sort' (Williamson *et al.*, 1975, p. 266). Thus Williamson's approach is very closely related to the ideas of Lazear and others (sections 5 and 6) on the incentive effects of a rising profile of earnings over time. The additional element is an explanation of the hierarchical characteristic that each individual is not treated as a special case but, at any one time, is the holder of a 'standard' contract applying to a particular grade. From this perspective, it no longer follows therefore that firms will finance specific training. If the worker accepts a lower wage at first, which reflects his or her lower productivity as s/he gradually becomes acquainted with the idiosyncrasies of the task, s/he effectively 'posts a bond', as discussed at length earlier. In so doing s/he is forced to trust the firm. Why, though, should we expect the employee to trust the firm rather than the other way around?

For any exchange transaction to take place, even of the most basic 'bread for beer' variety, someone has to trust someone else. At the end of section 5 it was shown that the firm's 'reputation' would suffer in the long run if it cheated on its implicit agreements. A strand in the argument was missing at that stage, however. In principle, the same 'reputation-protecting' argument could be applied to employees to show that *they* might lose in the long run if the firm trusted them and they cheated. Clearly 'reputations' in the labour market may be important, and we shall see later that some writers have used this possibility as a limiting factor to managerial cheating of shareholders (Fama, 1980). However, it is usual to argue that, for most types of employee, 'reputations' are difficult; that is, costly to create. As Klein (1984) puts it, 'A firm generally has lower costs of creating brand name capital and hence contract fulfilment credibility because of its increased repeat purchase frequency' (p. 333). In other words, a single firm's integrity is tested each period in its dealings with each of its employees. Because it is a 'central contractual agent' it is party to many contracts, whereas each employee is party to only one. Further, the working lifetime of a joint-stock firm is not limited in the same way as the working lifetime of employees (although bankruptcy can 'terminate' a firm's life). Thus, 'cheating firms are likely to become known more quickly than cheating workers, reducing the short-run cheating potential of firms relative to workers' (p. 333). A single employee may only serve a few customers (employers) in a lifetime, and although a good 'track record' of reliability is not worthless, the difficulties of communicating such a record to potential employers (the source of the adverse selection problem) imply high costs of creating this type of 'brand name capital' as Klein calls it. Contrary to conventional human capital theory, therefore, 'the worker can be expected to make much of the specific investment and the firm guarantee that it will not hold up the worker by reducing his wage below the value of his marginal product' (Klein, 1984, p. 333).

We should not necessarily presume that the worker will implicitly finance *all* the specific human investment in the firm. Some sharing of the initial burden might occur, especially if the investment is so substantial that the temptation to the firm to renege is a serious one. Note that although both the 'bond-posting' and 'specific-human-capital' approaches to wages suggest that they will be observed to rise with length of tenure, the two theories differ in important respects. In the bond-posting or deferred compensation scheme, wages rise faster than the productivity of the worker – starting out lower and finishing higher than actual productivity. Where worker and firm share in the finance of specific human capital, wages will rise less fast than productivity – starting out somewhat higher (though below the 'market wage') and finishing lower (as the firm takes a return on *its* share in the human capital formation). Further, because the wage finishes below productivity according to the human capital view, it is not so necessary to insist on retirement at a particular date. Thus, whether a person is seen as receiving 'enforcement rents' or 'rents on specific human capital' makes a difference to the time path of wages.[31]

9.3 Behavioural Norms and Perceptions of Fairness

Williamson (1975, pp. 37–8) argues that 'atmosphere' and 'supplying a satisfying exchange relation' are part of the economic problem. The governance structure of the firm therefore aims not only to develop an environment of trust but also to generate a desire to act cooperatively in the interests of the team effort. There are close parallels here with the 'human relations school' of organisation theory mentioned briefly in section 1. The British system of relying on voluntary blood donors is a much-discussed example of the importance of establishing emotionally satisfying arrangements. A market in blood could be established, but would affect the individual's perception of the act of supplying blood. Titmus (1970) argues that the gift relationship is not only a worthy ideal in itself, but may also produce in certain circumstances a more effective system. The argument is of far wider significance than the blood example alone suggests. Akerlof (1982, 1984) applies the idea of 'gift exchange' to the whole area of labour contracts. Employers pay workers more than market-clearing wages (a gift) and in return they hope for a gift of greater loyalty and effort than would otherwise be forthcoming. He cites evidence from social psychology (Adams, 1965) indicating that people regarding themselves as 'overpaid' are more productive than those merely receiving 'the rate for the job'. The approach is thus a variety of the 'efficiency-wage' theory but relies on the existence of behavioural norms which require reciprocity.

Many analysts of labour markets have argued that observed behaviour is difficult to explain without reference to some notions of 'fairness' and implicit mechanisms of the 'gift exchange' kind. Schlicht (1992) uses the idea of 'wage generosity' and gift exchange to explain the fact that collectively set wages at the industry level in Germany are usually well below those actually paid by firms. Yet, bargaining over the collective norms is often tough and changes do feed through to actual wages paid. No firm likes to be seen as falling short of established standards and most prefer to be generous. Solow (1990) emphasises the development of norms of fairness in explaining the functioning of labour markets. As in the exchange game set out in Chapter 1, and the Hawk–Dove game of Chapter 4, norms of behaviour can evolve in a repeated game setting. These norms may prevent unemployed workers from trying to undercut the employed, or firms from trying to grab an unacceptably large share of the rents available. Solow argues (p. 23) that, 'norms of behaviour can be modelled as constraints on decisions', but, as Alchian notes in the quote at the head of Chapter 4, constraints on decisions can be modelled as property rights. Governance structures, by contributing to the establishment of prevailing norms of behaviour, are implicitly supporting the property claims of workers to income flows that are otherwise vulnerable to opportunism.

9.4   Company Unions and Disputes Procedures

Behavioural norms cannot cover every set of circumstances. The internal labour market reduces the return to opportunism and encourages cooperation by replacing individual bargaining with a set of standard contracts and the promise of promotion. These standard contracts, concerning as they do the relationship of employer and employee over a substantial period of time, cannot be comprehensive in their provisions because of the problem of bounded rationality. As time advances, therefore, disputes will arise concerning the precise interpretation of the vague terminology of the standard contract. In my own case, for example, a contract requires that as a professor of economics I 'perform the duties which are customary for such posts in universities in Great Britain and shall include teaching, research, examining, and if so directed administration'. Whether a daily chore of making the tea for the vice-chancellor could be considered as 'administration' or 'research' would have to be settled by arbitration procedures. The establishment of these arbitration and grievance procedures is thus an integral part of the internal labour market, and is closely associated with the role of trade unions or other associations of employees. Trade unions can be seen as monitoring the firm's commitment to its implicit obligations (Malcolmson, 1982), making 'shirking' by the firm less likely and increasing the confidence of employees in the working of the internal labour market.[32]

10.   THE JAPANESE FIRM

The ideas introduced in this chapter have recently been widely discussed in the context of the contrast between hierarchical structures in Japan and those in the United States and other Western countries. We cannot offer a survey of what is now a very large literature.[33] However, even a cursory sketch reveals how closely the debate follows the theoretical issues. The Japanese system is characterised by three important features:

1.   Japanese workers expect to remain with their employer for longer than do workers in the United States. The name given to this system of 'lifetime employment' is something of a misnomer, since Japanese workers do move when young and face mandatory retirement at a relatively early age.[34] However, Hashimoto and Raisian (1985) found

that a Japanese male worker would typically hold 4.9 jobs before retiring compared with eleven jobs in the case of a typical male worker in the United States. Continuous employment is fostered also by substantial separation payments which vary according to whether the separation is a result of 'private' or 'company' reasons. At the time of mandatory retirement, the separation payment represents, on average, seventy per cent of the present value of retirement benefits provided by companies.[35]

2. Earnings rise with tenure in Japan as in other countries, but the relationship is stronger in Japan than in the United States. Comparing the effect of general labour market experience and firm-specific experience, Hashimoto and Raisian (1985) found that firm-specific experience was more important in Japan as a determinant of earnings, whereas the reverse was true of the United States.

3. Japanese unions are not the industry-wide, general or craft-based unions, common in other countries. They are mainly enterprise unions.[36]

The general significance of these bald observations for our purposes here is simply that they relate closely to the characteristics of internal labour markets discussed earlier. They suggest that Japanese governance arrangements put greater emphasis on the *continuity* of relationships than is the case in the United States. There is a suggestion that either because of greater trust or because of greater investment in specific human capital the relationship between tenure and wages is more pronounced. There is also an implication that the enterprise union plays an important part in monitoring the very specific circumstances of the firm; an undertaking that 'outside' institutions are less well equipped to perform. The role of the union is to mediate on the distribution of rents in an environment where returns to specific human capital are very significant and where the quit threat is worthless.[37]

Differences in institutional structures do not in themselves lead to straightforward inferences about relative efficiency. Not only is the information about institutions continually changing, but varying possible interpretations can be put upon it. Clark and Ogawa (1992), for example, have recently cast doubt on the conventional wisdom about the wage–job tenure relationship in Japan. They show that considerable changes to the wage–tenure relationship have occurred in recent decades as the population has aged, the retirement age has risen, and productivity growth has declined. 'By 1986, the value of an additional year of general experience exceeds the gain from a year of job tenure' (p.344). Further, as Aoki (1990, p.12) argues, how far seniority payments reflect learning (human capital) and how far 'bonding' for diligence, is still not empirically settled.

Another aspect of the Japanese system, which has interested students of business structure, relates not to the role of the firm as a monitoring system but as a means of generating new information. Aoki (1986) contrasts the system by which jobs are defined by function and controlled by a vertical hierarchy according to fixed rules, with a system in which people are expected to accumulate knowledge of a wide range of jobs and take responsibility for coping with emergent events.[38] The former situation (which he admits is overdrawn) represents the American or 'A' firm. The latter is the Japanese or 'J' firm. The American system encourages specialisation and the development of outside markets in these specialist types of labour. The Japanese system encourages wide knowledge of the operations of a particular firm, a great emphasis on learning on the job, and the willingness to act flexibly and cooperatively.[39] Employees see themselves as members of a team rather than of a trade.

This argument of Aoki that the J firm is characterised by horizontal coordination while the A firm represents a system of rational 'hierarchical' control relates closely to the encouragement of entrepreneurship within the firm. The local knowledge accumulated by people in the J firm along with the ability to make suitable minor adjustments to production plans means that it is an excellent vehicle for the small-scale Cassonian entrepreneur and makes good use of 'tacit knowledge'. Information is generated and disseminated to those who will find it useful and continual flexibility at this level is achieved. The rents generated by this type of knowledge are really entrepreneurial in nature. Seniority payments and promotion as a reward for good cooperative performance may then be seen as ways of distributing these entrepreneurial rents between the various members of the team. Small-scale adjustments to evolving conditions are well handled by the J firm according to Aoki. It is not so clear whether the J firm has a similar advantage in the realm of larger scale changes of the Schumpeterian variety. Where old bonds have to be broken, a system which is designed to nurture and protect them may confront awkward choices. This is, however, an issue that is more conveniently discussed in Chapter 7.

11. CONCLUSION

Moral hazard, adverse selection and bounded rationality imply that all transactions must involve trust, and that all transactions involve problems of policing and enforcement. The firm can be seen as a highly developed mechanism of contract enforcement and adjustment to new circumstances – a 'governance structure' (Williamson, 1979, 1985). Governance mechanisms will vary with the type of contract involved and the hazards to which it gives rise. Some transactions are highly standardised and involve limited problems of moral hazard. In Chapter 2, we discussed Alchian's (1979) rationalisation of money as a device to 'standardise' transactions through the use of a medium about which everyone was well informed. Thus, traditional markets are a form of governance structure appropriate for the exchange of money and other standard products. As Williamson (1979) puts it: 'highly standardised transactions are not apt to require a specialised governance structure' (p. 248). Where very idiosyncratic transactions are concerned and knowledge is asymmetrically distributed or continually changing, exchange may be inhibited unless confidence can be established. This confidence requires a continuing association between the transactors, and where recurrent transactions are possible to arrange, a 'highly specialised governance structure' (p. 248) called the firm can develop.

Before leaving the subject of hierarchies and the internal labour market it is necessary to suppress any impression that the firm 'solves' the transactional problems we have been considering. Examples of rent seeking in hierarchical organisations are hardly unknown, and a cooperative attitude, though it may complement an entrepreneurial one, is clearly not the same thing. Williamson, as we have seen, includes as a type of 'cooperation' the use of 'judgement' which, for Casson (Chapter 3) is the defining characteristic of the entrepreneur. The J firm is widely supposed to inculcate this type of cooperation. Yet cooperative people are not always those who take initiative and use judgement, and those who use their judgement are not always very cooperative. Cooperative people 'toe the line' instead of confusing matters by suggesting different lines to toe or arguing that everyone should be pulling in a different direction. The internal labour market may encourage cooperation, but it is much less clear that it encourages initiative of the more disruptive variety.

In a hierarchical organisation, the returns to 'consummate cooperation' have long been recognised. Sir Joseph Porter KCB was certainly very cooperative. Indeed, it would be difficult to imagine cooperation more consummate than was Sir Joseph's:

> I always voted at my party's call,
> I never thought of thinking for myself at all,
> I thought so little they rewarded me,
> And now I am the ruler of the Queen's Navy.

NOTES

1. Alfred Marshall (1925), *Principles of Economics* (8th edn), Book IV, p. 138.
2. From 'HMS Pinafore'.
3. For an excellent overview for the uninitiated see Jackson (1982), Chapter 2. The chapter is specifically designed as a means of giving the economist some background information on the organisation theory literature.
4. Studies undertaken at the Hawthorne works of the Western Electric Company in the late 1920s and 1930s.
5. This approach has been developed more recently by Calvo and Wellisz (1978) and Calvo (1979).
6. Prendergast (1999) provides a recent review of the literature on incentives within firms. See also Lazear (1995) and (2000a).
7. Note that all through this section the outcome is perfectly observable and hence the usual objection to piece-rates, that quality will suffer, does not follow. Where output is not perfectly observable and is subject to quality variations, the quota piece-rate has obvious disadvantages and requires costly quality-control procedures. These are briefly discussed in section 3.1. If customers are well informed about quality, however, and franchise arrangements can be instituted, observability will not present a problem, as we saw in Chapter 5. Workers will have an incentive to maintain quality.
8. In this model, therefore, high-quality workers prefer steeper payment schedules. This is not always the case. In section 3, below, a case is discussed in which the workers are risk averse and higher 'quality' implies greater effort efficiency. A given level of effort is then achievable with lower incentives (and hence lower risk-sharing losses) with high-quality rather than low-quality workers. Here we are assuming that output is linearly related to quality. Low-quality workers are never as effective as high-quality ones no matter how hard they work, and we are abstracting from questions of risk.
9. So-called 'leniency bias'. See Prendergast (1999) for a review of these issues.
10. Further comments on opportunism and 'rent-seeking' in hierarchies can be found in section 8.
11. Lazear (1995), Chapter 2 provides an accessible model of the gains to worker sorting.
12. We are assuming, of course, that there are no 'consumption' benefits to be had from acquiring the relevant qualifications.
13. An intuitive discussion of this situation can be found in Hirshleifer and Riley (1979, p. 1407).
14. Duration of unemployment will have a geometric distribution with mean $1/p$ where p is the probability of finding a job in a given period.
15. 'The type of unemployment we have characterised here is very different from search unemployment. Here, all workers and firms are identical. There is perfect information about job availability. There is a different information problem: firms are assumed (quite reasonably in our view) not to be able to monitor the activities of their employees costlessly and perfectly' (Shapiro and Stiglitz (1984), p. 439.
16. Higher unemployment pay will reduce the incentive effects of a given wage level. Firms will raise wages in order to maintain incentives and a larger unemployment pool will result – see Shapiro and Stiglitz (1984), p. 439).
17. Another version is that of Salop (1979) who argues that higher wages reduce labour turnover and reduce recruitment and training costs to the firm. For a review see Yellen (1984).
18. See again, Chapter 2, note 2.
19. Lazear (2000a, pp. 618–19) uses his database on pay and productivity at the Safelite Glass company to show that, during the period that workers were paid by time-rates, earnings per day were much more strongly related to tenure (measured by years of service) than to output per day. A study of self-employed and employed people undertaking similar tasks showed the time profile of the former to be flatter. See Lazear and Moore (1984).

20. One mechanism for inducing the firm to monitor honestly is 'up-or-out' promotion. Under this system, the firm commits not just to promoting a given fraction of the workforce but to dispensing with the services of those it does not promote. If termination implies a period of unemployment, this system will increase the risk-bearing costs of employees. It will also force the firm to 'waste' any specific human capital built up by those it does not promote.

21. Anecdotal evidence suggests that this is not impossible in certain circumstances, as when a bureaucracy promotes someone to reduce the damage they are inflicting in their present job. Presumably this is more likely in a non-competitive environment.

22. The discussion below is informal. An appendix at the end of this chapter provides a more technical justification for some of the reasoning.

23. It turns out that the second-order conditions require that $a > \pi^*$.

24. Lazear and Rosen (1981) discuss the case of a tournament with risk-averse contestants.

25. See also Frey (1993a) and Frey (1993b).

26. Further discussion of related issues can be found below in subsection 9.3 and in chapters 10 and 11 on profit-sharing and non-profit enterprise.

27. It is worth emphasising that this concept of rent seeking as the pursuit of transfers by the challenging of property rights is not intended to be normative. It in no way follows that entrepreneurship is desirable and rent seeking undesirable by definition. To take an obvious example, a slave who challenges his master's rights by running away is a rent seeker, while the trader in slaves could be an entrepreneur. Clearly, the desirability of a given system of property rights is a conceptually separate issue from that of determining whether someone is attempting to undermine them or is accepting them as a framework for his or her transactions. The identification of rent seeking does require, however, that the status quo is well defined, and this may not always be the case.

28. There is an analogy here with the problem of public sector contracts. 'Cost-plus' agreements run the risk of encouraging rent seeking. 'Fixed-price' agreements imply greater risks for the contractor and require the product to be closely specified, but they encourage entrepreneurship. More detailed discussion of these issues can be found in Chapter 15.

29. This statement requires qualification. Becker (1965, p. 154) recognises that certain features of employment contracts suggest that firms hedge their bets. Thus, 'incompletely vested pension plans may be used because they help to insure firms against a loss on their specific investment'. This, though, represents a method of binding the employee to the firm as a long-term commitment with remuneration rising over time (see the arguments of Lazear (1979, 1981) reviewed in section 5.2). It is thus really a way of making employees pay for specific training by posting a bond to be repaid later.

30. It is important to remember that property rights are not dependent entirely on legislation. Property rights 'are to be construed as supported by the force of etiquette, social custom, ostracism, and formal, legally enacted laws supported by the state's power of violence or punishment' (Alchian, 1965, p. 129).

31. Hutchens (1989) provides a review of the theory and evidence on 'seniority' payments. See also Carmichael (1989).

32. A less positive view can be taken of union activity in an internal labour market. Siebert and Addison (1991) discuss the role of unions in extending the internal labour market.

33. See Hashimoto (1990) for a general review of Employment and Wage systems in Japan. Aoki (1989) investigates a whole range of institutions from the point of view of incentives and bargaining. Other general references include Dore (1986) and Yasuba and Yamamura (1988).

34. In the United States, the Age Discrimination in Employment Act (1978) and (1986) makes mandatory retirement rare.

35. Aoki (1989, p. 58). Carmichael (1989) notes that as a result of reform in the United States, the complete vesting of pension rights means that even dismissed workers receive a pension. There is thus no contingent payment to motivate workers as they approach retirement. If pension rights are based on final salary, however, promotion shortly before

36. At 23 per cent of the workforce in 1985, the rate of unionisation was not notably high.
37. See Aoki (1989, pp. 86–94) for a discussion of the role of the enterprise union in Japan.
38. Koike (1990) emphasises the role of intellectual skill and the ability to cope with changes on the shop floor.
39. It is the flexibility and horizontal coordination of Japanese firms, according to this view, that explains their success with 'just in time' stock-control systems which rely on highly decentralised responsibility for ordering parts.

Note: the line "retirement will be an incentive. A few years of shirking at the end of a successful career could be viewed as part of the prize." belongs to footnote 35 continued above footnote 36.

APPENDIX

The first-order condition for maximising expected benefits of effort for person j will be

$$\pi^* \partial p / \partial e_j = C'(e_j) \tag{6.4}$$

The dependence of p (the probability of winning the tournament) on j's effort now requires closer investigation.

Let e_j^* be the monitor's observation of j's effort. This is subject to an error θ_j with mean zero. Thus

$$e_j^* = e_j + \theta_j$$

Person j wins the prize π_1 if $e_j^* > e_k^*$ where e_k^* is the monitor's observation of person k's effort. We suppose that the error (θ_k) associated with observation of person k is distributed in exactly the same way as that associated with observing person j. Thus:

$$e_j^* - e_k^* = (e_j + \theta_j) - (e_k + \theta_k) = (e_j - e_k) - (\theta_k - \theta_j)$$

and

$$p(e_j^* > e_k^*) = p(\theta_k - \theta_j < e_j - e_k).$$

The probability that j will be observed to work harder than k therefore depends upon how hard he or she really does work relative to k. The larger is $e_j - e_k$ the less likely it is that observational errors will be big enough to cause a perverse result to the tournament. This is what gives person j the incentive to exert effort.

Assume the distribution of θ_k and θ_j is uniform (rectangular). It is sketched in Figure 6.6. The distribution $f(\theta)$ is assumed to range from $-\frac{1}{2}$ to $+\frac{1}{2}$. Thus it is possible (though very unlikely) that person j may be

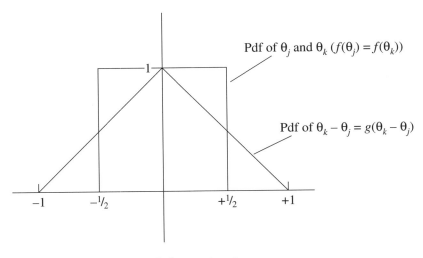

Figure 6.6   Distribution of observational errors

observed to have exerted effort $e_j + \frac{1}{2}$ or $e_j - \frac{1}{2}$. The probability is 0.5 that person j will be observed working harder than he or she does in fact work, and 0.5 that s/he will be observed working less hard.

Person j will be concerned with the distribution of $(\theta_k - \theta_j)$; that is, the *difference* in observational errors. Clearly, person j will not mind if the monitor underestimates how hard s/he is working if the monitor also underestimates how hard person k is working by an equivalent or bigger amount. The distribution $g(\theta_k - \theta_j)$ is shown in Figure 6.6. Its shape may be intuitively understood by taking a discrete example and assuming that the monitor's errors will be either $-\frac{1}{2}$, 0, or $+\frac{1}{2}$ with equal probabilities. Clearly, if $\theta_k = \frac{1}{2}$ and $\theta_j = -\frac{1}{2}$, $\theta_k - \theta_j = 1$. This is the biggest value that $\theta_k - \theta_j$ can take, and is very unlikely since there is only one way it can happen. A value of $\theta_k - \theta_j = \frac{1}{2}$ is more likely, since there are two ways this might occur ($\theta_k = \frac{1}{2}$, $\theta_j = 0$; and $\theta_k = 0$, $\theta_j = -\frac{1}{2}$). Finally, there are three ways $\theta_k - \theta_j = 0$ can occur (the monitor makes the same or no error for both persons j and k, $\theta_k = -\frac{1}{2}$, $\theta_j = -\frac{1}{2}$, and so on).

Figure 6.7 sketches the cumulative distribution function $G(\theta_k - \theta_j)$; that is, it indicates the probability of $\theta_k - \theta_j$ being less than or equal to the specified value. Clearly $\theta_k - \theta_j$ is certain to be less than or equal to $+1$ and cannot fall below -1. The function cuts the vertical axis at $p = \frac{1}{2}$ since $p(\theta_k - \theta_j < 0) = \frac{1}{2}$.

In general, $G(e_j - e_k)$ will give the probability of person j winning the tournament at the specified effort levels of persons j and k. That is, it will give us $p(\theta_k - \theta_j < e_j - e_k)$. The *change* in the probability of winning the

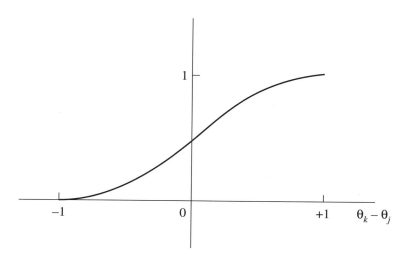

Figure 6.7   Cumulative distribution function of $\theta_k - \theta_j$

tournament brought about by an extra unit of effort will therefore be $G'(e_j - e_k) = g(e_j - e_k)$.

From Figure 6.6 it can be seen that the equation of $g(e_j - e_k)$ can be written $1 - (e_j - e_k)$ for $e_j > e_k$ and $1 + (e_j - e_k)$ for $e_j < e_k$. Thus the first-order condition 6.4 can be written $\pi^*[1 - (e_j - e_k)] = ae_j$ for $e_j > e_k$ and $\pi^*[1 + (e_j - e_k)] = ae_j$ for $e_j < e_k$.

7. Integration and the visible hand

'The forces determining the shape and size and activities of industrial
organisations do not hammer them out like the Brigade of Guards.'
(R.S. Edwards and H. Townsend)

1. THE VARIETY OF BUSINESS ENTERPRISE

The firm investigated in Chapter 6 was beginning to take on some of the
characteristics of hierarchical organisations and to reflect a few of the
structural features associated with modern business enterprise, but our discussion of internal structure is hardly complete. We have presented various
attempts at rationalising employment hierarchies, yet many other characteristics of the firm remain to be considered. In this chapter we consider
explicitly the question of the determinants of the size and scope of firms.
Firms, as was noted at the very beginning of Chapter 1, vary greatly in size
from organisations of tens of thousands of employees which generate
income for those involved equivalent to the national income of some independent nation states, to small local business enterprises, one-person businesses and partnerships. Why do we observe this variety? If hierarchies have
the incentive properties noted in Chapter 6, why not organise the whole
economy as one gigantic hierarchy? What forces determine the limits of the
firm and at what point do alternative contractual arrangements begin to
reassert themselves?

Pure size is not the only matter of interest. Size is related to, and perhaps
even the outcome of, decisions concerning the scope of the firm. Some
firms are highly specialised while others undertake an apparently diverse set
of activities. This diversity of activity is usually reflected in three dimensions – vertical, lateral and geographical.

1.1 Vertical Integration

Production of final output usually requires materials to be transformed
through many intermediate stages. In some instances, a single firm will
attempt to integrate these stages, even where quite different technical

problems may be encountered at each stage. Historically well-known examples of 'spectacular' backward vertical integration are the acquisition by Lever in the early twentieth century of raw material investments in West Africa in order to supply his requirements for vegetable oils used in soap and margarine manufacture. Dunlop also integrated backwards into rubber plantations, Guest Keen and Nettlefolds and Tube Investments (the engineering companies) into steel production in the 1950s, and General Motors (in the USA) into the production of motor-car bodies and other components (1929). The last case was mirrored later in the UK with the acquisition by Ford of Briggs Motor Bodies Ltd, and of Fisher and Ludlow Ltd by the British Motor Corporation in 1952, and it has been the focus of some theoretical interest in recent years (section 5.4). Examples of forward vertical integration include the ownership by brewers of public houses ('tied houses') or of petrol stations by oil refiners, and also special links between motor manufacturers and dealers.

Examples can be found, however, of companies that have not integrated backwards or forwards in this way, or at least have remained specialised at a particular stage for a substantial period of time. From the late eighteenth century to the 1950s, for example, Guinness specialised in what used to be called porter and is now known to most people only as 'Guinness'. In 1951, a director of Guinness could write[1] 'Nothing in the nature of either vertical or horizontal trustification was attempted.' Guinness produced only a little malt – 'just enough to give them a clear insight into all the problems of barley and malt'. They owned no retail outlets. 'They have done just one thing and done it better than anyone else. That policy has been fixed at the top and has run right through at all levels.' Until the last quarter of the twentieth century, therefore, a deliberate business strategy of specialisation was adopted at Guinness. At the retail level, a similar strategy appears to be pursued by most chain stores. Again, in the mid-1950s Dr A.J. Sainsbury wrote that[2] 'It has never been our policy to manufacture a considerable proportion of the goods we sell', while other famous stores in the UK such as Marks and Spencer also purchase their wares on the open market. The rise of 'own brands' by which Sainsbury's, Tesco and other chain stores vouch for the quality of some item but arrange for its manufacture by an 'independent' firm is, however, an interesting form of 'integration' which highlights the difficulty of distinguishing where in the spectrum of contractual arrangements the boundary between market and firm is to be found.

1.2   Conglomerate Diversification

Some firms, vertically integrated or otherwise, still operate within a limited sphere. This may be defined technologically in terms of a specific limited

type of output, or by concentration on products all derived from a particular input or particular industrial process. Thus, Edwards and Townsend
(1967) write of the history of Pilkington Brothers up until the mid-1950s
as follows: 'Pilkington Brothers have grown by stretching backwards into
earlier stages of production, forwards into processing and distribution of
glass, and sideways into the manufacture of additional glass products; their
growth has taken them all over the world but it has always been concerned
with glass' (p. 60). Other firms seem capable of undertaking operations in
apparently 'distant' areas. Products may be quite different both in terms of
the market served (with very low cross-price elasticities of demand) and of
the technology and inputs required. The growth of these 'conglomerate'
organisations was a notable feature of the four decades up to the mid-1980s
and the links between the component parts of such enterprises are not
always very obvious. The history of Guinness is an interesting example of
the changing patterns of recent business enterprise. From the textbook
example of a specialised firm, strategy changed radically, and in the mid-
1980s, Guinness became involved in a notorious takeover battle for
Distillers, and extended its interests into other areas. The goal became the
development of 'an international brand-orientated consumer products
business'.[3]

The great variety of activities undertaken in a conglomerate does not
imply that there is no underlying logic to its development, and the history
of each enterprise usually reveals the sometimes surprising links between
apparently quite different industrial processes. Technological developments
and marketing skills clearly play an important role in moulding the modern
conglomerate. Guinness, to pursue this example further, has always been
celebrated for its advertising and its skill in marketing a 'branded' product.
It may be that this expertise which can be applied in other areas, rather than
detailed knowledge of the properties of stout or porter, is the more valuable under modern conditions and is to form the foundation for future
developments. Knowledge not of a particular product but of how to
develop and sell new ones must feature prominently in any attempt to make
sense of the widely diversified corporation. An important objective of this
chapter will be to discuss why firms rather than markets may be an appropriate institutional response to the problem of coordinating resources in a
world of continual technical change.

1.3 International Integration

Another form of integration which has developed rapidly in recent years is
geographical integration; the combining in a single firm of operations in
many different locations and often in different countries. Standard theory

is hard pressed to explain this phenomenon. It may, of course, be a simple consequence of vertical integration, if raw material supplies are derived from different countries. The structure of many multinational enterprises, however, cannot be explained in this way, and once again it is to the problem of information that modern analysis has turned, in an attempt to find the forces which encourage the development of this geographically dispersed type of corporation.

2. STRATEGY AND STRUCTURE

The degree of vertical, lateral, conglomerate or international integration reflects the firm's strategic development. Another important feature of the firm is its internal administrative structure. In Chapter 6, we investigated the incentive properties of simple hierarchies, but we did not consider in what ways administrative systems might differ and whether any differences between firms might be explicable using the framework of transactions costs. Just as, at the beginning of Chapter 6, it was to the literature on management science that we turned for the early analysis of hierarchies, so it is to the business history literature that we must refer for the first attempts to analyse developments of business structure and to consider possible links between changes in structure and changes in strategy.

Chandler (1977) considers the impact of the railroad and the telegraph on business organisation in the United States during the nineteenth century. Although economic historians have hardly overlooked the importance of the railroad, the purely administrative achievement which they represented is not something that has been emphasised. Chandler points out that before the 1840s there were no business hierarchies in the United States and no middle managers. A railroad, however, requires a relatively complex administration to undertake the function of scheduling the trains, contracting for fuel and other supplies, maintaining rolling stock and track, selling tickets to passengers or arranging for the carriage of freight and so forth. In short, 'the operational requirements of the railroads demanded the creation of the first administrative hierarchies in American business' (p. 87). The typical administrative solution adopted during the nineteenth century, both in the US and in the UK, to the problems encountered as the scale of operations grew was the so called 'functional' or 'unitary' (U)-form. Although the scale of business enterprise developed rapidly, its scope remained limited. The improvements in communication brought about by the railroad and telegraph encouraged forward vertical integration into wholesaling for some branded goods, and even into retailing with the development of 'new complex, high priced machines that required specialised marketing services – demonstration, installation, consumer credit, after-sales service and repair' (p. 288); but the typical firm was not highly diversified and the U-form was the standard corporate structure.

Figure 7.1 illustrates the structure of a U-form enterprise. It is centralised and divided into departments which specialise in certain enterprise-wide functions. For illustrative purposes, the functions identified are the conventional production, sales and finance; but we might also have added other possible functions depending upon the character of the enterprise, such as research and development, personnel and distribution. This U-form structure reflects the advantages of arranging both for managers to specialise in the problems of a particular function and for communication to be established mainly along functional lines. Production managers communicate primarily with other production workers and, for the most part, do not require detailed information about finance or marketing. Given the bounds on the individual's information-processing capacity, each manager is left to concentrate on specific links that are expected to be most important for his or her particular purpose or function.

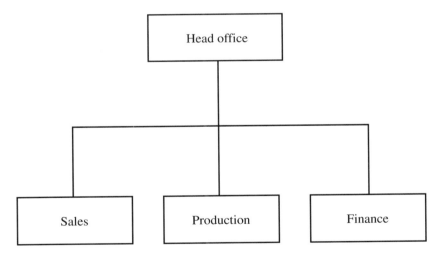

Figure 7.1   The unitary form

For enterprises with a limited scope, this system had (and has) definite advantages. Problems were encountered only when the firm began to undertake an increasing variety of activities and operate in many different geographical locations. The production and marketing problems arising in the field of one product may have very little connection with the production and marketing problems arising in another. In consequence, functional managers begin to become overloaded, attempting to make sense of flows of information which do not have many links between them. A firm manufacturing products such as shampoo, hair dyes and ethical drugs may find, for example, that the sales effort needs to be 'divisionalised'. Ethical drugs may be marketed by visits to doctors and hospitals by a specialised staff of trained representatives. Shampoo requires large-scale advertising and may be sold through thousands of retail outlets. The same management team will find it difficult to cope with the problems of both sectors simultaneously.

The gradually extending scope of the firm during the 1920s and 1930s in the United States led to experiments with different administrative structures and ultimately to what is now termed the multidivisional or M-form. Chandler traces these developments to a few major firms, such as Du Pont and General Motors. The innovation consisted of a set of 'divisions' based upon products or geographical areas, with a management organised within each division on functional lines to take responsibility for short-run operational decisions. Over these divisions was a 'general office' with the task of planning long-term strategy and monitoring divisional performance. Figure 7.2 illustrates the 'pure' case of the multidivisional structure in the context of the 'conglomerate'. Many intermediate cases could be envisaged, of course, and it would be a mistake to consider the business history of the last seventy years simply as comprising the general gradual adoption of the 'superior' M-form of organisation. The M-form structure is better adapted than the U-form to a particular type of strategic development, especially conglomerate and multinational expansion, and the diversified corporation could not have reached the stage that it has without this organisational innovation, but firms adopting a more specialised strategy will not necessarily be divisionalised, or may adopt a hybrid organisational form.

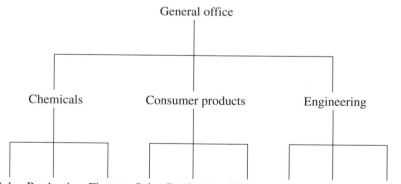

Figure 7.2   The multidivisional structure

Underlying the choice of organisational structure are the same considerations which have proved important throughout this book. Information must be collected and deciphered, responses put into effect, and inputs policed. If information about the market in hair dyes, shampoos, setting lotions and the like is jointly produced, it is reasonable to prevent duplication and to attach responsibility for these products to a single office. On the other hand there may be almost no connection between the market in shampoo and that in cough mixture and even less with drugs which can be obtained only from a doctor. In these circumstances, sales might be divisionalised into consumer products, patent medicines and ethical drugs. Research and development, on the other hand, might not be divisionalised and serve the entire organisation, depending upon perceptions about possible links between research into cough mixture and other drugs. Figure 7.3 illustrates the corporate structure of an entirely imaginary corporation, specialising in chemical products that are all more or less related to 'personal health'. If it were the case that the same production lines could be used to make and pack shampoo as could make and pack cough mixture, production would not be controlled by the divisions but would become 'functionalised', and the company would become increasingly U-form.

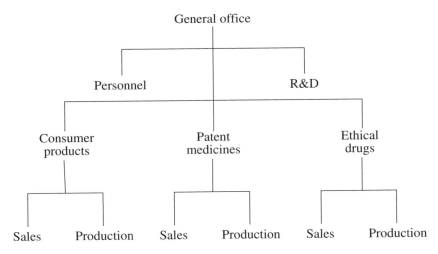

Figure 7.3   A hybrid form

Economies in the collection and use of information therefore represent an important determinant of organisational structure. Kay (1982, 1983) presents an analysis of structure based squarely on informational links: 'Wherever a potential link exists it may give rise to a potential economy; for example by facilitating specialisation and division of labour, or by improved exploitation of an indivisible resource' (1984, p. 95). Information which may have consequences for a number of different activities is just such an 'indivisible' resource. Communicating information to others can present severe problems (a factor which will be of great importance in section 6), and this leads to the boundaries between decision units being drawn 'to minimise necessary exchanges of information' (p. 102). 'Strategy thus determines structure; the extent and content of links dictate the appropriate form of internal organisation' (p. 103). In the context of the large, complex corporation, the M-form, in Williamson's words 'served both to economise on bounded rationality and attenuate opportunism' (1981, p. 1556). Kay (1983, Ch. 6) concentrates on information-handling economies and bounded rationality; problems that would exist even in the absence of opportunism, though Williamson's reference to opportunism reminds us that corporate structure will also affect the ability to police inputs.

Because the staff at the general office are relieved of day-to-day operational responsibilities, much of their time is spent in considering strategic alternatives and monitoring the divisions. Two significant theoretical propositions have flowed from this observation.

1. If the general office is seen as charting the overall progress of the corporation, it will have control over investment resources, which it will allocate to the various divisions. In Chapter 6, we considered Williamson's idea of the firm as an 'internal labour market'. Here, in Chapter 7, we come across the idea of the firm as an 'internal capital market'. In both instances, the words 'allocation mechanism' might be more appropriate than the word 'market', since the whole point is that pure market forms of contract are superseded by 'non-market' forms. The terminology, however, is now quite well established. This idea of the firm as a response to transactions costs in the capital market will be considered in greater detail in sections 4 and 6.

2. The existence of a group of general managers monitoring the divisions may increase the efficiency of operations and induce greater effort. This has been termed the 'M-form hypothesis'. Organisation along M-form lines 'favours goal pursuit and least cost behaviour more nearly associated with the neoclassical profit maximisation hypothesis than does the U-form organisational alternative' (Williamson, 1975, p. 150). The M-form represents a more efficient monitoring environment and the gains, it is argued, will be reflected in the profitability of the firms which adopt it. This hypothesis has stimulated a number of empirical studies. Armour and Teece (1978), for example, studied a sample of petroleum firms covering the period 1955–73 and found a positive relationship

between M-form structure and profitability 'during the period in which the M-form innovation was being diffused' (p. 106). In the period 1969–73, however, differential performance between M-form organisation and other forms was not observed and the authors inferred that 'the sample firms were, in general, appropriately organised' (p. 118). Thus, there is no assumption that M-form organisations are more efficient under all circumstances, but merely that for certain types of firm the M-form innovation was profitable. Over time, imitation reduces the profits accruing to the innovating firms.

Another study by Teece (1981) covered a wider range of industrial activities. It involved identifying the first firm in an industry (in the case of conglomerate enterprise this is, of course, not an easy concept to define) to adopt the M-form of organisation. This firm was tagged 'the leading firm' and its performance was compared with a second firm 'the control firm', as close to the leading firm as possible in terms of product range and size, which adopted the M-form later. Performance was compared in two time periods. In the first, only the leading firm was organised in an M-form. In the second, both firms were M-form. The economic hypothesis was that the 'control' firm would improve its performance relative to the 'leading' firm in the second period. Two statistical tests rejected the 'null hypothesis' that there was no effect on performance of organisational form (that is, that the probability of observing an 'improvement' in the second period was the same as the probability of observing a 'deterioration' on the part of the 'control' firm).[4]

In the UK, adoption of the M-form took place later than in the USA (Channon, 1973). ICI was evolving a divisionalised structure as early as the 1930s (Hannah, 1983a, pp. 81–5) and this was fully established by the mid-1950s, described in such textbooks as Edwards and Townsend (1967, p. 67). This experience, however, was not typical. Just as the UK lagged by several decades in the merger movement which established the framework of the 'corporate economy' at the end of the nineteenth century and the very beginning of the twentieth century in the USA, there was a similar lag in the development of managerial structures to cope. Between the two World Wars, many firms in the UK were 'loosely run confederations of subsidiaries with little central control' (Hannah, 1983a, p. 87). As was reported in Chapter 4, Chandler identifies family management and the absence of a managerial class as reasons for UK backwardness. In the USA, adoption of the M-form of organisation and the rapid development of conglomerate and multinational enterprise were associated with the 1940s and 1950s. In the UK (and other European countries), these changes appear to have been delayed until the 1960s and 1970s. When they did arrive, the evidence of studies by Steer and Cable (1978) and Thompson (1981) is that the organisational changes had substantial effects consistent with the M-form hypothesis.

3. VISIBLE AND INVISIBLE HANDS

3.1   The Boundary of the Firm

From sections 1 and 2 of this chapter we have seen that the 'visible hand' can guide the process of resource allocation and integrate vertical, lateral, conglomerate or international transactions using a variety of corporate structures. As has been remarked in earlier chapters, however, the distinction between visible and invisible hands is less clear than the terminology suggests. As Klein, Crawford and Alchian (1978) put it 'the conventional sharp distinction between markets and firms may have little general analytical importance' (p. 326). When thinking about the firm, it is natural to envisage the factory and office buildings, the machines and equipment, the signs proclaiming the company name, and perhaps even the wrought-iron gates confidently symbolising the idea that there is a clear boundary to be drawn between what goes on inside and what goes on outside. Begin to think in terms of the transactions involved, however, and the buildings and offices look increasingly 'open plan', the gate is perpetually ajar, and the evanescent firm appears to have all the substance of the residual grin on Alice's Cheshire cat. It would, however, be prudent to avoid the fate of the unfortunate sheepdog in Hardy's novel[5], which, concluding that it was employed to run after sheep, drove them over a precipice and was shot for its pains, a result 'which so often attends dogs and other philosophers who follow out a train of reasoning to its logical conclusion'. Our aim is to pursue the firm in an attempt to learn more about it; not to hound it to existinction.

Nevertheless, a transactions cost approach to economics does make a clear definition of 'the firm' difficult, and theorists have avoided the problem by concentrating instead on the question of why contractual arrangements differ as circumstances differ. In some cases, 'market-like' contracts are adopted; in other cases, contracts are more 'firm-like'. 'Firm-like' contracts, it will be recalled, govern the transactions between the parties involved over a long period of time. They are also, because of bounded rationality, *incompletely specified* and leave many obligations implicit. 'Market-like' contracts, by contrast, are (in the purest case) *completely specified*, with obligations perfectly understood and explicit. Because of bounded rationality, such contracts can involve only the simplest transactions and relatively short periods of time. So clearly is the contract specified and so easily is it policed that the identity of the buyer or seller is of no consequence and transactions can be almost 'anonymous', as when someone purchases a raw material such as copper of verifiable quality on a specialised market.

The first stage in the substitution of 'firm-like' for pure market relationships occurs, therefore, when the specific identity of buyers and sellers begins to matter. In a very stable, unchanging environment, information asymmetries and adverse selection might inhibit trade, but the development of specialised dealers in the various goods and services with a valuable 'reputation' to protect (as described by Alchian, see Chapter 2) will enable exchange to proceed. Any 'reputable dealer' will suffice for the purposes of buying or selling, and there will be no particular reason for always using the same one. Static conditions therefore greatly favour the use of markets and correspondingly restrict the scope of the firm. Where contractual requirements are complex and uncertain, bounded rationality leads both to implicit contracts and a much increased scope for moral hazard and the exercise of opportunism. It then becomes advantageous to develop a continuing trading relationship with particular suppliers. These suppliers (like the labour force in Chapter 6) gain in the experience of perceiving what the customer wants, satisfying a particular customer's changing requirements and coping with the idiosyncrasies of the tasks in hand. A continuing relationship is also central to the problem of policing the behaviour of suppliers. Thus, as Spence (1975) remarks, 'many of the structural features of resource allocation problems appear similar in markets and in organisations' (p. 171).

The requirements of a continuing association able to respond flexibly to new circumstances, and capable of providing incentives leading to cooperation instead of opportunism, gives rise to the 'firm'. As we saw at the end of Chapter 6, Williamson (1979) refers to the firm as a governance structure. However, the boundaries of such a structure, and the boundaries of the firm as defined by the law, will not necessarily coincide. Continuing relationships, embodying procedures for adjudicating in the event of disputes and including monitoring and incentive devices, can evolve between legally quite separate firms. The governance structure idea has something in common with Edwards and Townsend's definition of the firm as 'an area of unified business planning' (p. 64) although it is important not to interpret this as implying that each firm is a miniature 'command economy'. Some firms may adopt procedures which are quite decentralised, as was seen in section 2.

3.2 Arm's Length and Obligational Transactional Relations

The contrast between 'firm-like' and 'market-like' transactional arrangements is sometimes linked to the idea of 'obligation'. It is often argued, for example, that contracts in the United Kingdom and the United States are arm's length whereas in Japan they are obligational. These concepts are not simply related to 'internal' and 'external' transactions, however. It does not follow, for example, that Japanese firms are more highly vertically integrated than are those in the United States. Indeed, the contrary seems to be the case. The greater continuity and trust associated with obligational transacting in Japan results in a generally lower level of vertical integration. 'Outside' contracts can achieve levels of coordination in Japan that require integration and 'inside' contracts in the United States.

It would be a gross oversimplification, however, to think that arm's length contracting does not occur in Japan or that obligational relationships are never to be found in the United States or the United Kingdom. There is a spectrum of contractual relationships. Sako (1990), in a study of buyer–supplier relations in Japan and the United Kingdom, contrasted various characteristics of the contracts which she found in the electronics industry. Suppliers in the UK tended to have larger numbers of customers, with a lower level of dependency on any particular one. British suppliers could not count on repeat orders to the same extent as companies in Japan. Transactions tended to be more 'legalistic', with written documents playing a greater role in the United Kingdom. Trust, as measured by the willingness of suppliers to manufacture in advance of receipt of an order or by the willingness of buyers to forgo quality inspection, was generally lower in the United Kingdom. In other words the conventional contrast in transactional styles was supported by the evidence, but it was also true that variations occurred within each sector and that relationships between some buyers and suppliers could have pronounced obligational features even in the United Kingdom.

More recent work by Helper and Sako (1995) and Sako *et al.* (1998) has investigated supplier relations in the automotive industry. They find that supplier–customer relations in this industry are becoming more 'relational' and less 'arm's length' in the United States and the UK, although survey responses provided little evidence that suppliers felt their customers were becoming more trustworthy. The average length of contract offered to suppliers in the UK rose from one year in 1990 to three years in 1994. Similarly the median length rose from one year to one and a half years in the US (Sako *et al.*, 1998, p. 183). This might be interpreted as a sign of greater 'commitment' between suppliers and customers. In Japan, there was a slight move towards 'exit' rather than 'voice' relationships but it was not clear whether this represented the beginning of a long-run trend or a response to a cyclical contraction.[6] Empirical studies of buyer–supplier relations are playing an important role in the discussion of different theories of economic organisation. In particular, these studies have cast doubt on both property rights and transactions cost theory. Japanese subcontracting seems to indicate that the existence of transactional hazards can be handled using methods short of the common ownership of the assets (as in the Grossman–Hart framework) or the establishment of 'unified governance' within a single firm (as in the Williamson framework). Instead, the importance of repeat dealing and the evolution of trust between legally separate firms in a durable relationship is emphasised.[7]

3.3 The Franchise Chain

A set of 'outside' contracts which produce a form of economic organisation similar to a single 'firm' is the franchise chain. In a typical franchise contract, the franchisee pays a fee to the franchisor for the right to market a particular 'branded' product or service. The franchisee agrees to run the business in the manner stipulated so that product, price, hours of operation, personnel policies and so on may be standard throughout the chain. The franchisor may provide assistance in the form of managerial training or site selection, and the franchisee will usually pay a royalty in the form of a percentage of sales. Rubin (1978) notes that a common explanation for these arrangements is that outside capital is attracted, and that franchising is a method of tapping the capital provided by the franchisee. However, the explanation is clearly suspect since, if the franchisee is risk averse, s/he would prefer a 'share' in the profits of the entire franchise chain rather than the right to the return from a single outlet in the chain. Risk-spreading considerations would therefore work against the franchise as an efficient form of economic organisation unless franchisees are all risk neutral. Yet the success of franchising in particular areas suggests that it has its advantages. The explanation favoured by Rubin is in terms of monitoring and control within the firm. Usually, the franchisee is physically removed from the franchisor (as, for example, in a fast-food chain) and detailed monitoring would be extremely costly. Incentives can be provided instead by paying a franchise fee for the right to run the business for some period of time.

If the franchise chain is an institutional response to the incentives problem, why do not franchisees keep all the profits attributable to their business? Why does the franchisor typically receive a royalty? Rubin argues that the franchisor also requires incentives. The profitability of a given outlet does not depend exclusively on how that particular outlet is managed. It also depends on the image of the product generally with potential customers, and this 'goodwill' is the primary responsibility of the franchisor. The franchisor is responsible for policing quality, and ensuring that each franchisee maintains the correct standards. Through advertising, the franchisor also attempts to keep the distinctive features of the product known to the consuming public. Without the royalty, the franchisor would have a smaller incentive to pay attention to these activities. Thus, Rubin concludes (p. 230) that,

> in those businesses where there is much managerial discretion, we would expect a higher percentage of the revenue of the franchisor to come from the initial fee and a relatively lower percentage to come from royalties . . . Second, where the trademark is more valuable we would expect more of the franchisor's revenue to come from royalties, for this would create an incentive for him to be efficient in policing and maintaining value.

Martin (1988) takes the analysis further by investigating industries with differing proportions of managed and franchised operations in the United States. He argues that young firms may grow by franchising, not because of capital constraints but because franchising economises on management resources which would otherwise be very stretched. As firms mature, franchise contracts expire and direct monitoring may replace them. The proportion of company-owned outlets, in other words, should increase with the age of the chain. This 'life-cycle hypothesis' does not imply, however, that franchising is always simply a transitory form of organisation. In some circumstances, it will be a stable organisational form. High costs of monitoring will obviously militate against the managed outlet, and very 'noisy' (in a statistical sense) or uncertain environments will therefore favour franchising. Urban environments make monitoring more reliable because results are more predictable. Rural locations are more variable, which reinforces the franchising solution. The greater incidence of repeat buying in rural areas also favours franchising because the franchisee will have a smaller incentive to free ride on the brand-name capital of the chain.[8]

3.4 Quasi-vertical Integration

A further case of interest, which will be considered again in section 5, is a transaction which involves the buyer of an input providing the supplier with raw materials or important items of equipment necessary for its production. This has been termed quasi-vertical integration. Quasi-vertical integration has been defined by Monteverde and Teece (1982b) as 'the ownership by a downstream firm of the specialised tools, dies, jigs and patterns used in the fabrication of components for larger systems' (p. 321). The buyer contracts 'in the market' for the supply of the desired input but has property rights in the equipment necessary for production to take place.

Another form of quasi-vertical integration, undertaken for rather different reasons, occurs when a company trains specialist staff necessary to sell its goods effectively, but then uses the premises and other inputs of an independent retail store. In this case, the company is attempting to gain greater control over the 'human' rather than the 'physical' capital. Examples would include the use of a particular area in a department store for the sale of glass, chinaware or cosmetics, supplied by specialist companies and staffed by their trainees. A further option is the use of a franchise contract which gives the holder of the franchise an incentive to market a product with enthusiasm, if not always with the greatest care. The 'firm-like' features of this contract have already been discussed in subsection 3.3.

Integration, whether horizontal, vertical or geographical, may therefore be effected using a range of contractual mechanisms. The choice of contract will reflect the attempt to cope with the information problem. Earlier in this book it was found convenient to distinguish three facets to this problem and these will form the subject matter of the next three sections, but, first, a brief summary of each.

1. *Coping with a changing environment* There is first the problem of bounded rationality; the impossibility of predicting and specifying the appropriate response to every conceivable contingency. This leads to *the firm as a device for handling change*, for increasing flexibility and adaptability in the face of new circumstances. Here, the firm is closely connected to the entrepreneurial function identified by Casson and Knight; the exercise of judgement in the face of environmental uncertainty.

2. *Policing transactions in the presence of opportunism* A second facet to the problem is that of establishing and enforcing property rights. Property rights are insecure and, in the extreme case, worthless, if they cannot be enforced and protected. Enforcement requires, however, that infringements are detected, and detection requires information. This leads to *the firm as a monitoring device* to cope with moral hazard and adverse selection. The focus of attention is on information concerning the behaviour and performance of the various parties to a contract. It was this conception of the firm which underlay much of the analysis of Chapters 5 and 6.

3. *Generating new knowledge* The third facet is the problem of perceiving (Kirzner), creating (Shackle) or forcing through (Schumpeter) new opportunities and new information. This leads to *the firm as the instigator of change* and is most closely associated with the view of entrepreneurship espoused by Schumpeter.

In sections 4, 5 and 6, each of these facets will be examined in turn to see how they are reflected in the structure of firms. We will attempt to show how modern theorists have linked the information problem to the organisational form adopted and especially to the extent of vertical, horizontal, conglomerate and geographical (especially multinational) integration.

4. INTEGRATION, COMPLEXITY AND ENVIRONMENTAL UNCERTAINTY

After reviewing the literature on corporate strategy and structure, Caves (1980) remarks that much of it seems implicitly to be concerned with the concept of an 'organisational production function'. The 'inputs' into this function, he argues, are resources devoted to collecting and analysing information and coordinating other factors of production. The 'output' is the ability to 'reallocate . . . in response to unexpected disturbances' (p. 89). The mode of expression betrays Cave's neoclassical standpoint, and in Chapter 3 it was seen that many would dispute the ability of the neoclassical paradigm to cope with the truly 'unexpected' as distinct from the statistically 'risky'. Nevertheless, the inputs into his 'organisational production function' are Casson's entrepreneurs. Casson is quite clear that the entrepreneur can be an employee (pp. 213–15) and that the institutional setting of the firm will be one of the factors underlying the 'supply' and 'demand' curves of Figure 3.1.

4.1 INTEGRATION, COORDINATION AND COMPLEXITY

Notwithstanding Williamson's view reported in Chapter 2 that the distinction between complexity and uncertainty is inessential since both give rise to the problem of bounded rationality, we will consider separately the influence of each on the firm. Very close and complex technical relationships between processes and products may imply high costs of transacting in the market because of bounded rationality, but it is not clear that coordinating these processes necessarily requires great entrepreneurial as distinct from technical judgement. It may be perfectly obvious what actions need to be taken in any given set of circumstances, even if the exhaustive enumeration of all the possibilities in a state-contingent market contract is not feasible.

This is the situation which underlies some of the 'conventional' explanations of integration within the firm. Within the neoclassical tradition of the 'firm as production function' mentioned at the beginning of Chapter 6, it is natural to look for explanations of horizontal integration in the pursuit of economies of scale; or of conglomerate integration in technical complementarities or economies of scope; or of vertical integration in the close technical connections between one stage of production and the next. The objections of the transactions cost school to this way of thinking are most succinctly summed up in Williamson's (1975) aphorism: 'technology is no bar to contracting' (p. 17). Let us interpret this point in more detail and consider its applications to horizontal and vertical integration.

4.1.1 Horizontal integration

This is the most familiar case considered in elementary textbooks. By integrating within a single firm the resources required to produce larger quantities of a single output, costs may decline if there are economies of scale. A falling average cost of production with higher output is ultimately traceable to 'indivisibilities' associated with the various inputs. A particular item of capital equipment; for example, a ship for transporting cargo in bulk; will have associated with it a level of utilisation which minimises costs per tonne mile. If the ship is not fully laden, costs obviously will rise. On the other hand, tonne miles can be increased by reducing the time spent at ports or in maintenance. Such continuous operations may increase staff costs as crews, maintenance engineers, and administrative personnel are augmented. This example is therefore just a special case of the economist's familiar idea of increasing and then ultimately diminishing returns to a fixed factor.

Now suppose that there are five firms each shipping a particular type of cargo (let us say grain) between two countries. They each purchase the grain from suppliers, store it in warehouses, transport it in their own ships across the ocean, and distribute it to wholesalers at the other end. It is clear, however, that the actual process of shipping is unnecessarily costly with five crews and five small ships. A single large ship would enable advantages of scale to be achieved.[9] Does this imply that the five firms should merge their operations? 'Common sense' suggests that this would not be unreasonable, but, in principle, there are other options open. The most obvious alternative is that a new specialist ship-owner enters the market with a giant grain transporter, and the five grain buyers and distributors contract with the ship-owner for cargo space on the larger ship. In a world of zero transactions costs, in other words, indivisibilities might just as reasonably lead to 'disintegration' and the entry of a new specialist firm as 'integration' and the creation of a single firm out of the five existing ones. The purely technical advantages associated with particular bits of equipment do not automatically require reduced numbers of firms for their realisation. They may lead to integration, but the hidden and unspoken assumption in the 'common-sense' view is the (very often correct) one that transactions costs will inhibit the 'market-like' solution.

All 'economies of scale' involve an indivisibility of some form. Two further examples, taken from Hay and Morris (1979, pp. 44–5) may be useful. Larger size, it has been argued, will lead to economies in the use of maintenance staff. If a breakdown in any particular item of equipment is a random variable with a certain probability distribution, the larger the number of items of such equipment the less is the variation in the average number of breakdowns per period.[10] It then turns out that a given standard of service (in terms of the probability that a breakdown will occur with no staff available to cope with it) can be achieved at lower cost per machine as the number of machines increases. Although technically flawless, we can not deduce from this that larger 'firm' size is encouraged. Many small firms could, in principle, use an independent maintenance firm to cope with breakdowns, just as coffee machines, domestic appliances and office equipment are frequently serviced and mended by outside contractors. This could either be done on the basis of a payment per visit; or each small firm could pay the maintenance company a retainer, which would effectively represent an insurance premium, and the company would pool the risks. Either way, economies in maintenance do not logically imply the amalgamation of small firms, though the transactions costs associated with contracting in the market may, of course, produce such an effect.[11] Similar reasoning can be applied to the case of economies of purchasing inputs. If there is a fixed or overhead element associated with the cost of effecting each order, independent of the size of the order, it is clear that costs per unit will decline as the average size of purchase increases. This seems to favour large firms, but it is important to identify clearly the source of any advantage. The overhead element independent of the size of the order is nothing other than a simple representation of a 'cost per transaction in the market'. If there are transactions costs associated with market exchange, reducing the number of such transactions will be encouraged. The economies thus identified are transactions cost economies. If, for example, this transaction cost were peculiar to the bulk order of supplies of a particular input and did not apply to the transactions between the purchasing firms, a set of small firms could band together and order in bulk, rather as a group of students might combine to order a magazine or newspaper. 'Integration' would then occur only at the single specific level of transactions with this particular supplier and not more generally.

4.1.2 Vertical integration and technical links

Technological considerations have traditionally been seen as an important force leading to vertical integration in some industries. The case of the iron and steel industry is perhaps the most often cited. Thus, 'the later stages of production are bound to the earlier by many specially close technological links. In particular a great waste of heat can be avoided' (Robertson and

Dennison, 1960, p. 27). From our discussion of horizontal integration the objection to the view that vertical integration is a purely technological phenomenon will be clear. The question is simply whether the close technological links should be coordinated within the firm or by market transactions. Contracts might be drawn up which would permit the process of steel making to proceed with the steel maker purchasing iron in molten form. So detailed is the coordination required, however, that this is clearly not going to be the favoured procedure, and the entire process is more conveniently brought under a single administration in the firm. In cases like the production of iron and steel, the advantages of vertical integration are so obvious that it appears somewhat pedantic to drag transactions costs into the discussion. Yet, logically, nothing can be deduced about the organisation of production without reference to transactions costs because the organisation of production concerns precisely the choice of contractual arrangements best suited to a particular set of technical circumstances.

4.2 Integration, Coordination and Uncertainty

4.2.1 Generating information within the firm
In a continually changing environment, entrepreneurs gather information, interpret it to discover the opportunities latent in it, and act upon it. Acting on the basis of entrepreneurial judgement requires command over resources. It does so because the market value of an entrepreneur's knowledge cannot itself be appropriated simply by trading it in the market. A buyer would require the information before an assessment of its value was possible, but once in possession of the information there would be no need to purchase it.[12] The firm responds to this problem by screening for entrepreneurial talent, placing entrepreneurs in circumstances likely to produce a flow of information suitable for the exercise of entrepreneurial judgement, providing them with resources to back their judgement, and instituting a reward system which enables those with a flair for these decisions to benefit from them. On this interpretation, the firm represents an internal capital market, a method of allocating scarce resources amongst competing uses on the basis of entrepreneurial judgement.[13] The job is done internally because of the problems associated with transactions in markets for information.

From a property rights perspective, however, this rather rosy view of the 'internal capital market' requires some qualifying. Manager-entrepreneurs will be much better able to pursue their ideas and respond to unfolding events if they have the residual control rights in the assets they are using. In a multi-divisional firm, however, this will not be the case. It is the managers at headquarters who can implement a new idea without local approval rather than the other way around. As Bolton and Scharfstein (1998, pp. 107–8) put it 'the same control that gives HQ the incentive to monitor has an adverse effect on the incentives of division managers to act in an innovative or entrepreneurial fashion'. As was seen in Chapter 4, concentrating control rights in the hands of a single manager will reduce the incentive to others to make specific investments and act entrepreneurially. Independent owner-managers financed by bank lending would seem to give greater incentives to entrepreneurial alertness if the transactional problem between entrepreneur and capitalist could somehow be mitigated.[14]

4.2.2   Vertical integration and information

Integration of activities to take advantage of internally generated information would still seem to imply a fairly specialised firm. Vertical integration may be seen as a way of gaining from the improved communication of information from upstream to downstream firms. Arrow (1975) considers better information about the supply (and hence the future price) of an upstream good, leading to more appropriate input decisions by a downstream firm, as a motive for vertical integration. Integration into closely related products or processes may be favoured because information concerning markets or production is not totally specific, and may have wide-ranging implications.

4.2.3   The chain store

A useful example of integration, both as a means of discovering and analysing information, and as a means of using this, is the chain store. Many chain stores have benefited from the development of knowledge concerning customer wants and the identification of gaps in the market. This has not necessarily led to backward vertical integration into manufacturing, since the links between market information and production information may not be very important. The store concentrates on the entrepreneurial functions of identifying demands and then contracts with manufacturers directly to arrange supply. This, of course, implies that information about what is wanted can be cheaply and clearly communicated to potential suppliers. If the request is too innovative, it may be difficult to arrange supply from independent contractors, and backward vertical integration may occur. In section 6, we will consider the relationship between integration and innovation in more detail.

Information generated within the firm about markets can therefore be used to contract with suppliers, and the benefits derivable from this entrepreneurial information can then be used in every branch of the chain. A similar point could be made about information concerning the actual operation of the stores, the handling of goods, layout, warehousing, pricing, and so forth. New information can be used quickly throughout the chain of stores. As Edwards and Townsend recognised in their explanation of the growth of the chain store 'the main advantage lies in the fact that there are large indivisibilities in knowledge' (p. 296). As will be seen in section 5, the multinational enterprise can also be seen as a means of exploiting the use of knowledge throughout a geographically dispersed firm. In this section, however, we have been emphasising the ability of a firm to adjust and to capitalise flexibly on a flow of new information. Section 5 considers more generally the ability of the firm to exploit its non-tradable resources by means of internal expansion.

4.2.4 The conglomerate, information and uncertainty

Conglomerate firms are much more difficult to explain on the basis of the use of internally generated information. Instead, the emphasis switches to diversification as a means of coping with unexpected events. A neoclassical approach would see the firm as holding a portfolio of risky prospects so designed to maximise the value of expected wealth (in the case of risk neutrality) or, more generally, expected utility (in the case of risk aversion or risk loving). This 'portfolio' could involve the firm undertaking projects in many different product areas. A serious difficulty, however, is to understand why risks should be pooled within the firm instead of in the markets for financial claims. In a neoclassical world with low transactions costs, risks could be pooled as effectively by people holding claims to the returns from a variety of independent but specialised firms operating in different areas, as claims to the returns from a single suitably diversified firm. Thus, individual people through their portfolio of *financial* assets could select a desired risk-return profile, and this could be done independently of any decisions concerning the appropriate administrative framework for coordinating the *physical* assets concerned. If the firm itself takes on a risk-pooling role, it is once more to the transactional problems of the alternative institutional arrangements that we must turn for an explanation.

One obvious candidate for consideration is that people lack the information to take complex portfolio-building decisions, and that the transactions costs involved in holding a large number of different financial claims would prevent risk pooling. This problem, however, would appear to be met by developments within the financial markets themselves; developments such as the growth of unit and investment trusts which give people access to specialist information and, through the use of an intermediary, once more reduce transactions costs. A more persuasive explanation for diversification within the firm concerns the use of the physical assets, human capital and firm specific 'know-how'. As was seen in some detail in Chapter 6, within the firm, information about members of the team is collected, inputs are monitored and complex hierarchical incentive structures are instituted. Many of the skills absorbed are firm specific rather than product specific and relate to the ability to communicate and to get on with colleagues. Further, incentives require that the firm is perceived as having effectively an indefinite 'life' and is unlikely to go bankrupt. At the same time, they imply that, for a portion of a person's career, remuneration will exceed anything available on the 'open market'. In these circumstances, the ability to relocate resources from stagnant to growing sectors is essential. Bankruptcy or stagnation and decline in a specialist firm are of no consequence in a neoclassical world of full information where laid-off resources are immediately reabsorbed elsewhere at the going market rate. However, in the context of the analysis of Chapters 5 and 6, it is clear that the consequences of decline for the operation of the internal labour market or the tournament could be very severe and imply a renunciation of the firm's 'implicit' obligations.

Rapidly changing and uncertain conditions will therefore lead to conglomerate diversification and an M-form corporate structure. The head office monitors each division's performance and, through the internal capital and labour markets, reallocates resources towards growing and away from declining areas. This strategy is not, therefore, simply a matter of pooling risks. If it works, it will do so because the firm's structure permits flexibility and encourages adaptation to conditions more correctly viewed in Knight's terms as 'uncertain'.[15] Kay (1983) in his explanation for the conglomerate emphasises this point. The firm will make use of information flows from 'richly linked' product markets, but this implies that 'where links exist they may create mutual or common vulnerability' (p. 96). In very static environments, this may not be of great concern[16] but in other areas the danger of 'technological mugging' may lead to conglomerate diversification. For Kay, neoclassical portfolio theory is not the appropriate tool for understanding this phenomenon: 'The decision-maker faces a truly uncertain situation in which there is an asymmetric emphasis on the possibility of life cycle decline rather than life cycle growth . . . All we assume the decision-maker is able to do is to order the environment in terms of surprise potential' (p. 98).[17] Environments in which surprise potential is great will lead firms to diversify into areas which are not strongly linked, in order to reduce the damage that might result from a sudden mugging.

5. INTEGRATION, INTERNALISATION AND MARKET FAILURE

In this section, we consider integration in the context of market failure. The analysis runs parallel to that of Chapter 6 on the policing of labour contracts, but here the emphasis is on the problem of contracting with buyers or suppliers of non-labour inputs. Integration as a means of overcoming transactional hazards is sometimes called the 'internalisation' approach to the firm. Where markets fail, an alternative form of organisation is substituted and the market transaction is 'internalised' within the firm. Usually, this process is seen as increasing economic efficiency. Subsection 5.2, however, outlines cases in which the pursuit of monopoly advantages can be viewed in a transactions costs framework and may or may not lead to greater economic efficiency.

5.1 Monitoring Input Quality

If the quality of inputs is observable at very low cost, we could expect market transactions to be used for recurrent purchases of 'standard' items.[18] Even where quality is costly to monitor, full integration within the firm is only one of several options available. The continuing use of a particular supplier with a good 'reputation' to protect is a possible response to adverse selection. 'Cheating' on the part of such a supplier would be costly if discovered and 'the discipline of continuous dealings' with the implied threat of terminating the association following unsatisfactory performance may provide a 'solution' to the incentive problem. Clearly, this relatively simple response to adverse selection and moral hazard requires both the existence of 'reputable' suppliers, and at least some 'informative signal' about quality in order that a 'monitoring gamble' can be constructed. Obviously, the more informative the signal used, the more effective the monitoring of the input will be. Information is valuable to the buyer and may be sought in a variety of ways depending upon the costs involved.

It may be, for example, that simple inspection of the input is sufficient to ascertain its quality and reliability, and that staff with specialist knowledge can be employed simply to undertake this task. On the other hand, inspection of the input itself may not provide, at reasonable cost, information about quality. Knowledge of production conditions may be important. If this is so, a number of consequences follow. The first possibility is that detailed environmental circumstances, to which all producers are subject, may have important effects, and that these can be appreciated only by practical experience. This might result in a buyer integrating backwards into the production of an input simply to acquire this kind of information and thus to remove the information asymmetry associated with dealings with other suppliers. The objective is not to produce one hundred per cent of requirements of the input, but to produce information. An example already quoted is that of the interest of Guinness in malt production. Similarly, the history of Sainsbury provides a number of cases: 'Before the war we were very large buyers of beef cattle in Aberdeenshire, through our Northern agent, and it was our desire to get direct experience of rearing and fattening costs . . . that led to our farming enterprise.'[19] A second possibility is that quality is determined primarily by the efficiency of the production operation run by the supplier. This might lead to arrangements for technical inspection and direct monitoring between independent firms. Finally, where the detailed specification of the input is continually subject to change, technical inspection may give way to full internal integration within a single firm.

Forward vertical integration of manufacturers into retailing involves a similar range of options. Where one manufacturer's product is indistinguishable from another's, the use of market contracts and an independent wholesaler is suggested. The wholesaler develops contacts with retail outlets and supplies them with a variety of products from his stock. The transactional economies involved in employing an intermediary are clear since the alternative is that each manufacturer must develop links with each retailer. Problems arise, however, when it is no longer a matter of indifference to the manufacturer where his goods are sold, how they are treated and how presented. Faulty handling or poor presentation in the wrong environment may affect the brand image of the manufacturer's product. Complex products or new products require that consumer confidence is established, and once again this involves the development of a 'reputation' which is attached to a brand name. Manufacturers may respond to this problem in a number of ways. The first option is to establish a sales force to sell direct to retailers and monitor performance, presentation and general quality of the store. This is the policy adopted by Yardley and Co., the manufacturers of perfumery and cosmetics in the 1930s and 1940s. Selling more complex commodities may require a knowledgeable person to communicate with each potential customer, and, here, forward integration by the manufacturer can range from the direct training of the sales force and the use of space in a department store or (more recently) 'shopping mall' through franchising, to full integration.

Etgar (1978) reports that full or 'partial' vertical integration (franchising) into retailing is common in the USA. It is a system through which 'more than one-third of products and services is currently distributed' (p.249). He argues that forward vertical integration is 'motivated by a desire *to achieve product differentiation in the ultimate market*' (emphasis in original). If a distributor represents several suppliers, all will benefit by better service, whereas exclusive distribution is required to tie a good image to a particular brand. Etgar therefore formulates the hypothesis that 'suppliers who forward integrate from a competitive level into a competitively structured distributive level will provide more services' (p.251). This hypothesis is tested using data from the property and casualty insurance industry. In this industry, the system of independent insurance agents has been challenged since the war in the USA by the direct writing system (using either employees or franchisees). Etgar isolates twenty-one service variables (such as degree of home inspection, and time taken to settle the majority of claims) and compares the performance of the vertically integrated and non-integrated distributors. Significant differences were detected in eleven of the service areas, and eight out of these eleven service variables showed a higher quality performance by vertically integrated distributors.

5.2 Internalisation and the Multinational Firm

In our discussion of the economics of the chain store in section 4 we emphasised economies in the use of information gathered throughout the chain. This leads conveniently to the problem of the multinational firm. In both cases, the same fundamental phenomenon requires explanation – the integration of geographically dispersed operations in a single firm. Traditional theory has addressed the problem of explaining the geographical dispersion of production (for example, Heilbrun, 1981). In essence, the analysis derives from the location theory of Weber (1929), Alonso (1964) and others, as well as the 'central place theory' associated with Christaller (1933) and Losch (1954). In this theory, the advantages of concentration (mainly economies of scale) are traded off against the advantages of dispersion (mainly savings in transport costs), and a 'least cost' spatial pattern of establishments is derived for a given distribution of demand over the area. There is no clue here, however, as to why the establishments so distributed are integrated within a single firm in some instances but not in others. Similarly, in the international setting, static theory does not explain why production is undertaken by indigenous firms in some cases and by affiliates of a multinational corporation in others.

Dunning (1973) surveys not only location theory but also traditional trade theory in an attempt to highlight the ultimate source of multinational enterprise. He concludes that neither have any relevance to the issue. If the affiliates of a foreign firm have advantages over indigenous firms, this must have something to do not with advantages associated with the country concerned but rather with advantages specific to the multinational enterprise. The character of these advantages is important: 'Essentially, they are enterprise-specific, that is they are not transferable between firms, and are a function of their character and ownership' (p. 314). The multinational enterprise, according to this view, possesses a resource not available to the indigenous firms and for which there is no effective market, so that acquisition of the resource through the process of exchange is ruled out. Special skills and technical 'know-how' clearly come into this category. Knowledge acquired by pure experience at doing the job is entrepreneurial in character and impossible to market. It is specific to the firm because it is generated by the entrepreneurial talent of the people who happen to be working in it. Use of this firm-specific information may then result in multinational expansion.

Dunning's explanation of multinational production is sometimes called the 'eclectic' or 'Ownership–Location–Internalisation' (OLI) theory. Location advantages are necessary simply because without some reason to locate facilities in differing countries a firm would simply produce at a single location and export to the various markets around the world. Clearly transport costs, tariff or other barriers, economies of scale or varying factor prices give rise to location advantages. Ownership advantages are necessary because without them the firms located around the world could all be independent of one another. The exploitation of a firm-specific resource, such as a patent, a brand name, a set of marketing or production skills, managerial and organisational structures or 'know-how', helps to explain why firms located in many different countries are under common ownership. Internalisation advantages are necessary to explain why a firm with ownership advantages does not simply capitalise on them by contract rather than ownership. In other words the firm might license the use of its patented techniques or set up management advisory services to market its organisational expertise. Some 'market failure' or prohibitive transactional hazard explains the use of the firm rather than the market.[20] Further discussion of this approach to the multinational can be found in section 6.1.2.

5.3   Integration and Market Power

5.3.1   Monitoring restrictive agreements

Integration in pursuit of monopoly profits has been considered a primary determinant of industrial structure for many years. Even in this familiar area, however, it is necessary to understand the implicit assumptions about transactions costs which underlie the conventional theory. The advantages to be gained from 'combinations' have been recognised in every age. In a famous passage, Adam Smith writes that 'people of the same trade seldom meet together, even for merriment and diversion, but the conversation ends in a conspiracy against the public, or in some contrivance to raise prices' (p. 130). 'Integration', however, can take many forms other than the creation of a single firm, and the choice of institutional arrangements will depend upon transactions costs. A voluntary agreement between all existing producers covering prices to be charged and quotas to be produced would fulfil the same objectives as a complete merger. In a world in which information were perfect and transactions costs zero there would be no reason for preferring one method of monopoly creation over another from the point of view of the producers. If integration within a single firm is the strategy followed, this will be because the costs of monitoring and hence of ensuring compliance in the market exceed the costs of internal organisation.

As Stigler (1964) remarks 'no conspiracy can neglect the problem of enforcement' and he bases his theory of oligopoly squarely on the problem of acquiring information about the behaviour of other independent producers. A rapid and accurate flow of information about the compliance of others with the provisions of a restrictive agreement will render integration by merger less necessary as a means of securing monopoly advantages. It is interesting to note that economists have traditionally been sceptical about the stability of restrictive agreements and have noted the incentive to cheat on their provisions. This scepticism may explain the suspicion with which horizontal mergers are often regarded, internal control being substituted for external agreements.

5.3.2 The multinational and market power

Multinational integration may be seen as a means of establishing and consolidating monopolistic positions. An early proponent of this view was Hymer (1976). A firm with some advantage over foreign competitors would not have to expand into foreign markets if it could sell this advantage (perhaps a patented process or product) at a price determined on a competitive market. Where overseas firms are few in number, however, the transactions costs involved in agreeing the terms of a licence could be substantial. In order to capitalise upon a special advantage in overseas markets, integration with a foreign firm might then be necessary. Hymer's analysis at this point can be seen as a precursor of the more modern transactions cost school, although the nature of the advantages possessed by a multinational firm would be more likely to be described as 'competitive' than 'monopolistic' by members of this school. Hymer's awareness of transactional considerations is emphasised in a recent contribution by Yamin (1991, pp. 74–5).

A second motivation for multinational expansion is simply to remove the potential for conflict with competing suppliers. Again, Hymer emphasised that with very numerous competitors and standardised products multinational links between firms would not be so advantageous. With a few oligopolists, however, agreements to limit damaging price wars would be sought and collusion across national boundaries could result in higher joint profits. However, enforcing such collusive agreements requires good information about a rival's behaviour, and a full merger which creates a multinational firm can be seen as a method of overcoming this problem. A more recent and extended elaboration of this view can be found in Cowling and Sugden (1987). 'Transnationals arise because they are a means of consolidating or increasing profits in an oligopoly world' (p. 20).

The possible collusive advantages of multinational expansion are not confined to the product market. Building on the work of Marglin (1974), Cowling and Sugden (1987, pp. 62–70) suggest that multinational production gives a firm bargaining advantages over workers in the labour market. For Marglin, the demise of the 'putting-out system' and the rise of the factory system in England at the end of the eighteenth century was not simply the substitution of a more for a less efficient mode of production. Factory production gave the entrepreneur and capitalist much greater 'control' over the workforce. No doubt, there were important efficiency consequences, but there were also great *distributional* consequences. Sugden (1991) argues that the multinational enterprise also has notable distributional effects. In particular, the multinational can threaten workers in one country with the location of new investment in another country. This strategy is termed 'divide and rule'. 'By dividing workers into country-specific groups employers improve their bargaining position, thereby gaining *at the expense* of workers' (p. 179, emphasis in original). If the multinational form can arise from a distributional squabble, it may be as reasonable to regard it as a vehicle for rent seeking as a means of capitalising on entrepreneurial alertness. As mentioned in Chapter 6, it is often difficult to distinguish rent seeking from entrepreneurship, and the various interpretations of the multinational encountered here provide another example of this general problem.

5.3.3   Vertical integration and price discrimination

The costs of monitoring restrictive agreements in the market are also reflected in some other 'conventional' explanations of internal integration. Consider the argument that an upstream monopolist will integrate vertically with a downstream buyer to correct for the tendency of the independent buyer to substitute other inputs for those supplied by the monopolist if there are technical opportunities for doing so (Vernon and Graham, 1971; Schmalensee, 1973). A vertically integrated concern would, it is argued, increase combined profits by using more of the internally supplied input in the downstream production process. Figure 7.4 illustrates the point using the traditional isoquant–isocost diagram of neoclassical theory. The input of the monopoly supplier is measured along the horizontal axis and 'other inputs' on the vertical axis. Given a monopoly price P_m, the downstream producer will adopt the combination of inputs at a, where the line of constant outlay (slope $-P_m/P_n$) is tangential to the isoquant labelled $\bar{q}$. An integrated producer will be interested not in the monopoly price but in the marginal cost of production of input *m* labelled C_m. Clearly, the cost of *q* will be lower at point *b* than at point *a* for the integrated producer, and more of input *m* will be used.

This argument is impeccable from the point of view of neoclassical theory but, once more, it does not address the question of why market alternatives to vertical integration are not adopted. If substitution against the monopolist is severe, why does the monopolist not adopt a two-part tariff? Under a two-part tariff, the buyer would pay an initial lump sum and then a price per unit of the input purchased. The system is often used for such items as telephone, gas or electricity services, with a 'quarterly rental' for the telephone in addition to a price per call. A sufficiently low price per unit would solve the problem of substitution of other inputs by the buyer, and an appropriate 'standing charge' would give the monopolist his or her profit. As Figure 7.4 indicates, the resource savings available from moving to point *b* imply that some two-part tariff arrangement could benefit both monopolist and buyer. Only the bargaining costs associated with implementing it would appear to stand in the way.

The main difficulty of the two-part tariff arrangement is in ensuring that the buyer does not purchase the product on behalf of others and then resell it. If this happened on a large scale, the monopolist would miss out on the

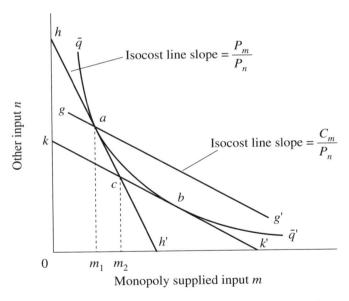

Figure 7.4 *Price discrimination is required if a monopoly supplier is to prevent substitution away from input* m *by downstream buyers*

lump-sum payments which buyers would otherwise have to pay. This, of course, is a problem faced by any scheme of price discrimination. A price of P_m for the first m_2 units of the input purchased (Figure 7.4) and a price of C_m for any further purchases would, for example, be an alternative system which would increase the profits of the monopolist seller and not harm the buyer, whose total costs would remain unaltered. Once again, resale from one purchaser to another would completely undermine the monopolists's position.

Forward integration in this case, therefore, is really a method of policing a system of price discrimination which might otherwise not be possible in the market. Formally, it involves the same reasoning as that used by Perry (1980) to explain the process of forward vertical integration by Alcoa in the years 1888–1930. The standard analysis of price discrimination tells us that if there are several different markets for a product with different price elasticities of demand, a profit-maximising monopolist will charge a higher price to the buyers with the relatively *inelastic* demand. Preventing arbitrage between the markets is the major problem and it is for this purpose that forward vertical integration may be undertaken. By integrating with the buyer who has the most elastic demand, the monopolist can charge a higher price to other buyers without fear of resale. Perry identifies five major markets for aluminium – as a reducing agent used in the production of iron and steel, and as an input in the manufacture of cooking utensils, electric cable, automobile parts and aircraft. On the basis of the price discrimination hypothesis, 'we expect Alcoa to have been more extensively integrated into those downstream industries with relatively more elastic derived demands for primary aluminium' (p. 44), and this is the pattern which Alcoa apparently followed. The argument, however, depends heavily on unstated assumptions about the transactions costs of alternatives to integration, and other theorists have interpreted the evidence very differently (for example, Silver, 1984, reported in section 6).

5.4 Transaction-Specific Investments and Opportunistic Recontracting

5.4.1 Hold-up and vertical integration

In Chapter 6, section 8, the problem of opportunistic recontracting and 'hold-up' was discussed in the context of the supply of labour when the latter acquired highly specific skills. A precisely equivalent problem can arise with the supply of other physical inputs or services to the firm. A supplier of a specialised component may have to cooperate closely with the purchaser, and over time gains a great deal of detailed knowledge of the particular 'idiosyncratic' problems associated with this contractual relationship. In other words, the supplier gains 'first-mover advantages' and a complex bargaining situation arises. As was seen in Chapter 6, the financing of this specialised know-how puts one or other contractor at a disadvantage. If the buyer, early on in the life of the contract, purchases the services of the seller on the basis of the seller's initial or pre-experience efficiency, he or she runs the risk of 'hold-up' later. The seller could attempt to recontract and extort the difference between the value of his/her services and those of the next-best outsider. Assuming that this threat was lifted by the seller 'posting a bond' and accepting lower remuneration in the first pre-experience period, the buyer might then act opportunistically by refusing to repay the bond. Contractors wishing to protect a 'reputation' will have reasons not to act opportunistically in this way, as was seen in earlier chapters. Nevertheless, the greater the appropriable quasi-rents available (that is, the greater the difference between the value of a particular supplier's services and the next-best outsider) the greater is the incentive to act opportunistically and the bigger the contractual problem.

Monteverde and Teece (1982a) use this framework to formulate the following hypothesis in the context of the automobile industry: 'The greater is the application of engineering effort associated with the development of any given automobile component, the higher are the expected appropriable quasi rents and, therefore, the greater is the likelihood of vertical integration of production for that component' (p. 207). They measure 'engineering effort' by the cost of development of a component and also take account of 'the degree to which any given component's design affects the performance or packaging of other components' (p. 210). Each component is coded according to whether it is produced in-house or supplied by an outside contractor. Monteverde and Teece are then able to show statistically that vertical integration and 'development effort' are positively and significantly related for their sample of components.

The existence of 'appropriable quasi rents' is not a product only of acquired 'know-how'. It may also derive from transaction-specific physical investment. In order to supply a particular component to a firm, a producer may have to invest in equipment which is more or less specific to this transaction. Once more this gives rise to quasi-rents because the value of the equipment in an alternative use may be well below its value in the manufacture of the component for which it was designed. In the extreme case, the equipment may be totally specific to a given transaction, and the alternative to using it for this purpose is simply to sell it for scrap. An opportunist buyer, under these conditions, might attempt to recontract with the supplier and seize these quasi-rents. Once the physical investment has been made, the supplier is 'locked-in' to a particular buyer and therefore faces the danger that the buyer will adjust the terms of the contract unfavourably.

This argument clearly relies for some of its force on the existence of changing, uncertain conditions. In a static world with contractual obligations closely specified over a long period of time, the possibility of 'recontracting' is ruled out. Property rights are clearly defined and obligations are spelled out as far into the future as is necessary. No problem of bargaining over quasi-rents then arises. As has frequently been asserted, however, the existence of bounded rationality will usually prevent a comprehensive agreement of this type, and the terms must of necessity leave much that is 'implicit'. Explicit sanctions imposed by a third party in the event of some contravention of the provisions of a contract are often costly to arrange and require very simple, unambiguous contract terms. Most complex contracts rely on trust between the parties and the threat of termination and loss of reputation. In these circumstances, the possibility that a buyer will act opportunistically must be a matter of concern to the supplier.

5.4.2   The case of General Motors and Fisher Body
Klein, Crawford and Alchian (1978) argue that the avoidance of opportunism deriving from specific investments will lead to vertical integration. They use the historical example of relations between General Motors and the Fisher Body Corporation to illustrate the difficulties of market contracts and the tendency towards integration. In 1919, the Fisher Body Corporation agreed to supply General Motors with closed car bodies. To do this, Fisher Body had to undertake highly specific investments in body presses and dies. The contract specified a price for car bodies of cost plus 17.6 per cent (no capital costs were included). In 1926, the two companies merged their operations fully. Over the intervening years, the demand for closed bodies had risen above expectations and General Motors felt the price they were paying was too high in the new conditions. Further, because capital costs were not included in the agreement, Fisher had an incentive to use techniques embodying as little capital as possible. Transport costs, on the other hand, were included and this gave Fisher little incentive to relocate their operations near General Motors; a move which the latter tried to encourage.

The case of General Motors and Fisher Body is a complex one and involves considerations other than the mere *specificity* of the capital investment required. Uncertain, changing conditions will favour full integration with a regular supplier, as was argued in section 4. Focusing on the issue of transaction-specific capital alone, it is possible to argue that opportunistic behaviour can be overcome by quasi-vertical integration, and that full integration therefore is not necessary. Thus, Monteverde and Teece (1982b) suggest that 'what Klein, Crawford and Alchian have offered is not a theory of vertical integration, but a theory of quasi integration' (p. 323). If specific investment is required, opportunism can be prevented by making the buyer finance it. The buyer of the input acquires property rights in the equipment necessary for its manufacture and grants certain rights of use to the seller. A relationship similar to that of landlord and tenant described in Chapter 4 is established with respect to property rights in the equipment. The seller of the input supplies the resources which are less specific and can be turned quickly to other uses and are thus less subject to 'hold-up'.

It is worth noticing that, in the case of physical equipment, financing the investment does not subject the buyer to the risk of 'hold-up' as it did in the case of 'know-how'. A buyer that finances the acquisition of non-patentable special skills and 'know-how' may be threatened by a seller who then has first-mover advantages. But a buyer who finances physical equipment is not subject to this threat, assuming that property rights can be policed and enforced at relatively low cost. The use of the physical assets can be transferred to another supplier in the event of threats from an existing one: the use of non-patentable 'know-how' cannot. This is the essential difference between the two cases and explains why, in principle, transaction-specific physical capital leads to quasi-vertical integration and not necessarily to full vertical integration.

The GM and Fisher Body merger has become one of the most intensively scrutinised 'case studies' in organisational economics. Some writers, for example Coase (2000), deny that Fisher Body ever made an attempt at 'hold-up' before 1926. Casadesus-Masanell and Spulber (2000) argue that coordination of production and inventories was a more important consideration in motivating the final merger (the forces discussed in section 4 above) and that transactional relations between 1919 and 1926 were characterised by a high degree of trust. Freeland (2000) emphasises the importance of access to the human assets represented by the Fisher brothers and points to the transactional problems encountered there. In 1934, the brothers threatened to leave if they were not granted options on GM common stock – a successful hold-up of GM which 'derived from their human assets – their specialized knowledge of the body business and its management' (p. 58). Against these criticisms, Klein (2000) defends the original interpretation. Relations between Fisher and GM might have been harmonious until 1924 but a sudden increase in vehicle production by 42 per cent in 1925 and another 48 per cent in 1926 tested the original cost-plus agreement to destruction. Fisher's refusal to develop a body plant at Flint, close to GM's Buick assembly plant, and its insistence on continuing to supply from Detroit was, for Klein, a clear case of hold-up.

In order to test the theory that specific physical capital encourages quasi-vertical integration, Monteverde and Teece (1982b) took a sample of components from two divisions of a US supplier of automotive products. Potential quasi-rents were calculated by taking two measures – the simple dollar cost of specialised equipment and an 'estimate of the percentage of original tooling costs which would be required to convert the tooling to its next best use' (p. 325). They found a significant positive relationship between their measure of appropriable quasi-rents and the occurrence of quasi-vertical integration, but the general explanatory power of their estimated equation was low.

5.5 Enforcing intertemporal commitments

Subsection 5.4 was concerned with the problem that the parties to a contract might attempt to 'renegotiate' it as time passed. A particularly extreme example would be that of a buyer who terminates the association and contracts with a new supplier after a certain period of time has elapsed. Considerable attention has been given to the incentive properties of terminating an agreement in earlier sections and chapters, and it may therefore come as a surprise that there are circumstances in which a buyer may wish voluntarily to 'disarm' and forgo this threat of termination. It may, in other words, be necessary for the buyer to 'tie him or herself down' and promise not to use alternative suppliers. Clearly, a buyer who does this will wish to monitor the operations of his or her supplier very closely and vertical integration is the likely result.

Goldberg (1976a) argues that granting a producer the 'right to serve' a constituency may be in the interests of the buyers if uncertainty about the introduction of new technology and the possible obsolescence of specific capital equipment renders the producers unwilling to undertake the required investment in the absence of some assurance about continuing outlets. The problem is not that the buyer might attempt to capture the quasi-rents associated with transaction-specific capital (as under subsection 5.4), but that s/he might desert the supplier entirely in favour of a new entrant using superior technology. Although, in the short run, it will always be in the buyer's interests to maintain the freedom to contract with anyone who offers the most favourable terms, 'the effective achievement of their long-term interests requires that barriers be erected to their pursuit of short-run self-interest' (Goldberg, 1976a, p. 433). Unfettered freedom to contract with anyone else at any time will not be in the buyer's interests if the supplier is thereby rendered unwilling to undertake the necessary investment.[21]

These ideas were developed primarily as an approach to the theory of regulation and were elaborated more formally by Ekelund and Higgins (1982). Public regulation, particularly of 'natural monopoly' markets, sometimes involves restrictions on new entrants, and this has been widely criticised by economists as suppressing competition and innovation. Goldberg does not dispute that giving the supplier a 'right to serve' could adversely affect incentives and suppress innovation, but in a very dynamic uncertain environment the total absence of such a right could also suppress innovation and prevent entry. He points out that private contractors will often voluntarily attempt to restrict their future options through long-term arrangements. Interpreted in this way, the firm operates like a 'thermal' type of nuclear reactor, increasing the chance that innovations will be 'captured' by using a 'moderator' to slow them down. Innovations which are, so to speak, 'uncontrolled' may be lost. It is a paradox that Schumpeter's 'gale of creative destruction' if too severe, could lay waste all plans to innovate.[22] The firm encourages change by simultaneously moderating its force, and assists new entry by restricting the scope for further entry. Further discussion of this question in the context of government regulation can be found in Chapter 15.

That restrictions on future freedom of contract do not necessarily prevent entry can be seen by considering the problem faced by a firm wishing to encourage the production of a component at present being supplied by a monopolist. It could be argued that the downstream purchaser will have an incentive to produce the upstream component within the firm in order to obtain it more cheaply. The problem with such reasoning is that it is not clear why if the downstream firm is capable of producing the component in this way, some other independent supplier cannot enter the market and compete with the monopolist. One possible answer is that the new entrant will take time to learn the techniques of production involved, and the established monopolist may have firm-specific cost advantages (that is, there are barriers to entry). In this situation, faced with the monopolist's threat to retaliate by cutting price in the event of new competitors entering the market, a potential new supplier would look for assurances from the downstream buyer that a continuing outlet would be provided at agreed prices. 'Firm-like' long-term arrangements therefore emerge, and possibly full vertical integration.

6. INTEGRATION AND INNOVATION

The ideas of Goldberg and others on the role of long-term commitments in coping with specific capital investments in the context of technical change lead naturally to an appraisal of the firm as a device for initiating change. In subsection 4, our attention was focused on flexibility and adaptability in the face of an exogenously changing environment. Here we see the firm not as a passive response to the environment but as an active determinant of the technical conditions prevailing.

Invention, the perception of new technological possibilities, is inevitably the product of personal insight and personal circumstances. Although it is possible to argue that invention may be stimulated by bringing together within the firm groups of ingenious people, all with the characteristics of curiosity and technical knowledge, many of the inventive insights appear still to originate from people outside (Jewkes *et al.*, 1969). However, to go from a new concept and perhaps a working model to the launching of a commercially viable product or process, usually requires the close cooperation of many people over long periods and involves the exercise of entrepreneurship of the Schumpeterian variety. Innovation and the firm are therefore intimately associated. Perhaps the most famous historical example concerns the association between James Watt, who appears to have had a working model of his steam engine operating as early as 1765, and Matthew Boulton, whose entrepreneurial flair and financial assistance were required before the first commercial engine was installed in 1776. Development expenditures amounted to at least sixty man-years of skilled labour (Scherer, 1980, p. 412).

6.1   Research and Development

6.1.1   Innovation and scale

Enormous institutional changes have occurred since those early years of the industrial revolution, and, in the modern world, research and development expenditure amounting to many billions of dollars is undertaken every year.[23] In fields such as chemicals, drugs, electronics, communications, instrumentation, aircraft, and electrical and mechanical engineering, investment in research and development commonly exceeds three per cent of sales revenue. Other industrial groups, such as food, textiles or paper, undertake much less research and development as a percentage of sales revenue, but individual firms assigned to these industries may vary considerably in research effort.

The effects of continuing innovation within the firm on its size and structure have been debated fiercely for many years and a full review cannot be attempted here.[24] It has been argued that large firms are required for successful innovation, reasons given being: (i) innovation is now beyond the resources of smaller enterprises; (ii) there are 'economies of scale' associated with research and development (sophisticated scientific equipment is 'indivisible' as is the knowledge to which its use may give rise); (iii) large size permits the pooling of risks over many projects, and (iv) market power is required to produce an environment sufficiently stable to provide the long-term confidence necessary for the innovator.[25] Others have pointed out that a flow of small to medium-scale innovations well within the capacity of firms of moderate size to undertake continues from year to year, and that only in the 'spectacular' fields of nuclear power, weapons and space research (mostly government funded) is very large size a prerequisite. Smaller firms may be more flexible and less prone to bureaucratic inertia, while the risks associated with innovation will vary widely and may, on many occasions, be perceived as not all that great. Most businessmen and women will try to ensure that the majority of significant technical problems have been satisfactorily resolved by relatively inexpensive research before the start of full-scale development.[26] Several smaller competing firms may provide an environment more stimulating to the pace of innovation than a single large firm by increasing the incremental reward attached to a more rapid completion of a project, but, as already noted in subsection 5, too many potential imitators or improvers may have an adverse effect and reduce the scope for profitable innovation.[27]

6.1.2 Innovation and the multinational

From the point of view of the transactions cost approach to the firm, the implications for firm structure of research and development expenditure depend upon the ability to trade in the information to which the research gives rise. Where the information is difficult to communicate simply, or where licensing the use of the information exposes the firm to opportunism, we would expect the firm to achieve its return by expanding internally. It is this reasoning which forms the basis of the theory of multinational enterprise associated with Dunning (1981), Buckley and Casson (1976), Hymer (1976) and Rugman (1980). Information, to quote Rugman, 'is the oil that lubricates the engine of the multinational enterprise' (p. 368). Firm-specific information which cannot be traded and which cannot be used to increase direct exports (perhaps because of tariffs, quotas, transport costs or other barriers to trade) will lead to geographical expansion.

At first sight, the above paragraph might appear simply to reiterate the 'internalisation' rationale for the multinational. Because markets in information are exposed to hazards, information is exploited within the firm. 'Internalisation' on its own explains why, *given* some informational advantage, a firm may become a multinational. In this somewhat static context, the relevant 'advantage', coming as it were from 'nowhere', is easily perceived as 'monopolistic' in nature. This is precisely how Hymer interpreted the situation, as mentioned earlier in section 5.3.2. However, the emphasis in this section is on the *generation* of new information. The ability to discover new information within the firm is itself a type of 'advantage'; an advantage which may require a firm to adopt a multinational strategy if it is to be fully exploited. The dynamic nature of this 'advantage' means that it can fit into an analytical framework of Schumpeterian competition rather than static monopoly.

This view of multinational production has been termed the 'eclectic approach' because it combines the 'internalisation' theory with that of the generation of 'competitive' or 'ownership advantages'. Dunning (1991) is particularly associated with the development of the eclectic paradigm. Cantwell (1991, p. 32) sums up the eclectic view by arguing that 'innovation and the growth of international production are seen as mutually support-ive'. Indeed the ability to transfer knowledge within the firm may be seen not only as a means of making the most of existing information but also as an important prerequisite for producing yet more innovations. The gener-ation and use of new information is at the heart of what Chandler (1990) calls 'organisational capabilities'.

Some link is therefore expected to exist between research and develop-ment expenditures and international and conglomerate expansion. Wolf (1977), for example, finds a statistically significant relationship between the extent of multinational operations and technical capability defined as the percentage of scientists and engineers in total employment. Vaupel (1971) found for a sample of 491 US companies, divided into national, transna-tional (operating in under six foreign countries) and multinational classes, that research and development expenditure as a proportion of sales was 2.4 per cent for multinationals, 1.6 per cent for transnationals and 0.6 per cent for national enterprises. Similarly, Dunning (1973) reports the results of his own study of US affiliates in the UK: US affiliates tend to be more con-centrated in faster-growing and export-oriented industries. They are also attracted to the technologically advanced industries and to those where both capital and advertising expenditure are slightly above average (p. 322). Pavitt (1987) similarly argues that the accumulation of technological knowledge within the firm is closely linked with the process of multina-tional expansion.

Markusen (1995, 1997) uses these results in his incorporation of the multinational firm into the theory of international trade. Multinational firms are characterised by a relatively high ratio of R&D expenditure to value of sales; a large proportion of professional and technical staff; significantly high levels of advertising and product differentiation; frequent introduction of new and complex products; and a high value of intangible assets to total market value. All these features can be seen as indicating significant 'ownership advantages' and thus as supporting a theory of the scope of the firm based upon the exploitation of firm-specific resources.[28]

6.1.3   Innovation and the conglomerate enterprise

Evidence is less clear in the case of conglomerate diversification. Wolf (1977) again finds evidence that domestic diversification is related to tech-nical capability as defined above, but, as Scherer (1980) points out (p. 422), studies of very broad diversification (across two-digit industry groups) do not reveal a close positive relationship with research and development expenditure. This may indicate that most research and development is product- or process-specific and does not typically confer benefits on activities in many different product markets.[29] If this is so, conglomerate diversification cannot generally be explained in terms of economies in the use of research and development resources, and might be better viewed, as in section 4, as a defensive response to the possibility of technological 'mugging'.

Innovation is not only about R&D however, and companies with internal 'resources' such as management skills, marketing expertise, valuable brand name recognition and so forth could use these resources by moving into differing markets – just as the Virgin brand has supported operations as different as cola, music stores, a radio station, an airline and rail transport. In other words, the arguments used to explain multinational expansion could be deployed also in the context of diversification into different markets. Thus, the use of firm-specific and non-tradable resources might still be an element in an explanation of conglomerate diversification.[30]

6.1.4 Vertical integration and innovation

Another attempt to study the association between integration (this time, *vertical* integration) and research, is that of Armour and Teece (1980). They hypothesise that vertical integration will increase the productivity of resources devoted to research, essentially because of improved flows of information between stages of production. In a sample of petroleum firms for the period 1954–75, vertical integration was measured by the number of primary production process stages undertaken (for example, crude production, refining, transport and marketing). Other 'exogenous' variables included size, cash flow and diversity (the number of activities in which the firm was engaged; for example, coal, uranium exploration/milling/mining, shale reserves, and so on). Their results indicated that 'vertical integration significantly influences . . . basic and applied research expenditures' (p. 473). Thus the direction of 'causation' is seen by Armour and Teece as flowing from 'strategy' to research expenditure rather than from research expenditures to 'strategy'. In principle, of course, both factors will react on one another and it may be misleading to consider that one 'causes' the other.

6.2 Schumpeter's Entrepreneur

As was seen in Chapter 3, Schumpeter argued that large corporations 'ousted' the entrepreneur and technical progress developed a momentum of its own. Thus, the influence of research and development on firm structure and strategy can be seen as part of a theory of the development of these mature corporations which have managed to 'institutionalise' technical change. In this subsection, however, we return to the original Schumpeterian vision of the innovating entrepreneur forcing through technical developments. Some theorists, and especially Silver (1984), have used this view of the entrepreneurial process to explain vertical integration.

Firms integrate forwards or backwards not merely to protect the information at their disposal from alert opportunists (as under subsection 6.1) but to force through changes which others are insufficiently alert to appreciate or who steadfastly refuse to be convinced of the need for them. The difficulties faced by an entrepreneur in convincing a financier of his or her ability and judgement were mentioned in Chapter 3, and the advantages of the entrepreneur having access to private resources were recognised, but this problem does not stop at the stage of finance. An innovating entrepreneur will have to persuade all the people playing a part in his or her plans that s/he has the skill and expertise to carry them through, and that s/he can fulfil his/her promises to suppliers and potential customers alike. Many of these may be suspicious of new ideas and doubtful about the possibilities of success. A supplier may be particularly reluctant to cooperate if heavy transaction-specific investment is involved. This is not simply because of the recontracting problem discussed earlier or the fear of further technical change. Even abstracting from these problems, the supplier would need to be reassured that the innovating entrepreneur had plans which were commercially viable.

Silver (1984) argues that much historical experience of integration is consistent with this view of the entrepreneurial process. New ideas are implemented by aggressive forward or backward integration and, after they have become accepted and information about the new ways of doing things has become more widely available, disintegration may occur and the 'invisible hand' may begin to reassert itself. Note that vertical integration, far from being to *restrict* access to information, is, in this view, a device to *disseminate* information which would otherwise simply not get across.

When the meat packers of Chicago wished to transport meat to the eastern cities of the USA they integrated forwards into retailing and wholesaling. Local wholesalers were initially unwilling to risk the introduction of refrigerated warehouses for handling large transhipments of meat, as they had no experience of what quality could be expected or of consumers' reactions. Once markets had been tested and established, independent wholesalers were willing to enter the trade and the meat packers withdrew entirely from retailing. A similar story can be told concerning the forward integration of oil refiners into the retailing of gasoline in the USA. We are so familiar with the service station, designed specifically for the motorist, that it is easy to forget how novel the idea must have seemed eighty years ago when gasoline would have been purchased from a general-purpose store. Once the construction of a network of outlets was complete, a move towards dis-integration could occur, mainly through franchise arrangements.

A notable example from British economic history of the resistance to new ideas, which Schumpeter's entrepreneur overcomes, is provided by the introduction of Henry Bessemer's process for making steel. When first announced, unexpected difficulties were encountered because Bessemer had unwittingly used low-phosphorus iron in his experiments and the process turned out to be unsuitable for the high-phosphorus pig-iron used by most manufacturers. Bessemer discovered the source of the problem and by using non-phosphoric pig-iron imported from Sweden was able to reduce the cost of steel from £50 to £7 a ton. In spite of these technical developments: 'I was paralysed for the moment in the face of the stolid incredulity of all practical iron and steel manufacturers . . . None of the large steel manufacturers of Sheffield would adopt my process, even under the very favourable conditions which I offered as regards licences, viz. £2 per ton.' Bessemer responded 'by adopting the only means open to me – namely, the establishment of a steel works of my own in the midst of the great steel industry of Sheffield'.[31]

Each of the examples cited thus far has concerned developments of some historic importance. The argument is applicable in many other areas, however. When efforts were made to redevelop a British watch industry in the decade after 1945 (apparently as part of the defence programme), man-ufacturers were forced to undertake the production of components and tools. As a result, the structure of the industry was quite different from that found in Switzerland at the time, where many firms were highly specialised (see again note 13). A process of very gradual historical evolution may produce a complex pattern of market cooperation between independent firms. Rapid development is rarely compatible with such a structure, and integration is required to marshal the available technical knowledge and disseminate it. To quote Edwards and Townsend once more, 'an industry cannot be started by the integration of a large number of small firms across the market if few people have the necessary technical knowledge, organis-ing knowledge and enterprise' (p. 242). In another case study, the managing director of Aero Research Ltd, a company mainly concerned with devel-oping glue (and acquired in the 1950s by Ciba Ltd), emphasised the impor-tance of 'customer education'. Although full forward integration to overcome this problem did not take place, measures were required such as the installation at cost price of tanks and apparatus at customers' works to permit bulk delivery of the new materials, the production of a monthly technical bulletin, and the running of summer schools.[32]

A final example concerns the case of Alcoa, already discussed in section 5. There it was seen that Perry (1980) explains Alcoa's strategy of forward integration as a means of instituting a regime of price discrimination. Silver (1984) argues, however, that the evidence can be interpreted in a different light. Alcoa integrated forwards into those areas where they could assist in establishing new uses for aluminium. Perry dismissed this kind of explanation as 'naive' but, as Silver points out, Perry's evidence is not sufficient entirely to discredit it.

7.   CONCLUSION

Firms differ. Even those selling in closely related markets vary considerably in size and structure. Conventional theory is not well equipped to explain this variety and predicts instead that there will be convergence to some optimal size and scope, depending upon technical conditions and the resulting cost curves. The approach surveyed in this chapter suggests, in contrast, that firms differ because the information problems with which the visible hand is designed to cope will alter over time and vary between firms. Integration may reflect a desire to protect and restrict the flow of information to others. It may represent an attempt to disseminate new information to potential customers or suppliers. It may occur as a defensive response to technical change, or as a means of developing and nurturing new ideas. It can be seen as a way of monitoring and enforcing contracts in the face of potential opportunism, or of achieving bargaining advantages in labour or other markets. Each of these possibilities has been discussed. They do not represent mutually exclusive and rival hypotheses, but may all play a part in making sense of the complex and changing patterns of integration observed in practice.

NOTES

1. Quoted in Edwards and Townsend (1967), pp. 45–6.
2. Edwards and Townsend (1967), p. 301.
3. *The Times*, 12 July 1985, p. 19, report of an analysis by Hoare-Govett.
4. There are many interesting problems associated with this type of work – the identification of industries and firms, the suitability of the statistical tests, and so on – but a detailed appraisal of the empirical work would take us too far from the main theoretical purposes of this chapter.
5. Thomas Hardy, *Far From the Madding Crowd*, edited by Ronald Blythe, Penguin, p. 87.
6. The 'exit' and 'voice' terminology is due to Hirschman (1970). See also the discussion of 'bank' versus 'market' systems of corporate governance in Chapter 9. Arm's-length contracts use termination as a means of exerting pressure on a contractor – the contractors 'exit' from the relationship if dissatisfied. Longer-term relational contracts imply the use

of 'voice'; that is, the provision of information or advice so that problems can be corrected and improvements realised.

7. Holmstrom and Roberts (1998) discuss the consequences of observed transactional relations for both the property rights theory and transactions cost theory of the firm.

8. Rubin (1978) and Martin (1988) both see franchising as a response to moral hazard. In contrast, Dnes (1992) provides an analysis of franchise contracts in terms of adverse selection and the screening out of low-quality potential franchisees. Minkler (1992) emphasises the entrepreneurial role of franchisees in discovering information about local conditions.

9. Sometimes the technical economies here are linked to the fact that the volume of a container (such as a box or a cylinder) increases as a proportion of its surface area as the sides of the box or the radius of the cylinder are increased. If costs are proportionally related to surface area, while output is more closely related to volume, average costs will fall as dimensions increase.

10. This is simply an application of the 'law of large numbers'.

11. Geographical proximity might be important but again does not, in principle, preclude the use of markets.

12. This is sometimes called Arrow's paradox (see Arrow, 1962). Kay (1983) links Arrow's paradox to the general phenomenon of 'closed loops'. Information is required to make a decision, but it is only by making the decision that we can find out the information required to guide our decision-making (pp. 68–9).

13. Entrepreneurship within the firm has been increasingly recognised and has recently been given the name 'intrapreneurship'. See N. Macrae (1976); also G. Pinchot III (1985).

14. See again Chapter 4, section 8.2 for the property rights analysis of the finance of the entrepreneur.

15. A single conglomerate enterprise might be perceived as ineffective where links between areas are insufficiently rich or where internal methods of capital allocation work against one of the divisions. In 1992, the pharmaceuticals operations of ICI were transferred to a separate firm (now called Zeneca).

16. Kay (1983) gives the example of the Swiss watch industry before the coming of electronics. Firms were highly specialised and vulnerable. Edwards and Townsend (1967) refer to the same case (pp. 237–40). The latter used the Swiss industry as an example of a case in which market transactions were important, and contrasted this with the British watch industry, where operations were more integrated (pp. 240–2). This contrast suggested that the degree of integration was not merely a technological matter but depended upon the process of development and 'maturity' of the industry; a point taken up further in section 6.

17. The use of a non-probabilistic approach to expectation and the concept of 'degree of surprise' is associated especially with G.L.S. Shackle (1970, Ch. 5).

18. This argument was used by Robertson and Dennison (1960) to explain the separation of spinning and weaving in the cotton industry in the UK but not in the wool industry: 'The various kinds of cotton yarn are much more uniform and easily standardised products than those of "woollen" yarn, and the cotton weaver is more certain of being able to satisfy his exact requirements in the open market, and has therefore less inducement to spin for himself.' (p. 27).

19. Edwards and Townsend (1967, p. 302).

20. Casson (1987) points out that internalisation may reduce the costs of transacting even in the absence of ownership advantages. Coase's original conception of the firm, for example, was about economising on transactions costs but he did not emphasise ownership advantages. 'Dunning thus uses Coasian theory in a thoroughly non-Coasian way' (p. 35).

21. This theme recurs at regular intervals. In Chapter 9 it arises in the context of takeovers. In Chapter 15 a similar problem of intertemporal commitment is discussed in the case of the intertemporal sustainability of 'natural monopoly'.

22. This statement is perhaps a little strong. If capital fixity combined with a rapid flow of potential new innovations meant that no one was willing to adopt an innovation, it

would follow that each individual could then innovate, secure in the knowledge that no one else would. The situation is similar to the paradox of voting. Given the minute chance of affecting the outcome of an election it is easy to show that 'rational abstention' is the best policy for the individual who faces positive costs of becoming informed or casting a vote. However, if everyone is in this position, each will reason that, since no one else is going to vote, a trip to the voting booth would be well worthwhile, since it will determine the outcome of the election. Owen and Grofman (1984) present a model in which individuals determine an optimal probability of voting to resolve this paradox.

23. In 1989, OECD figures record that gross expenditure on R&D was $89.8 billion in the United States, $33.7 billion in Japan, $16.6 billion in the Federal Republic of Germany and around $12 billion in France and the United Kingdom (all at purchasing-power-parity exchange rates).

24. Scherer (1980, Ch. 15) provides an overview and references to many of the fundamental contributions. For more recent theoretical developments see Tirole (1988).

25. Galbraith (1952, 1967) is particularly associated with these views.

26. Mansfield *et al.* (1971)

27. Scherer (1980) calls this the 'market room' effect, which, he argues, works in the opposite direction to the 'stimulus' effect (pp. 426–30). It is possible to argue that innovation will be 'too fast', if it occurs at all, in circumstances of great rivalry. The situation is analogous to the rapid exploration of an area in the hunt for minerals. Mineral rights can be secured only when discovered, and this will cause resources to be expended in 'discovering' deposits of minerals in advance of the date which would have been the outcome of a development process based upon secure property rights.

28. For an extensive review of the theory and evidence, see Caves (1996).

29. Nelson (1959) advanced the hypothesis that conglomerates might have an advantage in basic research; that is, research which might throw up unexpected results of importance to different products or processes.

30. See Montgomery (1994) for a review of the evidence on corporate diversification.

31. Bessemer's description of his problem is taken from his autobiography and quoted in Edwards and Townsend (1967, pp. 11–12).

32. Edwards and Townsend (1967, p. 110).

8. Corporate governance 1: managerial incentives

'Tho' love, friendship, esteem, and such like, have very powerful operations on the human mind; interest however, is an ingredient seldom omitted by wise men, when they would work others to their own purposes.'
(Henry Fielding)[1]

1. WHO CONTROLS THE JOINT-STOCK FIRM?

The firm, according to the paradigm that we are exploring in this book, is a *nexus of contracts*. These contracts establish an allocation of property rights among the individuals who comprise the firm. They may include rights to monitor, to administer resources, to receive income flows, to hire and fire, and so forth. In Chapter 6, we investigated how transactional hazards affect labour contracts and hierarchical arrangements within the firm, while in Chapter 7 attention was focused on contracts between buyers and suppliers of intermediate inputs and on the determinants of organisational scope. In Chapters 8 and 9, we address the problem of the relationship between the capitalist; that is, the supplier of *finance*; and the firm. This relationship has been traditionally intimately associated with questions of corporate governance. Where are the rights of *control* over the corporation ultimately held? What are the forces which determine the location of these rights? As will be seen, the association of finance with control is a close one, but the reasons are not as straightforward as is sometimes supposed, and the claims of other resources to rights of control will be considered at various points.

Fundamental to any discussion of business governance are distinctions between *control* rights, *decision* rights, and *residual* rights. Clearly, *decision* rights are often dispersed widely throughout an organisation. Workers and managers may be authorised to make a wide range of decisions about the best use of a company's resources. *Residual* (that is, profit) rights in the joint-stock company, as described in Chapter 4, are held by shareholders who may have no individual decision rights over the use of the assets of the company. *Control* rights are ultimately about the power to appoint the top managers of an enterprise. Again, there may be many individuals in an organisation who are empowered to negotiate on behalf of the firm and to contract with third parties. In this sense they may be thought to exercise control of the firm. However, this function is exercised on behalf of shareholders who may terminate the arrangement if they feel it is not being discharged in a satisfactory manner. The control rights of managers are thus delegated rights and can be alienated without their agreement. Ultimate control is exercised by holders of rights to appoint and dismiss directors and to approve their contractual terms; rights which cannot be alienated by the decision of some other contracting party.[2]

It would be quite mistaken to conclude from the above paragraph that there is anything 'absolute' about control rights. In the first place, the definition of control rights suggested above does not imply anything about their value and effectiveness. Property rights are never perfectly defined and costlessly enforceable. A notional control right that was too costly to exercise would be worthless, while a decision right that could not be removed from the existing holder would be a valuable asset even if it could not openly be traded. In other words, the fact that rights of control can be located and assigned to particular people in no way implies that those people are actually in control. 'De facto' control may lie with decision-makers even if 'de jure' rights of control rest elsewhere. As we shall see, the costs of enforcing and policing property rights lie behind many of the debates about corporate governance.

A second complexity is that control rights can be reassigned other than by simple exchange to different parties in certain circumstances. Debt holders, for example, do not have control rights under normal trading circumstances, but if the company defaults on its debt, control passes out of the hands of shareholders and bondholders acquire the right to intercede to protect their interests. In the literature, these rights of control are sometimes rather confusingly called *residual control rights*. The word residual, in this context, does not refer to the financial surplus of the firm but to the circumstances in which control rights can be exercised.[3]

2.   FOUR VIEWS OF CORPORATE CONTROL

2.1   Control and the Shareholder – the Traditional View

Essentially the traditional approach asserted that rights of 'control' in a joint-stock enterprise will be associated with risk taking and the provision of finance in the form of common stock. Shareholders are the claimants of all rents and are expected to exercise their rights to control the firm's resources so as to maximise this rental flow. One of the clearest statements of the traditional view of Corporate Governance can be found in Robertson and Dennison (1960). The proposition is stated in the form 'where the risk lies, there lies the control also – a proposition so important that it has sometimes been described as Capitalism's golden rule' (p. 75). By 'risk', however, Robertson and Dennison meant more than simple variability of return. The concept also embodied the notion of *team dependency*. Resources whose value depends on the success or otherwise of the team as a whole are team dependent. The importance of this idea is reflected in their analogy with control of a ship at sea. 'Those who can with honour leave the sinking ship are ultimately in a stronger position than the captain who must go down upon the bridge, and have less claim therefore to the manipulation of the wheel' (p. 78).

Underlying this traditional position was the assumption that all other members of the team – workers, managers, bondholders or the suppliers of any other inputs – could find ready alternative outlets for their services at the going 'market' rate. It was explicitly recognised that workers might be adversely affected by changes in the demand for their particular occupational skills and that this market rate might vary over time. However, this *market dependency*, while it implied that a portion of the worker's remuneration was a quasi-rent on the sunk human capital invested in acquiring occupational skills, did not make the worker dependent on the firm in which he or she worked. Nor, in the absence of monopsony power, could control of the firm in which they worked influence the overall market demand for their services. *Market dependency*, in other words, was not relevant in determining the assignment of rights of control within the firm. *Team dependent* shareholders were, by implication, those who were expected to exercise control, since failure could mean the extinction of the entire value of their 'equity'.

In subsection 2.4 we will see how the traditional view has been adjusted to take into account the existence of *transaction-dependent* resources. As it stands, the traditional view is inconsistent with much of the analysis of Chapters 6 and 7, where the significance, in modern conditions, of encouraging the accumulation of firm-specific human capital was emphasised. Further, the importance of alertness and the generation of entrepreneurial rents throughout an organisation is something which the traditional approach ignores. Entrepreneurship is simply associated with the provision of equity capital and control of the firm. Other factors receive rewards in straightforward neoclassical fashion according to their marginal productivity. The connection between the entrepreneur and the governance of the firm is discussed in subsection 2.3. Before coming to these questions, however, we discuss in subsection 2.2 the managerial critique of the traditional view of corporate control.

2.2   The Managerial Interest and the Berle–Means Critique

By the early 1930s, certain characteristics of the corporate economy were becoming difficult to reconcile with the traditional approach to corporate governance. In 1932, A.A. Berle and G.C. Means published their book *The Modern Corporation and Private Property* in which the role of the shareholder as a source of corporate control was called into question. Their thesis was based around two propositions. The first was that firms in the United States were becoming very large and that aggregate concentration was increasing. By 1930, according to Berle and Means, the two hundred largest corporations in the United States (other than banking corporations) controlled 49.2 per cent of corporate wealth, 38 per cent of business wealth and 22 per cent of national wealth (p. 33). A trend of increasing concentration had transformed the US economy in the early years of the twentieth century and seemed to show no sign of abating.[4]

The second proposition was that these large corporations were inevitably associated with highly *dispersed* shareholdings and that this made it unlikely that shareholders would exert significant control over managers. Berle and Means defined a stock interest as 'important' if it exceeded twenty per cent of the voting shares. Corporations with no single 'important' stock interest were classed as 'management controlled'. 'Control' was defined (p. 66) as 'the actual power to select the board of directors (or its majority)'. Later, in section 4, more modern thinking on what constitutes an 'important' stockholding will be discussed. By the Berle–Means criterion, however, 58 per cent of the assets of the two hundred largest non-financial corporations were classified as management-controlled in 1929. By 1963, Larner (1966) calculated that this percentage had risen to 85 per cent. 'It would appear that Berle and Means in 1929 were observing a 'managerial revolution' in process. Now, thirty years later, that revolution seems close to complete, at least within the range of the two hundred largest non-financial corporations' (pp. 786–7).

The continued importance of 'private' limited companies in the UK until the years following the First World War (see again Chapter 4) suggests that the trend towards dispersion was slower than in the USA. The inter-war years, however, saw a substantial move towards 'public' companies and the diversification of shareholdings. Between 1911 and 1960 'the minority of wealthy families no longer held their wealth in single companies in which they were also directors, choosing instead to spread their wealth over a wider range of assets' (Hannah, 1983a, p. 57).

By the middle of the twentieth century, therefore, the dispersed joint-stock corporation appeared to dominate many sectors of industry and commerce. For many observers, the consequences were expected to be far-reaching. Berle and Means (p. 116) summarised their findings using allusions to a process of imperial expansion: 'The concentration of economic power separate from ownership has, in fact, created economic empires, and has delivered these empires into the hands of a new form of absolutism, relegating "owners" to the position of those who supply the means whereby the new princes may exercise their power.' The managers of joint-stock corporations were thus invested by Berle and Means with princely authority over vast dominions – authority which, the word 'absolutism' suggests, is untrammelled by constitutional or other restraints. Galbraith (1967) has been one of the most effective modern exponents of this thesis, and has termed the managerial elite which is said to govern much of industry 'the technostructure'. Masters of new technologies and methods, members of the technostructure have replaced the old landed gentry and the more recent Victorian capitalists as the ruling class.

To a student of economic organisation, the Berle–Means critique is not without its difficulties. To pursue the Robertson and Dennison metaphor, the shareholders seem to have abandoned the bridge to highly paid officials who have access to excellent and conveniently located life-rafts in order to carouse away a dangerous voyage below decks. One might be forgiven for doubting the survival value of this particular institutional set-up. It is certainly difficult to see how capitalism's 'golden rule' can have any validity if the Berle and Means conception of events is correct. Two responses are possible. The first is that Berle and Means have misinterpreted their evidence and that, if not on the bridge, the shareholders are still able to exert their ultimate control over the management of the ship. In sections 3 to 6 we will investigate the mechanisms through which this control may be exercised. The second and more radical response is to accept the demise of shareholder control but to question the existence of shareholder dependency. If shareholders are no longer on the bridge, could it be that they have jumped ship entirely and are warm and safe in a dockyard hostelry? It is this idea which underlies subsection 2.3.

2.3   Entrepreneurship and a Neo-Austrian Critique

In Chapter 3, the idea that the modern joint-stock corporation could be viewed as a means of supplying capital to pure entrepreneurs was introduced. Kirzner mentions this interpretation as a possibility, but the theorist who develops it most fully is Wu (1989). Wu argues that the corporation represents the final stage of a long historical process during which land, labour and capital markets have become ever more developed and specialised. Whereas an entrepreneur would have once supplied his or her own labour and capital, the refinement of these markets now permits the exercise of 'pure entrepreneurship'. Capitalists are gradually becoming mere lenders of funds and risk bearers, leaving the control of the production process in the hands of the pure entrepreneurs. Firms are coalitions of entrepreneurs who control resources, claim the pure profits (entrepreneurial rents) generated by their activities, and bargain over how these rents should be distributed between them.

Wu attempts to circumvent the moral hazard problems that beset the relationship between financier and firm by appealing to the power of reputation. As information-flows improve in the capital market, any attempt to cheat the shareholders by failing to pay a satisfactory return will damage the future viability of the firm. 'In order to avoid jeopardising the firm's ability to raise funds in the capital market, the entrepreneurs must protect the value of shares as jealously as the capitalist would and must offer a satisfactory rate of return' (p. 227). The existing power of the shareholder collectively to influence decisions and change the team will become unnecessary because there is no shareholder dependency. As the capital market becomes increasingly efficient, argues Wu, 'Shareholders' veto power over the entrepreneurs' decisions will become superfluous' (p. 253). The Berle–Means 'division of ownership from control' becomes through Wu's radical reconceptualisation merely the division of capitalist from entrepreneur.[5]

Corporate governance for Wu is therefore entirely concerned with bargaining over entrepreneurial rents generated by the coalition of entrepreneurs that comprises the firm. It is the entrepreneurs who are the *team-dependent* resources while the highly developed capital market permits providers of finance to reduce their dependency on any particular team to negligible proportions. By spreading their stockholdings widely, the capitalists avoid team-specific risks and are left bearing the unavoidable risks associated with the 'market portfolio'. The returns to shareholders no longer include entrepreneurial rents but merely quasi-rents on capital because the physical resources financed by the shareholders will continue to supply their services in the short run irrespective of the return that is paid. Although the receipt of quasi-rents implies a type of dependency, the competition for shareholders' finance and the pursuit of good reputations by entrepreneurs will ensure that the potential for opportunism is not abused and shareholders can expect to receive the 'market rate' for their services. The *team dependency* of the classical capitalist is thus transformed into a form of *market dependency*. Like the occupation-specific labour discussed in subsection 2.1, the return from which was a quasi-rent dependent on general market conditions, so the capitalist can be seen as in a similar situation. A bearer of risk, the shareholder can nevertheless derive no advantage from the control of any particular team.

There is an important aspect of Wu's approach which must be explicitly recognised here, although more detailed discussion will not take place until Chapter 12. The theory has an inevitable evolutionary basis. In Chapter 3, the problem of supplying entrepreneurs with the resources necessary to back their judgements was noted. The hazards associated with the capitalist–entrepreneur relationship were seen to be so severe that throughout history the two functions have been closely integrated. Separating them out requires the generation of trust and the development of reputational capital. This is not a question of contractual design or legal innovation. It is a question of the passage of time. Only over time can firms develop reputations for integrity and reliability which can then be used to achieve ends which would otherwise have been impossible. Only over time can cultural norms develop which reduce the fear of opportunism. As Casson (1991) emphasises (see again Chapter 1), business culture is an important determinant of economic performance and a suitable culture cannot be created quickly. The approach to corporate governance explored by Wu is not therefore a straightforward rational choice approach. It is a system that is compatible with the rational behaviour of individuals, but it is the end result of a long process of historical evolution.

Capitalism's 'golden rule' is not overturned by this conception of the joint-stock corporation. In some ways it seems to apply with even greater purity. With the bearing of risk now quite separate from the receipt of entrepreneurial rents the rule can simply be reformulated as 'where the team dependency lies, there lies the control also'. Team-dependent people are the entrepreneurs – claimants to the pure profits which remain after payment of wages, interest, dividends and rents to non-dependent suppliers of factors of production.

There is, however, a further difficulty to discuss. Are the entrepreneurs the only team-dependent people, or are there other non-entrepreneurial inputs that are nevertheless dependent on the team and likely to be claimants to some control of its operations? It is this issue which comes to the fore in subsection 2.4.

2.4 Contractual Incompleteness, Dependency and Control

People who have claims to the pure profits generated by a team are clearly *team dependent*. There is, however, another form of dependency discussed in Chapters 6 and 7 which is relevant to the issue of corporate governance. If resources receive quasi-rents on *firm-specific* capital which they have financed, they may become vulnerable to 'hold-up'. Examples include implicit bond-posting arrangements which support monitoring arrangements within the firm and investments in human capital which have a payoff to a given team but not elsewhere. The quasi-rents which accrue to such resources are derived from the value created by the team, but they are not necessarily entrepreneurial in nature and do not imply any claim on the team's residual.[6] As was seen in earlier chapters, incentive devices involving the creation of dependency can be analysed in a rigorously neoclassical setting. They rely on trust in the firm's integrity, but (in the absence of bankruptcy) do not imply that the relevant resources are dependent on the team's *performance* as a whole.

We will term recipients of quasi-rents on firm-specific capital *transaction-specific* resources and the accompanying dependency on the goodwill of the firm *transaction dependency*. It is important to realise that transaction dependency does not derive from an assumption that the firm is unreliable. On the contrary, the state of dependency exists only if the firm is perceived as sufficiently reliable. As Alchian and Woodward (1987) put it 'a resource is "dependent" when it would lose value if separated from the team'. Any firm which stole the quasi-rents on transaction-specific resources would free those resources from further dependency since they would now lose nothing by deserting the team. A trustworthy firm is therefore required to create dependency and the quasi-rents associated with it.

Nevertheless, transaction-specific resources might still feel vulnerable to breach of trust or even managerial incompetence and this might be expected to influence the governance of the firm. 'Firm-specific[7] dependent resources will be the parties who place the highest values on the right to administer . . . In general, whoever has a value that has become firm specific will seek some form of control over the firm' (Alchian and Woodward, pp. 119–20). According to this approach, therefore, the controlling interest in a firm will not be associated with particular specialised functions (discussed in subsections 2.1 to 2.3) such as shareholding, managing, or entrepreneurship, but may include any resource which is firm specific and receives rent from its participation in the team activity. Transaction-dependent labour may, for example, form unions to monitor the adherence of firms to their implicit obligations. Representation on company boards might be a means of protecting vulnerable specific assets. If takeovers are perceived as a threat to firm-specific quasi-rents, modification to company constitutions may be sought to make takeovers more difficult. These possibilities will be taken up at various points later in this chapter and in Chapter 9.

The ideas explored in this subsection are related to those of subsection 2.3. Entrepreneurs must control resources in order to back their judgement and derive the profit from them. As claimants to entrepreneurial profit they are dependent on the performance of the team and are therefore holders of the team's *equity*. In a world in which reputation was powerful enough to reassure transaction-dependent resources that the value of their assets was safe from opportunism and rent seeking, governance mechanisms giving an element of control to these resources would not be necessary and pure entrepreneurs could be the sole holders of the team's *equity* and the associated rights of control. In the messier world of uncertainty, bounded rationality, and contractual incompleteness in which we live, control rights will be sought by all holders of dependent assets, and corporate governance will be a compromise between the interests of many different parties. Manager-entrepreneurs will fear raids on entrepreneurial rents by workers or shareholders; workers will expect their quasi-rents to be stolen by shareholders in takeover raids; shareholders will contemplate the possibility that managers will renege on their obligations to provide a suitable return on their capital. When we observe the governance structures that actually exist, therefore, we should not expect them to look like any of the 'pure cases' covered in this section.

3.   CORPORATE GOVERNANCE AS A PRINCIPAL–AGENT PROBLEM

No relationship in business life is more subject to transactional hazards than that between the financier and the managers of a joint-stock corporation. As we saw at the end of Chapter 4, the inability of the financier to observe the behaviour of managers gives rise to the problem of moral hazard. Managers may divert resources to their own personal ends, and, as Adam Smith expressed it, look with less 'anxious vigilance' over the shareholders' wealth than they would do over their own. Only if granted a monopoly or 'exclusive privilege', argued Smith, could the joint-stock form of enterprise hope to prevail over the 'private adventurer'.[8]

Hidden action is not the only problem with which contractors are faced, however. In an uncertain and complex environment it will usually be difficult for an outside financier to evaluate managerial competence and to distinguish good decisions which turned out badly from poor decisions which stood only a small chance of success in the first place. Because managers are much better *informed* about the affairs of the company than are financiers, the hidden information or adverse selection problem is serious.

For centuries, therefore, economists have observed the joint-stock enterprise and wondered at its survival potential. At the time of the Joint Stock Companies Act 1856 in the UK, it was by no means obvious that this form would come to dominate industrial and commercial life. The rest of this chapter concerns the ways in which these glaring problems of inducing managerial efficiency have affected the governance of the joint-stock enterprise. This is attempted by applying the theory of principal and agent to the relationship between financier and firm, just as in Chapters 6 and 7 it was applied to the analysis of labour contracts and the firm's relationships with suppliers.

The most systematic exposition of the idea of the firm as a 'legal fiction which serves as a nexus for contracting relationships' is to be found in Jensen and Meckling (1976, p. 311). Their discussion of 'ownership structure' in the corporation is based entirely on the concept of 'agency costs generated by the contractual arrangements between the owners and top management of the corporation' (p. 309). This conception is not entirely uncontroversial, however. To a lawyer, for example, the shareholder's relationship with the firm cannot be regarded as a contractual one. Neither is it true that shareholders have contracts with managers. This has led some theorists to argue that the principal–agent paradigm is not appropriate in the context of shareholder and manager. Clark (1985, p. 56), for example, objects to the use of the terms 'principal' and 'agent': 'The core legal concept implies a relationship in which the principal retains the power to control and direct the activities of the agent.' The shareholder's powers in a corporation, however, are limited, and 'the officers and directors are "fiduciaries" with respect to the corporation and its stockholders'. They have various responsibilities and duties but they are not agents.[9]

Accepting that managers are not, legally speaking, agents of shareholders, it is still reasonable to argue that the manager does have a contract with the firm, that the provisions of this contract and the incentive devices built into it will crucially influence the willingness of people to hold the financial instruments of the company, and that in assessing the likely effectiveness of these contracts the shareholder and bondholder will presumably have the same factors in mind as in an assessment of an agency contract. If it were objected that few shareholders would have detailed knowledge of managerial contracts in a firm, the defence must be similar to that advanced by Stiglitz in the context of the discussion of piece-rates and time-rates in Chapter 6. Over time, the competitive process selects those arrangements with survival value and these will look, in the end, like a 'solution' to an agency problem.

According to the nexus of contracts approach, we would expect the structure of rights within the corporation to reflect the hazards to which the contributors are subject. Shareholders will be aware that managers may shirk or may use profits to finance investments with low net present values rather than to pay higher dividends. Bondholders will know that shareholders' may be induced to endorse more risky projects because the benefit from successful (if rather lucky) outcomes will accrue entirely to share-holders rather than the recipients of fixed interest, while limited liability provides a floor to possible shareholder losses in the event of bad luck. Managers and workers who have accumulated much firm-specific expertise and are vulnerable to opportunistic recontracting (for example, after a takeover) will look for ways to defend their interests. These observations suggest that different conditions will be conducive to different contractual arrangements and differing financial structures. Sections 4 to 9 investigate responses to the agency problem in more detail. As Fama and Jensen (1983, p. 345) express it, 'we explain the survival of organisational forms largely in terms of the comparative advantages of characteristics of residual claims in controlling the agency problems of an activity'.

In Chapter 5, the major forces moulding relationships between principal and agent were set out. The 'observability' of effort; the cost of monitoring; the availability of informative signals concerning the agent's behaviour; the efficiency of effort; the degree of risk aversion of the contractors; the uncertainty of the environment; the durability of the relationship – all these matters were expected to play a part in establishing the contractual outcomes. In the following sections, the same considerations will be discussed in the context of corporate governance. Section 4 investigates incentive contracts for managers on the assumption that their actions are unobservable. In section 5, the role of monitoring is discussed. Is it true that shareholders have no incentive to monitor managers? Are there informative signals about managerial effort available? Are there ways that influence can be exerted even with dispersed shareholdings? The use of information on the relative performance of managers facing similar environmental conditions, and the role of the managerial labour market as a provider of incentives is covered in section 6. The constraining and stimulating influence of competition in the product market is the topic of section 7.

4.   MANAGERIAL INCENTIVE CONTRACTS

4.1   Managerial Incentives and the Theory of Principal and Agent

When the provider of capital appoints a manager to decide how it should be used, an agency problem arises. In Chapter 5, it was seen that the nature of a contract between principal and agent will depend upon what can be observed, by whom, and at what cost. Let us suppose that the manager's effort and the environment or 'state of the world' in which he or she is operating are unobservable to outsiders. The contract will then depend upon the 'outcome' alone, and the provisions for sharing the outcome between two parties will depend upon the risk preferences of each. In other words, if a manager is to be given an incentive his or her reward must depend upon the outcome; in this case, the overall profit of the firm.

Figure 8.1 applies the theory of principal and agent to the relationship between the outside shareholder (in this case the principal) and the manager (here seen as the agent). If shareholdings are widely dispersed, S can be regarded as a 'typical shareholder' who is risk neutral in so far as the operation of the firm is concerned. The shareholder is interested only in the expected value of his or her profits from the firm. The manager (M) is risk averse and is, by assumption, unable to find insurance in the market because of the inability of insurers to observe states of the world any more easily than shareholders. This rules out contracts between α and t along the manager's certainty line. Although ideal from the point of view of risk sharing, contracts on the manager's certainty line will not induce effort. There may, however, exist a contract along the locus xw which will induce effort e from the manager of the shareholders' funds. Contracts along xw imply some form of profit-related pay or stock ownership on the part of managers. If managers are risk averse, they will never take the entire risk, and hence we will not observe the manager effectively holding all residual claims and the provider of capital turning into a bondholder and lending at fixed interest (as at point ϕ in Figure 8.1). Thus, the concentration of all

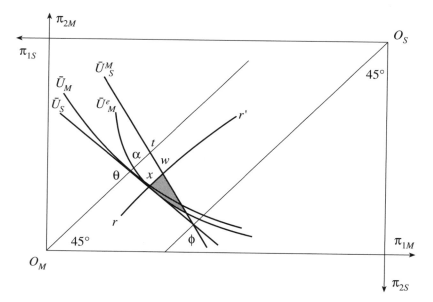

Figure 8.1   Shareholder and manager as principal and agent

residual claims in the monitor, as in the classical capitalist firm, is likely to exist only where capital requirements are small and monitors are risk neutral (see again the discussion of the single proprietorship in Chapter 4).

Contracts which link managerial rewards to profits will only work, of course, if the individual manager's effort is actually capable of influencing the overall performance of the firm. In a 'team' environment where the individual contribution of each manager cannot be identified, the 'public good trap' will lead to shirking, and, as was seen in Chapter 4, contracts based upon 'effort' will be instituted. 'Monitoring gambles' and the hierarchical structures associated with them will become important, as described in Chapter 6. Eventually, however, the problem must be faced of who monitors the effort of the most senior managers? If shareholdings are dispersed the answer seems to be no one, and the house of cards erected in Chapter 6 falls down as predicted by Adam Smith. However, by giving senior managers at the apex of the hierarchy compensation packages which depend upon overall performance, effort incentives are provided. A manager low down the hierarchical structure will not find the holding of shares a great incentive to effort because the total profit of the enterprise may be imperceptibly affected by his or her behaviour. Senior managers are like the keystone in an arch, however. Take them away and collapse ensues; in place, the whole structure stands. Thus, the effort of top managers clearly will influence outcomes, and changes in the intensity of monitoring will permeate through the hierarchical structure. This argument is therefore based upon Alchian and Demsetz's (1972) observation that monitors need an incentive to monitor, but it does not lead to the conclusion that the residual must be completely undiluted and assigned to a single person. All that is required is that incentives to top management are good enough for the joint-stock form, with its benefits of risk spreading and large team operations to prevail over alternative available institutional forms.

4.2 Some Early Studies of Managerial Contracts

The remuneration of senior executives is clearly a matter of great importance, and the evidence concerning the incentives built into various payment packages is still in dispute. At the heart of this long-running issue is disagreement about whether the interests of senior managers and directors are clearly associated with those of stockholders (for example, through direct stockholdings, stock options, pension entitlements, profit-related bonuses and so on) or whether, as Berle and Means asserted, managers have little reason to consider the shareholders and can pursue their own agenda. Early work by Sargant Florence (1961) for the UK and Villarejo (1961) for the USA pointed to the small percentage of shares held by directors in very large companies. The median holding was between one per cent and two per cent in the early 1950s. Managerial shareholding rose during the 1950s and 1960s, however, and the *combined* interest of corporate directors and management is often considerable. Demsetz (1983) reports that in the years 1973–82 the ownership interest of corporate directors and management was 19.3 per cent for the middle ten firms in the 1975 Fortune 500 list. For ten randomly selected firms too small to be included in the Fortune 500, the managerial interest was 32.5 per cent. It was in the very largest size range (the top ten firms), as would be expected, that the percentage interest of managers and directors fell to 2.1 per cent. Thus, 'a substantial fraction of outstanding shares is owned by directors and management of corporations in all but the very largest firms' (p. 388).

From the point of view of incentives, neither the combined shareholding of management nor the proportionate holding of senior managers is the most important factor, however. Of greater significance is the nature of the remuneration package of the most senior managers. Work in the early 1960s suggested that management income was more closely related to company size as measured by total sales than to company profits.[10] McGuire, Chiu and Elbing (1962), for example, reported statistical correlations between executive compensation, profits and sales in a cross-section of firms in the period 1953–59. Their evidence supported a relationship between sales and executive incomes, although they cautiously warned that statistical problems meant that their tests 'do not completely rule out the possibility of a valid relationship between profits and executive incomes too' (p. 760). By the early 1970s, cross-section studies of this nature were subjected to considerable criticism.[11]

Given the hierarchical structure of large firms, the internal incentive arrangement might be expected to result in a different scale of prizes for the contestants in a big tournament than a smaller one. This, though, would not permit us to deduce that, for a manager at the top of a given firm, an overriding incentive existed to increase the size of that particular hierarchy. A further criticism concerned the measure of executive incomes used. By concentrating on salaries, other important components were overlooked.

Masson (1971) constructed a measure of executive compensation which included deferred compensation such as stock options and retirement benefits as well as stock ownership, salary and bonuses. His sample consisted of the top three to five executives of thirty-nine electronics, aerospace and chemical companies for the years 1947–66. From these data, Masson concluded that executives receive a positive reward for increasing stock value, that changes in stock value are more important to the executive than changes in profit earned, and that the hypothesis that executives were paid to expand sales was rejected. Similar conclusions were reported by Lewellen (1969). In a survey of fifty of the largest five hundred US firms, Lewellen found that only about one-fifth of the total remuneration of the top executive came from salary. This study was followed by a further enquiry by Lewellen and Huntsman (1970). One of their measures of executive compensation included the 'current income equivalent' of various deferred and contingent pay schemes. In the case of a pension plan, for example, the extra salary necessary to buy equivalent cover from an insurance company was estimated and included as part of the comprehensive measure of managerial compensation. Their results indicated that 'reported company profits appear to have a strong and persistent influence on executive rewards, whereas sales seem to have little, if any, such impact' (p. 918). A surprising aspect of this finding was that it applied to the simpler measure of executive compensation (salary plus bonuses) as well as to the more sophisticated measure.

Meeks and Whittington (1975) concluded in contrast that managerial compensation was strongly correlated with sales in cross-section tests. Developing the point mentioned earlier, Meeks and Whittington did not, however, deduce from this that incentives are primarily in the direction of increasing size at the expense of profits. It is simply not open to managers or directors suddenly to choose to be as big as IBM or ICI in order to raise their salary. Although cross-section correlations are strong, large proportionate increases in size would be necessary to have a noticeable effect on a manager's income. In practice, the manager does not choose the size of the firm but may have some influence over the rate of growth. When Meeks and Whittington considered the relative influence of higher growth and higher profits on managers' rewards, however, their data suggested that profits were the more important.

4.3 Interpretative Problems and Some More Recent Studies

4.3.1 Executive stockholdings

More recent work, though increasingly sophisticated at a technical level, continues to reveal the difficulties of interpretation in this area. Cosh and Hughes (1987), for example, compare twenty-seven large UK companies from *The Times* 1000 with the same number of US companies from the Fortune list of the largest industrial corporations in 1981. The mean percentage of shares held beneficially and non-beneficially by Board Members was a mere 0.19 per cent in the UK sample compared with 5.7 per cent in the USA. These figures look small, especially in the UK. However, from a motivational point of view, small percentage holdings in extremely large companies can represent large personal wealth. Cosh and Hughes report that, in the USA 17.5 per cent of executive directors and 15.5 per cent of all directors were (pound sterling) millionaires simply through holdings of stock in the companies concerned. These figures rose to 33 per cent and 21 per cent respectively when stock options were included in the calculations. Directors in the USA can hardly be characterised as propertyless functionaries according to this evidence. On the other hand, it is clear that the situation in the UK in the early 1980s differed considerably from that in the USA. 'In general, US CEOs (Chief Executive Officers) receive over 40 times the dividend income of their UK counterparts and the average director about 10 times as much' (p. 303). Conyon and Murphy (2000) use 1997 data to confirm the finding that US chief executives receive higher total remuneration than those in the UK.[12] The sensitivity of CEO remuneration to shareholder wealth was also higher in the USA, with the median CEO receiving around 1.5 per cent of increases in shareholder wealth compared with 0.25 per cent in the UK.

An important study of the US position is offered by Jensen and Murphy (1990b). In their sample of firms, the median holding of common stock by CEOs was 0.25 per cent. When the value of other components of the remuneration package such as bonuses, salary revisions, stock options, and performance-based dismissal decisions were added, Jensen and Murphy estimated that the CEO receives $3.25 for every $1000 increase in shareholder wealth.[13] As a result of this low sensitivity of CEO remuneration to changes in shareholder wealth, 'we believe that our results are inconsistent with the implications of formal agency models of optimal contracting' (p. 227). Quite simply, the observed contract point seems too close to the CEO's certainty line out of O_M in Figure 8.1. Alternatively the 'profit share' or 'piece-rate' seems too small in terms of Figure 6.2 to be an optimal response to the principal–agent problem. This finding of a very small 'pay-performance sensitivity' is confirmed also in UK studies.[14]

Jensen and Murphy consider various escape routes from this quandary. Perhaps CEOs are easy to monitor after all and the shareholders have effective mechanisms for exerting direct control. We will be looking at this possibility in section 5. Perhaps CEOs cannot very much influence the welfare of shareholders by their efforts or their performance depends more on innate ability than on incentives. This, argue Jensen and Murphy, is inconsistent with evidence such as stock-price reactions to changes in CEOs which at least imply that the personality and efficiency of the CEO is important to the success or failure of the team. Perhaps the takeover threat is sufficient to motivate managers. But takeovers 'may be a response to, instead of an efficient substitute for, ineffective internal incentives' (p. 253). Unable to accept any of these explanations, Jensen and Murphy offer instead a 'political' answer. Sensational stories in the press and on television about 'excessive' executive compensation act as a disincentive to the introduction of suitable management contracts.

It is possible to argue, however, that Jensen and Murphy are too precipitate in their rejection of observed contracts as efficient responses to an agency problem. Cosh and Hughes' point about the reaction of individual CEOs to absolutely large wealth effects (even if small in relation to the capitalisation of the company as a whole) needs to be taken more seriously.

Consider Figure 8.2. A risk-averse agent (manager) runs a small company. Possible profit outcomes are Q_1 (good) and Q_2 (bad) respectively. Effort e, which, as in chapter 5, has the effect of increasing the probability of the good outcome, will be exerted by the agent at points along and to the right of the locus rr'. A contract prevails at c midway along the diagonal $O_M O_S$. Assume this is an optimal contract. It implies that the agent (manager) holds fifty per cent of the shares of the company. Now let the company double in size with the profit outcomes $2Q_1$ (good) and $2Q_2$ (bad). Under what circumstances would the contract at c still be an optimal contract? Suppose that effort level e had the same beneficial effect on the probability of the good outcome in the case of the big company as for the small company. The locus rr' would be unchanged and c would confer the same expected utility to the manager whether he or she were in the big or the small company. The contract at c would be optimal in both cases. Yet, in

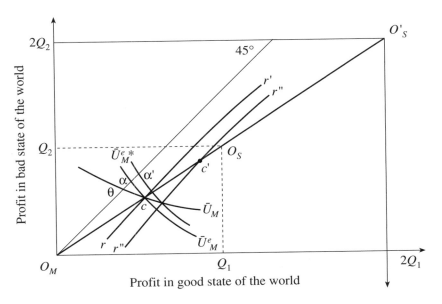

Figure 8.2   Management shareholdings and firm size

the case of the big company, the agent (manager) holds only 25 per cent of the shares. Indeed, we might imagine the large company being one hundred times bigger than the small. In that case, on the assumption that effort e affects the probability distribution of the outcomes in the same way in large and small companies, a shareholding of 0.5 per cent would be optimal.

It will rightly be objected that the above model is oversimplified in its assumption of a dichotomous choice of 'effort' or 'no effort' on the part of the agent. However, the crucial assumption driving the result is, of course, that effort level e produces the same rise in the probability of the 'good' outcome in both large and small firms, even though the absolute size of the potential gain from achieving the good outcome is obviously much greater in the former compared with the latter. Effectively, the expected return to the team as a whole from the effort of the CEO is assumed to rise in proportion with the size of the firm.[15] This permits the CEO to achieve the same expected *personal* return with a declining proportion of the outstanding shares. If the higher probability of the good outcome required *more* effort on the part of the CEO in the big compared with the small firm (let us say effort level e^*), the locus rr' would shift further away from the manager-agent's certainty line (for example to $r''r''$) and the optimal contract might involve greater risk-sharing losses. The cost of effort would now be represented by distance $\theta\alpha'$. Even in this case, however, a contract at a point such as c' in Figure 8.2 would imply a declining proportion of the firm's shares held by the manager as the company grew.

The CEO's effort can be regarded as a resource which reaches out through the organisation, increasing the productivity of the entire team. In the simplest formulation, a unit of CEO effort is a necessary ingredient to the more effective running of large and small teams – an overhead which is the same size for all firms. This might be rationalised in terms of strategic decision taking which may involve similar skills and effort in very different sizes of firm. To revert to the analogy of the ship at sea, the captain of a large oil tanker may use skills of a very similar order to those required on a smaller freighter, but the possible consequences for good or ill of his or her decisions will not be of the same order of magnitude. Alternatively, we might see the CEO as a motivator of others and a crucial influence on the 'culture' of the entire firm.[16] The point here is that the CEO's effort can produce indirect effects at some distance from the point of its initial application. The CEO sets a chain of events in motion by prodding into action the material closest to hand. The system as a whole gains momentum as limiting friction is overcome and each member of the team begins to exert force on the others.

Whether the above reasoning explains anything about the governance of the modern joint-stock enterprise is as much an empirical as a theoretical question. It does suggest the importance of recognising, however, that if CEO effort is highly effective at improving the probability distribution of outcomes, efficient personal incentives may be compatible with very small stockholdings as a proportion of the total stock issued. Haubrich (1994), for example, simulates 'optimal' contracts on the basis of plausible assumptions about risk preferences and effort costs and finds that 'principal–agent theory *can* yield quantitative solutions in line with the empirical work of Jensen and Murphy' (p. 259).

If effort is allowed to vary continuously, it might be expected that an efficient effort level for the CEO would be higher in a large firm than a small one. However, if the efficiency of effort is great in both cases, the optimal contract will be close to the agent's certainty line (see Chapter 5). Now suppose there is: (i) rapidly falling marginal productivity of further effort (in terms of its effect on the probability distribution of possible outcomes); (ii) rapidly rising marginal disutility of effort; and (iii) risk aversion on the part of the CEO. All these factors will imply that a given rise in effort will require big shifts to the right in the locus rr' of contracts capable of inducing it. As demonstrated in Chapter 5, these conditions are likely to imply the absence of Pareto improvements available from such contracts.

The above paragraphs have concentrated on reinterpreting the Jensen and Murphy findings in order to see whether they can after all be made compatible with principal–agent theory. However, some students of corporate governance cast doubt on the low pay–performance elasticity estimates of Jensen and Murphy. Hall and Liebman (1998) for example, use data on CEO compensation packages from the largest US firms. They report very high values of pay–performance sensitivity compared with Jensen and Murphy. Indeed, their median elasticity of compensation to firm value is 3.9 for 1994 – implying that a one per cent increase in firm value would result in a 3.9 per cent increase in CEO remuneration. The main factor driving this result appears to be the increase in the award of stock options during the 1980s and 1990s in the USA. The popularity of stock options during the 1990s is perhaps understandable given that the S&P 500 index rose by three hundred per cent during the decade.[17]

Stock options as a method of aligning the interests of managers with those of shareholders have been subject to some criticism, however.[18] An option gives a manager the right to purchase stock at an agreed exercise price during a specified period of time (after which the option lapses). Permitting the manager to determine the date of exercise of the option thus gives him/her a chance to speculate on general market movements, taking his/her profit while options are 'in the money' and when s/he judges conditions to be favourable. The incentive effects of this instrument are not, therefore, very focused. Further, there is a paradoxical side to the operation of stock options. If they are expected to motivate managers successfully, the present value of expected future profits will rise and so also will the value of the firm on the market. However, where a manager can exercise his/her options fairly soon after they have been granted, s/he might realise his/her gain quickly before much of his/her anticipated effort has been made. Presumably, an efficient market would allow for this effect in evaluating the incentive effects of the options in the first place, but options are clearly not a simple method of aligning managerial and ownership interests. Critics have suggested, for example, that an exercise date should be specified in the contract and that the value should be linked to relative performance against other firms in the same sector.[19]

Stock options can also be criticised from precisely the opposite perspective compared with Jensen and Murphy. In other words, they can imply a contract point too far from the agent's certainty line rather than too close. If an agent is risk averse, there will be a risk-bearing cost to this uncertainty. Especially where the riskiness of the stock is very great, the value of options to a manager can be well below the cost to the firm of awarding them. Outside equity holders in the firm might be well diversified whereas a manager whose remuneration depends substantially on stock options is not.[20]

4.3.2   Trading on inside information

At this point, it is convenient to look briefly at another possible incentive device – trading on inside information. The law takes a dim view of such activities in many countries and it is widely considered that insider dealing is undesirable. The Criminal Justice Act in the United Kingdom, for example, makes it a crime to deal, or to procure or encourage another to deal, on the basis of inside information.[21] The United States has a similarly restrictive legal background while the European Community has issued an important Directive on Insider Dealing.[22]

Justifications for this restrictive legislation are based on grounds of efficiency, the protection of property rights, and of straightforward fairness. If market makers dealing in stocks and shares frequently face better-informed 'insiders', it is claimed that they risk losing heavily in their trading activities with these parties and will be inhibited from trading.[23] Adverse selection will mean that the market will be less developed than it would be with symmetrical information – an application of the 'lemons' principle which was introduced in Chapter 2. The property rights argument relies upon a traditional view of the joint-stock enterprise (see again section 2.1) with shareholders as the rightful 'owners' of information accruing to the employees and managers in the course of their duties. According to this argument, insider dealers are attempting to steal some of the profits that belong rightfully to the shareholders. Finally, the idea of better-informed traders gaining at the expense of the unwary or misinformed by buying or selling assets at prices they know to be 'false' is not acceptable to some people, even when the trading is conducted on vast and impersonal stock markets.

Each of these arguments is open to serious objections. Firstly, restrictions on insider dealing could mean that the prices of assets on the stock market do not reflect the full information potentially available and that market efficiency is thereby impaired.[24] A celebrated exposition of this view can be found in Henry Manne (1966). Secondly, if shareholders wish to negotiate contracts with their managers permitting them to trade on inside information as part of an incentive package, breach of trust would not be involved. Finally, all entrepreneurial activity and the social benefits deriving from it relies on some people thinking they have better information than others. To abolish trade in the presence of asymmetrically distributed knowledge would be to abolish the entrepreneurial process entirely.[25] Indeed, the more we are inclined to accept Wu's conception of the firm as a coalition of entrepreneurs, the more important it becomes to provide a mechanism which enables them to claim entrepreneurial profits. Manne (1966) argued, for example, that 'profits from insider trading constitute the only effective compensation scheme for entrepreneurial services in large corporations' (p. 116). However, the logic of Wu's approach would not seem to suggest the use of insider trading. If shareholders receive a regular flow of dividends and have no claim to the 'pure entrepreneurial profits', share prices would be expected to be fairly stable, and surplus profits would presumably be received by the entrepreneurs in the form of bonuses, profit-related pay, pension rights and stock options.

Even in the context of the agency model of the joint-stock company, allowing insider dealing as a means of giving incentives to managers is not a straightforward way of aligning managerial and shareholder interests. Profits are made on securities markets by having better information than other people, but this applies to information about bad financial results as well as good results. The ability of an informed insider to profit from advance knowledge of bad trading results by a policy of selling the shares short would not be compatible with providing incentives to managers to avoid these results. Shareholders would presumably wish managers to benefit from diligence and skill in their jobs rather than from the simple privilege of gaining access to information first. Stock options, or the ownership of stock with *restrictions* on the right to trade for a specified period of time would therefore appear to be more effectively structured incentive devices. Managers can then only gain from ensuring a *rise* in the price of the stock over the long run.

5.   MONITORING MANAGERS

5.1   Do Shareholders Monitor Managers?

The analysis of section 4 applied to the standard case in which the effort of the agent was 'unobservable'. Could it be, however, that some monitoring of managers by shareholders is feasible? Let us envisage that managerial services are purchased from specialist suppliers. The nature of the service is highly complex and costly to monitor, but let us further suppose that shareholders through specialist advisers, journalists, independent auditors and other personal contacts are able to form some assessment of the competence and dedication of the management. They have, in the jargon of Chapter 5, some 'informative signal' at their disposal. Incentives could then be given to the top management, not only through the direct ownership of shares, or the offer of options and bonuses, but through a type of 'monitoring gamble'. This system has traditionally been regarded as inapplicable to the joint-stock form of enterprise, and it is interesting to consider whether the traditional approach is justified.

Shareholder intervention is usually expected to founder on the prisoner's dilemma. In a dispersed corporation, there is no single shareholder in a position to monitor the management and enforce the terms of any monitoring gamble. A penalty for 'shirking' could be imposed only through the mechanism of the shareholders' meeting, and we have already drawn attention to the lack of any incentive for the small individual shareholder to attend, or even to become acquainted with whatever 'informative signal' might be relevant. Further, in the unlikely event of a substantial shareholder revolt, it has usually been assumed that the incumbent management has an advantage because of the system of 'proxy' votes.[26] Uninformed shareholders may simply permit the managers to vote on their behalf. Persuading them to act for themselves by informing them of the evidence of managerial shirking may be a very costly undertaking, and if any single shareholder or group of shareholders attempted it they would effectively be supplying a public good (information) free of charge to the rest of the shareholding body. Thus, except in the special circumstances of low costs of acquiring a sufficiently informative signal and low participation costs at shareholders' meetings, shareholder monitoring might appear to be of little practical importance.

This view, however, has to be qualified in important respects. Whether shareholders monitor managers will depend upon the balance of private cost and benefit. We may agree that monitoring will be lower in a dispersed corporation than in one with concentrated shareholdings, for the reasons discussed in the previous paragraph, but the extreme conclusion that no monitoring will take place relies on the assumption that all shareholders are alike in holding a negligible fraction of the outstanding equity and thus will receive a negligible benefit. In practice, however, non-negligible blocks of shareholdings exist. This can affect incentives substantially, both by encouraging monitoring and playing a role in the takeover mechanism (see Chapter 9).

5.2 The Costs of Monitoring

The cost of monitoring will be influenced by three major factors:

1. Economic environments that are unpredictable and 'noisy' in a statistical sense may reduce the information content of a signal so much that its value falls short of the costs of observation and enforcement. In our discussion of the franchise chain, in Chapter 7, it was observed that outlets in urban centres (where trade was more predictable and comparisons could be made between similarly placed establishments) could be managed while rural outlets were franchised. Similarly, in stable businesses and those which give scope for performance comparisons between firms, monitoring costs will be lower than in highly unstable areas.

2. Monitoring costs will be lower the fewer the decision options between which managers can choose. Some assets give managers enormous scope for exercising discretion, others give only limited possibilities for management choice. Alchian and Woodward (1987) argue that where the assets of the firm allow for only a limited range of possible uses, the monitoring problem will not be severe. They call such assets *implastic* assets. Conversely, 'We call resources or investments "*plastic*" to indicate there is a wide range of legitimate decisions within which the user may choose, or that an observer can less reliably monitor the choice' (p. 117). The oil well, for example, is considered an *implastic* asset. In spite of the risks associated with fluctuating oil prices, oil recovery is easy to monitor and permits, they argue, a high level of debt finance in that particular business.

3. Receiving useful information is one thing; enforcing a change in policy or management is another. The costs of *enforcing* the shareholders 'control rights' will depend upon the minimum size of the coalition required to unseat the incumbent management. It was the assumed enormous size of this coalition which lay behind the argument that shareholder monitoring would not take place. In the following subsection, the question of whether shareholders can enforce their control rights is considered in more detail.

5.3   The Degree of Shareholder Control

5.3.1   Measuring the degree of 'control'

As was seen in section 2.2, Berle and Means assigned companies to 'control types' on the basis of criteria which were ultimately somewhat arbitrary. If a stock interest in excess of twenty per cent of the voting shares existed in a company with otherwise dispersed shareholdings, that company was classified as 'minority controlled'. 'Management-controlled' companies were those with no single important stock interest and so forth. This type of study continued to be important for many years but the problem of establishing agreed criteria is reflected in Larner's (1966) paper which, while following Berle and Means in most particulars, argued that 'minority control' might be achieved with as little as ten per cent of the shares.

An alternative tradition has therefore developed for studying 'ownership structure' which relies on measures of concentration. The idea is that the degree of 'control' exercised by shareholders will depend not merely on the size of the largest holding but on the concentration of voting power more generally. It might be, for example, that two large shareholders, each with 18 per cent of the shares will be more influential than a single shareholder with 21 per cent. Yet, by the Berle–Means criteria, the former situation would be defined as a case of 'management control' and the latter as 'minority control'. Students of corporate governance have therefore investigated the ratio of the outstanding shares held by the largest two, three, four shareholders and so on. These 'concentration ratios' then provide numerical measures of 'ownership structure' without requiring that each firm is definitively described as under the full 'control' of any given interest.

Concentration ratios on their own, however, are still not fully adequate as measures of shareholder influence, for the influence of any given coalition of shareholders, it could be argued, will depend upon the degree of dispersion of the remaining shares; that is, those held outside the coalition. Two shareholders, each with 18 per cent of the stock, will between them exert more authority if no other shareholder exists with more than a minute fraction of the company's shares than if many other shareholders have significant holdings. For this reason, Cubbin and Leech (1983) developed a measure of 'degree of shareholder control' which, for a coalition of the largest k shareholders, depends (positively) on the proportion of shares held by the group and positively also on the degree of dispersion of the remaining shares.[27] By this measure, possession of a fairly small proportion of the issued shares can give a high degree of control if the remaining shares are sufficiently dispersed.

It might be objected, of course, that although it is possible for a small coalition to exercise a high degree of control and that the *costs* of coalition formation may therefore not be great, the *benefits* to the participants will also diminish as the proportion of shares held declines. If five per cent of the shares can, in certain circumstances, confer considerable power over a corporation, it still remains true that 95 per cent of any benefits accruing to the exercise of such power will be received by passive shareholders who play no part in the monitoring process. How do we know that, even with a substantial degree of control by the Cubbin–Leech measure, minority shareholders will have an incentive to *exercise* their power?

This problem is precisely the same as that explored in section 4 in the context of managerial incentive contracts. There, we distinguished between the percentage of the shares held by an individual (which might be small) and the impact on the individual's wellbeing of the value of those shares (which might be very great). It was the latter, we argued, that would determine the influence of shareholding on a person's effort. Although effort would always be less than would occur in an ideal world of perfect observability and zero transactions costs, and certainly less than would occur if a single person held the entire equity, the latter would stimulate too great a level of effort while the former is not relevant to institutional choice which must be concerned with potentially realisable alternative arrangements rather than imaginary ideal states.

Behind arguments that corporate control can be exercised with small fractions of the stock, therefore, are assumptions that the quantitative stake is large enough to induce substantial monitoring effort. In large corporations we would then expect a highly diversified 'ownership structure' to be compatible with a high degree of control by the Cubbin–Leech measure. In small corporations, on the other hand, the 'ownership structure' would be expected to be less diversified, as monitoring incentives require shareholders to hold a higher fraction of the total stock. These hypotheses are supported by Leech and Leahy (1991) who, in a sample of 470 UK listed companies, find that measures of 'ownership concentration' (that is, concentration ratios) depend (inversely) on firm size but that measures of 'control classification' based on the Cubbin–Leech approach are not related to firm size. 'Control is exogenous while ownership concentration is endogenous, variations in the latter not necessarily having any implications for the former' (p. 1435).

In general, recent scholarship has tended to cast doubt on the Berle–Means thesis about the power of management *vis-à-vis* the shareholder. Leech and Leahy (1991), for example, calculate for their sample of large UK companies the size of coalition that would be necessary to give shareholders a degree of control of 99 per cent by the Cubbin–Leech measure. They concluded that a potential controlling coalition of three shareholders or fewer existed in 252 firms, or 54 per cent of their sample. Controlling coalitions of ten shareholders or fewer existed in all but one case. Looked at from this particular point of view, therefore, ownership 'control' could be argued to be almost universal.

Similar conclusions were drawn by Cosh and Hughes (1987). They used a variety of different approaches to assessing the control classification of a company. In particular, they distinguished between shareholdings of Board members and 'Off Board' holdings. Information flows to Board members might be expected to be better than to non-Board shareholders, thereby providing a bigger incentive to act in defence of shareholders' interests.[28] The existence of family connections between shareholders may increase the coherence and influence of shareholders as a group; a point emphasised in Nyman's and Silberston's (1978) study of the UK. Cosh and Hughes also draw attention to the importance of financial institutions in the UK and the USA in the case of non-Board holdings; a topic to which we will return in Chapter 9. Shared directorships with financial institutions are also important. 'This recurring intimacy between relatively small numbers of giant financial and industrial concerns is clearly a significant feature of the contemporary anatomy of corporate control' (p. 302). Taken all round, Cosh and Hughes conclude that their results, 'especially for the US, are not very comforting for the managerialist position' (p. 311).

Much modern research seems to suggest, therefore, that perceptions of the powerlessness of shareholders in the Berle–Means tradition may have been overdone. The costs of forming a coalition of some influence with access to information (either through Board members, or family or other business connections) and with an incentive to monitor performance are not necessarily prohibitive in spite of a generally dispersed structure of shareholding. It is worth noticing that the incentive to monitor does depend, however, on establishing an implicit differential in the value of control rights for different shareholders. In some countries, this phenomenon is so pronounced that family control of corporations is widespread even though these families hold only a small fraction of the shares. Claessens, Djankar and Pohl (2000), for example, report that 'when control is defined as a twenty per cent ownership threshold, sixty to seventy per cent of companies are family controlled in Indonesia, Malaysia, Hong Kong and Thailand'.[29] This far-reaching influence of families is not necessarily advantageous and has given rise to the term 'crony capitalism'. In Chapter 4 we noted that the influence of family control in the UK in the first part of the twentieth century hindered the development of the professional management required for the modern corporate economy. There, however, it was the private company which was the vehicle for family control and over the course of the century family influence declined, companies adopted the public form, and were floated. Under 'crony capitalism' families extend their control over the public corporate economy through pyramid structures (one firm owning another) or through shares carrying multiple voting rights.

5.3.2   Control rights and profit rights

Shareholders with minute proportions of a company's shares will have little incentive to become informed or to take part in elections. Their control rights are worthless. Rational abstention on the part of these shareholders means that the influence of minority shareholders is potentially greater than the bald proportion of shares held might suggest. There is a tendency, in other words, for the value of control rights to be more concentrated than the actual distribution of shares. Were control rights to be separately tradable, we might expect to see small shareholders maintaining their residual rights but selling their control (that is, voting) rights to a significant (though minority) shareholder.[30] More realistically, it would be possible for a substantial minority shareholder to be given authority by other shareholders to exercise their votes by proxy. The transactions costs of such an arrangement are likely, however, to be substantial.

As will be seen in section 9, there are systems in which these transactions costs have been reduced and where the overt concentration of control rights separate from residual rights is more common. In Germany, for example, the voting rights associated with shares deposited at banks can be exercised by the banks on behalf of the shareholders. In effect, the voting rights are clearly separate from residual rights and can be exercised by the bearer. This gives the banks an influence greater than would be expected on the basis of their shareholdings alone, and combined with their representation on company boards suggests that banks may perform important monitoring services in that system. The absence in the USA and the UK, either for legislative or historical reasons, of substantial holdings of shares in commercial companies by the banks, has meant that a similar system has not developed. In these countries, as mentioned above, it is the financial institutions (pension funds and insurance companies) that are the main shareholders and the extent to which they fulfil a monitoring role in the corporate economy is a controversial question.

The incentive effects produced by shareholder monitoring of managers will depend upon the structure of the monitoring gambles involved. In Chapter 5, it was seen how risk bearing costs, effort costs, and the reliability of information combined to influence the structure of monitoring gambles. Thus far in this section, we have concentrated mainly on discussing the costs to the monitor of collecting information and exercising a collective voting or 'control' right. Any benefit from incentive effects, however, will derive from the penalty associated with poor managerial performance, and the nature of this penalty has yet to be spelled out.

5.3.3   Measures of management performance

One possibility is that managerial remuneration can be linked to qualitative measures of performance based on the achievements of other executives in the same industry. Alternatively, various accounting measures of performance might be used to determine the level of bonus received by the senior managers. Empirical studies have failed to establish the importance of such bonus payments, however. Jensen and Murphy (1990b), for example, find that 'it does not appear that relative performance is an important source of management incentives' (p. 247). The median CEO bonus was fifty per cent of base salary in their sample but they argue that the year-to-year stability of this payment tells against linking it with substantial performance incentives. There are also dangers of distorting effort into manipulating the accounting system or producing deceptively good values for whatever signal is used to calculate the bonus. This, however, is a general problem with the use of any 'informative signal'.[31]

It is not immediately obvious why Jensen and Murphy should infer the absence of incentive effects from the stability of a bonus. If the probability of misperceiving the effort level of an industrious executive is small, while the chance of misperceiving the effort level of an idle executive is substantial, then, if the cost of effort is significant, we would expect a large bonus to be paid for effort. It can be large because the industrious executive does not fear being mistakenly deprived of it, and the potentially idle executive requires a sufficiently unfavourable gamble to induce effort. In other words the bonus will be large and stable. This in no way implies that the incentive effects are small.

Consider Figure 8.3, which is based on the same structure as Figure 5.8. It illustrates the extreme case in which a manager exerting effort level e will always be correctly observed and will receive a bonus. The indifference curves of the industrious manager will be horizontal straight lines. A typical indifference curve for expected utility level U_M is shown in the figure cutting the certainty line at a. In contrast, information if the manager is idle is very 'noisy'. Indeed, the probability of being observed idle is the same as that of being observed to exert effort e (both equal to 0.5). The slope of the manager's indifference curve if he or she chooses not to exert effort will therefore be -1 where it cuts the certainty line. Now, suppose the cost of effort is given by distance ab. A contract at c (where the manager's 'no-effort' indifference curve intersects his or her 'with-effort' curve with the same expected utility index) will be required to induce effort. This contract involves a fixed payment of W and a bonus of B when effort is observed.

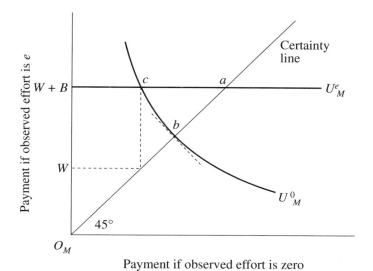

Figure 8.3 Managerial incentives: the case of the stable bonus

Note: With zero effort, the manager is equally likely to be observed working or shirking. With effort *e*, the manager is certain to be correctly observed. The cost of effort is distance *ab*.

The bonus will always induce effort and will always be paid, but if the bonus were incorporated into basic pay, the manager would shirk. Thus, instability of a bonus is not a necessary condition for that bonus to have large incentive effects.[32]

Another type of incentive discussed in Chapter 6 was the ranking hierarchy and the use of promotion as a type of monitoring gamble. The problem in the present context is that for managers at the very top of the hierarchy there appears to be no further prospect of promotion. Any appeal to this mechanism requires, therefore, a redefinition of the hierarchy. Aoki (1989) confronts this very problem when discussing top management incentives in Japan. The possibility of appointments to positions of social distinction within the industry after retirement are significant, he argues, and exert an important influence. This, however, is to see the industry rather than the individual firm as the relevant hierarchy. Within Aoki's framework for analysing the Japanese situation, this may not be inappropriate. As we saw in Chapters 6 and 7, much emphasis is placed by the Japanese system on cooperative relationships within the firm and with outside suppliers. Managers are rewarded for seeking and achieving consensus. Top managers are regarded by Aoki (1984) as mediators between potentially conflicting interests within the firm and are not simply agents of 'sovereign' shareholders. Managers at the top of a firm in such a system will be interested in their reputation in the industry as a whole. The incentives produced by this mechanism, however, are clearly not aimed at increasing the shareholders' influence on management.

Within the agency costs tradition which we are primarily expounding here, top management incentives derive not merely from internal 'monitoring gambles' but also from the operation of the outside 'managerial labour market'. It is the operation of this mechanism which is investigated in the next section.

6.   THE MANAGERIAL LABOUR MARKET

There are two different strands of thought in the literature on the managerial labour market, which are central to our discussion here. There is first the idea of the labour market as *complementary* to the internal incentive and monitoring systems of the firm. A second distinct theme is the labour market as a *substitute* for internal control by shareholders.

The first view of the managerial labour market links in with the incentive properties of labour markets generally discussed in Chapter 6. If acceptable monitoring gambles cannot be constructed internally, termination of an agreement will be the mechanism used for penalising poor performance. The penalty will take the form either of a downward revision in salary or of a period of job search. Again, empirical estimates suggest that wealth effects from 'performance-related dismissal decisions'[33] are not great for CEOs and that therefore they are unlikely to be an important determinant of senior managerial effort.

The second view of the managerial labour market is more far reaching. Attempts have been made to see it as a means of circumventing the moral hazard problem entirely. The difficulties, outlined in section 5, of monitoring management effort will obviously be much less significant if alternative methods exist of ensuring compliance with shareholders' wishes. Not surprisingly, the argument relies on the repeated game and the economics of reputation. As we saw in Chapter 5, an agency game that is repeated into the indefinite future enables the principal to judge performance against the average that would be expected if the agent is providing a given level of effort. In reality, of course, agency situations are not repeated indefinitely and neither do the conditions of the game remain unaltered over time. However, the theoretical background does suggest the point that repetition changes the nature of the game substantially and permits contractors to achieve agreements that would not be possible in the single game setting.

The use of information on an agent's past performance can also be used in the repeated game setting. Further, if this past performance is known publicly it can be used in contracts with new principals. It is this mechanism that forms the basis of Fama's (1980) model of the managerial labour market. In this model, a manager's wages fall if he or she is associated with failure and rise if associated with success. Fama argues that managerial labour markets may result in a form of *ex post* 'settling up' whereby shirking is punished by future losses of income equivalent to the resulting shortfall in performance. Managers will then have an incentive to maintain their value on the labour market and will not shirk. The argument is similar to that developed by Alchian (1969). Much of the effort of academics in the fields of publication and research, he pointed out, is not the result of a desire to enhance the prestige of the institutions which employ them, or to serve the interests of the taxpayer, but derives from attempts to increase the value of the individual in the academic labour market. Thus, taxpayers or shareholders do not need to exercise close monitoring but can rely on market incentives to induce effort.

For this '*ex post* settling-up' mechanism to work, it has to be assumed that managers recontract period by period and that they are effectively always selling their services on an external market. The whole of Chapter 6, however, was dedicated to the proposition that incentives required *long-term commitments* and the formation of *internal* labour markets. Further, it was there argued that reputations and 'brand name capital' were more costly for individual managers to establish than for firms. Is it possible to reconcile these points of view? The answer is that incentives based upon hierarchies and internal labour markets will develop in conditions of information asymmetry and task idiosyncrasy, but that eventually all such arrangements confront the central problem of this chapter – who monitors the person at the top? To this question there are several possible responses. The first is that the person at the top, whether a dominant shareholder or a manager, has a personal interest in the residual great enough to induce effort and ensure the viability of the organisation. This is the answer explored in section 4. The second response is that the top managers are constrained by shareholders who have access to informative signals and present top managers with appropriately structured monitoring gambles. This is the answer explored in section 5. Finally, there is the argument that managers will be subject to impersonal 'market pressures'. 'The market' will force a penalty for poor performance. This is the answer suggested by Alchian and Fama, and reported in this section. Essentially, an appeal is made to some *external* force to restrain the behaviour of senior managers; in the case considered above, the force of competition in the managerial labour market.

The mechanism by which competition influences behaviour is still somewhat mysterious, however. We are asked to imagine a world in which a group of elite senior managers take a succession of posts and build up reputations for high-quality service which then become a valuable component of 'human capital'. Intuitively plausible though this may be, there is a difficulty. Assume for the purposes of this paragraph that shareholders find it too costly to monitor managers and that the mechanisms explored in sections 4 and 5 are not operating. Managers in a dispersed corporation will be appointed by other managers. If attention to shareholders' interests cannot be assumed on the part of managers promoted internally to the top of the hierarchy, there seems no good reason to assume that in their screening of senior managers from outside they will be any more efficient. Good outside applicants might simply highlight the shortcomings of the established group. If, on the other hand, we assume that internally promoted managers at the top of the tree are by convention moved to positions where their ability to damage the firm is limited, and that all senior appointments are under the control of a mobile manager, it is still not clear that, in choosing a successor, such a manager would have an incentive to pick the best candidate. He or she might attempt to portray his or her 'reign' in the best light by picking a poor successor unless the managerial labour market is very sophisticated and penalises failure in this function as surely as failure in internal monitoring. Arguments which attempt to show the power of 'impersonal market forces' therefore appear incomplete. Ultimately, they seem to come down to the idea that a mobile manager who contracts on the labour market at frequent intervals will not shirk because s/he believes that other managers will penalise him/her later if s/he does. These other managers penalise him/her because they believe that if they do not do so they themselves will be penalised by other managers elsewhere who believe the same, and so on. The joint-stock enterprise survives through the power of shared beliefs, an institutional proof of the existence of collective levitation.

The power of shared beliefs is not to be underestimated, but we might expect these beliefs to be more durable if founded on something more substantial than thin air. Shareholders may not need to implement detailed monitoring to motivate managers but if they want managers to pursue shareholders' objectives they will have to be powerful enough to influence senior appointments and thus to ensure that it is *shareholders'* interests that are communicated through the managerial labour market rather than those of some other group.[34] This influence of shareholders on senior appointments may be exercised in the ways covered in sections 4 and 5, although, once more, it is widely considered to be ineffective. Shleifer and Vishny (1988) chart what they see as the general weakness of internal controls on management and specifically draw attention to the fact that the Board does not even exercise choice of the CEO at the point of succession. If this is so, some other force is required to induce managers to consider shareholders' interests. It is here that the role of the takeover mechanism enters the picture. General shareholder influence on appointments, it is argued, can be brought to bear through the threat of takeover by *new* shareholders rather than the direct influence of existing ones.

If senior managers are constrained by outside forces it is because they know that there are people outside the firm who are alert enough to spot a team operating short of its potential and with an incentive to act on that information. Competition is not an automatic impersonal force; it operates through the activities of the entrepreneur, and it is the entrepreneur with his/her accompanying threat of unexpected change who provides the managerial incentives. In Chapter 9, it is argued not simply that the takeover is an alternative to the managerial labour market as a device for encouraging profit-orientated behaviour, but that the effectiveness of that market can itself only be understood in conjunction with the possibility of entrepreneurial intervention and the restructuring of property rights which this can bring about. Before investigating the takeover, however, we look at competition in the product market as another constraint on managerial behaviour.

7.   THE PRODUCT MARKET

Competition in the product market is widely considered an incentive to effort. Monopolists are popularly supposed to take much of their profit in the form of a quiet life, while competition is expected to reduce the capacity of managers to indulge in discretionary behaviour. In the case of perfect competition, elementary textbooks imply that all discretion disappears. We do what must be done and survive, or we do something else and perish. This has led many neoclassical economists to assume that, provided product markets are competitive, problems of the division of ownership from control can safely be ignored.[35]

Behavioural theorists, such as Leibenstein, who coined the term 'X-inefficiency' to describe the achievement of less than the maximum output technically possible from given inputs, and who has developed his own approach to the internal workings of the firm, also assign a prominent role to competition. In Leibenstein (1979), the incomplete nature of employment contracts and the necessity for monitoring are recognised. A theory of average production costs is then developed. As the effort of workers increases, money costs per unit of output fall. Effort depends on 'pressure', either from peers (horizontal pressure) or from superiors (vertical pressure).

The degree of pressure is, in turn, a function of average costs. As costs rise, the survival of the firm is threatened and the pressure on the individual to 'pull his weight' is increased. Diagrammatically, Leibenstein's approach is summarised in Figure 8.4. Curve A shows how costs depend on effort. Curve $B(T_1)$ shows how effort increases as costs rise (because of more intensive monitoring or 'pressure'). The equilibrium is at point a with average costs C_1 and effort E_1.

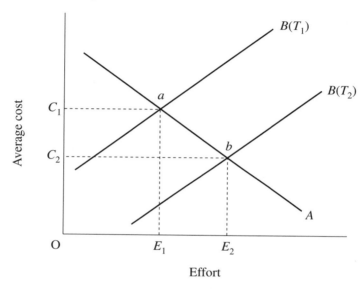

Figure 8.4   Leibenstein's X-efficiency theory of costs

Competition enters Leibenstein's theory in the form of 'environmental tightness', which influences the position of curve B. For any given level of average costs, 'pressure' and hence 'effort' will be lower the more protected is the firm from competition. Conversely, as 'environmental tightness' increases, effort will increase at each level of costs. If 'tightness' increases from T_1 to T_2, the new position of equilibrium will be point b. If effort increases to E_2, costs fall to C_2 and the firm becomes more 'X-efficient'. Leibenstein's approach has been subjected to much criticism by neoclassical economists (Stigler, 1976, De Alessi, 1983). First, they object to the idea that failure to 'maximise' output is in any sense inefficient. As we have seen, the existence of agency costs is perfectly compatible with efficiency if it does not benefit anyone to reduce them.[36] Second, they dislike Leibenstein's behavioural insistence that individual people facing problems of bounded rationality cannot be regarded as rational 'utility maximisers'.[37] Third, the ability of the theory to produce refutable predictions is questioned.[38]

For our present purposes, however, the relationship between 'environmental tightness' and monitoring 'pressure' is of central interest. The relationship has intuitive appeal but the mechanism is not clearly specified. If many firms in a particular market had dispersed shareholdings, for example, what would impel the managers to greater effort? Just because there are many firms, are we saying that property rights no longer matter, and that twenty nationalised firms in a market will behave like twenty joint-stock firms, or twenty closely held ones? Presumably this cannot be correct. As Jensen and Meckling (1976, p. 330) express it: 'the existence of competition in product and factor markets will not eliminate the agency costs due to managerial control problems . . . If my competitors all incur agency costs equal to or greater than mine I will not be eliminated from the market by their competition.' The argument is therefore identical to that used in section 6 to question the role of competition in the managerial labour market.

Once more our basic difficulty is caused by attempting to talk about competition without the entrepreneur. Our instinctive feeling that competition does matter requires a more detailed look at the types of firm that are involved in a particular market, and the provisions of the contracts offered to managers. This is attempted in a paper by Hart (1983). Hart starts by assuming that managers are extremely risk averse. Their preferences are such that the indifference curves illustrated in Figure 5.2 would be L-shaped. From the analysis of Chapter 5, it is evident that we cannot offer such a manager incentives based upon sharing the risk. If effort is unobservable, the best that can be done is to pay the manager a fixed time-rate conditional upon achieving some minimum level of performance (profit). Hart does not intend this to be realistic, but merely convenient for illustrating the working of his model. He then assumes that there are two types of firm: 'entrepreneurial'[39] and 'managerial'. The only difference between these two types is that managerial effort can be monitored in the 'entrepreneurial' firm. Achieving this monitoring potential is not costless, however, and, again for simplicity, Hart assumes that there are additional fixed costs incurred in setting up an entrepreneurial firm relative to a managerial firm.

Where people are able to set up either managerial or entrepreneurial structures, Hart shows that if v is the proportion of entrepreneurial firms, there is a market equilibrium with $v \neq 0$. There will, in other words, be both entrepreneurial and managerial firms in the market. The intuition behind this result is as follows. Suppose that $v = 0$ and only managerial firms exist, then agency costs will be great and considerable managerial shirking will occur. If this is so, however, it may be profitable to set up an entrepreneurial firm and accept the additional fixed costs necessary to reduce managerial shirking. The argument is similar to that used to demonstrate the potential benefits from a takeover raid (see Chapter 9), but here we are allowing for the possibility that instead of changing an existing managerial firm into an entrepreneurial one via a raid, we can simply set up a new firm. As new entrepreneurial firms enter the market, however, industry output increases and the price of the product falls. This makes it more difficult for managers to achieve their minimum profit constraint and their effort level will rise. The rise in managerial effort which accompanies a fall in product price implies that the industry will not necessarily come to be composed entirely of entrepreneurial firms. To see this, consider the case of $v = 1$. Managerial shirking is at a minimum and product price is at its lowest. The entry of a managerial firm might now be profitable since the low market price will ensure high managerial effort and the fixed costs of instituting monitoring devices can be dispensed with. Thus, managerial firms will displace entrepreneurial ones until an equilibrium position is reached.

Hart's model implies therefore that 'entrepreneurial firms provide a source of discipline for managerial firms'.[40] The market mechanism can indeed function as an incentive scheme but it does so through the medium of the entry of entrepreneurial firms which affect market price and induce greater effort from managers, who are assumed to have a rather special contract. As Hart points out, 'if managerial tastes are less extreme, ordinary salary incentive schemes will become more effective in reducing managerial slack, and competition will become less important' (p. 381). This possibility has already been discussed in sections 4 and 5.

Another mechanism by which competition might influence management behaviour is by providing comparators in the design of incentive contracts. Performance relative to other firms in an industry can be used as the basis of managerial remuneration. This sharpens incentives because general external 'shocks' which affect all firms in an industry similarly will no longer be attributable to managerial competence. Only relative performance will be rewarded or penalised. We have already observed that such contracts do not figure prominently in the remuneration of CEOs. However, in the absence of specific incentive contracts it is still possible that Fama's *ex post* settling-up mechanism in the managerial labour market (discussed in section 6) is more effective when there is product-market competition than when there is no competition. The information about managerial competence available to this market is better when it comes out of an environment in which each manager has been pitted against other managers facing similar 'general' environmental difficulties.[41] In a study of 670

UK companies, Nickell (1996, p. 741) found some support for the proposition that higher levels of competition (as measured by higher numbers of competitors or lower monopoly rents) were associated with higher rates of total factor productivity growth.

8. CONCLUSION

In this chapter, some of the main mechanisms for providing managerial incentives have been discussed. There is, however, another incentive device – the market in corporate control – that has become so significant in recent years, and is so closely associated with the problem of corporate governance, that a whole chapter has been assigned to it. The reader should always be aware that Chapters 8 and 9 are intimately connected in their subject matter. An attempt is made at the end of the next chapter (in section 11) to bring the issues together and to compare the characteristics of the system of corporate governance which exists in the United States and the United Kingdom with those associated with the different systems of Germany and Japan.

NOTES

1. Henry Fielding, *Tom Jones*, ([1749] 1955) Collins Classics, London and Glasgow, p. 354.
2. Such rights may, of course, be challenged and this paragraph should not be interpreted as meaning that the location of ultimate control rights is always clear. In Chapter 9, on takeovers, we will see how certain 'poison pill' provisions introduced by management can be seen as wresting rights of control from the shareholders.
3. See again the property rights theory of the firm introduced in Chapter 4. Hart (1995) points out that corporate governance is not a problem in a world of complete contracts. Governance is about the allocation of residual control rights and hence about who controls the assets when contract fails. Agency problems on their own could be overcome in a world of complete contracts.
4. The UK saw a similar dramatic rise in aggregate concentration during the twentieth century. Prais (1976, p. 4) records the share of the hundred largest enterprises in manufacturing net output. This rose from around 16 per cent in 1909 to approximately 42 per cent by 1976, most of the increase occurring after 1949. Utton (1982, p. 22) remarks that 'the great increase in the relative growth of the largest enterprises in the UK in the last twenty-five years has produced a manufacturing sector which is one of the most highly concentrated (if not the most highly concentrated) in the world'.
5. It is important to recognise that Wu does not assert that existing conditions have already reached the state in which corporations are run by coalitions of pure entrepreneurs. Neither does he assert that *all* corporations will eventually evolve to this state.
6. Rents associated with bond-posting and monitoring within the firm are called *enforcement rents* by Bowles and Gintis (1993). These are quite different conceptually from *entrepreneurial rents*.
7. Alchian and Woodward do not distinguish between team dependency and transaction dependency. Both may be seen as incorporated in their use of the term 'firm dependency'.

An entrepreneur who leaves a successful coalition would 'lose value' and is therefore 'dependent'. This loss of value in the entrepreneur's case is not reflected in an observable lower market price because entrepreneurial services cannot be traded and entrepreneurs do not receive a 'market price'. Nevertheless, claimants to the pure profits of a firm are team dependent. A worker who posts a bond as an assurance of good behaviour or invests in firm-specific skills, will also lose value if he/she is 'separated from the team', and is likewise 'dependent'. We have called such people *transaction dependent* in order to distinguish those with a claim to pure entrepreneurial profit (the team's residual) from those with a claim to quasi-rents which are not part of pure profit (that is, which provide a competitive return on sunk capital in the long run).

Control of the firm may be sought (i) to permit entrepreneurs to pursue and lay claim to entrepreneurial profit, and (ii) to permit dependent resources in a world of incomplete contracts to protect themselves from opportunism. At the conceptual level, the distinction seems worth making and is reflected in my use of the terms team dependency and transaction dependency. It is worth adding, however, that a particular person may be both transaction dependent and team dependent. One form of dependency does not preclude the other. Where people have accumulated specialised knowledge and skills over time, the returns could reasonably be regarded as returns to entrepreneurial alertness and the implied human capital as part of the firm's equity. These entrepreneurial returns may co-exist with returns to more conventional training in specific operations of the firm.

8. See *The Wealth of Nations*, Vol. 2, p. 233.
9. Supporters of the nexus of contracts approach recognise that the shareholder–manager relationship is not contractual from a legalistic point of view, but argue that it can be analysed as if it were. The contract is once again 'implicit'. Clark (1985, p. 61) replies that 'this extreme contractualist viewpoint is almost perverse . . . I would insist that the use of the term contract in connection with "implicit contracts" . . . is metaphorical, and . . . that the metaphor is seriously misleading'.
10. Roberts (1959), Patton (1961), McGuire, Chiu and Elbing (1962).
11. Notably by Lewellen (1969), Lewellen and Huntsman (1970), Masson (1971).
12. A major difference is the greater use of share option awards in remuneration packages in the USA compared with the UK.
13. It is worth noting that this small responsiveness of overall CEO remuneration to changes in the value of the firm on the stock market is quite compatible with Cosh and Hughes' observation that CEOs may be extremely wealthy through their holdings of stock.
14. See Conyon, Gregg and Machin (1995).
15. The *expected* return to effort level e is $(P_1^e - P_1)(Q_1 - Q_2)$ where, as in Chapter 5, P_1^e is the probability of the good state when the CEO exerts effort, P_1 is the probability of the same event when s/he does not exert effort, Q_1 is the good outcome, and Q_2 the bad one. Clearly if $(P_1^e - P_1)$ is the same in large and small firms while $(Q_1 - Q_2)$ is proportional to firm size (as measured, say, by capitalisation) the return to effort is proportional to firm size.
16. See again the review of Casson's ideas in Chapter 2.
17. In the UK, the trend in the 1990s was towards Long-Term Incentive Plans (LTIPs) rather than stock options. See Main (1999).
18. Abowd and Kaplan (1999) review the main questions arising from executive compensation.
19. For example Conyon, Gregg and Machin (1995) pp. 711–12.
20. Meulbroek (2000) argues that the difference between the cost to the firm of stock options and the value to the manager can imply a large deadweight loss – especially in high-risk areas such as Internet start-ups.
21. The Bill tightens the provisions of the Companies and Securities (Insider Dealing) Act 1985. Under this Act, an insider had to be in a position of trust with respect to the company. Under the Criminal Justice Act, an insider can be anyone who obtains information in the course of his or her employment or dealings with a company, which they know to be inside information. For a critical view, see Alistair Alcock (1993).
22. Directive [89/592/EEC].

23. Models relying on this adverse selection mechanism have been developed, for example, by Ausubel (1990) and Leland (1992).
24. For a fuller discussion of concepts of stock market efficiency see Chapter 9, section 7.
25. See again the discussion of rent seeking versus entrepreneurship in Chapter 6, section 7.
26. 'The proxy machinery has thus become one of the principal instruments not by which a stockholder exercises power over the management of the enterprise, but by which his power is separated from him.' (Berle and Means (1932), p. 129).
27. The Degree of Control is defined as

$$a_k = A \, (C_k \, / \, \sqrt{V_k})$$

where $V_k = \Sigma p_i^2$ $(i = k + 1$ to $N)$, p_i is the proportion of shares held by shareholder i, and C_k is Σp_i $(i = 1$ to $k)$; that is, the concentration ratio of the largest k shareholders. N is the total number of shareholders. A is the standard normal distribution function. For the largest shareholder, the degree of control would be

$$a_1 = A \, (p_1 \, / \, \sqrt{(H - p_1^2)})$$

where H is the Herfindahl concentration index defined as Σp_i^2 $(i = 1$ to $N)$.
28. Where the main Board shareholders are executive rather than non-executive directors, however, the incentives provided are aimed directly at executive effort (as in section 4) rather than at encouraging monitoring which is strictly the topic of this section.
29. As reported in *Economic Intuition*, Summer 2000, p. 9.
30. Blair, Golbe and Gerard (1989) consider the implications of the trading of voting rights separate from residual claims. They are mainly interested, however, in the impact on hostile takeovers rather than the direct control of managers.
31. There is a parallel here with Goodhart's Law in the field of monetary control. Rely on an established relationship (for example, between a given measure of the money supply and nominal income) to exercise control, and that relationship will change and become unreliable. Once people know what signals are being used by others to make certain judgements, they will attempt to manipulate those signals and anticipate the judgements. See also the problem of managerial incentives in non-profit enterprises, covered in Chapter 11.
32. In this rather extreme case, it might be noted that any contract to the left of point c, involving even larger bonuses, would be equally satisfactory. Because the manager can avoid all risk by exerting effort, the bonus can be as large as we care to make it as a proportion of total remuneration.
33. See Jensen and Murphy (1990b).
34. A highly influential managerial labour market is therefore quite compatible with powerless shareholders. Alchian's argument that academics strive to increase their market value by research, for example, ignores the point that the research they do will be designed to appeal to other academics or administrators in non-profit institutions who will appoint them. The academic labour market is widely considered effective as an incentive mechanism. David Lodge's 1984 satirical novel, *Small World*, is about the stimulating effects of this market and competition for the UNESCO Chair, a post entirely unencumbered with inconvenient responsibilities. It is also, though, about the importance of the preferences of those on the selection board which did not include representatives from the world's taxpayers.
35. A classic statement of this view can be found in Machlup (1967). In a competitive model 'Frankly, I cannot quite see what great difference organisational matters are supposed to make in the firm's price reactions to changes in conditions' (p. 13).
36. It is worth noting, however, that this type of neoclassical reasoning leads to the conclusion that anything which exists must be efficient, since it has not paid anyone to change it. From the point of view of normative theory, which we discuss in Part 3 of this book, this neoclassical position would appear somewhat inhibiting. See Culyer (1984) on these Panglossian issues.

37. We have deliberately avoided methodological disputes. Essentially, our approach has been to present the theory of the agency problem in terms of rational expected utility-maximising people, but to view the process by which 'solutions' are found as one not of calculation but of entrepreneurial discovery and trial and error.

38. The 'Austrian' theorists would not count this a great deficiency, since their subjectivism leads them to question the ability of any economic theory to produce truly refutable implications.

39. Note throughout this section on Hart (1983) that the word 'entrepreneurial' is used merely to signify the existence of monitoring by shareholders (or a dominant shareholder). Our use of the term in this book has, of course, been quite different. However, the competitive process implied by Hart's model does suggest that it is entrepreneurial in Kirzner's sense.

40. The entrepreneurial firm is responsible for an external effect by reducing shirking in managerial firms. These effects are not considered by the entrepreneur when making the initial entry decision, and it is thus possible to argue, using standard welfare economic theory, that entrepreneurial firms should be encouraged.

41. See Meyer and Vickers (1995).

9. Corporate governance 2: the takeover and capital structure

'There, I will stake my last like a woman of spirit. No cold prudence for me. I am not born to sit still and do nothing. If I lose the game it will not be from not striving for it.'

The game was hers, and only did not pay her for what she had given to secure it. Another deal proceeded . . .'

(Jane Austen)[1]

1. THE ENTREPRENEUR AND THE TAKEOVER

Inherently, a joint-stock firm is neither concentrated nor dispersed in the structure of its shareholdings. No document or constitution exists proclaiming that a particular company's shares will be dispersed widely. The degree of concentration or dispersion is capable of changing over time. It may appear at any given moment that shareholdings are dispersed and management has great discretionary power, but financial capital can congeal suddenly and unexpectedly. A dominant interest can emerge which changes the top management and consigns the existing top managers to the labour market. As with the model of Shapiro and Stiglitz (1984), reported in Chapter 6, the penalty involved in being fired will depend on conditions in this market. If all managers were identical, the penalty might be a period of unemployment (top managers' salaries are above market-clearing levels). Where managers differ in attributes and skills, the penalty might be extorted through downward revision of the wage, as suggested by Fama. This will occur because managers, fearing takeover themselves, will have a clear incentive to avoid appointing other managers with a poor record.

Fama (1980), however, explicitly rejects the influence of the takeover or the entrepreneur as necessary ingredients in an explanation of the operation of the labour market. Manne's (1965) description of management discipline as an 'entrepreneurial job' is criticised (p. 295) and the takeover is considered merely a 'discipline of last resort'. Instead, Fama prefers to rely on markets in outside directors (p. 294) who 'are in their turn disciplined by the market for their services which prices them according to their performance as referees'. Like a steeplejack gingerly edging further and further up an elaborate tower of indeterminate height, monitor stacked upon monitor, Fama is apparently determined not to look down. The whole argument is reminiscent of debates surrounding the survival of a paper currency. Once the psychology of acceptability has been established, no one bothers to present his or her paper to the issuer and demand the gold or other commodities promised. Yet many would still argue that the potential for convertibility would be important in maintaining confidence in circumstances where coercive power cannot compel acceptance of the currency. Similarly, in a free society, the survival of the dispersed joint-stock company ultimately depends upon a recognition that it can be turned into something else. The agents of any such transformation are Kirznerian entrepreneurs.

Where the management of a dispersed corporation is judged by an outside entrepreneur to be inefficient, the advantages of establishing a controlling interest are obvious. The gains from closer monitoring may outweigh the disadvantages of less-widely-spread risks and, if this is so, entrepreneurial rewards are available. To achieve these rewards, however, the entrepreneur must have knowledge which is not widely available to others. As was seen in Chapter 3, the entrepreneur will gain if his or her judgement is different from that of other people and it proves to be correct. However, where information is publicly available and capital markets are efficient in using this information for valuing assets such as equity shares, the scope for entrepreneurial action is much more limited. The difficulty is once more the free-rider problem.

2. THE TAKEOVER AND THE FREE-RIDER PROBLEM

As Grossman and Hart (1980) point out, if the public-good trap and the free-rider problem prevent internal monitoring by existing shareholders, it seems unreasonable to assume that the same problem would not be faced by outsiders. Specifically, any offer made by an outside bidder for the existing shares will not succeed because it will be in no individual shareholder's interest to accept the price and sell to the raider. Our Kirznerian raider is hoping to gain from the appreciation of the shares which s/he purchases, but any profit which s/he makes 'represents a profit shareholders could have made if they had not tendered their shares to the raider' (p. 43). A small shareholder will reason that whether or not they accept the raider's offer will not perceptibly affect the chance of the raid succeeding, and they will refuse in the hope of making capital gains.[2] The problem is similar to that encountered in Chapter 4 by the entrepreneur attempting to purchase communal rights to fish in the island lake. An existing holder of the communal right might 'hold out'[3] for a price which made the whole enterprise profitless.

Differences in information and expectations between raider and shareholders may permit profits to be achieved by the entrepreneur and hence takeovers to take place. However, if the threat of takeover is to exercise a disciplinary effect on managers we might argue that efforts to circumvent the free-rider problem will be sought by shareholders to encourage entrepreneurial intervention. To overcome free riding it is necessary to exclude non-payers. How can this be achieved? Grossman and Hart suggest that minority shareholders (that is, those who do not tender their shares to a raider and still hold shares in a company following a successful raid) might be excluded from the benefits brought about by the raider. Once a raider has control of fifty-one per cent of the shares, the assets or output of the company could be sold to another company owned by the raider at a price disadvantageous to minority interests. A constitution which permitted a raider to behave in this way would represent a 'voluntary dilution of (the shareholders') property rights' (p. 43) which was nevertheless 'essential if the takeover bid mechanism is to be effective' (p. 46). Shareholders face a trade-off. The greater the 'dilution' they permit, the more closely are managers constrained by the takeover threat, but the prospect of pecuniary gain arising out of a raid is reduced. The attitude of the law towards post-raid behaviour of the new majority shareholders, and the provisions of corporate constitutions, will therefore play an important part in determining the costs of pursuing a takeover. Managers of a dispersed corporation, if they wish to avoid the managerial labour market, must therefore exert a level of effort which leaves no scope for pure profit on the part of a raider after allowing for the costs which s/he will incur.

3.   MINORITY SHAREHOLDERS AND THE TAKEOVER

The Grossman and Hart paper clearly identifies an important problem, but as a description of the market in corporate control it seems to prove too much. Takeovers do take place on a substantial scale, and indeed the 1980s saw an upsurge in corporate restructuring which, if conditions reflected those assumed by Grossman and Hart, could hardly have taken place. As in sections 4 and 5 of Chapter 8, the influence of shareholders with a minority interest can prove decisive in certain circumstances.

Shleifer and Vishny (1986) present a model of takeovers in which a bidder accumulates a proportion (say five to ten per cent) of the target firm's stock prior to announcing the bid. It is assumed that the target shareholders (each of whom, with the exception of the bidder, holds insignificant amounts of stock) do not know the extent of the improvement in value that the bidder can achieve. Thus, there is an information asymmetry that allows takeovers to occur. If all the recipients of the offer have the same information about the firm, and if they are all risk neutral, they will accept any offer which equals or exceeds their *expectation* of the improvement in share value which will result from the takeover. Providing this *expectation* (which may be affected by the value of the bid) is less than or equal to the improvement actually achievable by the bidder, the latter can gain from this difference in value on his/her own stockholdings. It still remains true, of course, that 'bidders have to share a lot of the value gains with shareholders of the target firm'.[4]

Although the approach of Shleifer and Vishny succeeds in isolating and analysing some significant features of the takeover process it still results in some curiosities. Because all target shareholders have the same information, the predicted bid will equal their expectation of the value of an improvement achievable by a bidder. This implies that the *actual* size of the improvement achievable will not influence the bid. High improvement bidders will make the same offer as low improvement bidders. Further, observed bids will all just be sufficient to induce acceptance and therefore will not fail. These considerations led Hirshleifer and Titman (1990) to develop the Shleifer and Vishny analysis. They incorporate variation in the information about possible value improvements available to target shareholders. In these circumstances, the expected number of shares tendered to a raider will increase with the value of the bid. Risk-neutral raiders calculate the optimal bid which will maximise their expected return, but this bid will not absolutely *guarantee* success in terms of attracting a level of acceptance sufficient to give a raider majority control. Thus, some raids will be observed to fail. Because the cost of failure will be higher for bidders who might have achieved substantial increases in share value compared with those able to make improvements of only low value, the former are expected to make a higher offer than the latter. The optimal bid rises with the improvement achievable by the bidder. Further, a bidder who begins with a higher proportion of the shares will need to attract fewer acceptances to gain control. Thus, the probability that a bid will succeed rises with the size of the initial holding.

These features of Hirshleifer and Titman's analysis would seem consistent with the stylised facts about the market for corporate control. The main point of the model, however, is that it relies on the existence of minority shareholders to facilitate the takeover process. Holders of substantial blocks of shares confer benefits on other shareholders and it would be expected that share values would be higher where such blocks exist than where they do not. The free-rider problem is not completely solved, but it is in the interests of a minority shareholder to provide monitoring services, either directly or through the takeover mechanism, up to the point at which the marginal private benefits equal the marginal private costs.

4. HOLD-UP, BREACH OF FAITH AND THE TAKEOVER

Sections 1 to 3 have proceeded on the assumption that the takeover is a vehicle for *entrepreneurship* and the achievement of efficiency gains. There is another side to the takeover, however. This is the takeover as a vehicle for *rent seeking*, a challenge to insecurely held property rights and a cause of efficiency losses. As we noted in Chapter 6, although clear in principle, it is often difficult in practice to distinguish between rent seeking and entrepreneurship.

In the case of hostile takeover activity, the possibility exists that the raider gains by diverting income from other sources rather than by improving the efficiency of the firm and increasing total income. Shleifer and Vishny (1988) quote the case of Icahn's takeover of Trans World Airlines. It was estimated that the present value of the loss of wages to the three labour unions involved was greater than the takeover premium paid to TWA shareholders. TWA shareholders gained while TWA workers lost. The takeover was redistributive. This does not prove that there were no net efficiency gains resulting from this particular takeover, but it does suggest the possibility that large redistributive effects may encourage rent seeking at the expense of entrepreneurial initiative.

Raiders can gain by renegotiating contracts with suppliers of various inputs (especially, but not exclusively, labour). Clearly, they can only succeed in this attempt if the resources involved are *dependent* on the firm as discussed in section 2.4 of Chapter 8. The causes of dependency are then crucial to an assessment of the consequences of contract renegotiation. Suppose, for example, that the labour force in this particular firm had formed a strong union, had pushed up wages above those in competing firms (thus producing dependency), and had prevented managers from hiring labour from any other source. The return to shareholders had fallen and so had the price of the firm's shares on the stock market. Suppose that a raider now takes over the firm and breaks the union. The share price returns to the level associated with other firms in the industry. Assuming that production methods and the technical efficiency of the organisation are not affected (a somewhat unlikely situation) redistribution of income would be the exclusive consequence of the takeover. Resources invested in the actual takeover process would then logically represent social losses. The whole episode represents a fight over who receives the quasi-rents on shareholders' capital. Absence of agreement on this issue can be socially very destructive. Labour robbed capital. Capital then retaliated. In the process, resources were wasted.

Dependency, however, can result from sources other than collective action within the firm. Where the existence of dependency implies an expression of trust in the good faith of the firm, contract renegotiation after a takeover may result in social losses far in excess of the mere resources expended in the negotiations, for such behaviour destroys trust and with it the ability to contrive beneficial and efficiency-enhancing agreements in the future.[5] Willingness to invest in transaction-specific human capital, to transact with the firm by designing and supplying specialised inputs, and to accept incentive schemes based upon promises of rising future income will all be undermined if new 'owners' fail to honour the implicit obligations entered into by the firm in the past.

5.   ADVERSE SELECTION, SHORT-TERMISM AND THE TAKEOVER

A major question remains unanswered concerning the vulnerability of specific assets in the takeover process. If the 'goodwill' underlying these assets is so important to the long-run health of the firm, why would a takeover raider wish to destroy them? Would not such vandalism immediately be reflected in lower share prices as investors noticed how these actions were casting a blight on future prospects? At the heart of this question is the issue of the efficiency of the capital market. Clearly, if information about the behaviour of those who exercise the decision rights over the resources of a firm is publicly available, and if the implications of that behaviour can be interpreted at low cost, the prices of securities would move rapidly to reflect changes in conditions. If outside shareholders are less well informed than insiders, however, information asymmetries can radically change this perception of capital markets.

Leaving aside the possibility that valuable long-term assets might inadvertently be destroyed, either by the blind ignorance of a takeover raider or by the cunning that hopes to profit from the ignorance of others – perhaps by raising short-term profits and selling out to people who are unaware of the long-term cost; there is still the possibility that information asymmetry could lead managers generally to act in ways that are destructive of long-term value. This possibility does not derive from the moral hazard problem. Even where managers are fully devoted to shareholders' interests through stockholdings of their own (as in Chapter 8, section 4) short-termism may arise. The root of the problem is the existence of adverse selection.

In Chapter 6, it was seen that adverse selection could result in signalling. A signal is an action which is rational for one type of contractor but not for another. It enables separate contracts to be established for different types of contractor. An educational qualification, for example, may be a 'signal' if it separates labour of high from low innate ability. We also saw in Chapter 6 that signalling could be wasteful of resources. Although it might be in the private interests of the signallers, it was possible to construct cases in which, after allowing for the costs of signalling, social losses were the result. The gain to high-ability individuals of an educational signal, for example, might be partially offset by losses to those of low ability.

In the present context, the problem is that outside shareholders may not know the true internal state of a firm.[6] Managers of 'good-state' firms will want somehow to convey their status to the market. This 'true' information will benefit shareholders through a rise in share values and we are assuming here that managers have shareholders' interests at heart. If shareholders were unaware that the firm was in a good state, they might be prepared to accept a low offer from a takeover raider. It is not necessary to assume here that the raider is any better informed than the shareholder with respect to the existing misvaluation of the shares. It may be, for example, that there is a chance of a takeover occurring anyway because of real 'synergies' from combining the operations of two firms and that the raider will be pleasantly surprised to learn of the true situation after the takeover has been completed.

Managers cannot simply write a letter to shareholders, or prepare statements in the newspapers or on the Internet, declaring the health of the firm because managers of both 'good-state' and 'bad-state' firms can engage equally in these activities. Managers of 'good-state' firms require a signal. They may, for example, distribute a high level of dividends to shareholders. Assume that this possibility is denied to 'bad-state' firms and that it will convince the market that the firm paying high dividends is 'good'. The firm's share price will then reflect that 'true' information. A 'separating equilibrium' is established in which 'good-state' and 'bad-state' firms are distinguished by the market and gains (even inadvertent ones) to takeover raiders at the expense of shareholders no longer occur.

Although a system which permits the communication of valuable information about the true success of a firm to *existing* shareholders is beneficial to them, a wider perspective may reveal substantial disadvantages. In the model described above, the signal merely prevents a possible redistribution from existing shareholders to takeover raiders. The lower the costs of takeovers and the more likely they are to occur, the greater is the value to existing shareholders of the informative signal from the managers. On the other hand, the signal creates no new opportunities for efficiency gains, and transmission of the signal was not costless. Suppose that the payment of a higher present return to shareholders means that resources are diverted from long-term investments in research and development or prevents full advantage being taken of other investment opportunities. Such managerial 'myopia' or 'short-termism' will have efficiency reducing long-term consequences.

Shareholders as a group might have been better off had they somehow bound the managers not to signal. After all, once the belief is widely held that dividends are a signal, managers operating in the shareholders' interests have no option but to engage in signalling. Absence of a signal will be taken as a bad sign and the shares will be valued on the (possibly false) basis that the company is a 'dud'. If, on the other hand, shareholders believed that dividend decisions were *not* signals, the share price reaction to a low dividend would be less pronounced. Low present dividends might simply imply that resources were being used for investment rather than that a 'bad state' had occurred. Both good and bad firms would declare lower dividends (a pooling equilibrium). Although the share price of a good firm might be somewhat lower than would prevail in the context of a 'good-news' signal, any possible loss in the event of a takeover occurring might be more than outweighed by the eventual gains derived from the pursuit by 'good' firms of a long-term investment strategy.

The upshot of this type of reasoning, therefore, is that the existence of the takeover threat combined with information asymmetry can result in wasteful signalling and short-termism. If the costs of mounting a takeover are low and thus the probability of succumbing to a raid is high, managers will signal. If takeover costs are great and the probability of being taken over is very low, then signalling may reduce the return to shareholders. So-called 'pooling beliefs' about dividends may then be current (that is, shareholders will not necessarily view a low/high dividend as a signal of a bad/good 'state of the world'). Where managers are assumed to value their control of the firm for its own sake, and where raiders are assumed to share the inside knowledge of managers about the true valuation of the company, the temptation on the part of managers to embrace short-termism will be greater. Under-valuation of shares on the market will be less acceptable to managers the more likely is a takeover and the more pronounced are their personal losses associated with it. The existence of informed raiders and fear of job loss both push managers in the direction of greater market signalling.

6. MORAL HAZARD, MONITORING COSTS AND THE TAKEOVER

If adverse selection leads to the use of dividend payments for signalling and the possibility of short-termism, moral hazard has been seen by some theorists as producing somewhat different results. Suppose that information asymmetry prevents shareholders from monitoring and disciplining managers in the manner discussed in Section 5 of the last chapter. Suppose also that the costs of mounting a takeover are high. Providers of capital will require some assurance that the managers will not shirk or use the resources of the firm to pursue their own rather than shareholders' interests. A long-term commitment to pay a regular dividend can then be seen as a mechanism for inducing effort and assuring shareholders of a minimum return.

Economic theorists, working with the full information assumption, have in the past found it difficult to explain why firms are observed to distribute assets to shareholders. Where capital markets are well developed and information costs are low, a *requirement* to pay a dividend would not seem necessary. Especially when the tax systems of many major countries discriminate against distributions and when profitable investment opportunities are available to a firm, distributions of dividends would appear not merely unnecessary but irrational. Shareholders should logically prefer to avoid some tax on the profits of the firm and to take their income in the form of capital gains on the market value of their shares. The difficulty, of course, is that shareholders will only be prepared to accept such a policy if they have good information about managerial competence and the likely profitability of the investment opportunities available, and can always *enforce* distributions at low cost should they disagree with the managers' judgements. Where neither of these conditions exists, regular dividends can be seen as a means of building a long-run reputation.

One view is that dividend payments are a mechanism by which the managers commit themselves to use the capital market for new funds, thereby subjecting themselves to greater scrutiny from the providers of new capital (Easterbrook, 1984).[7] Given the initial assumptions of high monitoring costs and *plastic* assets, however, it is not clear why the providers of new capital should be any better informed than the existing shareholders. De Alessi and Fishe (1987) therefore prefer to regard dividends as a way of reducing information and monitoring costs to shareholders. Regular dividends represent 'a commitment of minimum performance on the part of the management' (p. 43). Just as buyers or suppliers can commit themselves to buy or sell at declared and relatively stable 'posted prices' rather than take advantage of every opportunity to renegotiate more favourable terms, so joint-stock firms with widely dispersed shares commit themselves to stable dividends and promise implicitly not to 'hold up' the vulnerable shareholders. This interpretation of dividend payments is similar to that of Wu (1989) discussed in section 2.3 of Chapter 8.

It should be clearly understood that this explanation of dividend payments does not rely on their acting as a 'signal'. The commitment is to a regular and relatively stable payout to encourage effort. In the 'signalling' world of section 5, a firm going through bad times cut its dividend. It did this because it was unable to fool the market into thinking it was 'good' (the truly 'good' firms would always signal in ways that the bad ones could not match). Maintenance of the dividend in the face of adverse results would therefore serve no purpose. In this section, however, there *is* a purpose to maintaining the dividend rather than reducing it. A reputation for regular payments is valuable to the firm. Cutting the dividend might destroy market confidence in the firm's ability to deliver minimum standards of performance in the long run.

The cost of mounting takeovers provides the important link between sections 5 and 6. In the case of the adverse selection problem, *high* takeover costs discouraged signalling and permitted resources to be devoted to long-term investment. *Low* takeover costs led to wasteful signalling and short-termism. In the case of the moral hazard problem, *high* takeover costs implied that a reputation for the payment of regular dividends was necessary to reassure shareholders. *Low* costs of asserting control and enforcing distributions when managers misuse funds would make such a reputation less necessary (see section 9). Thus, short-termism can be seen as the result of both high and low costs of mounting takeovers. Low takeover costs produce dividends as signals. High takeover costs may produce dividends as a commitment to minimum performance. Either way, asymmetric information has consequences for long-term investment.

7.   THE TAKEOVER AND CAPITAL MARKET EFFICIENCY

We have seen in sections 4 to 6 that takeovers may have a destructive as well as a constructive side. Some analysts have argued that they threaten firm-specific assets, and may lead to short-termism by inducing higher cash distributions and lower investment than is socially desirable. How far these criticisms are justified is an empirical rather than theoretical issue. It is important, however, to distinguish between various different propositions about capital-market efficiency.

1. There is first the assertion that the capital market makes systematic mistakes in valuing assets. Even in the context of publicly available information, the market might underestimate the productivity of long-run investments in physical capital or research and development, or fail to appreciate the adverse long-run consequences of stealing the quasi-rents from firm-specific assets. Capital markets may not satisfy the requirements of *fundamental-valuation efficiency* to use Tobin's (1984) terminology. Capital markets would be efficient in this sense only if the valuation of financial assets always reflected accurately 'the future payments to which the asset gives title – . . . if the price of the asset is based on "rational expectations" of these payments' (p. 126).[8]

2. There is second the possibility that, in a world of asymmetric information, capital-market pressures lead *managers* to act myopically. The implication is that managers take actions which are disadvantageous for society as a whole even though the value of shares may reflect the rational expectations of *traders in the market* about the firm's future payments to shareholders. Stock prices, that is, are rationally based on *available* information, but not on *full* information.

The distinction is important because a capital market that is perfectly efficient in valuing assets on the basis of existing publicly available information may nevertheless not produce efficient results where there are asymmetries in information availability. In general, attempts to *disprove*[2] market efficiency by showing that there exist ways of using available information systematically to make profits (that is, to 'outsmart' the market) have failed. Even studies of professionally managed funds have shown that they have not outperformed the market. Available information seems rapidly to become incorporated into the prices of traded shares and the possibility of using information about investment plans (for example, by buying shares in firms with high R&D expenditures, which the market, by hypothesis, undervalues) has not been confirmed.

Critics have argued, however, that studies showing a random pattern of price movements are testing a particular form of market efficiency – *information arbitrage efficiency*. A market may be efficient in this sense without, it is said, implying that it satisfies the requirements of *fundamental-valuation efficiency*. The latter implies the former. The former is necessary but not sufficient for the latter. In the extreme case, for example, all the information available to the market might be 'wrong' and prices would depart from the 'correct' efficient ones. Alternatively, the implications of correct information for the future of a firm might be 'wrongly' interpreted by stock market traders. In neither case would information arbitrage efficiency be ruled out, though prices might depart from 'true' fundamental valuations. The difficulty with these arguments is that objective knowledge of what constitutes 'correct' information or 'rational' interpretation of this does not exist. Any general demonstration that markets are either efficient or inefficient in terms of fundamental valuation is therefore impossible. All that can be done is to test *ad hoc* assertions about the nature of stock market irrationality against the evidence.

Claims that institutional investors pay exclusive attention to current dividend flows – for example, selling shares in companies who adopt long-term policies of investment, thus depressing their share prices and making them vulnerable to takeover – fail to attract much support in the empirical literature. A report by the Office of the Chief Economist of the United States' Securities and Exchange Commission (1985) found no relationship between the size of institutional shareholdings and vulnerability to takeover, or lower R&D expenditure. Higher R&D expenditure did not appear to result in a greater risk of takeover. Indeed, announcements of R&D expenditure were associated with stock price *increases*. Hall (1988) looked for evidence that acquisitions cause a reduction in R&D expenditure. She found that firms involved in mergers and those not so involved could not be distinguished on the basis of their pre- or post-merger R&D performance (p. 93). McConnell and Muscarella (1985) confirmed that higher planned capital expenditure was associated with increases in the value of common stock except in the cases of exploration and development in the oil industry (see section 9) and the regulated utilities, the profits of which are controlled.[10]

The fact that the capital market responds to available information in ways compatible with efficient forward-looking valuation of common stock does not, however, necessarily mean that it copes efficiently with the moral hazard and adverse selection problems associated with information asymmetry. Stock prices will not reflect 'inside' information and pressure from the takeover might theoretically result in *managers* acting in a short-termist way. Even those who are convinced of the efficient properties of capital markets with respect to publicly available information accept that signalling may be an important feature. Marsh (1991) writes, for example, that 'Current dividend announcements are thus an important signal of management's own (inside) knowledge and judgements about the longer-term future of the companies they manage' (p. 6). It was, though, precisely this incentive to signal when takeover costs are low that led to the diversion of resources away from investment towards distributions in Stein's (1988) model of *managerial* short-termism outlined in section 5.

If *fundamental-valuation efficiency* is interpreted to require symmetric and public information, few analysts would claim that stock markets were efficient. The very fact of large trading volumes could be used as evidence against the 'efficiency' of the market on the grounds that it must imply that large numbers of people *think* existing prices are 'wrong' and that they have better information about future prospects, or more developed analytical skills, or superior judgement, compared with other traders. A truly 'efficient' market would, if we were to follow this line of argument to its logical conclusion, be entirely 'non-speculative' (that is, it would be based on objectively correct and publicly available information). Yet a non-speculative capital market is a contradiction in terms. As we have seen elsewhere in this book, the economist's notion of efficient markets is quite capable of wiping out the entire trading system.

Demsetz's (1969) warning against nirvana economics must be remembered at this point. If stock markets are inefficient from a fundamental valuation point of view, so also is every other asset-price determination system yet devised. Available institutional responses to information asymmetry are the relevant comparisons to make. How they compare with a world of zero information costs is not the issue. Unfortunately, institutional comparisons are immensely complex and contentious. Three observations are pertinent here.

1. Adverse selection and moral hazard problems tend to pull in opposite directions in this field of takeovers. Restricting takeovers may reduce 'wasteful' signalling but is likely to increase 'managerial' behaviour more generally.
2. Information asymmetry is not necessarily correctly seen as a feature independent of the institutional means chosen to cope with it. For example, a system in which some major 'inside' shareholders were actively monitoring management behaviour would be less subject to information asymmetry problems than a system of widely dispersed 'outside' holdings. Of course, the former system would involve higher risk-bearing costs (see sections 10 and 11 below).
3. If takeover pressure is particularly disadvantageous to a firm (for example if it relies heavily on the accumulation of firm-specific human capital) there are various takeover defences that it can adopt. The nature of these defences is discussed in the next section.

8.   DEFENCES AGAINST HOSTILE TAKEOVERS

8.1   Supermajority Amendments

If shareholders believe that the risk of takeover could have adverse consequences for the value of the firm, they could make adjustments to their corporate constitutions. Changes in the composition of the Board of Directors or mergers would have to be approved by more than a simple majority of votes – perhaps two-thirds or more. In fact, such supermajority amendments are not common. Where they have occurred, the effect on stock prices appears to have been negative.[11]

8.2   Dual-class Recapitalisations

Stock can be issued which gives the holder a claim to the residual but only a restricted voting right. In the United States during the takeover boom of the 1980s, stock with enhanced or restricted voting rights became common enough for the New York Stock Exchange to petition the Securities and Exchange Commission to relax the requirement that each share traded on the exchange should carry one vote. Jarrell, Brickley and Netter (1988) comment that the 'typical dual class firm is already controlled by insiders and the recapitalisation provides a means to raise needed capital for positive Net Present Value projects without dilution of control' (p. 61).

8.3   Poison Pills

Sections 2 and 3 were concerned with the free-rider problem and the resulting tendency for takeover activity to be discouraged. Grossman and Hart suggested that a dilution of the existing shareholders' rights might encourage bidders. Bidders might be permitted to purchase remaining shares from shareholders on terms disadvantageous to the latter. If, on the contrary, takeover activity is considered to be too high for the reasons discussed in sections 4 to 7, it can be inhibited by 'negative dilution'. Existing shareholders, for example, can be given *enhanced* rights to sell their shares to the company at favourable prices following a raid. This is the essence of the so-called 'poison pill'. The pill contains provisions which make a company extremely unattractive to a takeover raider.

It is an interesting feature of poison pills in the United States that the courts have upheld the right of managers to introduce some varieties without the consent of shareholders. This position has been justified by the 'Business Judgement Rule' which is designed to prevent shareholders from questioning particular business decisions in the courts. Jensen (1988) argues that this position fails to distinguish 'decision rights', which shareholders delegate to managers, from 'control rights', which they keep for themselves. 'The Courts are effectively giving the agent the right to change the control rights unilaterally' (p. 43). In an analysis of the effects of takeover litigation in the courts, Ryngaert (1988) found that fifteen out of eighteen pro-poison-pill decisions resulted in negative effects on the stock price of the target firm. At present, therefore, it is far from clear that poison pills are being introduced with the consent of shareholders in the interests of protecting other stakeholders from 'hold-up' or as a weapon against 'short-termism'.

8.4   Greenmail

If a potential raider accumulates a certain fraction of a firm's stock, it may give the target management the option of repurchasing these shares at a premium in return for not pursuing the takeover. When the management of a firm makes such 'targeted repurchases' it is popularly said to pay 'greenmail'. This can hardly be regarded as a long-term policy of protection against takeovers. However, the question arises of whether greenmail payments are against the interests of target shareholders.

Clearly, if managers are inefficient and merely protecting their position in the firm, greenmail will deplete shareholders' funds and the price of the stock will end at or below its pre-raid level. Greenmail, in these circumstances, is a manifestation of the *moral hazard* problem. Shareholders would prefer managers to declare a policy of never paying greenmail. If, on the other hand, information asymmetries had resulted in a systematic undervaluation of a good firm's shares because a low dividend was wrongly interpreted as a bad signal, or 'pooling beliefs' on the part of shareholders had left the shares below their 'true' level, payment of greenmail would simply result in a correction of this false impression. The informed 'greenmailer' would be performing a useful public service in correcting a false stock market valuation, while target managers would be serving shareholders' interests by preventing them from accepting a low offer.[12] Here, the greenmail payment arises from the improvement in the information available and serves to mitigate the *adverse selection* problem.

Since the payment of greenmail uses cash, however, it might be argued that it represents a species of 'forced signal' and that the greenmailer's activities therefore exacerbate short-termism. If managers of good firms do not signal, raiders will do it for them, and managers will simply find themselves having to pay greenmail. There is an important distinction, however. In the greenmail case, it is an 'outsider' that has initiated the signal. The existence of outsiders who see the firm as in a good state will affect the ability of managers to raise new capital.[13] Stein's signalling model of short-termism, discussed in section 5, was based on the assumption that no ways of convincing the capital market of the long-term state of the firm existed apart from the wasteful use of capital. Firms who found themselves in the 'good' state could afford to waste more capital (by distributing it) than those who found themselves in the 'bad' state.[14] The greenmail case is different. If markets believe the greenmailer's assessment of the worth of the firm when he/she 'threatens' to bid for shares at a premium, real investment should not suffer when greenmail is paid because new sources of finance will be available.

8.5   Golden Parachutes

Instead of trying to resist takeover bids, a company which relies heavily on firm-specific human capital could reduce hold-up potential by establishing clear individual property rights to the returns from these assets. For top managers, the promise to make a large severance payment in the event of a successful takeover (that is, the provision of a 'golden parachute') can be seen as compensation for the loss of specific capital which might otherwise have been incurred by the managers. Fear of takeover should then, in theory, not discourage a manager from investing in firm-specific skills. The golden parachute removes the dependency that is otherwise associated with this type of asset. Similar protection for people at other levels in the organisation is difficult to contrive, however, short of adopting the quite different institutional structure of a cooperative or large partnership discussed in Chapter 10.

A golden parachute which compensates for the potential loss of firm-specific capital is one thing. A parachute which compensates for the search costs of the manager in the labour market and hence removes managerial dependency entirely would be another. The latter would encourage an entirely 'passive' attitude to takeovers on the part of managers. They would neither fight them nor embrace them. Some have argued that such managerial neutrality towards takeovers would be advantageous. It would certainly remove the conflict of interest which might otherwise be involved between shareholders and managers at the time of a takeover. The former are in line for a substantial bid premium to the share price. The latter are in line for the job market. Even where substantial commercial advantages could be expected from a takeover, managers would be expected to resist unless offered compensation. Full compensation for loss of position, however, would totally undermine the managerial incentive properties of takeovers. Only if it were possible clearly to distinguish takeovers aimed at removing inefficient managers from takeovers designed to achieve benefits of synergy from the combining of two firms' operations, could this dilemma be resolved.

9.   DO TAKEOVERS IMPROVE ECONOMIC EFFICIENCY?

9.1   The Takeover Wave of the 1980s

During the 1980s in the UK and the USA, conditions favoured a high level of corporate restructuring via takeovers, divestments, and management buy-outs (MBOs). The 'market for corporate control' appeared very active and led to a continuing debate about its effects. In the UK, the number of acquisitions is very variable, with sudden surges of activity. As a proportion of GDP, expenditure on acquisitions was one per cent or less in the mid-1950s and mid-1970s. However, in 1968, 1972 and 1988, the proportion rose to around five per cent or more of GDP. The USA also experienced a rise in expenditure on acquisitions as a proportion of national income in the 1980s. At five per cent of GNP in 1988, acquisitions were running at levels well in excess of post-war norms (though below estimates for the takeover booms of the 1890s and 1920s).[15] In contrast to the Anglo-American experience, the value of acquisitions in Japan remained below one per cent of GDP, even in 1988, and economies such as those of France and Germany were similarly less affected by takeovers. These differences will be taken up in section 11. For the moment, we briefly set out contrasting perspectives on the market in corporate control in the USA and the UK.

9.2 Moral Hazard and the Free Cash-Flow Theory

For agency cost theorists of corporate structure, the takeover is a mechanism for disciplining managers and reducing problems of moral hazard. Interpretation of events is complicated, however, by the fact that takeovers can be both a weapon against inefficient managers and an instrument of managerial inefficiency. Jensen (1988) argues, for example, that the loosening of restrictions on mergers in the USA, the movement towards deregulation in many industries (such as oil, gas, transport, broadcasting and financial services) and innovations in the financial field, all led to the necessity of considerable industrial restructuring. Often this would be opposed by managerial interests, especially if restructuring implied the shrinking of an organisation and the distribution of assets to shareholders. Rather than contemplate the orderly run down of activities and the distribution of surplus funds, managers were likely to engage in attempts to expand into new areas (often using the takeover as a mechanism) or to undertake imprudent investment projects.

Jensen gives as an example of the squandering of shareholders' resources, the tendency of oil companies to use cash surpluses to engage in further exploration activities even when excess reserves were a major problem. This exploration activity resulted in falling stock prices until it became cheaper to obtain reserves by buying other petroleum companies than by actual geological search.[16] Wherever managers had access to large cash reserves that could not productively be invested in established lines of activity, a potential problem existed. Broadcasters with valuable licences looking to diversify, or pharmaceutical companies with patents but uncertain about future technological developments, are other examples of potentially cash-rich companies with shareholders vulnerable to managerial opportunism. Shareholders face the problem of laying claim to the firm's resources and preventing wasteful 'managerial' investments from occurring. This explanation of takeover activity in the 1980s became known as the 'free cash-flow theory of takeovers'.

9.3   The Role of the 'Junk Bond'

A characteristic of the 1980s takeover boom was the use of the 'high-yield non-investment grade bond' popularly known as the 'junk bond'. This financial instrument is simply a commercial loan with a yield reflecting the associated risks which can be traded on secondary markets. Three consequences of the widespread use of junk bonds in takeovers are relevant here. Firstly, the ability of quite small firms to raise large amounts of money by the issue of such bonds made firms that had previously appeared immune from takeover vulnerable to a raid financed by bonds. Secondly, successful takeovers or management buy-outs financed in this way implied a move to a higher debt–equity ratio. With managers holding a larger proportion of the equity than before, restructuring might often be seen as moving away from the manager's certainty line towards the type of high-incentive contract discussed in section 4 of Chapter 8. Finally, in the absence of trust, bonds are a way of reassuring the providers of capital that cash will be distributed and not invested in low-yielding projects. A high debt–equity ratio can leave bondholders vulnerable to the taking of reckless risks by equity-holding managers[17] (as discussed in Chapter 4) but it leaves outside providers of capital less vulnerable to the retention by managers of the firm's resources.

Restructuring as a result of takeovers has been a matter of great public interest over recent years and subsection 9.4 considers some of the evidence. Using debt finance to take companies private through management buy-outs (often with eventual reflotation as a public company later on) has been less widely studied, though representing a significant proportion of the market in corporate control. Evidence from leveraged buy-outs in the United States during the 1980s suggested that performance improved significantly.[18] Similarly, in the UK, where MBO activity grew substantially in number and value[19] over the same period, Thompson, Wright and Robbie (1992) studied the returns to capital between the time of a buy-out and the following public share offering. The proportion of equity held by the management was found to be the main determinant of performance. 'The size and robustness of the management ownership effect in our results lends support to the views of those . . . who see corporate re-structuring primarily in terms of increasing managerial motivation' (p. 414). On the other hand, they found 'no support for the debt-bonding or free cash-flow hypotheses' (p. 428).

9.4 Gains to Target and Bidding Companies

Studies of share price movements at the time of a takeover indicate that the main beneficiaries are the shareholders of target companies. Bid premia averaged around thirty per cent in the period 1980–85 in the USA.[20] In the UK, evidence presented by Morgan and Morgan (1990) suggests bid premia of a similar size: 'In 1989 premiums averaged 29 per cent over the price ruling the day before the offer, and 37 per cent above the price a month before' (p. 72). The shares of acquiring companies, on the other hand, reveal low or zero gains on average (around two per cent or less). Supporters of the agency costs approach to takeovers argue that the stock-price reactions reflect the capitalised value of future returns and that, even allowing for some redistributional effects, the overall impact of takeovers is to increase economic efficiency. Jensen (1988, p. 23) writes that 'The market for corporate control is creating large benefits for shareholders and for the economy as a whole by loosening control over vast amounts of resources and enabling them to move more quickly to their highest-valued use.'[21]

The asymmetry in the distribution of the gains to acquirer and acquired firms is of interest in itself. Our discussion of the free-rider and the hold-out problems faced by bidders in sections 2 and 3 indicates why acquirers find it difficult to appropriate a large fraction of the gains available. There is, though, in addition a possible distortion introduced by the fact that some acquisitions are in any case 'managerially' motivated. The 'free cash-flow' approach implies that managers of cash-rich companies may tend to overbid for targets. If this is so, a further question suggests itself. Do companies that overbid or indulge in takeovers of which the markets disapprove, themselves become the targets of other more successful predators? A study by Mitchell and Lehn (1990) investigates this issue. For the years 1982–86, they divided a sample of firms into those that were at some point 'target' firms and those that were never the 'target' of a raid. They then looked for differences in the stock market reaction to announced takeovers by these firms. They discovered that 'The stock prices of targets decline significantly when they announce acquisitions . . . and the stock prices of non-targets increase significantly' (p. 375). The probability of being a hostile target over the period was inversely related to the stock market reaction to a firm's acquisitions. The authors argue that their results are supportive of the claims of Jensen and others concerning the role of takeovers as a disciplinary device.

Many writers take a more sceptical view of the evidence than has been reported thus far. Although all are agreed that the shareholders of acquired firms gain considerably, the effect on acquiring firms is seen by some as adverse and the existence of net social gains as dubious. Scherer's (1988) views have already been noted (see note 10). Morgan and Morgan (1990, p. 80) argue that the performance of 'acquiring companies' deteriorates during a two-year interval after a merger or takeover. They also cite the volatility of stock markets and the existence of merger 'waves' as evidence of irrational or 'faddist' influences. Hughes (1989), in a survey of the UK evidence, questions the use of changes in stock prices around the time of a takeover to measure efficiency gains, arguing that this amounts to little more than a declaration of faith. Similarly, Peacock and Bannock (1991) find 'no concrete evidence that takeovers are predominantly "successful" whatever measure of "success" (managerial perceptions, profitability, rates of return on capital, shareholder wealth) is used' (p. 62).

The reader will deduce from all this that, as usual in economics, empirical evidence seems incapable of settling anything. Our primary purpose here, however, is not to embark on a discussion of public policy towards takeovers, but to prepare the ground for a brief outline of the properties of different systems of corporate governance in section 11. Much of the confusion in the debate about the effects of takeovers derives from a reluctance clearly to specify the alternative set of institutional arrangements which are to be compared with the status quo. The idea that those defending takeovers believe that markets are efficient whereas those who doubt the value of takeovers believe that markets are inefficient is very wide of the truth. It would be bizarre to criticise (say) Michael Jensen for overlooking the possibility of inefficiency arising from information asymmetry and agency costs. Jensen, as we have seen, was a major architect of the modern agency cost theory of the firm.

Supporters of takeovers are likely to argue that moral hazard is a more significant problem than short-termism deriving from adverse selection; that, in a stock-market economy, takeovers place limits on managerial behaviour; and that to raise the costs of takeovers would lead to higher levels of managerial shirking. Note that all these propositions could be true even if no takeover was ever observed to take place or if the takeovers that did occur produced no rise in combined shareholder value. Managers might, for example, keep the costs of their shirking to levels below the transactions costs required to unseat them. Supporters of takeovers are implicitly offering a scientific prediction, which they would prefer not to see tested. 'Increasing the costs of takeovers while leaving institutional arrangements otherwise unchanged will reduce the productivity of economic resources.' The experiments reported in earlier paragraphs do not test this proposition.

Critics of takeovers are likely to argue that the adverse consequences of short-termism are substantial; that, in a stock-market economy, low takeover costs exacerbate this problem; and that higher takeover costs would produce social gains if the danger of moral hazard were countered by the more direct monitoring of managers. Critics are therefore implicitly offering a scientific prediction that they would be prepared to see tested. 'Increasing the costs of takeovers combined with an adjustment to the monitoring arrangements faced by managers will increase the productivity of economic resources.' The experiments reported in the previous paragraphs do not test this proposition. Both the prediction of the supporters of takeovers and the prediction of critics of takeovers could be simultaneously true. For completeness we should recognise that a strong opponent of takeovers might be prepared to predict a rise in productivity from their restriction, even without changes in the monitoring environment. This would produce a direct conflict in the predictions based upon different beliefs about the relative influence of the problems of adverse selection and moral hazard.

Although evidence on the effects of takeovers is difficult to gather and interpret, strong opinions are nevertheless expressed, both by way of criticism and support. This discussion of corporate governance derives much of its momentum from the fact that quite different systems can be observed in different countries and that this comparative experience is seen as relevant to the formulation public policy. A detailed appraisal of policy towards mergers and takeovers would take us beyond the scope of this book. Nevertheless, a brief outline of existing systems of corporate governance will enable us to link their characteristics to some of the theoretical issues which have been discussed so far. Before embarking on this discussion of comparative systems, however, it will be useful to discuss the connection between corporate governance and financial structure.

10.   CAPITAL STRUCTURE AND CORPORATE GOVERNANCE

10.1   The Modigliani–Miller Theorem

Throughout this chapter the agency problems of corporate control have been to the fore. Yet, although financial instruments such as ordinary shares and various types of debt have been mentioned and the consequences for incentives have been noted, we have not linked observed financial structure systematically to control problems. The question of what determines the capital structure of firms now comprises a substantial part of modern financial theory and the reader is referred to a specialised text for a more extensive treatment.[22] It is important to sketch the outlines of the subject, however, because the financial structure of a modern corporation can be seen as a response to some of the agency problems that we have been discussing.

Just as traditional neoclassical theory provided no satisfactory rationalisation of firms, the neoclassical theory of finance had little to say about the choice of financial structure. In a pathbreaking contribution to the theory of finance, for example, Modigliani and Miller (1958) showed that, under conditions of full information, the value of the firm would be independent of the means chosen to finance it. The debt–equity ratio would not influence the value of the firm.[23] The Modigliani–Miller theorem provides the same sort of benchmark in finance as the work of Ronald Coase provides in the theory of economic organisation (see, again, Chapter 2). With no transactions costs and full public information, organisational structure would be indeterminate because there is no organisational problem to solve. Similarly, with costless and perfect markets, the means of finance is irrelevant to the firm's valuation and there is no particular 'optimal' financial structure.

The Modigliani–Miller theorem seems, at first acquaintance, counterintuitive. There appears to be a deceptive implication that the riskiness of an asset will not influence its price. This, however, would be a complete misinterpretation. The theorem does not tell us that the market value of firms is independent of the risk and return characteristics of their anticipated net cash flows. On the contrary, the theorem asserts that it is precisely the nature of these anticipated cash flows that will determine the value of the firm and *not* the nature of the financial instruments issued by the firm to lay claim to them.

Consider two firms setting out the various 'states of nature' that might happen in the future and calculating the net cash flows that they would receive were those states of nature to materialise. Suppose the firms are identical except that one is financed entirely by equity while the other is financed with both equity and debt. Assume that the debt is risk free and that in neither firm does bankruptcy occur in any state of nature. The total market value of the outstanding claims must be the same for each firm. If this were not the case and the shares of the all-equity firm were valued, in total, more highly than the shares plus bonds of the firm with both equity and debt, profitable arbitrage possibilities would exist for holders of the securities. If, for example, a person held one hundred per cent of the shares of the all-equity firm, he or she would sell them and buy the shares plus bonds of the other firm. The claims to net cash flow represented by the mixed portfolio are (by assumption) the same overall as the claims represented by the all-equity portfolio. Thus, the market prices of stocks and bonds will so adjust that firms with the same risk and return characteristics will have the same total market valuation, irrespective of their financial structure.

Similar types of argument can also be used to show that the firm's policy on distributions will not affect its value. Whether a firm retains its earnings to invest in a project or distributes earnings and raises funds by issuing new equity, will not matter. In the former case, share prices will rise to reflect higher future cash flows from the investment. In the latter case, the greater value of the firm will be reflected in a larger number of outstanding shares. Individual shareholders will not be affected because they can always adjust their own portfolio of shares to neutralise the actions of the firm. If the firm finances an investment by retentions, for example, a shareholder who is unwilling to contribute can simply sell sufficient of his or her shares to offset the rise in their total value.

It is evident that a theory which explains the financial structure of firms cannot be based upon assumptions of costless and frictionless markets with full information. The final paragraphs of this section aim to describe how the information and agency problems discussed earlier relate to the choice of financial structure. As we have seen, moral hazard and adverse selection problems deriving from asymmetric information are at the centre of the stage. In addition, however, bounded rationality and the incomplete and imperfectly specified nature of contracts play an important part.

10.2   The Agency Costs Theory of Financial Structure

A formal analysis of the incentive problems associated with joint-stock enterprise is presented by Jensen and Meckling (1976). Their approach incorporates the use of debt instruments as well as equity in a sophisticated theory of 'ownership structure'. At this point we merely outline the simplest case, and consider the effect of outside-equity holders on the market value of the firm. Suppose that the firm is of a given size, that it is financed entirely by equity and that initially all the equity is held by a single manager or 'peak coordinator'. In Figure 9.1, the market value of the firm is measured on the vertical axis and the market value of the stream of 'expenditures on non-pecuniary benefits' is measured along the horizontal axis. The slope of the constraint VF is -1, indicating that expenditures on non-pecuniary benefits are at the expense of pecuniary benefits. A single proprietor will operate at point a, where his or her indifference curve U_1 is tangential to the constraint VF. The market value of the firm as a single proprietorship will be OV^*, and the non-pecuniary benefits available will have a value of OF^*.

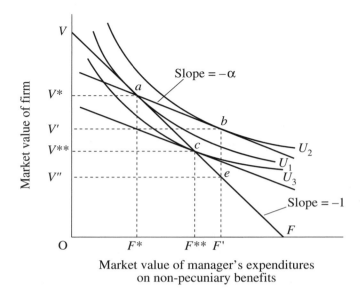

Source: Jensen and Meckling (1976), Fig. 1, p. 316.

Figure 9.1   The agency cost of outside equity

Now assume that the 'peak coordinator' can sell a fraction of his or her equity shares to outsiders. These shares, Jensen and Meckling assume, carry no voting rights. Suppose that the peak coordinator retains a proportion of the shares and sells a proportion $1 - \alpha$. Clearly the 'cost' to the coordinator of 'managerial' expenditures on non-pecuniary benefits will now only be a fraction α of the reduction in the market value of the firm which results. We would therefore expect the peak coordinator to indulge in more 'managerial' expenditures than before, and the market value of the equity shares will fall. This change in behaviour induced by the manager's smaller proportionate stake in the enterprise will be predicted by the outsiders who purchase equity from him/her and they will adjust downwards the price they are prepared to pay for the shares accordingly. An outside investor short-sighted enough to pay $(1 - \alpha)V^*$ for the shares offered would suffer a loss. The peak coordinator would not remain at point a with wealth V^* (made up of $(1 - \alpha)V^*$ in cash and αV^* of remaining equity) and with managerial perks of OF^*. S/he would increase his/her nonpecuniary expenditures to OF' and his/her private wealth would fall to OV'. The value of the firm would fall precipitously to OV'', but a fraction $(1 - \alpha)$ of this fall would be borne by the outsider, not the manager.

When the outsider purchases a fraction $1-\alpha$ of the equity, s/he will revise downwards the value of the firm to OV^{**}. Assuming the outsider's expectations about managerial shirking are correct, the manager will operate at point c in Figure 9.1. The total value of the firm's equity will be OV^{**} and the manager will indulge in OF^{**} of non-pecuniary benefits. Any higher initial valuation of the shares would result in the outsiders making a loss as already described, and any lower valuation would imply that the peak coordinator had sold for less than outsiders would have been prepared to pay. The distance $OV^{*}-OV^{**}$ is termed by Jensen and Meckling the gross agency cost of the move to a fraction $1-\alpha$ of outside equity. We should note that this fall in the value of the firm would not occur if an enforceable contract could be drawn up limiting the manager's non-pecuniary benefits to OF^{*}. Thus, even where monitoring is costly, some arrangement of this type might be in the interests of both parties.

If outside equity reduces the value of the firm and results in 'agency costs', why is it that all firms are not individually owned and managed? One answer might be that no single individual is wealthy enough to hold the entire equity. This does not, however, explain why, if this is so, capital could not be borrowed at fixed interest instead of raised by outside equity holders. The objection that proprietors would not like highly leveraged operations because of the risk of bankruptcy has less force in a world of limited liability than one of unlimited liability. Under limited liability, the problem is not the risk aversion of the owner-manager but instead the incentives that a highly leveraged structure will give to such a person to take very large risks. The costs of failure are borne by outside bondholders and the benefits of success go to the single equity holder. Clearly, there are agency costs associated with the use of debt as well as outside equity.

Given the inescapable agency costs of outside finance, Jensen and Meckling explain the existence of outside equity and debt holders primarily by reference to risk-spreading benefits. Selling equity claims to outsiders will reduce the value of the firm and hence the owner-manager's wealth, but if the benefits of a more widely diversified portfolio outweigh these agency costs, the owner-manager will still prefer to reduce his/her holding. The optimal amount of outside financing will be reached when the marginal benefits from increased diversification equal the marginal agency costs incurred.[24]

Figure 9.2 summarises the agency costs approach to capital structure. Let E be outside equity and D represent the issue of debt. Along the horizontal axis, the proportion of equity finance declines and the proportion of debt finance increases. We have seen that as the proportion of outside equity increases, managerial effort declines and gross agency costs of equity rise. This relationship is represented by the curve labelled EE' in Figure 9.2.

Similarly, as the proportion of bond finance rises and outside equity declines, the agency problems of debt become increasingly serious. Inside-equity holders have greater effort incentives, and bond finance ensures the distribution of cash from successful ventures, but bonds also encourage greater risk taking. This relationship is shown by curve DD'. Total agency costs are minimised at point P on TT'.

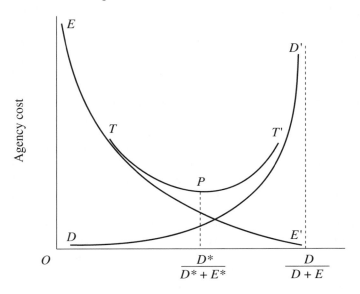

Source: Jensen and Meckling (1976).

Figure 9.2   Financial structure: the agency cost approach

10.3   Agency Problems, Debt and the Hart–Moore Theory of Financial Structure[25]

10.3.1   Non-contractibility and financial structure

In section 10.2, the use of debt was seen as constrained by the potential opportunistic behaviour of a few significant equity holders. Jensen and Meckling's theory therefore applies to situations in which owner-managers hold all the control rights and a significant portion of profit rights. In this subsection, agency problems remain to the fore, but we return to the main focus of Chapters 8 and 9 – the problem of controlling managers who may have negligible profit rights. In a modern joint-stock enterprise, we take it as given that equity holdings are widely dispersed, that incentive contracts will not always align managerial interests with those of shareholders and that managers therefore have considerable scope to indulge in discretionary behaviour. Debt instruments can then be seen as the means by which the diversion of resources towards managerial ends is controlled. Hart and Moore (1995) have developed this theory, which extends the type of reasoning explored in Chapter 4, subsection 8.2, on the finance of the entrepreneur. There, the contract of debt was a means of forcing the entrepreneur to disgorge revenue flows when these were assumed not to be *ex ante* contractible. Here, short-term debt can be seen similarly as a mechanism for forcing managers to distribute cash flows rather than wasting them on unprofitable projects.[26] Short-term debt also forces managers to liquidate investments when this is better than pursuing them further at a loss. Long-term debt can likewise be seen as a mechanism for preventing managers from undertaking loss-making new ventures, whilst permitting them to continue with profitable existing ones.

Suppose, adjusting the exposition of Chapter 4, that a project undertaken at the beginning of period 1 yields revenues of R_1 and R_2 at the end of periods 1 and 2 respectively. The liquidation value of the project at the end of period 1 is K_1. In the context of this chapter, the project is undertaken not by an entrepreneur but a 'manager'. The revenue stream is still not contractible because not verifiable but, unlike the model introduced in Chapter 4, we do not assume that the manager can simply steal these revenues and divert them to his or her own purposes. Instead, we assume that the manager gets private benefits from undertaking projects whether or not they are profitable. Revenue streams and cash flows from liquidation are received by outside equity holders or the holders of short- or long-term debt. For simplicity, the rate of discount is assumed to be zero.

10.3.2 Short-term debt and project liquidation

Financial structure, in this model, is about constraining managers. Clearly, if $R_2 < K_1$, it is efficient to liquidate the project at the end of period 1. Managerial interests, however, dictate that the project should go on if it can possibly be arranged. Managers cannot be controlled directly by the owners and told to liquidate such a project, because owners are dispersed and because a suitable contract to this end cannot be written. Short-term debt can be used in this situation to force liquidation. Suppose that the manager must make a payment to bond holders at the end of period 1 of P_1. A sufficiently large value of P_1 will force the manager either to liquidate the assets or to borrow sufficient new funds to permit the project to continue. In particular, if $P_1 > R_1$, the manager will have to default unless new borrowing can be arranged. Will the manager be able to borrow $P_1 - R_1$ so as to avoid defaulting on the short-term debt? Assume for the time being that there is no outstanding long-term debt with its associated obligations to repay at the

end of period 2. Managers will be able to raise new finance, providing $R_2 >$
$P_1 - R_1$. To prevent this happening, owners must set $P_1 > R_1 + R_2$.

If revenue flows are known with certainty at the beginning of period 1,
therefore, sufficiently high levels of short-term debt can force liquidation at
the end of period 1, if this is efficient. Bond holders would receive P_1 while
equity holders would receive $R_1 + K_1 - P_1$. Given that we are assuming that
$K_1 > R_2$, it is possible for equity to receive a positive return under these
circumstances. The problem, of course, is that revenues are not known with
certainty at the beginning of period 1. If we make the assumption that it is
only at the *end* of period 1 that managers and providers of finance will
know whether or not the project should be liquidated or continued into
period 2, the dangers of high levels of short-period debt become apparent.
The managers might be forced into liquidation even if it transpired that K_1
$< R_2$ and the project should continue. To avoid inefficient liquidation, a low
level of short-term debt is required. If we knew with certainty that $K_1 < R_2$
and that the project should continue, we could set $P_1 = 0$ and there would
be no role for short-term debt.

Suppose now that there are two possible scenarios for the outcome of the
project (scenario A and scenario B). Which scenario prevails will not be
known until the end of period 1. If both scenarios involve keeping the
project going to the end of period 2, it is easy to see that $P_1 = 0$ is the best
solution for short-term debt. Similarly, if the project should be liquidated
at the end of period 1 under both scenarios, a sufficiently high level of P_1
will be able to accomplish this. The more interesting cases involve $R_2^A > K_1^A$
and $R_2^B < K_1^B$. In other words, it would be best to continue to the end of
period 2 under scenario A, but liquidate the project at the end of period 1
under scenario B. Is there a level of P_1 which will force closure under scenario B and permit continuation under scenario A?

There are several possibilities to consider. Suppose first that revenue in
period 1 is higher in scenario A than scenario B ($R_1^A > R_1^B$). This implies
that we can set the level of short-term debt (say) P_1^* below R_1^A and above
R_1^B, thereby posing no financing problem to the managers at the end of
period 1 in scenario A while forcing them to seek new borrowing in scenario
B. How, though, can we be sure that the managers in scenario B will not
find willing lenders? Clearly, they might do so if revenue at the end of
period 2 exceeds the level of borrowing necessary to keep going ($R_2^B > P_1^*$
$- R_1^B$) and this possibility is not ruled out by any of our assumptions. One
way of preventing the managers successfully finding finance to continue the
project inefficiently in scenario B is to issue senior long-term debt repayable
at the end of period 2, or before if the project is liquidated. Potential lenders
at the end of period 1 will observe that there are already prior claimants to
some of next period's revenue. They will lend only if $R_2^B > P_1 + P_2 - R_1^B$,

where P_2 is the level of long-term debt obligations. While P_1 is constrained to be no higher than $R_1{}^A$, so that there are no impediments to continuing the project in scenario A, there are no such limitations on the level of P_2. The level of long-term senior debt can therefore be set at a level sufficient to prevent managers in scenario B extending the life of the project inefficiently.

What happens, however, if scenario A's revenue is lower than scenario B's in period 1 ($R_1{}^A < R_1{}^B$)? Setting the level of P_1 low enough not to inconvenience managers in scenario A will imply that it is also low enough to leave them unhindered in scenario B. If we are to control managerial behaviour in scenario B, we cannot avoid forcing the managers into the financial markets in *both* scenarios. This will not matter, providing the managers can successfully find the necessary finance to continue under A but are forced to liquidate under B. Thus, if $R_2{}^A > P_1 - R_1{}^A$ but $R_2{}^B < P_1 - R_1{}^B$, managers can find finance under A but not under B. These conditions can be satisfied if $R_1{}^A + R_2{}^A > R_1{}^B + R_2{}^B$. The level of short-term debt (say $P_1{}^*$) can be set below the present value of revenues in scenario A but above the present value of revenues in scenario B. This forces liquidation under B but not under A, as required.

The real problem case is where the present value of revenues under scenario B exceeds that under A, even though it is under B that the project should be liquidated at the end of the first period ($R_1{}^A + R_2{}^A < R_1{}^B + R_2{}^B$). Setting P_1 between the present value of revenue streams would simply force managers to liquidate the project under A but not under B – the reverse of what is required. The choice is therefore either to liquidate the project under both scenarios using a high value of P_1 or to continue it under both with $P_1{}^* = 0$. Clearly, the best policy will depend upon the probabilities attached to scenarios A and B respectively. The higher the probability of scenario A, the more likely it is that we will want the project to continue and the better it will be to opt for low levels of short-term debt. The greater the probability of scenario B, the more likely that we will wish to liquidate the project and the better it will be to opt for high levels of short-term debt.

10.3.3 Long-term debt and new investment

We have already noticed in subsection 10.3.2 that, under certain circumstances, the existence of long-term debt obligations might prevent managers from raising finance inefficiently to continue a project which should be liquidated. In this subsection, the same idea is used to show that long-term debt might control managerial behaviour when managers have opportunities for undertaking new investments.

Suppose, for example, that, at the end of period 1, managers can add to the investment in a project. This extra investment (I) will then produce additional revenue at the end of period 2 ($R_2{}^I$). Clearly, if $R_2{}^I > I$, it would be a good idea to add to the investment, while if $R_2{}^I < I$, it would be better if the managers were not able to go ahead. It is assumed that the potential extra investment is not a stand-alone project but an extension of the original one. To simplify matters, assume that short-term debt is set equal to zero because under no scenario should the project be liquidated at the end of period 1. The only issue is how to control managerial empire-building, since the managers will always want to invest if they can, and, although the project should not be liquidated early, the additional investment is not always profitable.

In the absence of short-term debt, managers will be able to invest if $R_1 > I$. They simply finance the investment out of period-1 revenue. This is bad news for shareholders since there is no way of checking inefficient investment. As we have already seen, short-term debt can serve to force managers to pay out 'free cash flow' rather than to dissipate it in unprofitable investments. Here, however, we merely illustrate the main argument of recent theory and assume that $R_1 < I$. Revenues in period 1 are not sufficient to cover the new investment, even when there are no short-term debt obligations to cover. Managers therefore have to borrow $I - R_1$. They will succeed if $R_2 + R_2{}^I > I - R_1 + P_2$; that is, if revenues in period 2 are sufficient to cover the repayment of period-1 borrowing plus the repayment of long-term debt.

Clearly, if we knew at the beginning of period 1 that $R_2{}^I > I$ we would not want to inhibit the management in any way and would put $P_2 = 0$. Conversely, if we knew that $R_2{}^I < I$, we would want to prevent the managers investing at the end of period 1 and could achieve this by setting a sufficiently large value of long-term debt obligations P_2. As with subsection 10.3.2, however, the problem is that we do not know, *ex ante*, which situation will prevail. A high value of P_2 (say $P_2{}^*$) risks preventing managers undertaking potentially profitable investments ($R_2 + R_2{}^I < I - R_1 + P_2{}^*$ even though $R_2{}^I > I$).[27] A low value of P_2 (say $P_2{}^{**}$) risks allowing managers to squander funds in unprofitable additional investments ($R_2 + R_2{}^I > I - R_1 + P_2{}^{**}$ even though $R_2{}^I < I$). Suppose, however, that, under scenario A, $R_2{}^I < I$, while under scenario B, $R_2{}^I > I$. Can we find a level of P_2 which will permit investment under B but deny it under A?

Using superscripts for scenarios A and B as before, the correct managerial responses require that $R_2{}^A + R_2{}^{IA} < I - R_1{}^A + P_2$ and $R_2{}^B + R_2{}^{IB} > I - R_1{}^B + P_2$. Revenues at the end of period 2 must not be sufficient to cover repayment of additional borrowing plus senior long-term debt obligations if scenario A occurs, but they must do so if scenario B occurs. Some straightforward rearrangement establishes that if $R_1{}^A + R_2{}^A + R_2{}^{IA} - I < R_1{}^B + R_2{}^B + R_2{}^{IB} - I$, it is possible to find a value of P_2, which will achieve our objective. We can set the level of long-term debt above the present value of net revenue flows in scenario A but below the level of net revenue flows in scenario B. If the inequality is reversed and the present value of net revenue is lower in B than in A we have to choose either to permit managers to invest in both scenarios or to stop them in both. Clearly, a sufficiently high probability of scenario B will lead to no long-term debt ($P_2 = 0$). Conversely, a sufficiently high probability of scenario A would recommend a level of P_2 large enough to prevent any new investment by managers.

10.4   Bounded Rationality and Financial Structure

Jensen and Meckling's agency cost approach to financial structure takes account of information problems but does so in a traditional neoclassical way. Given prohibitive costs of monitoring and control; given also attitudes to risk; and given the probabilities of certain states of the world occurring and so forth; an optimal response is calculated. Hart and Moore's incomplete contracting approach pays greater attention to the fact that capital structure to some extent reflects an intrinsic lack of contractibility over some matters. Their theory of debt has the advantage of explaining why firms issue short- and long-term debt and why default leads to 'bankruptcy' and a change of control rights from equity holders to bond holders. In neither of these theories do transactions costs figure prominently. Managers simply cannot contract to put in a specified level of effort in Jensen and Meckling's world. Similarly, they cannot contract to invest only in profitable projects in Hart and Moore's model. Capital structure is not so much about reducing transactions costs as adjusting to non-contractibility (effectively infinite transactions costs in certain areas). Agency models of capital structure draw on the theory of Chapters 4 and 5 rather than on the theory of Chapters 2 and 3.

The transactions cost approach of Williamson and others, in contrast, sees the firm as a means of responding to complex emerging events. It is not simply verifiability that prevents enforceable contracts but complexity and bounded rationality. Corporate governance and capital structure, according to this view of things, is about establishing rules which permit the intervention of different parties over time as the commercial environment unfolds. This kind of approach suggests, for example, that information flows are as important to bond holders as shareholders; that a lender who is well informed about a company will be more prepared to advance a loan than a lender who is more at 'arm's length'; and that lenders may feel more secure if they are also 'inside' shareholders and have the right to intercede in the management of an organisation at an earlier stage than would otherwise be possible. In section 11, some of these ideas are explored in the

context of the differing systems of corporate governance which prevail in
the United States, Europe and Japan.

11.   CORPORATE GOVERNANCE – BANK VERSUS MARKET SYSTEMS

11.1   The United Kingdom and the United States

In his study of financial systems, Berglof (1990) argues that there are essentially two models of corporate governance – market oriented and bank oriented. Using this taxonomy, both the system in the UK and in the USA fall
into the category of market oriented. A market-oriented system is characterised by 'outside' shareholders who play little part in monitoring management behaviour, prefer to spread their risks widely, and trade actively in
shares (selling them when dissatisfied with managerial performance).
Falling stock prices and the market for corporate control provide an important source of management incentives. To use Albert Hirshman's (1970)
terminology, 'exit' (that is, the severing of a relationship and the search for
new ones) is the preferred mechanism for exerting pressure rather than
'voice' (that is, investing time and effort in reforming the existing relationship).

The impersonal and distant relationship between the shareholder and
the firm in the market-oriented system is reinforced by several other factors.
Shareholders possess both control rights and residual rights. These are
rarely separated, so that widely spread residual rights result in equally
spread voting and control rights. The principle of equality of shareholder
status is also defended by regulatory bodies who try to ensure equal access
to information, prevent dealing by 'insiders' who may have privileged information, and insist on the disclosure of the build-up of large stakes in a
company. Further, trade in shares on the UK and US stock markets is dominated by institutions. These are financial intermediaries, such as pension
funds and insurance companies, owing a fiduciary duty to the people who
have entrusted them with their money. This does not entirely prevent them
from holding a stable portfolio of shares, but the prompt disposal of a
failing stock may well be considered a cheaper and safer way of protecting
the saver than embarking on a costly and possibly vain rescue attempt.

A central characteristic of market-oriented systems is therefore the low
incidence of direct monitoring by 'inside' shareholders. Section 5 of
Chapter 8 discussed the circumstances in which incentives to undertake
monitoring would exist in a market system even where shareholdings were
fairly dispersed. Accepting, however, that monitoring costs will limit the

extent of such activity, Boards of Directors will find themselves relatively free of direct shareholder intervention. Shareholders are able to appoint outside 'non-executive' directors to the Board of a company, and auditors owe a duty to the body of shareholders to prepare suitably informative accounts.[28] If, however, the appointment of non-executive directors and auditors is under the effective control of executive directors, and if the flow of information reaching auditors and outside directors is controlled by the management group, the effectiveness of these control mechanisms is open to question.[29]

Dimsdale (1991) and Sykes (1991) have discussed these problems in the context of the UK. The latter argues strongly for a greater commitment by institutional investors to monitoring and control. He suggests the use of managerial incentive contracts by which managers might hope to achieve ten to twelve times their annual salaries by way of stock options. These, however, would be tied to five to seven year performance targets. The stability of control required for the system to operate would be achieved by financial institutions combining to take significant (twenty per cent or more) stakes in a company. Sykes wishes to encourage three to five institutions to build up expertise and knowledge about the firm in which they are to take a long-term interest. He suggests that investment institutions should each establish a secretariat which would support non-executive directors nominated by the institution. His objective is clearly to move away from the market-oriented system towards an 'investment-institution'-oriented (though non-bank) one. This would re-establish some of the conditions of classical capitalism by providing significant shareholders with an incentive to become knowledgeable 'insiders'. He argues that agreements between financial intermediaries to build up expertise in specific areas, but outside these areas to spread risk widely, could limit the adverse consequences for risk pooling. Each financial institution would implicitly be conferring monitoring and control benefits on other institutions in its specialised field. The full benefits, therefore, would require an agreement by all institutions to participate and not simply free ride on the services of others. At present, there does not seem to be a working example of an 'investment-institution'-oriented system of corporate governance.

11.2   Japan and Germany

In earlier chapters, some of the characteristics of Japanese transacting have already been discussed. The flexible, long-term, non-specific and obligational aspects of transactional relations in Japan mentioned in the context of buyer–supplier relations (Chapter 7) and labour contracts (Chapter 6) can also be seen in the area of corporate governance. Shareholders in Japan are 'insiders'. Although institutional shareholdings make up a similar proportion of the total in Japan as in the UK (about seventy-five per cent in the late 1980s), the institutions concerned are not independent pension funds or insurance companies. Instead, shares are held by institutions the commercial operations of which may be quite closely intertwined. Shareholders may include banks who also provide loan finance, firms that are customers or suppliers, and other companies in 'Keiretsu' groups linked by cross-shareholdings.

As a result of these reciprocal long-term arrangements, trade in shares is far less active. Implicit agreements to hold shares as friendly and passive 'insiders' are widespread and the most active trading of shares therefore takes place in the household sector. This is quite different from the market-based system where institutional shareholdings are the most frequently traded. Because markets in shares are thinner and holdings are stable, continuity of control can be relied upon in Japan and the takeover is virtually unknown.

In Germany, there are no equivalent barriers to the transfer of shares that exist in Japan. In spite of this, continuity of control is greater than in a market-oriented system and changes in control are effected without frequent recourse to the takeover. A number of features of the German system produce these results. Public companies in Germany can issue non-voting stock up to an amount equal to all voting shares. Thus, it is possible, up to a point, to raise capital by means of an issue of non-voting shares without affecting the control of a company. Further, the banks in Germany are able to exercise by proxy the voting rights attached to shares deposited with them. This gives the banks an influence far in excess of that which would be expected solely on the basis of their own shareholdings.

As briefly mentioned in Chapter 8, section 5, monitoring incentives in the German and the Japanese systems seem to derive from a splitting of control rights from residual rights. Individual shareholders use other institutions not simply (as in the market-oriented system) to make trading decisions but to exercise a monitoring and control function on their behalf. The agency costs associated with this arrangement might be thought to be prohibitive, but the fact that the banks themselves hold a substantial minority stake in a firm[30], are providers of loan finance, and will often have seats on the Board means that they have the incentive and the influence to act as monitors of performance. In the Japanese context, Aoki (1989) sees the 'main bank' as implicitly providing monitoring and control services. He even argues that certain financial characteristics of the Japanese system, such as the tendency for firms to borrow more from the main bank than would be expected on the basis of normal commercial requirements, can be rationalised as a payment for monitoring services. 'The deviation from share price maximisation by the company at the sacrifice of individual stockholders and the phenomenon of overborrowing in the interests of the bank may in part be thought of as the "agency fee" paid by the individual stockholders to the bank for that service' (p. 148).[31]

It would be a mistake to oversimplify the nature of bank-oriented systems by forming the impression that they recreate the conditions of classical capitalism. Control rights may be more concentrated, and greater direct monitoring effort may occur through the 'Hausbank' in Germany or the 'Main bank' in Japan, but the conclusion that shareholder interests thereby dominate business decisions would be quite erroneous. In Japan, managers on Boards are mainly promoted internally through the ranking hierarchy described in Chapter 6. This mechanism is not designed to reward the singleminded pursuit of shareholder value. Indeed, Aoki (1984) sees managers in the Japanese system as mediators between the 'quasi-permanent employees' and the body of stockholders. The firm is a coalition of cooperating resources and a central managerial function is to make sure that the rents generated by the team are not dissipated in rent seeking. Instead, they are distributed according to a cooperative bargain mediated by the managers. This bargain is likely to involve higher growth rates and a greater concern for market-share objectives (in the interests of the promotion prospects of employees) than would be chosen by the stockholders alone.

The German system likewise gives voice to more than shareholder interests.[32] In particular, the two-tier Board structure is deliberately designed to provide a vehicle for worker representation. Membership of the Supervisory Board is divided equally between the representatives of shareholders and of employees. These Supervisory Boards appoint the Management Boards but they do not exercise very close control over day-to-day operations. They are there to oversee matters of broad policy and will not interfere unless business conditions deteriorate. However, clear institutional recognition of the claims of other 'stakeholders' in the firm is important. Vulnerable holders of firm-specific assets may feel more secure in a bank-oriented system with representation on supervisory boards than in a stock-market system where takeover by new owners is more likely.

11.3 Differences in Capital Structures

The protean nature of economic systems makes it advisable not to assume that observed differences in financial variables between countries are immutable. Nevertheless, bank systems and market systems do seem to be characterised by differing financial structures. Berglof (1990), for example, concludes that bank systems 'generally have higher debt/equity ratios, higher shares of bank credits in their liabilities, more concentrated holdings of both debt and equity, and a lower turnover of these holdings' (p. 257).

Studies of balance sheets indicate that companies in the UK and the USA have higher proportions of equity than do companies in Germany or Japan.[33] OECD data for 1975 to 1989 show the debt–equity ratio for non-financial enterprises in Japan falling steadily from 5.6 to 4.2. Over the same period, the German figures rose from 2.56 to 4.25. In contrast, the debt–equity ratio in the USA was much lower, although it increased during the 1980s. It rose from 0.52 to 0.82 (in 1989). The UK ratio was fairly stable at or just below 1.1 over the same period.

Care is required when interpreting this type of information, however. It certainly seems consistent with the contrast between 'bank-oriented' and 'market-oriented' systems. Greater stability, longer-term relations, better information flows and closer direct monitoring by banks would be conducive to a higher ratio of debt to equity. On the other hand, the nature of some of the 'debt' instruments is important. Much of the Japanese debt is made up of short-term trade credits between contracting firms. The close supply chain associations between Japanese companies and the lower degree of complete vertical integration was discussed in Chapter 7. These closer links and the high level of trust that is apparently engendered are reflected in the short-term credits that are advanced and which appear on both sides of Japanese balance sheets. The German case is complicated by the problem of pension provisions. Unlike 'arms-length' systems, where pension funds are governed by trustees who are independent of firms, in Germany pension contributions are retained by each company as a liability on their balance sheets. Financial ratios are very sensitive to the treatment of these provisions. Treating them as a form of debt produces a much higher ratio of debt to equity than treating the claims of pensioners as a form of equity stake.

If bank-oriented systems result in higher debt–equity ratios, market-oriented systems have certainly produced a greater incidence of takeover activity. The experience of the USA and the UK compared with Japan has already been mentioned in section 9 above. Franks and Mayer (1990) contrast Germany with the UK and argue that the influence of the banks reduces the level of contested takeover activity.

In sections 5 and 6, the possibility that dividends would be important in market-oriented systems either as signals or as commitments to minimum levels of performance was discussed. The evidence does suggest that dividend payout is higher in both the USA and the UK compared with Germany and Japan. In the late 1980s, the ratio of dividends to gross income was around forty per cent in the UK, compared with 28 per cent in the USA and only 10 per cent in Japan. Mayer and Alexander (1990) estimate that dividend ratios in the UK were more than double those in Germany during the 1980s.

12. CONCLUSION

Our discussion of the role of takeovers in corporate governance has revealed how complex is the problem of placing suitable limits on entrepreneurial intervention. The restless energy which leads to the establishment of new transactional relationships also destroys old ones. If every agreement in the market were made for the fleeting moment and no longer, changing patterns of cooperation would offend no person's reasonable expectations, but where agreements are made for the longer term, where their provisions are implicit, where transactors face dependency and hence where cooperation relies heavily on the existence of trust and obligation, the potentially harmful effects of disruption to established patterns of trade cannot be ignored.

Mary Crawford, in the passage from *Mansfield Park* quoted at the beginning of this chapter, represents an attractive, lively, individualistic, but ultimately meretricious, shallow and rootless commercial ethos which threatens the order and stability of an early nineteenth-century household. It is perhaps not very surprising that the power of individualistic forces to dissolve social ties and cast people adrift is a recurring theme in English literature. Yet the power of individual choice to cement ties and resist change is also central. 'We can set a watch over our affections and our constancy as we can over other treasures', writes George Eliot.[34] If this is so for our social and sexual relations, it is hardly likely to be overlooked where durable economic relationships are of value. The institutional means available to protect reputation and guard long-term assets has formed part of the subject matter of this chapter. Economic institutions embody responses to problems that are to some degree *constitutional* in nature.[35] They reflect our attempts to bind ourselves not to take actions which are destructive of our own long-term interests or of social capital more generally, while permitting actions which are individually and socially advantageous. An environment too protective of established relationships runs the risk of setting an expensive watch over worthless, if familiar, trinkets. An environment which is unprotective of established relationships may leave true treasures unwatched and vulnerable to the depredations of raiders or of the purveyors of enticing novelties.

We have seen in this chapter how systems of corporate governance differ between countries and imply differing degrees of exposure to these dangers. The discussion has, however, centred entirely on the public joint-stock limited-liability company. Many other 'constitutional' settings exist. Labour-managed or cooperative firms protect firm-specific capital from takeover raiders while facing other contractual and incentive problems. Non-profit and charitable enterprises are also important and may be analysed using principal–agent theory, the incomplete contracts framework and the transactions cost approach more generally. It is to an analysis of these institutional forms that Chapter 10 is devoted.

NOTES

1. Jane Austen, *Mansfield Park*, Penguin English Library (1966), p. 251. The game Mary Crawford was playing was called 'Speculation'.
2. As with the paradox of voting (Chapter 7, note 15) and the paradox of innovation, we should note here that a small shareholder could reason that, since a raid must fail through lack of support for the raider's offer from others, the best policy will be to accept with alacrity if the price includes any potential gains. Clearly, much will depend on the precise mechanism by which the offer is made. Grossman and Hart set up their model so that the only takeovers that occur are certain to succeed. This implies that none will take place. Existing shareholders will not tender their shares to a raider who is certain to succeed at any price less than the post-raid price. Any successful raid will therefore be profitless to the raider.
3. Not to be confused with 'hold-up'.
4. Shleifer and Vishny (1988), p. 12.
5. Shleifer and Summers (1988) are particularly associated with this point of view. 'Breach of trust through corporate takeover enables shareholders to capture the *ex post* rents from contracts with stakeholders, such as suppliers and employees' (p. 53).
6. The story set out in the next three paragraphs is based on the model presented by Stein (1988).
7. In subsection 10.3, the existence of debt obligations is rationalised in a similar way. There it will be assumed that reputational mechanisms are ineffective so that dividend payments cannot be used to control 'managerial' behaviour.
8. There is difficulty hidden in this definition. Expectations of the 'payments' to which a shareholder is 'entitled' will depend not only on the earnings of the firm in the future but on the ability of the shareholder to lay claim to them. The valuation of a share will therefore be influenced by factors such as the perceived likelihood that a takeover might be mounted to force distributions from a recalcitrant management (see section 9.2). This, in turn, might be related to such factors as the existence or otherwise of substantial minority shareholders (section 3). If share prices reflect the agency problems of corporate control, does this imply they are or are not *fundamental-valuation efficient*? Morgan and Morgan (1990) for example, interpret fundamental-valuation efficiency as requiring that stock prices reflect rationally expected future *earnings* of companies (p. 73), but *earnings* of companies are not the same as *payments* to shareholders, except in a world without problems of corporate control. However, the fact that stock prices may depart from 'fundamentals' because of agency problems, does not in itself establish that the system is 'inefficient' relative to available alternatives which confront the same problems of information and control.
9. It is, of course, impossible to prove directly that share prices incorporate all publicly available information. For a summary review of the literature on market efficiency, see Marsh (1991).
10. Not everyone is convinced by this type of evidence. Scherer (1988) criticises 'event studies' which simply look at immediate stock-price reactions to a particular announcement or 'event'. When the timeframe is extended, results can alter. The conglomerate

merger movement of the 1960s and 1970s, he argues, led to widespread failure in spite of positive market reaction at the time. However, it is always possible to be wise *after* the event. Supporters of the efficient markets hypothesis do not claim that markets are always right, merely that it is not possible, using the information available at the time, to show that they are wrong. Scherer also gives credence to the view that general market conditions are subject to fad-like movements which have little to do with underlying real conditions. Exaggerated movements over time can result in 'bargains' being available at particular points. The debate continues.

11. See Jarrell and Poulsen (1987).
12. Mikkelson and Ruback (1985) find a slight rise in stock prices over the entire period from the original purchase by the raider to the announcement of the payment of greenmail.
13. We are assuming here that collusion between incumbent managers and greenmailer to mislead the market is ruled out. It should also be recognised that the information provided by the greenmailer is not absolutely pure. Has the greenmailer discovered an idle and incompetent management or a firm whose stock is simply undervalued?
14. This signalling mechanism has affinities with Tullock's (1980a, p. 24) discussion of the 'potlatch' as a form of rent seeking. The 'Potlatches' of the Pacific North West of the USA were said to gain power and prestige by destroying valuable objects.
15. For more details see Bannock (1990).
16. It was T. Boone Pickens of Mesa Petroleum who is credited with first spotting the necessity of restructuring in the oil industry in the USA. He initiated a wave of takeovers, in the process of which large amounts of cash were disgorged to shareholders in payment for their shares. Supporters of this agency costs approach to the takeover wave argue that the distributed capital was available for more socially productive investments in other industries.
17. The use of 'strip financing' can be seen as a response to this problem. A firm may issue various types of security (for example, ordinary debt, subordinated debt, debt which is convertible into common equity in certain conditions, preferred equity and so forth). These may be sold not as independent instruments but in 'strips' which cannot be broken down into their component parts. Thus, an investor might hold one per cent of each type of financial instrument in a strip. The strip as a whole would be tradable. If a firm defaults on its ordinary debt, a strip holder might exercise his or her right to convert other debt into equity and intervene in the organisation.
18. For example Kaplan (1989) and Lehn and Poulson (1989).
19. MBOs accounted for around twenty per cent by value of the market in corporate control in the UK in the late 1980s. See Thompson, Wright and Robbie (1992, p. 415) table 1.
20. A summary of this literature can be found in Jarrell, Brickley and Netter (1988).
21. Jensen (1988, pp. 22–3) summarises previous work on takeovers. He argues that social gains are generated by the average takeover, amounting to about eight per cent of the total value of both companies involved.
22. Thomas E. Copeland and J.F. Weston (1988), *Financial Theory and Corporate Policy* (3rd edn), Addison-Wesley, Chapters 13 and 14.
23. 'The market value of any firm is independent of its capital structure and is given by capitalizing its expected return at the rate appropriate to its risk class' (Modigliani and Miller, 1958, p. 268).
24. See Jensen and Meckling (1976), pp. 349–51.
25. Hart presents this approach to capital structure in an accessible form in Hart (1995a), chapter 6.
26. See Jensen's 'free cash-flow theory' already encountered in subsection 9.2. In that subsection, it was the takeover that acted as a constraint on the wasteful internal use of cash. Here, it is short-term debt obligations.
27. This is sometimes called the 'debt overhang problem'.
28. This duty of care does not extend as far as making auditors liable for any losses that shareholders or non-shareholders might suffer from trading on misleading information supplied by the auditor. *See Caparo Industries plc* v. *Dickman and others* [1990] 1 All ER 568.

29. Dimsdale (1991) provides a survey of the problems of corporate governance associated with a market-oriented system. The British Unitary Board system is not entirely the same as that in the United States. The number of non-executive directors on Boards in the UK varies widely, while the USA is unlike the UK in that the majority of directors in the USA have no executive responsibilities.

     A report on *The Financial Aspects of Corporate Governance* published in December 1992 in the UK (the Cadbury Committee) recommends a voluntary Code of Best Practice concerning the appointment of non-executive directors, the establishment of remuneration committees to set executive contractual terms, and audit committees to ensure that auditors fulfil their obligations to shareholders. A statement of compliance with the Code will be a condition of continuing listing on the London Stock Exchange.

30. In Japan, equity stakes held by banks are limited to five per cent in any one company. German banks were estimated to hold about twelve per cent of equity in 1988.

31. In the case of Japan, there is also an important debate concerning industrial policy. Some have argued that the structure of industry described here favours the influence of state organisations such as MITI – the Ministry of Trade and Industry. In the 1980s, some writers credited the supposed benign influence of MITI, along with the binding force of nationalism, with supporting the 'long-termism' and competitiveness of Japanese industry. Williams (1994) takes this view. Others (as in the text) argue that the advantages experienced by Japan during the 1970s and 1980s were contractual and not inherently 'statist' in nature, and that the influence of MITI was not so important.

32. As in the case of Japan, the German or 'Rhineland' model has been supported on more general grounds. See Albert (1993).

33. More details can be found in Prevezer and Ricketts (1991).

34. In *Middlemarch*, ([1871] 1985) Penguin Classics, p. 625.

35. Gifford (1991) sets out a constitutional view of the firm.

10.   Profit-sharing, cooperative and mutual enterprise

'Thus there is de facto *some sort of profit-and-loss sharing between almost every business and its employees; and perhaps this is in its very highest form when, without being embodied in a definite contract, the solidarity of interests between those who work together in the same business is recognised with cordial generosity as the result of true brotherly feeling. But such cases are not very common; and as a rule the relations between employers and employed are raised to a higher plane both economically and morally by the adoption of the system of profit sharing . . .'*
(Alfred Marshall)[1]

1.   RESIDUAL CLAIMS AND ENTERPRISE GOVERNANCE

The joint-stock corporation is an immensely important institutional form, but it is not ubiquitous, and, as Chapters 8 and 9 have shown, it faces significant contractual problems. Given these problems, we might not expect the joint-stock enterprise to be better adapted than any alternative possible assignment of property rights to all conceivable situations. In this chapter, a variety of enterprises is discussed, enterprises which have the common characteristic that residual claims are held by people other than outside shareholders. Sections 1 through to 7 are concerned with enterprises in which residual claims are held by the workforce or, in section 6, shared between the workforce and providers of capital. Sections 8 through to 10 discuss enterprises in which consumers are residual claimants, while section 11 briefly reviews recent debates about 'stakeholding'. We delay until chapter 11 an analysis of the operation of non-profit enterprises – institutions without residual claims. Public enterprise is not considered until Part 3.

Because the number of possible bundles of property rights assignments is so great, and one type of enterprise shades into another, the nomenclature can become confusing. It will therefore be useful at the start to clarify the terminology that will be used and to define the distinguishing characteristics of the various enterprises that will be discussed.

1. *Profit-sharing enterprises*   Any enterprise that distributes to its workforce, or to some group other than the providers of capital, a share of the residual is engaging in profit sharing. Thus, a joint-stock corporation can be a profit-sharing enterprise. All the types of enterprise discussed in this chapter are profit sharing, according to this definition, including the retail cooperative.

2. *The management-owned firm*   Where all residual claims are held by several monitors of a team we term the enterprise a management-owned firm. Some of the features of this variety of enterprise were discussed in Chapter 4, although there the context was the traditional unlimited partnership. From a purely legal point of view, a company in which the management team holds all the equity capital is likely to be a private limited company. Management buy-outs, for example, frequently result in this form of organisation. The main points here are that the equity is held by a subset of people who work in the firm (the managers), the residual rights are not necessarily distributed equally among the holders, and the rights can be traded (though only with the agreement of other shareholders).

3. *The professional partnership*   Residual claims in this case are again held by a subset of those who work in the firm. Lawyers, management consultants, accountants and doctors are often organised in professional partnerships. In this case, the partners are not primarily engaged in a managerial role (though some management may inevitably be necessary) but as practitioners. Junior associates, secretaries and other assistants receive a wage or salary and are not residual claimants. One partner will not have hierarchical authority over another. The earnings of the partnership are distributed equally between the partners, with some allowance for age and experience. All partners do essentially the same job. Residual rights are not privately or collectively exchangeable.

4. *Worker ownership*   Where all workers share the residual, and either elect managers from their number or appoint managers on separate contracts from outside, we will refer to worker ownership. Under worker ownership, residual rights are collectively exchangeable. The workers collectively could decide, for example, to sell their firm to a single proprietor if the price were sufficiently attractive. The residual may be distributed on a basis of equality, but where individual output is easy to measure, remuneration may instead be determined by reference to such output. Taxi firms, for example, are often worker owned but the revenue is easily attributable to individual drivers. The drivers

benefit from the provision of central services such as marketing, reputation, and radio communications for which they pay a proportion of their takings. In contrast, the plywood industry in the United States, in which worker ownership has a strong tradition, operates on the basis of equal distribution of the earnings of the team.[2] Like taxi drivers, the workers do jobs that are similar to one another, but their individual productivity is not so easily gauged. Managerial skills for the firm are purchased from salaried 'outsiders'.

5.   *The worker cooperative*   The main difference between a worker-owned firm and a worker cooperative is that, in the latter, residual claims are non-tradable. A pure form of worker cooperative would distribute the net revenue of the team (that is, revenue after paying for intermediate inputs, interest on borrowed capital and allowing for maintenance and depreciation) equally between the members. There would, in other words, be no 'wage' element in the worker's compensation package. Rights to this stream of payments would be non-exchangeable and would depend upon continued membership of the team. Managers would be team members on the same terms as other workers.

In practice, of course, institutions called 'worker cooperatives' may have characteristics which depart from those of the pure case. Equal distribution of the net revenue, for example, will be unworkable where individuals with differing skills have opportunities outside the firm. Payment of a market-related 'wage' element might then be necessary, with the team's 'residual' defined in the same way as that in a private company. Where the legal 'ownership' of the enterprise is vested in the state (as was the case in the pre-civil war Yugoslavian system), George (1982) suggests the use of the term 'labour-managed firm'. The labour-managed firm was studied extensively in the 1970s.[3] Our interest, however, will primarily be in cooperative enterprise where the state plays no role in protecting or encouraging it.

6.   *Labour–capital partnerships*   In a labour–capital partnership, the residual is shared among workers and outside providers of equity capital. The situation differs from simple profit sharing (subsection 1) in that the division of the residual between labour and capital is not constant but will vary as employment rises or falls. When new capital is raised, new capital shares will be issued. Similarly, when labour is recruited, new labour shares will be issued. The 'dividend' on both types of share is the same. Capital shares are freely tradable on stock markets; labour shares are non-tradable. Thus, risk-bearing capital does not hire labour as in the traditional capitalist firm, nor does risk-bearing labour hire capital as in the worker-owned or cooperative firm. Labour and capital share the risk between them.

> This type of enterprise is, at the moment, more of theoretical than practical interest. James Meade (1985, 1989) is particularly associated with analysing the properties of labour–capital partnerships. Section 6 will be devoted to a brief summary of Meade's analysis because it helps clarify the theoretical issues surrounding the problems faced by other forms of profit sharing.

7. *Retail and wholesale cooperatives*   Although we are principally concerned in the main part of this chapter with profit sharing among workers, the possibility that buyers of goods may set up organisations and share residual profits in proportion to their purchases is discussed in section 8. Suppliers' cooperatives are covered in section 9.
8. *The mutual enterprise*   An important form of enterprise in many areas but especially in financial intermediation is the mutual. Ownership is shared between the users of the financial services who club together for the purposes of mutual provision and protection. Insurance companies and Savings and Loan Associations (Building Societies) have often been established as mutuals in the past and this form of enterprise is considered in section 10.

Our immediate objective is to look more closely at profit sharing from a transactional point of view. Even if full worker ownership is rare there are features of most firms which imply an element of cooperation, mechanisms for encouraging trust, for rewarding investment in firm-specific skills and so forth. The passage from Marshall's *Principles of Economics* which opens this chapter indicates that this has been recognised for many years, but how plausible is Marshall's Victorian view of the economic value of explicit profit sharing?

2.   PRINCIPAL–AGENT THEORY AND PROFIT SHARING

2.1   Type of Firm Classified by Distribution of Residual Claims

Some of the issues can be disentangled by considering once more the diagrammatic exposition of principal and agent introduced in Chapter 5. Consider Figure 10.1. Two parties are negotiating a contract. One is the 'outside' investor (I). The other is the 'inside' worker (W). The two outcomes represent the revenue of the firm after payment of intermediate inputs and raw materials and after providing for maintenance and depreciation on capital. In other words, the sides of the Edgeworth Box give the available distributable surplus to labour and capital depending upon which of two states of the world happens. As in other chapters, the probability of the occurrence of these states is influenced by the worker's effort. The problem is to share the surplus between the parties.

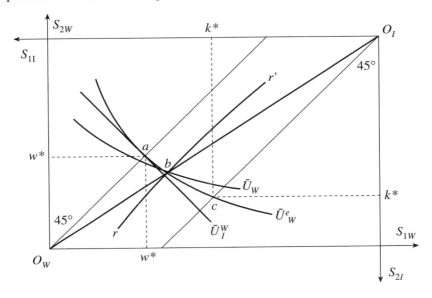

Notes:
1. a = Investor-owned firm.
2. b = Labour–capital partnership.
3. c = Worker-owned firm.

Figure 10.1   Firm type and the distributable surplus

A contract at point a in Figure 10.1 represents the traditional capitalist *investor-owned firm* (IOF). The figure is drawn on the assumption that the worker is risk averse while the investor is risk neutral. At point a, therefore, risk is shared efficiently. The worker receives a fixed wage w^* and the investor receives whatever remains. Thus, the investor can be seen as holding one hundred per cent of the equity of the firm. Because investors are able to spread their risks widely over many enterprises while workers are normally more restricted in the number of enterprises to which they can supply their labour, the above assumptions about risk preferences would seem plausible. As Meade (1972) argues 'this presumably is a main reason why we (traditionally) find risk-bearing capital hiring labour rather than risk-bearing labour hiring capital' (p. 426).

As we saw in Chapter 5, however, this solution is viable only if the worker can be monitored at low cost. Without information about the worker's level of effort, and in the absence of monitoring, the worker will shirk. Further, our justification for assuming investors are risk neutral implies that they are only minimally committed to any one enterprise and that they will not have an incentive to monitor effectively. Giving investors an incentive to monitor by concentrating their investments is likely to result in a degree of risk aversion on their part. Both risk aversion on the part of the investor and the provision of effort incentives unrelated to investor monitoring would require the worker to move away from the certainty line in the efficient contract. The firm, in other words, begins to take on profit-sharing characteristics.

Let us assume that monitoring is extremely costly and ineffective. Effort incentives for the worker require a contract along *rr'* in Figure 10.1. Let the diagonal through each origin in the diagram cut *rr'* at *b*. In this set of circumstances, the optimal contract yields a *labour–capital partnership*. The worker does not receive a wage but a share in the distributable surplus. The worker's share is $O_w b / O_w O_I$.

If effort costs are very great or worker risk aversion less pronounced, the locus *rr'* will move even further to the right. In the extreme case, we might envisage a contract at point *c* on the investors certainty line. This is the *worker-owned firm*. The outside investor receives a fixed payment for the use of his or her capital. Interest payments are given by distance $O_I k^*$. The worker receives no wage but the entire distributable surplus after interest payments. One hundred per cent of the equity is held by the worker. It will be recalled, however, that one of the results obtained in Chapter 5, section 4, was that an efficient contract could not occur along the principal's certainty line if the agent were risk averse. In the present context this implies that, if the worker is risk averse, a fully worker-owned firm cannot be an efficient response to this contractual problem.

Figures 10.2 and 10.3 illustrate other sharing arrangements short of complete worker ownership. Figure 10.2 shows an investor-owned firm but with profit sharing. The contract is at point *d*. It implies a fixed wage of *w'* and a share of the distributable surplus (now after the payment of wages) of gd/gO_I. There is no debt finance. By contrast, in Figure 10.3 the contract point is at *e*. It shows a mainly worker-owned firm with some outside debt and equity. The wage is zero. The worker has a share in the distributable surplus (now after interest payments) of $O_w e / O_w h$. The outside investor receives the remaining share of the surplus and an interest payment of $O_I k'$.

Already this simple analysis gives some clues about the conditions under which profit sharing will occur. In particular, it is consistent with the 'stylised facts' of market economies in suggesting that profit sharing is a rational response to particular circumstances but that full worker ownership is much less likely.[4]

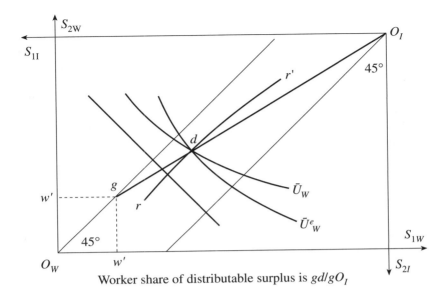

Figure 10.2   Investor ownership with profit-related pay

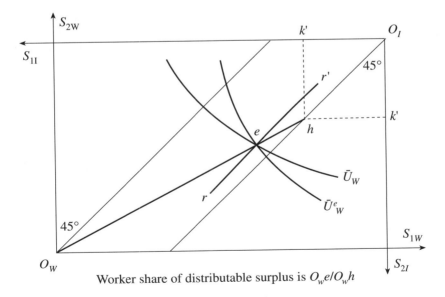

Figure 10.3   Worker ownership with debt and outside equity

1. If a large commitment to monitoring on the part of the investor yields only very noisy information about the worker's level of effort, monitoring gambles of the type discussed in Chapter 5, section 7, will not be acceptable and other types of worker incentive, including profit sharing, will be required.
2. If investors are risk averse because capital markets are undeveloped and do not permit risk spreading, profit sharing will be encouraged.
3. The less risk averse are workers, the more attractive will be profit sharing arrangements.
4. The greater the efficiency of effort (that is, the lower the effort cost of achieving the higher probability of the good state) the closer will be rr' to the worker's certainty line and the more likely it will be that a mutually acceptable profit-sharing contract exists.

The question of the efficiency of worker effort raises another fundamental problem with profit sharing. We have so far concentrated on the role of sharing the surplus between worker and outside capitalist, but where there are many workers employed in an enterprise the surplus will be shared between them, and the original Alchian and Demsetz analysis of the free-rider problem reasserts itself. If a large number of investors leads to a low incentive to monitor, large numbers of profit-sharing workers lead to a small incentive to work. As was pointed out in Chapter 5, in team environments the relationship between any individual worker's effort and the probability of good profit outcomes may be slight, even if *collectively* the relationship is strong. Moving away from the worker's certainty line will then not be an effective means, in itself, of inducing effort.

2.2   Monitoring Effort and the Profit-sharing Firm

This brings us to the role of monitoring in a profit-sharing or worker-ownership environment. Profit sharing, according to this line of reasoning, is not primarily about inducing effort *directly* from workers because it is in their individual interests. Profit sharing is about reducing the costs and increasing the effectiveness of monitoring both worker and management effort.[5] There are several ways in which this may be brought about.

1. Workers may monitor one another. This possibility will be explored in more detail in section 7.
2. Workers may feel a loyalty to their fellow profit sharers or cooperators that is absent in their dealings with outside investors. A satisfying 'contractual atmosphere', as Williamson terms it[6], may be important and may reduce the need for monitoring. The principal advantage of

the cooperative enterprise has long been considered the more positive motivation of the workforce and the absence of 'alienation' that is said to afflict workers in joint-stock enterprises.

3. Monitoring of managers by workers might be more effective than the monitoring of managers by outside investors. Workers might be more informed about company operations, face lower costs of taking part in collective decision-making processes, and have a greater individual stake in the enterprise than dispersed outside shareholders. These factors would tend to reduce the agency costs of the relationship between residual claimants and managers that we investigated at great length in the context of the joint-stock enterprise in Chapter 8. A worker-owned firm would represent the arrangement described by McManus (1975) and referred to in the organisational literature as 'the fable of the barge'. On protesting at the brutality of an overseer as he whipped a team of men pulling barges on the Yangtze River, an observer was informed 'those men own the right to draw boats over this stretch of water and they have hired the overseer and given him his duties'.[7]

As the fable suggests, however, the managers need a penalty to impose or a prize to offer if their monitoring is to be effective. Hierarchical incentive devices discussed in Chapter 6 do not sit easily with the egalitarian residual-sharing basis of cooperation, although the incorporation of such mechanisms into worker ownership or labour–capital partnerships is theoretically feasible, as will be seen in section 6. Managers might also be given the right to impose fines or to terminate a person's membership of a team. Given that managers are hired by the team and could themselves be fired for abusing their position, workers might be prepared to tolerate a significant degree of managerial discretion in the determination of rewards and penalties.

If the managers are salaried employees and do not share in the residual, an active managerial labour market and the protection of reputation would seem to be an important component of the incentive structure. Managers taken from outside the team might appear more 'neutral' and able to resist the subtle personal pressures and accusations of favouritism that otherwise might reduce the productive efficiency of their decisions. Where no tradable outside residual claims exist, however, the manager's ability to inform the managerial labour market of his or her ability is restricted. The prices of shares act as a means of conveying news of success or failure to others. Except where competing teams are operating in similar conditions and in close proximity so that reliable knowledge of managerial performance circulates easily, the absence of exchangeable residual claims may make it more costly to build managerial reputations in labour-owned or cooperative enterprises than in investor-owned enterprises. A prediction suggested by this reasoning is that salaried outside managers are more likely to be used in worker-owned enterprises (which can be transformed at low cost into investor-owned firms) than in pure cooperatives.

3.   PROFIT SHARING AND CONTRACTUAL INCOMPLETENESS

As has been emphasised on frequent occasions, information costs and bounded rationality mean that real world contracts are not fully specified. This contractual incompleteness leaves people vulnerable to opportunism and makes the assignment of residual control rights a matter of great importance. The governance structure of the worker-owned firm and the cooperative influences its ability to cope with these problems.

3.1   Debt Finance

A firm that is closed to outside equity holders and raises finance in the form of debt has a highly 'geared' or 'levered' capital structure. Other things constant, higher leverage would imply that bankruptcy is more likely; that is, there are more states of nature in which the firm will be unable to meet its contractual obligations than there would be if more equity finance were employed. It should be remembered, however, that, in the pure worker-owned firm and in the cooperative, labour receives no wage. Because payment of a wage to labour is not an inescapable obligation, as it is in the investor-owned firm, we should not assume that the cooperative enterprise is more vulnerable to bankruptcy. Workers are residual claimants and this will reassure providers of fixed-interest capital in that interest payments are senior to payments to labour.

There is an important caveat to the above argument, however. Workers are free agents and cannot plausibly bind themselves not to leave a cooperative. Thus, if their share in the cooperative falls substantially below the level achievable in other enterprises they will leave. As labour flees from poor results, the provider of fixed-interest capital will once more face the prospect of default. The cooperative, in other words, may be resilient in the context of adverse circumstances when workers are confident that these are merely temporary. Suspicion that problems are longer term, however, may lead to rapid desertion and uncontrolled decline.

Agency problems of outside debt are therefore as troublesome to a cooperative as they are to a joint-stock enterprise. There is still the moral hazard danger that the equity holders (in this case, the workers) will act in many ways contrary to the interests of bond holders. The danger is at its greatest if the workers are not transaction dependent; that is, if their human capital is very general in nature and their dependency on the firm is very low. Workers of this type would have very little to lose by taking large risk with the bond holders' resources in the hope of a large payoff. Bond holders, on the other hand, would not be unduly perturbed by this possibilty if the physical capital they were financing were similarly non-specific. In the event of the firm being wound up, the bond holders could always take control of these easily marketable non-firm-specific capital assets.

Mobile, non-dependent workers, therefore, will be able to form a worker-owned firm or a cooperative only where the capital requirements are small and can be raised internally, or where physical capital consists in non-firm-specific assets. Hansmann (1990) refers to the takeover of United Airlines by the pilots. Pilots are easily transferable between airlines and are unlikely to stay with an airline which yields them a low return just because it is worker owned. However, although aeroplanes are expensive, they are not firm specific, and represent satisfactory security for lenders.

Highly dependent labour embodying firm-specific skills and human capital, on the other hand, will be in a better position to persuade bond holders to finance some specific capital. To take an extreme hypothetical example, if the workers in a cooperative were so specific that their value elsewhere were zero, bond holders need not anticipate their desertion in the event of poor trading results. The probability of default is thereby lowered. We might surmise that the experimental and entrepreneurial role of cooperatives is related to this point. Groups of handicapped people, for example, whose productivity is systematically underestimated by outside employers, might find it possible and profitable to finance a cooperative. Over time, as other employers become more aware of the value of the services of handicapped people, greater mobility is possible, and the problems of running a cooperative are paradoxically increased.

The agency problems of debt thus lead us to two conclusions. Firstly, cooperative and worker-owned enterprise is assisted if human capital is firm specific while physical capital is non-specific. Secondly, cooperatives requiring highly specific capital assets are likely to be labour intensive with equity capital supplied internally by their members. Cooperatives requiring non-specific capital may be quite capital intensive operations.

3.2 Hold-up

One of the major theoretical advantages of worker ownership is that it mitigates the problem of opportunism where workers are dependent on the firm. If the equity is held by the workers and they all receive a share in the distributable surplus, it is clear that other parties cannot steal the quasi-rents on firm-specific human skills by downward revision of the wage. In practice, of course, things are unlikely to be so simple. Where there are several groups of workers with differing degrees of dependency and differing contracts, conflicts of interest might arise in the firm. Non-dependent workers with general skills would be expected to be paid a wage. Partners or worker-owners would be those people who were most firm dependent. This is consistent with assistants and secretaries in law firms receiving salaries while the more firm-specific partners receive a profit share.

Concentrating residual claims on the workers also overcomes some of the problems discussed at length in Chapter 9 related to the takeover. A worker-owned firm can only be taken over if the workers agree and sell their claims to a bidder. They presumably would not do this if the terms implied the expropriation of their firm-specific capital. Further, because all the holders of equity are 'insiders', there is no incentive to waste resources on signalling to the stock market, and this mitigates the short-termism problem. As will be seen in section 4, however, worker cooperatives face severe problems of short-termism of their own.

3.3   Bargaining Within the Firm

It is sometimes argued that the governance structure of a worker-owned enterprise lowers the costs of coming to agreements within the firm. Two reasons can be adduced in support of this proposition. Firstly, conflicts of interest between investors and workers are avoided (as noted in section 2). Secondly, information is likely to be more symmetrically distributed across the workforce and this would be expected to reduce adverse selection problems within the firm.

Although these points are plausible, they are by no means conclusive. Indeed, Hansmann (1990) points to the costs of collective decision-making within the worker-owned firm as a primary consideration explaining important aspects of its structure and governance. In the joint-stock company, equity holders may be expected to want to maximise the value of their stock. Although differing risk preferences, dealing costs, tax regimes and so forth can result in conflicts of interest even among shareholders, these are likely to be much less severe than the differences that can arise between groups of workers. If some workers receive a wage element in their remuneration and do very different types of job from others, tensions between groups will be likely. Hansmann notes that business decisions may involve closing some plants and opening others, investing in technology requiring new skills, deciding on the level of safety equipment, and adjusting any wage element of worker compensation to new circumstances. All these decisions are likely to prove contentious.

As numbers rise, the cost of direct democracy as a means of collective decision-making becomes onerous. Time and information costs increase while decisions may turn out to be very inefficient. The theory of voting indicates how, if voters are not sufficiently similar in their preferences, collective choices may result in paradoxes and collectively irrational decisions.[8] Representative democracy reduces some of the decision-making costs, but it neither removes the conflicts of interest nor ensures rational collective choices, while it recreates some of the conditions said to result in feelings of alienation on the part of labour in the joint-stock firm. Homogeneous interests are therefore important to a worker-owned firm if decision-making costs are to be kept under control. 'Worker ownership is extremely rare in firms in which there is any substantial degree of heterogeneity in the work force.'[9]

4. THE PROBLEM OF INVESTMENT DECISIONS

Short-termism is particularly associated with labour-managed and cooperative enterprises, though not for the same reasons adduced in the case of joint-stock firms. The problem ultimately derives from the lack of exchangeability of claims to the residual. We are therefore discussing, in this subsection, those profit-sharing enterprises in which residual claims cannot be traded. The analysis would not apply to labour–capital partnerships or (without some modification) to worker ownership, as these forms have been defined in section 1.

An elementary theorem in the theory of finance is that, with perfectly efficient capital markets, investment decisions will not be affected by the pure time preference of the particular people making the decisions. One person may be highly 'impatient' and disinclined to postpone consumption from one period to the next. His or her rate of 'pure time preference' may be high. Another person may have a very low rate of pure time preference and be disinclined to discount future utility just because it is in the future. Given the rate of interest prevailing in the market, these different individuals would be expected to come to quite different decisions about how to organise their time streams of consumption. The 'impatient' person will consume more 'now' and less 'later' compared with a 'patient' person with the same level of wealth. Both, however, will wish to maximise their wealth and will adopt all those investment opportunities that add to net present value. They will achieve their own preferred distribution of consumption over time through their borrowing or lending activities on the capital market.[10]

Conditions in the capital market do not, of course, accord with those required for this theorem to hold in its purest form. Rates of interest are not the same for borrowers and lenders and invariant to the size of the loan advanced. Future flows of income from investment projects are not known with certainty by all transactors in the market (the source of the signalling problem in Chapter 9). A particular problem with cooperatives, however, is that title to the intertemporal income flows is not clearly assigned. In the simple model outlined above, a person investing resources 'now' has an undisputed right to the returns that accrue 'later'. People are so confident of these rights that they can trade them on the capital market. They can, if they wish, borrow in the certain knowledge that their investment returns will enable them to repay their debts, or lend secure in the knowledge that a return will be paid. In a cooperative, a person who invests does not have an individually assigned right to a share of the full flow of returns. The returns are received in the form of a share in the distributable surplus for as long as a person remains with the cooperative. Thus, an investment which yields returns over a ten-year time horizon to the cooperative as a whole may yield returns for only two years to a worker who is due to retire two years hence.

Older workers in a cooperative may be expected, therefore, to oppose long-term investments financed from internal resources, and achieving agreement on an investment strategy within the firm will be difficult because different people face different rates of return from the same projects. It is very important to note, however, that by adjusting the structure of property rights, the interests of older and younger workers can change. Hansmann (1990), for example, mentions the case in which investment from internal resources is paid into a pension fund. Through the fund, a right to investment returns is conferred on retired workers. In the extreme case in which all internal investment was held by the pension fund, retired workers would implicitly be the holders of the rights to a return on internally financed investment. Young workers would then have little to gain from agreeing to finance the firm's investment, whereas those near retirement would favour larger payments to the capital fund at the expense of distributions to the workers.

In principle, making membership of a cooperative a tradable right would circumvent some of these problems. Cooperatives with a successful record of profitable investments would find that membership rights would trade at a premium compared with less successful cooperatives. Those leaving a cooperative could gain access to the present value of the returns from the investment they had financed. However, controlling the membership of the team may be important if the correct mix of skills and other attributes is to be achieved. The personal characteristics of shareholders are of no concern to a joint-stock enterprise and the rights can be freely traded. Where the success of the team is highly dependent on particular skills it would be difficult to introduce tradable rights in what would be a very 'thin' market.

Capital raised internally from the surpluses that would otherwise be distributed to the workforce has further risk-sharing disadvantages. Instead of using the capital market to spread their risks widely, workers in a cooperative who invest in the firm using part of their distributable surplus become dependent on a single firm for a return on their savings as well as on their labour and human capital. Rather than tolerate this dependency, we would expect a marked preference for the use of outside debt finance in cooperative and labour-managed firms. Individual members of the cooperative would save privately out of their share of the surplus and use outside financial intermediaries to spread their financial risks as widely as possible.

The agency problems associated with outside debt in the context of cooperative enterprise were discussed in subsection 3.1 above. Here, contractual incompleteness and agency problems are related to the determination of the firm's investment choices. In particular, the use of outside debt rather than inside funds does not solve the problem of diverging interests between members of the firm. The duration of bank loans, for example, will determine the payments that existing team members will have to make over whatever time horizon is appropriate to their individual circumstances. Rapid repayment of a loan, for example, will obviously be detrimental to the interests of a worker who is near retirement. Workers in general will prefer only to pay interest on borrowed funds and to leave repayment of the capital sum to a future generation, but this could result in the build-up of debt obligations and the bequeathing of a considerable burden on members of the cooperative in future years. It is for this reason that Pejovich (1992) argues that an efficient investment programme will be chosen by a labour-managed firm only if 'the labour-managed economy pushed the length of bank credits toward an equality with the expected life of capital goods to be purchased with those credits' (p. 37).[11] In a fully-fledged labour managed economy, Pejovich regards this result as a remote possibility since there appears to be little in the incentive structure to lead in that direction. Firms will want to extend the life of credit, while banks will face high information costs if they have to form judgements about the economic life of assets in every case.

5. THE SIZE OF THE TEAM

One of the most debated issues in the academic literature on profit sharing concerns its likely effect on the level of employment in a firm when compared with the norm of investor ownership. The answer depends crucially on what type of profit sharing is being analysed. There are two traditions which superficially appear to be mutually contradictory. The theory first advanced by Ward (1958), Vanek (1970), Meade (1972) and others with respect to the labour-managed firm suggests a generally restrictive impact on the size of the firm in the short run. Indeed their most famous result is that labour-managed enterprises may be expected to respond in a 'perverse' manner to changes in the price of their product under competitive conditions. Rising product prices will lead the team members to try to cut back on their numbers, and vice versa. In contrast, advocates of profit sharing have suggested that, in a share economy, employment would tend to expand. Weitzman (1984) is particularly associated with the view that pure investor ownership leads to insufficient wage flexibility and a high level of unemployment compared with profit-sharing alternatives. The essential difference which produces these contrasting predictions is that in the cooperative or labour-managed firm it is the workforce which controls its own size, whereas in Weitzman's share economy it is still the outside investors who determine employment levels in the firm.

5.1   Employment in the Labour-managed Firm

Assume that the surplus of a labour-managed firm, after capital charges and payments for intermediate inputs, is distributed equally among the workers in the team. Each person will therefore receive remuneration equal to the 'surplus per worker'. In the elementary theory of the labour-managed firm, workers are assumed to determine the size of the team so as to maximise the value of this 'surplus per worker'.[12] Thus, given the price for their product under competitive conditions, they will continue to welcome new members, providing that the value of the additional output produced by the extra labour (and hence revenue generated) exceeds the 'surplus per worker'. If the extra revenue generated by a new worker is greater than the payment he or she will receive (that is, the average surplus), the latter will rise as new workers are attracted and hence new workers will confer benefits on the existing ones. On the other hand, if the market value of extra output is less than the surplus per worker, there will be incentives to cut back on the size of the workforce.

It is this possibility which leads to the 'perverse' supply response of the labour-managed firm. If the size of the team is perfectly adjusted and the surplus per worker is equal to the value of the marginal product of labour, a rise in the price of the firm's product will disturb this relationship. This may be seen by considering the expression below where

$$(PQ - K)/L = P(MP_L)$$

P is product price, Q is output, K is the charge on capital, MP_L is the marginal product of labour, and L is the labour force. The term on the left-hand side is the surplus per worker. On the right is the value of the marginal product of labour. An increase of ten per cent in product price will increase the value of the marginal product of labour by ten per cent in competitive conditions. It will also increase total revenue per worker (PQ/L) by ten per cent. Capital charges per worker (K/L) will remain unchanged, however, which implies that the distributable surplus per worker will rise by *more* than ten per cent. With the value of the marginal product of labour now below the surplus per worker, there will be an incentive to reduce the size of the team in the face of an increase in demand for its product.

There are, of course, many reasons why the force of this theoretical result may be weakened in practice. If workers have the right to claim the residual they are unlikely to leave the team just when prices are rising and this residual is getting larger. It would still remain true, however, that there would be no real enthusiasm for recruiting new workers. Conversely, attracting new workers when prices have fallen might not be possible if earnings in the team have fallen below those available elsewhere. In the long run, any required expansion of output following an increase in demand has to come from the formation of new firms rather than increasing the size of existing ones. In this respect, however, the labour-managed economy would behave much like the textbook version of the competitive investor-owned economy. Where reputation and team-specific skills are important, reliance on new firm formation has distinct disadvantages, since these new firms will face the set-up costs associated with accumulating knowledge within the team and winning consumer confidence.

More recent theoretical work has suggested that labour-managed enterprises will produce the standard 'non-perverse' responses to price changes under certain conditions. Kahana and Nitzan (1993), for example, show that where the surplus per worker cannot fall below a level determined by alternative outside opportunities, lower product prices may cause workers to leave until the return in the labour-managed firm is equal to that available elsewhere. This flight of labour implies that the output of the firm varies directly with product price. The model is not entirely symmetrical in that the initial size of the workforce is assumed to be settled *before* the price of the product is revealed by the market. Workers may then leave. There is, however, no incentive for the cooperating group of workers to *add* recruits to their number *after* the price of the product is revealed, no matter how high the price of the product turns out to be, so that the restrictive nature of cooperative enterprise is still implicit.

Figure 10.4 may help to clarify the differences between the conventional analysis of Meade (1972) and that of Kahana and Nitzan (1993). Meade's analysis is presented in part (a) of Figure 10.4. The two curves $P^*Q(L)$ and $P'Q(L)$ show total revenue as the size of the team varies for two different price levels ($P^* > P'$). K represents fixed capital charges. The slopes of the straight lines out of point K through points a and b represent the distributable surplus per worker at those points. For price level P', this surplus per worker is maximised at b and the size of team is L'. For price level P^*, surplus per worker is maximised at a, where the size of team is L^*. The higher price level leads to a smaller firm.

The structure of part (b) of Figure 10.4 is precisely the same. In this case, however, it is assumed that the initial size of the cooperating group is fixed in advance before the price of the product can be known. It is also assumed that opportunities exist outside the firm and that these are given by the slope of the straight line KK. Suppose that the initial size of the group of cooperators is L^*. If the price of the product turns out to be P^*, returns to team members will be given by the slope of KK^* through point a. There is no incentive for any of them to leave, since their returns exceed those available elsewhere. A smaller team would increase the surplus per worker, but it could only be achieved at the expense of coercing members to leave, which is not compatible with the assumed voluntary nature of the cooperative association. Now assume that the price of the product turns out to be P'. A team of L^* workers would produce a return per worker lower than is available outside (point a'). Workers will leave until point b is reached and the size of the team has shrunk to L'. A still lower price of P'' would cause the team to shrink further to L''. No production would take place if returns within the firm fell short of outside opportunities at every firm size.

Clearly, Kahana and Nitzan's approach yields a non-perverse supply response to price changes on the part of labour-managed firms, but their generally restrictive employment consequences are still apparent. A cooperative group, once established, only sheds labour or maintains its size; it never grows.[13] Further, the determination of the initial size of the group is important. Kahana and Nitzan show that the higher the *expected* price of the product the smaller will be the initial size of the group. This would seem in accordance with the conventional analysis. Higher *actual* prices will lead people to wish they were in a smaller group, and higher expected prices might therefore lead them to opt to form a smaller group in the first place since forcing people out *ex post* is not possible. The negative association between group size and product prices is still there, but now dubbed a 'long-run' rather than 'short-run' phenomenon.

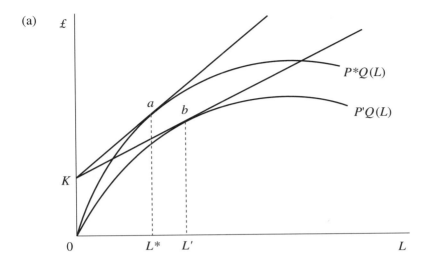

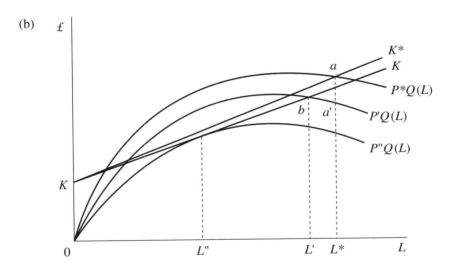

Notes:
(a) = Meade's analysis.
(b) = Kahana and Nitzan's analysis.

Figure 10.4   The size of the labour-managed firm

5.2   Employment and Profit Sharing

In contrast to the labour-managed firm, profit sharing is expected to have expansionary effects on employment where workers have no control over recruitment. Consider an extreme case in which the workers receive no wage but agree to share the distributable surplus with capital. For the sake of argument, suppose that fifty per cent goes to labour and fifty per cent to capital. With this arrangement, it will be in the interests of shareholders to recruit any worker who is capable of raising the distributable surplus by any discernible amount whatsoever. Fifty per cent of a small quantity is better (abstracting from recruitment costs) than nothing at all. From the workers' point of view, however, the recruitment of further members of the team will only benefit them if newcomers are capable of adding to the total distributable surplus an amount that is at least as great as the existing total distributable surplus per worker. Beyond a certain point, therefore, workers and shareholders will come into conflict over recruitment, because newcomers will dilute each person's share of the surplus.

Employment is encouraged by squeezing the earnings of labour. It does not follow, of course, that workers as a whole will necessarily be worse off in such a system. Although shareholders will be anxious to employ any remotely productive person, the return to labour cannot be reduced in any firm below what is available elsewhere or labour will desert the firm. Weitzman argues that the system is attractive because it gives such a strong encouragement to capital to employ labour. The share system, as was seen in section 2.1, implies that the payment to labour is more risky than it would be in the fully investor-owned firm where, traditionally, workers have received a fixed wage. However, although remuneration is more variable in the share system, employment is more reliable. A lower risk of unemployment is the prize for accepting greater income risk. It also permits longer-term and less-interrupted relationships between team members to develop – an important condition for the development of firm-specific skills.

With these apparently desirable properties it is a matter of some interest to know why the sharing form of enterprise is not more common, especially in the United States and the United Kingdom. Japanese enterprise, as noted in Chapter 6, does reveal sharing characteristics. Weitzman's answer to this quandary is that economic systems may become trapped in positions from which individuals or small groups cannot easily escape. Once a system of investor-owned firms paying wages has become established it may not be in the interests of wage earners to agree to a change in their contract independently of wage earners in other firms. Vulnerability to unemployment is not necessarily evenly spread across all wage earners. Many 'insiders' may feel relatively secure. These secure workers will associate profit sharing with the prospect of 'outsiders' being recruited to the firm, both lowering pay and making it less predictable. The possible overall benefits of the system, were it to be adopted widely, would not weigh very heavily with these 'inside' workers. In Chapter 12, we will take up in more detail the question of how far the structure of institutions might be influenced and constrained by evolutionary forces.

'Insiders' may, however, be prepared to choose a profit-sharing contract in some circumstances, in spite of their fears about new recruitment and falling remuneration. As Brunello (1992) points out, what is required is that 'insiders' should have something to gain from employment growth. The advantage that Brunello suggests is that, in a hierarchical enterprise, employment growth will lead to more senior posts and a higher probability of promotion. 'With internal promotion the bargained profit sharing parameter can be positive even if insiders face no unemployment risk' (p. 571). Clearly, this effect will only be felt if insiders are promoted to senior positions, as analysed in Chapter 6, and do not compete with outsiders.

6. THE LABOUR–CAPITAL PARTNERSHIP

Sections 4 and 5 have been concerned with the difficulties faced by cooperative and profit-sharing enterprises when confronting investment and employment decisions. The labour–capital partnership is a form of organisation which has some attractive theoretical properties and is discussed in detail by Meade (1989). It is distinguished from the worker cooperative in having outside holders of shares. It is distinguished from Weitzman's profit-sharing enterprise in that workers are issued with labour share certificates. The raising of more capital would require the issue of more capital share certificates, while the recruitment of more labour would involve granting the new workers extra labour share certificates. All share certificates would entitle the holder to the same dividend. In Meade's presentation, equal numbers of Board members are elected by the group of capital shareholders and the group of labour shareholders respectively.

Because capital share certificates are freely tradable, the time-horizon problem associated with pure worker cooperatives and labour-managed firms is circumvented. Any capital project which adds to the total distributable surplus more than is required to pay the dividend on the new capital share certificates, will be approved by all existing holders of capital and labour share certificates. Similarly, any extra worker who raises the distributable surplus by more than is required to pay the dividend on his or her labour share certificates will be unanimously approved. Tension between capital and labour over investment plans and team size is thereby reduced.

The 'perverse supply response' of the labour-managed firm in Figure 10.4(a) is also overcome. A rise in the price of the firm's product will not lead to a reduction of employment because existing employee-sharers have labour share certificates which entitle them to a dividend whether or not the firm makes use of their services. In other words, the firm cannot simply fire workers and reduce its size. Members have rights to a share in the residual, providing they are available for work. There would still be resistance to *increasing* the size of the team in the face of temporary price rises, however, because this would leave it too large in the long run. Since the employment of newcomers involves long-run commitments, the number of worker-sharers would be determined by long-run considerations. Greater short-run flexibility would require the firm to employ some people on short-term wage contracts, thus introducing two classes of worker.[14]

Favourable conditions which are not transitory will imply that new workers will require to be issued with fewer labour share certificates (since the expected dividends on all shares are higher). Existing labour sharehold-ers therefore do not have to give up a portion of the reward from past suc-cesses to newcomers and will be more inclined to accept them. All workers receive the same dividend on their certificates, but the number of certificates they hold will depend on when they joined the firm. This is why Meade refers to firms structured in this way as *discriminating* labour–capital part-nerships. Some of the return on the certificates of older workers may there-fore be seen as reflecting the build-up over time of their firm-specific human capital, a reward for participating in the development of a successful 'archi-tecture', and a return to entrepreneurship. It is possible to imagine a portion of a worker's labour share certificates being converted over time into capital share certificates in recognition of this process. However, if firm-specific human capital were represented by a tradable capital share certificate, the worker embodying that human capital would no longer be firm dependent. He or she could, without penalty, leave the firm for a job elsewhere and sell the capital share certificates on the capital market. In other words, this policy might lead to the dissipation of the specific human capital in the firm unless workers converting labour into capital share cer-tificates could bind themselves not to leave the team.[15]

Retirement of workers presents another difficulty for the labour–capital partnership. If the retiring worker's certificates are simply cancelled and new ones issued sufficient to attract a replacement, then to the extent that this procedure implies a net reduction in the outstanding shares, all contin-uing shareholders (both labour and capital) will benefit from the worker's retirement. In this way, the gains from any long-term profit opportunities discovered by workers 'leak away' to capital shareholders. This seepage could be prevented if the retirees were permitted to keep any share certificates in excess of those required to attract a replacement worker. The danger here is that the pure profits accruing to the firm at the time of a worker's retirement might turn out to be transitory. When the pure profits disappear, the distributable surplus of the team will fall and replacement workers will leave the firm unless they are issued with further labour share certificates to raise their incomes to the levels achievable in alternative positions. Thus, the total of outstanding shares increases and the providers of risk capital will find their capital share certificates 'diluted'. A further possibility is that any excess certificates available at the time of a worker's retirement could be redistributed to the rest of the labour force. This, however, would introduce an incentive to restrict the size of the team on the part of existing workers. In this way they would hope to gain more from the redistributed labour share certificates of retirees.[16]

The labour–capital partnership has theoretical properties which overcome some of the problems associated with worker cooperatives. It is a form of governance that, in principle, protects firm-specific human capital while permitting the use of outside financial capital with its risk-spreading advantages. The interests of capital and labour shareholders are cleverly aligned over such matters as employment and investment policy. Labour participates in the risk of the enterprise although the risk of unemployment is lower than in an investor-owned firm, while the risk of very low income is limited by the ability to move elsewhere.

On the other hand, any attempt to operate such an enterprise in practice would face some obvious difficulties. Investment, for example, must be financed by the issue of new capital share certificates and not from internally generated funds. The accounting problems of estimating the distributable surplus making allowances for the depreciation of capital and corrections for inflation are substantial. In an investor-owned firm, accounting conventions may be important for conveying a true impression of the state of the business, but the application of different conventions would not directly affect the position of labour or the underlying value of shareholders' claims.

Further, the ability of managers to discipline workers (and vice versa) in an environment of a high level of employment security and widely held residual claims is an open question. Hierarchical incentive devices such as those discussed in Chapter 6 are logically feasible (promotion would bring with it the issue of extra labour share certificates). In the absence of the takeover and of monitoring by outside capital shareholders, motivation of senior managers might require the issue of special bonus shares for good overall performance. The managerial labour market would also be a possible motivator because successful management would be communicated through the prices of the traded capital share certificates. 'Inside' worker-directors on the Board would be expected to offer some monitoring services, since they are likely to be well informed and have a significant personal interest in the distributable surplus. The closest monitoring of managers will be to no avail, however, if the managers have no mechanism for motivating workers. As already mentioned, a tournament structure might provide some leverage, even where the threat of termination is not significant, but an additional factor yet to be discussed is the role of peer-group pressure.

7.   THE ROLE OF PEER PRESSURE

With purely self-interested behaviour on the part of team members, effort is expected to decline as the residual is shared amongst an increasingly large number of people. Each person's private calculation is to equate the additional costs of effort with the *private* payoff. If the residual is shared equally, the private payoff will be $1/N$th of the payoff to the team as a whole where N is the size of the team. Where effort cannot be easily observed, measured and rewarded, therefore, the effectiveness of profit sharing as a means of providing alternative incentives will be severely limited by the free-rider problem. This is the conventional reasoning and it is the basic problem which permeates the entire theory of economic organisation.

7.1   Internal Pressure

Suppose, however, that people are capable of experiencing some disutility from a consciousness of having not performed well in a team endeavour. The first and simplest situation might be to assume that, even if their peers did not observe their shirking, free riders would experience some feelings of guilt. Guilt is unobserved or 'internal' pressure. Now, it could be argued that to assume the existence of 'internal' pressure or guilt is effectively to assume away the problem of economic organisation. Clearly, if everyone felt a strong social motivation not to shirk in any team activity or defect in any prisoner's dilemma, the world would be a much less interesting place. The assumption of a pervasive sense of guilt has seemed unreasonable to most observers of the social scene throughout the centuries. As Thackeray put it, 'We grieve at being found out, and at the idea of shame or punishment; but the mere sense of wrong makes very few people unhappy in Vanity Fair'.[17]

We may, however, accept Thackeray's tolerant realism without denying the existence of guilt in its entirety. Some down-to-earth observations of

Vanity Fair suggest that institutions exist which rely heavily on inculcating a sense of commitment to collective goals amongst their members. The most obvious example is that of military institutions, which invest heavily in building 'team spirit' and inculcating loyalty to the unit. Military units rely for their effectiveness on people behaving cooperatively, even in dangerous circumstances where they cannot be observed and where the incentive to defect would be compelling for most 'untrained' people. Assuming that human beings have the capacity to respond to some 'social conditioning', 'indoctrination' or whatever we choose to call investments in the generation of group loyalty, further questions of economic significance are suggested. Under what conditions will such investments be productive and where might they be expected to fail?

Investing resources in making workers feel loyalty to the shareholders of a joint-stock company would probably be considered by most people a waste of effort. For loyalty-building investments to be productive, the wellbeing of each member of the group must be mutually dependent, the activities of each member should be costly to monitor, and the group should be small and homogeneous enough for people to 'empathise' with the predicament of their colleagues.[18] If the actions of individuals in a group have no effect on the utility of other members, no guilt can accompany lack of effort. If actions can be monitored at very low cost, loyalty is unnecessary to achieve effort. If the return to loyalty building is low in the absence of natural 'empathy' then we would not expect to observe large investments in team spirit in heterogeneous groups. These factors are consistent with strong family or social links between partners, and with a greater investment in loyalty building where profits are shared than where they are not.

7.2 External Pressure

Guilt or 'internal' pressure is a valuable resource because it operates even in the absence of observability. Shame or 'external' pressure, requires that a person's actions are observable by his or her peers. Although the observability requirement restricts the range of circumstances in which shame can be effective, the pressure which it can exert when conditions are suitable is enormous. Adam Smith, in the *Theory of Moral Sentiments*, asks to what we can attribute all the 'toil and bustle' of the world. It cannot, he argues, merely be a desire to satisfy the basic needs of hunger or shelter. For people who have satisfied these basic requirements of existence the benefits of action are more social. 'To be observed, to be attended to, to be taken notice of with sympathy, complacency and approbation, are all the advantages which we can propose to derive from it. It is the vanity, not the ease, or the pleasure, which interests us.'[19] If Adam Smith is correct here in his assessment of human motivations, the potential (both productive and unproductive) of the crushing force of social disapproval as a means of inducing effort and compliance with group norms should not be overlooked.

For shame to be an effective motivator, actions must be observed. If peers are to monitor one another, there must be some payoff for doing so. Profit sharing is therefore a necessary condition for peer-group monitoring. If I am a wage earner and my colleagues' activities do not affect me, I will have no incentive to monitor them. Where their effort affects the size of my share in the team's residual, then an incentive will exist. As with the theory of Chapter 6, there must also be a penalty associated with being discovered shirking, which we may here envisage as social isolation and a sense of shame rather than a specific monetary penalty. We should also note once more that an ability costlessly to escape censure by leaving the group would be to remove the power of the group to inflict punishment. Some form of dependency is required even in profit-sharing groups and communities formed for collective purposes.[20]

With two identical profit sharers, the determination of the amount of monitoring and effort for each person is shown schematically in Figure 10.5. The figure is a much-simplified formulation of the arguments presented in Kandel and Lazear (1992).

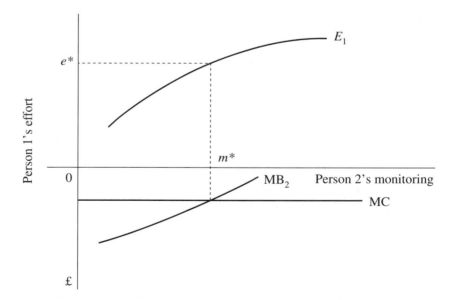

Figure 10.5   Mutual monitoring in a partnership

The effort of Person 1 increases with the monitoring of person 2 (curve E_1). We assume that extra monitoring increases the accuracy of observation. Greater work effort will be more effective at reducing peer pressure when observation is accurate than when it is inaccurate. Thus, person 1 will find it worthwhile to increase his or her effort in response to greater monitoring by person 2. Assuming that monitoring is not entirely costless, person 2 will monitor only to the point at which his or her private gains from person 1's extra effort (in this case one half of the additional output) equal the extra monitoring costs incurred (MC). With diminishing returns to effort, person 2's marginal benefit from person 1's extra effort is given by curve MB_2. In the context of identical individuals, both will monitor with intensity m^* and work with intensity e^*.

What happens as the number of people in the group increases? Up to a point, we might expect peer pressure to rise. Ten hostile or otherwise disapproving erstwhile colleagues might be worse than just a single one. Presumably, there are limits to this tendency, however, as relationships become more distant and detached as numbers rise above a certain point. Similarly, the incentive to monitor may rise over a certain range. Supposing that a given degree of monitoring intensity is as effective when spread over ten people as it is when applied to a single person (monitoring has public good characteristics for groups below a certain size) the private benefits from monitoring will increase. Again, however, there must be some limit. Presumably a person cannot monitor one hundred or one thousand people as easily as five or ten. A person's monitoring may be a form of 'joint input', but it will become subject to diminishing effectiveness after a certain point.

For relatively small groups, therefore, peer pressure deriving from mutual monitoring may be an important component of a satisfactory theory of profit sharing. It is even conceivable that the peer pressure generated may be substantial enough to result in a greater level of effort than the contractors would ideally prefer. Just as we saw in Chapter 6 that the wrong structure of prizes in a tournament could result in 'too great' a level of effort, an environment with excessive peer pressure might logically produce a similar effect. For very large groups, however, such an outcome would seem unlikely. A person will not monitor those in his or her peer group if the benefits flow away to people outside, while punishing people who are not cooperative is likely to become less certain as the size and complexity of the group rises.[21]

Peer pressure will be most effective when the size of the group is such that each individual can effectively monitor all the others. Further, monitoring will be more effective when each person has a good knowledge of the nature of the work they are observing and the skills required to do it effectively. This is another reason for expecting successful profit-sharing groups to be small and relatively homogeneous. As was noted earlier, Hansmann (1990) highlights the adverse effect on the costs of collective decision making of group diversity because of conflicts of interest. In contrast, Kandel and Lazear (1992) draw attention to the adverse consequences for the effectiveness of peer-group monitoring of heterogeneity amongst the profit sharers and hence of a low degree of observational accuracy. 'The grouping of partners by occupation is a direct implication of the mutual monitoring analysis ... Partnerships should be less prevalent in firms in which workers specialise in non-overlapping tasks' (p. 814).

Our discussion of the implications of various forms of profit sharing between workers, or between the workers and providers of finance in an enterprise, is now complete. As mentioned in section 1, however, there are occasions when consumers find it advantageous to band together to form a cooperative. Before leaving the subject of profit sharing, therefore, section 8 investigates the rationale and governance structure of the retail cooperative.

8.   THE RETAIL COOPERATIVE

8.1   Transactions Costs and the Retail Cooperative

Where consumers are poorly informed about the quality and reliability of the goods offered by suppliers, the formation of a cooperative may be seen as a response to the adverse selection problem. By setting up a cooperative, consumers establish an institution that can gain no advantage from delivering poor quality to its members. Further, if buyers suspect that established retailers or wholesalers are acting as a cartel and exploiting a monopoly position, they may attempt to circumvent these suppliers by combining together to deal directly with producers. This will be more likely where normal competitive processes are tardy or ineffective, perhaps because sunk costs prevent new firms from entering the market. A cooperative could be viewed as a method of binding buyers to remain loyal to a new entrant.

In the case of retail cooperatives, however, capital requirements are not great, nor is the physical capital highly firm specific. The risk-sharing disadvantages associated with worker cooperatives are also less pronounced in the case of consumer cooperatives. The average member of a consumer cooperative will have much less capital at risk and will not be entirely dependent upon a single enterprise for his or her purchases. On the other hand, the moral hazard problems of enterprise governance – of disciplining workers and managers – have still to be overcome. Assuming that the worker in a retail cooperative has little firm-specific capital at stake and may be monitored at low cost, the main problem will be providing incentives to directors and senior managers. It is hardly likely that personal membership of the cooperative will constitute a sufficient incentive. Nor would it seem reasonable to expect the monitoring of other members of the cooperative to be very rigorous. To some extent, a monitoring function might accompany the very process of shopping by members of the cooperative, but, with little capital at stake, the incentive to pursue a complaint through the collective choice process would appear to be negligible.

Peer pressure on senior directors of the cooperative may play a significant role. As will be seen in the next subsection, consumer cooperatives were often started by people from particular social 'groups' in society. Serious maladministration would then be expected to result in very significant loss of social esteem, or at least enough to induce a modicum of effort on the part of directors. While routine operations in fairly stable conditions could be carried out within the context of this property rights structure, the ability to stimulate and reward entrepreneurial flair internally is obviously limited. Whereas the setting up of a cooperative can be seen as an entrepreneurial act in itself on the part of consumers, with the objective of breaking a monopoly or improving information flows, the maintenance of this flexibility *after* the cooperative is established is a significant problem. Cooperative status can be important in the early days of an enterprise as a means of establishing a good reputation with consumers. If trust is important and consumer cooperatives have an institutional advantage in creating trust, we have the beginnings of an explanation of the role they played in late-nineteenth-century retailing, but if flexibility and adaptability are required, and if other institutional forms can gradually develop equally good reputations for quality and fair dealing over time, the cooperative will tend to be a transitory rather than a permanent feature of the institutional landscape.

8.2 Role of Retail Cooperatives in Nineteenth-century England

The potentially entrepreneurial character of cooperative enterprise can be seen in the transformation of the retail trade in the UK during the later part of the nineteenth century.[22] Until the mid-1860s, middle-class shoppers in London faced a multitude of specialised small establishments offering elaborate service and extended credit. They published no price lists and were widely assumed to charge different prices to different customers. Resentment was widespread. The demand for a new form of retail service was satisfied by the rapid growth of cooperatives, which initially catered to particular middle-class groups. The most successful of these consumer cooperatives was the Army and Navy Cooperative Society Ltd (A and N), which started trading in 1872. Membership was open to army and naval officers, and the initial capital consisted of 15000 shares of £1 each. Those eligible but unwilling to become members could nevertheless shop at the 'A and N' by purchasing an annual 'ticket'. The new societies offered low prices, assurance of quality, and much reduced service. They offered no credit and accepted cash only. They published price lists and distributed them four times per year to members. There were few shop assistants. Shoppers made out their own bill.

So successful were the new cooperatives that their competitors attempted to restrict them 'by political and other coercive action' (Hood and Yamey, 1957, p. 318). Given the membership of the cooperatives, these attempts were doomed to failure, and emulation of some of the societies' methods became the only rational response. By the early 1870s, the range of products sold by the cooperatives was enormous. 'The societies played a large part in bringing about other changes which have generally been credited to the ordinary department stores (that is, stores not organised on cooperative lines). It is probable that their shops were the first major department stores in England.' (p. 317). Thus it was that admirals and generals (who comprised five out of eight directors of the A and N in 1879) presided over a movement that, *The Times* insisted, 'threatens nothing less than a social revolution'. As time advanced, however, the societies themselves had to meet competition from stores offering low prices but greater services, including Whiteley's and Harrod's. Restrictions on membership were relaxed and the advantages of cooperative status became less clear. By the mid-1920s, societies had transformed themselves into joint-stock firms and their premises were open to all customers by 1939.

In the context of the earlier analysis presented in this book, it is interesting to consider why the cooperative form of enterprise proved so attractive in retailing during this period. First, as was noted above, consumer cooperatives suffer less from the risk-sharing disadvantages of producer cooperatives. Consumers are able to distribute their expenditure between establishments as they think fit, and the capital requirements of forming a retail cooperative are less of an obstacle. Most fundamentally, the societies provided consumers with information about the wholesale costs of various products and were in a good position to establish a reputation for quality and fair dealing. It is no accident that they started out with a membership taken from fairly closely defined professional groups and that their achievement was to let people know 'what things cost, and what they ought to cost'.[23] Their very success produced the conditions in which competitors could also build up this kind of reputation by matching the societies' prices and emulating their methods.

When expansion was called for, the restrictive tendencies of cooperative enterprise with respect to capital investment became apparent. A and N shareholders[24] refused to sanction an increase in capital to permit the premises to be extended in 1879. This led to the establishment of the Junior Army and Navy Stores by members of the armed services unable to join the A and N. After the profitability of the new retailing methods had become fully demonstrated, it was the joint-stock enterprise that was best equipped to raise the capital to exploit them. Further, the accumulated profits held by the societies were a constant temptation to 'shareholders' to establish the exchangeability of residual claims and to realise the full present value of their entrepreneurial gains, instead of reducing prices and sharing them period by period with the rapidly expanding body of 'ticket holders'.[25] The history of the cooperatives represents, therefore, a case study of the continuing process of competition between organisational forms.

9. MARKETING AND SUPPLY COOPERATIVES

9.1 Marketing and Distribution

It is not only at the retailing end of the supply chain that cooperative enterprise has played a historically significant role. In retail cooperatives, the buyers became owners. Sometimes, however, sellers face the monopsony power of buyers or confront other significant transactional hazards. In these cases, there is a possibility that ownership by the seller will raise efficiency. Hansmann (1996, p. 120) reports, for example, that in 1991 there were 2 400 cooperatives in the USA, marketing farm products. Membership totalled 1 840 000 farmers. Some are simply bargaining cooperatives. Here sellers are banding together in order to create monopoly power as a countervailing force to the monopsony power of the buyer. Most, however, actually market and even process their members' output. Over the course of the twentieth century, the share of agricultural output marketed by cooperatives in the USA rose from six per cent (in 1913) to thirty per cent (in 1982). In other countries, such as France and Germany, the share of the cooperatives in the marketing of agricultural output is even higher (over forty per cent), while in Sweden it reaches eighty per cent.

Hansmann considers various explanations of the success of supply cooperatives. Policies against monopoly and against agreements to fix prices have not been used to suppress supply cooperatives.[26] Perhaps they are simply ways of raising prices against buyers and avoiding antitrust legislation? Cooperatives also have various tax advantages relative to investor-owned companies. In particular, the income is not taxed twice – once as 'corporate profit' and then again when income is distributed to the membership as in an investor-owned firm. There is a mechanism which aims to tax the cooperative's income once only, with distributed income taxed at the marginal rate of each member. However, fiscal advantages and the pursuit of monopoly power do not stand scrutiny as decisive and exclusive explanations for the success of agricultural supply cooperatives. Basically, this is because most cooperatives have open membership and contracts which last for only one year, suggesting that their power to limit long-run supply is negligible. Further, the dominance of cooperatives in certain important areas predates the introduction of the income tax. The Sixteenth Amendment permitting Congress to collect taxes on incomes was not ratified until February 1913, yet Hansmann (p. 134) notes that half the California citrus crop was marketed by cooperatives in 1906.

In Chapter 4, subsection 7.2, we have already introduced Hansmann's theory of ownership. Ownership rights, he argues, will be assigned so as to economise on the costs of ownership plus the costs of transacting. 'Patrons' who face high costs of transacting (relative to other patrons) are therefore likely to be prime candidates for the ownership role, providing that the costs of ownership are not also relatively high. In the case of agricultural supply cooperatives, the existence of monopsony power and the importance of the correct storage and treatment of the crops presented clear transactional hazards. It is the relatively low 'ownership costs' of the cooperatives, however, that Hansmann argues is the key to their long-run survival. Monitoring of the management of a cooperative is undertaken by informed local farmers. These farmers produce a limited range of crops about which they are very knowledgeable. Further, collective decision making is facilitated by the fact that the interests of the membership are very homogeneous. 'The scarcity of co-operatives that handle more than one commodity is strong evidence of the importance of this homogeneity of interest' (p. 136).

Transactional problems between a processor or distributor and a farmer can be overcome by the farmer owning the distributor, but why should the farmer own the distributor rather than the other way around? Hansmann argues that farmers are low-cost owners because homogeneity of interest makes collective decision making easy. The investors in a joint-stock distributor might, however, also face low costs of collective decision making. Why cannot they own the farms? Presumably the difference is that the costs of monitoring and management are different. Investors in a marketing and distribution firm would make poor monitors of farmers, while farmers make quite reasonable monitors of distribution and marketing managers. We can also use an argument based upon Hart's theory of ownership to establish a similar result. Transferring the ownership of land from farmer to a combined marketing and farming company, owned by an investor, would adversely affect the farmer's non-contractible investments in the farming activity while not improving marketing and distribution. Transferring distribution and marketing assets to the farmer increases the farmer's incentives without diminishing those of the distribution manager. The assets are to some degree complementary and should be held by the farmer.

Although collective ownership by farmers of marketing activities is therefore common, large-scale collective farms themselves have had a much less successful, not to say disastrous, record for many of the reasons explored earlier in this chapter. Agricultural marketing cooperatives as well as agricultural supply cooperatives (for fertilisers, seeds and other farm inputs) thus enable the small-scale family-controlled farm to coexist with much larger scale supply and distribution activities which might otherwise wield great localised market power over the farmers.

9.2   Supply Cooperatives and the Utilities

The analysis of supply cooperatives mirrors closely that of the marketing cooperatives. Wherever contracting costs are high or monopoly power is strong, consumer or supply cooperatives are an important response. Agricultural supply cooperatives in the United States received one quarter of farm production expenditure in 1990.[27] Once again, the ownership interests (the farmers) are sufficiently homogeneous to keep decision-making costs down. For similar reasons, one half of farm households in the United States were supplied with electricity by cooperative companies in 1980, and cooperative provision of telephone services covered over one million subscribers in 1989.[28]

Consumer ownership of the public utilities would indeed seem to be a predictable way of responding to the problems of 'natural' monopoly which beset the provision of electricity, gas, water, telephone and other 'network' services. A more extended discussion of the regulation of natural monopoly and the policy issues which surround it can be found in Chapter 15. In the context of consumer ownership, the main factors preventing cooperative solutions seem to have been the heterogeneous interests of consumers in urban areas. Where networks serve consumers of very differing incomes or service requirements, consumers become, in Hansmann's terms, high-cost owners. Some will be industrial users, others residential and yet others commercial. Some will have large and predictable requirements while the demands of others will be small and unpredictable. Some will be users at peak times and others at off-peak times. Collective decision making becomes problematic under these circumstances. Indeed municipal ownership and cooperative ownership will be quite similar in urban areas except that the major interest groups will have somewhat different political influence. In a consumers' cooperative, control rights and rights to the residual could be distributed in proportion to each member's purchases. Industrial interests (or large commercial consumers) might then be expected to be more powerful than under municipal ownership where residential consumers would make up the bulk of the voting population and decisions would be mediated by politicians. Another important problem with consumer ownership of the utilities in urban areas is that high levels of mobility would both reduce the incentive to monitor the management of the utility and require the continual transfer of ownership rights from one person to another. The valuation of these rights would be a problem unless means could be found to make them tradable.

10.   MUTUAL ENTERPRISE

Where people form a 'club' to provide various forms of financial protection, we refer to 'mutual enterprise'.[29] Mutuals have played an important role in insurance and banking in the past and still feature significantly in many countries in spite of considerable 'demutualisation' in the 1990s, especially in the UK. The basic explanation for mutual enterprise is that it economises on the high transactions costs that are associated with certain financial markets. In Chapter 2, the concepts of adverse selection and moral hazard were introduced, using examples from the world of insurance, and it is not surprising therefore that many early insurance companies and savings banks were structured as mutuals. Lenders would want to ensure that borrowers were of good character and likely to repay loans; providers of fire insurance that those insured would take reasonable precautions, and so forth. A club with a membership sufficiently well known to each other to take advantage of mutual monitoring, local information and the use of some social pressure to control opportunism was a natural response. The provision of life assurance was another area in which the mutual enterprise played an important role.

The Amicable Society for a Perpetual Assurance Office (which later became the Norwich Union) was founded in London in 1706. It established a simple mechanism for providing security for orphans or other family members after a person's death. Each year the members paid a sum of money into a fund which was securely guarded. At the end of the year, the contents of the fund were distributed to the survivors of those who had died. Clearly, the sum assured was not guaranteed and would vary according to the number of club members that happened to die during the year. In the absence of mortality tables and in a world still subject to epidemics of life-threatening diseases, life assurance would have been difficult to arrange by any other means. By the 1770s, however, advances in statistical knowledge and in financial investment techniques had led to recognisably modern arrangements. The Society for Equitable Assurances on Lives and Survivorships, established in 1756, had introduced level premiums paid throughout life, varying with age at entry and with a specified sum assured.[30] However, the mutual form of enterprise was still important for this development in life assurance. The financial calculations involved were so uncertain that investor-owned institutions offering similar promises of sums assured in exchange for premiums paid might find themselves either bankrupt and unable to honour their promises, or hugely profitable. A club could simply set the premiums at a prudently high level and then distribute any surpluses to the membership as time advanced (or add periodically to the sums assured).

During the nineteenth century in the UK and the USA, investor-owned life assurance companies developed and competed with the mutuals. In the UK, investor-owned institutions incorporated profit sharing for the reasons outlined in the last paragraph. The Deed of Settlement of the Prudential[31], as amended in 1853, for example, provided for five per cent interest to shareholders with periodic valuations of new profits. Eighty per cent of new profits were to go to policyholders as bonuses and twenty per cent to shareholders.[32] In the USA, investor-owned life insurance companies developed in the early nineteenth century but failed to overcome the problems of trust that confronted them. The first mutual life insurance company was set up in 1843. By 1849, there were nineteen mutuals and all but two of the investor-owned companies had withdrawn from the business by 1853.[33] The mutuals were able to offer longer-term whole life policies compared with the shorter-term policies (one to seven years) offered by the investor-owned companies. After the coming of state regulation of insurance companies in the 1850s and 1860s, joint-stock life insurance companies recovered, although they remained more risky than the mutuals. Hansmann (1996, p. 274) reports that of the 205 stock companies existing in 1868, 61 per cent had failed by 1905 compared with 22 per cent of the mutuals. Perhaps because of this record of relative safety, or because of the 'muck-raking' journalism of the Roosevelt years exposing scandals in the life insurance business, or because managers wished to avoid being taken over, conversions to mutual status were significant in the first forty years of the twentieth century. Only in the second half of the century did the joint-stock companies gain a definite advantage in the USA.

By the last decade of the twentieth century, pressure to 'demutualise' insurance companies was strong in the UK, although mutuals still have a significant presence in the market.[34] A similar trend towards demutualisation has also occurred in the building societies (savings and loan associations). Other areas of demutualisation include stock and commodity exchanges (historically owned by their members) and automobile breakdown services. There are several differing explanations of this trend. As insurance companies and banks grew larger and less local, the ownership advantages of mutual status were substantially reduced. Monitoring managers by the members of a society is no less costly than monitoring managers by shareholders once an organisation becomes sufficiently big. Similarly, where the major transactional problem is lack of trust in borrowers or fire insurance policy holders, the advantages of scale and widely dispersed risk might outweigh the monitoring advantages of local mutual arrangements. Against these arguments, there remains the point that the existence of shareholders could encourage a riskier investment strategy than managers in a mutual would find attractive. Managers in a mutual (with no takeover pressure to consider) might be expected to be less cost efficient, more cautious and more inclined towards in-kind benefits. If financial prudence is to be encouraged, however, these consequences of 'low-powered incentives' might be a price worth paying.

Hansmann's framework of analysis would suggest that either the relative ownership costs of mutuals or the relative transactions costs have risen. As we saw with the history of retail cooperatives in the UK, the gradual decline in transactions costs with consumers probably played a major part in their eventual eclipse. This might plausibly also have happened in the financial sector, with the evolution of greater trust and reputational capital in investor-owned insurance companies and banks. Similarly, on the ownership side, the inherent disadvantage of large mutual organisations is the likely heterogeneity of holders of control rights. Savers will have different priorities from lenders, old members of an insurance society might favour different investment strategies from younger members, married people might be more risk averse than younger single people and so forth. Even in the case of stock exchanges, differences in interests between large institutions and smaller stockbroking firms can be important. The high cost of collective decision making has been cited as an important contributory factor in the demutualisation of stock exchanges.[35]

Changes in government fiscal and regulatory policies might also have had a significant influence on the fate of the mutuals in the financial sector. If both mutual and investor-owned organisations face similar regulatory oversight, this will subtly undermine one of the principal advantages of the mutual – the fact that 'ownership' by members and lower-powered incentives to managers are conducive to greater 'trust'. Consumers of financial products will not pay any price for extra security if they think that government regulation makes all financial institutions equally reliable. Matters of governance then become arcane issues for lawyers and of no day-to-day significance for prudent consumers. The mutual form of enterprise becomes a victim of adverse selection and a form of Gresham's law – 'bad governance drives out good' – comes into operation. Similarly, if governments regulate utility companies, the option of consumer ownership is subverted; if they regulate healthcare services, non-profit governance structures have their advantages eroded; and if they regulate takeovers, private responses to vulnerability in the form of partnerships or worker control are discouraged. This is not to argue that government regulation is always undesirable but merely that its costs can take many important and hidden forms. The role of regulation in influencing enterprise governance seems to be an under-researched area in economic organisation.[36]

Rent seeking can also undermine mutual status in the financial sector. Over many years the mutual societies have built up valuable brand-name capital. In addition, conservative valuation policies and the tendency of managers to accumulate reserves within the mutual rather than to distribute them fully to policyholders have encouraged members to establish privately exchangeable claims to these reserves by means of demutualisation. As a member of a Society, a person can gain from collectively held reserves, but people may judge that establishing a private and exchangeable right in their share of this 'inheritance' is more valuable than taking the benefit in the form of a higher return on their premiums over the period of their membership. The value of a higher return on their premiums is uncertain, subject to dilution from new members, vulnerable to further diversion in favour of managerial interests, and dependent on the expected duration of membership. The single 'windfall' gain that accompanies demutualisation is often preferred to the continuing flow of benefits associated with remaining in a mutual society.[37]

11. STAKEHOLDING

We have seen that firms are usually owned by investors but may also be owned by consumers, workers or other users of the firm's services. We have also seen that ownership is usually assigned to a single relatively homogeneous group and we have reviewed Hansmann's explanation of this observation. Homogeneity of the ownership interest economises upon collective decision-making costs. Some writers, however, have advocated sharing ownership rights among wider groups of patrons. Hutton (1997, p. 9), for example, argues that 'corporate governance (should be) reformed to reflect the various interests that converge on the firm – suppliers, workers and trade unions, banks, as well as shareholders and directors. This is the central idea of the stakeholder economy.'

Writers taking this position on corporate governance tend to do so not on grounds of economic efficiency but on rather wider grounds of political or, more specifically, democratic principle. The governance of the firm is, for these writers, a sub-branch of politics. Hutton (1995, p. 294) writes that 'the constitution of the British firm . . . self-consciously reproduces the unwritten British constitution'. He advocates the 'democratisation and republicanisation of the state' (p. 286) and the reform of corporate govern-ance to reflect what he sees as similar (stakeholder) principles.

From the point of view of the theory of economic organisation, the problem with stakeholder analysis is that it does not at any point confront the issues of transaction and ownership costs. It might be argued, for example, that transaction costs prevent stakeholder firms being formed and that, although social gains are potentially available from such governance arrangements, they can only be achieved through the intervention of the state. In societies such as the UK and the USA, however, where the legal system is flexible enough to permit considerable experiment with govern-ance arrangements, it is not clear that costs of transacting are so great as to prevent the emergence of stakeholder-controlled companies. As has been seen, cooperatives and mutuals have been established and have thrived in the past. An alternative view would be that stakeholding has never emerged spontaneously because it incurs levels of collective decision-making costs which render it vulnerable to investor-owned competition.

Consider the history of the retail cooperatives again. These were origi-nally local societies. They attracted support from socialist thinkers and were considered to be 'good employers'. Yet, as Robertson and Dennison (1960, p. 91) observe, 'the relations of the co-operative societies with their workpeople are almost precisely similar to those of capitalist indus-try . . . The building of the bridge between consumption and control has left the gulf between day-labour and control nearly as wide as ever.' The pioneers and those that followed in the cooperative movement seem intui-tively to have recognised that extending control rights to labour would complicate matters without conferring any additional advantage. Life was complicated enough as it was. The cooperative was a response to transac-tional hazards in consumer markets. It was therefore logical to give control rights to consumers, providing ownership costs could be kept within bounds. If there were no significant hazards in the market for local retail labour there was no point to extending ownership in that direction. Robertson and Dennison write that the cooperators' 'shrewdness' was thus carried to 'disappointing lengths', but the pursuit of purely ideolog-ical goals requires very special conditions to be successful in a market setting.[38]

Similar comments could be made about the failure of labour–capital partnerships to evolve in spite of the attractive potential properties discussed in section 6. Although Meade cleverly aligns the interests of labour and capital using a neoclassical framework, the possibilities for disagreement among the labour force deriving from differing levels of skill, differing trades, geographical locations and ages would still be substantial. If, on the contrary, the labour interest were plausibly homogeneous, there might then be no advantage to giving outside investors control rights. Small amounts of equity capital could be financed internally while a requirement for non-firm-specific capital assets could be debt financed. For labour–capital partnerships to evolve, we would have to imagine large transactional hazards in both labour and capital markets combined with low collective decision making and monitoring costs for the outside investors and inside workers.[39]

12. CONCLUSIONS

Economic analysis indicates that generalisations about the effect on performance of profit sharing are not possible. Everything will depend upon the precise specification of property rights and the detailed circumstances of each case. In some institutions, *all* residual claims are held by workers and are not tradable. In others, the residual claims are held by a subset of workers. In yet others, the residual is shared between consumers or club members. Other possible governance arrangements mentioned above include capital–labour partnerships (Meade), consumer–labour cooperatives (Robertson and Dennison) or, indeed, 'stakeholder' firms (Hutton). Theory predicts that the behaviour of such differently structured enterprises will be dissimilar, even though they may all be said to embody an element of profit sharing.

Survival of the various possible forms will depend upon the economic environment in which they are placed. What transactional hazards are faced by the patrons of a firm? Are monitoring costs high? Does the controlling group have diverse interests or is it homogeneous? Are conditions appropriate for mutual monitoring to be effective? Are large quantities of capital required? Is this capital firm-specific or entirely non-specific? How important is the generation of firm-specific human capital to the success of the firm? In this chapter, we have seen how these and other factors will influence the ability of a profit-sharing firm to survive against the competition of alternative forms.

Some institutions, however, do not merely share profits widely; they abjure them entirely. Given the importance which has been attached throughout this book to the allocation of rights to the residual as a means of inducing effort, it is, at first, surprising that some firms might deliberately sacrifice all incentives from this source. Yet the non-profit sector is a substantial one in most economies. Chapter 11 is devoted to a discussion of the rationale and characteristics of the non-profit enterprise.

NOTES

1. *Principles of Economics* (eighth edn), (1925), London: Macmillan, p. 627.
2. See Hansmann (1990) for further discussion of these cases.
3. Important contributions were made by Ward (1958), Vanek (1970, 1975, 1977), Furubotn and Pejovitch (1970), Meade (1972), Chiplin, Coyne and Sirc (1977), Sirc (1979), Moore (1980), among many others.
4. The simplicity of the model should be emphasised here. I do not wish to imply that worker ownership will never be an effective institutional form; merely that the factors so far discussed militate against it.
5. Weitzman and Kruse (1990) survey the empirical evidence on the relationship between profit sharing and productivity.
6. Williamson (1975, p. 37) considers the importance of 'supplying a satisfying exchange relation' though not in the context of worker ownership or cooperatives. See also Chapter 6, section 8.
7. An interesting critique of the fable of the barge can be found in Garvey and Swan (1988).
8. A simple example of the 'paradox of voting' is given in Chapter 4, section 7.2.
9. Hansmann (1990), p. 169.
10. Readers may recognise in this paragraph a purely verbal exposition of Fisher's 'separation hypothesis'. Any textbook on intermediate microeconomic theory will provide a more formal discussion.
11. Even here it is also necessary to assume that the time horizon of the individual decision-makers in the labour-managed firm is no less than the life of the assets being financed (unless the net returns are assumed to be constant throughout the assets' life).
12. Furubotn (1976) presents a long-run analysis in which the maximand of the firm is a welfare index of a particular group of workers rather than 'surplus per worker'.
13. It is not clear whether, in a multi-period analysis, Kahana and Nitzan would envisage original group members being permitted to rejoin a labour-managed firm if product prices recovered. Without such a right, group size would presumably continue to ratchet downwards over time. On the other hand, one might expect 'returners' to be unwelcome, as they will dilute the earnings of those who stayed with the team. Efforts to maintain secrecy about high surpluses would be predictable.
14. If the labour market were so efficient that workers could costlessly and immediately find employment at a competitive rate of remuneration, these conclusions would require amendment. Faced even with a short-run rise in the price of their product, existing worker partners would be happy to see others recruited at a competitive rate in the knowledge that the issued certificates would immediately be cancelled and the new workers would leave when the price (and hence the distributable surplus) fell back to its normal level.
15. In Meade's analysis, most attention is directed at the possibility that entrepreneurial gains may not be permanent. If a portion of the worker's labour shares is converted into tradable capital share certificates then, when the profits disappear, the remaining labour shares will not yield a return as great as that available in other firms. More labour share certificates would then have to be issued to prevent labour leaving (Meade, 1989, p. 10). As pointed out in the text, however, even if the converted capital certificates represent gains that are 'permanent' in some sense; that is, they reflect long-run competitive advan-

tage deriving from the accumulation of specific human capital, there is still a problem associated with making them tradable, for then dependency will be reduced.

16. For a much fuller explanation of these possibilities see Meade (1989), pp. 14–18.

17. William Makepeace Thackeray, *Vanity Fair* ([1848] 1987), Penguin Classics, p. 497.

18. These are the factors isolated in Kandel and Lazear (1992), p. 808.

19. Adam Smith, *The Theory of Moral Sentiments*, (1767), (3rd edn), Part 1, p. 84. The quote is perhaps slightly out of context since Smith is trying to explain why people bother to strive for positions of distinction, wealth, and public office. Nevertheless, the implications for other contexts would seem clear.

20. For a full exploration of the view that 'intentional communities' (that is, those groups which form in order to achieve particular collective purposes such as religious communes or political parties) rely on imposing a degree of dependency on members in order to maintain discipline and achieve their goals, see Michael Hechter (1987), *Principles of Group Solidarity.*

21. If members of the group are not prepared to punish observed shirking, the effectiveness of mutual monitoring will be fatally undermined. To play their part in the imposition of punishment, people will have to believe that failure to punish will itself be punished. A structure of these beliefs may be self-supporting, but also may be fragile and inclined to unravel. The situation is entirely analogous to that analysed in Chapter 8, section 6, with respect to the managerial labour market. 'The punishment dilemma' is discussed in detail by J.M. Buchanan (1975), *The Limits of Liberty*, University of Chicago Press, Chapter 8, in the context of mechanisms for the governance of entire states rather than of individual firms.

22. The following account relies completely on Hood and Yamey (1957).

23. *The Times*, 31 January 1873, quoted in Hood and Yamey (1957), p. 314.

24. Each member had one vote, and interest on 'shares' was, in practice, a steady five per cent per annum.

25. Hood and Yamey (footnote 1, p. 320) indicate that the management of the enterprises resisted the demands of the 'shareholders' and supported 'ticket holders'. In 1874, half the Civil Service Supply Association (CSSA) management resigned in protest when shareholders moved to increase their proprietary rights. They formed another society, the New Civil Service Cooperative Ltd, to maintain the 'spirit of cooperation'. Eventually they were taken over by the CSSA in 1906.

26. Anti-monopoly policy is considered in more detail in Part 3.

27. Hansmann (1996), p. 149.

28. Hansmann (1996), p. 168.

29. Sometimes the term 'mutual' is used wherever an enterprise excludes outside investors from governance. Thus, the worker and consumer cooperatives discussed above would be termed 'mutuals' as would the non-profit enterprises investigated in Chapter 11. In this section, we are mainly concerned with the financial sector. A more detailed discussion of mutual enterprise widely defined using historical examples from the UK can be found in Ricketts (1999). Leadbeater and Christie (1999) investigate the present role of mutual enterprise, also in the UK. They emphasise that mutual enterprise is still quantitatively significant and that in certain areas of welfare provision is growing.

30. See Raynes (1964), Chapter 6.

31. The Prudential operated with unlimited liability until 1881.

32. Dennett (1998), pp. 35–6.

33. Hansmann (1996), p. 266.

34. Scottish Widows, originally established in the early nineteenth century to improve the financial position of the survivors of deceased clergy and teachers, was demutualised in 1999. In 1997, it had funds under management of £28 billion. Standard Life fought a successful battle to resist demutualisation during 2000. Equitable Life, one of the oldest surviving mutuals in the UK, has faced serious financial problems after the directors were held to have exceeded their lawful powers in determining the allocation of final bonuses to the members. Unfortunately, they had given 'guarantees' to a subgroup of members which created a conflict of interest with those without 'guarantees'. This

interesting case is discussed in Ricketts (2000). It suggests that the directors had not considered that mutual status might limit what promises could be made to particular people.
In terms of the theory of economic organisation, the distinction between an ownership
relationship and a purely contractual relationship appears to have been hopelessly
muddied.

35. Davies (1998) quotes George Moller of the Amsterdam Exchanges (AEX) as follows:
     'Now, once we have consulted the market users, we make a decision. But for a mutual it
     is very hard to make any decision – you get an awful lot of lobbying from your members.'
36. The possibility that state regulation might have reduced the competitive advantage of
     mutual governance in the post-1860s US life insurance industry has already been men-
     tioned above. Leadbeater and Christie (1999) observe that the state as a regulator 'has
     frequently played a critical role, tipping the balance in competition between mutuals and
     investor-owned companies' (p. 21).
37. Claims to reserves built up over the history of life insurance companies give rise to prob-
     lems in investor-owned companies as well as mutual companies. Axa, the French insu-
     rance group, has recently been involved in litigation over the distribution of a two billion
     pound 'orphan estate' that it acquired when it took over several UK companies.
     Prudential, the UK's largest life assurer faces, at the time of writing, a similar problem
     deciding on the distribution of a four billion pound fund between shareholders and
     policy holders.
38. See, for example, the section on 'intentional communities' in Chapter 11, subsection 4.4.
39   Furubotn (1988) discusses different models of codetermination and the circumstances
     in which they might be expected to succeed.

11.   Non-profit and charitable enterprise

[At an eleemosynary feast] '*it is well known, that the entertainer provides what fare he pleases; and tho' this should be very indifferent, and utterly disagreeable to the taste of his company, they must not find any fault . . . Now the contrary of this happens to the master of an ordinary. Men who pay for what they eat, will insist on gratifying their palates, however nice and even whimsical these may prove; and if every thing is not agreeable to their taste, will challenge a right to censure, to abuse, and to d--n their dinner without controul.*'

(Henry Fielding)[1]

1.   THE NON-PROFIT ENTERPRISE

Institutions which cannot distribute residual profits and issue no exchangeable or non-exchangeable claims to profits are non-profit enterprises. Non-profit enterprises have a board of trustees who are responsible for appointing managers to run the day-to-day administration, and for ensuring that the activities of the enterprises are compatible with the purposes for which they were established. They are frequently observed in areas such as education and health provision or where charitable (that is, redistributional) objectives are being pursued.[2]

A difficulty with the definition of non-profit enterprise suggested above is that it would appear to include organisations of the state which provide services free to consumers. Every state-run school, for example, might be considered a non-profit enterprise. It is therefore useful to distinguish institutions that sell their output in the market from those that are in receipt of subsidies and may provide services free of charge. Hansmann (1980, 1987) suggests the term *commercial* non-profit enterprise, where sales of goods or services provide the major source of revenue. Enterprises in receipt of subsidy are called *donative* non-profit firms. Again, it is useful to distinguish subsidies which derive from the state and those that are provided from voluntary private giving. The former defines a situation of *bureaucratic supply*.

Sales of services, financial assistance from the state, and donations from private sources can vary widely as a proportion of total revenue, and it will always be possible to argue about the point at which a *bureau* becomes a *non-profit enterprise*, or where a *donative* non-profit firm becomes *commercial*. Nevertheless, the terminology reflects distinctions which are of great importance for incentives and behaviour.

Another significant issue concerns the governance of the non-profit enterprise. Some non-profit institutions give their *patrons* collective rights to nominate trustees and thereby to determine the general policy of the firm. These enterprises are called *mutual* non-profit firms. In giving voice to the mutual interests of their patrons, they resemble cooperatives, but, unlike the cooperative, they are unable to distribute residual profits to their members. Other non-profit institutions have a board of trustees that is self-perpetuating – making appointments and accepting resignations. Because 'control' of these non-profit firms is dependent upon the character of board members, Hansmann (1980) calls them *entrepreneurial* non-profit organisations.[3]

Nationalised firms present a further problem for terminology. It might be argued that the absence of residual claims combined with the sale of its output means that the nationalised firm is in the *commercial* non-profit category. This would clearly be unsatisfactory since, amongst the objectives set for them, managers of nationalised firms may be asked by the responsible ministers of state to meet a profit target. Rather than regarding the nationalised firm as being without residual claims, therefore, it may be more suitable to see these claims as non-exchangeable and spread over the entire body of the tax-paying public. Profits and losses accrue to taxpayers. This implicit sharing of the residual amongst taxpayers puts the nationalised firm in a category of its own. Bureaucratic supply will be considered later in this chapter (in section 5) while a fuller discussion of public enterprise is delayed until Chapter 13 in Part 3.

2.   GOVERNANCE PROBLEMS AND THE NON-PROFIT ENTERPRISE

It will be evident from the brief description of the governance arrangements in non-profit firms in section 1 that effort incentives are likely to present a serious problem and that managerial discretion will be substantial. An analysis based upon the property rights theory of Chapter 4 would predict a low level of productive efficiency in non-profit enterprise. Trustees will have no pecuniary incentive to monitor the effectiveness of managers. Managers cannot be given incentive payments based on profit sharing, holdings of common stock, or stock options. Bonuses based upon other dimensions of performance are costly to contrive in service industries where output is difficult to measure objectively and 'team production' is often important. The takeover threat does not operate. At first sight, these features would appear to be a serious handicap and to suggest poor survival qualities on the part of non-profit enterprise in the competitive battle between institutional arrangements.

Managers might be expected to have considerable discretionary power under these circumstances, and theories of the activities of non-profit institutions have been developed in this 'managerial' tradition. Nicols (1967) argues, for example, that mutual (that is, non-profit) savings and loan associations in the USA will behave differently from stock (that is, for profit) associations. Depositors in mutuals receive 'shares' but 'typically surrender their proxies to management on opening an account' (p. 337). The result is a diffused 'ownership', but 'control' concentrated in management. Nicols describes management at one point as 'a self-perpetuating autocracy' (p. 337). Managers can divert the resources of mutuals for their own benefit, he argues, by inflating expenses. Where new entry is restricted, managers may operate a policy of creating artificial shortages and then 'ration' loans to those who purchase insurance or other services from private companies in which they have a personal interest. Nepotism is likely to be higher in mutual than in stock associations; a proposition Nicols tested by the simple expedient of checking the names of chief executive officers and other officers to see how frequently officers had the 'same name'.

A similar type of analysis is presented by Newhouse (1970) in his model of a non-profit hospital. Trustees, administrators and medical staff will inflate the quality of medical services provided in the interests of prestige. Expensive medical equipment will be under-utilised, while Newhouse uses 'accreditation' as an index of quality and notes that 'there is a lower percentage of accreditation among the proprietaries than among the voluntaries' (p. 69). We will discuss Newhouse's model briefly again in section 4. For now it suffices to note that the view of non-profit institutions taken by Nicols and Newhouse suggests that they can survive only in a protected environment. Both are explicit about this: 'The mutual is an institution which can survive only at the cost of continued governmental restriction of competition' (Nicols, 1967, p. 346). Similarly, Newhouse explains the non-profit hospital by reference to legal barriers to entry and favourable tax status. Thus, both writers take the same position with respect to non-profit enterprises as Adam Smith took with respect to the joint-stock firm. They can survive only with an 'exclusive privilege'.

Property rights are undoubtedly attenuated within the non-profit firm, but, for a variety of reasons, it would be wrong to deduce that effort incentives are entirely absent.

1. Trustees, for example, have legal obligations which the state may enforce (even if imperfectly). Because non-profit enterprises often face a lenient tax environment, the tax authorities have an interest in ensuring that the non-profit firm does not abuse this position. Some monitoring from this source can therefore be expected.

2. Further, non-profit firms may employ people who gain satisfaction from the knowledge that they are engaged in some 'higher' purpose than the simple pursuit of monetary reward. This might logically result in the existence of a degree of peer pressure. As was seen in Chapter 10, peer pressure requires participation in a collective outcome. In the context of a profit-sharing enterprise the outcome was the firm's residual. If a non-profit firm produces a good which confers joint benefits on its workers (such as the successful achievement of charitable or public objectives), a similar mutual interest in the collective result will exist. That incentives of this type are important is suggested by the large amount of voluntary labour that is used by non-profit firms and by the fact that non-profit firms pay lower wages to people of similar skills than do profit-making firms.[4] It has been suggested that non-profit firms 'screen' for a particular type of person. Someone who gains satisfaction from 'high quality' output will be willing to work for a lower wage in a non-profit than in a profit-making firm providing that the former produces 'higher quality' services than the latter (at least as perceived by the worker). The worker's interest in quality of output *per se* will then provide an incentive to monitor peers. As we saw in Chapter 10, however, a fairly small scale of operation is likely to be necessary if this mechanism is to be effective.

3. Competition in the product market is another force which will operate on the non-profit firm. Non-profit firms can become bankrupt. Providing that the managers and staff are to some degree dependent on the firm and cannot costlessly and immediately find equivalent employment elsewhere, bankruptcy is something they will try to avoid. Competition with other non-profit enterprises which face similar incentive and control problems is not predicted to be effective. However, as Hansmann (1980, p. 863) points out 'commercial non-profits almost always operate in competition with proprietary firms that provide similar services, suggesting that the competing advantages and disadvantages of the two types of firms are closely balanced'. The incentive mechanism is therefore similar to that analysed by Hart (1983) and discussed in Chapter 8, whereby proprietary firms provide incentives to 'managerial' or, in this case, non-profit firms. Government suppliers are also often active in the areas served by non-profit enterprises, such as hospitals, educational establishments or research organ-

isations. There is evidence that costs are higher in government than in other forms of enterprise. In nursing homes in the United States, for example, one study indicates[5] that employees were paid 6.6 per cent more than in profit-making establishments and ten per cent more than in church-related non-profit nursing homes. Steinberg (1987, p. 130) comments that 'it seems unlikely that governmental competition provides the same spur to efficiency that for-profit competition does'.

4. Another incentive mechanism discussed in Chapter 8 was the managerial labour market. The absence of tradable residual claims makes it more difficult to signal good managerial performance in the context of non-profit enterprise. Information about managerial competence is more likely to be 'impacted' within the firm and the overall performance of management is very difficult to measure effectively when objectives are complex. There are situations, however, in which objectives are fairly clear and success is easily signalled. Donative non-profits require the services of fund-raisers. Success in this area can easily be signalled in terms of amounts of money raised during particular time periods. Good fund-raisers can be sought by non-profit firms and a market in their services can develop. People with fund-raising skills can form consultancy firms which operate on a profit-making basis, selling their services to non-profit firms.

Although monitoring by the tax authorities, peer pressure, competition from other firms, and competition in the labour market may all play a part in mitigating the adverse effects on work incentives of non-profit status, it is still not clear what are the advantages of the non-distribution constraint. Unless we can point to some specific comparative institutional advantage associated with non-profit status, Nicol's (1967) assertion that profit-oriented firms will put non-profit firms out of business when the latter are not protected by the state would appear well founded. What does the non-distribution constraint enable a non-profit enterprise to achieve which could not equally be achieved by a profit-making firm, a partnership, or a cooperative?

3.   THE RATIONALE OF THE NON-PROFIT ENTERPRISE

3.1   Contract Failure

Recent work in the transactions costs tradition suggests that non-profit status is partly a response to the adverse selection problem. The non-distribution constraint acts as a crude, but possibly effective, consumer protection device. Papers by Hansmann (1980), Easley and O'Hara (1983) and Holtmann (1983) explore the idea that non-profit enterprises are a response to particular kinds of information problem and thus 'contract failure'. Consider once more the non-profit firm in the context of the principal–agent problem of Chapter 5. Easley and O'Hara (1983), following the work of Hansmann (1980), discuss the circumstances in which a non-profit organisation 'can be at least partially described as the solution to an optimal contracting problem' (p. 531). In their formulation, the consumer becomes the principal and the firm or manager becomes the agent. A profit-making firm faces no constitutional constraints on the payment of executives, production techniques, or profits distributed. Providing the consumer is supplied with the benefits for which he or she has contracted, the manager of the firm is left to arrange production by any means deemed appropriate. Diagrammatically this is equivalent to the consumer (principal) receiving a definite payoff, and the manager (agent) bearing the entire risk (point ϕ in Figure 5.5). In contrast, a non-profit firm is constrained to pay 'reasonable' compensation to its executives and cannot distribute any profits. This might be interpreted as the manager receiving a definite, constant, payoff and the consumer bearing the risk by receiving variable benefits depending upon the state of the world (point θ in Figure 5.5). Assume that consumers can observe neither the effort of managers nor the state of the world, then if consumers are risk averse and managers are risk neutral a first-best position will be achieved with a for-profit institution (at ϕ in Figure 5.6). This approach would suggest that non-profit institutions merely cope with managerial risk aversion, and, to the extent that this can be achieved by other methods, it implies a limited role for the non-profit firm.

There is, however, another possibility that consumers cannot observe the benefits which they hope they are buying. If I buy medical care, I may not be in a position to judge whether the services were really delivered or not. This is obvious if my purchase is on behalf of someone else who is not capable of reporting to me, but it might also apply to my own purchases. Whether the treatment I am being offered is really in my best interests or merely serves to increase the profits of the supplier may be very difficult to determine. A profit-maximising agency employed to transport food to the starving would have an incentive to pocket all charitable donations if the actual delivery of food could not be monitored. In circumstances such as these, the ability to control the supplier's remuneration may be valuable. Where benefits are completely unobservable, a profit-maximising firm will produce no benefits at all. A non-profit firm will operate at minimum effort, but, providing this minimal effort results in some positive output, it may nevertheless permit activities not possible under alternative institutional arrangements.

Complete 'unobservability' of output is an extreme assumption designed merely to illustrate the 'contractual' approach to non-profit institutions. In less extreme conditions, a profit-oriented firm would have to worry about the loss of reputation if it cheated its customers, and this may be a constraint on managerial rent seeking which is as effective as restricting managerial remuneration. We do not observe non-profit garages, for example, even though customer ignorance may be substantial. The consequences of using a poor garage may be expected to be less severe than a poor hospital, and the discipline of continuous dealings is likely to be more significant. In the case of hospitals, therefore, a bias in favour of high-quality service for the managerial reasons mentioned by Newhouse (1970) might be precisely the type of bias that customers would prefer.[6]

Commercial non-profit enterprises will always be subject to competition from profit-making firms who can try to develop reputations for fair dealing and high-quality performance over time. Wherever *donations* are an important source of funds, however, non-profit status would appear to be necessary to reassure contributors that their money will not simply be used to augment profits.[7] Similar comments apply to the suppliers of volunteer labour. Were these volunteers to believe that their efforts left service quantity or quality unaffected and merely raised the profits of the proprietor or the shareholders, their commitment would presumably rapidly wane. Non-profit status is a mechanism for ensuring that all resources are used within the organisation and cannot be distributed outside. Resources may be used inefficiently relative to some ideal, but they may be more likely to be used to the donor's satisfaction than in a for-profit enterprise.

3.2 Government Failure

Weisbrod (1975) was among the first to propose that non-profit enterprise enabled adjustments to be made to the quantity of public goods produced by governments. In Chapter 2, the role of political institutions in the provision of public goods was discussed. Markets, it was argued, would fail to produce an efficient quantity of these goods because of the free-rider problem. Here the standpoint is reversed. When collective choices are made concerning the quantity of public goods to finance using the political process, it would be unlikely that all the citizens in a jurisdiction would express themselves satisfied with the result. Some would have preferred a greater quantity of public goods to be provided (given the methods of taxation used to finance them) and others might have preferred less. Where tastes and incomes vary, dissatisfaction is the inevitable outcome of any political decision.[8] Voters wishing to receive *greater* quantities of public goods than provided by the state could band together to make marginal adjustments. This private provision of additional public goods could be effected through non-profit firms.

In this model, non-profit firms grow up to pursue the collective purposes left unsatisfied by the government. They take non-profit form because they rely on voluntary donations to finance their activities. In this respect, Weisbrod's approach to non-profit firms is complementary to Hansmann's contractual failure approach. Weisbrod is simply exploring the ultimate source of the demand for the services of non-profits. He still requires Hansmann's analysis to explain why cooperatives, partnerships, or other types of firm could not be used for the provision of additional public services.[9]

Clearly, the existence of *donative* non-profit enterprises with charitable or other public objectives contradicts the pure free-rider model of individual decision making. Apparently people *are* prepared to contribute to certain public causes even when uncoerced. Some of this giving may be explained by reference to the pursuit of status, prestige or a good reputation; that is, indirectly to self-interested motives; but it is also possible to model donor behaviour on the assumption of a degree of altruism and truly philanthropic motives. People might care about the consumption levels of certain goods experienced by others.[10] Even in this case, however, the free-rider problem would inhibit donations unless the very act of giving conferred a degree of satisfaction.[11] Models of donor behaviour (for example, Steinberg, 1985) therefore assume that donors gain satisfaction both from provision of the public good and the personal act of giving. For our purposes here, however, the main thing to note is that the existence of commercial non-profit enterprise can be explained without reference to altruistic or other ethical responses. Donative non-profit enterprises providing non-excludable public goods, on the other hand, do seem to imply a degree of altruistic behaviour by donors, although purely self-regarding motives can be invoked even in this case.[12]

3.3   Tax advantages

Non-profit enterprises receive favourable treatment by the state in most countries. This may take the form of exemption from sales, property or income taxation (as in the United States at the state level) and may include other advantages, such as privileged postal rates, preferential regulatory treatment, the issue of tax-exempt bonds, the use of public contracts to favour non-profit firms and so forth. Some economists have argued that much of the recent growth in non-profit enterprise can be attributed to these advantages rather than to the inherent ability of the form to cope with contract failure.

Steinberg (1987) reports that tax advantages do result in a larger share of non-profit enterprise. Hansmann (1980, p. 881) argues, however, that 'tax considerations are probably far less important than is commonly thought'. In support of this conclusion, Hansmann argues that non-profit firms were well established in certain fields before the era of public sector growth and high taxation. Further, tax and regulatory advantages have tended to follow the expansion of non-profit enterprise into a field rather than vice versa. A more recent contribution by West (1989) takes a far more sceptical view. Tax and other advantages, he argues, can be converted into benefits for those who work in non-profit firms. The 'self interest theory of non-profit formation predicts a larger ratio of non-profit to for profit firms in jurisdictions where tax rates are high' (p. 170). Non-profit status can be used as a means of shielding the income from non-tax-exempt activities. Commercial research, for example, might easily be passed off as charitable activity, thus giving an advantage to non-profit- compared with profit-oriented research organisations.

West (1989) offers a public choice view of the growth of non-profit enterprise. It is the suppliers, in his view, who gain from non-profit status and therefore lobby governments to achieve this end. Consumers of the output of commercial non-profit firms are dispersed and much less influential. West argues that consumers may have a prejudice against profit making in certain areas of activity and may not be inclined to resist the spread of the non-profit firm. If this 'prejudice' were related to an implied appreciation of contract failure on the part of consumers, Hannsman's view of the growth of the non-profit sector would be supported. In the area of commercial non-profit enterprise, however, West doubts that adverse selection leading to contract failure is sufficiently serious to give the non-profit firm an advantage over the profit-making firm.

4. EXAMPLES OF NON-PROFIT ENTERPRISE

The following four subsections offer a short discussion of non-profit enterprise in particular areas from the perspective of the theory of contract failure.

4.1 Hospitals

In the United States, two thirds of employment in the short term and general hospital sector is in non-profit enterprises. As we have seen, discussion of hospitals has formed a major part of the debate over the rationale and efficiency of non-profit firms. On the one hand, the dominance of non-profit hospitals can be seen as an efficient response to consumer ignorance by providing a form of quality assurance. Alternatively, it can be argued that the services provided by hospitals are purchased by medical practitioners on behalf of their patients and that these expert intermediaries are well able to assess hospital quality. Non-profit status might even result in quality which is excessive and which reflects the desire for professional standing of the medical staff.

Newhouse's model of the non-profit hospital is in this tradition. In Figure 11.1, the constraint qq' represents combinations of quantity and quality of service that can be offered while permitting the hospital to break even. At low levels of quality, demand for the hospital's services is oq'. Higher quality raises costs, but it also results in a rise in quantity demanded over a certain range. An administrator wishing to maximise demand for the hospital's services would pick point n on the constraint. Beyond this point, further increases in quality cause quantity demanded to fall. Higher quality is assumed to increase demand, but this effect is outweighed by the consequential rise in prices. If medical staff trade off quality against quantity in the way indicated in Figure 11.1 they will choose a point such as m.

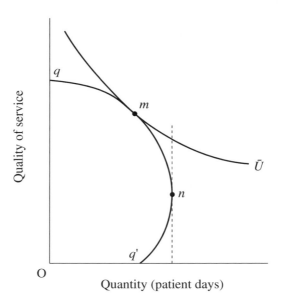

Figure 11.1   Newhouse's model of the non-profit hospital

The model implies, like all theory in the 'managerial' tradition (see again Chapter 4), that the hospital can exploit a degree of monopoly power. This is not entirely unreasonable because medical staff will have an incentive to lobby to restrict new entry. Wendling and Werner (1980), for example, study the use of 'certificate of need' regulation in some states in the USA. If new hospitals have to convince a regulatory agency that there is a 'health need' in the area before new capacity can be built, existing hospitals have an incentive to organise themselves politically to fight these proposals. With completely 'free entry' by proprietary as well as non-profit hospitals, staff in the non-profit hospital sector will themselves have to pay (perhaps be accepting lower remuneration) for increasing quality to levels in excess of those desired by patients. We would then observe the different types of hospital concentrating in different parts of the market. Non-profit hospitals would provide services of 'over-high quality' partly financed by their staff, while proprietary hospitals would provide the mainstream services.[13]

Assuming, for present purposes, that the unobservability of hospital quality is not a crucial problem for contracting, the dominance of the non-profit form of enterprise still requires an explanation. Hansmann (1980 and 1987) speculates that a historical lag is involved. In the nineteenth century, hospitals were less commercial and more donative in their financial structures. Redistribution was as important as the provision of technical services. As hospitals become more commercially oriented over time, they will find themselves, according to this view, increasingly threatened by proprietary organisations.

Another possibility is that there are public benefits associated with the activities of hospitals, even in the modern world, which attract voluntary donations and which therefore require non-profit status. A philanthropic concern for the medical care of poor people would certainly be included here, but, in addition, economists have isolated some other important issues. Medical facilities cannot be created quickly, for example, and some excess capacity can be seen as a form of insurance against the occurrence of serious disasters such as accidents or epidemics. The methods used to cope with similar problems in other markets (such as the laying down of electricity generation capacity to cope with a freak winter) involve the charging of higher prices, when this capacity is used in order to recoup the capital costs. In medical markets, however, the probability attached to future freak demands would seem even more difficult to assess, while the prospect of raising prices at a time of strain on resources might appear unacceptable. In these circumstances, donors can be seen as paying for excess capacity and thereby correcting for another form of contract failure.[14] Non-profit status provides assurance that funds are indeed used to produce additional medical capacity and are not distributed as profits.[15]

4.2   The University

The non-profit status of universities provides a similar type of puzzle to that discussed above. To the extent that universities exist to teach students, the contract failure approach to the non-profit enterprise would seem unlikely to apply. Students in higher education are able to judge the quality of their teachers and are intelligent and articulate enough to complain in terms at least as colourful as those used by Fielding's diners in the quote which opens this chapter. Adam Smith robustly supported the system of direct payment of lecturers by their students in order to provide clear incentives to the staff to maintain quality.[16]

Research activity at universities presents a more promising area for the discovery of contract failure. The results of research activity do not necessarily lead to easily appropriable and marketable 'discoveries'. They may simply contribute to a general climate of scholarship. This can be seen as having a value in itself. It can also be seen as providing the background of work and ideas which may 'pay off' at some future point, even if no one has yet quite perceived the ways in which this will happen. Research of this type is a form of public good, and its finance raises all the usual free-rider problems in addition to intractable problems of valuation. Given that individuals are prepared to donate resources for 'pure research', a good reputation for high-quality results and non-profit status would appear necessary to reassure benefactors.

Where research work is commercially oriented, however, some form of professional partnership would be predicted to be the preferred institutional form. Steinberg (1987, Table 7.1) reports that in 'basic research', 67 per cent of expenditures in the United States are accounted for by non-profit institutions. In 'research and development', 72 per cent of expenditures occur in the for-profit sector. From this evidence, we might be tempted to deduce that universities which concentrate on teaching and on commercial research have little to gain from non-profit status and that pure research provides the only serious source of contract failure.

Once again, however, Hansmann in his extensive (1980) survey of the role of non-profit enterprise suggests another interpretation. He notes that many colleges in the United States do little research of the public good variety but that donations are still very significant. These donations come largely from the alumni of the colleges. They enable colleges to educate students at lower fee levels than would otherwise be possible. In effect, the colleges can be seen implicitly as running a voluntary and spontaneous student loans system. Students receive, through below-cost fees, an implicit loan which many of them repay much later in their lives by donating funds to their old college. The reasons for voluntary compliance with this system are the same as those mentioned in section 3(2). This explanation for non-profit status is in the contract-failure tradition because it is a response to the hazards that otherwise beset the financing of human capital. Commercial loans are difficult to raise for educational purposes. The lender cannot establish control over human capital assets in the event of default by the borrower. Student loans schemes which use private sources of finance in 'the open market', therefore, usually require the state to act as a guarantor. Individual non-profit colleges, on the other hand, can be seen as creating the conditions required for voluntary compliance on a much smaller scale.

4.3 The Arts

Why are many performing arts groups organised along non-profit lines? Arguments for state subsidies have been developed based upon the public benefits thought to be associated with a lively performing arts sector. A paternalistic desire to encourage people who are ignorant of the arts to sample them and develop their taste has also played a part. Charitable objectives such as bringing 'high' culture within the price range of the relatively poor are frequently voiced. The relevance of these aims to the institutional structures adopted by the suppliers is not obvious, however. They might all be pursued within the context of profit-making, cooperative, or non-profit arts organisations.

As with hospitals and universities, the ability to attract private donations for the various charitable or public purposes mentioned above could be affected by whether or not a theatre or other group of performers is allowed to distribute its surpluses. However, the idea that private donations have much to do with redistributional or educational objectives is difficult to accept. Audiences are still made up of relatively affluent people, even after private donations have reduced the price of tickets. Indeed, many of the affluent people attending performances will be those who have also donated funds.

An alternative explanation of donations in the contract-failure tradition draws upon the cost characteristics of theatre and opera productions.[17] The overhead costs of mounting a theatre production will often be large, while the marginal costs of serving an extra member of the audience at a point short of the full capacity of the house may be close to zero. Average costs per attender will therefore decline as audience size rises. It is possible, however, that there is no single price for tickets that will permit the theatre company to cover its costs. This could be so even if the sum total of willingnesses to pay by all the members of the audience were more than sufficient to justify the performance.

A method of increasing revenue from the sale of tickets is for the theatre to introduce a system of price discrimination. More comfortable or conveniently located seats may carry higher prices in the hope that those members of the audience with the greatest willingness to pay will be induced to choose them even though their valuation of the extra comfort may fall short of the price differential. Considerations of social status may also enable the theatre to charge differential prices for seats in different parts of the house. The situation is illustrated in Figure 11.2. Curve cc' traces the average cost per member of the audience for a theatre performance. Curve dd' is the market demand for the performance. It requires differential pricing of p' and p'' for the company to break even. No single price will suffice.

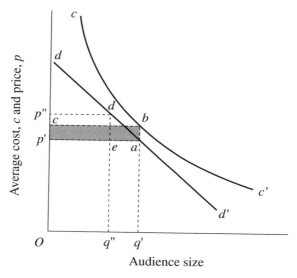

Note: Area $p''dep'$ is equal to area $cbap'$

Figure 11.2   Donation as a method of voluntary price discrimination

Supposing, however, that the company finds it impossible, even by introducing gradations of comfort and social status, to discriminate sufficiently between people to cover its costs; voluntary donations might still enable a production to take place. Donations, in other words, function as a voluntary system of price discrimination. By revealing their high willingness to pay for live theatre performances, donors help to finance the overhead costs which are strictly joint to all the audience members. Non-profit status encourages such donations because it ensures that money is used to lower seat prices or finance the costs of performance and is not distributed as profit.

In circumstances where demand for live performances is sufficiently great so that a theatre can operate at close to full capacity over a long run of performances, donations and voluntary price discrimination schemes will be unnecessary. Thus, in the United States and the United Kingdom, there is a large for-profit theatre sector which produces popular plays and musical shows. It is in the 'higher culture' sector where audiences are smaller that donations become a significant part of theatre finance and non-profit status is more common. Modern and experimental artistic work is also likely to be pursued within a non-profit institutional framework.

The role of the state as a major 'donor' to non-profit enterprises in the arts is also of great significance. It is perhaps no surprise that the analysis of non-profit institutions in the performing arts reported above was developed in the United States. There, public support comes indirectly via tax deductions for donations. In continental Europe, *direct* government support is much higher. Frey and Pommerehne (1989, p. 22) report that 'in the case of theatres, governments typically provide more than 80 per cent of the cost, and in France more than 90 per cent'. In the United States, the figure for direct government support is five per cent. The United Kingdom is located somewhere in between these positions. The overwhelming level of state support in continental Europe is also reflected in the structure of theatre companies. 'The system of state opera and state theatre is not restricted to such famous institutions as La Scala of Milan, the Paris Opera and the Vienna Burgtheater, but applies equally to hundreds of theatres and operas in the capitals and provinces' (Frey and Pommerehne, p. 41). In other words, the performing arts sector in some countries is effectively part of the public administration. The supplying institutions are nearer to *bureaucracies* than to commercial or even donative non-profit enterprises. Bureaucratic supply will be discussed briefly in section 5.

4.4   The Club

Clubs form to provide collective goods for their membership. In circumstances where it is possible to exclude non-payers, goods consumed jointly by groups of people can be produced by competing clubs. Buchanan (1965), for example, investigates a situation in which some excludable public good can be produced within a club. For a *given* size of club, the members will have to agree about how much of the jointly consumed good to finance. If they agree to share the cost equally between them, and if the members have similar tastes and incomes, they will all agree to improve club facilities up to the point at which the marginal private benefit to each member equals the extra club fee that is implied. Conversely, for each level of service provision in the club, there will be an optimal membership size.

New members will benefit existing ones by contributing a share towards the cost of club facilities. On the other hand, if facilities are subject to 'crowding', new members will, after a certain point, reduce the service flow experienced by the established group. The club will expand to the point at which these additional 'crowding costs' just equal the benefits from lower fees.

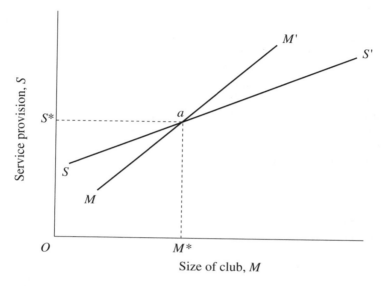

Figure 11.3   The optimal club: Buchanan's analysis

Figure 11.3 summarises the above argument. Curve SS' traces the chosen level of service provision at each club size. Curve MM' traces the chosen club size for each level of service provision. If existing members do not wish to change the level of provision or the membership size, the club is operating at its optimal point. This is point a in Figure 11.3, with membership M^* and service level S^*. As we saw with worker-owned firms, decision-making costs will be much lower if the club has a fairly homogeneous membership. Further, there will be a tendency for clubs to cater for particular income levels. Rich people will be dissatisfied with the level of service provision if other club members are much poorer, whilst the poorer members will chafe at the fees imposed in rich clubs.[18]

Buchanan's analysis does not, however, explicitly address the question of why provision of club services should be organised in non-profit ventures. Proprietary organisations, it might be argued, could provide a range of services for different classes of consumer. In principle, there is no reason why tennis or other sports facilities, for example, should not be produced by for-profit organisations. High-service-level, high-fee, low-crowding institutions would compete in the market with other firms offering different attributes. Health clubs are often profit-making entities. Arguments for non-profit status based upon consumer ignorance or the attraction of charitable donations would appear somewhat forced. Club-type facilities which require investment in large amounts of capital equipment would seem to favour for-profit enterprise unless (as in the theatre argument) viability requires a system of voluntary price discrimination and the market is not large enough to permit the formation of many institutions catering for particular client groups.

An exception to this reasoning occurs when clubs form not merely to *finance* an output of joint benefit but actually to *produce* the output. A social club, for example, produces an output which derives from the activities and interaction of the members themselves. As a group they produce a 'social milieu' which confers satisfaction on each person. Such clubs will be non-profit enterprises. If social clubs were run along proprietary lines, the members would be vulnerable to 'hold-up'. The benefit that they receive from club membership is a form of rent which derives from the special conditions which the club creates. A proprietor, having established these conditions, would be tempted to increase the membership fee so as to appropriate some of the value of the social environment which is actually created by the members. Even allowing trade in membership rights might be resisted on the grounds that the acceptability of a new member will not necessarily be simply related to his or her willingness to pay.

Club goods of the social variety take us to the very margins of the subject matter of this book. Nevertheless, it is important to appreciate the great range of institutions within which 'business', broadly defined, is conducted. The social club has a place in a spectrum of institutions, which ranges from the private firm at one end to what sociologists call 'intentional communities' out in the furthest reaches at the other. Hechter (1987, p. 148) defines 'intentional communities' as 'obligatory groups whose members seek to produce joint goods – like a sense of community, friendship, love, and the feeling of security – all of which flow from the existence of social harmony'. People who form groups to produce joint goods take their 'profit' in the form of the subjective net benefits which accompany membership. Profits do not take a monetary form and cannot by definition be distributed to outsiders. The very nature of the institution enforces the non-distribution constraint.

It would be a mistake to assume that obligatory groups are of no economic importance. There is an element of the 'intentional community' in many contexts. A university, for example, may be seen as creating a 'scholarly atmosphere' which appeals to its staff members and represents a joint 'club-like' good. No doubt, this is a somewhat feeble echo from the past under modern conditions, but from a historical point of view the communal side of university life could be a significant explanation of its non-profit structure. It is also worth noting that incentive and control problems afflict 'intentional communities' as much as the other institutional forms we have been studying. Such communities will often expect a great deal from their members and will enforce compliance by ensuring that members are dependent on the group and have a great deal to lose from expulsion. Hechter shows, for example, that successful groups (as measured by the duration of their survival) are characterised by hierarchy (monitoring), cultural homogeneity, limits on privacy, group rewards, and public sanctions. He comments that commitment to the group is not a matter of socialisation or identification. Rather, the structure of a communal institution 'may reveal its doubts that such identification is likely to develop at all' (p. 165).

5.　BUREAUCRACY

A bureaucracy can be viewed as a form of non-profit enterprise with the government acting as the main or even exclusive provider of funds. Because the output of a bureau is not marketed, competition in the product market is weak. Indeed, it is usual to assume that a bureau has a monopoly of the supply of some service. The threat of bankruptcy is also removed, since the state stands ready to finance deficits and will often directly employ the staff of the bureau. Bureaucrats are less constrained, therefore, than the managers of commercial non-profit enterprises or non-profit firms that rely on donations from the private sector.

Niskanen's (1968) model of bureaucracy is a managerial model. He assumes that bureaucrats maximise their budget in the ultimate interests of power, status or prestige and are constrained only by the demand curve for the services they provide. The situation is illustrated in Figure 11.4. Curve MV is the demand curve faced by the bureaucrat. It shows the marginal willingness to pay for output by the bureau's consumers. The ultimate consumers may be taxpayers, but their demands are reflected through a political process so that MV really represents the valuations of politicians. Curve MC is the marginal cost curve. As drawn, bureaucratic output will be ON, at which point the total benefit derived from the output will be equal to the total costs incurred. The bureaucrat's budget will be given by area $abNO = dcNO$. The total willingness to pay for service level ON is extorted from the 'consumer' in the manner of a perfectly discriminating monopolist. Niskanen's approach to bureaucracy therefore gives all the bargaining power to the bureaucrat. The justification for this rather extreme assump-

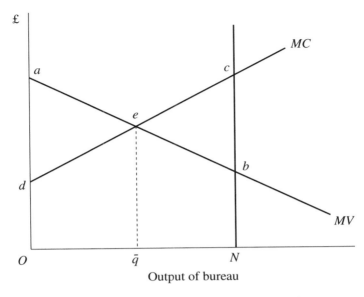

Figure 11.4   Niskanen's model of the budget-maximising bureau

tion is that only the bureaucrat knows the true position of the marginal cost curve and is capable of exploiting the ignorance of politicians.

Clearly, this is a rather special set of circumstances, and Migué and Bélanger (1974) amended Niskanen's approach and presented a more general managerial discretion model. They first calculated 'the margin of discretion enjoyed by the manager' (p. 30) as 'the excess of revenue over minimum cost'. This is the curve *ON* in Figure 11.5. They then assume that the manager 'can choose to divide his discretionary profit between only two desired goods: output and a combination of other expenses' (p. 31). The size of the bureau is still important but it is now combined with other possible items yielding managerial satisfaction. Niskanen's early work implied that bureaucrats would operate in a technically efficient way. Economic inefficiency resulted entirely from the 'over-expansion' of services. Migué and Bélanger imply that managers will take their rewards in other 'cost-increasing' ways, such as unnecessarily large numbers of staff, lavish equipment or 'on-the-job leisure'. The manager's utility function can be represented conventionally as a set of indifference curves, and the final position is at point *m* in Figure 11.5.

A feature of each of these models is that the monitoring of bureaucrats by their 'principal' is nowhere explicitly discussed, and the precise nature of the bureaucrat's contract, incorporating as it might various incentive

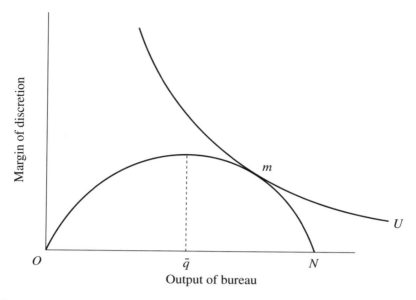

Figure 11.5   Migué and Bélanger's bureaucrat discretion model

devices, is ignored. This led Breton and Wintrobe (1975) to criticise Niskanen's assumption that bureaucrats are perfectly discriminating monopolists constrained in their depredations only by the maximum total willingness to pay for each level of service. Instead, they argue that 'politicians are able to enforce their preferences by the use of control devices' (p. 206). These control devices are used to gain information and reduce 'over-expansion'. They are worth instituting up to the point at which the additional costs of control equal the marginal benefits from control. Musgrave (1981) also disputes the bureaucratic over-expansion hypothesis, which he argues largely follows from the behavioural assumptions of Niskanen's model and which disregards checks built into the budgetary process.

The explicit incorporation of monitoring into models of bureaucracy has been attempted by a number of theorists. Lindsay (1976) compares the problem of monitoring a manager of a joint-stock firm with monitoring a bureaucrat. Monitoring financial statements will not be appropriate for a government enterprise if output is not marketed or if the manager's job is to modify market outcomes in the interests of social policy. Lindsay concludes that crude 'performance indicators' will be established relating 'output' to total costs. Output, however, is often very difficult to define and measure, and may be multidimensional, and thus 'the output of government enterprises will, in general, contain fewer of those attributes which are "invisible" to Congress, that is, whose presence and quantity are not measured' (p. 1066). 'Observable' attributes, on the other hand, will be overproduced, with the result that the average cost of these 'observable' attributes is predicted to appear lower in government enterprises than in proprietary enterprises. Managers in government enterprises (for example, in Veterans Administration Hospitals) have less incentive to incur staffing costs to produce non-observable benefits such as reassurance to patients, closer attention to personal comfort and so forth, compared with proprietary hospitals.

Property rights theory predicts that production within a bureau confronts greater problems of incentives and control than does production in any of the other institutional arrangements discussed so far. Empirical studies which attempt to estimate the technical and economic inefficiencies of bureaucratic supply, however, face considerable methodological problems. If a bureaucracy really does produce a non-excludable public good, state-financed zero-priced provision would seem the only institutional form capable of delivering substantial output. The crucial question is then whether *all* the units of the public good should be produced by a *monopoly* supplier staffed by employees of the state, or whether a set of suppliers competing for public contracts is a feasible option. Defence, for example, has long been considered an archetypal public good. Yet it does not follow that the inputs into 'defence production' must all be organised within state bureaucracies. Military aircraft, tanks and other weaponry are produced within private firms; maintenance of equipment can be undertaken by private contractors; food can be delivered by private caterers and so forth. Most of the cost comparisons that have been made have therefore concerned the relative efficiency of bureaucracies and other types of institution when contracting out is possible. A fuller discussion of the problems of contracting with the public sector appears in Chapter 15.

6. CONCLUSION

A great range of different institutional structures has been discussed in this chapter. It is also apparent that the institutional arrangements which exist at any one time are far from immutable and that quite radical changes can occur over a period of time. The 1980s saw a ferment of institutional change in many countries of the world (not least in the countries of the old Soviet Union). However, how far the economic theory which has been reviewed in this book helps us to understand the forces making for institutional change or provides us with opportunities beneficially to influence institutional change is still an open question. In Chapter 12 we look at various approaches to the analysis of institutional change including the evolutionary perspective. A more detailed appraisal of public policy towards some important areas of economic organisation is attempted in Part 3.

NOTES

1. Henry Fielding, *Tom Jones* ([1749] 1955), Collins Classics, London and Glasgow, p. 33.
2. Rudney (1987) estimated that the non-profit sector in the United States accounted for eight per cent of the labour force in 1982 and (because of the service industry bias of non-profit firms) for thirteen per cent of all jobs created between 1972 and 1982. Healthcare accounted for fifty per cent of all 'philanthropic employment'. Education and research absorbed a further twenty per cent.
3. The term reflects the influence of Board members who are not required to consult outsiders – rather like the members of a private company. There is no implication that firms structured in this way will necessarily be entrepreneurial in the sense discussed in Chapter 3.
4. Rudney (1987) estimated that volunteer labour amounted to about 8.4 billion hours in the United States in 1980 with a value of $62.6 billion. The average wage in the philanthropic sector was about three-quarters of the average wage for all employees (p. 59). Borjas, Frech and Ginsburg (1983) found that non-profit nursing homes (especially those with religious affiliations) pay substantially lower wages to comparably skilled workers.
5. Schlenker and Shaughnessy (1984).
6. In the case of hospitals, some theorists find arguments for non-profit status based upon adverse selection unconvincing. It is the services of the medical practitioners rather than the hospitals which are difficult to assess by the lay person. See section 4 below.
7. Steinberg (1986) points out that donations might be used in efforts to raise even further donations and this would be difficult to police. Indeed, in a donative non-profit enterprise, it will pay to spend an additional dollar on fund raising if it raises any sum greater than a dollar. The marginal donative product of fund raising should therefore equal 1. Steinberg shows, however, that small donations will not affect the total expenditure on fund raising undertaken by the non-profit enterprise and that such donors will reasonably assume that the full amount of their donation is available internally for service provision.
8. In some circumstances, it is possible to show that the outcome of a public choice process will be the one preferred by the median voter. However, as mentioned in Chapter 10, collective choices can be unstable and paradoxical.
9. James and Rose-Ackerman (1986, pp. 19–31) survey theories of non-profit enterprise formation and the empirical evidence for Weisbrod's hypothesis. Studies have attempted to link indicators of heterogeneity in communities with the share of non-profit enterprises in particular sectors.
10. When person A gains utility from person B's consumption of a good, an external benefit is associated with higher consumption levels on the part of B. Externalities of this type are sometimes called 'distributional externalities' by economists. See Hochman and Rogers (1969).
11. Sugden (1984) argues that people may feel an obligation to donate if others do. If one person's donation to a good cause indirectly benefits me I will feel obliged to reciprocate. It is difficult to explain the 'stylised facts' of charitable giving without recourse to some such mechanism. If people cared only about the total final income of a charity, news of a large donation would tend to reduce the donations of others. Charities would then have an incentive to keep large donations secret. In certain contexts this may happen, but news of success in fund raising is often seen as encouraging new donors. Subventions from the

state for certain public purposes may 'crowd out' private donations to non-profit enterprise, but where state subsidies are interpreted as a signal of competence, 'negative crowd-out' (that is, a rise in private donations) is a possibility. For a review of the empirical evidence up to 1986 see Steinberg (1987, p. 132).

12. Corporate donations to charitable causes will be mainly concerned to advertise the product and create a suitable image. The donation of a person's time may yield social and even economic payoffs (via experience and the development of productive skills) in the future.

13. The reader should not deduce from this that proprietary hospitals will not care about quality. It is merely that they will only care to the extent that patients are attracted. They may, for example, be much better than some non-profits at the more 'non-technical' (but to patients extremely important) aspects of quality such as the provision of reassurance and emotional support. *Donative* non-profit hospitals, especially those financed by the state, may be particularly poor at producing these dimensions of quality both because of the difficulty of objective measurement in these areas and because adverse patient reactions and complaints are commercially less important. See Lindsay (1976), reported in more detail in section 5.

A final sophistication is worth noting for completeness. It would theoretically be possible for a proprietary hospital to provide the high-quality services by agreeing with staff to introduce better medical facilities in exchange for lower wages. Such an agreement would require the staff to trust the proprietary hospital not to divert their lower wages into profits instead. It is this lack of trust which ultimately leads to the non-profit hospital.

14. Theoretically, consumers of medical care might buy options to hospital care at various dates in the future, contingent upon the occurrence of certain events. Clearly, the transactions costs discussed at length in Chapter 2 would impede these arrangements.

15. Frank and Salkever (1994) review the size and scope of the non-profit health sector in the USA.

16. Rosen (1987) investigates the economics of teaching in more detail. Smith's comments on educational institutions occur in Book 5 of *The Wealth of Nations*.

17. Hansmann (1981) discusses the rationale for non-profit status in the performing arts.

18. Tiebout's (1956) theory of local governments as competing providers of public services to a mobile population is in the same tradition as Buchanan's analysis of clubs.

12. Evolution and economic organisation

'The fact is, human reason can carry you a little too far – over the hedge, in fact. It carried me a good way at one time; but I saw it would not do. I pulled up; I pulled up in time.'

(Middlemarch)[1]

1. THE VARIETY OF THEORETICAL APPROACHES

Over the last ten to twenty years, institutional change has proceeded at a rapid pace in many countries. The wholesale collapse of the organisational structures of the planned economies of Eastern Europe is of obvious importance, but even in Western countries, which could loosely be described as 'market-oriented' and 'capitalist', changes have occurred which few would have predicted in the 1970s. The privatisation of industry; the experiment with new contractual methods in the public sector; attempts to stimulate competition and liberalise entry in certain industries; the setting up of new regulatory agencies; an upsurge in takeovers, management buy-outs and buy-ins; unprecedented interest in different models of corporate governance – all these features have been characteristic of recent years.

An introductory appraisal of some of these developments and of public policy in the sphere of economic organisation can be found in Part 3. It is clear that the economic analysis of institutional structure cannot be regarded as a somewhat peripheral or secondary part of economics. On the contrary, it is central to our understanding of how economic systems actually operate. In spite of this pivotal role, a fully developed theory of economic organisation has yet to emerge. As we have seen in earlier chapters, there exist many different strands of thinking which can be observed woven together in varying combinations. Two very broad approaches can be distinguished, however, and the tension between them can be found running through much of the economic writing about economic organisation. For simplicity, they are referred to below as the *neoclassical* and the *radical* approaches respectively.

1.1 Neoclassical Analysis of Organisations

In Chapter 1, the impossibility of a theory of organisational structure built upon the assumptions of full information and costlessly enforced contracts was demonstrated. A world with these characteristics – the 'general equilibrium' world of Arrow and Debreu – would be free of organisational structures, although there is an implied assumption that a perfectly effective state acts as a costless enforcer of contracts. Recognising that the world is one of imperfect information and imperfectly enforceable property rights does not mean that the neoclassical research programme becomes obsolete and that a 'paradigm change' is inevitable, for neoclassical microeconomics is built, not on any particular assumptions about the costlessness of information or the economic environment of transactors, but on the technique of constrained maximisation. Applying this technique to situations in which information is distributed asymmetrically between contracting parties, in which the environment is risky, in which people will behave opportunistically if that proves to be in their own interests, and in which enforcement is part of the problem of optimal contract design, has ensured an ample supply of new contributions to economics journals in the neoclassical tradition. The archetypal form of this analysis is the theory of principal and agent, which was reviewed in Chapter 5 and applied in many different contexts throughout Part 2.

A major problem with neoclassical analysis of this type is that it suffers from several of the weaknesses which motivated the development of institutional economics in the first place. Transactors may not have *full* information, but in calculating the optimal response to particular circumstances they seem to have access to vast quantities, nevertheless. If the principal cannot observe the agent with perfect reliability and at zero cost, both parties know the characteristics of the monitoring technology, the probability distribution of states of the world, the influence of the agent's effort on this probability distribution, the degree of risk aversion associated with each contractor and so forth. Where agents differ from each other and the adverse selection problem arises, further contractual problems are confronted. The existence of transaction-specific capital (either human or physical) complicates the issue further.

In spite of this complexity, the theory has been used extensively to explain institutional structures. Again, in Chapters 6 and 7 we saw how asset specificity combined with opportunism influenced hierarchical incentive structures within the firm and relationships with suppliers. Principal–agent models were also used to cast light on management incentives (Chapter 8), the financial structure of the corporation (Chapter 9) and on other types of enterprise (Chapters 10 and 11). On the other hand, application of the theory to particular circumstances confronts substantial methodological problems. Unless concepts such as asset specificity, risk aversion and monitoring costs can be objectively identified there is a danger of rationalising all observed institutional structures as an efficient response to transactional problems. Economists' efforts in this area then call to mind Tristram Shandy's father who 'like all systematic reasoners . . . would move heaven and earth, and twist and torture everything in nature, to support his hypothesis'.[2] Simon (1991, p. 27) expresses this point when he comments that while the New Institutional Economics is 'compatible with and conservative of neoclassical theory, it does greatly multiply the number of auxiliary exogenous assumptions that are needed for the theory to work'.

1.2　Radical Approaches to Organisations

Critics of the neoclassical paradigm argue that the approach is flawed at a very fundamental level. It provides a theory of contracts but not of organisation. In neoclassical theory, people choose optimal contractual arrangements in stochastic environments where information can be generated by monitoring or search using a known technology. Differing circumstances will produce differing optimal solutions for the contractors. The contracts chosen will not be 'first best'. Indeed, from the point of view of traditional theory there may be many 'inefficiencies' associated with the contractual outcome. In Chapter 6, we saw how the payment of 'efficiency wages' might lead to unemployment and, in general, how effort incentives could lead to 'bond-posting' or the taking of 'hostages'. These contractual devices produced dependency on the firm and implied that payment was in part a rent on resources sunk in the relationship – an *enforcement rent*. However, although such contracts may be far from 'first best', it is not clear that they must necessarily be 'incomplete'. For the critics, though, organisations are inextricably linked to contractual incompleteness.

Radical schools of institutional economics all have as their basic starting point the idea that organisations exist in order better to handle change and uncertainty. This includes adaptation to events outside the organisation, and the devising and initiating of new developments within. As explained at length in Chapter 6, contracts in the face of continual change and uncertainty are 'relational' rather than 'classical'. They are loosely specified and operate within the context of some 'governance structure'. Although Williamson falls within the neoclassical camp with his great emphasis on the problems posed by opportunism and asset specificity (and hence contract enforcement), the plain problem of coordinating resources and establishing valuable information flows in a world of continual change is enough to require some form of 'organisation'.

Indeed, for the radical critics, the firm as a means of generating and using information is a more significant concept than the firm as a means of contract enforcement. The primary purpose of economic organisation, in the radical view, is to provide a vehicle for entrepreneurship and a system capable of generating, coordinating and using new knowledge. The focus of attention, in other words, is less on the contractual necessity of introducing *enforcement rents* and more on the creation of *entrepreneurial rents*; a distinction which has been emphasised at several points throughout the text, especially in Chapter 7 and the first sections of Chapter 8.

The neoclassical and radical research programmes both contribute to the study of economic organisation, and individual scholars often appear to be looking for a place in both schools. Williamson's work, for example, sometimes has a neoclassical flavour in its emphasis on the problem of contract enforcement in the presence of opportunism, but the underlying acceptance of bounded rationality means that the firm as a device for coping with change and uncertainty is perhaps more central to Williamson's overall scheme. The problem with taking this idea seriously, however, is that a different analytical framework from the one that most economists find familiar is required. People cannot be seen as constrained maximisers in a world where there is true uncertainty (as defined by Knight)[3], where information about constraints has to be discovered, and where the ability of the human mind to see the possible implications of a piece of information is bounded. It is for this reason that theorists wishing to develop the more radical research programme in economic organisation have found it useful to adopt a more evolutionary perspective.

2. THE RESOURCES OF THE FIRM

Use of the term 'radical' to describe the evolutionary research programme should not be taken to imply that the ideas are extremely recent. It is true that neoclassical theory has dominated the discipline for many years, but the founders of modern economics such as Marshall and Menger were well aware of the tensions that we have been discussing. The rhetoric of Marshall's *Principles of Economics* has a strong evolutionary bias which reflects a clear recognition of the importance of the growth of knowledge in economic development.

> Capital consists in a great part of knowledge and organisation . . . Organisation aids knowledge; it has many forms, e.g. that of a single business, that of various businesses in the same trade, that of various trades relatively to one another, and that of the State . . . The distinction between private and public property in knowledge and organisation is of great and growing importance: in some

respects of more importance than that between public and private property in material things; and partly for that reason it seems best sometimes to reckon Organisation apart as a distinct agent of production.[4]

For Marshall, therefore, as for many more recent scholars of economic organisation, the main resource possessed by a firm is knowledge. Further, this resource was not conceived of as limited to technical knowledge possessed by employees, but also encompassed tacit knowledge, and knowledge concerning the wants of customers and the reliability and flexibility of suppliers. 'External economies are constantly growing in importance relatively to Internal in all matters of Trade-knowledge.'[5] Loasby (1991) draws attention particularly to Marshall's treatment of the external relations of the firm. 'By his use of the term "external organisation" to describe a firm's network of contacts, Marshall had defined the management of this network as a normal business activity' (p. 84). The notion of a network as an intermediate form of organisation between the firm and the entirely arm's-length market transaction has become of great interest and concern to business analysts recently, but it has a very long pedigree.[6]

The special knowledge embodied in each firm's resources, procedures, contacts, team relationships and so forth, produces what Chandler (1990, 1992) calls 'organizational capabilities'. The relationships established by each firm enable it to do things which other firms cannot do, or cannot do so well, or so quickly or so cheaply. Organisational capabilities take time to replicate. They permit the firm to be 'more than the sum of its parts' (1992, p. 86). Other writers use slightly different terminology, but usually they are driving at the same basic point. Porter (1990) uses the notion of 'competitive advantage' which can derive from a variety of possible strategies, such as the search for cost-reducing methods, greater product variety, high product quality and so forth. Which strategy a firm will pursue, however, is determined by the capabilities of its resources. Teams that are used to concentrating on improving product quality will find their routines, procedures, contacts and technical knowledge inappropriate for the search for cost reductions or entirely new products. Kay (1992, p. 119) sees the distinctive capability of a firm as determined by its 'architecture'.

> Architecture is the most subtle and elusive source of competitive advantage. It is a feature of the set of contracts taken as a whole, and it emphasises the relational rather than the classical aspects of these contracts; by its nature, a classical contract can be written down, and what can be written down can be replicated.

If organisations create competitive advantage from the generation of knowledge, the link between entrepreneurship and organisational structure is a close one. In Chapter 3, we saw how Kirzner interpreted the entrepreneurial function entirely in terms of intermediation in the market. The modern conception of the firm as the creator of competitive advantage implies that entrepreneurs gain from working in groups, and that Wu's idea of the firm as a group of cooperating entrepreneurs is closer than Kirzner's to recent work in business strategy. On the other hand, Kirzner's view of the entrepreneur as gradually uncovering the possibilities latent in a given set of circumstances does have close affinities with that of Marshall and does lend itself to evolutionary analysis. By looking at the firm as a coalition of Kirznerian entrepreneurs, an evolutionary theory of the firm can be developed which does not draw on neoclassical principles of maximisation. Shackle's world of boundless possibilities and 'the anarchy of history' precludes analysis. Kirzner's conception of a world of continual but marginal discoveries might at least be compatible with historical evolution – a process which may be seen as neither totally anarchic nor totally predictable.

3. EVOLUTION IN ECONOMICS

3.1 Biological Analogies

Biological analogies have a long history in Economics. Marshall (1925, p. 240) specifically mentions the influence that Malthus's writing on population is said to have had on the development of Darwin's thinking.[7] Most of Marshall's analysis of economic organisation is couched in the language of evolution and the 'struggle for survival'. The most famous of his biological analogies concerns the life cycle of firms which he compares to the trees in a forest (pp. 315–16). As saplings, the trees compete for light and air against their larger neighbours and many fail to develop and die. Later, the more successful ones grow rapidly until they dominate the environment. The years of this domination are numbered, however, and they eventually atrophy and are replaced by younger more vigorous trees. Modern scientific understanding of genetics and ecology has advanced greatly since Marshall's time so that the analogy now seems extremely loose. Where in a joint-stock company, for example, is the genetic material which condemns it to inevitable decline? Penrose (1952, p. 804) was induced to complain that 'biological analogies contribute little either to the theory of price or to the theory of growth and development of firms'. The analogies are descriptive rather than exact.

One may sympathise with Penrose's irritation with loose descriptive connections between the natural and economic worlds, but the problem of providing a coherent intellectual framework capable of explaining the behaviour of the firm as a generator and interpreter of information remained. It was Alchian (1950) who suggested a systematic incorporation of the ideas of evolution and natural selection into economics. The economic system, he argued, could be interpreted as 'an adoptive mechanism which chooses among exploratory actions generated by the adaptive pursuit of "success" or "profits"' (p. 16). People are not maximisers. They merely wish to survive and, in the economic context, this implies making positive profits. Those who do not make positive profits are selected out by the economic environment. Survival invites imitation by others, who use those procedures that are thought to ensure it.

Penrose argued that if conscious imitation in pursuit of survival qualities is admitted, the analogy with biology breaks down. Firms might then attempt not merely to adapt to a given environment but to change the environment in their favour. This might be accomplished, for example, through political pressure or by some startling innovation. In terms of the analysis of Chapter 3, we might see a Kirznerian firm as adapting to a given environment but a Schumpeterian firm as actively creating the conditions necessary for its future progress. Whatever their formal relationship to biological models of evolution, however, economic models have been developed in recent years by Boulding (1981) and most notably by Nelson and Winter (1982).

3.2 The Evolution of the Firm

At the heart of Nelson and Winters' approach is the assumption that the firm has, at any given time, a set of 'decision rules' and 'routines'. These 'routines' might be regarded as the genetic material of the organisation. As in the system proposed by Alchian, routines and decision rules which produce profits lead the firms which have adopted them to grow relative to other firms experiencing lower profits. Nelson and Winter simulate evolutionary change by linking profits to investment in the firm and hence to its rate of growth. In addition to the mere use of existing routines, search takes place within the firm for new or adjusted routines. 'Our concept of search obviously is the counterpart of that of mutation in biological evolutionary theory' (p. 18). Search and selection then results in an evolutionary time path.

It is an interesting aspect of Nelson and Winters' approach that 'search' and the implied entrepreneurial activity is itself seen as bound up with 'routines'. 'Problem solving efforts that are initiated with the existing routine as a target may lead to innovation instead' (p. 130). Kirzner would be sure to point out that no routine can produce innovation automatically. A machine-repair person who notices, while applying a routine procedure, that a cheap alternative to this procedure would be possible, is alert in Kirzner's sense. Noticing such improvements requires the exercise of a human faculty quite distinct from following routines. However, what Nelson and Winter emphasise is that the established routines may condition the scope for successful search by determining the likely information sources that people will encounter. Routines which acquaint people with different activities within the firm, for example, may be more likely to produce ideas for improvement than routines which confine people within a more limited sphere.[8]

Successful routines, argue Nelson and Winter (p. 119), will lead the firm to expand into areas where the success can be replicated. 'A firm that is already successful in a given activity is a particularly good candidate for being successful with new capacity of the same sort.' Chandler (1992, p. 93) strongly supports this view and suggests that it was precisely these advantages of experience and learning which led to the growth of many of the major firms who were 'first movers' in chemicals, electrical engineering, motor cars, telephony and office machinery after the First World War. 'Such growth was driven much less by the desire to reduce transaction, agency and other information costs and much more by a wish to utilize the competitive advantages created by the coordinated learned routines in production, distribution, marketing, and improving existing products and processes.' His argument supports the view of the firm as a means of making use of information – not simply of the technical variety, but of the accumulated experience of the resources of the firm which become embodied in its routines. Further, it is not simply access to particular pieces of information that confers competitive advantage on the firm, but the ability to *generate* such information. The entrepreneurial function of the firm is thus central to this conception.[9]

3.3   Market Relationships and Evolution

Evolutionary forces can be seen as of wider-ranging influence than the establishment of routines within the firm, however. Relationships with suppliers, customers and workforce may also be affected by perceptions of reliability, reputation, trust, expertise, and so forth which have evolved over a long period of time.

3.3.1   Trust

At many points in earlier chapters the importance of establishing trust between trading partners has been emphasised. Firms that were trusted by their workers could institute hierarchical incentive systems involving bond-posting which would be unavailable to other firms (Chapter 6). Trust in suppliers could result in a less vertically integrated industrial structure (Chapter 7). Firms with a good financial record and close contacts with their financiers would find it cheaper to raise finance for further expansion (Chapter 9). In other words, a reputable history is a valuable asset that cannot be wished into existence. Creating a reputation requires a degree of continuity over time and continual reinforcement in repeated deals. Marshall (1925, p. 198) noted the potentially disruptive consequences of lack of continuity in exchange relationships, when he wrote 'change may be carried to excess; and when population shifts so rapidly, that a man is always shaking himself loose from his reputation, he loses some of the best external aids to the formation of a high moral character'. Our ability to transact with others profitably in the present thus depends to some extent upon the history of our relationship with them.

Modern treatments of the process of innovation emphasise the importance of collaboration between firms. Collaborative ventures grew in importance during the 1980s in areas such as biotechnology, microelectronics and information technology. In the United States, the Microelectronics Computer Corporation (formed jointly by 19 firms) played a part in persuading Congress to exempt joint research ventures from antitrust legislation such as the Sherman Act. In Europe, the European Computer Research Centre also represented an attempt to share the costs and results of research between a group of member firms. These cooperative associations require the development of trust and experience over time. Metcalf (1992, p. 226), in a review of types of collaboration in the innovation process, emphasises that 'collaborations involve more than contracts; they involve interactions between the organisations to alter the behaviour of at least one of the parties'. Firms, by their collaborative associations become part of an evolutionary process of 'group selection'. Survival depends not merely upon the existing capabilities of a firm and selection in the market (the first level of competition), but also on the ability to generate new capabilities (the second level of competition). This type of competition can involve the formation of collaborative associations with other firms in a group. 'Collaborative R and D is a prime example of group selection at the second level of competition' (p. 223).

3.3.2 Codes of conduct

Market transactions rely on the existence of codes of conduct which limit uncooperative behaviour. As was seen in Chapter 1, it is possible to construct repeated games in which self-interested responses on the part of individuals produce cooperative outcomes. These games rely on a high probability of repetition of a transaction or on the ability to recognise characteristics likely to correlate with a transactors's trustworthiness. Again, biological analogies can be used. The Hawk–Dove game[10] indicated how, over time, the equilibrium proportion of those playing an aggressive non-cooperative strategy might be determined. Where a Hawk can be identified in advance, the payoff to the Hawk strategy will be reduced. Hawk strategies will be met with Hawk strategies, and the resulting conflict will be dis-advantageous. Aggressive non-cooperation is only a good survival strategy in a world in which most other individuals are cooperative and cannot modify their strategy according to the characteristics of their opponents.

Once we admit the possibility of informative signals about the reliability of transactors in a market, conventions and codes of conduct supportive of cooperation can evolve.[11] Conventions are rules of behaviour which are self-enforcing in that it is in each person's individual interests to recognise them and comply with them. Sugden (1986, p. 8) argues that these conventions may take on a moral dimension. When people fail to meet our expectations and breech some time-honoured convention, we complain of injustice. 'Some of our ideas of rights, entitlements and justice may be rooted in conventions that have never been consciously designed by anyone. They have merely evolved.'

These conventions have the added advantage of economising on decision-making costs. Bounded rationality implies that our decisions will often be made on the basis of 'rules of thumb' or historical precedents. Following conventions and adopting behavioural patterns that other trans-actors see as reliable and honest have the advantage of making no demands on a person's decision-making powers. It is perhaps not sufficiently empha-sised in the recent economics literature that bounded rationality places limits on opportunistic behaviour. 'Plotting covetousness and deliberate contrivance in order to compass a selfish end, are nowhere abundant but in the world of the dramatist; they demand too intense a mental action for many of our fellow-parishioners to be guilty of them.'[12] Covetousness and contrivance play an abundant role in the world of the institutional econo-mist, as we have seen, but it is interesting that, even in a social world small enough for its inhabitants still to be called 'parishioners', George Eliot emphasises not the peer pressure leading to cooperative behaviour but the plain mental effort required in planning anything else. Once social evolu-tion has produced a functioning set of conventions or norms, therefore, inertia can protect them from systematic challenge over long periods of time.

3.4 An Ecology of Institutions

Interdependencies between institutional structures provide another analogy with the natural world. At several points in earlier chapters, the consequences for one organisational structure of the existence of another have been commented upon. Absence of firms with sufficient information about new methods to act as reliable suppliers leads to vertical integration at one time followed by disintegration as the new structures are developed (Chapter 7); competition from the proprietary firm constrains the managers in a dispersed joint-stock firm through competition in the product market (Chapter 8); the takeover threat and hence the viability of the dispersed joint-stock enterprise depends upon the existence of concentrations of private wealth capable of intervening in the market for corporate control (Chapter 9); the managerial labour market which gradually develops to serve the large dispersed corporations may later be used by worker-owned firms to recruit managers (Chapter 10); the performance of public enterprises may be assessed and incentive packages constructed using comparative information generated in other sectors (Chapter 11). Although analytical tractability often requires it, a given institutional form cannot, therefore, be seen as entirely independent of the environment of other existing institutions or of the time path followed by their development.

4.   EVOLUTION AND EFFICIENCY

According to the radical evolutionary thinking set out in section 3, the organisational structures that exist at any one point in time cannot be explained entirely by reference to conditions prevailing at that time. Instead, they must be seen in the context of the evolutionary time path that has produced the search routines, networks of contacts, cultural norms, conventions, and informal enforcement mechanisms that accompany institutional developments. Institutional structures are *path dependent*. Further, it is not clear that the path is leading anywhere in particular.

Again, it is possible to discern two different views about the direction of the evolutionary path. Some theorists such as Demsetz and Williamson, being closer to the neoclassical world of optimisation than many others, tend to take an optimistic view. In Chapter 4, Demsetz's view that property rights tend to develop in a way conducive to the realisation of efficiency gains was discussed. Similarly, Williamson (1993, p. 107) takes the view that evolutionary processes will produce institutions which economise on transactions costs. 'I hold only that the institutions emerging from the competitive process will be *comparatively* efficient; and I eschew reference to minimising and maximising.' The path may not always be ideal, and it may not lead to a land of perfect efficiency, but on the whole there are social benefits attached to moving on.

Others are more sceptical. At the purely theoretical level, it is easy enough to construct game-theoretic models which are consistent with the evolution of inefficient self-enforcing conventions.[13] Further, all are agreed that the 'survival of the fittest' in no way implies that those that survive are perfectly suited to their environmental niche.[14] Some historians of economic development take a notably pessimistic view of the evolutionary process. North (1991, p.98) argues that most economic history concerns the failure of economies to develop a beneficial evolutionary time path. 'When economies do evolve, therefore, nothing about that process assures economic growth.' He contrasts the history of the English colonies in America with those of Spain. The centralised structures imposed by sixteenth-century Spain at the time of Philip II led to a time path of evolution which was inimical to economic development. By contrast, those established by seventeenth-century England at the time of the Civil War and the struggle between Crown and Parliament permitted the evolution of more secure property rights and the ability to experiment with new ideas on the part of economic agents. The initial conditions proved to be far more favourable.[15]

It is interesting to note, however, that the liberating forces which underlay economic development in the United Kingdom and the United States have recently become the subject of suspicion. The fluidity and individuality which permitted experiments to be undertaken and new deals to be struck has been seen as now fatally undermining cooperative efforts. Marshall (1925, p.197) was well aware of the tensions involved. 'Changes in work, of scene, and of personal associations bring new thoughts, call attention to the imperfections of old methods, stimulate a "divine discontent", and in every way develop creative energy.' Yet, as we have already noted, such continual changes of personal association 'shake a person loose' from their reputation. Some things require trust to accomplish rather than mere energy.

A study of the United States by Dertouzos, Lester and Solow (1989) draws particular attention to what it sees as lack of training for the workforce, poor coordination of research effort, an inability to foster teamwork, and failure to agree upon common technical standards. British students of their domestic economic situation have been reading similar lists for years. The point is simply that each of these areas is thought to play a vital role in modern economic development but each confronts the decentralised market with substantial difficulties. If human capital is more significant than physical capital for economic growth; and if new knowledge is a more influential determinant of 'competitive advantage' than 'factor endowments', it is sobering to reflect that these areas are precisely those in which transactional hazards abound. Markets in human capital and information are, to a greater extent than most others, prone to information asymmetry, vulnerable to opportunism, and dependent for their effective operation on suitable 'organisation'.

The view is widely held that countries such as the United Kingdom and the United States with their decentralised and individualistic traditions are at a disadvantage in matters of economic organisation. As Adam Smith predicted, the United States evolved into the world's richest country, yet now, according to some commentators, it faces the consequences of being a 'low trust economy'.[16] The ability of individuals to escape from the coercive influence of conservative social interests that see all innovation as a threat, so necessary to the initial stimulation of new methods, carries with it disadvantages which become evident only as time advances. Sen (1987, p. 18) remarks, for example, that 'in the case of Japan, there is strong empirical evidence to suggest that systematic departures from self-interested behaviour in the direction of duty, loyalty and goodwill have played a substantial part in industrial success'. Japan, in other words, has a competitive advantage in 'organisation', an advantage which cannot be replicated easily by other countries because it rests upon an evolutionary time path which happens to have produced favourable results in the post-war era. Even for Japan, however, advantageous factors at one point in time may become disadvantageous at another. Opportunity costs are attached to strong and durable contractual bonds. Such bonds involve sacrificing the flexibility and fluidity of weaker, less durable, associations.

5.   CONCLUSION

How far people are at the mercy of the forces of economic evolution in the development of institutional structures, and how far they are able, by the exercise of reason, to mould these structures efficiently or influence the future time path, is a complex and important issue. As the countries of Eastern Europe attempt to reform their systems of economic organisation, and as other countries consider institutional innovations in areas such as the provision of public services or corporate governance, the question becomes of more than merely philosophical interest. Policy is no longer about planning good results; it is about jolting an economy from a disadvantageous evolutionary path on to a more favourable one. The very attempt has ironic connotations. If reform in Eastern Europe, for example, marks a recognition and repudiation of Hayek's (1989) 'fatal conceit' that the results of human reason and design would always be superior to those of a 'spontaneous order'; there would nevertheless appear to be plenty of room for conceit in the claim that a beneficial evolutionary time path might be ensured by the establishment of appropriate initial conditions. Such a project seems to require God-like wisdom in a rather modern sense.

The liberal school of political economy contains a strand of thought, however, which regards the preconditions for economic development as uncomplicated even if rarely occurring. Adam Smith wrote that 'little else is required to carry a state to the highest degree of opulence from the lowest barbarism, but peace, easy taxes, and a tolerable administration of justice; all the rest being brought about by the natural course of things'.[17] As we have seen, it is likely that an economist of the modern evolutionary school would regard this position as over optimistic. The behavioural norms which enable a market economy to develop may themselves take a long period of time to evolve. Further, an entirely individualistic, decentralised, market-trading economy might not develop those behavioural norms required to support it. Bowles and Gintis (1993, p. 96) argue that the Walrasian model of the economy (see, again, Chapter 1) is flawed not simply because of the informational assumptions that underlie it but because it is internally inconsistent. It assumes that transactors can rely on the integrity of other people in the market, yet the assumed impersonal and anonymous structure of exchange relations 'would provide little evolutionary support for anything but *homo economicus* with a vengeance'.[18]

Evolutionary approaches to economic organisation do not lend themselves to the easy identification of public policies which will affect beneficially a time path of development. On the contrary, they serve to confront us with the bounds on human rationality and human knowledge. It is the problem of coping with these bounds which lends the subject of economic organisation its peculiar fascination, and results in a wide range of contributions from differing schools within economics and from other disciplines. This can be frustrating, but there is as yet no theory of economic organisation which can claim to be complete and general. Until there is such a theory, we will have to be content with trying to reconcile and use various bits and pieces from different traditions. In Part 3, therefore, neoclassical, transactions cost, property rights, public choice and Austrian perspectives are all used to discuss the role of public policy in some important areas of economic organisation.

NOTES

1. George Eliot, *Middlemarch* ([1871] 1965), Penguin Classics, p. 39. The character quoted is Mr Brooke who was 'fond of going into things' but 'not too far'.
2. Lawrence Sterne, *The Life and Opinions of Tristram Shandy* ([1759–67] 1985), Penguin Classics, p. 80.
3. See again, Chapter 3.

4. Alfred Marshall (1925), *Principles of Economics* (8th edn), Book IV, pp. 38–9.
5. Op. cit. p. 284.
6. For example, Bureau of Industry Economics (1991), *Networks: A Third Form of Organisation*, Discussion Paper No. 14. Australian Government Publishing Service, Canberra.
7. Schumpeter (1954, pp. 445–6) warns against reading too much into the connection between Malthus and Darwin. 'I wish to comment on Darwin's remark to the effect that he derived inspiration from Malthus' theory of population. It seems very hazardous, to be sure, to dissent from a man's statement about his own mental processes. But quite insignificant events or suggestions may release a given current of thought . . .'
8. The Japanese system of training people to undertake a range of jobs and encouraging them to gain experience of different departments in the firm may be seen as an application of this principle (see Chapter 6).
9. Penrose (1959), in spite of her suspicion of evolutionary analogies, presented a view of the growth of the firm which concentrated on the generation and use of knowledge. Loasby (1991, pp. 59–64) argues that Penrose adopted a thoroughly Marshallian approach to the firm in her emphasis on the heterogeneous resources available to each firm, the fact that time and experience differentiate resources further, and that opportunities are gradually uncovered in the course of everyday business.
10. See again Chapter 4, section 3.
11. See also Witt (1986) on the evolution of cooperation and (1985) on the evolution of individual preferences through cultural influences.
12. George Eliot, *The Mill on the Floss* ([1880] 1979), Penguin Classics, p. 75.
13. A rule that traffic on a wide and fast road should give way to traffic on a minor road wherever such roads crossed might be self-enforcing once it had become established. It is unlikely that it would prove efficient.
14. Marshall (1925, p. 248) was himself at pains to point out this fallacy. 'The argument that if . . . a change had been beneficial, it would have been already brought about by the struggle for survival, must be rejected as invalid.'
15. Witt (1989) argues that societies can remain stagnant for centuries and then enter a phase of rapid change and innovation (p. 425). Baumol (1990) draws particular attention to the allocation of entrepreneurial talent between productive and unproductive activities. For most of human history the 'rules of the game' have channelled entrepreneurial energies into war or other forms of rent seeking. The point at which true entrepreneurship became a rational response to the set of rules and conventions that had evolved was thus of pivotal importance in industrial development.
16. See, again, Casson (1991).
17. From Dugald Stewart, *Account of the Life and Writings of Adam Smith LL. D* (1793), reprinted in Bryce and Wightman (eds) (1980).
18. It has even been argued that market systems historically have required a period of mercantilism to establish certain prerequisites for their successful operation. Baron and McGarvey (1993) have suggested that this applies to Russia under present conditions. Bowles (1998) provides a wide-ranging discussion of the interdependence between preferences and institutions.

PART THREE

Public Policy and Economic Organisation

'So that if we turn to the nagging enigma, how far do the size and form of institutions influence their effectiveness in action, it is the ecology of the matter that counts; it is the right combination of sizes and forms which should be sought for'.
(John Jewkes)[1]

13. Economic organisation and the role of the state

1. INTRODUCTION

The activities of the state can have profound effects on business. Notwithstanding Adam Smith's famous dictum that 'there is a deal of ruin in an economy' the history of the twentieth century seems to have shown conclusively that the wrong type of government action is easily capable of achieving this result. The wreckage of large-scale efforts by governments to organise major economies using a central plan during the early and mid-years of the twentieth century is strewn across the international landscape as the twenty-first century begins. Even where state intervention has been more limited than wholesale attempts to plan entire economies, governments have found that the results of their well-intended policies have frequently been disappointing.

If governments have great destructive potential it is, conversely, also true that appropriate institutions, sometimes buttressed by state power, are a necessary condition for economic advance. 'A tolerable administration of justice' sounds rather undemanding as a policy objective until it is realised that the absence of this condition is a major cause of poverty over large areas of the globe.[3] As was seen in Part 1 of this book, the gains from trade and the growth of enterprise cannot take place without clearly defined, secure and exchangeable property rights. It was also noted in Chapter 2 (pp. 42–43) that the state itself can be seen as a response to transactional difficulties in the provision of public goods. Although private substitutes may evolve when the state fails in its fundamental task of providing public goods – as, for example, when individuals band together to protect their own persons and property by hiring guards – these measures are unlikely to provide security services and other public goods as cheaply as a well-functioning state.

To cover comprehensively the entire range of public policy as it relates to business cannot be achieved in a few chapters. Instead, the objective of Part 3 of this book is to investigate some issues of critical importance; issues closely connected to the material covered in Parts 1 and 2. The objective is to consider some of the principal implications for public policy of the 'New Institutional Economics'. Attention will be focused not on highly detailed descriptions of particular government policies in different countries, since these policies are multifarious and the details change by the day, but on important issues of general principle which will be illustrated with some historical examples. We will be mainly concerned with government regulatory activity; that is, government intervention using non-fiscal instruments. This regulatory activity influences the structure of economic organisations and also concerns the methods used to influence decision making within these organisations. Organisational structure has for at least fifty years been regarded as an important determinant of economic welfare, and the state is often deeply involved in attempts to improve it.

2.   THE NEOCLASSICAL TRADITION

In traditional public finance theory, the existence of 'market failure' provides the main (though not exclusive) justification for government intervention.[4] We saw in Chapter 1 how a perfect market (with zero costs of transacting) would result in all potential gains from trade being achieved. In welfare economics, the exhaustion of all possible gains from trade is described as a state of 'Pareto efficiency' after the Italian economist Vilfredo Pareto (1848–1923). Given this ideal yardstick, it is tempting when confronted with the fact of transaction costs to argue that markets 'fail' and that the state should attempt to 'correct' for these failures. Notice that, at this very general theoretical level, the 'private' institutions and organisations (the origins and structures of which we have been discussing in Parts 1 and 2 of this book) and the 'state' activities (which form the subject matter of Part 3) are responses to the same problems – information and transactions costs. Thus the intervention of the state in the face of 'market failure' often acts as a substitute for private action and the crucial question is to determine the circumstances in which the displacement of private action will be beneficial. This requires the comparative analysis of institutions and organisational structure.

Much of the public policy literature of the 1950s and 1960s, however, failed to consider transactions costs in a systematic way. Instead of regarding state action as one possible organisational response to information and transaction costs, there was a tendency to make the unwarranted and usually unstated assumption that government action could somehow avoid such costs altogether. This approach was criticised by Demsetz (1969) as 'the Nirvana fallacy' – the assumption that governments had access to costless information not available to others and could thus achieve some idealised state of perfect efficiency. It could produce optimal amounts of public goods[5], calculate 'ideal' prices for publicly produced private goods, and impose 'efficient' taxes and subsidies to correct for 'external' effects.[6] By ignoring the information problem, this early type of neoclassical analysis therefore tended to lead to almost unlimited recommendations for state intervention. If actual markets face transactional difficulties while government action is costless, the substitution of the latter for the former in the pursuit of a Pareto-efficient allocation of resources will necessarily always seem to be advantageous. The same point can be restated by observing that costless government makes true comparative institutional analysis redundant (government is always best) – just as costless market transacting was seen in Chapter 1 to leave no scope for institutions or organisations. Take away transaction costs and all institutions are equally efficient. Assume one organisation (the state) can avoid information and transaction costs entirely and it sweeps the board.

3. THE NEW INSTITUTIONAL ECONOMICS AND PUBLIC POLICY

To criticise the naïve neoclassical approach to policy is one thing. To offer an alternative framework for public policy which allows for ubiquitous transactions costs and boundedly rational transactors is quite another. In Chapter 11, it was argued that a competitive market was likely to lead to a structure of organisations that economised on transactions and ownership costs. Further, in Chapter 12 it was seen that some theorists had argued that the institutions emerging from a competitive market process would be 'comparatively efficient'[7] – that is, there would be a tendency for more efficient structures to replace less efficient structures. Neither of these propositions, however, implies that market processes will tend towards the same 'equilibrium' irrespective of the starting point, and policy makers therefore have to face the daunting problem of working out how their interventions are likely to influence a whole time path of development. Economics, at present, offers only limited help.

Students of 'chaos theory' and complex dynamic processes have shown how even fairly simple deterministic models can generate dynamic paths which are highly sensitive to the assumed starting conditions and which have the appearance of randomness to people who are 'boundedly rational' and who do not have the computing power to calculate the predetermined path.[8] In the light of this complexity, some have argued that governments have a role in trying to limit uncertainty and dynamic fluctuations, while others argue that, in the nature of things, governments will not be able to calculate the results of their interventions and might actually make things worse.

3.1   Establishing External Institutions

One response to these conundrums which accords with much of the work we have been reviewing in this book derives from modern Institutional Economics. Economic change cannot be predicted in detail, but an important determinant of the time path of development will be the institutional context. Institutions may be conceived as 'internal' (evolved spontaneously by the inter-reaction of people) or 'external' (imposed by outside authority).[9] The role of the state is to establish and enforce those 'external' institutions which permit a desirable time path of development to take place. External institutions can be divided into several categories. External rules of conduct are universally applicable and can be found in the system of civil, commercial and criminal law operating in a country. They do not aim at particular ends but simply permit individual people to interact more productively. In contrast, purpose-specific directives 'instruct public or private agents to bring about predetermined outcomes' (Kasper and Streit, 1998, p. 109). Examples would include regulations which insist on the introduction of particular technology, which impose particular contractual terms, or which lay down specified standards of safety or environmental quality. Such institutions 'place high requirements on the knowledge problem because they are prescriptive'.

Some institutional structures tend to produce better results than do others over the long run in terms of the economic wellbeing of the people who operate within them. The institutions of private property, exchangeability of property rights, freedom of contract, the rules of honest dealing, freedom of movement and so forth, produce very complex systems, the precise time path of which is impossible to predict. These institutions are 'end-independent' and not designed to achieve particular goals. However, historical evidence combined with the '*a priori*' type of reasoning introduced in Part 1 of this book provide some confidence that, whatever path the economy takes, it is highly likely to be better than the path traversed by certain alternative systems. Alternatives based on purpose-specific directives, government ownership, restrictions on trade, non-exchangeability of property rights, and immobility of labour (both occupationally and geographically) have been observed to perform poorly in terms of most measures of welfare over long periods of time.

We have already seen in Chapter 3 how a free system can be thought of as displaying powerful 'equilibrating' forces through the self-interested actions of Kirznerian entrepreneurs. We also saw how entrepreneurial intervention could be characterised as 'destabilising' or Schumpeterian. Formal analysis cannot apparently resolve the question of which force will dominate, and from a philosophical point of view the question may not be all that meaningful. All that can be said is that 'the real world apparently has mechanisms which keep economies within certain bounds most of the time, if not necessarily convergent on equilibria, much less optimal equilibria'.[10] The modern institutional economist would argue that these 'mechanisms' are nothing other than the prevailing institutions, both internal and external, which govern the economic system, and that institutions which facilitate exchange and entrepreneurship have a better track record than others.

3.2 The Normative Hobbes and Coase Theorems

This distinction between specific intervention by government to achieve particular ends, and the establishment by government of legal systems enforcing end-independent rules of conduct is an important one. The former approach sees 'policy' as the achievement of desirable equilibrium outcomes. The latter sees policy as the enforcement of transactions cost reducing institutions.

3.2.1 The Coase Theorem
The modern transactions cost school of economic organisation derives from Coase's 1937 paper on 'The Nature of the Firm', a paper discussed in some detail in Chapter 2. Coase can also be seen as the founder of the sub-discipline of 'Law and Economics', which evolved out of an equally

path-breaking paper published in 1960. In 'The Problem of Social Cost', Coase considered the nature of external harm. If a person (N) creates an unwelcome noise and upsets her next door neighbour (P) she thereby imposes an 'external cost'. This is, of course, the sort of case which might be dealt with under the law of 'private nuisance'. Before the publication of Coase's paper, economists had tended to assume that government intervention in the form of taxes or other regulatory activity would be required to solve the problem of social or external cost. Using examples of cases from English common law, however, Coase showed that people might be expected to bargain with each other and thereby achieve an efficient allocation of resources.

Suppose, for example that the neighbour (P) likes peace and quiet and is very sensitive to noise. He can erect screens to insulate himself from the noise, or bribe his neighbour to reduce her noisy activities or to confine them to particular hours in the day. In principle, bargaining will proceed until the maximum that the neighbour (P) is prepared to pay for noise reduction (either via technology such as screens or behavioural adjustments by person (N)) is just equal to the minimum that person (N) is prepared to accept. In this way, person (N) faces a cost of creating her noise. When she creates noise, she sacrifices the payment that (P) might have made to persuade her to abate the noise. Where there are no transactions costs, bargaining will continue until all the 'gains from trade' are exhausted.

To the objection that the law should not be structured in this way and that person (P) should not have to buy his peace and quiet, Coase replies that, with no transactions costs, the final allocation of resources will be efficient, however we structure the law. Suppose person P has an enforceable right to peace and quiet. Relaxing one day, listening to the grass grow, he is outraged by person (N)'s din and is granted an immediate injunction by a court of law. Person (N) is now free to erect soundproof screens and offer bribes to person (P). Once more, bargaining continues for so long as person (N)'s valuation of an extra unit of her noise is greater than person (P)'s valuation of an extra unit of his peace and quiet. Obviously a system which gives people the right to make a noise is preferred by person (N), and a system which protects the right to peace and quiet is preferred by person (P). The assignment of rights affects the distribution of income, but efficiency in resource allocation is achieved in either case providing that transactions costs are zero.

Notice the connection between this result and the analysis of Coase (1937). In 'The Nature of the Firm', Coase argued that, in the absence of transactions costs, organisational structure is indeterminate and there is no rationale for the firm. Similarly, in 'The Problem of Social Cost' Coase argued that, in the absence of transactions costs, any initial assignment of property rights is efficient. Property rights must be clearly assigned and accepted by participants in the market, but irrespective of the initial assignment of these rights, the process of exchange will result in their reallocation until efficiency is achieved and the gains from trade are exhausted. It is even possible to show that, in the case of persons (N) and (P) above, the amount of noise finally agreed upon will, under certain conditions, be independent of the initial assignment of rights.

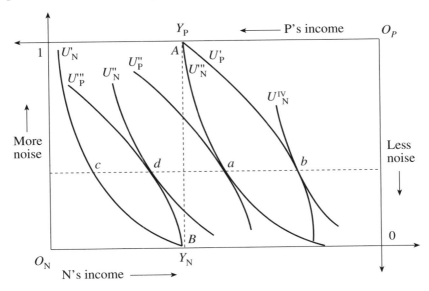

Note:
Whether the initial assignment of rights is at *A* or *B*, the two contractors bargain to an efficient outcome along *ab* or *cd*. Where the marginal valuation of noise depends upon the amount of noise but does not depend upon the transactors' incomes, a single 'efficient' amount of noise exists.

Figure 13.1   The Coase theorem

Figure 13.1 illustrates the case in which the transactors will agree upon the same amount of noise irrespective of the initial assignment of rights. The utility levels of persons (N) and (P) are assumed to depend upon 'income' and 'noise'. The combined income of the two people is measured along the horizontal dimension of the box. Noise is scaled along the vertical dimension and is assumed to vary between zero and unity. Noise confers positive utility on person (N) but negative utility on person (P). Thus, for any given income level, person (P) becomes better off as the common amount of noise goes from unity to zero, whereas person (N) becomes better off as the amount of noise goes from zero to unity.

A legal system which gives person (N) the right to make as much noise as she likes would imply an initial assignment of property rights at a point such as A. Person (N) has income $O_N Y_N$ and makes noise level unity. Person (P) has income $O_p Y_p$ and experiences noise level unity. The bargaining process by which person (P) persuades person (N) to reduce her noise is represented by a move from point A to somewhere on the arc ab. Along the arc ab, both contractors are better off than they were at A. Points on the arc ab are also efficient. No further gains from trade are possible. The indifference curves of person (N) are tangential to those of person (P) along the arc ab. Person (P) has less income because he has purchased a certain amount of peace and quiet from (N). Person (N) has accepted more income in return for reducing her noise.

A legal system which gives person (P) the right to peace and quiet would imply an initial assignment of rights at a point such as B. Person (P) and person (N) now start off with noise level zero but with the same incomes as before ($O_N Y_N$ and $O_p Y_p$). The bargaining process by which person (N) persuades person (P) to accept her noise is represented by a move from point B to somewhere on the arc cd. Points along cd are efficient just as were those along ab. Further, as the figure is drawn, the final amount of noise agreed by the transactors does not depend on whether we start from point A or B. The legal system affects the final distribution of income between the transactors but it does not affect the amount of noise that takes place. This is a special case that arises when the slopes of the indifference curves depend entirely on the amount of noise – each curve is a horizontal displacement of the others. The amount of money for example, that person (P) is prepared to pay for a reduction in person (N)'s noise is independent of his income. The greater the noise to which he is subjected, the greater the amount of money he is prepared to offer in exchange for a marginal remission (his indifference curves are convex). But (P)'s willingness to pay for extra peace and quiet does not change with his income for any given amount of noise.

In practice, of course, we would not expect these preferences to be common. It is more natural to suppose that peace and quiet is a 'normal' good to person (P) and that he will value it more highly at the margin as his income rises. Similarly, we might expect person (N) to value her right to make extra noise more highly at higher levels of her income. Where income effects are powerful, it no longer follows that the final amount of noise will be independent of the initial assignment of property rights. The 'strong' version of the Coase theorem will not hold. The 'weak' version remains intact, however. With zero transactions costs, efficiency is achieved through the process of exchange, whatever the initial assignment of property rights.[11]

3.2.2 The Normative Coase Theorem

In principle, the Coase theorem proper is a 'scientific law' rather similar to the laws of physics which apply in their purity only in 'unrealistic' conditions such as the rate of acceleration of a falling body in a vacuum or in the absence of friction. In a world of ubiquitous transactions costs, however, the assignment of property rights will not be irrelevant to the achievement of economic efficiency. The normative Coase theorem is a proposition about what is 'desirable' when the influence of transactions costs cannot be ignored. It states that the law should be structured 'so as to remove the impediments to private agreements'.[12] The statement that it is 'desirable' to reduce transactions costs where possible has a similar status to the claim that to reduce friction in a piece of machinery would be desirable. Actually, of course, this may not always be true. It depends what we are trying to achieve. In Chapters 10 and 11, we observed that voluntary restrictions on the tradability of property rights are sometimes observed. Nevertheless, the normative Coase theorem is an assertion that, in social life, structuring the law so as to reduce transactions costs is generally beneficial.

Consider, for example, a dispute between two people over the use of some land. Suppose that one person is crossing another person's land in order to take a 'short cut' to some destination. The 'owner' of the land sues the trespasser. It is a fundamental insight of the study of 'Law and Economics' that, where information costs facing a court exceed the expected transactions costs faced by litigants, the court should grant an injunction to the complainant, and then leave the litigants to bargain. If the person against whom the injunction is granted (in this case the 'trespasser') wishes to continue with the activities which induced the complaint (taking the short cut), he or she simply has to purchase the complainant's consent (that is, buy the rights to cross the land from the owner). The lower the costs of transacting in property rights, the more effective will the process of bargaining become. From the point of view of economic efficiency, the court does not have to invest time and resources in determining what precise final disposition of rights in the land would be best. This can be left to 'the market'; that is, to private agreements.

3.2.3 The Normative Hobbes Theorem

Suppose now that transactions costs are high and seriously confine the scope for private agreements. Suppose further that the opportunity for reducing these costs of transacting is limited. In these circumstances, it matters how rights are assigned. The normative Hobbes[13] theorem states that the law should be structured 'so as to minimise the harm caused by failures in private agreements'.[14]

If information about who values a resource most highly is cheaply available to a court and is less than the transactions costs facing the disputants,

economic efficiency requires that the court should allocate the legal rights
to the person who values them most. The reason is simply that efficiency
(the allocation of the resource to the highest valued user) is thereby
achieved more cheaply than by means of bargaining. If the court simply
grants an injunction, it saves information costs but runs the risk that, if the
'wrong' party is granted rights over the disputed resource, transactions
costs will prevent their reallocation to the party who values them more
highly. Even if transactions costs are not high enough to prevent successful bargaining, efficiency will have been achieved at an 'unnecessarily' high
cost.[15] In our example, the trespasser may have some special reason for
placing a very high value on the right to cross the land and might be more
than able to compensate the owner. If transactions costs exceed the potential 'gains from trade', however, agreement will not be forthcoming and
'efficiency' is sacrificed. Under such circumstances, the court would do
better not to grant an injunction but to award 'damages' to the complainant.[16] Where there are only two transactors and the dispute is relatively
simple, the remedy of an injunction is likely to be efficient (and is usually
observed). On other occasions, however, especially where large numbers of
people are involved, transactions costs could prevent the achievement of
desirable agreements, which then have to be imposed.[17]

These ideas have a wide application to the problem of public policy. The
government is seen as operating on two fronts. Firstly, it should try to
assign property rights in ways which 'simulate a perfect market' and
produce outcomes which would be chosen by transactors if the costs of
transacting did not get in the way (the normative Hobbes theorem). Here
the government is assumed to be able to act 'in the public interest', as
explained in section 4 below. Secondly, it should try, by establishing appropriate legal rules and procedures, to reduce the costs of transacting in property rights so as to permit the greatest scope for private bargaining and
hence for the correction of 'errors' (the normative Coase theorem). Here
the government is assumed not to be able to calculate the ideal outcome
either because it does not have access to the necessary information or the
rationality to process it, or both. It has to operate at the 'constitutional
level', establishing rules of the game which encourage private agreements
between economic agents and the discovery of the gains from trade.

Note that the normative Hobbes theorem is closely allied to the neoclassical view of policy. The 'Sovereign' is assumed to be powerful, well
informed and benevolent. The normative Coase theorem is more closely
allied to the New Institutional Economics because it is rooted in a recognition that information and transactions costs exist, information is scattered,
and the gains from trade arise from the process of bargaining and agreement between agents. Note again, however, that Coasian reasoning does

not lead to the conclusion that decentralised bargaining is always preferred to direct state intervention. The normative Coase theorem is not that decentralised bargaining is always best; it is that lower costs of transacting are to be preferred to higher costs of transacting. As was seen in Chapter 2, it was Coase himself who rationalised 'the firm' as a response to transactions costs in the market. If the costs of market transacting are too great relative to information costs and other 'costs of ownership', Coasian logic leads us to expect bargaining in decentralised markets to be replaced by 'authority' – even, perhaps, by government authority.

This contrast between the normative Hobbes and Coase theorems is explored further in subsections 4 and 5 below. The public interest approach to running publicly owned firms outlined in subsection 4 is based squarely on the Hobbesian premise that 'failures in private agreements' (market failures) are serious and amenable to correction by the intervention of the state. The criticisms of this position outlined in subsection 5 are based on the Coasian premise that 'impediments to private agreements' (transactions costs) should be discouraged so that markets can function more effectively.

4. THE PUBLIC INTEREST APPROACH

The influence of neoclassical welfare economics could be seen in many areas of policy in the 'mixed economies' after the Second World War. Nowhere was this more apparent than in policy towards nationalised firms in the UK during the period up to 1980. The managers of nationalised industries were instructed to operate resources under their control 'in the public interest'. In theory, political intervention was supposed to be limited and public enterprise was governed through 'Boards', which were kept at 'arm's length' from direct government interference. A classic example of this arrangement can be found in the Coal Nationalisation Act (1948), which gave the Coal Board the responsibility to 'secure the efficient development of the mining industry'. It was then enjoined to 'make supplies available of such qualities and sizes, in such quantities and at such prices, as may seem to them best calculated to further the public interest in all respects'.

To run a firm so as to make a profit is an aim that is not difficult to understand, even if it is frequently not all that easy to bring about. To further the public interest, on the other hand, leaves a fair amount of room for interpretation. What could it possibly mean? Neoclassical economics provided an intellectually enticing option. To further the public interest could be seen as an instruction to operate so as to achieve Pareto efficiency. Pareto efficiency required that the marginal social benefits (MSB) of an activity should equal the marginal social costs (MSC).[18] Clearly, if the marginal social benefits from producing extra output are greater than the marginal social costs, there would appear to be net social gains available from going ahead – the gains from trade discussed in Chapter 1. 'Social' benefits are seen simply as the sum total of all the individual 'private' benefits that might derive from extra output. In the case of a strictly 'private' good, therefore, social benefit and private benefit are the same. Where there are 'spillover' or 'external' effects on people other than the direct consumer, the value of these (positive or negative) has to be added to calculate net 'social' benefit.

From the simple proposition that social efficiency is achieved where $MSB = MSC$, a number of 'rules' appeared to follow. Where the price of a unit of output could be taken as a reasonable measure of the marginal social benefit derived from it – and this would be so for all purely 'private' goods which confer no benefits and impose no costs on others – managers of public enterprises could achieve 'efficiency' by continuing to supply extra output until the marginal social cost of doing so equalled the maximum price at which it could be sold. This came to be called the 'marginal cost pricing rule' and was discussed and elaborated at great length in the literature on public enterprises in the 1960s and 1970s, although it derives from a much earlier theoretical debate.[19]

Closely associated with the marginal cost pricing rule was an investment rule. Managers were advised to undertake all projects for which the net present value was positive. The rationale was essentially the same as that which justified marginal cost pricing. Each 'project' could be considered as a marginal increase in capacity. Revenues in future time periods could (again in the absence of external effects) be taken as measuring the resulting future streams of social benefits. If the value of these benefits, discounted to the present, exceeded the present discounted value of the stream of costs, there would be social gains from going ahead with the project. Thus, where the consumers' willingness to pay for the output of a new project exceeded the compensation required by the owners of the resources used then, at least in principle, everyone might be better off as a result of undertaking the project.

If this description of the case for marginal cost pricing sounds similar to the case for competitive markets reviewed in Chapter 1, that is no accident. What managers of public enterprises were being asked to do on the recommendation of neoclassical theory was to 'simulate a "perfect" market'. Indeed, from the late 1930s onwards, 'market socialism' was a powerful intellectual force associated with writers such as Abba Lerner and Oscar Lange.[20] Managers would be asked to adjust for so-called 'market failures' by taking into account the 'external' benefits and costs of their actions. They would also discount future streams of net benefits at lower 'social' rather than 'market' rates of interest so as to take advantage of the state's supposed greater ability to spread risks. These activities, however, could be seen as merely attempting to replicate what a complete and perfect set of markets would achieve were they to exist.

Industries subject to increasing returns to scale and hence declining average costs were regarded as particularly appropriate candidates for the introduction of public enterprise and the marginal cost pricing rule. These were 'natural monopolies' because a single supplier could provide output at lower cost than any combination of two or more suppliers. The industry's structure would therefore tend towards monopoly, and this was not entirely undesirable since a set of competing firms would sacrifice scale economies and operate at higher costs. All the main public utilities were assumed to fit into this category since the duplication of networks of pipes, cables or tracks was considered to be self-evidently wasteful. Public ownership would, according to the public interest theory, permit efficient marginal cost pricing. However, there was a catch. If average costs are falling, every principles of economics textbook teaches that marginal cost must be less than average cost. Setting price equal to marginal cost therefore must imply that price is less than average cost, and, if price (average revenue) is less than average cost, financial losses must be the result. Apparently, the socially efficient price of a good subject to 'natural' monopoly conditions might give rise to financial losses. Figure 13.2 illustrates the case.

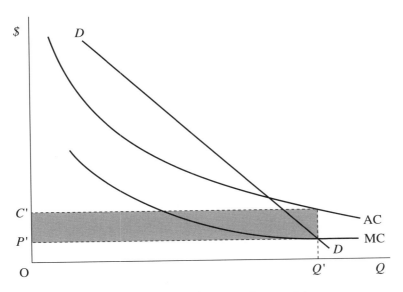

Figure 13.2   Economies of scale and marginal cost pricing

With declining average costs, application of marginal cost principles gives rise to financial losses. An 'optimal' price of P' results in a deficit of $(C' - P') \times Q'$. The loss is represented by the shaded area in the diagram.

Purists offered two 'solutions' to the financing of losses. Social efficiency required that marginal social benefits be equal to marginal social costs. The price paid by the consumer for additional units of output might be a good measure of marginal social benefits, but no efficiency principle held that this marginal price must equal average revenue. If average revenue could be increased, not by raising the price paid at the margin but by the imposition of 'overhead charges' or by increasing the prices paid on 'intra-marginal' purchases, costs could be covered and financial losses eliminated without infringing the efficiency conditions. Managers were here implicitly being asked to replicate the results not of a perfectly competitive market but a perfectly discriminating monopolist. A monopolist who can costlessly deal separately with each potential consumer and can prevent arbitrage will have an incentive to increase output until the gains from trade are exhausted.

An alternative 'solution' is to cover the losses of public enterprises from taxation. Taxes, however, are as likely to result in the contravention of the conditions for efficient resource allocation as the departure of public enterprise prices from marginal costs. In the absence of some 'ideal' lump sum tax which leaves marginal costs and benefits unchanged everywhere, there would appear to be no theoretical assurance that marginal cost pricing for the public utilities and tax-induced distortions in labour or other product markets would be better than (say) average cost or break-even pricing for the public utilities and no taxes. Coase (1946), for example, argued that a break-even objective and average cost pricing was desirable, not only because losses would require tax finance but because average cost prices would at least provide a rough practical *ex post* check that total social benefits (TSB) were as great as total social costs (TSC). The condition that MSB = MSC was, Coase pointed out, a necessary but not sufficient condition for Pareto efficiency. There was the troubling possibility that the marginal condition might be fulfilled but that total social benefits might still fall short of total social costs. In other words, the maximum net social benefit available from an activity might be negative and in those circumstances the nationalised firm should simply be closed down.

5.   CRITICISMS OF THE PUBLIC INTEREST APPROACH TO POLICY

Like general equilibrium theory from which it derives, the public interest approach to public policy represented a significant (and seductive) intellectual achievement. It was flawed, however, because of the complete absence of institutional and organisational content. The vision was that of the frictionless world of Chapter 1, the outcomes of which public officials had somehow to simulate. There was no explicit reference to the informational and transactional difficulties the public officials would face, no reference to their implied role as substitutes for the process of entrepreneurial discovery, no consideration of the structure of property rights within which they would be operating and no attention paid to the principal and agent problems which might be expected to characterise their relations with politicians and the public. In short, the issues introduced in Chapters 2 to 5 in Part 1 of this book were entirely absent from the public interest theory of public policy. The theory was Platonic in every sense. Applicable to the world of the forms, policy was discovered and intended to be implemented by disinterested philosopher kings.

5.1   The Austrian Critique

5.1.1   The marginal cost pricing debate

Although events at the end of the twentieth century have made some of the objections to the public interest theory of policy rather apparent, it was not always so. At the very beginning of the marginal cost pricing debate and the dispute over 'market socialism' in the late 1930s and 1940s, however, the essential weakness of the argument had been exposed by Hayek, Coase and others in the 'Austrian' school. The main distinctive features of the 'Austrian' school are its acceptance of continuous disequilibrium and its commitment to subjectivism. Benefits and costs are not 'objective' pieces of information, which can be observed and measured according to some universal measuring rod. Just as my evaluation of an extra unit of good x (the amount of some other good, y, I am prepared to sacrifice) is a matter of my own subjective judgement, so the 'cost' of an extra unit of x is likewise a matter for subjective evaluation. We do not know with certainty what opportunities we are sacrificing when we produce more x and thus the 'marginal costs' which determine our choices are inevitably subjective in nature.

In spite of familiarity with the paraphernalia of indifference curve analysis, with its clear implication of subjective value, economics students still often find Austrian subjective cost theory hard to accept. Two factors help to explain the difficulty. The first is that the neoclassical theory of supply is presented in terms of the 'production function'. This function represents the terms upon which inputs can be transformed into outputs given the existing known technological possibilities. In other words, unlike 'utility functions' in consumer theory, which are easily understood to represent subjective evaluations that will vary between people, 'production functions' are presented as technologically given and independent of the individual decision maker's subjective assessments. There is an element of 'objectivity' on the supply side of the market in conventional treatments of microeconomics which does not appear on the demand side.

The second feature, which makes subjective cost theory difficult at first, is the tendency to think in terms of equilibrium states. If I have to spend $10 to get a painter to paint my door, it is 'natural' to think that the 'cost' of the painter is $10 and that this is both observable and 'objective'. Market prices are indeed 'objective' pieces of information. It is also true that, 'in equilibrium', the $10 price would represent cost in terms of opportunities forgone. This is because, 'in equilibrium', if we were to ask what is the most some other employer of the painter (out of a large number of potential alternative employers) might have been prepared to pay for his or her services (and hence what is the value of the marginal displaced work) the answer would be a figure infinitesimally less than $10. If it were more, the marginally excluded employer should have used the painter and I should not have done so. If we were to ask what value I place on achieving a different possible objective over the same period of time – say mending a window – the answer, given a large number of alternative projects, would similarly be just short of $10. If it were more, I should have had the window mended instead of having the door painted. 'In equilibrium', therefore, in a world of many possible alternative uses of resources which people can rank in order of importance to them, prices represent marginal costs to producers and marginal benefits to consumers.

For the 'Austrian' theorist, however, this is a misleading way of looking at economic life. The economy is not 'in equilibrium'. The gains from trade are never completely exhausted. Existing prices may be 'objective' (after they have been found) but they cannot be taken as representing actual marginal costs and benefits. Transactors are always comparing existing prices with their own subjective assessments of marginal benefits and marginal costs. Opportunity costs are what determine choice of action, but these costs are not objective – they are 'in the mind' of the decision maker as he or she compares the possible consequences of various courses of action. It is this process of comparison which drives economic change by holding out the prospect of entrepreneurial profit. In Chapter 3, we discussed at some length the way that potential gains from trade (efficiency gains) will encourage entrepreneurial intervention. That whole analysis could be recast in terms of attempts to uncover new opportunities where the price of output exceeds subjective assessments of marginal costs.

Wiseman (1953, p. 118) represented this 'process' view of economic life when he wrote that 'in conditions of uncertainty . . . the marginal cost rule . . . gives no clear guidance' to policy makers. 'It is no longer possible, once uncertainty is admitted, to interpret the opportunity cost problem as one of scarcity alone . . . Opportunity cost decisions involve uncertainty (and therefore judgement) as well as scarcity' (p. 122). Anticipating the 'bounded rationality' argument of behaviouralists and others, Wiseman went on to point out that only a limited number of alternative plans of action could realistically be assessed; different people would take different views of these alternatives; and it was not clear how the process of selection was to be carried out. Neither was it obvious that different individuals could reasonably be expected to reach the same decisions 'even in the unlikely event of their acting on the basis of identical data' (Wiseman, 1957, p. 69).

Appearing in professional economics journals and discussing the subject matter in a somewhat abstract and generalised way, the practical importance of this work was completely overlooked. It is a curious feature of 'Austrian' economics that it is at once so consonant with 'common sense' and practical business experience and yet can appear so 'high flown' when presented in an academic treatise. The result seems to be that the bits that are understood are dismissed as 'obvious', while the important general consequences of accepting these obvious bits are missed entirely. Far from suggesting a few 'obvious' points about the practical difficulties of running nationalised industries, the Austrian critique was actually devastating. It was saying that there existed no mechanism for running them effectively. The difficulty, argued Wiseman (1957, p. 71), 'is the discovery of an incentive to efficient *ex ante* planning activity that will replace the association of reward with achieved net revenue generally used in private industry'. Go for advice to the box marked 'the theory of public utility price' and, as the title of Wiseman's paper makes clear, it will be found to be empty.

Over twenty years later, the failure of marginal cost pricing principles to give effective guidance to the managers of public enterprises was apparent in the UK. A National Economic Development Office Report (NEDO, 1976) found that the marginal cost pricing principle 'has been followed to a negligible extent in the four corporations we have studied in detail' and that 'only a limited proportion of investment in nationalised industries is subject to full investment appraisal using the test discount rate' (p. 31). The criticism here might be interpreted as a technical failure of management to plan according to the guidelines laid down by Parliament; something that might be corrected by changing the management. A more telling comment came from Littlechild (1979a, p. 18). 'An industry could defend virtually any pricing and investment policy it wished to adopt as being a reasonable interpretation of the rules and consistent with its own view of the future.' This was precisely Wiseman's point. In a world of change and uncertainty the 'cost' of a course of action was a matter for subjective judgement. Any outsider questioning a particular investment or pricing policy might try to claim they were merely checking that marginal cost principles were being applied – a purely technical task. In fact, they would simply be substituting their own subjective judgements about the future for those of the existing managers.

5.1.2   The 'competence' argument

In the 1990s, 'Austrian' analysis has emphasised a different strand of the argument. The exercise of judgement and entrepreneurial skills is inescapable. As discussed in Chapter 3, however, some people are more 'competent' at organising economic resources than others. Further, the allocation of entrepreneurial and decision-making talent to the 'control' of other resources is a crucial determinant of economic success. Human skills, effort and application can come to very little if they are misdirected – the 'wrong' industries developed, the 'wrong' techniques adopted, the 'wrong' markets served. When this happens, the collective frustration reveals itself in cynicism, exhaustion and a feeling that honest commitment is a sucker's game, since it is always profitless. Perhaps the most basic intellectual error of the supporters of central planning and of large areas of state production within an otherwise 'mixed economy' was the implied view of production as merely a 'technical' problem that officials could deal with using rational principles. It turned out, as Hayek recognised early on, that effective production was mainly a problem of making the best use of scattered information. Assigning resources to those who have the information to use them most effectively – linking resources to 'competence' – is the big problem.

At this point, it is worth clarifying our use of the word 'competence' in this context. In Chapter 12, it was seen that 'radical' – Austrian and evolutionary – approaches to the firm emphasised that the learned routines and other firm-specific human skills, which could not be transferred to others on the open market at low cost, represented the source of competitive advantage. Some writers refer to this firm-specific knowledge as a type of capital asset which leads to the ability to do things other firms cannot do. It represents their 'core competencies'. This is to use the term 'competence' to describe the outcome of a process of learning over time. Experience, repetition and experiment over time lead to a certain level of 'competence', and this 'competence' may be seen as applying to an individual or to a group of people working together. In this section, however, the word 'competence' is used to indicate 'talent', 'innate inability' or 'alertness'. Pelikan (1993, p. 355) refers to our present usage as 'the competence to learn competence'.

Granted that the competence to manage resources is scarce, the mechanism chosen to allocate it becomes of economic importance. It is socially wasteful if relatively incompetent individuals are managing large quantities of resources while competent ones have little or no control. An important part of management is therefore to recognise competence and assign it to suitable environments. This involves considerations of neoclassical 'incentives', as we saw in Part 2 of this book. Managers must have some personal reason for correctly assessing the competence of others and for exercising their delegated decision rights effectively (see, again, Chapter 8). Competent managers will be required to select competent managers. At the top of every chain of delegated managerial authority, however, there is an 'owner' – a person or group of people possessing residual control rights and responsible for appointing the most senior managers. These senior managers were described in Chapter 8 (p. 273) as like the keystone in an arch, without which the rest would be in danger of collapse. It is the 'owners' who are responsible for selecting this keystone and it is of crucial economic importance that the job is well done.

The selection of 'owners' is not a matter for some supercompetent person, however. If such a person existed, they would effectively be acting as a single overall 'owner' on which the whole system depended – a situation approximated perhaps by Joseph Stalin's Soviet Union and one that is most unlikely to make the most of scarce resources of competence. The question of what constitutes a 'good' mechanism for assigning ownership rights is quintessentially a constitutional one. Looked at from the 'competence' perspective, the great advantage of privately exchangeable property rights is their ability to be reassigned through a competitive process to those who think they are the most 'competent' owners. These will be entrepreneurs who cannot benefit from their insights and 'competence' without gaining ownership rights over resources. As we saw in Chapter 3, this process is not perfect. Some entrepreneurs may lack financial resources and be 'unqualified' in Casson's sense (pp. 71–76) even though they may have access to potentially valuable information and be highly 'competent'. Similarly, in Chapter 9, the role of the takeover in reassigning ownership through entrepreneurial intervention was discussed. There were theoretical circumstances (public information) in which the free-rider problem inhibited takeovers. Nevertheless, in a world of information costs and privately exchangeable rights, the incentives to overcome these problems will be considerable. Foss (1993, p. 136) concludes for example, that 'utilization of entrepreneurial competence thus requires a firm with the entrepreneur as residual claimant'.

Non-exchangeable and collective rights, on the other hand, permit changes of control to occur only through political and bureaucratic processes. They also provide little incentive for the possessors of potentially valuable information to seek out control rights, since they can benefit only by very indirect means – political honours, social status, or promotion to a higher salary range. Even these potential rewards might easily be blocked by vested interests opposed to the changes proposed by the entrepreneur. Thus, Pelikan (1993, p. 381) concludes using similar arguments that 'private and tradable ownership of firms is a necessary condition for efficiency of supply. More wasteful production must be expected if firms are owned by governments or other politically established bodies.' The system of privately exchangeable rights leads to a much more rapid recognition of failure and reassignment from less to more competent owners.

Before leaving the Austrian critique of public enterprise it is worth noting some close connections between the subjective-cost arguments of the 1950s and the allocation-of-scarce-competence arguments of the 1990s. Wiseman's basic argument was that managers were being asked to do the impossible when told to equate prices to marginal costs. The latter could only be revealed in a process of ongoing discovery. If managers were to simulate market outcomes, they would have to undertake the entrepreneurial function which neoclassical analysis ignored. This was not something that could be accomplished by following a few simple rules, however. Entrepreneurship requires the services of entrepreneurs, not public officials. Thus the objections raised in the 1990s that public ownership is inimical to the use of entrepreneurial knowledge and competence is intimately connected with Wiseman's case against marginal cost pricing. Similarly, both warn against the errors that can arise from assuming the existence of equilibrium. In equilibrium, argues Pelikan (1993, p. 358), where there is an ideal assignment of owners and competence,

> owners need not do much more than hold their optimal portfolios, receive dividends, and remain silent . . . This silence can then easily be confused with insignificance. It is only where the actual (assignment of competence) more or less deviates from the ideal that the social importance of the ownership role can properly be assessed.

Our discussion thus far in subsection 5.1 has concerned the 'radical' critique of public enterprises and emphasised the problem of discovering new knowledge and handling change. Even within the neo-classical framework of analysis, however, the structure of nationalised firms became subject to criticism from the 1970s onwards. The problem was that of contracting with managers. The public interest argument was naïve in assuming that there was a class of persons who could simply be asked to pursue a rather vague public interest objective and then get on with it. It is not that honest people do not exist. It is that people face a complex world of conflicting pressures (both moral and economic) and will therefore usually find it possible to associate the public interest with decisions which do not greatly threaten their own.

The following subsections consider the contractual context of state enterprise. Subsection 5.2 concentrates on the interests of the 'contractors' and briefly surveys the political pressures to which they are subjected. The question is asked: Who are the principals and what do they want to achieve? Subsection 5.3 comments briefly on the particular problems that arise with respect to contracting in the public sector, even on the assumption that a benevolent government is pursuing the public interest.

5.2 The 'Public Choice' Critique

Like the 'Austrian' critique of public enterprises, the principal–agent framework also has several sub-strands. The public choice tradition emphasises the fact that whereas the principal–agent approach to the public company assigns the role of principal to the 'shareholder', there is an extra complication in the case of public enterprise. There are two possible candidates for 'principal'. We might think, in a representative democracy, of 'politicians' or 'government ministers' as the ultimate 'owners'. Alternatively, we might envisage the 'principal' in the relationship to be the whole body of citizens. In this case, the analysis of public enterprise really requires us to study two principal–agent relations – the first between citizen and politician and the second between politician and manager.

Public choice theory has generated a large literature on the connection between citizens' preferences, constitutional conventions, voting systems and policy outcomes.[21] For our present purposes, the main point is that the translation of individual voter preferences into policy outcomes is very unreliable. There are two major reasons for this.

First, a famous result of 'social choice' analysis is that it is impossible under certain general conditions to talk meaningfully about a consistent set of 'social preferences' being derived from the preferences of all the individuals who make up the community (Arrow, 1951). There may be acceptable ways of making social choices (for example, through majority voting or other means) but these choices will sometimes be 'paradoxical'. There is no assurance that, as a group, we will not vote for option A over option B followed by option B over option C, only to find that we then vote for option C over option A. The apparent collective irrationality of such 'voting cycles' can be ruled out only if people have sufficiently similar preferences.[22]

Arrow's so-called 'impossibility theorem' has some important implications. If all the citizens of a country are seen as 'owners' of a public enterprise, then, with sufficiently diverse opinions about the purposes of the enterprise, it may not be technically possible (even where information about individual preferences is assumed to be costlessly available) to formulate a coherent set of social objectives for managers which can be said to reflect the wishes of the citizens. Very diverse ownership makes collective decision making costly, as was discussed in Chapters 10 and 11, and the population of an entire country is likely to contain groups with very differing ideas about the purposes of public enterprise. It might be objected that Arrow's theorem applies to all social choice contexts and not just that of a nationalised industry. The shareholders of a public limited company would also face the same problem. Shareholders are all holders of exchangeable residual claims, however, and this is likely to lead to greater harmony of interest. The desire to maximise the market value of their shares may not be universal among shareholders, but it is likely to be sufficiently dominant to make the interests of the 'owners' clear to managers. Indeed, as was seen at the end of Chapter 11, it is precisely this relative homogeneity of interest, and the lower decision-making costs that are implied, which constitutes a major part of Hansmann's (1996) explanation for the dominance in modern Western economies of the investor-owned joint-stock enterprise.

A second relevant strand of public choice analysis is the theory of pressure groups. Not all citizens are equally well placed for influencing political decisions – including those related to the control of public enterprise – and most may have little personal interest in doing so. Some producer groups, however, may have strong reasons to want to influence policy and may have the organisational coherence to make their interests count. The labour that actually works in the industry may be one such group, but other interests could include the suppliers of complementary inputs and local or regional groups. Following the logic of Mancur Olson (1965), producer groups will be more influential than consumers because they are more geographically concentrated, more substantially affected by particular decisions and better able to overcome the free-rider problems which beset pressure-group formation.

The result of 'public choice' pressures is that managers of nationalised industries are unlikely to be free to pursue neoclassical notions of the 'public interest'. If investment decisions have important consequences for employment in particular areas (especially if the balance between competing political parties happens to be a fine one) political 'interference' can be expected. This became apparent in the United Kingdom in the period up to 1980. Politicians used the nationalised industries to impose 'price freezes' as part of their 'anti-inflation' policies. They interfered in the type and location of investment. Public sector unions used their power to maintain employment and raise wages, a form of pressure which managers had little incentive to resist. In short, nationalised industry is always in danger of becoming a vehicle for 'rent-seeking' behaviour – lobbying government for favours and undermining potential competitors (chapter 6, pp. 199–203). 'Owners' or 'principals' in the shape of government ministers are like no other ownership group. They have virtually no personal stake in the business and possess the power to use tax revenue to cover losses. In these conditions, political rather than economic considerations are expected to dominate.

Public Choice pressures are emphasised in a paper by Boycko, Shleifer and Vishny (1996) in their analysis of the effects of privatisation. They argue that 'the critical agency problem that explains the inefficiency of public firms is the agency problem with politicians rather than that with managers' (p. 318). Political influence leads to excess employment and inefficient operations. Why, however, should privatisation have any effect on political influence? Politicians might, after all, still use the tax system to subsidise private firms. The answer suggested by Boycko *et al.* is also in the tradition of public choice. The forgone profits of inefficiently run public enterprises are largely 'invisible' to other politicians and other interest groups, whereas subsidies to private firms have explicitly to be sanctioned by the treasury and are seen by others. The political cost of subsidies to private firms is greater than the political cost that results from the inefficient operation of public enterprise. Thus, privatisation is expected to result in restructuring and less political interference.

5.3   Contracting and the Property Rights Critique

The principal–agent critique of state ownership, however, rests on more than a recognition of the theoretical impropriety of assuming that people are different when they operate in the public rather than the private sector. In Chapters 8 and 9, we observed that there were great agency problems involved in the operation of the public limited company. Governance arrangements could be seen in terms of principal and agent. The shareholder (principal) often did not have the private interest to act as a direct monitor of managerial (agent) behaviour. Shareholders were numerous and shareholdings dispersed. Free-rider and 'rational ignorance' problems existed. If responses to these problems are possible in the private sector, the question arises as to why they cannot be used in the context of the public sector. Might it not be feasible, for example, to construct an incentive contract which would induce effort from managers; to use the managerial labour market; to encourage or otherwise simulate competition between public enterprises in product markets; or to monitor managerial performance more directly?

Incentive contracts can indeed be devised to motivate managers and others in the public sector. As we have seen repeatedly, however, economic organisation is about the ways in which 'ownership' and 'contract' are combined. Broadly speaking, we expect that the greater are the transactional hazards confronting governments in their relations with suppliers, the greater the case for state ownership. Conversely, if contract is as effective in many spheres of government activity as it is in the private sector, the case for the government actually owning assets is much reduced. Contract and ownership are thus substitutes – just as Coase originally proposed.

5.3.1 Property rights theory – specific investments and hold-up

The property rights theory of the firm developed by Grossman and Hart, and Moore[23] provides a useful way of conceptualising the problem. Where contracts are incomplete, 'ownership' matters because vulnerable specific investments made by an 'owner' are less subject to 'hold-up' by another party. In the presentation of this theory in Chapter 4, the assignment of two assets between two people was discussed following Hart (1995a). Here we can simply envisage two transactors – a 'manager' and a 'government' – and a single asset. The government wishes to achieve some 'outcome'. To accomplish this outcome it must contract with a 'manager'. The manager will have to use the 'asset', but which of the parties – government or manager – should 'own' the asset?

Assume that the 'outcome' is observable but not verifiable for both the government and the manager. Assume also that the outcome depends upon management and government 'effort' in the form of specific *ex ante* investments in human or 'intangible' capital. The asset might, for example, represent a defence facility for building warships. The 'outcome' is a class of warships with certain technical specifications and qualities that cannot be exhaustively described and listed. The *ex ante* 'non-contractible' investments are expenditures on research and design work by the manager, and up-front investments by the government in providing training for the eventual commissioning of the warship. After investing in design work, the manager fears 'hold-up' by the government. Assume that the work cannot be transferred to others at low cost but is largely embodied in the 'human capital' of the manager. It could, however, be used (with some modifications) to produce a new type of fast civilian passenger ferry. The 'manager' can produce the ferry if he or she owns the construction facility but not otherwise. The net benefit to the manager will be less than would have been achieved if the agreement with the government had not foundered. On the side of the government, investments in specific training have increased the benefit derivable from the manager's ship and the manager may attempt to lay claim to some of these rents. However, we assume that there exists another supplier of ships which, when suitably modified, can serve the government's purposes. Again, the modifications can be carried out by the government if it owns the facility but not otherwise. The payoff to the government will be less than would have been the case if the original agreement with the manager had succeeded.

This story of warship design and construction is obviously very stylised. It does, however, contain the main elements of the property rights theory of the firm. Each contractor – government and manager – makes an up-front specific investment. Each knows that there will be renegotiation after these investments have been made. Each expects that this bargaining will be efficient and that the end result will be an equal sharing of the gains from achieving a (post investment) agreement. The ownership of the asset is significant because it affects the relative 'outside' opportunities available to the parties if they fail to agree. In the efficient bargain, each will receive this 'outside' or 'threat value' plus one half of the potential gains available from an agreement.[24] Ownership of the asset determines the threat values. If the manager owns the asset, he or she can construct a ferry and thus make use of some of the earlier human capital investments. In the absence of ownership, we assume that the up-front investments of the manager are a total loss and failure to agree with the government will result in a simple write-off. Similarly, if the government owns the asset, it can construct a warship even without the manager, but one with qualities that do not benefit from the application of the manager's human capital. In the absence of ownership, the government simply loses its initial training investments if the agreement with the manager fails.

Ex ante investments by both parties are expected to be less than optimal under these circumstances. The return to an investment that raises the surplus from agreement by one dollar will be shared equally between the contractors and hence will benefit each by only half a dollar.[25] However, the total of the investments made by the two parties will depend upon how the ownership of the asset is assigned. The property rights theory of the firm assumes that the return to each party's initial investment will be greater if they have control of the asset than if they do not. If ownership is assigned to the manager, there will be greater investment in ship design and less by the government in up-front training than if the ownership rights are reversed. At the level of pure principle, therefore, the 'correct' assignment of ownership will depend upon the relative sensitivity to ownership of *ex ante* investments by the two parties.

Suppose, for example, that ownership by the government of the defence facility makes very little difference to the payoff to its *ex ante* investment in training if agreement fails. The returns are much the same whether or not the government owns the asset. This would be the case if the possibility of modifying another supplier's ship in the government-owned shipyard was minimal or highly costly. Under these circumstances, it is not ownership of the asset that influences the productivity of the government's investment but use of the manager's human capital in conjunction with the asset. The manager's human capital and the physical asset are perfectly complementary.

A successful agreement secures the manager's future participation and raises the return to the government's *ex ante* investment. Without such an agreement, it makes no difference whether or not the government owns the asset – the return is the same in either case. The manager's human capital is thus said to be 'essential' to the more productive use of the physical asset. Suppose now that the manager's investment is highly sensitive to ownership and that the return to his investment is much greater when he or she owns the asset than when s/he does not. Even without an agreement, and therefore without the benefit of the the government's participation, the manager can use the asset to raise the productivity of his/her up-front investments in design. The manager is then the best owner of the asset.

If the government starts off owning the defence facility, a transfer of residual control rights to the manager will be advantageous. Non-contractible investment in design will be encouraged while investment in training by the government will not suffer. To reverse these conclusions, it would be necessary to think of a situation in which it is the government's 'intangible' capital that is 'essential' and in which the manager's non-contractible *ex ante* investment is not sensitive to ownership. As Shleifer (1998) points out, the scope of such activities is likely to be severely limited. Governments do not typically invest in ways that are 'essential' to the productive operation of physical assets. Even in the case of a benevolent government conceived unrealistically as a single contractor and aiming to produce a classic public good (defence) the nature of governmental *ex ante* 'investments' will not normally be 'essential' in the technical sense used here.

To illustrate the point, government efforts to build suitable military alliances, to come to defence agreements with other countries and to train military personnel, may greatly increase the social benefit derived from a successful agreement with a warship supplier. However, if in the event of failure to finalise an agreement with the supplying 'manager' the government gains nothing from its ownership of the warship facility, its *ex ante* 'intangible' investments are not 'essential'. It is the manager who is most intimately acquainted with production processes and who therefore might be expected to be in the best position to invest in ways that improve the quality of output or lower production costs. Further, if the manager, failing an agreement with the government, gains a great deal from ownership of the warship facility, ownership of this asset by the manager will greatly increase his or her bargaining power and hence his/her incentive to invest in innovations, cost reductions and so forth. In short, the manager's human capital is 'essential' since, without it, the government gains nothing from ownership of the shipyard. The government's intangible capital is not 'essential' because, even without it, the manager gains substantially from ownership of the shipyard and the complementary use of his or her own human capital.

5.3.2 Property rights and bargaining costs

A curious feature of the property rights theory of the firm as revealed in the above subsection is that transactions costs do not play a significant part. By assumption, there exist certain non-contractible activities that add to the gains potentially achievable from an agreement. We might perhaps interpret this as a statement that it is infinitely costly to transact over these activities. On the other hand, *ex post* bargaining occurs, which is efficient and costless.

As has already been seen in section 3.2, however, one important approach to the assignment of property rights is founded on the idea that transactions are not costless. Even in a world where there were no *ex ante* specific investments to be undertaken by the transactors, the assignment of ownership rights might still be important. Imagine that the manager has some idea for a cost-reducing innovation that arises not from an investment programme in research but as a result of pure alertness. S/he simply notices this opportunity in the manner described in Kirzner's theory of the entrepreneur reviewed in Chapter 3. If the exploitation of this innovation requires the use of the assets in ways not covered in his/her contract, s/he will have to approach the holders of the residual control rights to get their permission to introduce the innovation. This would not be a problem in a world of costless bargaining, and the Grossman–Hart–Moore theory reviewed above would simply assign half the gains to the innovator and half to the government. Where the bargaining process is itself costly, however, we cannot be sure that the gains from the innovation will be achieved.

Persuading others of the merits of an innovation can be a costly and difficult business, as was argued in Chapter 7 where it was seen that this problem could lead to vertical integration. Once we depart from the single contractor model of government and take account of the multiple interests involved and the low-powered incentives within bureaucracies and government departments, the potential importance of bargaining costs becomes apparent. Further, where an idea is not securely embedded in a person's human capital and is easily picked up and used by others, the innovation is very likely to prove profitless to the innovator unless he or she can act quickly using the assets at his or her disposal.

The more costly it is to bargain with government, the more important it will be to assign property rights 'correctly' to begin with, since the process of *ex post* bargaining cannot be relied upon to sort things out. This is, of course, an application of the normative Hobbes theorem. If it is the suppliers who are better placed to discover new opportunities, the residual control rights to the assets will be more socially valuable if assigned to them because then the bargaining costs with government are avoided and a greater number of productive ideas are successfully introduced. Ownership economises on the need for contract. Assets are put under the control of people with knowledge concerning how they can be used most productively. Only when it is desirable for the government to be able to change things frequently without recourse to bargaining with suppliers will the advantage tend the other way and towards public ownership. On the whole, for example, we would expect governments to 'own' their warships rather than to lease them from private suppliers. Even in the field of defence equipment, however, leasing is sometimes considered appropriate. The Royal Air Force in the UK plans to lease four C-17 strategic transport aircraft from Boeing. Under the terms of the lease, certain types of operation are ruled out, but the lease includes an option to buy the aircraft outright at any point. The leasing by the government of fisheries protection vessels has also been considered in the UK.

5.3.3 Non-contractible quality

The vulnerability of specific investments to *ex post* recontracting when contracts are incomplete is the foundation of the property rights approach to ownership (subsection 5.3.1). The cost of bargaining when control rights are 'wrongly' assigned underlies transactions-cost analysis (subsection 5.3.2). Other contractual issues are also significant, however. Consider the case in which the 'output' desired by the government is extremely complex, multifaceted and difficult to measure. Even in the absence of the *ex ante* specific investments in human capital considered above, contracting with a supplier is difficult because compliance is non-verifiable. We have already discussed in Chapter 11 the circumstances in which rights to the residual and the 'high-powered incentives' which go with them can be disadvantageous. Some contractual relationships require 'low-powered' incentives, and non-profit enterprise emerges as a result. Residual rights of control (ownership rights) in the firm's non-human assets tend to be dispersed widely in a non-profit firm. This dispersion of control rights also reflects the requirement for low-powered incentives. Logically, it is possible to imagine profit rights being suppressed while residual control rights are concentrated. The problem in such an arrangement, of course, is that the 'owner' would have an incentive to divert the use of the asset away from the assumed non-contractible objectives of the non-profit enterprise towards his/her private purposes.

Where there are important issues of non-contractible 'quality' at stake, therefore, it is possible to make a case for keeping control rights and profit rights out of the hands of suppliers. Whether the assignment of control rights to the government (still here assumed benevolent) is desirable depends upon other transactions-cost issues. Where competition between suppliers is possible and consumers are frequently in the market and able to make their own judgements about quality, the case for government ownership is weak. Indeed, it is even possible for profit-oriented firms to survive in such circumstances. Where infrequent purchases by consumers unable to judge quality are the norm, government and non-profit solutions are more evenly balanced. However, the possibility of competition between suppliers and the building of 'reputations' would still favour the non-profit solution over government monopoly. Competition between government-owned suppliers is feasible but with no obvious advantages over competition between non-profits and some disadvantages once the assumption of government benevolence is dropped. The competitive process and government ownership of assets seem antithetical, except perhaps in truly federal and decentralised political systems.

These considerations led Shleifer (1998, p. 140) to conclude that government ownership was only likely to be efficient where considerations of non-contractible quality were important; where the possibility of cost reduction via innovation was not great; where competition was limited; and where the building of reputations was costly and ineffective. After allowing for the possibility of non-profit enterprise Shleifer summarises by reflecting on 'how tenuous, in general, is the normative case for government production'.

6. CONCLUSION

In this chapter the theoretical analysis developed in Part 1 has been used to discuss one of the great problems of political economy – the appropriate scope and nature of government intervention in the organisation of economic activity. Neoclassical, Austrian, public choice, property rights and transaction cost approaches have been briefly reviewed.

The last twenty-five years have seen the substitution of contract for state ownership the world over, and it is to a closer examination of this trend that the next two chapters are devoted. Chapter 14 considers privatisation and the trend away from government ownership. Chapter 15 investigates the regulatory issues that have accompanied privatisation, and the enormous increase that has occurred in the use of contract in the achievement of public purposes.

NOTES

1. Jewkes, J. (1964), *Public and Private Enterprise*, The Lindsay Memorial Lectures, Routledge and Kegan Paul, London, p. 90.
2. Adam Mickiewicz, *Pan Tadeusz*, translated by Kenneth Mackenzie, Polish Cultural Foundation, London, 1999 (p. 88 and p. 92).

3. Kasper and Streit (1998).
4. Musgrave (1959) for example, refers to the 'allocation' branch of the budget in the context of government activity aimed at correcting for 'market failure'.
5. See again, Chapter 2, pp. 42–3.
6. See Chapter 4, pp. 97–8.
7. Chapter 12, subsection 4.
8. For a recent review see Barkley Rosser Jr (1999). See also Parker and Stacey (1994).
9. See Chapter 1, section 8, for a discussion of the evolution of 'internal' institutions.
10. Barkley Rosser Jr. (1999), p. 186.
11. See, again, Chapter 4 on the establishment of property rights. The diagrammatic exposition of the Coase Theorem used here can be found in Varian (1999, pp. 573–5).
12. Cooter and Ulen (1997), pp. 89–90.
13. After Thomas Hobbes (1588–1679), English political and legal theorist, author of *Leviathan* who argued that people accept a powerful 'Sovereign' in order to escape the terrors of a 'state of nature' and a war of all against all.
14. See, again, Cooter and Ulen (1997), pp. 89–90.
15. Readers requiring a more extended presentation of these arguments should consult Cooter and Ulen (1997), Chapter 4, section IV.
16. By assumption, these damages can be computed by the Court at low cost.
17. See, again, Chapter 2, section 3.2 where Hume's example of draining a meadow is discussed. Transactions costs are likely to be significant where large numbers of contractors lead to problems of free riding.
18. This idea has already been encountered in Chapter 4, pp. 85–9. As will be seen, MSB = MSC is a necessary but not a sufficient condition for Pareto efficiency.
19. Coase (1946) reviews some of this earlier literature.
20. Lerner (1944); Lange (1936).
21. See Mueller (1996). Classic references include Buchanan and Tullock (1962), Downs (1957) and Breton (1974).
22. See, again, Chapter 4, section 7.2.
23. See, again, Chapter 4.
24. See, again, Chapter 4 for the Nash solution to a bargaining game.
25. An application of the $1/N$ problem once more.

14. Private and public enterprise: the ownership of business

> *'It were good, therefore, that men in their innovations would follow the example of time itself; which, indeed, innovateth greatly, but quietly, and by degrees, scarce to be perceived.'*
> (Francis Bacon)[1]

1. INTRODUCTION

In this chapter, the public- versus private-enterprise debate is reviewed in more detail. Section 2 sketches some historical background and section 3 reviews the empirical literature on the performance of public enterprise in the 1970s and the suggestions that were made for the reform of managerial incentives. Sections 4 and 5 discuss the process of privatisation in the 'mixed economies' since 1980 and the policy dilemmas that were confronted. Mass privatisation in the old centrally planned economies since 1990 is the subject of section 6. Recent empirical studies that attempt to measure the effects of these changes in ownership on performance are discussed in section 7. Brief concluding comments make up section 8.

2. SOME HISTORICAL BACKGROUND

2.1 The Growth of Public Enterprise in the UK to 1980

Consider a brief history of public ownership in the United Kingdom and in other industrialised countries in the twentieth century. In the mid years of the century the nationalisation of enterprise became extensive in the UK. Between 1946 and 1949 the coal, electricity, gas, postal, telephone, rail transport and iron and steel industries were all brought into 'public ownership'. These added to the pre-war stock of nationalised assets which included the Port of London (1908), the Central Electricity Board (1926), London Transport (1933) and the British Overseas Airways Corporation (BOAC) (1939). Several reasons were advanced for this policy of state ownership. There was the need to control 'natural monopoly' in the cases of public utilities such as gas, railways and electricity. The desire to placate vested interests, particularly labour, was important in the cases of the Port of London and the coal industry. The exigencies of war played a part, as in the case of BOAC. Finally, there was the simple desire, according to the generally interventionist sentiments of the time, to control 'the commanding heights of the economy' in the interests of economic planning. It is instructive for a twenty-first-century reader to note that the 'commanding heights' of the UK economy in 1949 included the coal and the steel industries whose remnants (in the guise of RJB mining and Corus) no longer feature in the top fifty firms on the London Stock Exchange.

During the 1970s, the drift towards further public ownership continued and reached sectors far distant from the original public utilities and heavy industry. The nationalisation of shipbuilding (1977) and the rescue of British Leyland (a car company) in 1974 were responses to industrial decline and lack of international competitiveness. The crash and subsequent reconstruction of Rolls Royce (1971) and the formation of the 'National Enterprise Board' (NEB) in 1975 gave the government a stake in many individual firms. The NEB provided loans and equity finance to failing firms needing to restructure (such as Alfred Herbert, a machine-tools manufacturer) or those unable to raise finance from private sources on 'acceptable' terms. Further, the political obsession with the 'commanding heights' of the economy had given way to a new obsession with 'high technology'. Much of the assistance given by the NEB went to microelectronics and biotechnology companies. Indeed, the NEB was renamed the British Technology Group in 1981 after it merged with the National Research Development Corporation (NRDC). The government interest in 'high technology' can also be seen in the nationalisation of much of the aerospace industry and the creation of British Aerospace in 1977. Finally, the discovery of large petroleum deposits in the North Sea and the prospect of gaining access to natural resource rents for the public sector led to the establishment of the British National Oil Corporation in 1976.

2.2 Public Enterprise in Other Mixed Economies

By 1980, therefore, the UK government held a vast portfolio of assets. The nationalised sector employed over two million people, undertook over sixteen per cent of gross fixed capital formation and produced about eleven per cent of gross domestic product (GDP) at factor cost. Neither was this untypical of the so-called 'mixed economies' of the time. A paper produced for the International Monetary Fund (Short, 1983) noted that it was in the manufacturing sector rather than the public utilities that public enterprise was growing fastest in the 1970s. The public enterprise sector accounted on average for about 9.5 per cent of GDP in the industrialised countries in 1980 and about fifteen per cent of gross fixed capital formation. In Australia, the proportion of gross fixed capital formation undertaken by public enterprises was 19.2 per cent in 1979. The great exception was the United States where the share of public enterprises in gross fixed capital formation was about 4.4 per cent in 1978.

2.3 Reform after 1980

Even as Short was preparing his paper for the International Monetary Fund, an avalanche of reform was gathering pace. First, under the Thatcher government in the UK, but then spreading rapidly across the world, including the planned economies of Eastern Europe, enterprises were returned to the private sector on a massive scale. By 1998, the share of gross fixed capital formation undertaken by non-financial public corporations had fallen to 2.9 per cent in the United Kingdom and the share of gross value added at market prices to 3.8 per cent.[2] Almost one million jobs were transferred to the private sector in the years to 1993. In other countries, the banking, electricity and telecommunications industries were privatised on a very large scale. The Deutsche Telecom share offering in 1996, for example, was valued at a gigantic $13,300 million. Worldwide, the pace of reform in the mid-1990s seemed to have intensified as the process subsided in the UK. D'Souza and Megginson (1999) report sales of public enterprises totalling $161 billion in 1997 and almost $140 billion in 1998, with some commentators predicting $6 trillion of sales over the next two decades.

3. PUBLIC VERSUS PRIVATE ENTERPRISE

3.1 Empirical Studies in the 1970s

The period since 1979 has thus seen an upsurge in organisational reform the world over. The collapse of the planned economies in Eastern Europe and the disposal of state property to the private sector in the East and West have been dramatic changes in direction. This shift away from public enterprise, however, probably did not occur because policy makers rediscovered Austrian economics, property rights analysis or contract theory. The theoretical work simply helped to explain empirical observations that were beginning to accumulate.

By the mid-1970s it became clear, for example, that productivity growth in the public enterprise sector in the UK was poor relative to that achieved in the 1960s and relative to the manufacturing sector as a whole.[3] Academic studies at the time attempted to isolate the impact of property rights structure on the performance of firms by comparing public and private enterprise. This usually involved comparing public and private firms operating in otherwise 'similar circumstances'. Comparisons, it was argued, should involve firms of roughly similar size (to control for technical economies of scale), producing similar output, operating in similar market structures (to control for monopoly power), and facing the same prices of inputs, but with a different 'ownership structure'. Attention was then focused on factor productivity or costs of production in the different enterprises. The null hypothesis was that managers of public enterprises have greater discretion than those in private enterprises and that costs will be higher because of the absence of shareholder monitoring, the takeover threat, and managerial incentives related to stock prices and options.

Evidence from this academic work was mixed but ultimately seems to have helped the case for reform. Davies (1971, 1977) compared the performance of competing airlines (one public, one private) in Australia and found the private carrier more efficient in terms of freight tons per employee and passengers carried per employee. Similarly, Pryke (1982) compared the record of public enterprises such as British Airways, Sealink (a ferry company operated by British Rail) and Gas and Electricity retail outlets with private sector equivalents such as British Caledonian, European Ferries and Currys and Comet. Public enterprise, he concluded, 'has performed relatively poorly in terms of its competitive position, has used labour and capital inefficiently and has been less profitable' (p. 70). Other studies supporting this view include Crain and Zardkoohi (1978) for water utilities in the USA, Ahlbrandt (1973) for fire services, Bennett and Johnson (1979) for garbage collection, and Frech III (1976) for the processing of medical insurance claims.

Some work of this period runs counter to these findings of public sector inefficiency. Caves and Christensen (1980) compare the Canadian National railroad (public) with the Canadian Pacific Railroad (private). They calculate measures of total factor productivity and compare their growth over time and between firms. The public firm appears to have exhibited a lower level of productivity in the early 1960s but to have caught up with Canadian Pacific by 1967. Caves and Christensen therefore conclude that 'public ownership is not inherently less efficient than private ownership' (p. 974) although they accept that the existence of competition between the two railroads might provide an explanation of the performance of Canadian National. Electricity companies in the United States have provided another useful field for comparative institutional analysis. Meyer (1975), Neuberg

(1977) and Pescatrice and Trapani (1980) all found lower costs in publicly owned utilities but found it difficult to interpret the results. The private enterprises involved were operating under regulatory constraints on rates of return which could induce private companies to inflate their costs artificially.[4]

3.2   Reform of Public Enterprise

One response to the evidence of poor performance on the part of public enterprise was to consider reforms which altered the 'contractual' environment of managers but which fell short of privatisation.[5] As has been seen in Chapter 13, the property rights theory of organisation shows that the efficient assignment of ownership rights and the hazards which face people in a world of contractual incompleteness are interdependent. Once contractual innovations began to be widely discussed and introduced, the case for a change in the assignment of residual control rights and residual (profit) rights inevitably arose. In subsection 3, however, the focus is on the problems of contracting in the public sector where physical assets are held by the state and residual (profit) rights do not exist. The process of privatisation will be considered in subsection 4.

3.2.1   Financial targets

One option is to monitor certain indicators of performance. Instead of being asked to pursue the 'public interest', managers could be given more detailed financial objectives such as a target return on capital or a break-even constraint which they are asked to satisfy. Such objectives have the advantage of being reasonably clear and relatively easy to measure. The break-even objective is simple and provides, as noted in Chapter 13, a crude check that total benefits outweigh total costs. It is sometimes also claimed that managerial morale is higher when targets are financial in nature, straightforward and verifiable. Under 'public interest' conditions, managers find themselves swamped in controversy whatever outcomes occur. At least the achievement of a given financial target has the merit of being relatively objective.

Although financial targets are widely used as an instrument of public enterprise control, critics point to several problems. If managers are operating 'natural monopolies', achieving some basic financial targets may not be particularly demanding. It may be easy to exploit a monopoly position to achieve break-even or a specified rate of return on capital. Hitting a financial target is therefore only a very indirect and ineffective way of encouraging the efficient control of resource inputs where managers have the commercial freedom to set prices. Financial targets also ignore the wider social or environmental objectives of public enterprise, unless these can be separately accounted for. In effect, the setting of financial targets calls into question the reasons for the public sector status of the firm. If the firm is supposedly owned by the state to control a possible abuse of monopoly, and to ensure that social as well as private costs and benefits are taken into account in decision making, financial targets on their own seem ill-designed for these purposes. Further, the setting of financial targets involves a bargaining process between politicians and managers. Managers will be far better informed about the state of the enterprise than will politicians and this will give them an advantage. Bargaining will be considered in more detail in Chapter 15, where the relationship between the regulatory authorities and the managers of privatised firms will be discussed.

3.2.2   Efficiency targets

Because of the limitations of financial targets in the context of nationalised industries, they have been supplemented by separate 'efficiency targets'.[6] Efficiency here refers not to full Pareto efficiency but to lower-level targets for technical or cost efficiency. These can take the form of a given 'cost per unit of output' or a standard of service which managers must aim to achieve. To be effective, these efficiency targets must be simple and verifiable. However, simplicity runs the risk of producing a distorting influence on management decisions. Where there are many dimensions to 'output', the imposition of targets often results in the selection of a few relatively easily observable variables to monitor, which are then achieved at the expense of other important elements.[7] The 'output' of bus services, for example, could be measured in passenger miles, but the safety of the service, the courtesy of the staff, the comfort of the buses, the reliability of the service, and the convenience of the timetable, along with many other possible factors, will also go towards the satisfaction of the consumer. A bus service with low 'costs per passenger mile' will not necessarily represent the ideal service to consumers if it is unreliable and uncomfortable. Make 'reliability' a target, however, and managers will have an incentive to set undemanding timetables. As the targets proliferate and increase in complexity, managers begin no longer to be 'agents' exercising their judgement and using their knowledge and experience in the interests of the principal. Instead, the principal effectively takes over the task of the manager.

A report from the Monopolies and Mergers Commission (1988) provides an example of the difficulty of devising efficiency targets in the case of over-the-counter services at post offices in the UK (such as buying stamps or savings bonds). The General Post Office (GPO) faced the objective of achieving an annual percentage reduction in real unit costs. The unit of output was defined in terms of a 'basic transaction hour'. Transactions included paying pensions, motor taxation, receiving parcels for the post and so forth. Output was then defined as the number of transactions effected multiplied by a 'standard time' per transaction. Thus, two transactions taking one minute each would be equivalent to one (different) transaction taking two minutes. This was certainly one way of aggregating many differing activities into a single measure of 'output', but the implications for managerial incentives were not all benign. If managers succeed in thinking of ways to reduce the time taken per transaction for some or all of the categories, while the number of transactions remained unchanged, output would be recorded as having fallen. Yet, for most people, a generally faster service would mean a better one and hence a sign of higher output. Another problem related to the 'costs' which were considered. Some transactions were far more costly in terms of 'back-office support' than others, but this support did not figure in the calculation of basic transaction hours. A rise in business involving transactions which used little counter time but large amounts of back-office support could then result in a misleading impression about costs per transaction hour.

Financial targets and 'efficiency' targets are simply attempts to find an 'informative signal', in the jargon of Chapter 5, subsection 5, which will permit monitoring to be an effective spur to managerial effort. The criticisms mentioned above can be regarded as casting doubt on the quality of the information revealed. If it is too 'noisy', that is statistically unrelated to true management effort in pursuing the ultimate aims of the enterprise, information about particular components of 'costs' or 'output' will be of little use in raising performance. Further, the absence of privately assigned residual claims reduces the incentive to monitor performance, even if an informative signal is theoretically usable. The introduction of partial private ownership can be seen therefore as a means of encouraging sources of efficiency monitoring other than those emanating from government.

3.2.3   The Mixed Enterprise

Monitoring pressure plays a central part in Eckel and Vining's (1985) approach to the mixed enterprise. A mixed enterprise has a proportion of its equity shares held by the state and a proportion held by private individuals. Eckel and Vining suggest that this particular 'mixed' form of enterprise has advantages in certain circumstances over purely public or private forms. Suppose the government wished to ensure that a firm produced a certain 'social output' in addition to its usual 'private output'. Some modification of the firm's activity is required, in other words, in the public interest. The government might regulate the private firm, but this would require the devising of costly monitoring procedures to check performance in the achievement of social goals. Alternatively, it might nationalise the firm, but in so doing it would leave the managers relatively free from pressure. The 'mixed' enterprise gives the government an influential position and may permit minority or perhaps majority 'control'. But, as Eckel and Vining argue, 'Partial private ownership provides an alternative source of pressure for efficiency, lessening the need for efficiency monitoring by government' (p. 92).

As we saw in Chapters 8 and 9, the existence of exchangeable residual claims plays an important role in theoretical discussions of managerial incentives. Senior executives can be given incentives based on the performance of the shares, the share price provides concise information to the managerial labour market, and individual monitoring by shareholders is always a possibility. The government itself may be constrained not to push its demands for social output too far because of the effects on the share price and the difficulties which that might imply for the raising of further capital. The effect of selling equity shares to private buyers is to make managers more 'profit conscious'. This approach indicates, therefore, that achieving a given target level of 'social output' may be accomplished more efficiently by the state buying shares in an enterprise than by outright nationalisation.

Where monitoring is very costly relative to the value of the information gathered, the joint-stock company responds by using alternative incentive devices. Shareholders do not set objectives for cost per unit or attempt to set output targets. Instead, principal–agent theory predicts that we will observe agents (managers) taking some of the risks of the enterprise and being rewarded with a share of the actual outcome. In the private sector (see Chapter 8, subsection 4) this takes the form of profit-related pay, managerial stock ownership, stock options and other deferred compensation related to stock-market performance. The question therefore arises: in the absence of cheap and accurate information, is the public sector capable of devising equivalent incentive contracts for managers?

3.2.4   An incentive contract for managers of public enterprises

In principle, it is possible to imagine a contract between government and managers of a public utility which reflects the terms of the pure agency contract outlined in Chapter 5. With risk-neutral managers, for example, the contract would involve the managers (agents) paying a fixed fee to the government (principal) in return for the right to use the physical assets and to keep the final outcome. If Pareto efficiency is the objective, this final 'outcome' would have to be interpreted not simply as achieved profit from market sales, since this would result in the agents behaving like profit-maximising monopolists. Instead, the 'outcome' would have to represent the full net 'social' value of the firm's product (Loeb and Magat, 1979).

In terms of the 'box diagram' that we have been using to illustrate

contract theory, the dimensions of the box would have to represent net
social gains in two possible states of the world and management effort
would, as usual, be interpreted as increasing the probability of the 'good'
state. The optimal contract would be on the government's 45° line as illustrated in Figure 14.1. Were it practically possible to implement such a
scheme, the firm would operate efficiently because it would always receive
the full marginal social benefit deriving from its activities and would therefore maximise its expected profit by equating expected marginal social benefits to expected marginal costs.[8] The government (principal) would
negotiate with the managers over the fixed fee, which could be anything
between zero and some maximum amount that would just permit the firm
to make a 'pure' profit of zero on all its assets including the fee.

This 'ideal' scheme clearly overcomes the moral hazard problem and
means that the monitoring of managerial effort is not necessary. The practical difficulties, however, are clear. Payments must be made to the firm
not just from its customers but also from the government. Government

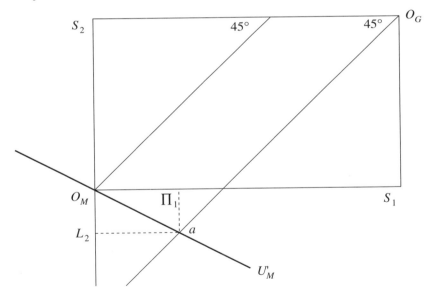

Note: S_1 and S_2 represent the net social surplus from the activities of the public enterprise
in the 'good' and 'bad' state respectively. A contract at *a* will give the risk-neutral managers
high-powered incentives to exert effort. They will earn pure profits of Π_1 in state 1 but make
losses of L_2 in state 2. They are assumed to achieve their reservation utility of U'_M. At *a* the
government receives the entire expected net social surplus from the enterprise given optimal
effort from the managers and the managers bear all the risk.

Figure 14.1   An optimal contract for public enterprise managers

payments to the firm would represent the excess of what consumers are prepared to pay over the price the firm actually charges them. In other words, the firm receives the full marginal social value attached to its output. From the customer it receives a price and from the government it receives a payment equal to the consumer's surplus. Like the perfectly discriminating monopolist mentioned in section 4 of Chapter 13, therefore, the firm receives the full social value of its output. Thus, although this contract means that information about managerial effort is of no value to the government, information about the 'outcome' is clearly crucial and must be observable if the contract is to work. Detailed information, however, about the maximum willingness of people to pay for additional output of the public enterprise (its full marginal social benefit) is unlikely actually to be available to the government.

A further difficulty concerns the negotiations over the level of the fixed fee. From the point of view of Pareto efficiency it does not matter what the level of the fee turns out to be providing that it is not so excessive that it actually causes the firm to close down – a contingency which is presumably unlikely to happen. The size of the fee determines not the level of efficiency but the income of the managers who effectively have become 'franchisees' of the government for the duration of the contract. Their knowledge of the business would be expected to give them a bargaining advantage and might lead them to exaggerate their prospective costs in order to negotiate the fee downwards. A government that put a higher value on benefits to consumer-citizens than to enterprise managers would obviously prefer a higher to a lower fixed fee. A competitive auction of the franchise is a response to this problem but a more detailed consideration of franchising as a response to the 'natural monopoly' problem must await Chapter 15.

Notice finally that contract theory does not explicitly consider the role of property rights. The managers lease the assets from the government. The government retains 'residual rights of control'. It is implicitly assumed that this retention of residual control rights by the government does not influence management incentives – a stark contrast with property rights theory. Presumably the rights in the physical assets transferred to the managers are assumed to be sufficiently comprehensive and clear to permit most innovations to take place without having to renegotiate with the government. The general inappropriateness of this assumption in a world of contractual incompleteness was considered in some detail in Chapter 13.

3.3   The Forces of Competition

The idea that by pitting groups of managers against one another in a competitive auction of a franchise, information about costs might indirectly be revealed to the government is important. For our purposes in this chapter it raises the more general question of how competitive forces might be used within the public enterprise sector to encourage and constrain managers.

3.3.1 The product market

The context of public utilities and 'natural monopoly' makes the use of competition in the product market problematic. If effective competition is possible, one of the main reasons for having public enterprise in the first place is absent. Sometimes, however, a 'natural monopoly' has associated with it many activities, which could be supplied competitively (and privately), and it will be seen in Chapter 15 how regulators have attempted to encourage competition wherever possible. However, the question of whether competition between public enterprises is likely to be effective as a spur to improved performance is an interesting one in itself. Neoclassical textbooks often try to separate out the influence of 'competition' from the influence of 'property rights' on a firm's behaviour, and it is sometimes argued that 'competition' is more important than 'ownership' in determining performance. This question can be approached as a purely empirical matter, and studies have been conducted into private and public enterprise in 'monopolistic' and 'competitive' circumstances respectively to see how measures of efficiency are effected. Such studies, however, tend to skate over some important theoretical matters.

It is not clear that property rights considerations and market competition can correctly be regarded as independent influences on a firm. This point was discussed in detail in Chapter 8, subsections 6 and 7. Quite apart from 'Austrian' objections related to 'competition as a process of discovery', plain neoclassical reasoning suggests difficulties, summarised in Jensen and Meckling's (1976, p. 330) observation: 'If my competitors all incur agency costs equal to or greater than mine I will not be eliminated from the market by their competition.' A town full of 'competing' publicly owned restaurants is not likely to produce a similar level of service to an identical town full of private restaurants. Competition in the product market cannot simply 'trump' the 'ownership' issue, rendering it of no real importance. Of course, a gourmet-led secret service might shoot the staff of the worst-performing restaurant each year and thereby induce competition (at least to satisfy the tastes of the secret service personnel), but this simply throws into relief the point that competition works in conjunction with other factors related to ownership and contract.

A more benign socialist regime could franchise the restaurant facilities for a period. The buildings and equipment might then be publicly owned and restaurants might be thought of as public services, but competition would work because the franchisees would have high-powered incentives to compete with others over the franchise period. Given the existence of competition, the importance of non-contractible quality, the likelihood of repeat purchases by individual consumers and the potential for reputation building, the advantage of state ownership of the physical assets is extremely unclear under these circumstances. The assets of private-sector franchised restaurants are normally held by the franchisee rather than the franchiser. However, the logical possibility of combining high-powered incentives with public ownership of assets, where it is possible to measure quality at low cost or where product market competition is strong, is one to which we will return in Chapter 15.

Similar points apply to the case of competition between public and private enterprises. The fact that, over a certain period of time, a public enterprise is found to match the performance of a private enterprise operating in the same market cannot lead to the conclusion that a system of competing public enterprises is likely to be as effective as a system of competing private enterprises. As was seen in Part 2 of this book, one type of firm can impose external benefits or costs on other types. In this context, suppose that private firms face lower agency costs than public firms. Their performance then acts as a benchmark against which the performance of the public enterprise can be compared. This type of competition is sometimes called 'yardstick competition'. Information about the performance of other types of enterprise, or about the performance of similar types of enterprise in different regions, states or countries can be used to motivate managers. Such information represents another 'informative signal' that enables the principal to assess the effort of managers and to agree suitably constructed incentive contracts. Use of 'yardstick' competition in the public sector is an important incentive mechanism, but it can be understood only when placed in the context of the contracting problem. Implicitly or explicitly, public sector managers must believe they have something to gain by matching or outclassing the competition – that they are engaged in a tournament with other management teams elsewhere.

An attempt to isolate the influence of competition in the product market on public enterprise efficiency can be found in Primeaux (1977), in the context of the electricity supply industry. Primeaux compared a set of municipally owned firms in a monopoly market with a set of municipally owned firms facing some competition from alternative private-sector suppliers. Competing and non-competing municipal firms were then matched together in pairs. Each pair had to be in the same state, with the same primary source of energy, and of approximately equal size. A cost function was then estimated from the entire sample using independent variables such as sales, fuel cost, market density and dummy variables to reflect location and the presence of competition. Primeaux found that average cost in competitive firms was lower at the mean by 10.75 per cent. Further, 'even though scale economies exist, the benefits of X-efficiency outweigh them until very large output levels are reached' (p. 107). Pressure from the product market seems to be established in this case, although there is no attempt to relate this pressure to the detailed provisions of the contracts held by public-sector managers.

3.3.2 The managerial labour market

Incentives can also be derived from the managerial labour market if participants in the market can assess performance and managers can recontract with sufficient regularity. The problem for public enterprise managers is that the more varied objectives typical of the sector and the greater problems of measuring 'success' or 'failure' mean that conveying information to the managerial labour market is more difficult than for managers in the private sector. In the private sector the level of profits and the stock-market valuation of a company are more 'objective' and easily observable tests of performance than those that are used in the public sector. For this reason, it will be difficult for a 'successful' public-sector manager to use his or her track record to raise their value in the private sector. The use of information generated in the private sector to select managers for the public sector is not unknown, however, although appointments from the public sector have often in the past signalled the adoption of corporate status on the part of a public enterprise, the introduction of financial targets and the eventual flotation or sale of the enterprise.

3.3.3 The market in corporate control

Perhaps the main difference between competitive forces in the public and private sectors is the absence in the former of the takeover threat. Without exchangeable ownership rights, the market in corporate control cannot operate. Most of Chapter 9 was devoted to an extended discussion of the takeover as a managerial incentive mechanism in the private sector. There it was seen that the agency costs resulting from dispersed ownership and managerial 'shirking' could not exceed the cost faced by an entrepreneur of reasserting control by acquiring a dominant interest in the stock. The difficulties of achieving a successful takeover were substantial (paradoxically, especially when information was assumed to be comprehensive and publicly available) but the takeover is nevertheless an important characteristic of modern Anglo-American Capitalism. From the perspective of 'Austrian' economics, the takeover is a significant mechanism by which successful or 'competent' entrepreneurs wrest control of resources from the less successful.

In some situations we have seen that the possibility of takeover might be suppressed for good economic reasons – for example, the protection of specific human capital from opportunist 'raiders' under conditions of asymmetric information. Wherever this happens, however, including the public sector, a price is paid in the form of lower incentives for managers to operate in a cost-efficient manner and of reduced chances of resources being reallocated from less to more competent owners. These dynamic advantages of private property in providing incentives to innovation and in facilitating the transfer of assets to the most productive owners have recently led to privatisation on a large scale. As we saw in Chapter 13, it is only where transactional difficulties are very great and where attempts to suppress dysfunctional high-powered incentives are necessary that public ownership can be advantageous. On the whole, the world has recently judged that it is a more desirable and tractable 'problem' for governments to wrestle via regulatory contracts with the effects of the high-powered incentives created by private ownership than to wrestle via managerial incentive contracts with the low-powered incentives created by public ownership. Subsection 4 investigates some of the policy issues which are associated with this process of privatisation.

4. THE PROCESS OF PRIVATISATION IN THE 'MIXED ECONOMIES'

The policy decision to transfer assets from the public to the private sector is conceptually simple but raises subsidiary policy issues of great importance relating to the methods used. Privatisation occurs when collective, non-exchangeable property rights held by the state are replaced by exchangeable, privately assigned rights. This can be brought about in various ways.

4.1 Stock Market Flotation

In the 'mixed economies', the primary method of privatisation is to create a public company (assuming that the public enterprise does not take this legal form to begin with) followed by a stock-market flotation of the shares. The offer of shares to individual members of the public can be at a 'fixed price' or may be a 'tender offer'. In the case of a fixed-price offer, a price is set by the government or its advisers. The decision of the private investor is simply to decide how many shares to purchase at the fixed price. The problem for the government is to assess the 'market' value of the assets. For reasons of political 'credibility', governments may tend to shade down the fixed-offer price in order to ensure that the flotation is seen as a 'success', although a flotation would normally be underwritten by financial institutions. In the case of excess supply of shares, the underwriter agrees for a fee to purchase the shares not taken up by the public. Where there turns out to be excess demand for shares at the fixed price, investors may be rationed and receive only a proportion of the shares they wanted.

In the case of a tender offer, judgement about how much the shares are likely to be worth on the market is transferred to the individual investor who tenders a price at which he or she is prepared to buy a specified quantity. The shares are then allocated to those who tendered the highest prices. Sometimes the investor will pay the price tendered. However, this type of system may lead to the withdrawal of all but the most sophisticated and knowledgeable investors. To avoid this eventuality, it is possible to sell the shares at the 'striking price' – the price at which all the available shares can be sold to the people tendering for shares. Individual investors then pay this 'striking price', rather than the price that they have tendered. Providing they have tendered a price above the eventual striking price, they will receive shares. Small investors can then be given the opportunity to buy some proportion of the shares 'at the striking price'. It is possible also to combine a fixed price offer for a portion of the shares with a tender offer for the rest. In the case of British Telecom (1987) for example, a proportion of the shares was available to overseas and institutional investors as a tender offer. In contrast, the general public faced a fixed-price offer.

4.2   The Employee Buy-out

Instead of selling to the general public or to financial institutions, some privatisations have been effected via management or employee buy-outs. Managers will often have the most intimate knowledge of a business and be in the best position to assess its future prospects. Concentration of ownership rights in the hands of a small number of senior managers will concentrate risk but provide high-powered incentives. Another consideration might also be vulnerability to 'hold-up' of firm-specific human capital. It is these conditions, as noted in Chapter 10, which favour constitutional arrangements which limit the power of outside investors. Establishing a price for the shares, however, requires bargaining between government and workers or managers, and is obviously less 'transparent' as a method than the stock-market flotation. Political considerations are also important in some contexts. Sale to the workforce may be the only politically acceptable way of 'privatising' assets and gaining the support of a powerful interest group.

4.3 The Private Sale

Private sale – that is, the sale of an enterprise as a single entity to another firm – is suitable where the assets are highly complementary to those under the control of the buyer and it is therefore efficient for them to be held together. The mechanism here is equivalent to a takeover of the hitherto public firm by a private one willing to offer the most attractive price. A number of companies which had become part of the public sector in the 1960s and 1970s in the UK were privatised by this means; for example, the sale of Rover cars to British Aerospace.

4.4 Voucher Privatisation

If assets are 'publicly owned', it might be reasonably asked why privatisation should necessarily proceed by share flotation or private sale. Since the people implicitly already 'own' the assets in an inefficient collective form, all that is required, it might be argued, is to make their rights tradable. The assets will then effectively have been privatised. This is the idea which lies behind voucher privatisation, a method used extensively in the transition process of Eastern European economies in the 1990s. Voucher methods of privatisation will be considered in more detail in section 6.2 below. In essence, however, rights to the assets (or the means to acquire such rights – vouchers) are simply distributed throughout the population on the basis of some equitable principle and individual trading is then allowed to proceed freely.

In the mixed economies, a number of considerations seem to have prevented the use of vouchers. It could be argued that, where assets had not been confiscated in a revolution but acquired by the public sector and the owners 'compensated', the public debt issued at the time should be redeemed when the process is reversed at privatisation. Further, in so far as public firms were profitable and these profits were part of public sector receipts, taxes would have to rise to replace this revenue if the assets were simply given away. A reasonable case could therefore be made for the sale of public-sector assets and the use of the proceeds to redeem public debt. Taxpayers as a whole would then benefit from the lower cost of financing the debt. The distributional consequences, however, were obviously very different from those that might have accompanied voucher privatisation. Vouchers were used extensively where the restructuring of entire economies was being attempted, where extreme disruption made the valuation of assets very speculative and uncertain, where capital markets were relatively unsophisticated and undeveloped, and where political interest groups were powerful.

5.   PRIVATISATION – POLICY DILEMMAS

5.1   The Austrian View

The means of privatisation adopted by different governments can be seen as reflecting the issues discussed in Chapter 13. From the perspective of 'Austrian' economics, the main objective is to create exchangeable private property rights in hitherto state-owned assets so that people have the incentive to discover how to use them most effectively and to permit the most 'competent' owners to gain control. Thus, privatisation *per se* is an important objective of policy. The final disposition of the assets and their ultimate value cannot be known in advance and so policy must simply concentrate on establishing the economic system which will allow this dynamic process to take place. An 'Austrian' policy would have used a competitive tender system to allocate privatised assets to the highest bidders and would have removed all restrictions on trade in privatised assets and on potential and actual competition.

There are additional twists even to this simple message, however. In particular, voucher privatisation 'qualifies', in Casson's sense, a wider group of people to take part in the privatisation programme. Auctioning state assets for cash might well be expected to produce a different evolutionary time path of subsequent trades than auctioning them for vouchers. By issuing vouchers, the distribution of wealth is changed, and a form of 'capital' is placed in the hands of a large number of people through which they can compete for control of the newly privatised assets. It can be argued that this enlarges the pool of talent from which new entrepreneurs can emerge.

5.2   The Public Choice View

The evidence from actual privatisation programmes suggests, however, that the considerations mentioned in section 5.2 of Chapter 13 were equally important. The methods of privatisation adopted often betray the fact that public choice pressures, corporate governance arrangements and the establishment of particular structures for the privatised industries played their part in determining the nature of privatisation policy. Governments did not, in other words, confine themselves to establishing new rules of the game but actively encouraged particular outcomes.

Support for wider share ownership, for example, was a significant objective of British government policy. Partly this may have been a matter of political and social policy – the judgement that citizens should have a basic grasp of how, in a free-market system, public companies operate, and that holding shares is more likely to impart this understanding than months of economics lectures. It was also, though, about public choice and the problem of how to make the privatisation programme politically difficult to reverse. Just as the UK government privatised a large part of municipal housing by selling the houses at below-market prices, it privatised the nationalised industries in a way which usually ensured a quick capital gain for small shareholders. As mentioned in subsection 4.1, fixed-price offers were usually set below estimates of market-clearing prices to ensure excess demand and to encourage small investors who could benefit quickly as 'stags'. In some privatisations, investors could pay for their shares in two or three 'instalments', thus making any post-privatisation premium on the share price even more attractive relative to the amount of capital that had to be committed in the first instalments. To encourage small investors actually to hold their shares rather than to sell them, other devices such as 'loyalty bonus shares' were tried.[9] The political appeal of renationalisation was unlikely to be very great among large numbers of small investors who held shares on which significant capital gains had been made.

Hostility to privatisation from employee interest groups was another public choice consideration. Support was sometimes 'purchased' by special treatment such as the offer of 'free' shares or shares at a fraction of the 'fixed' offer price. Employees were also given priority when an issue of shares was oversubscribed (as would usually be the case). Special arrangements of this nature figured in UK privatisations such as British Airways, British Gas, British Telecommunications and Amersham International (an oil company).

The interests of management and employee groups were also reflected in the way firms were structured at privatisation. In general, these groups felt less threatened by privatisation the more monopoly power they were granted. No doubt the new owners would try to pressure managers into operating more cost-effectively than before, but given the dispersed nature of shareholdings and the associated agency costs, the managers could hope to direct a portion of the monopoly rents towards 'internal' interests. Privatising fully fledged monopolies also tended to make projections of revenues more certain than would have been the case if large-scale restructuring had been attempted prior to flotation. The lower was the level of anticipated competition in the privatised market, the higher was the expected revenue raised by the sale of shares. Politicians wanting a 'successful' launch, bureaucrats interested in raising revenue, and managers wanting as little disruption as possible but happy to contemplate their new incentive packages were thus able to make common cause against radical changes in the industrial structure of the public utilities. British Gas (privatised in 1986) and British Telecom (1984), for example, were initially sold as integrated concerns with very little restructuring. As will be seen in Chapter 15, however, considerable structural change was introduced at a later date in these industries and the electricity and rail industries were privatised in the 1990s in a more 'disintegrated' fashion.

5.3 Privatisation and the Normative Hobbes and Coase Theorems

Outside the integrated public utilities, management and labour interest groups were smaller and less powerful. Privatisation still required some judgement to be made about organisational form. Unipart, for example, was separated from British Leyland (the nationalised car firm) and privatised as a management/employee buy-out. Sealink (a ferry company) was hived-off from British Rail and disposed of as a private sale. Austin Rover (a car firm) was sold to British Aerospace[10] and British Coal to RJB. The National Bus Company was sold in a series of no less than 27 separate privatisations, and management buy-outs were common in this area. Clearly, government policy seems to have been about more than simple privatisation. It was also about detailed questions of organisational structure.

In competitive conditions, the value of state assets on the market can be used as an indicator of the form in which they should be privatised. A government might divide up its assets into packages and sell these by means of buy-outs, trade sales or flotations according to which method maximises its proceeds. Strong complementarity between the assets and those held by other companies would tend to favour a trade sale. High levels of firm-specific human capital would suggest an employee buy-out, although the government might be tempted to act opportunistically, sell to outsiders and implicitly 'hold-up' the employees. A large requirement for outside equity capital would favour the stock-market flotation. Again, however, the information problem is confronted. The government could not realistically be expected to know what value the 'market' would put on the assets in all the varying circumstances that are possible. It might, for example, mistakenly divide up a hitherto vertically or horizontally integrated enterprise into separate companies, when the integrated business would have been more valuable. Alternatively, the government might sell an integrated business that should have been broken up or privatise a business by means of a buy-out when a flotation would have yielded greater revenue. Are such 'mistakes' a serious problem?

Transaction costs are once more central to the argument. In a world of negligible transaction costs it really would not much matter in what form public sector assets were privatised. The 'Coase theorem' could be invoked to show that, once property rights in the assets were exchangeable, they would at low cost rapidly be assigned to those who valued them most highly. This would be true whether the assets were given away, sold at auction as private companies, handed over to workers as independent cooperatives, or floated on the stock market. This theoretical proposition is of limited interest in the present context, however, because in such a low transaction-cost world, as we established in Chapter 1, organisational form is hardly a problem in the first place. Where transaction costs and ownership costs are negligible, we have no means of explaining the scope and ownership of enterprise. Given, therefore, that transactions costs are not negligible and represent a central organisational problem, decisions about the way firms should be structured at privatisation are likely to be important and might be expected to influence the way privatised firms adjust their organisation over time.

In the mixed economies of the West, the existence of highly developed capital markets and a long-established framework of company law helped both to identify owners who placed the highest value on resources at privatisation and to permit restructuring afterwards. In the jargon of Chapter 13, section 3, the institutions of Western capital markets provided information to the government (thus assisting the application of the normative Hobbes theorem) and lowered the cost of transacting in property rights after privatisation (thus assisting the application of the normative Coase theorem). A firm 'wrongly' floated as an independent company could fairly rapidly be acquired in the market for corporate control, while conversely another firm privatised with too many associated diverse activities could be expected to dispose of them in trade sales, 'spin-offs', or buy-outs. These were advantages not available to many of the countries in Eastern Europe during their privatisation programmes, and it is to a brief discussion of their problems that the next subsection is devoted.

6.   MASS PRIVATISATION

Reform of the former centrally planned economies confronted policy makers with a problem in political economy of the greatest complexity. Transition from one economic system to another is not something that could be planned. As many economists in Eastern Europe recognised, if it were possible to plan the transition it would have been possible to plan the economy. From a position in which virtually no private business enterprise existed, the economies of the East were to be transformed into functioning market systems. Detailed consideration of this huge subject is clearly beyond the scope of a few pages, but the normative Hobbes and Coase theorems do provide a framework for considering the main features of the process in various countries.

The first point to note is that the absence of market prices in the planned economies deprived the governments there of a source of information. The 'Austrian' economist might insist that all economic systems are in disequilibrium and that prices cannot be taken as objective measures of costs and benefits. From a practical point of view, however, it is clear that Western governments could form a much clearer assessment of the likely future market value of state assets than could the governments of Eastern Europe. This greatly reduced the scope for applying the normative Hobbes theorem. If the government has not the slightest idea how existing assets would be allocated in a long-established market system it can hardly structure its reform programme so as to 'minimise the harm done by failures in private agreements'. Nevertheless, the Hobbesian problem – to whom should the newly created private property rights initially be allocated? – could not be avoided. Indeed, because commercial and corporate law, along with the law of property and contract, were underdeveloped, and because legal processes (institutions) had not yet gained the confidence of contracting parties, transaction costs were likely to be significant. Reliance on the Coase theorem to sort things out after privatisation was therefore a less persuasive policy stance than in the economies of the West. Higher transactions costs, at least initially, made the normative Hobbes theorem more important, while the degree of dislocation of the economy made it simultaneously more difficult to apply.[11]

6.1 The Political Economy of Mass Privatisation

To establish clearly assigned, legally protected and privately exchangeable rights to resources was the first step towards reform. How should the new property rights be assigned? In Russia, for example, there was a possibility that politicians or state officials who had some 'de facto' control over the use of resources might gain 'de jure' property rights. This became known as 'nomenklatura privatisation'. It had three crucial disadvantages. Firstly, it would have been perceived as very 'unfair' and hence illegitimate – tantamount to legalised corruption. Secondly, firms would have remained 'politicised' rather than being 'depoliticised' and placed under the control of professional managers or entrepreneurs. Thirdly, politicians and state officials could not be expected necessarily to be the most 'competent' owners. This third objection would not be important if transaction costs were low enough and the process of reallocation to competent owners through exchange was anticipated to be sufficiently rapid. The first and second objections, however, made such an outcome unlikely.

Another possibility was to condone 'spontaneous privatisation' and let managers gain the control and residual rights to state property. A manager might, for example, set up a private company and then sell the property of the state enterprise to his or her private company at 'knock-down' prices. Basically, this would be to condone a form of theft and would not augur well for the future acceptability of the system. What was required was a legally acceptable process that held out the prospect of gain to a wide enough coalition of interests to make mass privatisation difficult to reverse. Boycko, Shleifer and Vishny (1995) describe the system adopted in Russia by which managers, workers, local officials and the general public were given a combined interest that eventually triumphed over the politicians and functionaries at the central ministries.

Small firms were sold in the form of proprietorships by local governments for cash. For larger organisations with a national scope and importance, however, cash sales were not considered appropriate. Although such sales would raise revenue for the government, the enormous scale of privatisation would have made the pace of change through cash sales too slow. There was also the danger that buyers would be bureaucrats suspected of corruption, gangsters or foreigners. Although the latter might, in principle, have much to offer, politicians did not relish the political consequences of selling a high proportion of state assets to foreign interests. Larger organisations were therefore privatised using the method of vouchers.

State-run organisations were first 'corporatised'; that is, turned into the legal form of joint-stock companies fully owned by the government. This is, in itself, interesting from the point of view of the normative Hobbes and Coase theorems. Legally, the reformers in Russia tried to ensure that the corporations that were to be privatised were 'open' companies. This ensured that shareholdings could not be restricted to 'inside' groups of workers and managers. A Hobbesian judgement was made that it was better to create 'open' rather than 'labour-managed' or 'cooperative' enterprises with the associated problems of collective decision making and the raising of capital to which (as was seen in Chapter 10) these are prone. There would, in other words, be fewer 'mistakes' in enterprise governance by making them 'open' than 'closed'. Further, from a Coasian viewpoint, the transactional impediments to recreating worker-owned enterprises later (that is, after privatisation) where they had advantages were likely to be far less severe than the transactional impediments to creating 'open companies' out of worker cooperatives. Thus, privatising 'open' companies rather than worker-owned 'closed' companies represented both a judgement about what would be best 'in the absence of further private agreements' (Hobbes) and a judgement about what would reduce transactions costs and hence 'most facilitate further private agreements' (Coase).

As with many privatisations in the West, workers and managers were given privileged access to shares. Under one option, it was possible for managers and workers to buy fifty-one per cent of the voting equity at 1.7 times the July 1992 'book value' – an almost arbitrary value with little necessary connection to the eventual (unknown) market value. As emphasised above, however, workers exercising this option had to own their shares as individuals and were free to sell to 'outsiders' whenever they wished. This policy reflected, therefore, the 'Austrian' argument that the allocation of competence to resources is of prime importance to economic development and that more-efficient owners should be able to gain control from less-efficient owners through private agreements and through the market in corporate control.

6.2   Vouchers and Privatisation

The general public was given an interest in privatisation through the use of vouchers. Firms being privatised sold 29 per cent of their shares in voucher auctions. All citizens were offered vouchers with a denomination of 10 000 rubles. These were tradable on the open market without restrictions. The 'value' of 10 000 rubles was arbitrary. It would have been possible simply to denominate the vouchers in terms of 'points'. From a strictly economic perspective – with citizens who fully understand the mechanism – both systems should produce the same outcomes. The 'perceptions' of the citizens of the two systems, however, were not likely to be identical. 'Points' denomination would have avoided the risk that the vouchers might trade at a discount to their face value and lead to people feeling 'cheated'. On the other hand, vouchers with a face value 'look like' securities. From a political point of view it would be more difficult to reverse the policy and 'cancel' paper assets 'worth' 10 000 rubles than to cancel books of 'points'.

More important than the denomination of the vouchers was the fact that they were tradable. Objections to this policy were mainly based on paternalistic considerations. In a society unused to trading paper assets, rich and sophisticated investors might take advantage of poorer less-well-informed ones. There was also the risk that speculative activity could lead to instability in the value of vouchers. Again, from a purely economic point of view, transition to a market system was sure to involve radical reassessments of the value of assets, and a degree of instability was inseparable from this process. Nevertheless, making the market economy 'acceptable' to a decisive coalition of interests was the central political problem, and very great instability in the market valuation of vouchers would be expected to undermine this objective.

A number of political arguments could be advanced for allowing trade in vouchers. If trade were forbidden, a 'black market' would certainly develop in which prices (because of the risk) would be lower and less transparent compared with open trade. Poor people deciding to sell under these conditions would be likely to gain less from their vouchers, while the buyers would tend to be gangsters rather than entrepreneurs. The overwhelming economic advantage of permitting trade in vouchers, however, was that entrepreneurs and larger investors could have a greater influence on the process of privatisation. Citizens could place their vouchers with investment funds controlled by professional managers or sell to entrepreneurs who would then have the means to acquire greater control over firms at privatisation. This relates to Pelikan's (1993) observation that voucher systems which permit individual citizens to trade vouchers or bid at auction result in a wider pool of talent competing for control of resources. 'The competence argument recommends investment vouchers because they broaden the starting field for market selection, and thus decrease the probability that some scarce competence or talents will be wasted' (p. 385). The case for permitting trade in vouchers is also clearly an application of the normative Coase theorem. By lowering transactions costs (that is, by removing restrictions on the right to trade vouchers) the aim is to free the channels by which resources come under the control of the owners who value them most highly.

Voucher auctions thus had some clear advantages for mass privatisation. The nature of the auctions varied between countries.[12] Under the Czech system, for example, shares in 1300 firms were offered in the first 'wave' of privatisation. The system was centralised, with shares floated at fixed 'prices' calculated using a computerised model.[13] If demand exceeded supply at the stated fixed price, shares were allocated pro rata, while if supply exceeded demand people received their bids and the remaining shares were auctioned in the next round at a lower price. Investment funds developed spontaneously as people preferred to use the services of intermediaries rather than to bid personally, and these funds came to hold the majority of shares. Under the Russian system, privatisation of firms occurred in a more decentralised and piecemeal way. The mechanism was simple. A given number of shares were offered. People tendered vouchers for the shares. A person tendering one per cent of the vouchers would receive one per cent of the shares. Boycko *et al.* (1995, p. 91) point out that the system had the advantages that small investors would always receive some shares, all investors paid the same 'price', and it was difficult for bureaucrats to sabotage. Technically, of course, there were disadvantages in that the 'price' paid by a bidder would depend on how many vouchers were tendered by other people. It was therefore possible, under a so-called type-2 bid, for bidders to place an upper limit on the price they were prepared to pay if they so wished.[14]

6.3 The Governance of Enterprise after Mass Privatisation

In the Czech Republic, the result of the privatisation process has been a concentration of ownership rights in the Investment Funds. Managers of enterprises should therefore theoretically be subject to some 'outside' monitoring. Since the funds are often run by state-owned banks, however, and because the managerial labour market and the takeover mechanism are undeveloped, it is not clear that constraints on managers have become as tight as was intended. In Russia, privatisation has left most enterprises initially under the control of 'insiders' because of the advantageous terms offered to workers and managers as described above.[15] Whether the 'open' nature of the firms and the tradability of shares will result in further restructuring and changes in ownership patterns, as presumably intended by the reformers, remains to be seen. Hare *et al.* (1999, p. 19) argue that the problems of productive inefficiency have not really been addressed by mass privatisation because the new owners are still not motivated to initiate change. 'In particular, there is little reason to expect profound changes from inside owners – either managers or workers – whose jobs and livelihood will be put at risk by deep restructuring.' There is, of course, some reason to expect change, since improved efficiency will benefit all owners, even if some have to become 'outsiders' and take jobs elsewhere. The somewhat pessimistic assessment of Hare *et al.* (1999) implies (perhaps correctly) that entrepreneurship will not create new opportunities sufficiently quickly to entice insiders to accept change, and that transaction costs will prevent the joint benefits from higher productivity being achieved. In spite of the efforts of the reformers to permit free exchange of shares and thus to reduce transactions costs, the supporting institutions of capitalism are simply not developed enough, according to this view, to ensure continued movement in the direction of higher efficiency.

It was precisely this thinking that led the Polish government to adopt a different scheme of mass privatisation; one that can be interpreted as an application of the normative Hobbes theorem. In Poland, fifteen national investment funds were set up managed by investment banks. Each firm would be allocated a 'lead fund' that would have a controlling block of shares. Other funds would hold shares but would be minority shareholders. Polish citizens received one tradable share in each of the funds. The advantage of this scheme is that it ensures ownership by 'outsiders' and introduces professional oversight of managers from the beginning. It 'addressed the corporate governance issue head-on' (Boycko *et al.* 1995, p. 82). As with most privatisation programmes, employees were given special advantages, although there were efforts to ensure that employee ownership was discou-

raged. Fifteen per cent of the capital of state enterprises in the mass privatisation programme was reserved for employees.[16]

The state is here exercising its judgement about the 'best' governance
arrangements and imposing this system rather than permitting choice in
the market to determine outcomes. The disadvantage is that the citizens are
entirely passive recipients of their vouchers in the funds and cannot use
them to bid directly for control of privatised assets. From an 'Austrian'
point of view the system does not permit the tapping of a big enough pool
of potential entrepreneurial competence. Pelikan (1993) for example, predicted that the Polish method of privatisation might be more successful in
the first few years and that more errors would occur under the Czech
system. In the long run, however, 'the Czech method is predicted to select
more true industrial "champions", and thus result in a more advanced
industrial structure' (p. 386). From a Coasian point of view, the transactions costs of arranging future restructuring will depend upon the rules
governing takeovers, the terms upon which the funds can relinquish their
holdings of shares to others, whether the funds themselves are effectively
competitive, and so forth.

7.   THE EFFECTS OF PRIVATISATION

Has privatisation been a successful policy? The question is more complex
than it looks and the empirical work required to provide an answer encounters substantial methodological problems. In the first place we have already
seen that governments were pursuing multiple objectives when they chose
to privatise state-owned assets and a single measure of 'success' is difficult
to contrive. A second problem is that the policy of privatisation was linked
to many other changes introduced at virtually the same time – including
changes to the regulatory structure and the legal framework more generally. A third problem, inseparable from any empirical work in economics, is
that it is difficult to control for factors other than the policy of privatisation. Time moves on. Exogenous changes in technology, the terms of trade
facing a country's exporters and importers, the prices of important inputs
– all these factors will influence the position of a firm, whatever its ownership status. 'Holding other things constant' so as to isolate the impact of a
change in ownership is therefore not an easy task.

7.1   Comparisons between Firms of Differing Ownership Types

One type of study tries to isolate the impact of 'ownership' at a given point
in time by using multiple regression techniques. It does not test directly for
the effects of privatisation on performance but infers from the results what

these effects are likely to be. Picot and Kaulmann (1989) for example, hypothesise that managers in public enterprises will be less closely constrained both by direct monitoring and by market pressures. The threat of takeover will be smaller and the bankruptcy constraint less severe than for managers in the private sector. From this they expect to observe lower levels of productivity, lower rates of return, higher gearing (ratio of debt to total assets) and a smaller responsiveness of profits to firm size in the public compared with the private sector. Fortune's 'The Foreign 500' for the years 1975–84 provides observations on private and government-owned corporations from six Western countries (excluding the USA and Japan). Picot and Kaulmann try to relate 'performance variables' such as sales per employee to 'independent variables' representing national origin, size of firm, industrial sector and 'ownership'. Their investigation is confined to corporations acting in unregulated markets and exposed to national and international competition. They conclude (p. 312) that 'the differences in performance between government-owned and privately-owned large industrial corporations that property rights theory would predict are confirmed by empirical evidence, especially with respect to differences in productivity and profitability, but also with respect to size effects'.

Using the same type of method, Frydman *et al.* (1997) use data on a large sample of mid-sized firms in the Czech Republic, Hungary and Poland to investigate the comparative performance of privatised and state-owned firms in transition economies. Both state and private firms face the powerful 'shock' of 'marketization' but Frydman *et al.* find that private firms are significantly better at generating sales and hence employment than are state firms. Both types of firm engage in removing 'the rather obvious cost inefficiencies inherited from the past' although private firms still have an advantage. The performance of firms with 'outside' owners is superior to those with 'inside' owners and employee control 'appears to offer no advantages over state ownership on any measure and creates a distinct disadvantage in terms of employment performance'.

7.2 Case Studies of Firms' Performance before and after Privatisation

An alternative approach is to study particular enterprises which have changed their 'status'. The performance of the 'same' organisation is compared 'before' and 'after' a change in property rights structure. An example of this approach is Parker (1994). Parker identifies six organisational types ranging from bureaucracies with the lowest-powered incentives, to owner-managed firms with the highest-powered incentives. In between these extremes, Parker places agencies at arm's length from the government departments[17], public corporations (nationalised firms) and joint-stock companies with and without a significant government interest. He investigates historical examples in which the reform of organisations moves them along this spectrum towards higher- or lower-powered incentives. He also classifies the moves according to whether they are changing to a more or less 'competitive' environment. His central hypothesis is that efficiency gains can be expected from organisational moves to higher-powered incentives and to more competitive conditions. The examples are taken from different industries and time periods, though all are from the UK. Until the mid-1970s, examples could be found of moves from higher- to lower-powered incentives. In 1970, for example, London Transport changed from a Public Corporation to a Local Government Department. Similarly, in 1971 Rolls Royce changed from a joint-stock company to public ownership. Later on, of course, all the moves were in the other direction. For example, British Aerospace was privatised in 1982 and National Freight in 1982. The results of this investigation 'do not contradict the view that privatisation improves performance . . . and political intervention . . . damages efficiency' (p. 166). Further 'the independent effect of product market competition on efficiency seems to have been borne out' (p. 167).

Investigating the performance of particular firms pre- and post-privatisation is a method which typically produces conclusions which are far from decisive.[18] Another paper on the British experience by Parker and Martin (1995) yielded very variable results. They examined the performance of thirteen firms privatised between 1981 and 1988 to see whether labour productivity or total factor productivity had improved relative to trends in the rest of the economy and relative to trends in the manufacturing sector. In each case the historical experience of the company was divided into five sub-periods – nationalisation, pre-privatisation, post-announcement, post-privatisation and recession.[19] Often large efficiency gains could be found in the period immediately preceding privatisation but not afterwards.[20] Interpretation then depends on how far the prospect of privatisation is seen as a necessary condition for the productivity improvement and how far these gains might have been achievable in any case. Parker and Martin (p. 217) confine themselves to the non-committal remark that 'privatisation does not guarantee good performance'. In general, the case-by-case type of investigation does not lend itself to robust statistical conclusions.[21] Each firm has its own story to tell about technical changes, market conditions, legislative interference, inspired or poor leadership, and other historical circumstances which apparently defies attempts at generalisation.

7.3   Econometric Studies of the Effects of Changes in Governance

Larger-scale econometric studies attempt to circumvent these problems. Some are concerned with particular industries. Others cover many different industries in different countries. Barberis *et al.* (1996) study the effects of privatisation on a sample of 452 Russian retail shops. An interesting feature of their results was that value-enhancing changes (including renovating shops, changing suppliers, increasing opening hours and laying off workers) were associated with new owners and managers, not with equity ownership by the existing workers. In the Russian context, therefore, the importance of entrepreneurial knowledge and of the marrying of resources with 'competence' (much emphasised by the 'Austrian' theorists) seems to be supported by this evidence. Giving effort 'incentives' through stock holdings, as in classic agency theory, is less important than permitting people with knowledge and drive to gain control of the enterprise.

The importance of the normative Hobbes and Coase theorems is demonstrated in this paper. Barberis *et al.* point out (p. 772) that 'if privatized shops can always be sold or equity stakes can always be redivided, then as long as privatization puts the shop in the private sector, who owns it does not matter'. This is simply a statement of the Coase theorem. At the time of their survey, however, 'resale of Russian shops was virtually impossible and never happened in our sample' while ownership structures 'could not be easily altered'. Given high transactions costs, the normative Hobbes theorem became more significant. Avoiding 'inside' ownership as a matter of policy might have been justified – although other considerations such as the political acceptability of the privatisation process may have been decisive as we have seen. On the other hand, reforms to encourage restructuring via takeovers, proxy fights, and bankruptcies are also important. 'If privatization were designed from scratch, these strategies should have received more attention than they have' (p. 789). In other words, policy makers did not consider the normative Coase theorem seriously enough at the time of privatisation.

The issue of corporate governance after mass privatisation has been investigated in a series of World Bank Policy Research Working Papers. Claessens (1995) finds that concentrated ownership raises the market value of privatised firms. In the Czech and Slovak Republics, following the 1992 mass privatisation programme, Claessens found that, controlling for sector-specific variables, majority ownership raises firm value, while firms with many small investors have lower prices. Similarly Claessens, Djankov and Pohl (1997) use a cross-section of 706 firms from the Czech Republic for the period 1992–95 to show that concentration of ownership and market valuation are positively related. They argue that the Czech privatisation process helped to improve management by encouraging concentrated ownership via the use of investment funds.

In contrast, Ellerman (1998) doubts the long-run governance advantages derivable from the investment funds. Fund managers will neglect the 'real industrial sector' and favour the 'financial sector'. Enterprise managers will look for the usual bonuses and perquisites of office. 'The most likely results of the strategy of voucher privatisation with investment funds may be a two-sided grab fest by fund managers and enterprise managers.' Gray (1996) is less pessimistic, although she accepts that 'initial results of privatization programmes are only part of the picture. How they foster further evolution of ownership is equally important.' Here 'the initial weight of evidence seems to favor significant reliance on voucher privatization'.

7.4   Econometric Studies of Privatisation using Multinational Data

D'Souza and Megginson (1999) use data from 85 companies privatised between 1990 and 1996 by means of public share offerings. Their sample includes companies from 28 countries (15 classified as 'industrialised' and 13 as 'developing') and 21 industries. They compare observations of profitability, operating efficiency, capital investment spending, employment, financial leverage and dividend payments for the three years before privatisation with the three years after privatisation. They also split their sample into sub-samples to compare privatisations in 'competitive' with 'noncompetitive' industries; privatisations where the government retains a majority stake with those where it does not; privatisations in industrialised and non-industrialised countries; and privatisations involving large changes to the board of directors and/or a change in the chief executive officer. For the full sample they find statistically significant increases in profitability, sales, operating efficiency and dividend payout. Significant decreases occur in leverage. In their sub-samples, output, operating efficiency and dividend payout rise in all, while profitability rises and leverage falls in all but a few cases. D'Souza and Megginson argue that higher profitability is not the result of higher prices and the exercise of monopoly power by privatised utilities. Their results confirm those from earlier studies[22] and they conclude their paper with the following sentence. 'Privatization "works", and it works in almost every institutional setting examined' (p. 1434).

8.   CONCLUSION

In a recent review of the 'public- versus private-ownership' debate, Shirley and Walsh (2000) remark that there is 'greater ambiguity about the merits of privatization and private ownership in the theoretical literature than in the empirical literature'. The empirical literature 'strongly favors private ownership in competitive markets over the state-owned counterfactual'. Perhaps this is to be expected. The point about theory is that it provides an 'engine of analysis'. It establishes a set of concepts and helps to clarify how 'exogenous' changes in one thing will influence other things. It cannot be used to prove the universal supremacy of one form of organisation over all others. Instead, as was shown in Part 2, theory suggests that many different forms may have their advantages in different circumstances.

Combine economic theory with a few common-sense empirical observations about the world, however, and the likely failure of government ownership relative to many available 'private' alternatives in most circumstances is apparent. In practice, the conditions in which economic theory might suggest that the 'low-powered incentives' of public ownership would confer net advantages – ignorant consumers facing prohibitive information costs, lack of competition, little prospect of technological innovation, high costs of contracting over 'quality' – these conditions are not as common as was once thought. This is, indeed, what the empirical work to date seems to bear out. The results of mass 'privatisation' in Eastern Europe and Russia, however, involve adaptations to radical and sudden systemic changes. Bacon's advice at the head of this chapter has not found a ready market in the twentieth century in those countries. Assessment of these huge social experiments would take us outside the scope of this book. Further, the results of the privatisation programmes in the 'mixed economies' are really the outcome of changes to property rights combined with changes to the regulatory system. These changes and the increased use of regulatory 'contracts' by governments to influence the activities of private firms make up the subject matter of Chapter 15.

NOTES

1. 'Of Innovations' in P.E. and E.F. Matheson (eds) (1924), *Bacon: Selections*, Oxford University Press, p. 69.
2. National Income and Expenditure, HMSO 1999.
3. Influential studies in the UK were by the National Economic Development Office (1976) and Pryke (1981).
4. See Chapter 15 on rate of return regulation.
5. Rees (1984) considers the control of public enterprises from a game theoretic point of view.
6. In the UK, for example, efficiency audits for the nationalised industries were introduced by the Competition Act 1980. They are undertaken by the Monopolies and Mergers Commission – since 1998 renamed the Competition Commission.
7. See again, for example, Lindsay's (1976) paper on Veterans Administration Hospitals in Chapter 11, pp. 324–5.
8. We are here assuming that private and social marginal costs are the same. Either the firm imposes no external costs on others via pollution or these costs are effectively 'internalised' via tax payments to the government.
9. People who held on to their stock for more than a certain minimum length of time were offered bonus shares.

10. Rover was later acquired by BMW. In the year 2000, BMW sold Rover to the Phoenix Consortium for £10.
11. Williamson (2000, p.609) comments, for example, on the nature of the privatisation process in Russia that 'Had the Boycko *et al.* team consulted the new institutional economics, a more cautious and selective program of privatization with greater attention to implementation would have resulted.'
12. See, for example, Estrin and Stone (1996).
13. Unlike Russian vouchers, Czech vouchers were denominated in points.
14. Details of the Russian voucher auction mechanism can be found in Boycko *et al.* (1995) pp.85–95.
15. Earle and Estrin (1996) report that 83 per cent of Russian privatised firms were majority owned by insiders in 1994.
16. See Nuti (1999, p.84).
17. Examples in the early 1970s included Her Majesty's Stationery Office (HMSO) and the Royal Mint.
18. Sometimes the results are so startling that it is difficult not to accept the existence of a 'privatisation effect'. Ramamurti (1997) studied the privatisation in 1990 of Ferrocarilla Argentinos – the railway system in Argentina. Labour productivity rose by 370 per cent and employment declined by 79 per cent. However, academic purists would still be reluctant to generalise from this experience. In Britain, very large productivity changes have occurred in some industries in the period before actual privatisation.
19. Britain experienced a severe recession in 1991. The separate treatment of this period represented an attempt to distinguish cyclical effects from those attributable to changes in ownership.
20. British Steel and British Coal greatly increased labour productivity in the years before privatisation. It is perhaps no accident that productivity in the coal industry (not part of Parker and Martin's study) rose rapidly after the defeat of a protracted strike in 1984. In the ports industry, productivity rose most significantly after privatisation but also after the end of the National Dock Labour Scheme which had determined pay and conditions in the industry and had suppressed competition between rival ports. Attributing separate effects to labour market reforms and privatisation when the two occurred over similar time periods presents obvious technical problems.
21. An exception to this is the ingenious methodology employed by Eckel, Eckel and Singal (1997) in which the effect of privatisation on efficiency is inferred from the impact on the stock prices of other firms in the same industry. This study finds that the privatisation of British Airways (BA) reduced the stock prices of competitors by seven per cent, presumably because BA was expected to be a more formidable rival.
22. Papers using a similar methodology were Megginson, Nash and van Randenborgh (1994) and Boubakri and Cosset (1998).

15. Economic regulation and the structure of business

'It is perhaps necessary to remark, that the state may be the proprietor of canals or railways without itself working them; and that they will almost always be better worked by means of a company, renting the railway or canal for a limited period from the state.'

(J.S. Mill)[1]

1. INTRODUCTION

The regulatory activity of government is so extensive that only a few of the major policy areas can be considered in this chapter. Our main objective is to examine the 'contractual' issues that arise when business is subject to regulatory intervention. More detailed consideration of specific areas such as environmental regulation, health and safety, equal opportunities and so forth would take us outside the main lines of enquiry that we are pursuing. There are, however, some general problems that are common to all forms of government regulation and these will be investigated in the context of an area of policy that impinges most closely on business structure – the regulation of the 'public utilities'. Sections 2 and 3 discuss the problem of distinguishing 'natural' from other forms of monopoly and the general case for government action to support competition. Section 4 outlines the main factors that influence the bargaining environment between regulator and regulated and discusses some of the main forms of utility regulation from a transactional point of view. Section 5 looks specifically at the role of franchising in the regulation of natural monopoly, while section 6 summarises the advantages and disadvantages of an array of organisational arrangements that can be observed in different industries and countries. Section 7 briefly surveys the effects of economic 'deregulation' in the United States.

Similar themes to those which appeared in Chapters 13 and 14 should be discernible running through this chapter. There is the 'optimal contracting' view of government–industry relations in which principal–agent theory dominates the analysis. A benevolent government principal transacts with a self-interested firm over the provision of some 'public' output. There is the transactions-cost view in which the 'governance' of a very durable 'relational contract' between regulator and firm is at the centre of attention. There are 'public choice' considerations relating to the special interests of pressure groups, firms, regulators and politicians. There are also the usual 'Austrian' themes about encouraging the discovery of new ways of doing things, the impossibility of regulators being fully informed and the central importance of the competitive process.

2.   THE 'NATURAL' MONOPOLY PROBLEM

2.1   Definition of 'Natural' Monopoly

In some circumstances, monopoly can take on the appearance of 'inevitability' – as if the laws of 'nature' herself make the competitive supply of a service unsustainable. Where, for example, economies of scale lead to declining costs per unit of output over a very large range relative to market demand, a single producer might be able to serve the market at a lower cost than a combination of producers. To insist on 'competitive' supply would be to sacrifice economies of scale. This is the classic case for government intervention in the control of the 'public utilities'. Where large fixed investments in 'infrastructure' are required, such as networks of cables, pipes, wires or track, duplication of such assets can be seen as 'wasteful' and unnecessary. Technically, in neoclassical theory, an industry is naturally monopolistic where its total cost function is sub-additive that is, where

$$C(Q) < C(q_i) + C(q_j) + \ldots + C(q_k) \qquad (15.1)$$

for all q_i, q_j, q_k such that $Q = q_i + q_j + \ldots + q_k$. In the above expression, Q is total industry output, q_i represents the output of individual firm i, and C is the total cost function. A continuously declining industry average cost curve is a sufficient condition for sub-additivity. However, condition (15.1) can be satisfied at some levels of total output even if average cost begins to rise after a point.

An important feature of this conventional approach to 'natural monopoly' is that technology dominates the analysis. The cost functions are derived from production functions. Production functions map inputs into output. They define the quantity of 'output' that will be achieved when specified amounts of inputs are used in a production process. In other words, they define the production possibilities available and assume a given state of scientific and technological knowledge. If technology dictates a single supplier, the public interest requires, according to conventional doctrine, that only a single supplier should operate. To prevent abuse of the monopoly position, however, regulators whose job it is to ensure efficient pricing and output should supervise the single supplier.[2]

There are at least three significant objections to this rather static view of 'natural monopoly'. The first is that costs are not determined entirely by technology. Organisational considerations are also important. Lack of competition might reduce the incentive to discover and implement the lowest-cost method of production and this 'X' inefficiency will tend to offset any technological advantages from scale effects.[3] The regulatory system itself might distort the operation of the industry (subsection 4) and public choice pressures might influence the objectives of the regulators and result in inefficient modes of operation. Secondly, technological innovation of the Schumpeterian variety is a form of dynamic competition that threatens even the most apparently entrenched 'natural' monopoly. Neoclassical competition – the entry into an industry of new firms producing an identical product using identical methods to an incumbent – may seem wasteful, but the entry of firms producing a 'new' product, which turns out to be highly substitutable for the output of the incumbent, is another matter. The growth of airlines undermined the railroads. Cable and satellite technology subverts the 'natural monopoly' of terrestrial broadcasting. Mobile telephony challenges conventional 'fixed link' telephone services. Thirdly, fixed costs leading to scale economies are not exactly the same thing as sunk costs. In certain restricted circumstances the force of 'potential competition' may be effective even when a single supplier serves the entire market. The aim of encouraging Schumpeterian innovation and 'potential competition' has supported the case for 'deregulation' over the last quarter of the twentieth century rather than regulation. Thus, as will be seen in more detail below, there is a tension between the claims of static efficiency and those of dynamic competition that runs through the debate about the role of utility regulation.

2.2   Contestability

The fact that a single supplier exists in an industry does not altogether rule out competitive pressure. 'Potential competition' – the threat from potential entrants – has long been recognised as a significant restraining force. Marshall wrote of the danger to a monopolist of 'spoiling the market' by overcharging and encouraging the entry of competitors. In the late 1970s, economists began to think more formally about this type of competition. Clearly, if a monopolist expected that, as soon as a profit opportunity existed, outside competitors would instantly move in to take advantage of it, the monopolist would not be able to earn more than a 'normal' competitive return. Such a market is now termed 'perfectly contestable'.

The conditions for perfect contestability are very demanding. Information must be costlessly available to potential entrants, there must be no sunk costs, and an incumbent firm must not be able instantly to match a new entrant's price. The first assumption ensures that outsiders will notice the chance of making a profit. The second assumption permits 'hit-and-run' entry. A newcomer can enter the market, supply the good or service for a short period of time and escape without loss when the incumbent firm retaliates. If the entrant had to invest in capital that was highly specific to the industry, this 'sunk' capital would be irretrievable at the point of exit and would constitute an effective 'barrier to entry'. The third assumption ensures that there is some period of time over which an entrant can make profits. An incumbent firm that could always precisely and instantaneously 'match' an entrant's terms and retain its existing customers could deny the entrant all prospect of gain.

In principle, therefore, it is possible to imagine a market that is both a 'natural monopoly' and 'perfectly contestable'. Consider the case in which average costs decline continuously over the relevant output range. Let three buyers (persons A, B and C) face three potential suppliers (X, Y and Z). Each buyer wants precisely one unit of output. The suppliers all face the same cost conditions given below.

$$C(1) = 19; \ C(2) = 30; \ C(3) = 39.$$

Average costs (AC) and marginal costs (MC) are therefore

$$AC(1) = 19; \ AC(2) = 15; \ AC(3) = 13$$

and

$$MC(1) = 19; \ MC(2) = 11; \ MC(3) = 9.$$

Notice that this cost function is sub-additive. If three units of output are to be produced, it is best that a single supplier should produce them. Three separate suppliers producing one unit each would cost $3 \times 19 = 57$. A combination of two suppliers would cost $19 + 30 = 49$. A single supplier faces total costs of 39.

Let the benefits to each consumer be as follows:

$$B(A) = 20, \ B(B) = 15, \ \text{and} \ B(C) = 10.$$

From a social point of view the best outcome would be for each of the three consumers to buy their unit of output from a single 'natural monopolist'. Total benefits are then 45 and total costs are 39. The social surplus of six is a maximum.

Now consider the organisational options.

1. If supplier X were a conventional monopolist (a price setter) with no threat of competition from the others and unable to discriminate in price between the consumers, s/he would sell a single unit of output to person A at a price of twenty. Supplier X would make a profit of one, in this case representing the entire social surplus. To sell two units the monopolist would have to reduce his/her price to fifteen (person B's maximum willingness to pay) at which point his/her profit would be zero. To sell three units, price would have to be ten, and losses would be made.

2. If supplier X were a contestable monopolist so that suppliers Y and Z could enter the market costlessly, s/he would sell two units of output at a price of fifteen. She is now constrained to offer an average cost price in order to forestall entry by other suppliers. A single unit of output sold to person A at a price of nineteen would also yield profit of zero but would attract entry from suppliers Y or Z offering to supply both persons A and B at a price of fifteen. Social surplus rises to five – this time accruing entirely to person A.

3. If supplier X were a monopolist, secure from new entry, but able to bargain costlessly with each consumer s/he would produce three units of output. Assume that the surplus is shared equally between consumer and producer. Person A will pay a price of 19.5 (midway between A's willingness to pay and the marginal cost of supplying him). Person B will pay a price of thirteen (midway between his/her benefit of fifteen and the marginal cost of eleven). Person C will pay 9.5. Supplier X's profit will be three. (Total revenue is 42. Total cost is 39). Consumers between them will gain a surplus of three. Gains from trade are maximised and the situation is 'efficient'. The Coase theorem is again vindicated. Where bargaining costs are zero, contractors achieve efficiency.

4. If supplier X were a contestable natural monopolist and all transactors could bargain costlessly, efficiency would again be achieved. This time, however, the possibility of costless entry would influence the bargaining process. There must be no incentive for a buyer or a coalition of buyers to desert supplier X in favour of Y or Z. If each buyer pays the marginal cost of their supply this condition will be satisfied. Person A pays nineteen, person B pays eleven and person C pays nine. Person A

cannot gain by contracting with another supplier for a single unit of output. Neither is it possible for A and B together to gain by contracting with Y or Z for two units of output. Supplier X makes zero profits and the consumers gain the entire social surplus. Person A gains a surplus of one; person B a surplus of four and person C a surplus of one.

This example illustrates some basic propositions about contestable markets. In the presence of natural monopoly, the threat of entry will constrain the incumbent firm and permit additional gains from trade to be achieved, all accruing to the consumers (compare 1. and 2. above). Although the 'contestable' position improves on monopoly, it does not achieve all possible gains from trade (compare 2. and 3. above). Individual bargaining at zero cost, as usual, yields efficient outcomes. This is so in both contestable and non-contestable markets. In a world of no transactions costs, contestability influences the distribution of the gains from trade, not the sum total of those gains.[4]

2.3 Sustainability

There are cases, however, in which natural monopoly exists but contestability will not produce such benign results. A slight adjustment to the example we have been investigating can be used to illustrate the point. Three consumers each wish to purchase one unit of output and are willing to pay a maximum price of twenty. There are three suppliers, each facing a total cost function as follows:

$$C(1) = 19; \; C(2) = 30; \; C(3) = 48.$$

Thus the average cost (AC) and marginal cost (MC) functions are now as follows:

$$AC(1) = 19; \; AC(2) = 15; \; AC(3) = 16.$$
$$MC(1) = 19; \; MC(2) = 11; \; MC(3) = 18.$$

The industry remains a 'natural monopoly' because the cost function is still sub-additive. If each supplier produced a single unit of output, total costs would be $3 \times 19 = 57$. If one supplier produced two units of output and another produced a single unit, total costs would be $30 + 19 = 49$. If one supplier produced all three units, total costs would be 48. Notice that the 'best' solution for this group of contractors as a whole is that a single supplier (either X or Y or Z) should provide three units of output (one each to persons A, B and C). Net social benefits will be $20 - 19 = 1$ if one consumer is served, $(2 \times 20) - 30 = 10$ if two consumers are served, and $(3 \times 20) - 48 = 12$ if all three are served by a single supplier.

Suppose now that the industry is 'contestable'. Supplier X (the incumbent) contracts to supply one unit of the product to each buyer at a price of sixteen per unit. This price equals the average cost of supplying three units of output and supplier X therefore makes no pure profit. Consumers A, B and C each gain a surplus of $20 - 16 = 4$. Social surplus in this particular case is maximised. The situation, however, is not sustainable.

Producer Y could offer to supply two consumers (say A and B) at a price of fifteen. This would permit Y to break even and would result in a gain of one each to A and B. Person C would be left to contract with another supplier at a price of nineteen. Social surplus will have declined from twelve to eleven. In this case, therefore, contestability undermines efficiency. According to our assumptions, natural monopoly exists and it is socially efficient for production to be undertaken by a single firm. The ability of new firms to enter at zero cost, however, makes it impossible for a single firm to serve the entire market even if it adopts a price that yields no pure profits. The natural monopoly can be 'unsustainable'.

Given the Coase Theorem, it is tempting to argue that this inefficiency is the result of some hidden 'cost of transacting'. With zero costs of transacting, would not our consumers and suppliers bargain to an efficient solution, one that would involve production within a single firm? What would happen, for example, if the firms could discriminate in price and bargain costlessly with all consumers? It turns out that the absence of transactions costs will not help. The problem here is not that agreements are costly but that there is no 'core' to the exchange game. In Chapter 1, we examined examples of a recontracting process which led to a solution that no individual person or group of people would have an interest in changing – a so-called 'core' solution. We observed there that a 'core' solution was not necessarily unique, although perfectly competitive general equilibrium analysis had managed to establish conditions under which the core contained only a single allocation of resources. Here, in contrast, we have a game that has an empty core.

Person C, for example, whom we last encountered paying a price of nineteen for his/her unit of output, would no doubt notice that producer Y could add him/her to his/her two existing customers at a marginal cost of only eighteen. By offering to pay a price of eighteen to producer Y, therefore, person C is better off and no one else is worse off. Persons A and B continue to pay a price of fifteen to producer Y and social efficiency is re-established – but not for long. Person C can do even better. An agreement between producer X and persons A and C by which A pays a price of fourteen and C pays a price of seventeen (a total of 31) would benefit both of these consumers and yield a pure profit for X. Indeed, it is easy to see that no set of prices exists which would sustain the natural monopoly position. For the natural monopoly to be sustainable it must break even. Thus

$$P_A + P_B + P_C = 48 \tag{15.2}$$

where P_A is the price paid by person A and so forth. It must also be impossible for an alliance of two of the consumers to come to a mutually advantageous agreement with a potential entrant. Thus sustainability requires that the following conditions are satisfied:

$$
\begin{aligned}
P_A + P_B &< 30 \\
P_A + P_C &< 30 \\
P_B + P_C &< 30
\end{aligned}
\tag{15.2}
$$

Adding the above inequalities we find

$$2(P_A + P_B + P_C) < 90$$

or

$$P_A + P_B + P_C < 45$$

which contradicts the break-even constraint (15.2). In the postulated conditions, the 'socially efficient' position, which involves a single supplier, cannot be sustained and is not a 'core' solution. At the same time, solutions involving more than one supplier cannot be in the core because agreements will then exist capable of making all contractors better off. There is no core and therefore low transactions costs are of no assistance in locating it.

The literature on contestability and sustainability has important though complex implications for public policy. In the first place, the role of potential competition as a force to control the exploitation of monopoly power leads to recommendations for lowering entry barriers and removing artificial restrictions on trade. The deregulation of Airlines and Trucking in the USA and long-distance bus services in the UK are examples of policy changes in the early 1980s which were encouraged by the idea that these markets could be seen as contestable. Trucks and planes are not specific to any particular route and can be moved at relatively low cost from serving one market to another. This reduces the problem of 'sunk cost' and means that incumbents are constrained in the margins they can earn even if there is no competitor actually operating in their particular market. Bailey and

Panzar (1981), for example, used data from the airline industry in 1979 and 1980 to show the restraining influence of potential competition. In the USA, the Airline Deregulation Act 1978 opened air routes to the threat of new entry and the Motor Carrier Reform Act 1980 allowed private and contract carriers to compete with common carriers. In the UK, the Transport Act 1980 removed restrictions on long-distance bus services and thereby opened up a market dominated at that time by National Express, a subsidiary of the National Bus Company.

What, however, of the danger that new entry will be destabilising and that restrictions are necessary to produce stability? There are both theoretical and empirical points at stake here. On the empirical side, non-sustainability is characterised by particular cost conditions that may or may not be very common. Our examples in subsections 2.2 and 2.3 indicate that the source of the unsustainability problem is the conjunction of sub-additivity (natural monopoly) with rising average costs. It is at least possible to argue that these conditions are rare, especially if average cost curves are expected to remain flat after a certain point with a large range of constant returns.[5] Against this position it can be argued that a particular form of unsustainability – 'intertemporal unsustainability' – might occur regularly. It turns out that unsustainability in a multi-period setting is possible even with continuously declining average costs.[6]

2.4   Intertemporal Unsustainability

Intertemporal unsustainability refers to a situation in which a natural monopoly supplier of a good for which demand is growing cannot find an investment plan that prevents entry as time advances. Suppose that one unit of capacity is necessary to provide one unit of output. There are two periods – period 1 ('now') and period 2 ('later'). The costs of installing capacity are as follows:

$$C(1) = 10, \ C(2) = 16.$$

Average costs of building capacity are therefore falling:

$$AC(1) = 10, \ AC(2) = 8.$$

Unlike the situation examined in subsections 2.2 and 2.3, these capacity costs are assumed to be sunk. In the single-period analysis, the existence of sunk costs makes the position of an incumbent monopolist more rather than less sustainable. In the intertemporal case, sunk costs no longer protect against entry.

Suppose the rate of discount (r) is one hundred per cent. There are three people. Person A wishes to consume one unit of output in period 1. Persons B and C each wish to consume one unit in period 2.

There are two ways of satisfying this demand. The firm can build one unit of capacity in period 1 and another in period 2 or it can anticipate the rise in demand and build two units of capacity in period 1. The advantage of the first plan is that the costs are delayed until the period when capacity is required. The advantage of the second plan is that the firm gains economies of scale from building two units of plant. The present value of the costs of each plan is as follows:

$$PV(\text{Plan 1}) = 10 + 10/(1+r) = 15.$$
$$PV(\text{Plan 2}) = 16.$$

With a rate of discount of one hundred per cent, it is better to delay construction of the second unit rather than to build in advance.

Unfortunately, it is possible to show that plan 1 is unsustainable if entry of new firms is possible. Let P_1 and P_2 be the prices charged in periods one and two respectively. If the incumbent firm is to break even, we have:

$$P_1 + 2P_2/(1+r) = 15.$$

The present value of revenues must equal the present value of costs. With $r = 1$, this reduces to

$$P_1 + P_2 = 15. \tag{15.2'}$$

For the position to be sustainable, however, it must not be possible for another firm to make profits by entering the market in period 2 and building two units of capacity from scratch. If the price charged in period 2 is to prevent this possibility we must have:

$$2P_2 < 16 \text{ or } P_2 < 8. \tag{15.3'}$$

It must also not be possible to make profits by simply building one unit of capacity in period 1, using it also in period 2 but not adding to it. Thus

$$P_1 + P_2/(1+r) < 10 \text{ or } P_1 + 0.5P_2 < 10. \tag{15.4'}$$

As can be seen from Figure 15.1, it is impossible to satisfy the sustainability constraints (15.3') and (15.4') and simultaneously satisfy the break even constraint (15.2'). A firm offering a price in period 2 less than the cost of building an additional unit of capacity (10) will find that it cannot break even without charging a price in period 1 that will attract entry. On the other hand it *must* offer a price in period 2 less than the cost of a single extra unit capacity if it is to avoid entry in period 2 by a firm building two units of capacity from scratch and offering a price of eight.

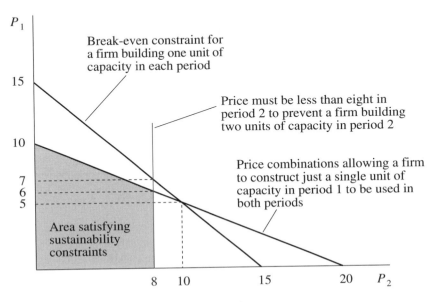

Figure 15.1   Intertemporal unsustainability

Once more it is possible to view the problem as a cooperative game with no 'core'. In this case, we imagine the contractors coming to agreements in period 1 concerning production and consumption levels in both periods 1 and 2. Persons B and C together will not pay more than sixteen for their consumption in period 2 (a present value of eight) because between them they can contract with a supplier now to build two units of capacity in period 2. Similarly, an alliance of A and B or A and C will not pay a present value of more than ten or they will contract with a supplier who will build just one unit of capacity (joint to both consumers) in the first period. As a last resort, each contractor can deal on his or her own with a supplier. Person A, for example, could pay a supplier ten in period 1 just to serve him or her and then scrap the capacity. Person B consumes 'later' so that a payment with a present value of five will secure him or her capacity in period 2.

The present values of the costs faced by all possible groups are recorded below. It is easy to check that there is no allocation of the cost between its participants that will prevent a coalition breaking up as people defect to alternative groupings. The grouping AB, for example, could allocate costs so that person A paid a present value of six and person B paid a present value of four. Person C would then be on his/her own paying five. This would be an 'efficient' position, since costs are minimised at fifteen.[7] In such a case B and C could get together and reduce the combined costs they face (four plus five) from nine to eight, leaving A to fend for him or herself at a cost of ten. A could then strike back by offering a deal with C. A very small positive contribution by C would reduce the cost borne by A and make both better off. This would in turn be vulnerable to some other coalition, and so on 'ad infinitum'.

Table 15.1   The present value of the cost of satisfying the demands of each possible 'coalition'

Possible groupings	PV of costs to group
A	10
B	5
C	5
AB	10
AC	10
BC	8
ABC	15

The potential instability of intertemporal investment plans is a possible argument for regulatory intervention to restrict the scope for 'disruptive recontracting'. We noted in Chapter 7 (section 5.5) that the problem of enforcing intertemporal commitments might lead to unwillingness on the part of producers to invest in sunk capital subject to obsolescence (Goldberg, 1976a). Here we have a related problem of scale economies and 'sustainability'. The connection with the problem of multi-period contracts can be seen if we imagine that person B in our example is in fact an older person A. If people contract period by period, the sustainability problem will still arise as in Figure 15.1, but, providing intertemporal contracts between firms and consumers can be negotiated and enforced, there is no longer a problem. The potential 'alliance' between persons B and C in period 2, which was the source of the disruption in our example, is neutralised.

If B is simply an older person A, we might expect this person (AB), when considering at the beginning all the two-period contracts s/he might make, fully to take into account the consequences of his/her commitments for period 2 for his/her younger persona. From the table above, person C cannot face a price of more than ten in period 2 (a present value of five). Similarly, person (AB) can always buy one unit in each period for a present value price of ten. The price pair $P_1 = 5$ and $P_2 = 10$ for person (AB) cannot now be improved upon. Person C might suggest to person (AB) that they jointly pay a price of sixteen to a period-2 entrant for two units of output, but person C will only gain from this if person (AB) pays a period-2 price in excess of six (a present value of three). Person (AB) will reject this option because s/he will not be able to find a firm to supply him/her in period 1 (but not period 2) for less than ten and thus the present value of his/her outlays will have risen by three to thirteen. To construct one unit of capacity in the first period and another two units by a different firm in the second period increases the present value of costs from fifteen to eighteen. In other words, the cost of the inefficiency implicit in person C's proposal, which involves excess capacity in period 2, is now fully borne by person (AB).

The argument can also be presented in terms of sustainable prices in the two periods. In Figure 15.1, a price combination $P_1 = 5$ and $P_2 = 10$ will enable the firm to break even and provide the incentive to build an extra unit of plant in period 2. It is also now 'sustainable'. The $P_2 < 8$ constraint no longer applies because consumer (AB) is committed not to deal with a new firm in period 2. Without person (AB)'s promise of loyalty, no price combination for the two periods will permit firms to break even while providing the efficient investment programme. With (AB)'s intertemporal commitment, a firm can set $P_2 = 10$ for both customers without attracting entry in period 2.

As an alternative scenario, consider the case of $P_1 = 7$ and $P_2 = 8$, with one unit of capacity built in each period. This also would enable costs to be covered by a single firm. In our simple arithmetic example, however, this solution is not in the core and is not 'sustainable'. Person (AB) would be paying $7 + 8/(1 + r) = 11$ for his/her output and would therefore recontract with another firm at a present value of ten. $P_1 = 7$ and $P_2 = 8$ is not a sustainable price combination, even with enforceable intertemporal contracts, because person C wants his/her output only in period 2. It would imply the following deal. Person (AB) promises to pay seven in period 1 and not to desert to a new entrant in that first period. The firm promises to invest in additional capacity in period 2 even though that period's price is less than the cost of additional capacity. However, another firm offering the price combination $P_1 = 5$ and $P_2 = 10$ would win (AB)'s custom in both periods and could not be undercut by another firm for person C's custom in period 2.

The root of the problem therefore turns out to be the cost and enforceability of this type of long-term exclusive contract. We have shown that there are circumstances in which the Coase theorem applies, the 'core' is not necessarily empty, and low-cost multi-period contracts solve the problem of 'intertemporal unsustainability'.[8] They do so, however, effectively by the contractors agreeing to abolish 'intertemporal contestability'. The market is 'contestable' at the beginning of period 1, when any firm can offer to serve the market over a certain number of future time periods, but it is not contestable thereafter because contracts prevent consumers from defecting.[9] Firms effectively compete for a franchise at the beginning of period 1. If high transactions costs inhibit the spontaneous emergence of such multi-period contracts with consumers, regulatory intervention may theoretically be necessary to prevent the threat of disruptive entry.[10] Paradoxically, however, contracts tying consumers to one supplier over time are usually considered highly suspect by antitrust authorities. The difficulty of distinguishing between restrictive contracts that enhance efficiency and those that simply foreclose competition is perhaps *the* fundamental problem in regulatory economics and can cause tensions between different regulatory agencies.

Indeed, as will be seen in section 5, one method of regulation of natural monopoly relies on the method of state franchising. Given our discussion here of 'sustainability', it should not be surprising if the two problems of the length of the franchise and the durability of sunk capital will turn out to be important issues. Note, however, that consumer ownership might also be a response to this problem. Consumers commit to deal over time with the same firm, not through contract but by owning the firm.[11] It is important always to be aware that government regulation, even where theoretical cases can be made out in its favour, will usually substitute for private action and that policy is about comparing feasible alternative institutional arrangements. Finally, if period-2 transactors are a different population from period-1 transactors, even zero transactions cost may not produce stability because of the absence of a 'core' to the exchange game. There is a sense in which the government, in this context, could be seen as providing a necessary link between the generations; a link without which firms in certain technological conditions would not have the confidence to invest.

3.   ORGANISATIONAL STRUCTURE AND COMPETITION

3.1   Vertical Disintegration in the Public Utilities

The literature on 'natural monopoly' and 'contestability' has had an important influence on the evolution of regulatory arrangements. On the one hand, it has led to attempts on the part of regulators to isolate the 'natural' monopoly element in the public utilities from the activities that are not naturally monopolistic. On the other hand it has, through state franchising, attempted to introduce 'contestability' into some areas that are naturally monopolistic. The result has been a surge in government involvement in the actual organisational structure of industry. Broadly speaking, it has led to vertical disintegration, the substitution of contract for ownership and much greater intervention in the process of mergers and acquisitions.

The gas, electricity, telecommunications and rail-transport industries developed historically as vertically integrated concerns. In Chapter 7, attention has already been drawn to Chandler's (1977) characterisation of the American Railroads as the first modern business hierarchies. The forces leading to vertical integration were clearly substantial in these areas. As Joskow (1997, p. 122) reminds us 'A free flowing AC network is an integrated physical machine that follows the laws of physics . . . When a generator turns on and off, it affects system conditions throughout the interconnected network.' On the face of it, transactions costs between different parts of this system might have been expected to recommend vertical integration and common ownership. Regulators in recent years have preferred to contrive a structure which introduces as much competition as possible into the system.

In gas, the pipeline represents the natural monopoly element in the industry while production and supply (that is, retailing) can be competitive. Similarly, the generation and retailing of electricity can be competitive while transmission and distribution are naturally monopolistic because of the network of cables involved. In telecommunications, the market in equipment and in services can be considered competitive while the network of wires is again a natural monopoly. In railroads, the provision of the actual track is monopolistic whereas competitive forces can be introduced into the running of trains and the provision of equipment. The tendency for regulators to break up these industries into their component parts means that contract rather than organisation is increasingly used as a coordinating mechanism

Encouraging competition, both actual and potential, where conditions are appropriate, has clear advantages for incentives. Aspiring entrants are encouraged to monitor the performance of incumbent firms in case entry into the market becomes profitable. The regulator is not involved in the detailed analysis of production processes, rates of return on capital or prices, but uses the market process itself to reveal the best services to be supplied and the most effective ways of supplying them. In addition, there is the great 'public choice' advantage that the danger of 'regulatory capture' is reduced. Where officials and industry personnel meet regularly to discuss detailed matters of pricing or production methods, pressure from interest

groups is likely to be strong. As with managers of the nationalised industries[12] regulators pursuing 'public interest' objectives will be subject to
many forms of influence from outright corruption to more subtle pressures.
Stigler (1975, p. 114) argued that much regulatory activity made more sense
if it was interpreted as designed to help the established producer groups in
an industry rather than as a means of preventing monopoly power. 'As a
rule, regulation is acquired by the industry and is designed and operated
primarily for its benefit.' This proposition became known as the 'capture'
theory of regulation. A requirement upon regulators to encourage competition where possible makes it more difficult for them to favour labour or
other supplier interests within the industry without overtly contravening
their terms of reference.

The inevitable disadvantage of this approach is that the 'contract' versus
'organisation' question at the heart of this book is not itself settled by trial
and error or entrepreneurial judgement but, in important areas, is determined by regulators. The process of resource allocation becomes, to use
'Austrian' terminology, one of 'ordered competition' rather than a strictly
'competitive order'.[13] Before looking specifically at the regulation of public
utilities in section 4, therefore, the rest of section 3 considers competition
policy more broadly. The debate in political economy concerning the role
of the state in the maintenance of competition is both old and deep. It is
perhaps unlikely ever fully to be resolved but in section 3.2 we set out some
of the main lines of argument.

3.2   Competition Policy

3.2.1   The classical liberal position
In classical liberal circles a long tradition holds that it is one of the main
functions of the state to ensure a competitive environment for industry and
trade. Restrictive agreements to fix prices, to close markets to others, to tie
consumers to particular producers, to charge different prices to different
customers, to set output quotas and so forth are, *per se*, undesirable. Jewkes
(1964, p. 73) sees this area of policy as similar to the provision of law and
order, defence, standards of weights and measures, and other public goods.
'Anyone who seriously advances the virtues of a competitive system', he
argues, should accept 'the need for active intervention on the part of
governments to exercise a watch over the industrial system for the purposes
of discouraging monopoly'. The Ordo-Kreis or Neo-Liberals in Germany
in the late 1940s and 1950s, appalled at the cartelisation of the German
economy from 1871 to 1945 and anxious to secure an open trading
economy, took a strong line on the market-policing functions of the state.[14]
The goal, as they saw it, was the protection of individual freedom of action

against the concentration of economic power.[15] In the United States, an active policy against 'restrictive agreements' and monopoly was also the 'orthodox' position, but a less traumatic political history led to justifications based more on the achievement of economic efficiency than on the protection of individual freedom.

It is possible to view this traditional liberal position as simply an implicit application of the normative Coase theorem. If the state has erected barriers to trade or has enacted laws that make it costly for people to transact with each other, that give special privileges to particular groups, and that artificially restrict mobility or prevent newcomers from entering a trade, then these should be removed in the interests of competition. If the law is to be structured to 'remove impediments to private agreements' it will, by lowering the cost of transacting, tend to favour 'competition'.

Public policy, however, has not typically been justified on these grounds alone. Instead, competition policy has exemplified a profound suspicion of the uncorrected outcomes of market processes. Competition policy has tried to ensure the survival of a suitable number of firms in an industry and to prevent successful firms from becoming too 'dominant'. Contracts between firms are policed in case they are, in themselves, 'anti-competitive'. They might, for example, establish exclusive dealing arrangements. A further consideration is to ensure that access to special technology, trade knowledge or reputational advantages does not lead to 'profiteering'. The state's involvement in competition policy, in spite of rhetoric about establishing 'level playing fields' therefore, is not just about 'economic processes'. It is also about economic 'outcomes'. The important thing is not simply to draw up the rules and inspect the track; it is to ensure a large field and a close race. The competition authorities, on this interpretation, operate a giant handicapping system in the economic sphere.

The classical approach to competition recoils from intrusive government monitoring and control. The basic idea is to keep markets open to newcomers and to facilitate trade – the very opposite of government control. But there is an unresolved dispute concerning the ability of privately negotiated, uncoerced agreements to close markets. A robust tradition going back to Adam Smith is under no illusions about the tendency of all business people to conspire together against the public if only they can get away with it. There is less agreement, however, about their ability to monitor and police such agreements in the absence of support from governments. Once it is accepted that private agreements are capable of generating significant efficiency losses over substantial time periods by closing markets, regulatory scrutiny of these agreements can be recommended on 'public interest' grounds. This has indeed been the 'consensus' of free-market economists for many years.

Providing that restrictive agreements which represent rent seeking can be identified at low cost, the case for competition policy is strong. The law should then be able to define clearly the types of agreement which are socially undesirable, all contractors will operate under the same rules, and bureaucratic discretion will be minimised – thus mitigating 'public-choice'-type objections to state interference. Again, this is the traditional classical conception of 'antitrust' or competition policy. Unfortunately, much of this book has been devoted to showing how difficult it is to distinguish rent seeking from entrepreneurship[16] or, in this context, a conspiracy in restraint of trade from efficiency-enhancing cooperation. Acceptance of the efficiency properties of certain 'restrictive' contractual arrangements enormously complicates competition policy. The scope for summarising in relatively 'objective' and simple terms what constitutes unlawful arrangements declines as the scope for bureaucratic intervention and pressure-group activity increases. The following subsections explore these dilemmas in more detail.

3.2.2   The rise of antitrust policy

The country with the longest experience of competition policy is the United States. Section 1 of the Sherman Act of 1890 made every contract in restraint of trade a crime and section 2 outlawed conduct aimed at monopolising a trade. European countries were slower to police markets in this way, but after 1945 similar legislation appeared in Europe. The German Ordo-Liberal approach found expression in Articles 85 and 86 of the Treaty of Rome establishing the European Economic Community, a foundation which has been maintained in the subsequent treaties leading to the European Union. The dilemma facing antitrust authorities – to support a system of ordered competition or to encourage a competitive order – runs through the twentieth-century history of competition policy.

In the area of market dominance, the most famous early twentieth-century case was the break-up of the Standard Oil Company into 34 parts in 1911.[17] At the time, it controlled ninety per cent of refinery output.[18] After two unsuccessful attempts in 1913 and 1949, the Justice Department in 1984 forced AT & T to divest itself of the Regional Bell Operating Companies. The idea was that AT & T would have to compete with others in the provision of equipment or network services to these 'local natural monopolies'. Most recently, Microsoft has been threatened with a similar break-up after it was accused of using its dominant position to 'tie' customers into taking a whole range of software services. In each of these cases, the law is being used as an instrument of organisational restructuring. It is trying to order the competition in a particular way.

Critics argue that, providing state-supported restrictions on trade are avoided, competitive pressures will themselves undermine positions of dominance. An example of the force of this argument is the IBM case. This dragged on through the American courts for many years and was finally dropped after it became apparent that the company was on the verge of bankruptcy as a result of the decline of the 'mainframe' and the growth of the personal computer. In a competitive world, 'dominance' was not apparently forever, and could even be for a shorter period than the length of an antitrust investigation. Even in the famous Standard Oil case, critics have argued that the years of market dominance did not harm the public and that, by 1911, competition was making itself felt. Shenfield (1983, p. 22) argued that the erosion of Standard Oil's position

> was only partly due to the rise of companies based on the new fields of Texas, Louisiana and California. It was also due to the fact that Standard's arteries had begun to harden. The new men were becoming more efficient than Rockefeller. With or without the anti-trust case, the days of his monopoly were numbered.

Similar dilemmas arise in the field of restrictive contracts. If all restrictive agreements are *per se* illegal, it becomes impossible to achieve some gains from trade other than by 'internalisation'. The law is (contrary to the normative Coase theorem) making certain types of contract 'infinitely costly'. If I wish to protect my brand name or my proprietary information by imposing restrictions on people with whom I trade, I might find myself falling foul of the law. There may be instances where an agreement is 'obviously' not against the public interest, but ideas about what these 'obvious' cases are tend to change over time. In the years between 1914 and the mid-1930s, a case-by-case 'rule of reason' approach to antitrust predominated in the United States. The words 'every contract . . . in restraint of trade' in the Sherman Act were interpreted by the Supreme Court to mean 'every unreasonable contract' and, especially in the depression era, some surprising examples were approved.[19] From the late 1930s to the early 1970s, however, *per se* rules against horizontal price fixing[20], price discrimination[21], tying arrangements[22] and resale-price maintenance[23] were emphasised in the United States. This period was the heyday of the 'inhospitality tradition'. Instead of presuming that an agreement between two consenting agents is socially advantageous and treating it 'hospitably', as in the common-law tradition, the antitrust approach was to view all non-standard contracts 'inhospitably'.[24]

3.2.3   New Chicago and the Transactions Cost School

The two related ideas that contract and internal organisation are alternative means of coordinating resources and that effective organisation requires a balance to be struck between the costs of transacting and the costs of ownership began to be fully developed only in the 1960s and 1970s. As the implications of Coase's early work were explored by writers such as Demsetz, Alchian and Williamson, the consequences for antitrust policy of the literature reviewed in Part 1 of this book began to be appreciated. If the firm was a purely technological entity, the scale and scope of which were determined by the laws of engineering, all attempts to coordinate activities with other firms using non-standard 'non-arm's-length' contracts were highly suspect. The *per se* undesirability of such contracts seemed to follow ineluctably from the economic theory of the time. If, on the other hand, a range of organisational forms was possible – from arm's-length spot-market contracts, through longer-term associations and franchise contracts to full internal integration – the implications for antitrust policy were profound. A *per se* condemnation of non-standard contracts risked forcing economic organisation into one of two 'acceptable' straitjackets. Either a relationship was 'within the firm' and outsiders were entirely excluded or, alternatively, transactors agreed to use approved 'market' arrangements in which everyone dealt on exactly the same terms. Vertical agreements to control quality, the licensing of technical knowledge, the transfer of know-how across markets, cooperation on research, and the use of franchise contracts to exploit certain types of brand-name capital – all inevitably involve some restriction on the freedom of the parties to trade with others. The fact that certain trading partners are favoured over others is not in itself a sufficient proof of an undesirable restrictive practice.

Between the early 1970s and the 1990s, therefore, changes in the interpretation of antitrust law occurred in the United States which began to take greater account of transactions-cost thinking. Scholars in Law and Economics, such as Richard Posner and Robert Bork, translated the ideas of the 'New Chicago School'[25] into practice. Kovacic and Shapiro (2000, p. 53) summarise the influence of the new approach as follows. 'The new Chicago scholars emphasised efficiency explanations for many phenomena, including industrial concentration, mergers, and contractual restraints, that antitrust law acutely disfavored in the 1950s and 1960s.'

The approach to vertical agreements, in particular, changed considerably. A frequently cited contrast is that between the Schwinn judgement in 1967 and the case of Sylvania v. Continental TV in (1977). Schwinn was a manufacturer of high-quality bicycles with franchised outlets which were forbidden to sell to other non-franchised dealers. This restriction was held to be anti-competitive by preventing competing retailers from selling Schwinn bicycles. The importance to the manufacturer of maintaining a reputation for quality; the reduction in search costs for people looking for Schwinn bicycles; the requirement on the franchisees to offer aftersales service and so forth, were not deemed to be considerations of sufficient public concern to overturn the presumption against the restrictive nature of the agreements. In 1977, however, the Sylvania judgement explicitly accepted the social utility of some vertical restraints and rejected the *per se* approach exemplified by the Schwinn case.

These developments also had an impact on other jurisdictions. A consultative document in the UK in 1988 contained passages that might have been taken straight from the work of Oliver Williamson.

> In many cases [vertical] restrictions . . . are necessary to encourage the retailer to undertake investment to promote the product by giving him the assurance that other retailers . . . will not 'free ride' on the generated demand. As long as there is effective . . . inter-brand competition, the reduction in intra-brand competition arising from such practices should not matter.[26]

By 1993, the Monopolies Commission in the UK was defending similar restrictions in the fine fragrances market. 'Fine fragrances were luxury items and suppliers needed to be able to . . . protect their brand images, which consumers evidently valued.'[27] Again, under European Union Law, certain categories of agreement are permitted under a 'block exemption' system. Some types of agreement, far from being objectionable *per se*, may therefore be treated as acceptable or even desirable.

It would be wrong to conclude that transactions cost theory has simply led to a more permissive climate of antitrust interpretation and enforcement. An example of the new approach leading to a seeming tightening of antitrust law can be found in Eastman Kodak Co. v. Image Technical Services Inc (1992). The 'market power' problem concerned the spare parts and services for Kodak photocopiers. Although Kodak had a market share of only twenty per cent of new copiers, it was argued that it might still have the power to exploit the people who were dependent on Kodak copiers after they had been installed. In other words, *ex post* contractual opportunism might be a problem. Dependency on Kodak spare parts and servicing could be used to 'hold up' the buyers of photocopiers, and the Supreme Court indicated that this 'installed base opportunism' could be construed as an antitrust violation.[28] Kovacic and Shapiro (2000, p. 56) note that 'the Kodak case stands for the principle that strategic behavior, including conduct based on imperfect consumer information, must be examined in detail by the trial court'.

These examples taken from the history of antitrust law in the United States indicate the way that interpretation has evolved over time. Whether a 'rule of reason' or a *per se* legal environment exists; whether the dominant school is 'Old Chicago' or 'New Chicago'; it is clear that competition policy cannot avoid becoming embroiled in the assessment of particular contractual arrangements and sitting in judgement upon the history of particular businesses. This has led some writers to question the nature of antitrust law. If antitrust is really a branch of 'public interest' economics it will approve contracts that lead to gains from trade and condemn those that lead to social losses. Such an interpretation seems to imply, however, that the difference between efficient and inefficient commercial arrangements can be reasonably calculated by a court of law and can be reasonably inferred in advance by contractors. Members of the Austrian School would deny that either of these conditions applies.

3.2.4   The Austrian critique of antitrust

For radical 'Austrian' writers such as Shenfield (1983, p. 29), antitrust is in the 'public interest' tradition and has achieved little over the very long term. It is a recipe for a 'Fusspot State'. The state, in his view, should concentrate upon supporting private non-coerced agreements. 'The only proper function of Government when we trade is to guard us against force and fraud. And fraud means fraud. It does not mean non-fraudulent inequality of bargaining power or of information or of business acumen.' Hayek also was a sceptic concerning antitrust. Möschel (1989, p. 153) well summarises Hayek's position. Hayek did not believe that 'his idea of the rule of law as an abstract general framework for exploratory processes that arise out of free interaction, can be realised in competition policy'. The principle that the state should not hinder uncoerced private agreements is capable of being enforced in a court of law. The principle that the state should not hinder voluntary agreements that enhance 'economic efficiency' but should forbid those that are 'socially inefficient' or that 'detract from competitive pressure' cannot be turned into abstract universal rules equally binding on all economic agents. In practice, antitrust law turns into a game in which economic consultants engage in a continuing debate in an attempt to win over officials or judges on questions of the economic efficiency of various organisational arrangements. For philosophers of Hayek's persuasion, this might be 'antitrust', but it does not really fit their conception of what 'law' ideally should be.[29]

Some economists and practising lawyers would argue, however, that antitrust policy is capable of refereeing the game without dictating the outcomes. This is certainly the Ordo-liberal position. If 'Austrian' writers can claim that antitrust inevitably succumbs to the influence of pressure groups and special interests, the Ordo-liberals can reasonably ask the Austrians what prevents private interests coming to dominate the state in the absence of antitrust? In spite of their awareness of public choice pressures, the Austrians stand accused of a dynamic form of the 'nirvana fallacy' – not that government policy can costlessly achieve efficient outcomes (the traditional form of the fallacy) but that the conditions in which government activity is procedurally neutral can somehow be assumed. In their ideal world, the government would be neutral and would not be corrupted by powerful private interests. But, as Willgerodt and Peacock (1989) point out, the Ordo-liberals in Germany were particularly worried about the possibility of private economic power subverting the individual freedoms that were the ultimate values that they wished to protect. In a truly 'comparative-institutions' approach to policy, antitrust law might plausibly give better long-term protection against the political pressures of the powerful than a night-watchman state. Night watchmen in traditional liberal theory are strong and focused on their patch. In practice, however, if strong, the exploitation of the neighbourhood by the night watchman will surely follow and, if weak, the watchman is unlikely to be effective against sufficiently ruthless criminals. If, however, a 'neutral rule of law' (or at least some system which approximates neutrality) is deemed possible in the field of competition policy and simply implies curbing the inadmissible use of private power then 'there is practically no difference between Ordo-liberals and Austrian liberals such as Ludwig von Mises and his followers'.[30]

Certainly, the justification of antitrust activity offered by practitioners often has a strong Austrian influence. Bingaman (1994) argues that 'both our antitrust and intellectual property laws share a common objective: promoting innovation'. This is to take a view of the competitive process closely associated with economists such as Joseph Schumpeter.[31] Real competition is not about other people producing the same thing. It is about other people improving on your product or producing a different thing which undermines your entire market. Schumpeter referred metaphorically to competition as 'a gale of creative destruction'. Bingaman is arguing that the role of antitrust is not about achieving known ends, it is simply to keep the gale blowing lest business people find ways of suppressing or moderating it. This view seems, on the face of it, compatible with the Austrian emphasis on discovery, innovation and evolution.

The dilemmas implicit in this view of 'antitrust as a boost for innovation', however, have already been encountered in Chapter 7. The problem is that the process of innovation often requires long-term commitments. These can easily look restrictive of competition. They are, indeed, specifically designed to moderate the gale of creative destruction. Sometimes you need a break in the weather to get things done. Schumpeter, after all, did not find it helpful to use the metaphor 'the hurricane of creative destruction' or 'the tornado of creative destruction'. In these images, the element of oxymoron is simply too pronounced to convey the right meaning – we can certainly see the destruction but would need some convincing about the creative side of a tornado. Once again, we see the tension between private solutions to problems – via integration, merger or long-term agree-ment – and regulatory solutions via antitrust. Pursuing the Schumpeterian metaphor further, it is as if private arrangements may be permitted that moderate the wind from storm-force ten to gale-force eight, but not as far as a bracing breeze and certainly not down to a light waft of air. Unfortunately, reasonable as this sounds as a policy objective, decisions about the consequences of various contracts for the time path of innova-tion are entirely judgemental and subjective.

The 'rule of reason' or 'each case on its merits' would seem to be the only way of proceeding, and the chances of achieving a steady gale through a body of clear rules applicable to all would appear remote indeed. Bingaman (1994) reveals this problem when she writes 'I don't want to leave the impression, by talking about instances in which the Division has blocked a transaction in order to protect innovation, that we are oblivious to the fact that many transactions promote innovation.' Some mergers, for example, will facilitate innovation. Others will not. Antitrust is simply aimed at the latter. This, however, is law as a continual process of negotiation with offi-cials. As Kovacic and Shapiro (2000, p. 57) remark, 'In the Justice Department's battle against Microsoft, both parties depict themselves as champions of innovation.'[32]

3.2.5 Ordered competition in UK telecommunications

A case study might be useful at this point to illustrate the difficult judge-ments that competition regulators face in technically dynamic conditions. After the privatisation of British Telecom (BT) in the United Kingdom (1984–90) a 'duopoly policy' was followed in the telecommunications market. A competitor to BT, Mercury Communications (MCL) was per-mitted to enter and operate a fixed-link service. Over the same period, mobile telephony developed rapidly and here also the regulators followed a duopoly policy. The two mobile telephone companies were Cellnet, in which BT had a majority stake, and Vodaphone. Cable companies added a further complexity. These were laying new networks but were not permit-ted to enter telephony unless in partnership with BT or MCL. Conversely, BT was not permitted to use its network for the delivery of entertainment services. After 1991, the duopoly policy ended. TV and cable companies could offer telephony services and mobile telephone companies could offer fixed-link services. Owners of other networks of wires and pipes were also permitted to enter telecommunications, as existing ducting could often be used for establishing a cable network. On the other hand, BT and MCL were still prohibited from providing entertainment in competition with the cable companies. Only in 1998 was this restriction lifted.

An interesting aspect of this history is that regulators would, at each stage, have maintained that their policy was pro-competitive. The restrictions were there to encourage new entry by limiting the rate of new entry and to encourage newcomers by handicapping the incumbent. With a powerful company such as BT in existence, new entrants in the cable market required assurances that the dominant firm would not be able to respond in a predatory manner. Permitting cable companies to offer telephone services threatened the dominant BT, and forbidding BT to offer entertainment gave cable companies a greater incentive to enter the market. However, the policy was essentially Hobbesian rather than Coasian. This was not about removing impediments to private agreements and letting the market rip. This was about structuring the law to encourage particular outcomes, building up some contestants and hobbling others. The regulator over the period of time in question was as much a player in the game as a referee and the system much nearer one of 'ordered competition' than a Hayekian 'competitive order'.[33]

4.   REGULATING UTILITIES

4.1   Regulation as a Contract

We have seen in sections 2 and 3 above that the broad trend in policy with respect to the public utilities has been to isolate the 'natural monopoly' element at the core of the utility and introduce competitive pressures in the other areas. This has entailed permitting new entry and 'deregulating' the production and retail ends of the vertical production chain. In this section, our focus is on regulation where actual and potential competition cannot be relied upon. An extreme example is that part of a public utility's business which is 'naturally monopolistic' – usually a network of pipes, tracks, wires or cables.

Under these conditions it is convenient to regard the firm and the regulator as in a quasi-contractual relationship. All the transactional considerations that have proved important throughout this book are relevant to an analysis of regulatory contracts. We can look at the regulatory problem through the lens of formal principal–agent theory (with the regulator as the principal and the firm as the agent) or we can use a more informal transactions cost or incomplete contracts approach. In the latter case, the relationship between regulator and firm becomes a durable one and the regulatory system can be seen, in the tradition of Oliver Williamson, as a 'governance structure' to moderate the behaviour of potentially opportunistic contractors.

From Chapter 5, the main determinants of an optimal contract were the cost of observing the agent's 'output' or 'result'; the cost of monitoring the agent's 'effort'; the degree of risk aversion of both principal and agent; the level of 'environmental uncertainty' and the 'efficiency' of the agent's effort in raising the probability of good outcomes. In the transactions cost and property rights tradition, we should also consider the probability that the contractual relationship will be repeated and the 'hold-up' potential offered by specific assets when the contract cannot be complete. Let us consider each of these factors in turn.

4.1.1   What does the regulator want and can it be measured?

If the 'outcome' is observable by both regulator and firm and if the 'effort' of the firm is unobservable, we have the conditions of the classic principal–agent contract. With risk-neutral firms, maximum effort incentives can be achieved without risk-sharing losses by making them bear the entire risk. In Chapter 14, we introduced the Loeb and Magat (1979) method of utility regulation which is derived from this optimal contracting tradition. There (see again Figure 14.1), it was assumed that the social surpluses from output were observable at low cost – conditions which are unlikely to pertain in practice. Notice that we introduced the Loeb–Magat contract in the context of the control of 'public enterprise'. From the point of view of the pure theory of contracts, we have the same analysis whether the 'government' contracts with a 'manager' or whether the 'regulator' contracts with a private firm. It will be recalled that the inability of standard principal–agent theory to explain why property rights mattered was an important aspect of the incomplete-contracts critique.

Where output is difficult to measure and qualitative factors are important, the danger of using high-powered incentives is that effort will be distorted away from what is not measured towards what is measured and rewarded. If the regulator (principal) 'gets what s/he pays for' this will only be beneficial if s/he has a very clear idea what s/he wants and can measure it accurately.

4.1.2   How costly is monitoring?

Where firms are risk averse and regulatory monitoring is informative there may be a mutual interest in establishing information flows about the firm's activities. The firm gains by reducing risk-bearing costs while the regulator gains by ensuring compliance with regulatory objectives. A regulator wishing to ensure 'safety' might, for example, contract with a firm on the basis of the number of people harmed over a period of time. However, a risk-averse firm would prefer to be judged on its safety 'effort', if the latter can be observed at low cost. A freak accident would not then result in large losses to the firm providing its observed safety effort were satisfactory.

4.1.3 Risk aversion and uncertainty

In the absence of uncertainty and with a known technology relating the agent's actions to desired outcomes, the contracting environment would be simple. The regulator would simply pay for the desired outcome if it occurred and not otherwise. It is environmental uncertainty that makes it difficult to distinguish bad luck from non-compliance. This results in two offsetting influences on the optimal contract. As uncertainty and risk aversion increase, so do the risk-bearing costs of an incentive contract, and the firm will prefer to contract nearer its certainty line and will accept a greater amount of monitoring. Working in the contrary direction is the fact that monitoring is likely to yield noisier signals and hence will become more costly as environmental uncertainty rises. More costly monitoring would be expected to push in the direction of an incentive contract.

4.1.4 Effort efficiency

The greater is the efficiency of effort on the part of the agent the lower the risk-bearing losses that have to be sacrificed in an incentive contract. In a world of risk-neutral firms, this would not make any difference to the optimal regulatory contract but where regulators are dealing with risk-averse firms the firms will ideally bear less risk as their effort efficiency rises.[34]

4.1.5 Repeated games

Analysing regulation as a single-period contract enables us to concentrate on some important features of the regulatory problem. However, in a world of incomplete contracts and bounded rationality, the 'relational' aspects of the regulatory process are also significant. As was seen in Chapter 1, repeat dealing can give rise to cooperative behaviour in a game of exchange even when the single period payoffs would lead contractors to act uncooperatively. The accumulation of trust and reputation, as well as the gradual development of information exchanges between the contractors, can also play an important part in regulation, just as in other relationships.

4.1.6 Hold-up and specific assets

Specific assets are a significant contractual problem in the regulation of public utilities as well as in other areas of regulation. Much physical capital as well as accumulated 'know-how' will have a greater value inside the regulated firm than in alternative uses outside. Such capital is vulnerable to regulatory opportunism. The regulator of a utility might, for example, try to 'renegotiate' a regulatory bargain after a firm has invested in expensive and specific capital. Knowledge that this is a possibility will reduce the firm's incentive to invest in this type of capital in the first place and could conceivably render certain types of regulation impossible.

It is perhaps worth explicitly comparing this reasoning with the arguments presented in Chapter 13 on the property rights case for private rather than state ownership. There, the up-front investment took the form of non-transferable human capital and the argument was (loosely) that the physical asset should be 'owned' by the contractor whose human capital was 'essential' and whose outside opportunities in the event of contractual 'breakdown' were the best. We concluded at that point that property rights arguments would tend to favour private ownership of the asset and a contract with the government over the output. If the government wished to purchase military hardware for the navy, construction services for roads and bridges, computers for the tax gatherers, educational services for pupils, medical services for patients and so forth, there were strong arguments that it should avoid 'owning' the dockyards, diggers, electronics companies, schools or medical facilities required.

Here, however, the argument is that *physical* asset specificity will make contracting with the government or 'regulator' hazardous. This will tend to favour government ownership of transaction-specific physical assets unless contracts can be made verifiable and highly reliable. The difference between the present context and that of Chapter 13 is that investment is here considered to be in a physical 'asset' which is not specific to the supplier's human capital but *is* specific to the buyer's requirements, so that there is no opportunity to use the asset for purposes other than those agreed with the government. We saw in Chapter 7 how the danger of opportunistic recontracting under these circumstances might lead to quasi-vertical integration – the buyer leasing specific equipment to the supplier – so that it is not surprising that similar problems might arise in dealings with a government buyer or regulator and private-sector suppliers.

4.2   Regulation as Rent Seeking

The implication underlying subsection 4.1.6 that the government is not an entirely benevolent and reliable agent but is capable of reneging on agreements and acting in an opportunist way suggests that 'public choice' forces are important to a full understanding of regulation. Regulation is, from this perspective, simply a means by which interest groups lay claim to resources which would otherwise flow elsewhere.[35]

Consider, for example, the setting up of the Interstate Commerce Commission (ICC) in 1887 in the USA. At first sight, it is natural to assume that this was to protect consumer interests against the monopoly railroad interests. Similarly, the regulation of telecommunications, first by the ICC and, after 1934, by the Federal Communications Commission (FCC), would likewise be considered as a response to natural monopoly. Indeed, natural monopoly could also be used to justify and explain the federal regulation of interstate trade in electricity and natural gas by the Federal Energy Regulatory Commission (FERC) and the setting up of the Civil Aeronautics Board (CAB).

Historical research has indicated, however, that 'consumer protection' as an explanation for regulation is far from the whole story. In the case of the railroads, long-haul routes before 1887 were subject to intense bouts of secret price cutting.[36] These secret rebates often did not stay secret for very long and the profitability of the long-haul routes was always subject to erosion. Shorter-haul routes, mainly used by farmers, were less subject to competition before the rise of motor transport, and farming interests therefore lobbied strongly for regulation. The railroad interests were not entirely opposed to these developments, however. They gained from the reduction of price competition and could look forward to regulated rates which provided a higher return on long hauls to compensate for more moderate rates on shorter hauls.

Similarly, at the beginning of the twentieth century, the expiry of patents, which had acted as protection since the 1880s, left the Bell telephone system subject to increased competitive pressure from new entry. Bell refused to interconnect with the new companies. Some responded by wiring into areas served by Bell. In the face of this competitive threat, Bell supported regulation to restrict new entry.

In the case of airline regulation and the setting up of the Civil Aeronautics Board (CAB) in 1938, the surface arguments were about 'destructive competition' and safety. Protection from new entry was also a major consideration, however. Behrman (1980) observed that 'Few interest groups have ever been so overtly and incontestably pre-eminent in legislative proceedings as the airline industry was during the congressional deliberations that led to the passage of the (Civil Aeronautics) act.' In the twenty-five years between 1950 and 1974, no new entrant was granted permission by the CAB to start an interstate scheduled air service.

Given our preliminary discussion of public choice analysis in chapter 13 and Stigler's (1971) work on the capture theory of regulation cited in subsection 3.1, the importance of producer groups in the regulatory process should not be surprising.[37] However, producer interests can be ranged against one another. Peltzman's (1976) model of regulation in which vote-maximising politicians balance the power of opposing interests is ultimately more satisfactory than a model in which one interest 'captures' the regulatory machine entirely. Favoured groups of voters can also benefit at the expense of others. By charging prices above marginal cost to one group of consumers and cross-subsidising some other group of consumers, the regulatory system can be used as an implicit (and often hidden) tax and transfer system.[38] Deregulation and the encouraging of competition make this system of regulatory redistribution unworkable.[39] Subsidies to rural areas or to other special interests become explicit and observable and have to be channelled through taxes rather than regulated prices. As was also the case in the Boyko, Shleifer and Vishny (1996) theory of privatisation cited in Chapter 14, transfers to special interests carry a higher political price after the economy has been deregulated. Producer interests might, therefore, not always be decisive, as will be seen later in this chapter. Further, when information about prices or profits is widely available, pressure from consumers via the voting system can be significant and can lead to 'populist' responses by politicians and regulators. In the following subsections, a few of the more common types of regulation are considered from the perspective of the contractual issues raised in subsection 4.1 and the public choice pressures mentioned in subsection 4.2.

4.3   Rate of Return Regulation

Rate of return regulation is traditionally associated with the system of utility regulation in the United States. A natural monopolist would be prevented from setting prices which maximise profit and would instead be constrained to a 'fair' return on capital. From the point of view of contract theory, the system has affinities with a 'cost-plus' agreement with the regulator. Diagrammatically, we can envisage the regulatory contract as somewhere along the firm's certainty line, as in Figure 15.2. Whichever 'state of the world' occurs, the firm is permitted to keep profits representing a fair rate of return on its capital.

The obvious objection to this approach is that it gives the regulated firm little incentive to exert 'effort' in reducing costs and increasing the probability of 'good' rather than 'poor' outcomes. Further, if information about capital requirements is costly for the regulator to gather, the company will try to use excessive amounts of capital in order to 'inflate its rate base'. Clearly, if a regulator is controlling the ratio π/K where π is profit and K is capital stock, any given level of profit will be acceptable providing the level of K is high enough. Providing the regulated rate of return is higher than can be achieved in alternative competitive areas of business, the use of capital is encouraged. This might take the form of highly capital-intensive techniques of production or even the 'wasteful' use of capital – adding capital to the company merely to increase the rate base (K). Unnecessarily expensive equipment, much of it serving managerial interests rather than productive effectiveness (so-called 'gold-plating') is also a predictable outcome. The tendency of capital inputs to rise under rate of return regulation is known as the Averch–Johnson effect.[40]

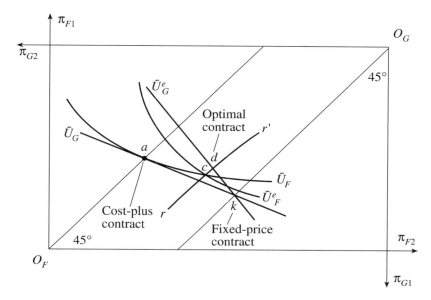

Figure 15.2   Government contracting: fixed price versus cost-plus

In order to counter the Averch–Johnson effect, even 'public-interest' regulators would be forced into a complex bargaining relationship with the firm. The regulator is forced to take an interest, not merely in the size of the capital base but in the techniques of production adopted by the firm. In the UK, for example, the Water Industry Act 1991 charges the regulator with ensuring that companies can make 'reasonable returns on their capital'. OFWAT scrutinises the investment plans of companies which have an interest in pressing for large increases in capital infrastructure, in water quality and in environmental standards.[41] Firms can be expected to try to mislead the regulator over the size of the rate base by classifying all sorts of expenditures as 'capital' subject to slow rates of depreciation. They would be expected to prefer investment in fixed assets such as reservoirs and new pipelines rather than in the maintenance and repair of old pipelines. They might conceal information about the uses to which items of capital are put in order to maximise allowable capital. In response, the regulator may threaten to reduce the allowable rate of return. An over-rigorous regulator, however, risks undermining the incentive to invest completely. The regulated company may find itself forced to borrow at fixed interest rather than to use equity finance. The specific nature of the long-lived assets employed in the water and other 'natural monopoly' industries raises the spectre of regulatory 'hold-up', however, and a zealous regulator is capable, paradoxically of raising the cost of finance.

Historically, it is not the danger of regulatory overkill but of regulatory capture that has been considered the bigger problem. The legislation requires the regulator to permit a 'fair' rate of return which can be interpreted as a constraint on regulatory 'hold-up'. Confiscatory measures would be subject to legal challenge. Over time, discussions between regulator and industry managers could lead to too much rather than too little mutual 'understanding'. The desire on both sides for a quiet life, as well as the possibility of subtle forms of corruption – such as post-retirement jobs in the industry for ex-regulators – could lead to regulatory capture. A classic early study of the effects of regulation over the long term was that of Stigler and Friedland (1962). They investigated electricity prices in regulated and non-regulated US states for the years 1912, 1922, 1932 and 1937. Their conclusion was that regulation seemed to have no impact after allowing for influences such as population density, per capita income and the proportion of power coming from hydroelectric sources. This and other studies, which appeared to indicate the general ineffectiveness of regulation, led Stigler (1971) eventually to formulate his capture theory.[42]

4.4   RPI Minus X

Price-cap regulation has been an important part of the regulatory system set up in the UK after the privatisations of the 1980s. In this system the regulator sets, for a specified period of time, a maximum price that the firm may charge for a service. This price may be increased each year by an amount equal to the rate of increase of the retail prices index (RPI). On the other hand, it must be reduced each year by an amount, agreed with the regulator at the beginning of the review period, which is supposed to be an estimate of the rate of productivity increase that might reasonably be anticipated – the mysterious factor 'X'. Because regulated firms are usually producing many different services, the regulated price is often actually an index of a 'basket' of services, produced by a regulated firm. The firm is then permitted to alter the prices of services within the basket; so-called tariff rebalancing; providing that the index does not infringe the RPI minus X constraint. Occasionally the formula also allows for the passing through into output prices of changes in the market price of an important input. The formula is then 'RPI plus Y minus X'. In the case of the UK water industry, for example, the enormous increase in investment required to meet regulatory environmental standards and quality objectives led to RPI plus K, where K was a capital cost factor. This later became RPI minus X plus Q where Q was the cost of quality.[43]

From a 'regulatory contracts' point of view, the advantage of RPI minus X is that it gives greater incentives for cost reductions and productivity improvements compared with rate of return regulation. It is nearer to the 'fixed price' contract than the 'cost-plus' variety. In terms of Figure 15.2, the contract might be seen as somewhere along the regulator's certainty line. The firm will receive the benefit from extra effort and the regulator receives a relatively 'certain' result. We might imagine some cost-reducing innovation which will increase the profits of the firm but will not change the benefits accruing to consumers. These are determined by the price agreed between the firm and the regulator. The firm bears the risk and has high effort incentives. Obviously, its profits would be expected to be more variable than under rate-of-return regulation.

In practice, of course, this contrast between rate-of-return regulation and RPI minus X is far less clear cut than the static analysis implies. Figure 15.2 represents a single-period 'contract'. Like all regulatory systems, however, RPI minus X involves a continuing association between firm and regulator. In the first place, the review period does not go on forever and setting an appropriate length of time is a very significant problem. If the period is too short, it reduces the return that the firm can expect on its cost-reducing ideas. On the other hand, if the period is too long it is possible that the firm will be observed enjoying very high (or low) profit levels for year after year. Quite apart from the conventional neoclassical objections to monopoly pricing which would then undoubtedly come into play, the pure public choice pressures unleashed cannot in practice be ignored. If the firm were so unprofitable that it was on the verge of collapse, renegotiation of the formula would be expected to occur. Similarly, large profits lead to political interference. In the UK, for example, the profits of some utilities, which were perceived as 'too high', led to the imposition of a 'windfall tax' in 1998. The tax was 'justified' by politicians on the grounds that the potential profitability at privatisation had been underestimated and that the assets had been sold at too cheap a price. Political pressures, therefore, restrict the regulatory bargains that can be delivered by the regulator and the incentive effects of the RPI minus X system are in this way to some degree undermined.

Another very fundamental issue concerns the method of determining the price cap at the point of renegotiation. If it is related to the prevailing costs of production, problems of information and bargaining resurface. The firm will have an incentive to distort upwards its reporting of existing costs and its estimates of future costs. In this way the regulator begins to get deeply embroiled in discussions of technology and costs just as rate of return regulators do. Knowledge that cost reductions will cause future price caps to be lower, clearly reduces the incentive to adopt improvements. This will particularly be so as the end of a review period approaches. Better for the present value of profits that any potential cost-reducing innovations are hidden from the regulator towards the end of a review period and introduced at the very beginning of the next.

Setting a value for 'X' is perhaps the most difficult part of the whole process. In principle, 'X' should be forward looking. If it simply looks back to the productivity improvements achieved in the past, the incentive properties of the system are once more subverted. Looking forward to the next period, however, requires that entrepreneurial judgements be made about opportunities ahead and it is not clear why the regulator will be in a good position to assess them. Certainly, there seems no reason to expect an entrepreneur/manager to explain his or her view of the future very clearly when the value of 'X' for the next review period is at stake. Once more the regulator and firm bargain, this time over competing views of future technological and market opportunities.

The difficulty of negotiating 'X' can be illustrated by the electricity-price review in the mid-1990s in the UK. The review was undertaken in 1994 and 'X' was provisionally set at two per cent per year. Early in 1995, however, Northern Electric, one of the companies subject to the review, was threatened with a takeover bid from Trafalgar House. The bid was resisted and shareholders were informed of hitherto unsuspected profit opportunities. The incumbent management promised cuts in costs, special payments to shareholders and increases in future dividends. Such was the public outcry that the regulator increased the value of 'X' from two to three per cent. This is an example of the market in corporate control revealing information about a company which had been successfully concealed from the regulator. A major advantage of rate of return regulation is that the rate of return which must be offered to attract capital to a particular line of business can be assessed by looking at actual capital markets. Prevailing rates of return in differing sectors may only be an imperfect guide, but they do represent a summary of market conditions. Under price-cap regulation, in contrast, 'when we turn to X we set sail on a sea of doubt'.[44]

A final problem which requires a specific mention is that of specifying the unit of output to which the price cap applies. The task of setting a separate price for each of many different services would be immense and we have already noted that a 'basket' of services is frequently used. There is also the question of 'quality'. In a technically dynamic industry, it is particularly difficult to specify an output precisely, but without an attempt there is a danger that the firm will meet the price cap and increase profits by reducing 'non-contractible quality'. Standards of service therefore form another component of the regulatory bargain.

In terms of practical effect, the differences between rate of return regulation and RPI minus X might be considered less pronounced than theory would suggest. To the extent that regulators extrapolate past trends in productivity into the future and seek to achieve reasonable profits for the regulated firm, the two systems would have much in common. A fixed duration for the regulatory settlement and the absence of a specific constraint over this period on the rate of return, however, do lead to a different bargaining environment in the case of RPI-minus-X regulation. The fundamental advantages attributed to it are that it allows entrepreneurial profits to be claimed for a fixed period of time and that it avoids the systematic bias in favour of capital implied by rate of return regulation.

Beesley and Littlechild (1988) argue that there is also greater scope for bargaining under RPI minus X. Because the regulator is forced to look ahead over a given time-horizon (an 'exogenous risk period'), and negotiates not just on prices but on the contents of the various regulated 'baskets' of output and on the value of 'X', the scope of the bargain is very broad. In the UK context, there is also the dubious advantage that regulators are less constrained by 'due process' legal restrictions on their activities than would be the case in the USA. 'The consequence of these four differences – exogenous risk period, forward looking approach, degrees of freedom, and less requirement to explain – is that there is greater scope for bargaining in RPI minus X than in rate of return regulation' (p. 461).

4.5   Sliding-scale Profits Tax

The political pressures that arise when regulated firms begin to make either very large profits or unsustainable losses tend, as we have seen, to undermine price-cap regulation of the type outlined in subsection 4.4. It has been suggested, therefore, that a profits tax levied on regulated utilities would be more sustainable and might still avoid the Averch–Johnson effects associated with rate of return regulation. In neoclassical theory, a tax on 'pure profit' is neutral. It does not affect an otherwise unregulated monopolist's decisions about what techniques of production to employ, what quantity of output to produce or what price to charge. Clearly, if pure profits are subject to a simple proportional tax, the policy which maximises pre-tax profit will also maximise after-tax profit.

To levy a tax on pure profit would divert part of the monopolist's profit to the government but it would not induce the monopolist to set prices equal to marginal cost and adjust output in line with the 'public interest' criteria. Further, to measure the level of pure profit requires information about all constituents of the 'costs of production'. In other words, the neutrality of a pure profits tax is a theoretical benchmark rather than a practical proposition. Recent work has therefore refined the profits tax so as to make it more attractive from a neoclassical public interest point of view.[45] The basic idea is that the rate of tax on profit should be linked to prices or output. The system has been called 'variable rate' or 'sliding scale' regulation. Turvey (1995) has shown that sliding-scale mechanisms were first employed in the British gas industry during the nineteenth century.

A utility subject to a sliding-scale profits tax would be able to reduce the rate of tax applicable to its profits by increasing its output (or lowering its price). It is possible, with sufficient information about demand and cost conditions, so to calibrate the schedule linking tax rates to output or prices that the firm is induced to operate efficiently from a 'public interest' point of view. It will maximise its post-tax profits by setting prices equal to marginal costs.[46] The idea is attractive because it incorporates a 'profit-sharing' element – both government and utility gain from higher profits deriving from greater efficiency, and an incentive is provided to increase output rather than to restrict it. On the other hand, the analysis is entirely in the marginal-cost-pricing tradition discussed in Chapter 13. In place of well-informed and benevolent nationalised industry managers we have well-informed and benevolent regulators.

The sliding-scale system can be defended from a slightly different perspective however. Burns, Turvey and Weyman-Jones (1998), for example, continue to assume a benevolent regulator interested in efficiency, but their regulator is not perfectly informed and public choice pressures are introduced into the analysis. The regulator expects that the high-powered incentives associated with price-cap regulation will elicit 'populist' responses leading to confiscatory measures in the future if regulated firms are too successful at raising profits. Thus, 'an intermediate incentive contract, whilst sacrificing some productive efficiency, can still be preferable to the highest-powered regime, if public and political pressure would otherwise force a change to cost of service, or rate of return regulation' (p. 134). It is possible to offer a somewhat crude illustration of this point using Figure 15.3. A contract between the certainty lines of the two contractors, implying less than the highest-powered incentives, can be optimal from a second-best point of view even with a risk-neutral firm. This is because there are political constraints on the amount of profit that can accrue to the firm in the 'good' state of the world.

In Figure 15.3 the firm is risk neutral. At point a it receives its reservation utility U and exerts minimal effort e_1. Using the same arguments as those in Chapter 5, a contract at b would just induce effort level e_2, thus raising the probability of the 'good' outcome and steepening the line of constant expected utility. A contract at c will just induce effort level e_3 and a contract at k effort level e_4. Taking the inner envelope of these lines of

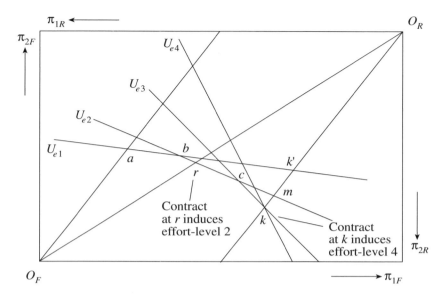

Note: A regulator constrained for political reasons to adopt 'profit-sharing' regulation will operate at point *r*. The firm is risk neutral. Locus *ak* traces contracts giving constant expected utility to the firm. Effort levels rise as the contract moves from *a* towards *k*. The firm receives its 'reservation utility' at point *r* which maximises the regulator's profit share.

Figure 15.3   A profit-sharing regulatory contract

constant expected utility applying to increasing levels of effort, we derive the locus *abck*. Point *k*, where this locus intersects the regulator's certainty line, would be the normal optimum contract. Whether the regulator was risk averse or, like the firm, merely interested in expected profit, point *k* would give a 'first-best' result. The regulator would have maximised the government's expected profit while bearing no risk and giving the firm its reservation utility.

The regulator may not be able to deliver a contract at *k*, however. Voters do not see the effort of the firm but they do see the large profits made by the firm if the 'good' outcome occurs. The firm expects this political pressure to result in regulatory 'post-contractual opportunism'. It will have no confidence in a contract at *k*. We might then imagine the regulator moving away from point *k* to a point such as *r*. With a risk-neutral firm, this would sacrifice effort incentives, but it would be better than a move all the way to point *a* which, by hypothesis, might otherwise occur. Point *r*, maximises the regulator's profit share ($O_R r / O_R O_F$) subject to giving the firm its reservation utility. If the regulator is risk neutral, the indifference curves in the figure can be read with respect to the O_R origin, gains to the firm implying equivalent losses to the regulator and vice versa. The regulator will wish to contract on an indifference curve which cuts his or her certainty line as far as possible from O_R Thus, in the absence of political constraint, point k is optimal. The 'cost' of meeting the political constraint is given by the distance km along the regulator's certainty line.

5.   FRANCHISING

5.1   Auctioning the Right to Serve the Market

One simple method of ensuring greater managerial efficiency in the provision of a natural monopoly service than could be expected from a public enterprise would be to auction the right to serve the market for a specified period. In the absence of competition *in* the market an auction would provide competition *for* the market. There would, of course, still be the sources of managerial shirking discussed at length in Chapters 8 and 9, but managerial constraints would be tighter than those associated with a public enterprise. The winning firm would receive the profits from the natural monopoly and distribute them between the various members of the coalition of interests which make up the firm. These profits would represent, however, a competitive return on the money invested in obtaining the franchise. The government would receive the expected present value of profits in the franchise bid and could, in principle, use these resources to finance tax reductions or for other public purposes.

It would remain true that the winning firm would charge monopoly prices and would restrict output below socially efficient levels. The system, in other words, would not produce full *economic* efficiency even in the most favourable conditions, but if gains in productivity are judged to be more significant than losses from output restriction, and if the costs of alternative regulatory systems are high, auctions might represent a suitable institutional framework for coping with natural monopoly. In terms of Figure 15.3, an auction system produces a contract along the government's certainty line at point k. We have already discussed some of the political disadvantages of such a high-powered arrangement. However, the auction system means that the regulator does not have to estimate where point k is and run the risk of offering a lenient contract at k'. The competitive auction process should itself force the firms to offer terms which are just sufficient to achieve their reservation utility (assumed above to be a 'normal' competitive return on their assets).

5.2   The Chadwick–Demsetz Auction

Output restriction can be countered by different auction systems, but only at the price of losing some of the essential simplicity of the above version. In a Chadwick or Demsetz auction, for example, bidders tender prices at which they are prepared to serve the market. Under competitive conditions, the bid prices should fall until they just enable firms to achieve a normal return on capital.[47] The system would produce a price equal to average costs of production rather than the marginal cost price favoured by standard welfare economic theory. However, once again, the informational requirements of the government appear superficially to be much reduced compared with the regulatory systems outlined in section 4.

In practice, however, this conclusion concerning the lower regulatory costs of an auction system is open to doubt. The issues are those that have concerned us repeatedly. Auctions require the writing of explicit contracts, and represent a form of market-like arm's-length contracting. Regulation is nearer to a variety of ongoing internal governance. In Chapter 14, the costs of internal controls within a nationalised structure were discussed. Here, we confront, once more, the costs of market contracting. Bidders in a Demsetz auction may shade their prices in the hope of receiving the franchise and then reduce the quality of service they offer at a later stage. Defining the product that is to be produced may be impossibly complex and leave plenty of scope for post-contractual opportunism. Bidders might also hope to gain from the accumulation of non-transferable know-how. Indeed there will be a tendency to 'over-invest' in cost-reducing but non-transferable assets during the course of a franchise period. The incumbent gains 'first-mover advantages' and challenges the regulator at the renewal date to 'waste' the returns from this past investment.[48] Further, the duration of the contract is important. Short time periods have the advantage of making the contract simpler, but the disadvantage of requiring frequent auctions with the attendant possibilities of disruption when assets are transferred from one firm to another. As contract duration lengthens, the franchisee will want protection against changes in demand and other conditions and the freedom to adjust the product. As we saw in Chapter 2, bounded rationality will inhibit these contracts as more and more contingencies are allowed for. On the other hand, vaguely phrased provisions may result in misunderstandings and costly litigation.

The award of television broadcasting franchises provides a classic case of some of these problems. Williamson (1985) provides a related example in the cable television industry. The franchise to lay a cable network in Oakland California was awarded to a company called Focus Cable. The duration of the franchise was 15 years and it specified the type and number of channels to be available, the rate of construction, the technical characteristics, the geographical coverage, the connection fee to subscribers and so forth. It turned out that progress was slower than anticipated and the company renegotiated the terms of the agreement with the city. The construction schedule was lengthened, penalty clauses were weakened and technical specifications changed. Had the city decided to hold the company to the original terms, bankruptcy would have ensued. New bidders could have been invited, but the problems of valuing the partially completed network would have been immense, litigation would have been expensive, and the final outcome perhaps no better for the city.

Asset valuation and problems of specific capital have already been mentioned in the context of contracting with government regulators. Where large quantities of highly specific and very durable capital are involved, as is often the case in the context of natural monopoly, the problems become very serious. The leasing solution, with a government agency operating the relevant network and leasing it to competing suppliers, mitigates the asset-valuation problem but creates other contractual difficulties concerning the link between the 'common carrier' and its users. Rail privatisation in the United Kingdom, for example, created a company to own and maintain the track and signalling equipment (Railtrack). Train-operating companies compete for the franchises to run trains over particular routes. These franchised train companies then contract with Railtrack for access to the rail infrastructure. A separate regulator mediates the terms of the contracts between train companies and the natural monopoly Railtrack. The necessary link between the two main elements (track and train) has thus become a matter of contract rather than a matter of internal organisation. Policy disputes in this and other similar areas[49] are therefore implicitly about the transactions costs involved in alternative institutional arrangements.

It is clear that many modern questions of policy are about institutional design. The market-oriented 'auction' approach to the provision of public services would seem appropriate where small amounts of non-specific capital are involved, where technology and market conditions are stable, where quality is cheap to define and police, and where penalties can be made clear and enforceable. Other forms of regulation are more likely to be observed as sunk costs become significant, uncertainty more pronounced, specific assets more dominant and contractual terms more costly to write and enforce. As Williamson (1985, p. 350) has put it 'franchise bidding requires the progressive elaboration of an administration apparatus that differs mainly in name rather than in kind from that, which is associated with the regulation that it is intended to supplant'. The continual renegotiation of franchise terms, in other words, turns franchise bidding into a regulatory system by another name.

6.   CONTROL OF NATURAL MONOPOLY NETWORKS – A SUMMARY OF ORGANISATIONAL MODELS

Many organisational responses to the 'natural monopoly' problem are possible. As we have seen, the trend in utility regulation has been to encourage a vertically disintegrated structure, encouraging competition where possible and subjecting the pure 'natural monopoly' assets to some form of public control. Interconnection charges for users of the network then become a primary problem. How will generators or consumers of electricity be charged for the use of transmission facilities? On what terms will the competing suppliers of telecommunications services gain access to local networks? How should train companies pay for the use of railway infrastructure? Is it technically feasible and not too costly for competing gas producers and suppliers to contract with a gas-pipeline operator? Would it be possible to separate the operation of water pipelines from the businesses concerned with retailing, collection, storage and the treatment of wastewater? The basic idea in all these cases is that the operator of the network should have 'common carrier' obligations and should deal with customers on an equal footing, although there are substantial differences in the technological context in each case.

A single model is unlikely to prove the most effective in all cases of natural monopoly. Even within a vertically disintegrated structure there are different ownership and contracting possibilities.

6.1   Government Ownership and Operation of the Network

The network assets might be owned by the state and run as a nationalised concern with a remit to provide access to customers at marginal cost prices along 'public interest' lines. It is possible to argue that the nationalised industries were a mistake in so far as they strayed far outside the limited 'natural monopoly' areas in which they might have been useful. With all the possible disadvantages, particularly with respect to public choice considerations and low-powered incentives, public ownership of certain network assets is not self-evidently worse than the alternatives. Lack of competition, little opportunity for innovation, substantial possibilities for cost savings by reducing non-contractible quality and the absence of pressure from loss of 'reputation' were the conditions highlighted by Shleifer (1998, p. 140) as identifying a residual case for ownership by a benevolent government. It is a matter of judgement whether, for example, if rail transport is vertically disintegrated, the provision of the track and signalling might fit this list and, if so, whether the public choice problems associated with special interests might still render state ownership less desirable than alternatives.

6.2   Government Ownership with Assets Leased to a Private Operator

The network assets might be owned by the state but leased to network operators. This is a variety of franchise contract solution. The advantages are that it permits Demsetz auction-type incentives to be achieved even when large quantities of specific sunk capital are required.[50] In other words, it avoids the capital valuation problems that would otherwise arise at contract renewal and reduces the fear of post-contractual opportunism or 'regulatory hold-up' by the government. A further advantage arises in the context of intertemporal non-sustainability. If the right to operate a 'natural monopoly' is auctioned periodically using a Demsetz framework, the analysis of section 2 indicated the possibility that no promised investment programme and pricing policy in period 1 might protect an incumbent from an invader in period 2 and permit break-even. Government ownership of the durable capital then produces the intertemporal continuity required for an investment programme to be undertaken. The disadvantages would be severe where the human capital of the network operators was highly specific and complementary with the physical assets owned by the government. In these circumstances, property rights theory suggests, as set out at the end of Chapter 13, that the operators should own the physical assets in order to encourage greater up-front investment in human skills and also to create greater scope for entrepreneurship. There are also moral hazard problems associated with the upkeep and maintenance of the capital which an operator might run down over the period of its franchise.

6.3   Network Assets Owned and Operated by a Franchisee

A third option is simply that the natural monopoly should be franchised with the assets owned by the franchise winner. Here the balance of advantages is the reverse of case 6.2. Capital valuation problems, regulatory hold-up and intertemporal sustainability might be serious concerns but ownership of the assets would encourage innovation. If the franchisee is to invest in large amounts of durable capital, the bidding process becomes more complicated as the investment programme must be agreed as part of the franchise deal rather than 'announced' by the government before bidding begins. Where the length of the franchise and the durability of capital can be equated, problems of asset valuation at the termination of the franchise are overcome. Each bidder starts from scratch at contract renewal. In situations where capital is not very long lived, where the environment is technically very dynamic, where human capital is highly complementary with the assets and where issues of non-contractible quality are not very serious, this straightforward franchising system would be favoured. An example might be the running of the National Lottery in the UK, although the competition for the renewal of that particular franchise during the year 2000 has led to great problems and has culminated in litigation. As Williamson's cable TV example illustrated, even bigger problems arise when dynamic uncertain conditions are combined with large amounts of highly durable and sunk capital. The more stable the environment and the less specific the capital, the longer can be the duration of this type of franchise solution.

6.4   Network Assets Owned and Operated by a Regulated Public Company

Purely regulatory solutions to the natural monopoly problem were discussed in section 4 above. Here, private sector companies own the physical assets but negotiate periodically with a regulatory agency over rates of return, prices charged for use of the network and other factors. The National Grid Company in the UK, for example, owns and operates the transmission network in electricity; Railtrack the physical railroad infrastructure; Transco the natural-gas pipelines; and British Telecom most of the local lines which connect local telephone exchanges to domestic users.[51] The operational difference between this 'traditional' regulatory arrangement and case 6.3 diminishes as the time period of a franchise lengthens. Over long periods of time, so many provisions in a franchise contract have to be loosely specified that the arrangements for 'governing' this contract look very similar to a conventional regulatory system. It was further noted above that over a time span of several review periods, RPI minus X and rate of return regulation can begin to approximate one another.

6.5   Network Assets Owned by a Network User but Leased to a Separate Company

Isolating the core 'natural monopoly' element in a public utility has been attempted in some cases at the time of privatisation. Electricity and rail privatisation in the UK were examples. Where utilities have not been broken up at privatisation, however, or have evolved over time as vertically integrated private concerns, as in the United States, complex regulatory restructuring is sometimes involved which can give rise to ownership arrangements subtly different from any so far discussed.

If electricity companies operate in generation and retailing as well as in distribution, the natural monopoly assets subject to regulation have somehow to be separated from those in non-regulated parts of the business. Rivals in generation or supply have to be given access to the transmission and distribution facilities similar to the access available to generators or suppliers within the integrated firm. One approach, short of complete structural separation, is to insist that the integrated firm 'unbundles' the services it supplies, costing the transmission part separately and posting prices which it then charges to both 'internal' and 'external' users. Regulatory enforcement of this system is difficult and costly. In the UK, for example, the telecommunications regulator has had considerable difficulty in arranging for British Telecom to open up its local networks to suppliers of high-speed digital services.

Another possibility is that the company itself leases the assets to a separate 'independent system operator' or ISO. Joskow (1997) reports that this is becoming a significant method of dealing with the control of jointly used networks in the electricity industry in the USA. This ISO could have a number of different governance structures. It could be state owned (as under 6.1); it could be a normal public company with leased assets (a variant of 6.2); it could be jointly owned by the network users; it could be owned by retail consumers as in a retail cooperative; but equally it could be a non-profit enterprise. The advantages and disadvantages of these different governance arrangements will vary with the contracting and ownership costs encountered. However, to the extent that cooperative and mutual arrangements are a substitute for government regulation, the continuation of regulation would tend to favour private ownership unless there are very specific reasons for wishing to suppress possible dysfunctional incentives.

6.6   Network Assets Owned and Operated by an Unregulated Public Company

For completeness, we should not omit another option. In spite of the theoretical arguments for regulating natural monopolies, there is always the possibility of leaving them alone and permitting them to structure their operations as they wish. In a world of second-best choices, an unregulated natural monopoly could be the least bad option. Subject to Schumpeter's destructive gale, the power even of the traditional utilities is always being eroded – maybe not visibly over months, but discernibly over decades, and almost certainly over a lifetime. Whether all the paraphernalia of modern regulatory mechanisms – the legal wrangling, the consultants' reports, the bureaucratic interests, the political pressures, the warping of economic organisations into special patterns to suit the latest regulatory theories –

whether these actually produce better results than would otherwise occur over the very long run is not as obvious as is sometimes assumed. It is probably the case, however, that doing nothing, while a theoretical option, is not a politically realistic one in any modern democratic state.

7. DEREGULATION

7.1 Production and Supply in the Public Utilities

The term 'deregulation' is usually applied rather generally to the process of encouraging competition and reducing the barriers to new entry. As we have seen, 'deregulation' and 'regulation' are somewhat paradoxically intertwined in the case of the public utilities. In these areas, the vertical disintegration of the various utilities has been pursued in the interests of the 'deregulation' of activities where competition can be encouraged or contestability is a feasible option. This 'deregulatory' policy is possible, however, only because regulators exercise their powers to keep the industries from reintegrating and because they intervene to ensure the availability of 'natural monopoly' or network assets on equal terms to competing users. In other words, 'deregulation' and the 'restructuring' of public utilities are intimately connected. It is unlikely that the restructuring which has occurred would survive complete deregulation.

In the case of the transmission of electricity, for example, very complex provisions have had to be developed to enable competing generators and suppliers to use the national grid while balancing the system as a whole. Until recently, the UK operated a system by which generators offered to deliver to a 'pool' specified amounts of electricity at specified prices during half-hourly time intervals.[52] The operators of the 'pool' would meet demand from electricity suppliers (retailers) by calling on generators in merit order (those generators offering the lowest price would be called upon first). The price which balanced supply and demand became the 'pool price' and this was the price actually received by all generators and paid by the suppliers. Generators and suppliers wishing to establish greater certainty in advance could, however, agree a 'strike price' between them and then, depending upon whether the 'pool price' turned out to be greater or less than the 'strike price', reimburse one another for the difference. Suspicion that a few large generators could manipulate the 'pool price' to their advantage at certain times has led to reforms which extend electricity trading arrangements further. It has also led regulators to attempt to add 'market abuse conditions' to the operating licences of generating companies (thus far successfully resisted by the companies). The National Grid Company is itself subject to RPI-minus-X regulation on its charges for maintaining and developing the transmission system.

Regulators have exercised their powers to prevent some vertical and horizontal mergers, although conglomerate mergers (for example, between gas, telephone and electricity retailers) are less suspect. The availability of enough points of comparison for 'yardstick competition' to be used in the regulatory process has been a significant reason for opposing mergers between regional companies in the water industry, where lack of metering and other factors make competition in supply less advanced. Conglomerate mergers can also make the separate accounting for 'regulated' and 'non-regulated' parts of the business a complex issue. Clearly, such businesses will have an incentive to make profits appear where they will not be subject to regulatory scrutiny. Deregulation and regulation have thus gone hand in hand.

In spite of these difficulties, considerable deregulation of production and supply has been achieved in many countries. In the UK, for ecample, competition between gas suppliers (retailers) has developed far enough for the regulator to remove RPI-minus-X restrictions from mid-2001. In telecommunications, services considered sufficiently subject to competition can be removed from the price-cap basket and replaced by a 'safeguard' cap of RPI minus 0. In electricity, full supply competition has existed in the UK since 1998. Joskow (1997) calls this the 'customer choice' model in comparison with the 'wholesale competition model'. Under the latter, supply would still be in the hands of local monopolies and the price would be subject to regulation, but these local monopolies would be able to procure their supplies competitively. In other words, the 'wholesale competition model' secures competition in generation (production) but not in supply.

Public choice pressures play a part in deregulation as well as in regulation. In the USA, for example, a major pressure for reform in electricity derives from large differences in regional electricity prices. Consumers in high-price states would clearly welcome the freedom to buy from producers in low-price states. These price differences, however, reflect to some degree the history of regulatory policy in each state. For example, regulators in some states encouraged utilities to buy on long-term contracts from generators using renewable fuels under the Public Utility Regulatory Policy Act of 1978. Some invested heavily in nuclear power. Opening the market to full competition could bankrupt the utilities with these historical obligations. The problem of allocating the burdens of this financial inheritance between the shareholders of existing utilities, consumers and taxpayers has been called the 'stranded-cost' problem. Industrial consumers in high-priced areas are pitted against the local utilities.[53] Deregulation can therefore be seen as driven not by 'public interest' considerations but by the usual battle between competing interest groups.

7.2 Deregulation Outside the Public Utilities

Restructuring and deregulation have not been confined to the traditional 'public utilities'. In section 2.3 we have already drawn attention to the deregulation of the airlines in 1978 and trucking in 1980 in the USA. In those industries, the carriers did not own the network assets (roads, airports and air-traffic control) so that deregulation could occur without raising difficult issues of vertical disintegration. The 1970s saw deregulation also in brokerage and banking. Fixed commissions were abolished on stock exchanges and greater competition introduced in financial services.[54] Similar changes were introduced in the UK in the 1980s. In the USA, price controls on domestic crude oil and on the wellhead price of natural gas were also removed in 1978. These had been introduced at the time of the 'oil crisis' of the early 1970s and had severely hampered the opening up of new domestic petroleum supplies.

In the United Kingdom local authorities are required to award contracts by competitive tender in certain areas of activity.[55] Directly employed staff of local authorities therefore have to compete with private contractors for most building and maintenance work, refuse collection, cleaning, catering, and ground and vehicle maintenance. Before 1988, local authorities could choose whether or not to adopt a policy of competitive tendering. This provided conditions suitable for estimating any cost advantages associated with contracting out. For example, a study by Cubbin, Domberger and Meadowcroft (1987) found that the mean technical efficiency of private contractors in refuse collection was 17 per cent higher than direct labour organisations in authorities that did not adopt a policy of competitive tender. Similarly, a study by the National Audit Office (1986) estimated cost savings in the area of support services in hospitals of around twenty per cent.[56] The Ministry of Defence in the UK has been notably active in reorientating itself towards the use of private contractors. Work placed competitively rose from 36 per cent by value in 1982–83 to 67 per cent in 1989–90. The proportion of cost-plus contracts by value over the same period fell from sixteen to four per cent.[57]

The effects of these deregulatory measures are difficult to assess for the usual methodological reasons already encountered in our discussion of the effects of privatisation. Working out what might have happened in the absence of deregulation can be a contentious undertaking.[58] However, Winston (1993, 1998) attempts to draw some general conclusions concerning US experience from a wide survey of the empirical literature. With the exception of petroleum and natural gas, where the removal of price controls might have been expected to lead to higher prices[59], the introduction of greater competition should have led to lower prices, higher output, greater technological innovation and lower profits. Winston finds that these expectations are not generally contradicted by the historical record. In the airline industry, for example, the evolution of the hub-and-spoke system has produced economies and increased flight frequency. Increased frequency was unexpected, as many analysts thought deregulation would reduce the general convenience of services as competition made cross-subsidies between routes more difficult. Airline fares had been falling in the decade before deregulation, mainly as a result of technological changes such as the introduction of wide-bodied jet aircraft. The contribution of deregulation to the continuing fall in prices is difficult to judge but Winston argues that it was significant. Morrison and Winston (1998) estimate that 59 per cent of the reductions in real fares since deregulation are the result of additional competition.

Allowing for losses to producers, mainly in trucking where wages and profits were expected to fall after the protection of regulation was removed, Winston (1993) estimated that overall gains to consumers from price reductions and quality improvements and to producers from changes to profits and wages were between 35.8 and 46.2 billion US(1990) dollars.[60] Moreover, these benefits were rising over time as further lagged adjustments took place. Winston (1998, pp. 101–2) concluded that 'a conservative estimate of the annual net benefits that consumers have received just from deregulation of intercity transportation – airlines, railroads, and motor carriers – amounts to roughly $50 billion in 1996 dollars'.

8.   CONCLUSION

The scale and scope of organisational and regulatory changes have been so extensive in recent years that a single chapter can only serve as an introduction to some of the main issues. Enough material has been covered, however, to indicate the ways in which transactions cost, principal–agent and property rights theory relate to economic regulation.

Competition policy and the regulation of public utilities impinge directly and obviously on the questions of economic organisation which are the subject matter of this book – market contract versus internal control, short-term contracting versus longer-term relational arrangements, high-powered versus low-powered incentives. Business enterprise, however, is faced with many other areas of 'social regulation' which also have organisational implications. The regulation of labour contracts directly concerns the ability of firms to provide the incentive contracts and governance arrangements discussed in Chapter 6. A fundamental debate in environmental regulation contrasts the Coasian approach (in which property rights in environmental resources are defined, privately assigned and made tradable) with a more Hobbesian approach in which solutions are directed and monitored using command and control methods. The regulation of financial markets raises questions about the ability of financial institutions to overcome the undoubted transactional hazards that exist in that area. Regulatory intervention can substitute for private responses such as reputational mechanisms or mutual ownership. Space constraints, however, prevent further investigation of these areas.

Readers may feel disappointed at the complexity of the organisational economics reviewed in Part 3 and the lack of clear policy guidance derivable from it. For every argument there appears to be a counter-argument. This would be to overlook the main point of the material, however. Organisational responses should adapt to differing circumstances. Sometimes the complexity of the circumstances can make organisational choice a matter of guesswork and entrepreneurial insight, but awareness that there is no single ideal set of organisational arrangements for all circumstances is important. It helps to insulate the student from the enthusiasms which can take over policy towards organisational questions from time to time. Rational planning by central authorities has been superseded by admiration for contract. As contract is pushed to breaking point, the false conclusion is likely to be drawn that only central administration can solve a country's problems. There was a time when 'central planning' was actually a sophisticated and 'modern' thing to support. The pendulum has swung, until any critic of contracting processes runs the risk of being thought primitive and dirigiste. The pendulum may yet swing back. No serious student of economic organisation has ever claimed that market contract is universally to be preferred to the firm. It was, after all, the founder of the transactions cost school who made the original gravid observation that it 'would seem to be that there is a cost of using the price mechanism'. That cost is endlessly changing. An economic system that gives opportunities to adjust to those changes and avoids imposing ideal organisational standards is likely to prove the one which is most resilient and productive over the long term.

NOTES

1. J.S. Mill, *Principles of Political Economy*, (People's edition) (1898), Book V, Chapter XI, 'Limits of the Province of Government', Longmans, Green and Co., p. 581.
2. See again the 'public interest' view of public policy and the marginal cost pricing controversy discussed in Chapter 13.
3. An extensive literature on 'X' inefficiency and monopoly developed in the 1970s. See Leibenstein (1976).
4. A perceptive reader might be wondering whether a world without transactions costs would not be contestable by definition. 'Hit-and-run' implies that agreements with

consumers are always for the moment and no longer. With no costs of transacting, however, the 'sunk costs' problem would be overcome anyway because agreements could be multilateral and could cover a time period long enough for capital costs to be retrieved. At this point in the text, however, I simply take it as given that consumer contracts are effectively spot contracts. I assume also that it makes sense to talk of these contracts as 'costless' while at the same time assuming that longer-term contracts with consumers are so costly that they are ruled out. At other points in the book, the longer-term perspective is investigated. Subsection 2.4 considers the problem of contracting over several time periods in more detail.

5. Baumol, Panzar and Willig (1982, p. 223) comment that 'the combination of natural monopoly and decreasing returns to scale must be considered unlikely'.

6. In the intertemporal setting, 'Unsustainability can come closer to being the rule rather than the exception' (Baumol, Panzar and Willig, 1982, p. 405).

7. Given that it is efficient to build a unit of capacity in each period, it does not matter whether one firm undertakes this construction or different firms are used. Thus, the groupings ABC, AB plus C, or AC plus B are equally 'efficient'.

8. This statement applies to the cost conditions examined in this example, not to all cost conditions. In other words, continuously declining costs of capacity do not lead to an intertemporal unsustainability problem if intertemporal contracts with people whose lives span the periods are possible. The conditions of subsection 2.2 are restored. Other cost conditions (considered in subsection 2.3) might still create difficulties, however.

9. The market is 'contestable' at the beginning of period 1 because agreements occur before any capital has been 'sunk'.

10. Clearly, the sustainability problem is bigger if we think of 'period 2' as peopled by the next generation in the distant future rather than the same generation in the fairly near future. Very long periods of time make the static assumptions about technology underlying sections 2.2 to 2.4 very unsuitable, however.

11. See, again, the discussion of the cooperative or mutual form of organisation as a response to the natural monopoly problem in Chapter 10.

12. See Chapter 13, subsection 5.2.

13. This terminology was introduced by Hayek (1949).

14. Important figures in this group were Walter Eucken, Franz Böhm, Friedrich A. Lutz, Fritz W. Meyer, Alfred Müller-Armack, Alexander Rüstow and Wilhelm Röpke. For an introduction to the political and economic thought of the German Neo-Liberals, see Barry (1989).

15. See Möschel, W. (1989) for a discussion of the philosophical basis of the Ordo view of competition policy.

16. See, again, Chapter 6, section 7.

17. *Standard Oil Co* v. *United States* (1911).

18. The reader should not assume that the Sherman Act was immediately effective against large companies. In the 1895 case, *US* v. *E.C. Knight* the Supreme Court permitted the continuation of a Sugar Trust controlling 98 per cent of refining capacity.

19. Most notably in *Appalachian Coals, Inc* v. *United States* (1933) which accepted as lawful a marketing agreement by a coal cartel. The Clayton Act was more explicit than the Sherman Act about the forms of behaviour which were objectionable. But it was not intended to be exhaustive and it prohibited only conduct expected 'to substantially lessen competition or tend to create a monopoly in any line of commerce'.

20. Found to be illegal *per se* in *United States* v. *Socony-Vacuum Oil Co.* (1940).

21. Prohibited in Section 2 of the Clayton Act (1914). Later replaced by section 1 of the Robinson–Patman Act (1936). The main objective of the Robinson–Patman Act was to protect small shops against the competition of national chains.

22. First specifically covered in section 3 of the Clayton Act (1914).

23. Found illegal *per se* in *Dr. Miles Medical Co.* v. *John D. Park & Sons Co.* (1911).

24. See Gilbert and Williamson (1998).

25. The 'Old Chicago School' was associated with the work of economists such as Frank Knight and Jacob Viner in the 1930s – for the most part supportive of antitrust inter-

vention to maintain competition. The 'New Chicago School' drew its intellectual influence from Aaron Director in the late 1940s, Ronald Coase's transactions-cost reasoning (Coase arrived at the University of Chicago Law School in 1964) as well as Stigler's work on regulation in the 1960s. Legal scholars 'translated' this work into applicable legal form – see, for example, Bork (1978) and Posner (1979).

26. Consultative Document Cm. 331 (DTI, 1988).
27. Office of Fair Trading (1993), p. 31.
28. The Supreme Court was not considering the case itself, but merely whether it should come to trial.
29. Hayek argued that agreements which restricted a person's ability to trade with others should not be illegal but neither should they be enforceable at law. See Hayek (1979).
30. Willgerodt and Peacock (1989), p. 8.
31. See again the summary of Schumpeter's ideas on entrepreneurship and competition in Chapter 3.
32. Schmalensee (2000) considers the Microsoft case from a Schumpeterian perspective. Fisher (2000) contrasts the Microsoft case with the IBM case of the 1970s mentioned above.
33. For a more extended discussion of UK regulation from this perspective see Burton (1997) and Robinson (1996).
34. In the interests of simplicity, the more analytical sections of this book have used a model with two levels of effort only. For the same diagrammatic apparatus used in the context of a continuum of effort levels, see Ricketts (1986). An indication of the method used can be found later in Figure 15.3.
35. Noll (1989) provides a review of the politics of regulation.
36. A study of early railroad regulation can be found in Kolko (1965). Further references can also be found in Noll (1989).
37. It is worth noting at this point that not all legislation can be plausibly explained by pressure group activity. Chandler (1990, p. 72) notes with respect to the Sherman Act that 'unlike the Interstate Commerce Act passed three years earlier, its enactment had not been demanded by a powerful group of shippers and wholesalers. Indeed, it was passed with relatively little debate and even less opposition.' It seemed more a simple expression of American values.
38. See Posner (1971), where regulation is seen as a form of taxation. See also Posner (1974).
39. Universal service provisions can still be incorporated in the licence conditions of franchised operators, of course, but these operators will then require protection from 'hit-and-run' competition confined to the surplus generating parts of their market.
40. See Averch and Johnson (1962).
41. See Glaister (1996). The system of water regulation in the UK is usually presented as a version of RPI minus X (see subsection 4.4). However, as Glaister points out, 'whether we like it or not, the system of price determination we have has a large element of rate of return regulation, albeit a forward looking one' (p. 36).
42. Joskow and Rose (1989, p. 1465) argue that Stigler and Friedland were actually observing the difference between municipal franchise regulation and state commission regulation (which tended to replace municipal regulation over the period) rather than the difference between regulation and no regulation.
43. See Byatt (1995), p. 26. Note that domestic consumers of water in the UK are still primarily charged by means of a tax on housing although the metering of water is gradually increasing. Thus, the regulator and the water companies are setting the level of a tax levied on households rather than a price per cubic metre of water consumed.
44. Steltzer (1996, p. 194).
45. See Burns, Turvey and Weyman-Jones (1998) for a description of the properties of various regulatory regimes.
46. Glaister (1996, pp. 51–7) describes this system. See also Glaister (1987).
47. See Demsetz (1968b). Demsetz acknowledges Edwin Chadwick as an early student of franchise arrangements for natural monopoly. Chadwick (1859) distinguished clearly between 'competition for the field' and 'competition within the field'.

48. See Scarpa (1994).
49. The relationship between electricity generators and the operators of the distribution network involves similar contractual problems as does the relationship between telecommunications networks and the providers of services which use the networks.
50. Demsetz (1968b, p. 63) considers public ownership of the distribution system. The installation of the system could still be achieved by means of competing bids and the assets then leased to a single franchised user. Demsetz does not appear to have considered in this paper the possibilities and problems of giving access to the distribution system to many competing users.
51. In the United States, local telephone operating companies, the 'Baby Bells', were separated from AT & T by antitrust action in 1982. This, of course, still gives these companies monopoly control of local networks.
52. See Newbery (1998) for a description of the 'pool' in the UK and discussion of suggestions for reform.
53. See White (1996).
54. Brokerage was reformed by the Securities Acts Amendments (1975) and Banking by the Depository Institutions Deregulation and Monetary Control Act (1980). In the UK, similar reforms to financial markets occurred with the 'big bang' in 1986.
55. Local Government Act 1988. In other countries, competitive tendering is common. The UK is unusual simply in *requiring* it for certain local services.
56. A recent review of the evidence concerning contracting out is provided in Carnaghan and Bracewell-Milnes (1993).
57. See Carnaghan and Bracewell-Milnes (1993, p. 113).
58. Joskow and Rose (1989) review the methodological problems of calculating the effects of regulation and deregulation. Clearly 'deregulation' is an even less precise term than 'privatisation' although the techniques that are available for assessing its effects are similar to those briefly covered at the end of Chapter 14. They include comparisons between regulated and deregulated industries or jurisdictions; time-series analysis in which performance is compared before and after some deregulatory change; case studies, and simulation exercises using estimated cost and demand functions.
59. Deregulation in fact coincided with lower 'world' energy prices, so that the predicted higher prices following deregulation did not occur.
60. Winston (1993), Table 6. Hahn and Hird (1990, p. 250) estimated that the regulation of US airlines, trucking, railroads, oil and natural gas imposed an efficiency cost of around $36 billion in 1977 – about half the total. Hahn and Hird included agricultural price supports and international trade barriers in their estimates of the total efficiency costs of regulation.

Bibliography

Abowd, J.M. and D.S. Kaplan (1999), 'Executive compensation: six questions that need answering', *Journal of Economic Perspectives*, **13** (4), 145–68.

Adams, J. Stacy (1965), 'Inequality in Social Exchange', in Berkowitz, L. (ed.) *Advances in Experimental Social Psychology*, Vol. 2, New York: Academic Press, p. 267.

Ahlbrandt, R. (1973), 'Efficiency in the provision of fire services', *Public Choice*, **16**, 1.

Akerlof, G.A. (1970), 'The market for "lemons": qualitative uncertainty and the market mechanism', *Quarterly Journal of Economics*, **84**, 488.

Akerlof, G.A. (1976), 'The economics of caste and of the rat race and other woeful tales', *Quarterly Journal of Economics*, **90**, 599.

Akerlof, G.A. (1982), 'Labor contracts as partial gift exchange', *Quarterly Journal of Economics*, **97**, 543.

Akerlof, G.A. (1984), 'Gift exchange and efficiency-wage theory: four views', *American Economic Review*, **74**, 79.

Albert, M. (1993), *Capitalism against Capitalism*, London: Whurr Publishers.

Alcock, A. (1993), 'Insider Dealing – an Unholy Mess', *New Law Journal*, 8 January, 21–2.

Alchian, A.A. (1950), 'Uncertainty, evolution and economic theory', *Journal of Political Economy*, **58**, 211.

Alchian, A.A. (1965), 'Some economics of property rights', *Politico*, **30**, 816.

Alchian, A.A. (1969a), 'Corporate management and property rights', in Manne, H. (ed.) *Economic Policy and the Regulation of Corporate Securities*, American Enterprise Institute.

Alchian, A.A. (1969b), 'Information costs, pricing and resource unemployment', *Economic Inquiry* (Journal of the Western Economic Association), **17**, 109.

Alchian, A.A. (1977a), 'Why money?', *Journal of Money, Credit and Banking*, **9**, 133.

Alchian, A.A. (1977b), *Economic Forces at Work*, Indianapolis, IN: Liberty Press.

Alchian, A.A. and H. Demsetz (1972), 'Production, information costs, and economic organization', *American Economic Review*, **62**, 777.

Alchian, A.A. and S. Woodward (1987), 'Reflections on the theory of the firm', *Journal of Institutional and Theoretical Economics*, **143**(1), 110–36.

Alonso, W. (1964), 'Location theory', in Alonso, W. and Friedman, J. (eds) *Regional Development and Planning*, Cambridge, MA: MIT Press.

Aoki, M. (1984), *The Co-operative Game Theory of the Firm*, Oxford: Clarendon Press.

Aoki, M. (1986), 'Horizontal versus vertical information structure of the firm', *American Economic Review*, **76**(5), 971–83.

Aoki, M. (1989), *Information, Incentives and Bargaining in the Japanese Economy*, Cambridge, MA: Cambridge University Press.

Aoki, M. (1990), 'Towards an economic model of the Japanese firm', *Journal of Economic Literature*, **28**(1), 1–27.

Archibald, G.C. (ed.) (1971), *The Theory of the Firm*, Harmondsworth: Penguin.

Armour, H.O. and D.J. Teece (1978), 'Organisation structure and economic performance: a test of the multidivisional hypothesis', *Bell Journal of Economics*, **9**, 106.

Armour, H.O. and D.J. Teece (1980), 'Vertical integration and technological innovation', *Review of Economics and Statistics*, **62**, 470.

Arrow, K.J. (1951), *Social Choice and Individual Values*, New York: John Wiley.

Arrow, K.J. (1962), 'Economic welfare and the allocation of resources for invention', in *The Rate and Direction of Economic Activity: Economic and Social Factors* (NBER), p. 609, Princeton, NJ: Princeton University Press.

Arrow, K.J. (1969), 'The organization of economic activity', in Joint Economic Committee, 91st Congress, 1st Session, *The Analysis and Evaluation of Public Expenditure: The PPB System*, p. 59.

Arrow, K.J. (1973), 'Higher education as a filter', *Journal of Public Economics*, **2**, 193.

Arrow, K.J. (1974), *The Limits of Organization*, New York: W.W. Norton and Co.

Arrow, K.J. (1975), 'Vertical integration and communication', *Bell Journal of Economics*, **6**, 173.

Arrow, K.J. (1985), 'The economics of agency', in Pratt, J.W. and Zeckhauser, R.J. (eds), *Principals and Agents: The Structure of Business*, Harvard Business School Press, pp. 37–61.

Audretsch, D. and J. Jin (1994), 'A Reconciliation of the unemployment–new firm start-up paradox', *Small Business Economics*, **6**, 381–5.

Auerbach, A.J. (ed.) (1988), *Corporate Takeovers: Causes and Consequences*, NBER University of Chicago Press.

Auster, R. (1978), 'Shirking in the theory of the firm', *Southern Economic Journal*, **45**, 867.

Auster, R.D. and M. Silver (1979), *The State as a Firm: Economic Forces in Political Development*, The Hague: Martinus Nihoff.

Ausubel, L.M. (1990), 'Insider trading in a rational expectations economy', *American Economic Review*, **80**(5), 1022–41.

Averch, H. and L.L. Johnson (1962), 'Behavior of the firm under regulatory constraint', *American Economic Review*, **52**, 1052.

Axelrod, R. (1984), *The Evolution of Co-operation*, Basic Books: New York.

Azariadis, C. (1975), 'Implicit contracts and under-employment equilibria', *Journal of Political Economy*, **83**(6), 1183–202.

Azariadis, C. and J.E. Stiglitz (1983), 'Implicit contracts and fixed price equilibria', *Quarterly Journal of Economics*, **98** (Supplement), p. 1.

Bacharach, M. (1976), *Economics and the Theory of Games*, London: Macmillan.

Bagwell, L.S. and J.B. Shoven (1989), 'Cash distributions to shareholders', *Journal of Economic Perspectives*, **3**(3), 129–40.

Bailey, E.E. and J.C. Panzar (1981), 'The Contestability of Airline Markets during the Transition to Deregulation', *Journal of Law and Contemporary Problems*, **44**, Winter, 125–45.

Baily, Martin, N. (1974), 'Wages and unemployment under uncertain demand', *Review of Economic Studies*, **41**, 37–50.

Bannock, G. (1981), *The Economics of Small Firms: Return from the Wilderness*, Oxford: Basil Blackwell.

Bannock, G. (1990), 'The Takeover Boom: an International and Historical Perspective', Papers prepared for the Inquiry into Corporate Takeovers in the United Kingdom, No. 2. The David Hume Institute, Hume Occasional Paper No. 15.

Barberis, N., M. Boycko , A. Shleifer and N. Tsukanova (1996), 'How does privatisation work? Evidence from the Russian Shops', *Journal of Political Economy*, **104**, 764–90.

Barkley Rosser Jr, J. (1999), 'On the complexities of complex economic dynamics', *Journal of Economic Perspectives*, **13**(4), 169–92.

Baron, T. and R. McGarvey (1993), '*The Creation of a Civil Economy in Russia: The Need for Mercantilism*', Economic Research Council Discussion Paper 239, Shaftesbury Avenue, London, WC21 8PJ.

Barry, N.P. (1989), 'Political and Economic Thought of German Neo-Liberals', in Peacock, A. and Willgerodt, H. (eds), *German Neo-Liberals and the Social Market Economy*, London: Macmillan, pp. 105–24.

Barzel, Y. (1989), *Economic Analysis of Property Rights*, Cambridge, MA: Cambridge University Press.

Baumol, W.J. (1959), *Business Behavior, Value and Growth*, New York: Macmillan.

Baumol, W.J. (1962), 'On the theory of expansion of the firm', *American Economic Review* (reprinted in Archibald, G.C. (ed.) (1971)).

Baumol, W.J. (1965), *Welfare Economics and the Theory of the State*, London: G. Bell and Sons Ltd.

Baumol, W.J. (1990), 'Entrepreneurship: productive, unproductive, and destructive', *Journal of Political Economy*, **98** (5), (part I), 893–921.

Baumol, W.J., J.C. Panzar and R.D. Willig (1982), *Contestable Markets and the Theory of Industry Structure*, New York: Harcourt Brace Jovanovich Inc.

Becker, G.S. (1964), *Human Capital*, New York: NBER.

Becker, G.S. (1965), 'A theory of the allocation of time', *Economic Journal*, **75**, 493.

Becker, G.S. and G.J. Stigler (1974), 'Law enforcement, malfeasance, and compensation of enforcers', *Journal of Legal Studies*, **3**, 1.

Beesley, M. and S. Littlechild (1988), 'The Regulation of Privatized Monopolies in the United Kingdom', *Rand Journal of Economics*, **20**, 454–72.

Behrman, B. (1980), in J.Q. Wibon (ed), *The Politics of Regulation*, New York: Basic Books.

Bell, D. and I. Kristol (eds) (1981), *The Crisis in Economic Theory*, New York: Basic Books.

Bennett, J.T. and M.H. Johnson (1979), 'Public versus private provision of collective goods and services: garbage collection revisited', *Public Choice*, **34**, 55.

Berglof, Erik (1990), 'Capital Structure as a Mechanism of Control: a Comparison of Financial Systems', in Aoki, M. et al. (eds), *The Firm as a Nexus of Treaties*, New York, Sage Publications, pp. 237–62.

Berle, A.A. and G.C. Means (1932), revised edn (1967), *The Modern Corporation and Private Property*, New York: Harcourt, Brace and World, Inc.

Bingaman, A.K. (1994), 'The Role of Antitrust in Intellectual Property', Address June 16, 1994 before the Federal Circuit Judicial Conference Department of Justice.

Binks, M. and J. Coyne (1983), '*The Birth of Enterprise: An Analytical and Empirical Study of the Growth of Small Firms*', Hobart Paper 98, Institute of Economic Affairs, London.

Blair, D.H., D.H. Golbe and J.M. Gerard (1989), 'Unbundling the voting rights and profit claims of common shares', *Journal of Political Economy*, **97** (2), 420–43.

Blanchflower, D.G. and A.J. Oswald (1991), 'What makes an entrepreneur?', Revised version of NBER Working Paper 3252.

Blaug, M. (1980), *The Methodology of Economics: or How Economists Explain*, Cambridge, UK: Cambridge University Press.

Bolton, J.E. (1971), *Small Firms*, Report of the Committee of Inquiry on Small Firms, Cmnd 4811, HMSO.

Bolton, P. and D.S. Scharfstein (1998), 'Corporate finance, the theory of the firm, and organizations', *Journal of Economic Perspectives*, **12**(4), 95–114.

Borjas, G.J., H.E. Frech III , P.B. Ginsburg (1983), 'Property Rights and Wages: The Case of Nursing Homes', *Journal of Human Resources*, **17**, 231–46.

Bork, R.H. (1978), *The Antitrust Paradox, A Policy at War with Itself*, New York, Basic Books.

Bothwell, J.L. (1980), 'Profitability, risk and the separation of ownership from control', *Journal of Industrial Economics*, **28**, 303.

Boubakri, N. and Jean-Claud Cosset (1998), 'The financial and operating performance of newly privatized firms: Evidence from developing countries', *Journal of Finance*, **53**, 1081–110.

Boulding, K.E. (1950), *A Reconstruction of Economics*, New York: Wiley and Sons.

Boulding, K.E. (1978), *Ecodynamics*, London: Sage Publications.

Boulding, K.E. (1981), *Evolutionary Economics*, Beverley Hills, CA: Sage Publications.

Bowen, A. and M. Ricketts (eds) (1992) *Stimulating Innovation in Industry*, London: NEDO/Kogan Page.

Bowles, S. (1998), 'Endogenous preferences: the cultural consequences of markets and other economic institutions', *Journal of Economic Literature*, **36**(1), 75–111.

Bowles, S. and H. Gintis (1993), 'The revenge of homo economicus: contested exchange and the revival of political economy', *Journal of Economic Perspectives*, **7**(1), 83–102.

Boycko, M., A. Schleifer and R.W. Vishny (1995), *Privatizing Russia*, Cambridge, MA: MIT Press.

Boycko, M., Shleifer, A. and Vishny, R.W. (1996), 'A Theory of Privatisation', *Economic Journal*, **106**, 309–19.

Breton, A. (1974), *The Economic Theory of Representative Government*, Chicago: Aldine.

Breton, A. and R. Wintrobe (1975), 'The equilibrium size of a budget maximising bureau', *Journal of Political Economy*, **83**, 195.

Brown, C.V. and P.M. Jackson (1986), *Public Sector Economics* (3rd edn), Oxford: Basil Blackwell, Chapter 4.

Brunello, Giorgio (1992), 'Profit sharing in internal labour markets', *Economic Journal*, **102**(412), 570–77.

Bryce, J.C. and W.P.D. Wightman (eds) (1982), *Adam Smith Essays on Philosophical Subjects*, Oxford: Oxford University Press.

Buchanan, J.M. (1965), 'An economic theory of clubs', *Economica*, **32**(1), 1–14.

Buchanan, J.M. (ed.) (1967), *L.S.E. Essays on Costs*, London: Weidenfeld & Nicolson.

Buchanan, J.M. (1975), *The Limits of Liberty*, Chicago: University of Chicago Press.

Buchanan, J.M. (1980), 'Rent seeking and profit seeking' in J.M. Buchanan et al. (eds) *Toward a Theory of the Rent Seeking Society*, College Station, Texas: Texas A and M University Press, p. 3.

Buchanan, J.M. and G. Tullock (1962), *The Calculus of Consent*, Ann Arbor, MI: University of Michigan Press.

Buchanan, J.M., R.D. Tollison and G. Tullock (eds) (1980), *Toward a Theory of the Rent Seeking Society*, College Station, Texas: Texas A and M University Press.

Buckley, P.J. and M. Casson (1976), *The Future of Multinational Enterprise*, London: Macmillan.

Bureau of Industry Economics (1991), Networks: A Third Form of Organisation, Discussion Paper no. 14, Australian Government Publishing Service, Canberra.

Burns, P., R. Turvey and T.G. Weyman-Jones (1998), 'The behaviour of the firm under alternative regulatory constraints', *Scottish Journal of Political Economy*, **45**(2), 133–57.

Burton, J. (1997), 'The competitive order or ordered competition?: The UK model of utility regulation in theory and practice', *Public Administration*, **75**(2), 157–88.

Byatt, I. (1995), 'Water: the Periodic Review Process', in Beesley, M. (ed.) *Utility Regulation: Challenge and Response*, Readings 42, IEA/LBS, pp. 21–35.

Calvo, G.A. (1979), 'Hierarchy, ability, and income distribution', *Journal of Political Economy*, **87**, 991.

Calvo, G.A. and S. Wellisz (1978), 'Supervision, loss of control, and the optimum size of the firm', *Journal of Political Economy*, **86**, 943.

Cantwell, J. (1991), 'A Survey of Theories of International Production', in Pitelis, C. and R. Sugden (eds) *The Nature of the Transnational Firm*, London: Routledge, pp. 16–63.

Carmichael, H. Lorne (1989), 'Self-enforcing contracts, shirking, and life cycle incentives', *Journal of Economic Perspectives*, **3**(4), 65–83.

Carnaghan, R. and B. Bracewell-Milnes (1993), *Testing the Market: Competitive Tendering for Government Services in Britain and Abroad*, Institute of Economic Affairs, Research Monograph 49, London.

Casadesus-Masanell, R. and D.F. Spulber (2000), 'The fable of Fisher Body', *Journal of Law and Economics*, **43**(1) (April), 67–104.

Casson, Mark (1982), *The Entrepreneur: An Economic Theory*, Oxford: Martin Robertson.

Casson, Mark (1984), 'The theory of vertical integration: a survey and synthesis', *Journal of Economic Studies*, **2**, 3.

Casson, Mark (1987), *The Firm and the Market: Studies on Multinational Enterprise and the Scope of the Firm,* Oxford: Basil Blackwell.

Casson, Mark (1989), *Alternatives to the Multinational Enterprise*, London: Macmillan.

Casson, Mark (1990), *Enterprise and Competitiveness: A Systems View of International Business*, Oxford: Clarendon Press.

Casson, Mark (1991), *The Economics of Business Culture: Game Theory, Transactions Costs and Economic Performance*, Oxford: Clarendon Press.

Caves, D.W. and L.R. Christensen (1980), 'The relative efficiency of public and private firms in a competitive environment: the case of the Canadian railroads', *Journal of Political Economy*, **88**, 958.

Caves, R.E. (1980), 'Industrial organization, corporate strategy and structure', *Journal of Economic Literature*, **18**, 64.

Caves, R.E. (1996), *Multinational Enterprise and Economic Analysis*, Cambridge Surveys of Economic Literature (2nd edn), Cambridge University Press.

Chadwick, Edwin (1859), 'Results of different principles of legislation and administration in Europe: of competition for the field, as compared with the competition within the field of service', *Journal of Royal Statistical Society*, **22**, 381.

Chandler, A.D. (1977), *The Visible Hand: The Managerial Revolution in American Business*, Cambridge, MA: Harvard University Press.

Chandler, A.D. (1980), 'The transnational industrial firm in the United States and the United Kingdom: a comparative analysis', *Economic History Review*, **33**, 396.

Chandler, A.D. (1990), *Scale and Scope: The Dynamics of Industrial Capitalism*, Cambridge, MA: Belknap/Harvard University Press.

Chandler, A.D. (1992), 'Organizational capabilities and the economic history of the industrial enterprise', *Journal of Economic Perspectives*, **6**(3), 79–100.

Channon, D.F. (1973), *The Strategy and Structure of British Enterprise*, Boston, MA: Harvard University.

Chiplin, B., J. Coyne and L. Sirc (1977), *'Can Workers Manage?'*, Hobart Paper 77, Institute of Economic Affairs, London.

Christaller, W. (1933), *Die Zentralen Orte in Suddeutschland*, Jena: Gustav Fischer.

Claessens, S. (1995), 'Corporate Governance and Equity Prices: Evidence from the Czech and Slovak Republics', World Bank Group, Policy Research Working Paper, No. 1427.

Claessens, S., S. Djankov and L. Lang (2000), 'The separation of owner-ship from control in East Asian corporations', *Journal of Financial Economics*, **58**(1–2), 81–112.

Claessens, S., S. Djankov and G. Pohl (1997), 'Ownership and the Corporate Governance: Evidence from the Czech Republic', Policy Research Paper No. 1737, The World Bank.

Clapham, J.H. (1922), 'Of empty economic boxes', *Economic Journal*, **32**, 305.

Clark, R.C. (1985), 'Agency costs versus fiduciary duties', in Pratt, J.W. and Zeckhauser, R.J. (eds) *Principals and Agents: The Structure of Business*, Boston, MA: Harvard Business School.

Clark, R.L. and N. Ogawa (1992), 'Employment tenure and earnings profiles in Japan and the United States: comment', *American Economic Review*, **82**(1), 336–45.

Coase, R.H. (1937), 'The nature of the firm', *Economica*, **4**, 386.

Coase, R.H. (1946), 'The marginal cost controversy', *Economica*, **13**, 169.

Coase, R.H. (1960), 'The problem of social cost', *Journal of Law and Economics*, **3**, 1.

Coase, R.H. (1970), 'The theory of public utility pricing and its applica-tion', *Bell Journal of Economics and Management Science*, **1**, 113.

Coase, R.H. (2000), 'The Acquisition of Fisher Body by General Motors', *Journal of Law and Economics*, **43**(1) (April), 15–31.

Committee on the Financial Aspect of Corporate Governance (1992), *Report of the Committee*, chairman Adrian Cadbury, Gee Publishing Ltd, December.

Conyon, M., P. Gregg and S. Machin (1995), 'Taking Care of Business: Executive Compensation in the United Kingdom', *Economic Journal*, **105**(430), 704–14.

Conyon, M.J. and K.J. Murphy (2000), 'The prince and the pauper? CEO pay in the United States and the United Kingdom', *Economic Journal*, **110**(467), 640–71.

Cooter, R. and T. Ulen (1997), *Law and Economics*, New York: Addison-Wesley.

Copeland, T.E. and J.F. Weston (1988), *Financial Theory and Corporate Policy*, (3rd edn), Reading, MA: Addison-Wesley, chs 13 and 14.

Cosh, A.D. and A. Hughes (1987), 'The anatomy of corporate control: directors, shareholders and executive remuneration in giant US and UK corporations', *Cambridge Journal of Economics*, **11**, 285–313.

Cowling, K. and R. Sugden (1987), *Transnational Monopoly Capitalism*, Wheatsheaf.

Crain, W.M. and A. Zardkoohi (1978), 'A test of the property rights theory of the firm: water utilities in the United States', *Journal of Law and Economics*, **40**, 395.

Cubbin, J. and D. Leech (1983), 'The effect of shareholding dispersion on the degree of control in British Companies: theory and measurement', Economic Journal, **93**(2), 351–69.

Cubbin, J., S. Domberger and S. Meadowcroft (1987), 'Competitive tendering and refuse collection: identifying the sources of efficiency gains', *Fiscal Studies*, **8**(3), 49–58.

Culyer, A.J. (1984), 'The quest for efficiency in the public sector: economists versus Dr Pangloss', in Hanusch, H. (ed.), *Public Finance and the Quest for Efficiency*, Proceedings in the 38th Congress of the International Institute of Public Finance, Copenhagen, 1982.

Cyert, R.M. and J.G. March (1963), *A Behavioral Theory of the Firm*, New York: Prentice Hall.

Davies, D.G. (1971), 'The efficiency of public versus private firms: the case of Australia's two airlines', *Journal of Law and Economics*, **14**, 149.

Davies, D.G. (1977) 'Property rights and economic efficiency – the Australian airlines revisited', *Journal of Law and Economics*, **20**, 223.

Davies, S. (1998), 'Trading on Borrowed Time', *Financial Times*, 24 March.

Davis, O.A. and A.B. Whinston (1961), 'The economics of urban renewal', *Law and Contemporary Problems*, **26**, 105.

Dawkins, R. 1986, *The Blind Watchmaker*, London: Longman.

De Alessi, L. (1969), 'Implications of property rights for government investment choice', *American Economic Review*, **59**, 13.

De Alessi, L. (1974a), 'An economic analysis of government ownership and regulation: theory and the evidence from the electric power industry', *Public Choice*, **19**, 1.

De Alessi, L. (1974b), 'Managerial tenure under private and government ownership in the electric power industry', *Journal of Political Economy*, **82**, 645.

De Alessi, L. (1980), 'The economics of property rights: a review of the evidence', *Research in Law and Economics*, **2**, 1.

De Alessi, L. (1983), 'Property rights, transaction costs and x-efficiency', *American Economic Review*, **73**, 69.

De Alessi, L. and R.P.H. Fishe (1987), 'Why do corporations distribute assets? An analysis of dividends and capital structure', *Journal of Institutional and Theoretical Economics*, **143**(1), 34–51.

Demsetz, H. (1964), 'The exchange and enforcement of property rights', *Journal of Law and Economics*, **7**, 11.

Demsetz, H. (1967), 'Towards a theory of property rights', *American Economic Review*, **57**, 347.

Demsetz, H. (1968a), 'The cost of transacting', *Quarterly Journal of Economics*, **82**, 33.

Demsetz, H. (1968b), 'Why Regulate Utilities?', *Journal of Law and Economics*, **11**(1) (April), 55–65.

Demsetz, H. (1969), 'Information and efficiency: another viewpoint', *Journal of Law and Economics*, **12**, 1.

Demsetz, H. (1970), 'The private production of public goods', *Journal of Law and Economics*, **13**, 293.

Demsetz, H. (1979), 'Ethics and Efficiency in Property Rights Systems', in Rizzo, Mario, J. (ed.) *Time, Uncertainty, and Disequilibrium: Exploration of Austrian Themes*, Lexington Books, Lexington, Toronto: D.C. Heath, p.97.

Demsetz, H. (1983), 'The structure of ownership and the theory of the firm', *Journal of Law and Economics*, **26**, 375.

Dennett, L. (1998), *A Sense of Security: 150 Years of Prudential*, Cambridge, UK: Granta Editions, Chesterton.

Dertouzos, M.L., R.K. Lester and R.M. Solow (1989), *Made in America: Regaining the Productivity Edge*, MIT Commission on Industrial Productivity, Cambridge, MA: MIT Press.

De Soto, H. (2000), *The Mystery of Capital: Why Capitalism Triumphs in the West and Fails Everywhere Else*, Transworld Publishers: Bantam Press.

Dimsdale, N. (1991), 'The Need to Restore Corporate Accountability: An Agenda for Action', Paper presented to National Economic Development Office Conference, Capital Markets and Company Success, 21–2 November.

Dnes, A.W. (1992), '"Unfair" contractual practices and hostages in franchise contracts', *Journal of Institutional and Theoretical Economics*, **148**(3), 484–504.

Doeringer, P. and M. Piore (1971), *Internal Labor Markets and Manpower Analysis*, Boston, MA: D.C. Heath and Co.

Dore, R. (1986), *Taking Japan Seriously*, London: The Athlone Press.

Downs, A. (1957), *An Economic Theory of Democracy*, New York: Harper and Row.

D'Souza, J. and W.L. Megginson (1999), 'The financial and operating performance of privatized firms during the 1990s', *Journal of Finance*, **54**(4), 1397–438.

DTI (1988), Review of Restrictive Trade Practices: A Consultative Document, Cm. 331, London: HMSO.

Dunning, J.H. (1973), 'The Determinants of International Production', *Oxford Economic Papers*, **25**, 289.

Dunning, J.H. (ed.) (1974), *Economic Analysis and the Multinational Enterprise*, London: Allen and Unwin.

Dunning, J.H. (1981), *International Production and the Multinational Enterprise*, London: Allen and Unwin.

Dunning, J.H. (1991), 'The Eclectic Paradigm of International Production: a Personal Perspective', in Pitelis, C. and Sugden, R. (eds), *The Nature of the Transitional Firm*, London: Routledge, pp. 117–36.

Earle, J.S. and Estrin, S. (1996), 'Employee Ownership in Transition', in Frydman, R. (ed.) *Corporate Governance in Central Europe and Russia, Vol. 2, Insiders and the State*, Budapest: CEU Press.

Easley, D. and M. O'Hara (1983), 'The economic role of the non-profit firm', *Bell Journal of Economics*, **14**, 531.

Easterbrook, F.H. (1984), 'Two agency-cost explanations of dividends', *American Economic Review*, **74**(4), 650–59.

Eckel, Catherine, C. and Aidan R. Vining (1985), 'Elements of a theory of mixed enterprise', *Scottish Journal of Political Economy*, **32**, 82.

Eckel, C.C. and Vermaelen, T. (1986), 'Internal regulation: the effects of government ownership on the value of the firm', *Journal of Law and Economics*, **29**(2), 381–403.

Eckel, C., D. Eckel and V. Singal (1997), Privatization and Efficiency: Industry Effects of the Sale of British Airways', *Journal of Financial Economics*, **43**(2), 275–98.

Edgeworth, F.Y. (1925), *Papers Relating to Political Economy*, London: Macmillan.

Edwards, R.S. and H. Townsend (1967), *Business Enterprise*, London: Macmillan.

Ekelund, R.B. and R.S. Higgins (1982), 'Capital fixity, innovations, and long-term contracting: an intertemporal economic theory of regulation', *American Economic Review*, **72**, 32.

Ekelund, R.B. Jr and R.D. Tollison (1980), 'Mercantilist origins of the corporation', *Bell Journal of Economics*, **11**, 715.

Ellerman, D. (1998), 'Voucher Privatisation with Investment Funds: An Institutional Analysis', *Policy Research Working Paper No 1924*, The World Bank Group.

Estrin, S. and R. Stone (1996), *A Taxonomy of Mass Privatizations* in *Transition*, Washington, DC: World Bank.

Etgar, M. (1978), 'The effects of forward vertical integration on service performance of a distributive industry', *Journal of Industrial Economics*, **26**, 249.

Evans, P. and B. Jovanovic (1989), 'An estimated model of entrepreneurial choice under liquidity constraints', *Journal of Political Economy*, **97**(4), 808–27.

Evans, P. and L. Leighton (1989), 'Some empirical aspects of entrepreneurship', *American Economic Review*, **79**(3), 519–35.

Fairburn, J.A. and J.A. King (eds) (1989), *Mergers and Merger Policy*, Oxford: Oxford University Press.

Fama, E.F. (1980), 'Agency problems and the theory of the firm', *Journal of Political Economy*, **88**, 288.

Fama, E.F. (1983), 'Agency problems and residual claims', *Journal of Law and Economics*, **26**, 327.

Fama, E.F. and M.C. Jensen (1983), 'Separation of ownership and control', *Journal of Law and Economics*, **26**, 301.

Fisher, F.M. (2000), 'The IBM and Microsoft cases: what's the difference?', *American Economic Review*, **90**(2), 180–83.

Flanagan, R.J. (1984), 'Implicit contracts, explicit contracts, and wages', *American Economic Review*, **74**, 345.

Forester, T. (1978), 'Asians in business', *New Society*, Feb 23.

Forsyth, P.J. and R.D. Hocking (1980), 'Property rights and efficiency in a regulated environment: the case of Australian airlines', *Economic Record*, 182.

Foss, N.J. (1993), 'Theories of the Firm: Contractual and Competitive Perspectives', *Journal of Evolutionary Economics*, **3**, 127–44.

Fox, E.M. (1981), 'The modernization of antitrust: a new equilibrium', *Cornell Law Review*, **66**, 1140–92.

Frank, R.G. and D.S. Salkever (1994), 'Nonprofit Organizations in the Health Sector', *Journal of Economic Perspectives*, **8**(4), 129–44.

Franks, J. and C. Mayer (1990), 'Corporate ownership and corporate control: a study of France, Germany and the UK', *Economic Policy*, April, 191–231.

Frech III, H.E. (1976), 'The property rights theory of the firm: empirical results from a natural experiment,' *Journal of Political Economy*, **84**, 143.

Freeland, R.F. (2000), 'Creating holdup through vertical integration: Fisher Body revisited, *Journal of Law and Economics*, **43**(1), (April), 33–66.

Freeman, R.B. and M.M. Kleiner (2000), 'Who benefits most from employee involvement: firms or workers?', *American Economic Review*, **90**(2), 219–23.

Frey, B.S. (1993a), 'Does monitoring increase work effort? The rivalry with trust and loyalty', *Economic Inquiry*, **31**(4), 663–70.

Frey, B.S. (1993b), 'Shirking or Work Morale? The Impact of Regulating', *European Economic Review*, **37**, 1523–32.

Frey, B.S. (1994), 'How intrinsic motivation is crowded out and in', *Rationality and Society*, **6**(3), 334–52.

Frey, B.S. (1995), 'On the Relationship between Intrinsic and Extrinsic Work Motivation', Institute for Empirical Economic Research, University of Zurich.

Frey, B.S. and W.W. Pommerehne (1989), *Muses and Markets: Explorations in the Economics of the Arts*, Oxford: Basil Blackwell.

Friedrich, C.J. (1929), (Translation) *Alfred Weber's Theory of the Location of Industries*, Chicago: University of Chicago Press.

Frydman, R., C.W. Gray, M. Hessel and A. Papaczynski (1997), 'Private Ownership and Corporate Performance: Some Lessons from Transition Economies', Policy Research Working Paper No. 1830, The World Bank Group.

Furubotn, E.G. (1976), 'The long-run analysis of the labor-managed firm: an alternative interpretation', *American Economic Review*, **66**(1), 104–23.

Furubotn, E.G. (1988), 'Codetermination and the modern theory of the firm: a property-rights analysis', *The Journal of Business*, **61**(2), 165–81.

Furubotn, E. and S. Pejovich (1970), 'Property Rights and the Behaviour of the Firm in a Socialist State: The Example of Yugoslavia', in Furubotn, E. and Pejovich, S. (eds.) (1974), *The Economics of Property Rights*, Cambridge, MA: Ballinger, p. 227.

Furubotn, E. and S. Pejovich (1971), 'Towards a general theory of property rights; in Furubotn, E. and Pejovich, S. (eds.) (1974), *The Economics of Property Rights*, Cambridge, MA: Ballinger, p. 341.

Furubotn, E. and S. Pejovich (1972), 'Property rights and economic theory: a survey of recent literature', *Journal of Economic Literature*, **10**, 1137.

Furubotn, E. and R. Richter (1997), *Institutions and Economic Theory: The Contribution of the New Institution Economics*, Ann Arbor, MI: University of Michigan Press.

Galbraith, J.K. (1952), *American Capitalism: The Concept of Countervailing Power*, Boston, MA: Houghton Mifflin.

Galbraith, J.K. (1967), *The New Industrial State*, London: Hamish Hamilton.

Galbraith, J.K. (1973), *Economics and the Public Purpose*, Boston, MA: Houghton Mifflin.

Garvey, G. and P. Swan (1988), 'The Fable of the Barge: Towards an Economic Theory of Authority', Australian Graduate School of Management Discussion Paper.

George, D.A.R. (1982), 'Worker participation and self-management', *Scottish Journal of Political Economy*, **29**, 310.

Gibbons, R. (1998), 'Incentives in Organizations', *Journal of Economic Perspectives*, **12**(4), 115–32.

Gibrat, R. (1931), *Les Inequalités Économiques*, Paris.

Gifford, A. Jr (1991), 'A constitutional interpretation of the firm', *Public Choice*, **68**(1–3), 91–106.

Gilbert, R. and Williamson, O. (1998), 'Antitrust Policy' in *The New Palgrave Dictionary of Economics and the Law*, Vol. 1, 82–8.

Glaister, S. (1987), 'Regulation through output related profits tax', *Journal of Industrial Economics*, **35**(3), 281–96.

Glaister, S. (1996), 'Incentives in Natural Monopoly: The Case of Water', in *Regulating Utilities: A Time for Change?*, Readings 44, IEA/LBS, pp. 27–62.

Goetz, C.J. (1984), *Law and Economics: Cases and Materials*, American Casebook Series, St Paul, MN: West Publishing Co.

Goldberg, V.P. (1976a), 'Regulation and administered contracts', *Bell Journal of Economics*, **7**, 426.

Goldberg, V.P. (1976b), 'Toward an expanded economic theory of contract', *Journal of Economic Issues*, **10**, 45.

Gordon, R.A. (1940), 'Ownership and compensation as incentives to corporate executives', *Quarterly Journal of Economics*, **54**, 455.

Gravelle, H. and R. Rees (1981), *Microeconomics*, London: Longman.

Gray, C.W. (1996), 'In Search of Owners: Lessons of Experience with Privatization and Corporate Governance in Transition Economies', Policy Research Working Paper No. 1595, The World Bank Group.

Grossman, S.J. and O.D. Hart (1980), 'Takeover bids, the free rider problem, and the theory of the corporation', *Bell Journal of Economics*, **11**, 42.

Grossman, S.J. and O.D. Hart (1986), 'The costs and benefits of ownership: a theory of vertical and lateral integration', *Journal of Political Economy*, **94**(4), 691–719.

Hahn, R.W. and J.A. Hird (1990), 'The costs and benefits of regulation: review and synthesis', *Yale Journal of Regulation*, **8**, 233–78.

Hall, Bronwyn H. (1988), 'Effects of takeover activity on corporate research and development', in Auerbach, A.J. (ed.), *Corporate Takeovers: Causes and Consequences*, NBER, Chicago: University of Chicago Press, 69–96.

Hall, B.J. and Liebman, J.B. (1998), 'Are CEOs really paid like bureaucrats?', *Quarterly Journal of Economics*, **113**(3), 653–91.

Hannah, L. (1983a), *The Rise of the Corporate Economy*, (2nd edn), London and New York: Methuen.

Hannah, L. (1983b), 'Entrepreneurs and the Social Sciences', An Inaugural Lecture, London School of Economics and Political Science.

Hannah, L. and J.A. Kay (1976), *Concentration in Modern Industry: Theory, Measurement and the UK Experience*, London: Macmillan.

Hannon, T.H. and F. Mavinga (1980), 'Expense preference and managerial control: the case of the banking firm', *Bell Journal of Economics*, **11**, 671.

Hansmann, H.B. (1980), 'The role of non-profit enterprise', *Yale Law Journal*, **89**, 835.

Hansmann, H.B. (1981), 'Nonprofit enterprise in the performing arts', *Bell Journal of Economics*, **12**, 341–61.

Hansmann, H.B. (1987), 'Economic Theories of nonprofit organisation', in Powell, W.W. (ed.), *The Nonprofit Sector: A Research Handbook*, New Haven, CT: Yale University Press, pp. 27–42.

Hansmann, H.B. (1990), 'The Viability of Worker Ownership: an Economic Perspective on the Political Structure of the Firm', in Aoki et al. (eds), *The Firm as a Nexus of Treaties*, London: Sage Publications, pp. 162–84.

Hansmann, H.B. (1996), *The Ownership of Enterprise*, Cambridge, MA: Harvard University Press.

Hare, P., J. Batt and S. Estrin (eds) (1999), *Reconstituting the Market: The Political Economy of Microeconomic Transformation*, Harwood Academic Publishers.

Harris, M. and A. Raviv (1978), 'Some results on incentive contracts with applications to education and employment, health insurance and law enforcement', *American Economic Review*, **68**, 20.

Hart, O.D. (1983), 'The market mechanism as an incentive scheme', *Bell Journal of Economics*, **14**, 366.

Hart, O.D. (1995a), *Firms, Contracts and Financial Structure*, Clarendon Lectures in Economics, Oxford: Clarendon Press.

Hart, O.D. (1995b), 'Corporate governance: some theory and implications', *Economic Journal*, **105**(430), 678–89.

Hart, O. and J. Moore (1990), 'Property rights and the nature of the firm', *Journal of Political Economy*, **98**, 1119–58.

Hart, O. and J. Moore (1995), 'Debt and seniority: an analysis of the role of hard claims in constraining management', *American Economic Review*, **85**(3), 567–85.

Hart, O. and J. Moore (1997), 'Default and Renegotiation: A Dynamic Model of Debt', Discussion Paper No. TE/97/321, Theoretical Economics Workshop, The Suntory Centre, London School of Economics.

Hashimoto, M. (1990), 'Employment and wage systems in Japan and their implications for productivity', in Blinder, A.S. (ed.), *Paying for Productivity: A Look at the Evidence*, Washington DC: Brookings Institution.

Hasihmoto, M. and J. Raisian (1985), 'Employment tenure and earnings profiles in Japan and the United States', *American Economic Review*, **75**(4), 721–35.

Haubrich, J.G. (1994), 'Risk aversion, performance pay, and the principal–agent problem', *Journal of Political Economy*, **102**(2), 258–76.

Hay, D.A. and D.J. Morris (1979), *Industrial Economics: Theory and Evidence*, Oxford: Oxford Univesity Press.

Hayek, F.A. (1937), 'Economics and knowledge', *Economica*, **4**, 33.

Hayek, F.A. (1945), 'The use of knowledge in society', *American Economic Review*, **35**, 519–30, reprinted in Townsend, H. (ed.) (1971), *Price Theory*, Penguin Modern Economics Readings, p. 17.

Hayek, F.A. (1949), *Individualism and Economic Order*, London: Routledge and Kegan Paul.

Hayek, F.A. (1978), 'Competition as a Discovery Procedure', in *New Studies in Philosophy Politics and the History of Ideas*, London: Routledge and Kegan Paul, p. 179.

Hayek, F.A. (1979), *Law Legislation and Liberty*; Vol. 3 *The Political Order of a Free People*, London: Routledge and Kegan Paul.

Hayek, F.A. (1989), *The Fatal Conceit*, London: Routledge.

Hechter, M. (1987), *Principles of Group Solidarity*, Berkeley, CA: University of California Press.

Heilbrun, J. (1981), *Urban Economics and Public Policy* (2nd edn), New York: St Martin's Press, chapter 4.

Helper, S.R. and M. Sako (1995), 'Supplier relations in Japan and the United States; are they converging?', *Sloan Management Review*, **36**(3), 77–84.

Hey, J. (1979), *Uncertainty in Microeconomics*, Oxford: Martin Robertson.

Hill, C.W.L. (1984), 'Organisational Structure, the Development of the Firm and Business Behaviour', in Pickering, J.F. and Cockerill, T.A.J. (eds), *The Economic Management of the Firm*, London: Philip Allen, p. 52.

Hindley, B. (1970), 'The division of ownership from control in the modern corporation', *Journal of Law and Economics*, **13**, 185.

Hirschman, A. (1970), *Exit, Voice, and Loyalty: Responses to Decline in Firms, Organizations and States*, Harvard University Press.

Hirshleifer, D. and S. Titman (1990), 'Share tendering strategies and the success of hostile takeover bids', *Journal of Political Economy*, **98**(2), 295–324.

Hirshleifer, J. (1983), 'From weakest link to best shot: the voluntary provision of public goods', *Public Choice*, **41**, 371.

Hirshleifer, J. and J.G. Riley (1979), 'The analytics of uncertainty and information – an expository survey', *Journal of Economic Literature*, **17**(4), 1375–417.

Hochman, H. and J.D. Rogers (1969), 'Pareto Optimal Redistribution', *American Economic Review*, **59**(4), 542–57.

Hollander, H. (1990), 'A social exchange approach to voluntary cooperation', *American Economic Review*, **80**(5), 1157–67.

Holstrom, B. (1979), 'Moral hazard and observability', *Bell Journal of Economics*, **10**, 74.

Holstrom, B. and J. Roberts (1998), 'The boundaries of the firm revisited', *Journal of Economic Perspectives*, **12**(4), 73–94.

Holtmann, A.G. (1983), 'A theory of non-profit firms', *Economica*, **50**, 439.

Hood, J. and B.S. Yamey (1957), 'The Middle-class Co-operative Retailing Societies in London, 1864–1900', *Oxford Economic Papers*, N.S, Vol. 9, p. 309.

Hughes, A. (1989), 'The Impact of Mergers: a Survey of Empirical Evidence for the UK', in Fairburn, J.A. and King, J.A. (eds), *Mergers and Merger Policy*, Oxford: Oxford University Press.

Hume, D. (1978), *Treatise of Human Nature*, P.H. Nidditch (ed.), Oxford: Clarendon Press, (first published 1740).

Hutchens, R.M. (1989), 'Seniority, wages and productivity: a turbulent decade', *Journal of Economic Perspectives*, **3**(4), 49–64.

Hutton, W. (1995), *The State We're In*, London: Jonathan Cape.

Hutton, W. (1997), *Stakeholding and Its Critics*, Choice in Welfare No. 36, Health and Welfare Unit, Institute of Economic Affairs, London.

Hymer, S.H. (1976), *The International Operations of National Firms: A Study of Foreign Direct Investment*, Cambridge, MA: MIT Press.

Iannacone, L.R. (1992), 'Sacrifice and stigma: reducing free-riding in cults, communes, and other collectives', *Journal of Political Economy*, **100**(2), 271–91.

Jackson, P. (1982), *The Political Economy of Bureaucracy*, London: Philip Allen.

James, E. and S. Rose-Ackerman (1986), *The Nonprofit Enterprise in Market Economics*, Harvard Academic Publishers.

Jarrell, G.A. and A.B. Poulson (1987), ' Shark repellents and stock prices: The effects of antitakeover amendments since 1980', *Journal of Financial Economics*, **19**(1), 127–68.

Jarrell, G.A., J.A. Brickley and J.M. Netter (1988), 'The market for corporate control; the empirical evidence since 1980', *Journal of Economic Perspective*, **2**(1), 49–68.

Jensen, M.C. (1988), 'Takeovers: their causes and consequences', *Journal of Economic Perspectives*, **2**(1), 21–48.

Jensen, M.C. and W.H. Meckling (1976), 'Theory of the firm: managerial behavior agency costs and ownership structure', *Journal of Financial Economics*, **3**, 305.

Jensen, M.C. and K.J. Murphy (1990a), 'CEO incentives', *Harvard Business Review*, **68**(3), 138–53.

Jensen, M.C. and K.J. Murphy (1990b), 'Performance pay and top-management incentives', *Journal of Political Economy*, **98**(2), 225–64.

Jewkes, J. (1948), *Ordeal by Planning*, London: Macmillan.

Jewkes, J. (1964), *Public and Private Enterprise*, The Lindsay Memorial Lectures, London: Routledge and Kegan Paul.

Jewkes, J., D. Sawyers and R. Stillerman (1969), *The Sources of Invention*, London: Macmillan (second edn).

Joskow, P.L. (1997), 'Restructuring, competition and regulatory reform in the US electricity sector', *Journal of Economic Perspectives*, **11**(3), 119–38.

Joskow, P.L. and N.L. Rose (1989), 'The Effects of Economic Regulation', in R. Schmalensee and R.D. Willig (eds), *Handbook of Industrial Organisation*, Vol. II, 1450–506, Elsevier Science Publishers.

Kahana, N. and S. Nitzean (1993), 'The theory of the labour-managed firm revisited: the voluntary interactive approach', *Economic Journal*, **103**(419), 937–45.

Kamerschen, D. (1968), 'The influence of ownership and control on profit rates', *American Economic Review*, **58**, 432.

Kandel, E. and F.P. Lazear (1992), 'Peer pressure and partnerships', *Journal of Political Economy*, **100**(4), 801–17.

Kania, J. and J.R. McKean (1976), 'Ownership, control, and the contemporary corporation: a general behaviour analysis', *Kyklos*, **29**(2), 272.

Kaplan, S. (1989), 'The effects of management buyouts on operating performance and value', *Journal of Financial Economics*, **24**, 217–54.

Kasper, W. and M.E. Streit (1998), *Institutional Economics: Social Order and Public Policy*, The Locke Institute, Cheltenham, UK: Edward Elgar.

Kay, N.M. (1979), *The Innovating Firm: A Behavioural Theory of Corporate R and D*, London: Macmillan.

Kay, N.M. (1982), *The Evolving Firm*, London: Macmillan.

Kay, N.M. (1983), *The Emergent Firm: The role of Bounded Rationality in Economic Organisation*, London: Macmillan.

Kay, J. (1992), 'Innovations in corporate strategy', in Bowen, A. and M. Ricketts (eds), *Stimulating Innovation in Industry*, NEDO, Policy Issues Series, London: Kogan Pape, 117–31.

Kim, Jae-Cheol (1985), 'The market for "lemons" reconsidered: a model of the used car market with asymmetric information', *American Economic Review*, **75**, 836.

King, R.G. and R. Levine (1993), 'Finance, Entrepreneurship and Growth: Theory and Evidence', *Journal of Monetary Economics*, **32**, 513–42.

Kirzner, I.M. (1973), Competition and Entrepreneurship, Chicago: University of Chicago Press.

Kirzner, I.M. (1976), *The Economic Point of View: An Essay in the History of Economic Thought*, Kansas City: Sheed and Ward Inc.

Kirzner, I.M. (1979), *Perception, Opportunity and Profit*, Chicago: University of Chicago Press.

Kirzner, I.M. (1980), 'The Primacy of Entrepreneurial Discovery', in Seldon, A. (ed.), *Prime Mover of Progress: The Entrepreneur in Capitalism and Socialism*, Institute of Economic Affairs, Readings 23, London, p. 5.

Kirzner, I.M. (ed.) (1982), *Method, Process and Austrian Economics*, Essays in Honor of Ludwig Von Mises, Lexington, MA: Lexington Books.

Klein, B. (1984), 'Contract costs and administered prices: an economic theory of rigid wages,' *American Economic Review*, **74**, 332.

Klein, B. (2000), 'Fisher-General Motors and the nature of the firm', *Journal of Law and Economics*, **43**(1) (April), 105–41.

Klein, B., R.G. Crawford and A.A. Alchian (1978), 'Vertical integration, appropriable rents, and competitive contracting process', *Journal of Law and Economics*, **21**, 297.

Klein, D.B. (1997a), 'Discovery Factors of Economic Freedom: Response, Epiphany and Serendipity', in J.R. Lott (ed.), *Uncertainty and Economic Evolution: Essays in Honor of Armen A. Alchian*, London and New York: Routledge, pp. 165–80.

Klein, D.B. (1997b), 'Discovery and the Deepself', Mimeo, Santa Clara University.

Knight, F.H. (1921), *Risk, Uncertainty and Profit*, Boston MA: Houghton Mifflin.

Koike, K. (1990), 'Intellectual Skill and the Role of Employees as *Constituent Members of Large Firms in Contemporary Japan*, in Aoki, M. et al. (eds) *The Firm as a Nexus of Treaties*, London: Sage Publications, pp. 185–208.

Kolko, G. (1965), *Railroads and Regulation 1877–1916*, Princeton, NJ: Princeton University Press.

Kovacic, W.E. and C. Shapiro (2000), 'Antitrust policy: a century of economic and legal thinking', *Journal of Economic Perspectives*, **14**(1), 43–60.

Lancaster, K.J. (1966), 'A new approach to consumer theory, *Journal of Political Economy*, **74**, 132.

Lange, O. (1936), 'On the economic theory of socialism', *Review of Economic Studies*, **4**(1), 53–71 and (2), 123–42.

Larner, R.J. (1966), 'Ownership and control in the 200 largest non-financial corporations, 1929 and 1963', *American Economic Review*, **56**, 777.

Lazear, E.P. (1979), 'Why is there mandatory retirement?', *Journal of Political Economy*, **87**, 1261.

Lazear, E.P. (1981), 'Agency, earnings profiles, productivity and hours restrictions', *American Economic Review*, **71**, 606.

Lazear, E.P. (1984), 'Incentives and wage rigidity', *American Economic Review*, **74**, 339.

Lazear, E.P. (1991), 'Labor economics and the psychology of organizations', *Journal of Economic Perspectives*, **5**(2), 80–110.

Lazear, E.P. (1995), *Personnel Economics*, The Wicksell Lectures, London and Cambridge, MA and London: MIT Press.

Lazear, E.P. (2000a), 'The future of personnel economics', *Economic Journal*, **110**(467), 611–39.

Lazear, E.P. (2000b), 'Performance Pay and Productivity', *American Economic Review*, **90**(5), 1346–61.

Lazear, E.P. and R. Moore (1984), 'Incentives, productivity and labour contracts', *Quarterly Journal of Economics*, **99**(2), 275–96.

Lazear, E. and Rosen. S. (1981), 'Rank order tournaments as optimal labour contracts', *Journal of Political Economy*, **89**, 841.

Leadbeater, C. and I. Christie (1999), *To Our Mutual Advantage*, London: Demos.

Leech, D. and J. Leahy (1991), 'Ownership structure, control type classifications and the performance of large British companies', *Economic Journal*, **101**(409), 1418–37.

Lehn, K. and A. Poulson (1989), 'Free cash flow and shareholder gains in going private transactions', *Journal of Finance*, **44**, 771–88.

Leibenstein, H. (1966), 'Allocative efficiency v. x-efficiency', *American Economic Review*, **56**, 392.

Leibenstein, H. (1975), 'Aspects of the x-efficiency theory of the firm', *Bell Journal of Economics*, **6**, 580.

Leibenstein, H. (1976), *Beyond Economic Man: A New Foundation for Microeconomics*, Cambridge, MA: Harvard University Press.

Leibenstein, H. (1978a), *General X-efficiency Theory and Economic Development*, New York: Oxford University Press.

Leibenstein, H. (1978b), 'X-efficiency Xists-reply to an Xorcist', *American Economic Review*, **68**, 203.

Leibenstein, H. (1979), 'A branch of economics is missing: micro-micro theory', *Journal of Economic Literature*, **17**, 477.

Leland, Hayne E. (1992), 'Insider trading: should it be prohibited?', *Journal of Political Economy*, **100**(4), 859–87.

Lerner, A. (1944), *The Economics of Control*, London: Macmillan.

Lewellen, W.G. (1969), 'Management and ownership in the large firm', *Journal of Finance*, **24**, 299.

Lewellen, W.G. (1971), *The Ownership Income of Management*, New York: Columbia University Press.

Lewellen, W.G. and B. Huntsman (1970), 'Managerial pay and corporate performance', *American Economic Review*, **60**, 710.

Lindsay, Cotton, M. (1976), 'A theory of government enterprise', *Journal of Political Economy*, **84**, 1061.

Littlechild, S.C. (1979a), 'Controlling the nationalised industries: quis custodiet ipsos custodes?', Series B Discussion Paper No. 56, University of Birmingham, UK.

Littlechild, S.C. (1979b), 'Comment on Shackle's "Imagination, formalism and choice": Radical Subjectivism or Radical Subversion?' In Rizzo, M.J. (ed.), *Time Uncertainty and Disequilibrium*, Lexington Books, Lexington, MA: D.C. Heath, pp. 32–49.

Littlechild, S.C. (1982), 'Equilibrium and the market process' in Kirzner, I.M. (ed.), *Method, Process, and Austrian Economics: Essay in Honor of Ludwig Von Mises*, Lexington, MA: Lexington Books, p. 85.

Loasby, B.J. (1976), *Choice, Complexity and Ingorance*, Cambridge: Cambridge University Press.

Loasby, B.J. (1982a), 'The entrepreneur in economic theory, *Scottish Journal of Political Economy*, **29**, 235.

Loasby, B.J. (1982b), 'Economics of Dispersed and Incomplete Information', in I.M. Kirzner (ed.), *Method, Process and Austrian Economics: Essays in Honor of Ludwig Von Mises*, Lexington, MA: Lexington Books, p. 111.

Loasby, B.J. (1984), 'Entrepreneurs and organisation', *Journal of Economic Studies*, **11**(2), 75.

Loasby, B.J. (1991), *Equilibrium and Evolution: An Explanation of Connecting Principles in Economics*, Manchester: Manchester University Press.

Loeb, M. and W. Magat (1919), 'A Decentralised Method for Utility Regulation', *Journal of Law and Economics*, **22**, 399–404.

Losch, A. (1954), *The Economics of Location*, translated by Waglam and Stolper, New Haven, CT: Yale University Press.

Luce, R.D. and H. Raiffa (1957), *Games and Decisions*, New York: John Wiley and Sons.

Machlup, F. (1967), 'Theories of the firm: marginalist, behavioral, managerial', *American Economic Review*, **62**, 1.

Macrae, N. (1976), 'The coming entrepreneurial revolution: a survey', *The Economist*, 25th December, p. 42.

Main, B.G. (1999), 'The Rise and Fall of Executive Share Options in Britain', in J. Carpenter and D. Yermack (eds), *Executive Compensation and Shareholder Value: Theory and Evidence*, Dordrecht: Kluwer, pp. 83–113.

Malcolmson, J.M. (1981), 'Unemployment and the efficiency wage hypothesis', *Economic Journal*, **91**, 848.

Malcolmson, J.M. (1982), 'Trade Unions and economic efficiency', Conference Papers (Supplement to the Economic Journal), Conference of the Royal Economic Society and the Association of University Teachers of Economics, ISER Reprint No. 360, University of York, UK.

Malcolmson, J.M. (1984), 'Work incentives, hierarchy, and internal labor markets', *Journal of Political Economy*, **92**(3), 486.

Malcolmson, J.M. (1997), 'Contracts, hold-up, and labor markets', *Journal of Economic Literature*, **35**(4), 1916–57.

Manne, H.G. (1965), 'Mergers and the market for corporate control', *Journal of Political Economy*, **75**, 110.

Manne, H.G. (1966), 'In defence of insider trading', *Harvard Business Review*, **44**, Nov.–Dec., 113–22.

Mansfield, E. et al. (1971), *Research and Innovation in the Modern Corporation*, New York: Norton.

Marglin, S.A. (1974), 'What do bosses do?', *Review of Radical Political Economics*, **6**, 60–112.

Markusen, J.R. (1995), 'The boundaries of multinational enterprises and the theory of international trade', *Journal of Economic Perspectives*, **9**(2), 169–89.

Markusen, J.R. (1998), 'Incorporating the Multinational Enterprise into the Theory of International Trade', in Mudambi, R. and Ricketts, M. (eds), *The Organisation of the Firm: International Business Perspectives*, Routledge Studies in Business Organisation and Networks, London and New York, pp. 79–98.

Marris, R. (1963), 'A model of the managerial enterprise', *Quarterly Journal of Economics*, **77**, 185.

Marris, R. (1964), *The Economic Theory of Managerial Capitalism*, London: Macmillan.

Marris, R. (1971), 'An Introduction to Theories of Corporate Growth', in Marris, R.L. and Wood, A. (eds), *The Corporate Economy*, London: Macmillan.

Marris, R. and D.C. Mueller (1980), 'The corporation, competition and the invisible hand', *Journal of Economic Literature*, **18** (March), 32.

Marris, R.L. and A. Wood (eds) (1971), *The Corporate Economy*, London: Macmillan.

Marsh, P. (1991), 'Market Assessment of Company Performance', Paper presented at National Economic Development Office Conference, Capital Markets and Company Success, November 21–2, London Business School.

Marshall, A. (1925), *Principles of Economics* (8th Edn), London: Macmillan.

Martin, R. (1988), 'Franchising and Risk Management', *American Economic Review*, **78**(5), 954–68.

Masson, R.T. (1971), 'Executive motivation, earnings and consequent equity performance', *Journal of Political Economy*, **79**, 1278.

Mayer, C. and I. Alexander (1990), 'Banks and Securities Markets: Corporate Financing in Germany and the UK', *Journal of Japanese and International Economies*, **4**(4).

McConnell, J.J. and C.J. Muscarella (1985), 'Corporate capital expenditure decisions and the market value of the firm', *Journal of Financial Economics*, **14**, 399–422.

McEachern, W.A. (1978a), 'Corporate control and growth: an alternative approach', *Journal of Industrial Economics*, **26**, 257.

McEachern, W.A. (1978b), 'Ownership, control and the contemporary corporation: a comment', *Kyklos*, **31**, 491.

McGuire, J.W., J.S.Y. Chiu and A.O. Elbing (1962), 'Executive incomes, sales and profits', *American Economic Review*, **52**, 753.

McManus, J. (1975), 'The costs of alternative economic organisations', *Canadian Journal of Economics*, **8**, 334–50.

McNabb, R. and K. Whitfield (1998), 'The impact of financial participation and employee involvement on financial performance', *Scottish Journal of Political Economy*, **45**(2), 171–87.

Meade, J. (1972), 'The theory of labour-managed firms and of profit sharing', *Economic Journal*, **82**, 402.

Meade, J. (1985), *Wage-fixing Revisited*, Institute of Economic Affairs, Occasional Paper 72.

Meade, J. (1989), *Agathotopia: The Economics of Partnership*, The David Hume Institute, Hume Paper No. 16, Aberdeen University Press.

Meeks, G. and G. Whittington (1975), 'Directors' pay, growth and profitability', *Journal of Industrial Economics*, **24**, 1.

Megginson, W.L., R.C. Nash and M. van Randenborgh (1994), 'The financial and operating performance of newly privatized firms: an international empirical analysis', *Journal of Finance*, **49**, 403–52.

Meiners, R., I. Mofsky and R. Tollison (1979), 'Piercing the veil of limited liability', *Delaware Journal of Corporation Law*, **4**, 351.

Menger, Carl (1950), *Principles of Economics* (translated and edited by Dingwall, Jones, and Hoselitz, Bert, F.), Glencoe, IL: Free Press.

Metcalfe, S. (1992), 'Competition and collaboration in the innovation process', in A. Bowen and M. Ricketts (eds) *Stimulating Innovation in Industry*, London: NEDO/Kogan Page, pp. 218–40.

Meulbroek, L.K. (2000), 'The Efficiency of Equity-Linked Compensation: Understanding the Full Cost of Awarding Executive Stock Options', Harvard Business School Working Paper No. 00-056.

Meulbroek, L.K., M.L. Mitchell, J.H. Mulherin, J.M. Netter and A.B. Poulsen (1990), 'Shark repellents and managerial myopia: an empirical test', *Journal of Political Economy*, **98**(5) (part 1), 1108–17.

Meyer, M.A. and J. Vickers (1995), 'Performance Comparisons and Dynamic Incentives', Discussion Paper No 1107, Centre for Economic Policy Research, London.

Meyer, R.A. (1975), 'Publicly owned versus privately owned utilities: a policy choice', *Review of Economics and Statistics*, **57**, 391.

Migué, I. and G. Bélanger (1974), 'Toward a general theory of managerial discretion', *Public Choice*, **17**, 27.

Mikkelson, W.H. and R.S. Ruback (1985), 'An empirical analysis of the interfirm equity investment process', *Journal of Financial Economics*, **14**(4), 523–53.

Mill, J.S. (1898), *Principles of Political Economy with Some of their Applications to Social Philosophy* (People's edition), London: Longman, Green, and Co. (first published 1848).

Millward, R. (1978), 'Public ownership, the theory of property rights and the public corporation in the UK', *Salford Papers in Economics*, no., 78-1.

Minkler, A. (1992), 'Why firms franchise: a search cost theory', *Journal of Institutional and Theoretical Economics*, **148**(2), 240–59.

Mirrlees, J.A. (1976), 'The optimal structure of incentives and authority within an organization', *Bell Journal of Economics*, **7**, 105.

Mises, L. (1945), *Bureaucracy*, London: William Hodge and Co.

Mises, L. (1949), *Human Action*, London: Hodge.

Mitchell, M.L. and K. Lehn (1990), 'Do bad bidders become good targets?', *Journal of Political Economy*, **98**(2), 372–98.

Modigliani, F. (1988), 'MM-past, present, future', *Journal of Economic Perspectives*, **2**(4), 149–58.

Modigliani, F. and M.H. Miller (1958), 'The cost of capital, corporation finance, and the theory of investment', *American Economic Review*, June, 261–97.

Monsen, R.J. Jr, J.S. Chiu and D.E. Cooley (1968), 'The effect of separation of ownership and control on the performance of the large firm', *Quarterly Journal of Economics*, **82**, 435.

Monteverde, K. and D.J. Teece (1982a), 'Supplier switching costs and vertical integration in the automobile industry', *Bell Journal of Economics*, **13**, 206.

Monteverde, K. and D.J. Teece (1982b), 'Appropriable rents and quasi-vertical integration', *Journal of Law and Economics*, **25**, 321.

Montgomery, C.A. (1994), 'Corporate Diversification', *Journal of Economic Perspectives*, **8**(3), 163–78.

Moore, J.H. (1980), *Growth with self-Management: Yugoslav Industrialization 1952–1979*, Stanford, CA: Hoover Institution Press.

Morgan, E. Victor and Anne D. Morgan (1990), 'The stock market and mergers in the United Kingdom', Papers prepared for the Inquiry into Corporate Takeovers in the United Kingdom, no. 10, David Hume Institute, Hume Occasional Paper no. 24.

Morrison, S.A. and Winston, C. (1998), 'Regulatory Reform of U.S. Intercity Transportation', in Gomez-Ibanez, J.A., Tye, W.B. and Winston, C. (eds), *Essays in Transportation Economics and Policy: A Handbook in Honor of John R. Meyer*, Washington, DC: Brookings.

Moschel, W. (1989), 'Competition Policy from an Ordo Point of View', in Peacock, A. and Willgerodt, H. (eds), *German Neo-Liberals and the Social Market Economy*, Macmillan, pp. 142–59.

Mueller, D. (1996), *Public Choice II*, Cambridge: Cambridge University Press.

Musgrave, R.A. (1959), *The Theory of Public Finance*, New York: McGraw Hill.

Musgrave, R.A. (1981) 'Leviathan Cometh – Or Does He?', in Ladd, H.F. and Tideman, T.N. (eds), *Tax and Expenditure Limitations*, Washington, DC: The Urban Institute.

National Audit Office (1986), Report by the Comptroller and Auditor General, *Competitive Tendering for Support Services in the National Health Service,* London, HMSO.

National Economic Development Office (1976), *A Study of UK Nationalised Industries*, London: HMSO.

Nelson, R. (1959), 'The simple economics of basic scientific research, *Journal of Political Economy*, **67**, 297.

Nelson, R.R. and S.C. Winter (1982), *An Evolutionary Theory of Economic Change*, Cambridge, MA: Harvard University Press.

Neuberg, L.G. (1977), 'Two issues in the municipal ownership of electric power distribution systems', *Bell Journal of Economics*, **8**, 303.

Neumann, J. Von. and O. Morgenstern (1944), *Economics and the Theory of Games*, London: Macmillan.

Newbery, D.M. (1998), 'Pool Reform and Competition in Electricity', in Beesley, M.E. (ed.), *Regulating Utilities: Understanding the Issues*, Readings 48, LBS/IEA, London.

Newhouse, J. (1970), 'Toward a theory of non-profit institutions: an economic model of a hospital', *American Economic Review*, **60**, 64.

Nickell, S.J. (1996), 'Competition and Corporate Performance', *Journal of Political Economy*, **104**(4), 724–46.

Nicols, A. (1967), 'Stock versus mutual savings and loan associations: some evidence of differences in behavior', *American Economic Review*, **57**, 337.

Niskanen, W. (1968), 'Non-market decision making: the peculiar economics of bureaucracy', *American Economic Review*, **58**, 293.

Niskanen, W. (1971), *Bureaucracy and Representative Government*, Chicago: Aldine.

Niskanen, W. (1973), *Bureaucracy: Servant or Master?*, Hobart Paperback 5, London: Institute of Economic Affairs.

Niskanen, W. (1975), 'Bureaucrats and politicians', *Journal of Law and Economics*, **18**, 617.

Noll, R.G. (1989), 'Economic Perspectives on the Politics of Regulation', in Schmalensee, R. and Willig, R.D. (eds), *Handbook of Industrial Organization*, Vol. II, Elsevier Science Publishers, 1254–87.

North, D. (1981), *Structure and Change in Economic History*, New York: Norton.

North, D. (1991), 'Institutions', *Journal of Economic Perspectives*, **5**(1), 97–112.

Nuti, D.M. (1999), 'Employee Ownership in Polish Privatizations' in Hare *et al.* (eds), *Reconstituting the Market*, 81–97.

Nyman, S. and A. Silbertson (1978), 'The Ownership and Control of British Industry', *Oxford Economic Papers*, **30**(1), 74–101.

Odagiri, H. (1980), *The Theory of Growth in the Corporate Economy: An Inquiry into Management Preferences, R and D and Economic Growth*, Cambridge: Cambridge University Press.

Office of Fair Trading (1993), *Annual Report*, London: HMSO.

Okun, Arthur M. (1981), *Prices and Quantities: A Macroeconomic Analysis*, Oxford: Basil Blackwell.

Olson, M. (1965), *The Logic of Collective Action*, Cambridge, MA: Harvard University Press.

Owen, G. and Grofman, B. (1984), 'To vote or not to vote: the paradox of nonvoting', *Public Choice*, **42**(3), 311–25.

Palmer, J. (1973a), 'The profit variability effects of the management enterprise', *Western Economic Journal*, **2**, 228.

Palmer, J. (1973b), 'The profit performance effects of the separation of ownership from control in large US industrial corporations', *Bell Journal of Economics and Management Science*, **4**, 293.

Parker, D. (1994), 'Nationalisation, Privatisation, and Agency Status within Government: Testing for the Importance of Ownership', in Jackson, P.M. and Price, C.M. (eds), *Privatisation and Regulation: A Review of the Issues*, London: Longman, 149–69.

Parker, D. and S. Martin (1995), 'The Impact of UK Privatisation on Labour and Total Factor Productivity', *Scottish Journal of Political Economy*, **42**(2), 201–20.

Parker, R.D. and R. Stacey (1994), *Chaos, Management and Economics: The Implications of Non-Linear Thinking*, Hobart Paper 125, London: Institute of Economic Affairs.

Patton, A. (1961), *Men, money, and Motivation*, New York.

Pauly, M.V. (1968), 'The economics of moral hazard', *American Economic Review*, **58**, 531.

Pavitt, K. (1987), 'International patterns of technological accumulation', in Hood, N. and Vahne, J.E. (eds), *Strategies in Global Competition*, London: Croom Helm.

Peacock, A.T. (1983), 'Public x-inefficiency: information and institutional constraints', in H. Hanusch (ed.), *Anatomy of Government Deficiencies*, Heidelberg: Springer Verlag.

Peacock, A.T. and G. Bannock (1991), *Corporate Takeovers and the Public Interest*, David Hume Institute, Aberdeen University Press.

Pejovich, S. (1992), 'A property rights analysis of the inefficiency of investment decisions by labour-managed firms', *Journal of Institutional and Theoretical Economics*, **148**(1), 30–41.

Pelikan, P. (1993), 'Ownership of Firms and Efficiency: the Competence Argument', *Constitutional Political Economy*, **4**(3), 349–92.

Peltzman, S. (1971), 'Pricing in public and private enterprises: electric utilities in the United States', *Journal of Law and Economics*, **14**, 109.

Peltzman, S. (1976), 'Toward a more general theory of regulation', *Journal of Law and Economics*, **19**, 211.

Penrose, E.T. (1952), 'Biological analogies in the theory of the firm', *American Economic Review*, **42**, 804.

Penrose, E.T. (1959), The Theory of the Growth of the Firm, Oxford: Basil Blackwell.

Perry, M.K. (1980), 'Forward integration by Alcoa: 1888–1930', *Journal of Industrial Economics*, **29**, 37.

Pescatrice, D.R. and Trapani, J.M. III (1980), 'The performance and objectives of public and private utilities operating in the U.S.', *Journal of Public Economic*, **13**, 259.

Picot, A. and T. Kaulmann (1989), 'Comparative performance of government-owned and privately-owned industrial corporations – empirical results from six countries', *Journal of Institutional and Theoretical Economics*, **145**(2), 298–316.

Pigou, A.C. (1949), *The Veil of Money*, London: Macmillan.

Pinchot, G.M. (1985), *Intrapreneuring: Why you don't have to leave the Corporation to become an Entrepreneur*, New York: Harper and Row.

Polanyi, M. (1958), *Personal Knowledge*, London: Routledge and Kegan Paul.

Polanyi, M. (1967), *The Tacit Dimension*, Garden City, New York: Doubleday Anchor.

Porter, M.E. (1990), *The Competitive Advantage of Nations*, London: Macmillan.

Posner, R.A. (1971), 'Taxation by regulation', *Bell Journal of Economics and Management Science*, **2**, 22–50.

Posner, R.A. (1974), 'Theories of economic regulation', *Bell Journal of Economics and Management Science*, **5**, 335–58.

Posner, R.A. (1979), 'The Chicago School of antitrust analysis', *University of Pennsylvania Review*, **127**, 925–48.

Powell, W.W. (ed.) (1987), *The Nonprofit Sector: A Research Handbook*, New Haven, CT: Yale University Press.

Prais, S.J. (1976), *The Evolution of Giant Firms in Britain*, London: Cambridge University Press.

Pratt, J.W. and R.J. Zeckhauser (eds) (1985), *Principals and Agents: The Structure of Business*, Boston, MA: Harvard Business School Research Colloquium.

Prendergast, C. (1999), 'The provision of incentives in firms', *Journal of Economic Literature*, **37**(1), 7–63.

Prevezer, M. and M. Ricketts (1991), 'Corporate Governance: The UK Compared with Germany and Japan', Paper presented to National Economic Development Office Conference, Capital Markets and Company Success, November 21–2.

Primeaux, W.J. (1977), 'An assessment of "x"-efficiency gained through competition', *Review of Economics and Statistics*, **59**, 105.

Progressio Foundation (1990), *Towards the Civic Economy*, Series Publication 1.

Pryke, R. (1981), *The Nationalised Industries: Policies and Performance Since 1968*, Oxford: Martin Robertson.

Pryke, R. (1982), 'The comparative performance of public and private enterprise' *Fiscal Studies*, July, p. 68.

Quirk, J. and R. Saposnik (1968), *Introduction to General Equilibrium Theory and Welfare Economics*, Economics Handbook Series, New York: McGraw Hill.

Radice, H.K. (1971), 'Control type, profitability and growth in large firms: an empirical study', *Economic Journal*, **81**, 547.

Radner, R. (1981), 'Monitoring cooperative agreements in a repeated principal–agent relationship', *Econometrica*, **49**, 1127.

Ramamurti, R. (1997), 'Testing the limits of privatization: Argentine railroads', *World Development*, **25**, 1973–93.

Rasmusen, E. (1989), *Games and Information: An Introduction to Game Theory*, Oxford: Basil Blackwell.

Raynes, H.E. (1964), *A History of British Insurance* (2nd edn), London: Pitman.

Redwood, J. (1984), *Going for Broke: Gambling with Taxpayers' Money*, Oxford: Basil Blackwell.

Redwood, J. and J. Hatch (1982), *Controlling Public Industries*, Oxford, Basil Blackwell.

Rees, H. and A. Shah (1986), 'An empirical analysis of self employment in the UK', *Journal of Applied Econometrics*, **1**, 95–108.

Rees, R. (1980), 'The Principal–Agent Relationship and Control of Public Enterprise', Paper presented to seminar on Regulation at the Centre for Socio-Legal Studies, Wolfson College, Oxford, March.

Rees, R. (1984), 'The public enterprise game', *Economic Journal*, **94**, 109–23.

Reid, G.C. and Jacobsen, L.R. (1988), *The Small Entrepreneurial Firm*, David Hume Institute, Aberdeen University Press.

Ricardo, D. (1891), in E.C.K. Gonner (ed.), *Principles of Political Economy and Taxation*, London: George Bell and Sons (first published 1817).

Richardson, G.B. (1956), 'Demand and supply reconsidered', *Oxford Economic Papers*, (New Series), **8**, 113.

Richardson, G.B. (1959), 'Equilibrium, expectations and information', *Economic Journal*, **69**, 223.

Richardson, G.B. (1960), *Information and Investment*, Oxford: Oxford University Press.

Richardson, G.B. (1972), 'The organisation of industry', *Economic Journal*, **82**, 883.

Ricketts, M.J. (1986), 'The geometry of principal and agent: yet another use for the Edgeworth Box', *Scottish Journal of Political Economy*, **33**(3), 228–48.

Ricketts, M.J. (1999), *The Many Ways of Governance: Perspectives on the Control of the Firm*, Social Affairs Unit, London.

Ricketts, M.J. (2000), 'Competitive processes and the evolution of governance structures', *Journal des Economistes et des Etudes Humaines*, **10**(2/3), 235–52.

Robbins, L. (1935), *An Essay on the Nature and Significance of Economic Science*, London: Macmillan.

Robertson, D.H. and S.R. Dennison (1960), *The Control of Industry, Cambridge Economic Handbook*, Nisbet, Cambridge: Cambridge University Press.

Roberts, D.R. (1959), *Executive Compensation*, Glencoe, IL: Free Press.

Robinson, C. (1996), 'Profit, Discovery and the Role of Entry: The Case of Electricity', in Beesley, M. (ed.), *Regulating Utilities: A Time for Change?* Readings No. 44, IEA/LBS, 109–40.

Rosen, S. (1987), 'Some Economics of Teaching', *Journal of Labour Economics*, **5**(4), 561–75.

Ross, I.S. (1982), 'Dugald Stewart's account of Adam Smith', in Bryce, J.C. and Wightman, W.P.D. (eds), *Adam Smith Essays on Philosophical Subjects*, Oxford: Oxford University Press.

Ross, S.A. (1973), 'The economic theory of agency: the principal's problem', *American Economic Review*, **63**, 134.

Rowley, C. and Elgin, R. (1985), 'Towards a theory of bureaucratic behaviour' in Shaw, G.K. and Greenaway, D. (eds), *Public Choice, Public Finance and Public Policy: Essays in Honour of Alan Peacock*, Oxford: Basil Blackwell.

Rubin, P.H. (1978), 'The theory of the firm and the structure of the franchise contract', *Journal of Law and Economics*, **21**, 223.

Rudney, G. (1987), 'The scope and dimensions of nonprofit activity', in Powell, W.W. (ed.), *The Nonprofit Sector: A Research Handbook*, New Haven, CT: Yale University Press, pp. 55–64.

Rugman, A.M. (1980), 'Internationalisation as a general theory of foreign direct investment: a reappraisal of the literature', *Weltwirtschaftliches Archiv*, III, 365.

Rumelt, R. (1974), *Strategy, Structure and Economic Performance*, Cambridge, MA: Harvard University Press.

Ryngaert, M. (1988), 'The Effect of Poison Pill Securities on Shareholder Wealth', *Journal of Financial Economics*, **20**(1/2), 377–417.

Sah, R.K. (1991), 'Fallibility in human organizations and political systems', *Journal of Economic Perspectives*, **5**(2), 67–88.

Sako, M. (1990), 'Buyer–supplier Relationships and Economic Performance; Evidence from Britain and Japan', PhD thesis, University of London.

Sako, M., Lamming, R. and Helper, S.R. (1998), 'Supplier Relations in the Multinational Automotive Industry', in Mudambi, R. and Ricketts, M. (eds), *The Organisation of the Firm: International Business Perspectives*, London and New York: Routledge, pp. 178–94.

Salop, S. (1979), 'A model of the natural rate of unemployment', *American Economic Review*, **69**, 117.

Samuelson, P.A. (1954), 'The pure theory of public expenditure', *The Review of Economics and Statistics*, **36**(4), November, 387–9.

Sappington, D.E.M. (1991), 'Incentives in principal–agent relationships', *Journal of Economic Perspectives*, **5**(2), 45–66.

Sargant, Florence, P. (1933), *Logic of Industrial Organisation*, London: Trench, Trubner & Co.

Sargant, Florence, P. (1961), *Ownership, Control and Success of Large Companies*, London: Sweet and Maxwell.

Say, J.B. (1803), *Traite d'economie politique*, 5th edition 1826, Paris.

Scarpa, C. (1994), 'Regulation as a bargaining process: negotiation over price and cost-reducing investments', *Oxford Economic Papers*, **46**, 357–65.

Schelling, T.C. (1960), *The Strategy of Conflict*, Cambridge, MA: Harvard University Press.

Scherer, F.M. (1980), *Industrial Market Structure and Performance* (2nd edn), Chicago: Rand McNally.

Scherer, F.M. (1988), 'Corporate takeovers: the efficiency arguments', *Journal of Economic Perspectives*, **2**(1), 69–82.

Schlenker, R.E. and P.W. Shaughnessy (1984), 'Case mix, quality, and cost relationships in Colorado nursing homes', *Health Care Financing Review*, **6**, 61–71.

Schlicht, E. (1992), 'Wage Generosity', *Journal of Institutional and Theoretical Economics*, **148**(3), 437–51.

Schmalensee, R. (1973), 'A note on the theory of vertical integration', *Journal of Political Economy*, **81**, 442.

Schmalensee, R. (2000), 'Antitrust Issues in Schumpeterian Industries', *American Economic Review*, **90**(2), 192–6.

Schumpeter, J.A. (1936), *The Theory of Economic Development*, Cambridge, MA: Harvard University Press.

Schumpeter, J.A. (1943), *Capitalism, Socialism, and Democracy*, London: Unwin University Books.

Schumpeter, J.A. (1954), *History of Economic Analysis*, London: Allen and Unwin.

Securities and Exchange Commission (1985), '*Institutional Ownership, Tender Offers and Long-term Investments*', Office of the Chief Economist, SEC study, Washington DC, GPO, April.

Sen, A. (1987), *On Ethics and Economics*, Oxford: Basil Blackwell.

Shackle, G.L.S. (1961), (2nd edn, 1969), *Decision, Order and Time in Human Affairs*, Cambridge: Cambridge University Press.

Shackle, G.L.S. (1966), *The Nature of Economic Thought, Selected Papers 1955–1964*, Cambridge: Cambridge University Press.

Shackle, G.L.S. (1970), *Expectation, Enterprise and Profit: The Theory of the Firm*, London: Allen and Unwin.

Shackle, G.L.S. (1972), *Epistemics and Economics: A Critique of Economic Doctrines*, Cambridge: Cambridge University Press.

Shackle, G.L.S. (1979a), *Imagination and the Nature of Choice*, Edinburgh: Edinburgh University Press.

Shackle, G.L.S. (1979b), 'Imagination, formalism and choice', in Rizzo, Mario, J. (ed.), *Time, Uncertainty, and Disequilibrium: Exploration of Austrian Themes*, Lexington Books, Lexington, Toronto: D.C. Heath.

Shackle, G.L.S. (1982), 'Means and meaning in economic theory', *Scottish Journal of Political Economy*, **29**, 223.

Shannon, H.A. (1931), 'The coming of general limited liability', *Economic History*, II, 267.

Shapiro, C. and J.E. Stiglitz (1984), 'Equilibrium unemployment as a worker discipline device', *American Economic Review*, **74**, 433.

Shavell, S. (1979), 'Risk sharing and incentives in the principal and agent relationship', *Bell Journal of Economics*, **10**, 55.

Shenfield, A. (1983), *Myth and Reality in Anti-Trust*, Occasional Paper 66, Institute of Economic Affairs, London.

Shirley, M. and P. Walsh (2000), 'Public versus Private Ownership: The Current State of the Debate', Policy Research Working Paper No. 2420, The World Bank Group.

Shleifer, A. (1998), 'State versus private ownership', *Journal of Economic Perspectives*, **12**(4), 133–50.

Shleifer, A. and L.H. Summers (1988), 'Breach of trust in hostile takeovers', in Auerbach, A.J. (ed.), *Corporate Takeovers: Causes and Consequences*, NBER/University of Chicago Press, 33–56.

Shleifer, A. and R.W. Vishny (1986), 'Large shareholders and corporate control', *Journal of Political Economy*, **94**(3), (part 1), 461–88.

Shleifer, A. and R.W. Vishny (1988), 'Value maximisation and the acquisition process', *Journal of Economic Perspectives*, **2**(1), 7–20.

Short, R.P. (1983), 'The Role of Public Enterprises: An International Statistical Comparison', International Monetary Fund Department Memorandum, No. 83, Washington DC.

Siebert, W.S. and J.T. Addison (1991), 'Internal labour markets: causes and consequences', *Oxford Review of Economic Policy*, **7**(1), 76–92.

Silver, M. (1984), *Enterprise and the Scope of the Firm*, Oxford: Martin Robertson.

Silver, M. and R. Auster (1969), 'Entrepreneurship, profit and the limits on firm size', *Journal of Business*, **42**, 277. (Reprinted in Auster, R.D. and Silver, M. (1979) *The State as a Firm*, p.111.)

Simon, H.A. (1957), *Models of Man*, New York: John Wiley and Sons.

Simon, H.A. (1964), 'On the concept of organizational goal', *Administrative Science Quarterly*, **9**, 1.

Simon, H.A. (1969), *The Sciences of the Artificial*, Cambridge, MA: MIT Press.

Simon, H.A. (1976a), *Administrative Behavior: A Study of Decision Making Processes in Administrative Organization*, (3rd edn), New York, NY: Free Press.

Simon, H.A. (1976b), 'From substantive to procedural rationality', in Latsis, S.J. (ed.), *Method and Appraisal in Economics*, Cambridge, UK: Cambridge University Press.

Simon, H.A. (1978), 'Rationality as process and as product of thought', *American Economic Review*, Papers and Proceedings, p.1.

Simon, H.A. (1979), 'Rational decision making in busines organizations', *American Economic Review*, **69**, 493.

Simon, H.A. (1991), 'Organizations and markets', *Journal of Economic Perspectives*, **5**(2), 25–44.

Singh, A. (1971), *Takeovers*, Cambridge, UK: Cambridge University Press.

Singh, A. (1975), 'Takeovers, economic natural selection and the theory of the firm: evidence from the post-war UK experience', *Economic Journal*, **85**, 497.

Sirc, L. (1979), *The Yugoslav Economy Under Self-Management*, London: Macmillan.

Sisk, D.E. (1985), 'Rent seeking, noncompensated transfers, and laws of succession: a property rights view', *Public Choice*, **46**, 95.

Slater, M. (1980), 'The managerial limitation to the growth of firms', *Economic Journal*, **90**, 520.

Smiley, R. (1976), 'Tender offers, transactions costs and the theory of the firm, *Review of Economics and Statistics*, **58**, 22.

Smith, Adam (1925), *The Wealth of Nations*, (4th edn), Edwin Cannan (ed.), London: Methuen and Co. (first published 1776).

Smith, J.M. (1982), *Evolution and the Theory of Games*, Cambridge: Cambridge University Press.

Solow, R.M. (1990), *The Labor Market as a Social Institution*, Oxford: Basil Blackwell.

Sorenson, R. (1974), 'The separation of ownership from control and firm performance: an empirical analysis', *Southern Economic Journal*, **40**, 145.

Spence, M.A. (1975), 'The economics of internal organization: an introduction', *Bell Journal of Economics*, **6**, 163.

Stano, M. (1976), 'Monopoly power, ownership control, and corporate performance', *Bell Journal of Economics*, **7**, 672.

Stanworth, J. and Gray, C. (eds) (1991), *Bolton 20 Years On: The Small Firm in the 1990s*, Small Business Research Trust, London: Paul Chapman.

Steer, P. and Cable, J. (1978), 'Internal organization and profit: an empirical analysis of large UK companies', *Journal of Industrial Economics*, **27**, 13.

Stein, J.C. (1988), 'Takeover threats and managerial myopia', *Journal of Political Economy*, **96**(1), 61–80.

Steinberg, R. (1985), 'Empirical relations between government spending and charitable donations', *Journal of Voluntary Action Research*, **14**, 54–64.

Steinberg, R. (1986), 'Should Donors Care about Fundraising?', in Rose-Ackerman, S. (ed.), *The Economics of Nonprofit Institutions: Studies in Structure and Policy*, New York: Oxford University Press.

Steinberg, R. (1987), 'Nonprofit organisations and the market', in Powell, W.W. (ed.), *The Nonprofit Sector: A Research Handbook*, New Haven CT: Yale University Press, pp. 118–38.

Steltzer, I. (1996), 'Lessons for UK Regulation from Recent US Experience', in Beesley, M. (ed.), *Regulating Utilities: A Time for Change?* Readings 44, IEA/LBS, 189–206.

Stigler, G.J. (1951), 'The divison of labour is limited by the extent of the market', *Journal of Political Economy*, **59**, 190.

Stigler, G.J. (1961), 'The economics of information', *Journal of Political Economy*, **69**, 213.

Stigler, G.J. (1962), 'What can regulators regulate: the case of electricity', *Journal of Law and Economics*, **5**, 1–16.

Stigler, G.J. (1964), 'A theory of oligopoly', *Journal of Political Economy*, **72**, 44.

Stigler, G.J. (1971), 'The Theory of Economic Regulation', *Bell Journal of Economics*, **2**, 3–21.

Stigler, G.J. (1975), *The Citizen and the State: Essays on Regulation*, Chicago: University of Chicago Press.

Stigler, G.J. (1976), 'The xistence of x-efficiency', *American Economic Review*, **66**, 213.

Stigler, G.J. and C. Friedland (1962), 'What can Regulators Regulate?: The Case of Electricity', *Journal of Law and Economics*, **5**, 1–16.

Stigler, G.J. and C. Friedland (1983), 'The literature of economics: the case of Berle and Means', *Journal of Law and Economics*, **26**, 237.

Stiglitz, J.E. (1975), 'Incentives, risk, and information: notes towards a theory of hierarchy', *Bell Journal of Economics*, **6**, 552.

Storey, D.J. (1982), *Entrepreneurship and the New Firm*, London: Croom Helm.

Storey, D.J. (1991), 'The birth of new firms – does unemployment matter? A review of the evidence', *Small Business Economics*, **3**, 167–78.

Storey, D.J. and S. Johnson (1987), 'Regional variations in entrepreneurship in the UK', *Scottish Journal of Political Economy*, **34**(2), 161–73.

Storey, D.J. and A.M. Jones (1987), 'New firm formation – a labour market approach to industrial entry', *Scottish Journal of Political Economy*, **34**(1), 37–51.

Sugden, Robert (1984), 'Reciprocity: the supply of public goods through voluntary contributions', *Economic Journal*, **94**, 772–87.

Sugden, Robert (1986), *The Economics of Rights, Co-operation and Welfare*, Oxford: Basil Blackwell.

Sugden, Roger (1991), 'The importance of distributional considerations', in Pitelis, C. and Sugden, Roger (eds), *The Nature of the Transnational Firm*, London: Routledge.

Swann, D. (1988), *The Retreat of the State*, Hemel Hempstead: Harvester Wheatsheaf.

Sykes, A. (1991), 'Rethinking Corporate Governance and Takeovers – A

Compact between Owners and Managers', NEDO Conference, Capital Markets and Company Success, 21/22 November.

Taylor, F.W. (1911), *The Principles of Scientific Management*, New York: Harper and Row.

Teece, D.J. (1981), 'Internal organisation and economic performance: an empirical analysis of the profitability of principal firms', *Journal of Industrial Economics*, **30**, 173.

Thompson, R.S. (1981), 'Internal organisation and profit: a note', *Journal of Industrial Economics*, **30**, 201.

Thompson, R.S., M. Wright and K. Robbie (1992), 'Management Equity Ownership, Debt and Performance: Some Evidence from UK Management Buyouts', *Scottish Journal of Political Economy*, **39**(4), 413–30.

Thünen, J.H. Von (1966), translated by C.M. Warenberg, *Von Thünen's Isolated State*, Hall, P. (ed.), (first volume of original published 1826, second part 1850), Oxford: Pergamon Press.

Tiebout, C. (1956), 'A pure theory of local expenditures', *Journal of Political Economy*, **64**, 416–24.

Tirole, J. (1988), *The Theory of Industrial Organization*, Cambridge, MA: MIT Press.

Titmus, R.M. (1970), *The Gift Relationship*, London, Allen and Unwin.

Tobin, J. (1984), Fred Hirsch Memorial Lecture, *Lloyds Bank Annual Review*.

Toma, E.F. (1990), 'Boards of trustees, agency problems and university output', *Public Choice*, **67**(1), 1–9.

Tullock, G. (1965), *The Politics of Bureaucracy*, Washington, DC: Public Affairs Press.

Tullock, G. (1980a), 'Rent seeking as a negative sum game', in Buchanan, J.M. *et al.* (eds), *Toward a Theory of the Rent Seeking Society*, College Station, TX: Texas A and M University Press, p. 16.

Tullock, G. (1980b), 'Efficient rent seeking', in Buchanan, J.M. *et al.* (eds), ibid., p. 97.

Tullock, G. (1980c), 'The welfare costs of tariffs, monopolies, and theft', in Buchanan, J.M. *et al.* (eds), ibid., p. 39.

Turvey, R. (1995), 'The Sliding Scale: Price and Dividend Regulation in the Nineteenth-century Gas Industry', NERA Topics Paper.

Urwick, L.F. (1943), *The Elements of Administration*, New York: Harper and Row.

Utton, M.A. (1982), *The Political Economy of Big Business*, Oxford: Martin Robertson.

Vanek, J. (1970), *The General Theory of Labour-Managed Market Economies*, Ithaca, NY: Cornell University Press.

Vanek, J. (1975), (ed.), *Penguin Modern Economics Readings in Self-Management*, Harmondsworth: Penguin.

Vanek, J. (1977), *The Labour Managed Economy*, Ithaca, NY: Cornell University Press.

Varian, H.R. (1999), *Intermediate Microeconomics* (5th edn), New York: Norton.

Vaupel, J.W. (1971), 'Characteristics and Motivations of the U.S. Corporations which Manufacture Abroad', Paper presented to Atlantic Institute, Paris, June 1971.

Vernon, J.M. and D.A. Graham (1971), 'Profitability of monopolization by vertical integration', *Journal of Political Economy*, **79**, 924.

Vickers, J. and G. Yarrow (1985), *Privatization and the Natural Monopolies*, Public Policy Centre, London.

Villarejo, D. (1961), 'Stock ownership and the control of the corporation', Chicago: New University Thought.

Walras, L. (1954), *Elements of Pure Economics* (translated by William Jaffé), London: Allen and Unwin.

Ward, B. (1958), 'The firm in Illyria: market syndicalism', *American Economic Review*, **48**, 566.

Weber, A. (1929), *Alfred Weber's Theory of the Location of Industries* (translated by Carl J. Friedrich), Chicago: University of Chicago Press.

Weber, M. (1947), *The Theory of Social and Economic Organization*, New York: Free Press.

Weisbrod, B. (1975), 'Toward a theory of the voluntary non-profit sector in a three sector economy', in Phelps, E. (ed.), *Altruism, Morality, and Economic Theory*, New York: Russell Sage.

Weisbrod, B. (1988), *The Nonprofit Economy*, Cambridge, MA: Harvard University Press.

Weisbrod, B. (1989), 'Rewarding performance that is hard to measure: the private non-profit sector', *Science*, 5 May, p. 244.

Weiss, L.W. (1983), 'The extent and effects of aggregate concentration', *Journal of Law and Economics*, **26**, 429.

Weitzman, M.L. (1984), *The Share Economy: Conquering Stagflation*, Cambridge, MA: Harvard University Press.

Weitzman, M.L. and D.L. Kruse (1990), 'Profit sharing and productivity', in Blinder, A. (ed.), *Paying for Productivity: A Look at the Evidence*, Washington, DC: Brookings Institution.

Wendling, W. and J. Werner (1980), 'Nonprofit firms and the economic theory of regulation', *Quarterly Review of Economics and Business*, **20**(3), 6–18.

West, E.G. (1989), 'Nonprofit organizations: revised theory and new evidence', *Public Choice*, **63**(2), 165–74.

White, M. (1996), 'Power Struggles: Explaining Deregulatory Reforms in Electricity Markets', Brookings Papers on Economic Activity: Microeconomics, pp. 201–50.

Whynes, D.K. and R.A. Bowles (1981), *The Economic Theory of the State*, Oxford: Martin Robertson.

Willgerodt, H. and A. Peacock (1989), 'German Liberalism and Economic Revival', in Peacock, A. and Willgerodt, H. (eds), *Germany's Social Market Economy: Origin and Evolution,* Trade Policy Research Centre, London: Macmillan, pp. 1–14.

Williams, D. (1994), *Japan: Beyond the End of History*, London and New York: Routledge.

Williamson, O.E. (1963), 'Managerial discretion and business behavior', in Furubotn, E. and Pejovich, S. (eds) (1974), *The Economics of Property Rights*, Cambridge, MA: Ballinger.

Williamson, O.E. (1964), *The Economics of Discretionary Behavior: Managerial Objectives in a Theory of the Firm*, Englewood Cliffs, NJ: Prentice-Hall.

Williamson, O.E. (1967), 'Hierarchical control and optimum firm size', *Journal of Political Economy*, **75**, 123.

Williamson, O.E. (1970), *Corporate Control and Business Behavior*, Englewood Cliffs, NJ: Prentice-Hall.

Williamson, O.E. (1975), *Markets and Hierarchies: Analysis and Antitrust Implications. A Study in the Economics of Internal Organization*, London and New York: The Free Press, Collier Macmillan.

Williamson, O.E. (1979), 'Transaction-cost economics: the governance of contractual relations', *Journal of Law and Economics*, **22**, 233.

Williamson, O.E. (1981), 'The modern corporation: origins, evolution, attributes', *Journal of Economic Literature*, **19**, 1537.

Williamson, O.E. (1983), 'Organization form, residual claimants, and corporate control', *Journal of Law and Economics*, **26**, 351.

Williamson, O.E. (1985), *The Economic Institutions of Capitalism: Firms, Markets, Relational Contracting*, London: Collier Macmillan.

Williamson, O.E. (1986), *Economic Organisation. Firms, Markets and Policy Control*, Brighton: Wheatsheaf.

Williamson, O.E. (1993), 'Contested exchange versus the governance of contractual relations', *Journal of Economic Perspectives*, **7**(1), 103–8.

Williamson, O.E. (2000), 'The New Institutional Economics: taking stock, looking ahead', *Journal of Economic Literature*, **38**(3), 595–613.

Williamson, O.E., M.L. Wachter and J.E. Harris (1975), 'Understanding the employment relation: the analysis of idiosyncratic exchange', *Bell Journal of Economics*, **6**, 250.

Winship, C. and S. Rosen (1988), 'Sociological and economic approaches to the analysis of social structure', *American Journal of Sociology*, (supplement on Organizations and Institutions), **94**, 1–16.

Winston, C. (1993), 'Economic deregulation: days of reckoning for microeconomists', *Journal of Economic Literature*, **31**(3), 1263–87.

Winston, C. (1998), 'US industry adjustment to economic deregulation', *Journal of Economic Perspectives*, **12**(3), 89–110.

Wiseman, J. (1953), 'Uncertainty, Costs and Collectivist Economic Planning', *Economica*, May, 118.

Wiseman, J. (1957), 'The Theory of Public Utility Price – An Empty Box', *Oxford Economic Papers*, **9**, 56–74.

Witt, U. (1985), 'Economic behavior and biological evolution', *Journal of Institutional and Theoretical Economics*, **141**(3), 365–89.

Witt, U. (1986), 'Evolution and stability of cooperation without enforceable contracts', *Kyklos*, **39**(2), 245–66.

Witt, U. (1989), 'Subjectivism in Economics – A Suggested Reorientation', in Grunert, K.G. and Olander, F. (eds), *Understanding Economic Behaviour*, Dordrecht: Kluwer Academic Publishers, pp. 409–31.

Wolf, B.M. (1977), 'Industrial diversification and internationalisation: some empirical evidence', *Journal of Industrial Economics*, **26**, 177.

Wu, Shih-Yen (1989), *Production and Entrepreneurship*, Oxford: Basil Blackwell.

Yamin, M. (1991), 'A Reassessment of Hymer's Contribution to the Theory of the Transnational Corporation', in Pitelis, C. and Sugden, R. (eds), *The Nature of the Transnational Firm*, London: Routledge, pp. 64–80.

Yasubu, Y. and K. Yamamura (eds) (1988), *The Political Economy of Japan*, Stanford, CA: Stanford University Press.

Yellen, J.L. (1984), 'Efficiency wage models of unemployment', *American Economic Review*, Papers and Proceedings, **74**, 200.

Yunker, J.A. (1975), 'Economic performance of public and private enterprise: the case of US electric utilities', *Journal of Economics and Business*, **28**, 60.

Index